THE PRINCIPLES OF THEOLOGY

THE
PRINCIPLES OF THEOLOGY

AN INTRODUCTION TO
THE THIRTY-NINE ARTICLES

BY THE LATE

W. H. GRIFFITH THOMAS, D.D.

*Formerly Professor of Systematic Theology, Wycliffe College, Toronto,
and sometime Principal of Wycliffe Hall, Oxford*

Wipf & Stock
PUBLISHERS
Eugene, Oregon

Wipf and Stock Publishers
199 W 8th Ave, Suite 3
Eugene, OR 97401

The Principles of Theology
An Introduction to the Thirty-Nine Articles
By Thomas, W.H. Griffith
ISBN: 1-59752-073-X
Publication date 1/26/2005
Previously published by Longmans, Green and Co., 1930

PREFACE BY THE REV. T. W. GILBERT, D.D.

THE death of Dr. W. H. Griffith Thomas removed from our midst one of the foremost Biblical scholars and teachers of our generation. His influence as parochial minister both at St. Aldate's, Oxford, and at St. Paul's, Portman Square, London, had marked him out as essentially a teacher, and it was this characteristic which led to his appointment as Principal of Wycliffe Hall, Oxford, and subsequently as Professor of Systematic Theology at Wycliffe College, Toronto. His many writings made his name well known to the Christian public, and the influence of such of his books as *The Catholic Faith* and *The Work of the Ministry* has been far-reaching. But important as all his previous writings have been, it is no exaggeration to say that all his earlier work will be surpassed by the volume which is now published.

It was known that Dr. Thomas was at work on the subject of the Thirty-nine Articles prior to his death, and fortunately the manuscript was completed before he was taken from us. Had he lived, the book would no doubt have been published ere this, but it is the privilege of some of his former colleagues and other friends to give to the public the work Dr. Thomas left behind.

The manuscript needed little but a few verbal alterations, and goes forth practically as it was prepared for the press by the author. Its exhaustive and penetrating treatment, its fidelity to the Bible, and its exact historical scholarship will ensure it a welcome from all who wish to know the basis of Christian doctrine in general and of the Anglican Church in particular.

T. W. GILBERT.

ST. JOHN'S HALL,
HIGHBURY.

PREFACE BY THE AUTHOR

It is believed that there is room for another presentation of Anglican Doctrine as embodied in the Articles. In the preparation of it all the important earlier works from Rogers down to modern days have been carefully considered and their vital points discussed as far as possible. The effort has been made to look at the Articles in the light of the historical circumstances which gave rise to them, and thus to derive the essential Anglican Doctrine from the known views of the times of their compilation and revision, and also of the men who were responsible for them.

The book represents the work of forty years from student days. It owes much to some notes of Lectures on the Articles received at King's College, London, from the Principals under whom it was my privilege to be a student, Dr. (afterwards Bishop) Barry and Dr. Wace, afterwards Dean of Canterbury. It is also deeply indebted to Litton's *Introduction to Dogmatic Theology*, which for clearness of view, firmness of grasp, balance of statement, and forcefulness of presentation, remains unsurpassed among works on Anglican Dogmatics. I must also mention another work which has been found of great value all through these years, Boultbee's well-known book on the Articles. The historical material in the introductory sections will be found supplemented by one of the ablest books of modern days, *History of Creeds and Confessions of Faith*, by W. A. Curtis ; while for detailed history of particular articles special mention must be made of some papers in the *English Churchman*, by Mr. W. Prescott Upton.

The manuscript has been read by three friends, whose full and accurate knowledge and clear judgment I greatly value, and to whom I owe several important suggestions. I must not omit to refer to an American book, *Outlines of Christian Doctrine*, by the late Dr. Pardington.

It has seemed best to keep as closely as possible to the Articles as the truest expression of and best guide to Anglican Theology, but those who wish to study the subject of Dogmatics from a wider standpoint will find in the Bibliography a list of various modern works.

W. H. GRIFFITH THOMAS.

FOREWORD BY THE
REV. CANON DYSON HAGUE, D.D.

ANY book by Dr. Griffith Thomas should command attention, and we think that in these unsettling and reactionary days there is peculiar need for a great work like this. The late Dr. Griffith Thomas was remarkable as a teacher and leader. His outstanding characteristic was clearness and forcefulness. He had the power of presenting every subject, whether with the pen or with the voice, with a singular conciseness of order and method. From his early college days in King's College, London, and Christ Church, Oxford, he lived a life of the most strenuous activity, and was ever a prodigious toiler.

This massive work was the harvest of many years of the widest reading and profoundest thinking. It constitutes in its entirety a complete armoury for the Churchman of to-day, ministerial, student, or lay. It covers, in a most comprehensive way, the whole field of Anglican Church teaching. There is scarcely a subject pertaining to the doctrine of our Church that is not exhaustively and conclusively treated. In fact, it is almost an Anglican Encyclopædia, a volume not so much for reading from cover to cover, but as a book of reference treating in the ablest possible manner those great principles of Christian dogmatics that must occupy the thought and reading of all earnest Churchmen.

A committee of Canadian Churchmen, consisting of four lecturers in Wycliffe College, Toronto, have gone through every section of the work. But, after careful perusal, they have come to the conclusion that emendations or amplifications were practically impossible. Though written ten or fifteen years ago, the work is so thoroughly done and the subjects treated with such carefulness and fidelity, that they are unanimous in the opinion that the work should be presented to the Church public as it came from the pen of Dr. Griffith Thomas himself, without abbreviation or radical alteration. Our hope is that it may stablish, strengthen, and settle.

For, after all, the Thirty-nine Articles still stand, not only as a great monument of the victories of the Reformation, but as an ever-steadfast bulwark of the true principles of the Church of England. It is the great historic Confession of the Faith, and to all conscientious sons of the Church they do contain the true doctrine of the Church of England agreeable to God's Word. Our heart's desire and prayer to God is that this monumental work will not only prove of inestimable value to the present generation of the clergy and laity generally, and especially to the divinity students in all the Theological Colleges throughout the Empire, but that it will remain as a standard for accuracy, suggestiveness, and fulness for future generations of English Churchmen.

DYSON HAGUE.

WYCLIFFE COLLEGE,
TORONTO.

CONTENTS

INTRODUCTION

INTRODUCTION

REVELATION[1]

THE word " Revelation " almost suggests its own meaning of the unveiling of something hidden. It corresponds to the Greek word " Apocalypse," or " Uncovering " (Rev. i. 1). In the present connection the word
refers to the Revelation of God, the " Unveiling " of the Unseen God
to the mind and heart of man. While the term is variously applied,[2]
there are certain specific uses which call for definite consideration. (1)
There is the Revelation of God through Nature, referring to the indications of wisdom, power, and purpose in the world around (Rom. i. 20).
(2) There is the Revelation of God in Man, referring to the traces of
God's " image and likeness " in man's conscience, emotional nature and
personality in general, involving the consciousness of obligation, the
desire for fellowship, and the craving for satisfaction. (3) There is the
Revelation of God in History, which means the marks of an over-ruling
Providence in the affairs of the human race, and the traces of a progress
in the history of nations and mankind in general. (4) There is the
Revelation of God in Judaism. The Old Testament involves and
records a special supernatural communication of God to man, a disclosure of His character and relationship. (5) There is the Revelation
of God in Christianity. This is the crowning feature of God's self-
manifestation in the Person of Christ for human redemption.

The problem of Revelation is the correlation of the supernatural
disclosure of the character, purpose, and grace of God with the historical
and fragmentary process by means of which this progressive revelation
has become a received tradition.[3] It is essential that justice be done
both to the supernatural fact and also to the human elements of the
Revelation. In the course of this we are brought face to face with the
antitheses of Revelation and discovery, of Revelation and speculation,
of Revelation and evolution; and while accepting to the full all historical
processes we are led to the conviction (1) that Christianity is only adequately explained as a Personal Revelation of God, Who used and guided
history for this purpose; and (2) that history, discovery, philosophy, and

---

[1] This section is summarised from the writer's article "Revelation," in Hastings'
One Volume Bible Dictionary. The subject is also treated with great fulness and force
in the earlier part of *Revelation and Inspiration,* by Orr.

[2] The widest use is found in Gwatkin, *The Knowledge of God,* Vol. I, p. 5, "Any fact
which gives knowledge is a revelation . . . the revelation and the knowledge of God
are correlative terms."

[3] 2 Cor. iii. 14 illustrates both aspects, objective and subjective, of the "unveiling."

xvii

evolution are simply the means or channels by which the Revelation has come.

The possibility of Revelation is based on two grounds : (1) The Being of God as Supreme (which for the moment we assume) must necessarily be able to reveal Himself. A Personal God necessarily involves the power of a self-revelation. Theistic belief makes Revelation possible. (2) The nature of man bears the same testimony, for the fact of his personality with all its desires and possibilities involves a capacity for communion with a being higher than himself.

The probability of Revelation is also based on two grounds : (1) Granted a Supreme Personal Being, we are compelled to predicate His willingness as well as His ability to reveal Himself. Even human personality with its desire for self-revelation makes a revelation of God antecedently probable. (2) The needs of man point in the same direction, for as man, and still more as a sinner, he needs a Divine Revelation to guide and guard, to support and strengthen him amidst the problems and dangers of life.

The proofs of Divine Revelation are varied, converging, and cumulative. (1) Speculatively, we argue that " the universe points to idealism, and idealism to theism, and theism to a Revelation."[1] (2) Historically, the Christian religion comes to us commended by the testimony of (a) miracle; (b) prophecy; and (c) spiritual adaptation to human needs. (3) Behind these are the presuppositions of natural religion, as seen in nature, man and history. (4) But ultimately the credibility of Christianity as a Revelation rests on the Person of its Founder, and all evidences converge towards and centre in Him. The fact that God has made other manifestations of Himself in the course of history does not set aside the culmination of Revelation in the Person of Christ. All truth, however mediated, has come from the primal source of truth, and the genuineness of Christianity does not set aside the genuineness of other religions as " broken lights." The real criterion of all religions claiming to be Divine is their power to save. Not truth in itself, but truth in life, and truth as redemptive, constitutes the final and supreme test of religion.

The method of the Christian Revelation is first and foremost one of *Life*; that is, it is a revelation of a Person to persons. Christianity is primarily a religion of facts with doctrines arising out of the facts. All through the historic period of God's manifestation, from patriarchal times to the period of Christ and His Apostles, Revelation was given to life and manifested through Personality. But the Divine life has been expressed in *Word*, first oral and then written. Both in the Old Testament and in the New Testament we see first what God was and did to men, and afterwards what He said. So that while we distinguish between the Revelation and the Record, the former being necessarily prior to the latter, yet the Revelation needed the Record for accuracy, and also for

---

[1] Illingworth, *Reason and Revelation*, p. 243.

accessibility to subsequent ages.   Then, too, Scripture is not merely a record of Revelation, for the history itself is a Revelation of God.   While from one point of view the Bible is a product of the Divine process of self-manifestation, on the other the Bible itself makes God known to man.   It is in this sense that Christianity, like Judaism before it, is a book religion (though it is also much more), as recording and conveying the Divine manifestation to man.   A Revelation must be embodied if it is to be made available for all generations, and the one requirement is that the medium of transmission shall be accurate.   Christ as our Supreme Authority needs for His manifestation to all ages the clearest and purest available form.

Revelation having been mediated through history has of necessity been progressive.   The first stage was primitive Revelation.   How men first came to think of God is, and probably must remain, a matter of conjecture, for as so little is known about primitive man there must also be little known about primitive religion.   One thing, however, is clear, that the terms " savage " and " primitive " are not synonymous, for the savage of to-day represents a degeneration from primitive man.   Analogy favours the idea that primitive Revelation was a sufficient manifestation of God to enable man to receive and retain a true relation with his Creator ; that man, when created, had an immediate capacity for entering into fellowship with God, and with this religious endowment we assume a measure of Divine Revelation sufficient to enable man to worship in an elementary way, and to remain true to God.   Some such assumption is necessary for the very conception of Revelation, unless we are to resolve religion into merely human conjectures about God.   There is no argument against primitive Revelation which is not valid against all Revelation, Christianity included.   Then followed in due course the Revelation of God in the Old Testament, and whatever views may be held as to its origin and character it is impossible to avoid being conscious of something in it beyond what is merely human and historical.   It does not merely represent human endeavours after worthier ideas of God ; it records a true idea of God impressed on the people in the course of history under definite direction.   The Old Testament presentation of God is so different from that which obtained elsewhere that apart from a supernatural Revelation it is impossible to account for so marked a difference between peoples who were in other respects so much alike.   The New Testament Revelation was the crown and culmination of the Divine self-manifestation.   It was given at a particular time, mediated through one Person, and authenticated by supernatural credentials.   In Jesus Christ the self-disclosure of God reached its climax, and the New Testament is the permanent, written embodiment of the uniqueness of Christianity in the world.   " God, who in ancient days spoke to our forefathers in many distinct messages and by various methods through the prophets, has at the end of these days spoken to us through a Son " (Heb. i. 1, 2 ; Weymouth).

The purpose of Revelation is also life, God's life, to be received and possessed by man. This practical character is marked everywhere. The "chief end of Revelation" is not philosophy, or doctrine, or enjoyment, or even morality. Christianity has these, but is far more than them all. It is the religion of Redemption, including Salvation past, present, and future. The "chief end" of God's self-manifestation is the union of God and man, and in that union the fulfilment of all the Divine purposes for the world. Man is to receive God's grace, recognise His will, reproduce His character, render Him service, and rejoice in His presence here and hereafter.

FAITH

Literature.—Moule, *Faith : Its Nature and Work*; Inge, *Faith and Its Psychology*; Johnston, *A Scientific Faith*; Edgehill, *Faith and Fact* (Index, s.v. "Faith"); Warfield, "Faith in its Psychological Aspects" (*Princeton Theological Review*, Vol. IX, p. 537); Mabie, *Under the Redeeming Ægis*, Ch. V.

The subject of Revelation naturally leads on to that of Faith, which is a matter of vital importance to Christianity and the Christian. Faith is the human attitude to the Divine Revelation, the attitude of the soul to Christ as the manifestation of God. Christ is the Way, the Truth, and the Life, and Faith is the means of man's coming to God by Him (Matt. xi. 27; John i. 18; xiv. 6). It is not difficult to understand the interest and importance of Faith. As it is the foundation principle of earthly life in every aspect of relationship, from that of childhood through school days to maturity, in personal, social, commercial, and national affairs, so it enters into religion, and we are thus able to see the meaning of the words, "Without faith it is impossible to please Him" (Heb. xi. 6). Trust is the only adequate answer to God's Revelation. Just as the absence of faith makes it impossible for human beings to have any dealings with each other, so the absence of faith in God makes it wholly impossible for us to have any association with Him. "He that cometh to God must believe" (Heb. xi. 6). Trust is thus the correlative of truth. Faith in man answers to grace in God. As such, it affects the whole of man's nature. It commences with the conviction of the mind based on adequate evidence; it continues in the confidence of the heart or emotions based on the above conviction, and it is crowned in the consent of the will, by means of which the conviction and confidence are expressed in conduct. This is perhaps the meaning of the words, "Faith is the substance of things hoped for, the evidence of things not seen" (Heb. xi. 1). The passage is not so much a definition of faith as a description of it in relation to life, and as such it is illustrated by the examples of faith throughout that chapter. Thus faith is the outgoing of the whole nature to what it believes to be true, or rather, to Him Who is held to be the Truth. It is this that Hooker meant when he spoke of faith as including (1) the certainty of evidence, and (2) the certainty of adherence. Faith is not blind, but intelligent, since it rests on the conviction of the authority of Christ as Teacher, Saviour, and Lord. The threefold Revelation of Christ as Prophet, Priest, and King, revealing, redeeming, and ruling, is met by the response of the whole life, intellect, emotion, and will. This combination of all the elements in human nature involves a moral decision which is illustrated in almost every part of the New Testament (Acts ii. 41; xvii. 11; 1 Thess. i. 5; Jas. i. 21).

But it is necessary to note that the word Faith is also used for the substance of doctrine as well as for the attitude of the soul, for *fides quæ creditur* as well as *fides qua creditur*. This is sometimes spoken of as "the Faith," meaning the Christian truth which is everywhere believed among Christians. It is seen in such expressions as "the faith which was once for all delivered unto the saints" (Jude 3, R.V.); "the common faith" (Tit. i. 4); "the faith of the Gospel" (Phil. i. 27). This twofold use of the term "Faith" necessitates the greatest possible care in distinguishing between believing truths and trusting a Person. The Church Catechism first of all refers to believing "all the articles of the Christian Faith"; that is, the various parts or points of the Christian religion. But this is only a means to an end, since the supreme object of Christian faith can be none other than God Himself. Consequently, the Catechism appropriately follows the rehearsal of the Creed by the Question and Answer, "What dost thou chiefly learn by these articles of thy belief?" "I learn to believe in God." It is only too possible to believe with an intellectual conviction the facts and truths of Christianity, and yet to fall short of full trust in God. When we read that the devils believe and tremble (Jas. ii. 19), we see the difference between intellectual conviction and personal trust. These two elements of faith are found from time to time in Holy Scripture. Thus our Lord speaks in one passage, first, of "hearing His Word;" that is, receiving and accepting intellectually what He said; and, then, of believing on God Who sent Him; that is, personal trust in God arising out of the acceptance of Christ's Word (John v. 24). Nothing short of the latter can satisfy the requirements of the Christian religion.[1] All facts and truths are intended as the food, warrant, and inspiration of full trust, and are intended only to lead to this outgoing of the whole soul in personal confidence in and dependence on God. Danger lies in the frequent implication that man only needs instruction, while overlooking the solemn truth that by reason of sin he needs illumination as well. So that while the intellect is not to be neglected, faith is very much more than knowledge. It is not mere belief in a thought, or conception, or idea. It is the expression of the whole nature of man in response to God's approach in Christ. As such, it involves personal committal and confidence. Conviction alone stops short with orthodoxy, and is liable to lead to formalism, but to be orthodox

[1] Bishop Pearson (*Creed*, Article I) quoting Durandus, says: "'*credere in Deum*' non est præcise actus fidei, sed fidei et caritatis simul."

is not to be saved. Faith is the surrender of the soul to God and the appropriation of the grace which saves. Correct views of Christ are essential and vital. It behoves us to be thoroughly acquainted with the facts and truths of the Christian religion related to the Person of Christ, His Resurrection, the Holy Spirit, the Bible, and all else. But it must not be assumed that all is settled when the facts of the Christian religion are guaranteed and understood. We may inspect the records and make sure of the history and all the while may only obtain information about God without a personal experience of Him in the soul. Intellectual beliefs are valuable as means to ends, but not as ends themselves. In all true faith, therefore, there will of necessity be the three elements of knowledge, assent, and confidence, and anything short of these will never give the full Christian trust. The knowledge of God consists in sympathetic understanding of His character. We only know our friends so far as mutual sympathy gives us insight into their real nature. There are certain distinctions in the original languages of the Creeds, the Latin of the Apostles' Creed and the Greek of the Nicene Creed, which help to make this clear. In Latin *Credo Deum* (*esse*) means, " I believe God exists "; *Credo Deo*, " I believe what God says "; *Credo in Deum*, " I trust God."[1]

When once we have learned that God is the True Object of faith and we have been made acquainted with the substance of Christian truth, we naturally enquire what precisely we are to believe about God as essential, as distinct from that which is purely accidental. Our enquiry is met by being directed to Holy Scripture. This is the guide and standard of our faith, and the supreme authority as to what we are to believe. We shall see in Article VI that this is the fundamental principle of the Church of England. " Holy Scripture containeth all things necessary to salvation; so that whatsoever is not read therein, nor may be proved thereby, is not to be required of any man, that it should be believed as an article of the Faith, or be thought requisite or necessary to salvation." God has given His people a written Revelation of Himself, and this tells us clearly all that it is necessary for us to know about God. The more we ponder this Revelation the more we shall learn to know and trust God Who is revealed here. " Faith cometh by hearing, and hearing by the Word of God " (Rom. x. 17). The Bible is therefore of first importance for Christian knowledge and life. In theological language it is " the Rule of Faith," affording us information about truth and preserving us against error. The Creeds which we accept and hold are summaries of what the Bible contains, and are subordinate to the Bible as a secondary Rule of Faith.

---

[1] "In every movement of faith, therefore, from the lowest to the highest, there is an intellectual, an emotional, and a voluntary element, though naturally these elements vary in their relative prominence in the several movements of faith. This is only as much as to say that it is the man who believes, who is the subject of faith, and the man in the entirety of his being as man" (Warfield, *Princeton Theological Review*, Vol. IX, p. 566).

DOCTRINE

The New Testament has two words for *doctrine*, διδαχή, and διδασκαλία (2 Tim. iv. 2, 3 ; Tit. i. 9). Both together they occur about fifty times. The word " doctrine " itself is colourless, and is therefore used for truth and error : (*a*) doctrine of God (Tit. ii. 10); of Christ (2 John 9); " sound " (1 Tim. i. 10); " good " (1 Tim. iv. 6). (*b*) Of men (Col. ii. 22); of demons (1 Tim. iv. 1); every wind (Eph. iv. 14); divers and strange (Heb. xiii. 9). This necessitates the use of the term " Christian " doctrine to express the truths of Divine Revelation, and perhaps we may define Christian doctrine as the fundamental truths of revelation arranged in systematic form. Dogma, like other Greek words in μα, stands for something fixed, completed, *quod statutum est*.[1]

THEOLOGY

The term " theology " is used for the scientific expression of all truths relating to divine revelation. Just as nature has to be distinguished from science, so has revelation from theology. Science is the technical expression of the laws of nature ; theology is the technical expression of the revelation of God. It is the province of theology to examine all the spiritual facts of revelation, to estimate their value, and to arrange them into a body of teaching. Doctrine thus corresponds with the generalisations of science. Theology, as the science of religion, is concerned with all the phenomena of revelation recorded in Holy Scripture.

Special attention has been given of recent years to what is now known as Biblical Theology, which means theology drawn direct from the Bible and formulated along the lines in which it is there presented. It possesses at once variety and unity ; variety, because it was not given all at once, but at stages ; unity, because the Bible is held to contain a complete view of theological thought. It is the work of Biblical Theology to set forth this variety and unity of truth.

Dogmatic Theology is the systematised statement of truth deduced from the Bible, the intellectual expression in technical language of what is contained in the Word of God. Martensen defines dogmatics as " the science which presents and proves the Christian doctrines regarded as forming a connected system."[2] Dogmatic Theology is not necessarily non-Biblical, and Biblical Theology itself depends on the standpoint of the writer.[3]

---

[1] "A dogma is not a δόξα, not a subjective, human opinion, not an indefinite, vague notion; nor is it a mere truth of reason, whose universal validity can be made clear with mathematical or logical certainty: it is a truth of *faith*, derived from the authority of the word and revelation of God;—a positive truth, therefore, positive not merely by virtue of the positiveness with which it is laid down, but also by virtue of the authority with which it is sealed" (Martensen, *Christian Dogmatics*, p. 1).
[2] *Christian Dogmatics*, p. 1.
[3] "Biblical or New Testament theology deals with the thoughts, or the mode of thinking, of the various New Testament writers; systematic theology is the independent

There is obvious danger in every attempt at systematising Christian
truth, as we may see from the great works of men like Aquinas and
Calvin.   The human mind is unable to find a place for every single
Christian doctrine, and it is far better to be content with " Articles," or
" points," with gaps unfilled, because it is impossible for thought to be
covered by them.   General lines of Christian truth are far safer and
also truer to the growth of thought and experience through the ages.
This method prevents teaching becoming hardened into a cast-iron
system which cannot expand.   It is the virtue of the Church of England
Articles that they take this line and do not commit Churchmen to an
absolute, rigid system of doctrine from which there is no relief and of
which there is no modification.

CREEDS, CONFESSIONS, AND ARTICLES

Faith is response to divine revelation, and confession is the expression
of faith.

" What song is to the victory it celebrates, confession is to the religious spirit.
. . . Religion, like Science, not only seeks and finds the hid treasures of truth,
but is fain to cry ' Eureka.' . . . Religion only betrays an instinct which is
universal throughout all the higher interests and activities of humanity when it
thus gives utterance, in language as august as lips can frame, to its mature
convictions."[1]

Every religion has a Creed in one form or another, and we are therefore not surprised to find that the confession of the Christian faith has
taken various shapes through the ages.   The Creed, properly so-called,
is a short, comprehensive statement of belief suitable for discipleship and
worship.   The earliest form of this was personal, expressive of personal
confidence in Christ ;   it was the natural outcome of the possession of
spiritual life.   But even here the intellect was necessarily involved, for
to believe in Christ was to take up some intellectual attitude in relation
to Him.   Very soon a more elaborate confession of faith was felt to be
necessary, and in due course enquiry and examination at Baptism led to
further tests and requirements.   Later on the pressure of various heresies
accentuated the need of a careful statement of the Christian position.
The making of Creeds may be said to have covered the first four
centuries of the Christian era, and then nothing of importance in this
respect happened until the dawn of new light and life in the sixteenth
century, when confessions of faith and full statements of specific belief

construction of Christianity as a whole in the mind of a later thinker.   Here again
there is a broad and valid distinction, but not an absolute one.   It is the Christian
thinking of the first century in the one case, and of the twentieth, let us say, in the
other; but in both cases there is Christianity and there is thinking, and if there is truth
in either, there is bound to be a place at which the distinction disappears" (Denney,
The Death of Christ, p. 5).

[1] W. A. Curtis, History of Creeds and Confessions of Faith, p. 2.

arose in connection with the Reformation movement. There had been debates and discussions in the Middle Ages, but they were not theological and Christological. There seems to have been no desire to reopen problems settled ages before by the great Councils, but there was much thought and no little discussion on such matters as the Church, Ministry, Sacraments, and personal religion. When, however, the various Reformed Churches broke loose from Rome it was found essential to state their position with reference to the specific reasons for protest. As a result we find entire agreement on fundamental facts with very different expressions of the specific applications of those facts.

Creeds and Confessions are sometimes contrasted to the detriment of the latter, but a study of the historical order of emergence of these documents of the faith suggests a comparison rather than a contrast. As we follow in order the three Creeds themselves, the Apostles', the Nicene, and the Athanasian, we find that there is a tendency to elaboration, to a fuller theological statement, and to an explanation of what is involved in the original summary of belief. The confessions of faith in the sixteenth century are really only an extension, prolongation, and development of the same process.

If it be said that these Articles and other documents of the sixteenth century are incomplete, and do not provide an adequate statement of belief, it may be pointed out that the same is true of the Creeds. There are many subjects unnoticed in the ecumenical documents of our faith, and we believe this is one of the instances in which the Church has been definitely guided by God. The Church Universal is only committed to a comparatively few fundamental realities, and we might as well complain of the incompleteness of any of the three Creeds as criticise the incompleteness of any of the sixteenth-century Confessions of Faith. They must be judged in the light of the circumstances which gave them birth, and with strict and constant regard to their specific purpose.

THE ANGLICAN ARTICLES

The Thirty-nine Articles have a threefold value and importance :—

(a) Historical : In relation to their origin. They are part of the Reformation position and protest. Definition was necessary on the part of all who differed from Rome, and as a result all the Reformed Churches drew up their protest in the form of Confessions, or Articles. Our Articles are thus not only analogous to documents of Continental Churches, but were also influenced by them. They cannot be separated from their historical root in relation to Rome. They mark the position of the Church of England as it was re-stated in the sixteenth century, and they are equally important now for the same reason. They still mark our present position and attitude.

Another aspect of the connection of the Articles with Rome lies in the fact that they were written by men who had been taught and trained in the system of Roman theology, and a knowledge of the Roman Catholic controversy is therefore essential to a full understanding of the Articles. But in addition to the necessity of declaring their attitude against Rome, the Reformers were compelled to take action against dangers from the opposite direction. The inevitable swing of the intellectual and moral pendulums had produced serious errors of many kinds, and these were being charged by Rome on all Reformers and attributed to the Reformation movement in general. It was therefore essential not only to define what the true Reformation position was, but also to do everything possible to safeguard its members from reactionary or other errors which had become rife in different localities.

(b) Doctrinal: in relation to Church doctrine. They are of supreme value as giving the standard of Church of England doctrine on (1) points identical with the doctrines of other Churches, and on (2) points characteristic of our own position. They give with exactness, balance, and fulness the supreme voice of our Church on all matters covered therein.

(c) Practical: in relation to the Christian life. The Articles express the intellectual position involved in being a believer, the explicit, intellectual sign of what is spiritually implicit from the first moment of faith in Christ. When He is accepted as Saviour, Lord, and God, everything else is involved and possessed in germ. We commence by *faith* and go on to *knowledge*. It is inevitable that we should think out our position. St. Peter tells us to be ready to give a reason for the hope that is in us (1 Pet. iii. 15), and we see the natural order of experience followed by expression. (1) Hope possessed; (2) having a reason for our hope; (3) giving a reason. The intellectual grasp of Christianity is essential for a strong Christian life, for giving balance and force to experience, for protection against error, for equipment for service. It is possible to be thought spiritual and yet to be only emotional without intellectual clearness and power. This will inevitably produce weakness and lead to the earnest soul becoming a prey to error from one side or another.

It is easy to decry doctrine, and yet the power of science to-day is in its dogmas, not in its generalisations. Great ideas, like the conservation of energy, gravitation, the indestructibility of matter, as held and taught by scientists, are a great power. In the same way Christianity must be strong in its ideas of the personality of God, the Person and Work of Christ, the Holy Spirit, and other related truths. If it be said that religion is possible without doctrine, it may be fully admitted, and yet the question at once arises of what sort will it be. It can only be suited to spiritual childhood, not manhood. Great music involves the theory of music, and a religion without theory will be like a babe with love, but with no ideas. It is doctrine that makes grown men. It is simply impossible to have a religion worthy of the name without some dogma.[1]

---

[1] "Undogmatic religion is, strictly speaking, a contradiction in terms. Dogma is not indeed like Faith, the living spirit of religion; but it is at least the skeleton of all

It is, of course, essential to remember that theology is not merely a matter of intellect, but also of experience. Theology is concerned with spiritual realities, and must include personal experience as well as ideas. *Pectus facit theologum.* This association of theology with experience will always prevent the former from continuing merely abstract and philosophical. Dogmatics, as Martensen points out, must come from within the Church, and not from outside. It is a science of faith, with faith as its basis and source.[1] In past days theology has been too closely limited to metaphysics, intellectualism, and philosophy. The Articles bear the marks of this tendency of the age which produced them. But while the intellectual element must necessarily always be at the basis of every presentation of Christian truth, the intellect is not the only, perhaps not the dominant factor, and other elements must enter. The feeling equally with the reason must share in the consideration of theology, because theology is of the heart, and the deepest truths are inextricably bound up with personal needs and experiences. The moral consciousness of man must also find a place and conscience be allowed to take its part in the provision of a true Creed. This is only one instance out of many which proves the impossibility of limiting ourselves to that which is merely rational, and also the absolute necessity of emphasising the personal and ethical in our discussion of theology. Time was when Dogmatics and Ethics were separated, and the latter regarded as subsidiary and supplementary to the former. But this is not possible to-day. A theology which is not ethical, while it includes ethics, cannot be rightly called theology.[2]

But here again we must not allow ourselves to go to the opposite extreme and refuse a place to metaphysics and philosophy in our consideration and construction of Christian theology. It is impossible to keep our view of Christianity in any watertight compartment, be it purely intellectual, or purely emotional, or purely ethical. As Christianity speaks to every part of our nature, so every part must take its share in the reception and expression of Christian theology.

Our study of doctrine must therefore include the consideration of

embodied religion, the framework, however transitory, of the physical organisation of its life. Faith that is real will out. Faith that is uttered in dogma, like life that is born, may perish; but it is the medium of a manifested spiritual life, mortal like flesh and blood, but like them with a sanctity of its own" (W. A. Curtis, *op. cit.*, p. 3).

[1] "It springs out of the perennial, juvenile vigour of faith, out of the capacity of faith to unfold from its own depths a wealth of treasures of wisdom and of knowledge, to build up a kingdom of acknowledged truths, by which it illumines itself as well as the surrounding world" (*op. cit.*, p. 3).

[2] Fragment of a conversation between a Professor of Moral Science in an American College and a student just about to graduate from a certain Theological Seminary:
Professor: "Are you entirely satisfied with your course in theology?"
Student: "No, the course has been of value to me, but it has one lack."
Professor: "What? I am interested."
Student: "In studying the Bible and Christian doctrine no connection was anywhere made with moral science."
Professor: "I am not surprised. The theologian is quite wont to forget that a sinner is a man" (O. A. Curtis, *The Christian Faith*, p. 2).

God as its Object of Faith, and the Standard of duty, and the relation between God and man must be shown to include both worship and work, attitude and action, creed and conduct. Our doctrine of Theism, of Christology, of the Holy Spirit, of Divine sovereignty, of the Atonement, of sin, of justification, and the rest, must be closely and constantly related to life in every part if it is to be of weight in modern days. While not making human feeling the sole standard of truth, or human duty the test of theological accuracy, we must certainly enquire whether our intellectual conception of truth possesses ethical vitality, whether it makes for practical righteousness. History in the past warns us against the tendency to allow the intellectual aspects of Christianity to become abstract. We see this in the dreary wastes of controversy which followed Chalcedon, and again in the era of Protestant scholasticism which followed the warm, living experience of the Reformation Age. On the other hand, recent theological discussions have given us an equally grave warning against the tendency to rest in anything merely emotional without satisfying ourselves of its intellectual validity. Modern impatience against dogma, whether on the part of the Ritschlian theologian, or of " the man in the street," springs essentially from the same fundamental source, and is a phase of that practical agnosticism which would insist that no valid knowledge of God and His truth is possible. We must therefore preserve the mean between these two extremes, neither excluding ethics from theology, nor regarding theology as " a footnote to morality." When Creeds, Confessions, and Articles are thus related to every part of personality—mind, emotion, conscience, and will—we may feel sure that our theology is what it ought to be.

The sole and sufficient guarantee of Christian doctrine being at once intellectual and experimental is its constant and close association with the Person of Jesus Christ. In order to avoid anything dry and lifeless we must relate every truth to the living Person of Him Who declared, " I am the Way, the Truth, and the Life." When it is realised that " Christianity is Christ," that Christ Himself is the substance, source, and spring of all doctrine, our theology will be truly Christian.

THE HISTORY OF THE ARTICLES

THE Thirty-nine Articles must be viewed as part of a large number of Confessions issued about the same time. Definition of their position was essential on the part of the Reformers, and our Articles were both suggested by Continental Confessions and also influenced by them. For centuries abuses in the Church had been recognised and almost wholly unheeded, but forces were at work which paved the way for Reformation.[1] The movement in the sixteenth century was a return to the pure and simple faith of Christianity as embodied in Holy Scripture.

There is no distinction in character between our Articles and the Continental formularies such as the Lutheran Confessions. Though Luther and Calvin each emphasised particular doctrines which had been overlain or misrepresented, our formularies show the general attitude of Reformed belief as against Rome. The Reformation was mainly personal, concerned with the application of truth, and there was no desire or intention of questioning the fundamental theistic articles of the Creeds.[2] Indeed, it is interesting to notice that while the Reformers insisted on the supremacy of Scripture they were anxious to show that their views were also in accord with, and so far subordinated to, the Creeds of the Church.

An additional need for the formulation of the Reformed position was found in the excesses of the Anabaptists and others. The Renaissance was an intellectual new birth, and it is not surprising that on the discovery that much which had hitherto been held sacrosanct was really spurious, some went to extremes and denied the fundamental faith as well as the accretions of Rome. Superstition produces infidelity by a natural reaction. It was therefore necessary for the Reformers to

---

[1] "Beneath the rigorously smoothed and levelled surface of mediæval Christendom there lay but thinly covered the fruitful seeds of the various outgrowths of the Reformation. It is easy now to discern how far-reaching was the doctrinal and practical preparation for the great movement. For centuries before the crisis was reached, over against the demand of the Roman Curia that all learning and all thought, as well as all political and ecclesiastical life, should be organised in subjection to it, influences had been at work to stimulate freedom of thought and action" (W. A. Curtis, *A History of Creeds and Confessions of Faith*, p. 126).

[2] "Not the Person and Work of Christ or of the Holy Spirit, not the doctrine of the Divine Trinity, but the doctrines of the means of grace, Church, Ministry, Sacraments, and Scripture, of the processes involved in personal salvation, and of the use of mediators other than the Son of God, were the themes at issue" (W. A. Curtis, *ut supra*, p. 127).

state their position, and in the face of enemies to distinguish themselves from those who went to the extreme of denial. Nor may we overlook the fact that some statement of Protestant belief was required for the guidance and test of those who were, or wished to be, ministers of the Reformed Gospel. To preach the truth men must know that for which our Reformers stood.

We must therefore judge the character of these formularies of the sixteenth century by the circumstances of their origin and composition. They were due to fierce current controversies, and any resulting disproportion must be taken into consideration.[1]

LUTHERAN CONFESSIONS

Literature.—W. A. Curtis, *A History of Creeds and Confessions of Faith*, Ch. VIII; Hardwick, *History of the Articles of Religion*, Chs. I and II; Maclear and Williams, *Introduction to the Articles*, Ch. II.

Luther's early efforts against Rome naturally involved an attempt at doctrinal formulation, and the way was gradually prepared for a detailed statement which sooner or later was inevitable. The Greater and Lesser Catechisms of Luther (1527-1529) had great influence in Germany, but something much more definite and theological was soon required. The older Creeds were mainly concerned with the doctrines of the Godhead, but as the Reformation was essentially personal in addition, a Confession of this type was needed. But a special cause was also at work. Some German States were in danger of suppression by the Emperor for their Reformed opinions. The Diet of Spires (or Speier), 1529, protested against any forcing of conscience in religious matters, and so in 1530 a Diet met at Augsburg and stated its beliefs. There had been two or three earlier, but more limited, statements like the Articles of Schwabach, 1529, and of Torgau, 1530, but the Confession of Augsburg was by far the most important document of the Reformation, and has attained a permanent position and value.[2] This was drawn up by Melanchthon and Luther, subscribed June 1530, and

---

[1] "They all bear the marks of their birth-time and birth-place, and it is to the distinctive and often transitory features in them that they draw our chief attention. It is unjust to judge them without regard to their origin and their purpose. Few, if any, of them were fair-weather or leisurely productions laid out for academic criticism or appreciation. Many of them were the work of hunted, outlawed men, and were sealed with martyr blood. They were literally *extempore*" (W. A. Curtis, *ut supra*, p. 128).

[2] "The 'Augustana' (or Confession of Augsburg) is the classical statement of Lutheran doctrine, and has remained to the present day the bond between all Lutheran Churches. Its dignified simplicity, its temperate tone, and its Christian spirit have endeared it to successive generations, and have made it the model as well as the mother of later Confessions. Portions of it have become obsolete. The piety and thought it has fostered have outgrown their original vestments. But its profound loyalty to the best traditions of the Catholic Church and the great Fathers, its faithfulness to Scripture, none the less impressive because it is unlaboured and unobtrusive, and its deep note of evangelical experience, have secured for it a sacred place, perhaps beyond all other Confessions, in the living faith of its ministers and people" (Curtis, *ut supra*, p. 142 f.).

publicly read. It consisted of two parts : (1) Faith, covering twenty-one Articles; (2) Abuses, covering seven Articles. Thus it is concerned with positive beliefs and protests against abuses. There was a strong desire for reformation within the Church, if at all possible.[1] But though signed by representatives of Church and State it failed to accomplish its purpose of producing peace, and soon gave rise to further developments in the reforming direction. Yet it left its mark on all subsequent documents, and abides to this day as a monument of influence in Lutheran Churches.

The next Reformation Confession is known as the Articles of Schmalcald, 1537, which have been described as " Luther's last contribution to the Confessions of Protestantism." There was the expectation of a Council at Mantua, summoned by Pope Paul III, and Luther prepared these Articles for presentation to that assembly. There was no intention on the part of Protestants to appear at Mantua, but it was thought necessary to state the Protestant view, and Luther did so without any qualification. This statement of belief did much to bring about the final separation.

Other documents were the Saxon Confession, 1551, and the Confession of Wurtemberg, 1552, drawn up respectively by Melanchthon and Brentius in view of the meeting of the Council of Trent. The latter consisted of Thirty-five Articles framed on the model of the Confession of Augsburg.

Of all these Lutheran documents the two of most importance for the Church of England were the Confessions of Augsburg and Wurtemberg. The former, as we shall see later on, influenced the Articles of 1553,[2] and the latter those of 1563.

Other Lutheran documents were subsequently forthcoming in connection with Reformation controversies which came to a head in the Formula Concordiæ, the authoritative books of the Lutheran Church. These deserve notice because, as will be observed, in them the doctrine of our Article XXIX of 1571 is clearly denied and denounced. Although never so authoritative as the Confession of Augsburg, the Formula Concordiæ is a document of great importance.

---

[1] "The whole Confession, . . . is eloquent of its author's yearning to promote the reunion of divided Christendom; it breathes the spirit of defence, not defiance. It enphasises points of agreement before it affirms points of conscientious difference. To many Romanists it was an amazing revelation of the essential Catholicism of Lutheran teaching. To all it was proffered as a *via media* between the paths of sharp divergence " (Curtis, *ut supra*, p. 149). Melanchthon wrote an "Apology" of it a year later.

[2] "That Confession is most intimately connected with the progress of the English Reformation; and besides the influence which it cannot fail to have exerted by its rapid circulation in our country, it contributed directly, in a large degree, to the construction of the public Formularies of Faith put forward by the Church of England. The XIII Articles, drawn up, as we shall see, in 1538, were based almost entirely on the language of the great Germanic Confession; while a similar expression of respect is no less manifest in the Articles of Edward VI, and consequently in that series which is binding now upon the conscience of the English clergy" (Hardwick, *ut supra*, p. 13).

c

"REFORMED" CONFESSIONS

Literature.—Curtis, *ut supra*, Chs. XII–XV.

While the Reformation in Germany was, as we have seen, largely subjective, that in Switzerland, under Zwingli and Calvin, was also objective. Although none of the documents connected with the "Reformed" Churches seem to have had a direct influence on our Articles, yet they are useful, if not essential, for comparison of views.

1.—*Creeds connected with Zwingli*

(*a*) The Sixty-seven Articles of Zwingli, 1523.[1]
(*b*) The First Confession of Basle, 1532.
(*c*) The First Helvetic Confession, 1536.[2]

2.—*Creeds connected with Calvin*

(*a*) Calvin's Institutes, 1549.[3]
(*b*) Second Helvetic Confession, 1566. The work of the great Henry Bullinger, "last and greatest in the Zwinglian series."[4]
(*c*) The Synod of Dort, 1619.
(*d*) The Westminster Confession, 1647.[5]

[1] "The Reformation produced no more impressive or thought-provoking document" (Curtis, *ut supra*, p. 195).

[2] "It owed its origination to the peace-making genius of the Strassburg theologians, Bucer and Capito, who made it their great aim to reconcile the Swiss and Lutheran schools of Protestant doctrine—and also to the prospect of an Ecumenical Council being convened at Mantua" (Curtis, *ut supra*, p. 203).

[3] "If it inspired instant alarm in Romanist quarters, or won converts from them, if its pellucid Latinity and its masterly theology won admiration alike from foes and from rivals, it became for Protestants of well-nigh every type a veritable oracle, a source from which confessional, catechetic, and homiletic wants were unfailingly supplied. In diction, in structure, in comprehensiveness, in sheer mass and weight, in unflagging interest and power, in dignity and severe simplicity, it has all the characteristics of a classic. While recognising that it can never be for us what it was to earlier centuries, we cannot but lament that, in an age which so freely proclaims its emancipation from its spell, so few should read it for themselves, so many should condemn it cheaply and at second hand. Signs are not wanting that at no distant time justice will be more generally done to Calvin as a prince among systematic theologians not less than a prince among Christian exegetes" (Curtis, *ut supra*, p. 20).

[4] Curtis, *ut supra*, p. 207.

"No other Confessions, save its immediate predecessor, the Heidelberg Catechism of 1563, has ever rivalled it in popularity or in authority among the Reformed Churches of the Continent. . . . It is no small tribute to its merits that its appearance was the signal for the cessation of theological controversy and unrest in Switzerland, and that it enjoyed, during so many centuries of eager thought and change, an unchallenged authority" (Curtis, *ut supra*, p. 208).

[5] "It marks the maturest and most deliberate formulation of the scheme of Biblical revelation as it appeared to the most cultured and the most devout Puritan minds. It was the last great Creed-utterance of Calvinism, and intellectually and theologically it is a worthy child of the *Institutes*, a stately and noble standard for Bible-loving men. While influenced necessarily by Continental learning and controversy, it is essentially British, as well by heredity as by environment; for not only is it based upon the Thirty-nine Articles, modified and supplemented in a definitely Calvinistic sense at Lambeth and at Dublin, but it literally incorporates Ussher's Irish Articles, accepting their order and titles, and using, often without a word of change, whole sentences and paragraphs" (Curtis, *ut supra*, p. 275).

Now although, as it has been said, no direct and specific influence, such as came from Augsburg and Wurtemberg, can be traced from these formularies in the wording of our Articles, the documents themselves are valuable as showing the essential harmony of doctrine among the Reformers amid many details of difference. Expressions on doctrine like Predestination differ, but the difference is one of degree rather than of kind. There is nothing more striking than the fact that while our Articles are often verbally identical with those of Augsburg, their doctrine of the Sacraments is, and always has been, of the " Reformed," not the Lutheran type. And in the reign of Elizabeth Convocation ordered Bullinger's Decades " to be read and studied by the clergy."

THE CHURCH OF ROME

Literature.—Curtis, *ut supra*, Ch. VII.

The Reformation movement could not help affecting Rome, and it had therefore been determined that Protestants were not to be conciliated, but, if possible, crushed. Hence came the exclusion of Protestants from the Council of Trent, which made it impossible to do justice to the Reformed position. The result was the Canons and Decrees of the Council of Trent, 1545-1563, of which it has been well said, " The decrees are the utterance of jealous defence, the Canons with their anathemas are the challenge of proud defiance."[1] These were followed by the Creed and Catechism of Pope Pius IV, 1564, intended for younger clergy and now used for Protestant converts to Roman Catholicism. These are all authoritative documents to-day. The Council met in December 1545, and sat until 1547, when it was suspended until 1551. Then it sat until April 1553, when it was suspended until 1562, and at length its deliberations were completed in January 1564.

There was a distinct alternation of views between Rome and Protestantism. The two parties worked in sight of each other, and everything done by the Council up to 1551 was in clear view of the English revisers in 1553.[2] That the Protestants were interested in and informed of what was going on at Trent is abundantly clear.[3] Further evidence

---

[1] Curtis, *ut supra*, p. 107.

[2] "In several letters of Reformers we observe the interest with which they were watching the contemporary disputations at Trent, especially in the course of the eventful year, 1551: *e.g.* Cranmer's *Works*, I, 346, 349" (Hardwick, *ut supra*, p. 84, footnote 1).

[3] "Cranmer, just before the issue of the revised Second Prayer Book in 1552, and the first appearance of the Articles in 1553, wrote to Calvin (20th March 1552): 'Our adversaries are now holding their Councils at Trent for the establishment of their errors; and shall we neglect to call together godly synod, for the refutation of error, and for restoring and propagating the truth? They are, as I am informed, making decrees respecting the worship of the host : Wherefore we ought to leave no stone unturned, not only that we may guard others against this idolatry, but also that we may ourselves come to an agreement upon the doctrine of this sacrament' (Cranmer, *Miscellaneous Writings*, p. 432—Parker Soc.). Sir John Cheke, tutor to the King, and one who had been consulted by Cranmer about the Articles before they were published, wrote to Bullinger on 7th June 1553, after their publication, saying that the King 'has published

will be given when particular Articles are considered, but whether or not our formularies refer to Trent, there is no question about the attitude of our Articles to Rome, and great care must be taken lest we obtain a wrong impression of their character.

THE EASTERN CHURCH

This Church has always prided itself on its steadfast adherence to the orthodox Faith, based on the seven General Councils, the Trullan Council, 692, and the Second Council of Nicæa, 787. But even this Communion could not help being influenced to some little extent by what was going on in Western Europe. Cyril Lucar, Patriarch successively of Alexandria and Constantinople, imbibed Calvinism in Switzerland in the seventeenth century, but he suffered by reason of his Protestant opinions.[1] The Eastern Church repudiated his teaching, publicly and formally, and it has since formally adopted the doctrine of Transubstantiation, so that its Confessions include not only the worship of Images, but Transubstantiation, both name and thing. Thus Cyril Lucar in no sense represents the teaching of the Eastern Church at the present day. The Eastern Church does not really abide by the ancient Councils, but even *since* the Western Reformation has modified its standpoint in a Romeward sense. The " unchanging East " has, in fact, altered its standards more recently than the Western Churches of the Reformation.

THE ENGLISH ARTICLES IN THE REIGN OF HENRY VIII

THE ENGLISH REFORMATION

Literature.—Hardwick, *History of the Articles of Religion*, Ch. I; Curtis, *A History of Creeds and Confessions of Faith*, Ch. XI; Maclear and Williams, *Introduction to the Articles*, Ch. III; Tyrrell Green, *The Thirty-nine Articles and the Age of the Reformation*, Ch. II; Gibson, *The Thirty-nine Articles*, Ch. I; Lindsay, *The History of the Reformation*, Vol. II, Book IV, Ch. I; Kidd, *The Thirty-nine Articles*, Ch. II.

THERE was a decided difference as well as a real oneness between the English and Continental Reformations. The latter were first religious and then political; the former was first political and then religious.

the Articles of the Synod of London, which, if you will compare with those of Trent, you will understand how the spirit of the one exceeds that of the other. Why should I say more? I send you the book itself as a token of my regard'" (*Original Letters*, p. 142).

[1] A clergyman of the Cypriote Greek Church told the writer in 1907 that Cyril Lucar was not really Calvinistic, and referred to *Revue Internationale de Théologie*, Avril–Juin 1906, No. 54, pp. 327–330, and No. 53, pp. 17–20. But see Curtis, *ut supra*, p. 253, and references in Note.

Up to the sixteenth century the English Church had long been virtually and for practical purposes a part of the Church of Rome, in the same sense that the Churches of the other nations of Europe were. Our Reformers were all priests of that Communion, and both in doctrine and organisation there was fundamental identity, the English Church, that is, the organised society of baptised people in England, being an integral part of the great Western Church. "No tie of an ecclesiastical or spiritual kind bound the Bishop of Chichester to the Bishop of Carlisle, except that which bound them both to French and Spanish Bishops."[1] The assertions of independence from time to time came from Parliament, but never touched questions of doctrine. On the eve of the Reformation this was the general situation.[2]

The movement in the reign of Henry VIII was very gradual, being almost wholly personal and scarcely at all doctrinal. But it was impossible to ignore what was going on in Germany and elsewhere on the Continent, as well as among the laity in England, in the direction of Reform, and though no doctrinal break with Rome was possible during the reign of Henry VIII there were forces at work tending to produce effects which would inevitably bring about great changes. It was four years after the Confession of Augsburg that Henry's final break with Rome took place. Yet this did not involve any breach of essential doctrine, but only the severance from Papal authority, the King being substituted for the Pope as supreme Head.

The break on personal grounds through Henry's divorce afforded the opportunity of realising the King's idea of making the Church as national and English as it had been Roman since the days of Alfred. But we must distinguish between the occasion and the cause. King Henry's domestic and dynastic circumstances were the occasion, but certainly not the cause of the Reformation, for there were forces at work which were all tending to produce far-reaching effects. The Reformation

"experienced at Henry's hands as much embarrassment as help, and, though his mind had many enlightened sympathies, the royal 'Defender of the Faith' was not the real inaugurator of Reform. The land of Magna Charta and of John Wyclif could not keep still while the rest of Northern Europe was in the throes of the struggle for religious liberty. It was not likely to submit for ever to an Italian Papacy in the realm of truth and order."[3]

[1] Maitland, *Canon Law*. See also, Smith's *Antiquities of Anglicanism*, and Child's *Church and State under the Tudors*.
[2] "We see the Church of England on its clerical side more and more separated from the civil power from the Conquest to the Reformation; more and more identifying itself with the Church of Rome from Henry I to the Reformation. The Crown had its share in encouraging Papal domination, from its being continually in need of the influence of the hierarchy; but Parliament, so far as its direct enactments went, resisted Papal usurpations, and was the only body in the Constitution that maintained a consistent attitude of independence in regard to the See of Rome" (Hole, *A Manual of English Church History*, p. 113; see also pp. 28, 53, 72 f., 83).
[3] Curtis, *ut supra*, p. 165.

Thus we may see two movements proceeding side by side; the spiritual and the political, quite separate and, during the life of Henry, actually opposed, yet each doing its own part towards freeing our country from the errors and chains of Rome. Cranmer, as Archbishop of Canterbury, was on the one hand a help towards Reformation, and yet on the other his relation to the King made it practically impossible for him to move far or fast. Cranmer's convictions, like those of Luther, were, as we shall see, very gradual, and though the Lutheran Reformation naturally affected the English, there was no slavish following of Luther, while Calvin had no influence until 1550.[1]

Speaking generally, the two greatest names are those of Cranmer and Ridley, whose connection with the Articles of 1553 was close and even predominant, but Parker, in 1563, and Jewel, in 1571, as the final editor, have very great weight. In all stages of the doctrinal movement in England these four men occupied a dominant position, and from their writings may be obtained a clear idea of their position, and consequently a guide to the interpretation to be placed on the formularies for which they were thus responsible.

THE TEN ARTICLES OF 1536

The position following Henry's severance from Rome was at once interesting and difficult. There were two parties, headed respectively by Gardiner and Cranmer. To Gardiner, who had been made Bishop of Winchester, 1531, the rejection of Papal supremacy was sufficient, and when he saw the endeavours being made towards Reformation he opposed them with all his power. Cranmer, on the other hand, as Archbishop of Canterbury, was the leader of the reforming opinions, and saw that in addition to the repudiation of Papal supremacy, doctrinal errors and moral abuses would have to be corrected. But the conflict between these two men was only the personal aspect of far deeper and greater issues. The progress of reforming opinions in England could not fail to be affected by similar movements in Germany, and in addition there were political influences at work which made Henry VIII look in that direction. He had quarrelled with Luther in 1521, but that trouble had passed with the years, and Henry was known to have formed a high opinion of Melanchthon, and he even invited him to England. The community of interests between England and Germany in regard to national independence of the Papacy was a special reason for Henry's

---

[1] "The English was essentially a native Reformation, though assisted from abroad. Much as the English Articles, accordingly, owed to Wittenberg and Switzerland, they retained a character of their own. Like the English Church organisation, service, and traditions, they are not to be summarily described as Lutheran, Zwinglian, or Calvinistic" (Curtis, *ut supra*, p. 165).

"It is abundantly clear that the Anglican Church, since its break with Rome, has been in profound sympathy with the great leaders of the Continental Reformation, both German and Swiss, but it is not hastily to be identified with either of the historic groups" (Curtis, *ut supra*, p. 166).

action, and we are therefore not surprised to find a delegation sent from England to Germany, 1535, the object of which was to find a basis for Henry's association with the German Princes. But Gardiner, then Ambassador at Paris, was the means of preventing any definite political action and also of making Henry hesitate, though the Conference of the English delegates with Lutheran theologians went on, Luther and Melanchthon being present.

The outcome was seen in the Ten Articles of 1536, two years after the separation from Rome, six after Augsburg, and three after the appointment of Cranmer to Canterbury. These Articles consisted of two parts; five dealing with Doctrine and Sacraments, and five with Ceremonies. They were proposed by the King to Convocation, and after much discussion were accepted and published by royal authority. They were entitled, " Articles to establish Christian Quietness and Unity among Us and to avoid Contentious Opinions." The Anabaptists had begun to be troublesome in England and were bringing the Reformation into disrepute, and these Articles were largely directed against them. They did not indicate any positive advance towards the Reformation, though they were clearly influenced by the Reform Movement, for they had three Sacraments, including Penance, which even Luther retained for a long time. There was also an attempt to remove abuses. No general subscription was required, though many Bishops accepted them. They represented a compromise between the old and the new. It was a period of transition, and these Articles showed the oscillation of views. Foxe described them as intended for " weaklings newly weaned from their mother's milk of Rome." While there were three Sacraments there was no mention of the word Transubstantiation, though a doctrine of " impanation " was clearly taught.[1] Images were regarded as representing the Godhead, but were not to be worshipped; saints were to be honoured, but not like God; prayers could be addressed to the saints, but as intercessors, not as redeemers. Papal supremacy was rejected and the royal supremacy substituted. Prominence was given to Holy Scripture as authoritative, the Rule of Faith being the Bible, the Creeds, the Councils, and the Tradition of the Fathers in harmony with Scripture. The following opinions of their character and tendency are worthy of notice :—

" It is only when these Articles are read along with the *Injunctions* issued in 1536 and 1538 that it can be fully seen how much they were meant to wean the people, if gradually, from the gross superstition which disgraced the popular mediæval religion. If this be done, they seem an attempt to fulfil the aspirations of Christian Humanists like Dean Colet and Erasmus."[2]

" The Ten Articles thus authoritatively expounded are anything but ' essenti-

[1] The Tenth Article affirms that "under the form and figure of bread and wine is verily, substantially, and really contained the body and blood of Christ, which 'Corporally, really and in very substance is distributed and received to *all* them that receive the said sacrament.'"

[2] Lindsay, *ut supra*, p. 334.

ally Romish with the Pope left out in the cold.' They are rather an attempt to construct a brief creed which a pliant Lutheran and a pliant Romanist might agree upon—a singularly successful attempt, and one which does great credit to the theological attainments of the English King."[1]

" These Articles, with all their caution, are unmistakably on the side of such reformation as Luther demanded. They were meant to unite old-school and new-school Christians, and to be tender towards everything hallowed by tradition, so long as superstition was not necessarily involved in it. Agreement on a more advanced basis of doctrine was at the time impossible. It is something that Transubstantiation was ignored, that the risks and fact of idolatry in church observances were proclaimed, and that in the *Injunctions* of 1538 a large public Bible was enjoined to be placed in every parish, within the reach of all."[2]

THE SIX ARTICLES OF 1539

In 1537 the Ten Articles were practically superseded by a book known as "The Bishops' Book," and called *The Institution (or Instruction) of a Christian Man.* This consisted of an exposition of the Creed, the Lord's Prayer, the Sacraments, the Ten Commandments, and other points. But as it was not authorised by Convocation or Parliament it only obtained the authority of its signatories, and so since it never received legal sanction the Ten Articles remained legally binding until the publication of the King's Book, 1543.[3] Meantime, after 1536, the parties of

[1] Lindsay, *ut supra*, p. 335.

[2] Curtis, *ut supra*, p. 168 f.

[3] It is necessary to observe carefully the circumstances of the publication of this Book. It was issued by Bishops for the very good reason that neither Parliament nor Convocation sat from July 1536 till March 1539, so that their "sanction" was out of the question. And it is clear that Henry VIII was never fully in accordance with this Book, though it is certain that passively, at least, he was concerned in its issue. The preface to the book is an address to the King, reminding him that "Your Highness commanded us now of late to assemble ourselves together, and upon the diligent search and perusing of Holy Scripture to set forth a plain and sincere doctrine"—they "most humbly submit it to the most excellent wisdom and exact judgment of your Majesty, to be recognised, overseen, and corrected." And to show their determination not to clash with the Royal Supremacy they "knowledge and confess that without the which power and licence of your majesty we have none authority either to assemble ourselves together for any pretence of purpose, or to publish anything that might be by us agreed on and compiled." When after this we find that the King's printer issued the work, we may be sure that while Henry would not commit himself to any responsibility for the statement of the Book as a whole, he permitted the temporary employment of it until a formal revision could be taken in hand. That this was his attitude we learn from the draft reply to the Bishop's address printed in Cranmer's *Works* (Parker Society), Vol. II, p. 469. The controversy between the King and the Primate on this work is given at pp. 83–114 of the same volume, and as Dr. Jacob observes (*Lutheran Movement in England*, p. 112), it shows the "essentially Romanistic" position taken up by the King. Cranmer claimed for the Bishops' Book that it was published by or with the Royal connivance at least. (Cranmer's *Remains*, P.S. page 16). And Bishop Bonner five years *after* the book had been issued required of his London clergy "that you and every of you do procure, and provide of your own, a book called 'The Bishops' Book,' and that you and every of you do exercise yourselves in the same, according to such precepts as hath been given before, or hereafter to be given" (*Formularies of Faith*, p. 382). It is important to recognise that both at the Visitations of the Bishops, in their synods and consistory courts, and also

Gardiner and Cranmer were engaged in an ever-increasing struggle, while political matters affected and complicated the issues. In spite of the failure of the negotiations between England and Germany in 1535-1536, at the King's request three Lutheran divines were sent over to England, and were met by a committee of three, nominated by the King, consisting of Cranmer and two other Bishops. It was hoped to arrive at some concordat, but in 1538 an entire change of the national situation took place by the excommunication of Henry by the Pope. This seemed to the King to necessitate his putting himself right in the eyes of Europe by a vindication of his essential orthodoxy, and under the growing influence of Gardiner a Roman reaction set in notwithstanding Cranmer's opposition. The Conference with the Lutherans resulted in Thirteen Articles, based partly on the Confession of Augsburg and partly on the Ten Articles of 1536, though going beyond the latter in the direction of reform. But they never saw the light till three hundred years later, or acquired any legal force, for the Roman reaction proved too strong.

The importance of the Thirteen, however, is very great as indicating the channel through which the Confession of Augsburg influenced each of the Forty-two Articles of 1553. The discovery of the Thirteen Articles among Cranmer's papers within the last fifty years is as interesting as it is significant. While Cranmer could not effect any doctrinal Reformation as long as Henry was alive, these Articles represent his views at the time of the Conference, and they were found among his papers by Canon Jenkyns and published under the title of *The Thirteen Articles of 1538*.[1] One interesting point is that "The only Article, namely, that on the Lord's Supper, which there is an opportunity of comparing with the conclusions approved by Fox and Heath in Germany, is word for word the same."[2]

But the Six Articles of 1539 shelved everything. They were essentially Roman, and the fact that Convocation passed them shows the revulsion of opinion. They maintained Transubstantiation, Com-

by the High Commission, many things not enacted by Parliament could be and were enforced without let or hindrance.

Dr. Lindsay says (*History of the Reformation*, ii. 336): "The King declined to commit himself, on the plea that he 'had no time convenient to overlook the great pains' bestowed upon the book, which bore the signatures of Lee, Gardiner, Bonner, and was itself the product of a Royal Commission. So that the book was issued by the body of Bishops and divines, whom the King had summoned to draft it, though the King refused to formally commit himself to some of its statements." (From the *Church Intelligencer*, June 1914, p. 94).

[1] Hardwick, *ut supra*, p. 60.

[2] Hardwick, *ut supra*, p. 60. An American writer, Professor Preserved Smith, in the New York *Nation*, 17th December 1914, pointed out that the Thirteen Articles, in turn, were dependent on Seventeen Articles formulated by Luther and Melanchthon at Wittenberg in 1536 and handed to the English Ambassadors, Fox and Heath. This derivation was hardly if at all realised until recent days. The bare existence of the Seventeen Articles had been known from Seckendorf's *Historia Lutheranismi*, 1596, who called them a *repetitio et exegesis confessionis Augustanæ*, but the document had been lost and was first rediscovered in the Weimar archives, published, and its relation to the Thirteen Articles demonstrated by Professor G. Mentz in 1905. This evidence of Luther's own work in England is particularly interesting.

munion in one kind, Celibacy of the Clergy, Vows of Chastity, Private Masses, and Auricular Confession. They were well called " The Whip with Six Strings." Then, in 1543, the Bishops' Book having been revised,[1] was re-published under the sanction of Convocation as the King's Book, or *The Necessary Doctrine and Erudition for any Christian Man.* The book is a further proof of Roman Catholic influence.[2] All this shows that there was no real Protestantism in Henry's reign. It was Roman Catholicism with the King instead of the Pope as supreme. But it is interesting and significant to observe that no trace of the language of the Ten Articles or the Six Articles can be found in our present Formularies, though there are clear indications of the influence of the Thirteen Articles of 1538.

THE ARTICLES OF EDWARD VI

IN view of Edward's accession in 1547 it has often been a matter of surprise that the Articles should not have been published for six years. The history of this period is somewhat obscure, but certain points stand out. Cranmer was indulging the hope of a united Confession of all the Reformed Churches, and it was only after strenuous effort that he had to abandon the project.[3]

But the Reformed party was at work, while the party headed by Gardiner became less and less influential. In 1547 the Six Articles Act was repealed, and in 1549 the First Prayer Book was issued. Cranmer, too, appears to have been preparing some Articles as a test of the orthodoxy of preachers, and it would seem as though these were the first drafts of several of the Articles of 1553.[4]

Another movement was an Act passed in 1549 for the Reformation of Church Law. A Committee headed by Cranmer drew up the *Reformatio Legum Ecclesiasticarum* which, though never set forth by authority, was in some respects the foundation of our present Articles, or at least it may be said that the doctrine found in the *Reformatio Legum* is in accord, and sometimes verbally, with that which is found in the Articles.[5]

---

[1] The Committee of Revision had been at work since 13th April 1540 when Cromwell announced its royal appointment to the House of Lords.

[2] "It may be said that it very accurately represented the theology of the majority of Englishmen in the year 1543. For King and people were not very far apart. They both clung to mediæval theology; and they both detested the Papacy, and wished the clergy to be kept in due subordination. There was a widespread and silent movement towards an Evangelical Reformation always making itself apparent when least expected; but probably three-fourths of the people had not felt it during the reign of Henry. It needed Mary's burnings in Smithfield, and the fears of a Spanish overlord, before the leaven could leaven the whole lump" (Lindsay, *ut supra*, p. 349 f.).

[3] Hardwick, *History of the Articles of Religion*, p. 70 f.

[4] Hardwick, *ut supra*, pp. 77–80.

[5] On the *Reformatio Legum*, see below, p. xlviii.

In 1551 certain Commissioners directed Cranmer to prepare a Book of Articles. A sketch was made and submitted to some Bishops, but the matter was not carried further until 1552. In May of that year the Council asked Convocation for them, and they were sent. These numbered forty-five, and their interest and value are that they were the draft of those eventually published a year later. They were returned to Cranmer and by him sent to the King. They were revised by the Royal Chaplain, reduced in number to forty-two, and published in Latin and English, May 1553. Their authors were mainly Cranmer and Ridley, but after consultation with many Bishops and Divines. Their composition was mostly that of Cranmer who, when examined in Mary's reign, acknowledged that they " were his doings."[1] He derived much help from the Confession of Augsburg: e.g. in Articles I, II, IV, IX, XIV, XVI, XXIII, XXIV, XXV, though the influence was apparently not direct, but indirectly through the Thirteen Articles of 1538.

It is still undecided whether these Articles were sanctioned by Convocation. Authorities differ widely; some arguing against, and others urging considerations in favour of their endorsement.[2] It is probable that the subject will never be settled, as the records of Convocation were destroyed by the Fire of London, 1666. Yet the question is now only one of historical interest, for nothing turns on it. The idea that if they were not sanctioned by Convocation the Church of England was not committed to them[3] is wholly wide of the mark in view of the close association of Church and State in those days. Whether they were sanctioned by Convocation or not they were put forth by royal authority, and became law for the short time that elapsed before the King's death.

The purpose of these Articles was, to use the doctrine of the Reformers, " for the avoiding of controversy in opinions and the establishing of a godly concord in certain matters of religion." There was obviously no idea, because no need, of a full or systematic statement of beliefs. Like most sixteenth-century documents, they " bore the marks of their birth-time and birth-place," and it is therefore " unjust to judge them without regard to their origin and purpose."[4] Nor have we any means of knowing what revision they would have received at the hands of their authors if opportunity had occurred. It is equally unfair to speak of them as " provisional or temporary,"[5] simply because they were issued only seven weeks before King Edward's death. They must be judged by their character and contents, and when this is done we see two things

[1] Harold Browne, *Exposition of the Thirty-nine Articles*, p. 6, Note 2.
[2] Against: Lindsay, *The History of the Reformation*, Vol. II, p. 364; Gibson, *The Thirty-nine Articles*, p. 15 ff.; Tyrrell Green, *The Thirty-nine Articles and the Age of the Reformation*, p. 10 f. For: Cardwell, *Synodalia*, p. 4 f.; Hardwick, *History of the Articles of Religion*, pp. 106–115; Curtis, *A History of Creeds and Confessions of Faith*, p. 171; Harold Browne, *Exposition of the Thirty-nine Articles*, p. 6.
[3] Kidd, *The Thirty-nine Articles*, p. 29.
[4] Curtis, *ut supra*, p. 128. See above pp. xxiv, xxv.
[5] Kidd, *ut supra*, p. 25.

quite clearly: first, Roman errors are definitely condemned (Articles XII, XIII, XX, XXI, XXII, XXIII, XXV, XXVI, XXXI); second, the Anabaptists who caused serious trouble by their excesses are also condemned (Articles VI, VIII, XIV, XV, XXXVII). So that the true and fair explanation is that these Articles represent the Church of England view of the time on the points treated in the light of the necessities of the Reformation. In opposition to Roman and Anabaptist errors they state the position of the Reformers.[1]

One thing calls for special attention. It has been represented by writer after writer that the Forty-two Articles represent Cranmer's view of the Holy Communion as Zwinglian, and therefore at its lowest.[2] But the fact is that Cranmer's view of the Lord's Supper was fixed as early as 1548, the year of the Great Debate,[3] and this alone proves that there is no inconsistency between the Article on the Sacraments (XXVI of 1553) and that on the Lord's Supper (XXIX).

For the same reason it is impossible to accept the view that " the opinions of the Edwardian Reformers, such as Cranmer and Ridley, on the subject of the Holy Communion have nothing more than a historical interest for us."[4] A truer view is that which regards the opinions of these two Reformers as of great importance for the proper interpretation of the Articles which they put forth.

" It is of consequence to remember these facts. For, if Cranmer and Ridley were the chief compilers both of the Prayer Book and of the Articles; although the Church is in no degree bound by their private opinions, yet, when there is a difficulty in understanding a clause either in the Articles or the Liturgy, which are the two standards of authority as regards the doctrines of the English Church, it cannot but be desirable to elucidate such difficulties by appealing to the writings, and otherwise expressed opinions of these two reformers. It is true, both Liturgy and Articles have been altered since their time. Yet by far the larger portion of both remains just as they left them."[5]

Then, too, the views of all the Elizabethan Bishops, with two exceptions (Cheney and Geste), were identical with those of Cranmer.

[1] Hardwick, *ut supra*, pp. 83–98.
[2] Gibson, *ut supra*, pp. 28, 643; Tyrrell Green, *ut supra*, p. 10; and apparently repeated by Kidd, *ut supra*, p. 35.
[3] Tomlinson, *The Great Parliamentary Debate*, p. 21.
[4] Gibson, *ut supra*, p. 647.   [5] Harold Browne, *ut supra*, p. 7.

THE THIRTY-EIGHT ARTICLES OF 1563

Literature.—Cardwell, *Synodalia*, p. 34 ff.; Gibson, *The Thirty-nine Articles*, p. 30; Curtis, *A History of Creeds and Confessions of Faith*, pp. 179–181; Lamb, *Historical Account of the Thirty-nine Articles*, pp. 9–24; Hardwick, *History of the Articles of Religion*, Ch. VI.

THE death of Edward VI might have been thought to put an end to the Reformation, and so it did for a time, until an event took place which more than anything else made the Reformation popular and universal. By a natural rebound the martyrdoms during the reign of Mary gave a depth and an intensity to religious feeling on behalf of the Reformation, which had never been experienced either under Henry, or even under Edward VI.[1]

On Elizabeth's accession, 1558, the great majority of the people accepted and welcomed the changes, and the Queen soon showed on which side she intended to be. The Forty-two Articles of 1553, though referred to in a document presented to the Queen in 1559, were not revived and made obligatory for some years, but a preliminary Eleven were issued of a very simple and practical nature. These never became legally binding, though in 1566 they were made legal for Ireland and remained so till 1615, when the Thirty-nine Articles became the legal Formularies for that land also.

Meanwhile, under Parker, the Forty-two were revised and corrected from the Confession of Wurtemberg, 1552, another interesting illustration of the way in which, while Lutheran Formularies were freely used in connection with our Articles, the sacramental teaching was throughout of the Swiss or Reformed, not the Lutheran type.[2] These revised Articles were submitted to Convocation, reduced to Thirty-nine, then one was omitted, almost certainly by the Queen, and finally they were published as Thirty-eight in 1563. The influence of Wurtemberg can be seen in several of the Articles, *e.g.* II, III, VI, X, XI, XII, XX.

The alterations were numerous and important.

(*a*) *Six Articles were omitted.*

Article X.—Of Grace.

Article XVI.—Sin against the Holy Ghost.

[1] "The event, which seemed to crush the Reformation in the bud, in fact gave it life. Neither clergy nor people appear to have been very hearty in its cause, when it came commended to them by the tyranny of Henry, or even by the somewhat arbitrary authority of Edward and the Protector Somerset. But when its martyrs bled at the stake, and when the royal prerogative was arrayed against it, it then became doubly endeared to the people as the cause of liberty as well as of religion" (Harold Browne, *Exposition of the Thirty-nine Articles*, pp. 7, 8).
"However paradoxical at first sight this statement may appear, nothing more effectually tended to the final establishment of the Protestant faith in this Kingdom, and to a deep and lasting aversion to the Roman Catholic Religion than the cruel and frequent executions of this reign" (Lamb, *The Articles*, p. 5).
[2] See articles in *The Churchman* for January 1920 and 1921, by W. Prescott Upton.

Article XXXIX.—The Resurrection of the Dead is not yet brought to pass.

Article XL.—The Souls of Them that do part this Life do neither die with the Bodies, nor sleep idly.

Article XLI.—Heretics called Millenarii.

Article XLII.—All Men shall not be saved at the Length.

(b) *Two were united into one (with parts omitted).*

Article VI.—The Old Testament is not to be Refused.

Article XIX.—All Men are bound to keep the Moral Commandments of the Law.

Together these form our present Article VII.

(c) *Four were added (by Archbishop Parker).*

Article V.—Of the Holy Ghost.

Article XII.—Of Good Works.

Article XXIX.—Of the Wicked which eat not the Body of Christ in the Lord's Supper.

Article XXX.—Of Both Kinds.

Of these Article XXIX was omitted, apparently by the Queen.

(d) *Clauses and words were omitted or added in many other Articles.* Details of these will be given in the separate Articles, but the following call for special attention.

Article XX.—Of the Authority of the Church. First clause added, presumably by the Queen, after the Article had left Convocation.

Article XXV.—Of the Sacraments. Several important changes and additions.

Article XXVIII.—Of the Lord's Supper. A change in clause three.

The history of each of these points will be given in connection with the Articles themselves.

It is now necessary to enquire as to the character of these Articles.

1. They represent a greater completeness of statement of doctrine by the Church of England, especially on fundamentals. This was felt to be necessary,[1] and circumstances were favourable to the realisation, for the Reformation settlement made it possible.

2. But there was no essential doctrinal difference, as the following points indicate.

(a) The Article on Justification represented Luther's views and also the Confession of Augsburg.

(b) The Article on Good Works, so far from correcting the Lutheran view of Justification, expressed Luther's own teaching. There was an Article on Good Works in the Confession of Augsburg, 1530.

(c) The omission of the reference to the *opus operatum* view of the Sacraments in Article XXV was due to the ambiguity of the phrase.[2] The other changes in the Article on the Sacraments were introduced to distinguish between Sacraments and other Ordinances, without calling the latter Sacraments, or Sacramental Rites.

[1] Cardwell, *ut supra*, p. 35.   [2] Hardwick, *ut supra*, p. 132.

(*d*) Article XXVIII was altered by Parker, who is known to have held (not Lutheran, but) Calvinistic views on the Lord's Supper, in harmony with Cranmer, of whom he was a devoted disciple.[1]

(*e*) But inasmuch as some endeavour was made to give a Lutheran interpretation to Article XXVIII, Parker introduced Article XXIX to safeguard the true doctrine.[2] The teaching of this Article is admittedly opposed to Lutheranism.

(*f*) The omission by the Queen of Article XXIX was almost certainly due to her desire to keep Lutheran Reformers in union with other Protestants in support of her Throne. There does not appear to have been any endeavour to favour the Roman Catholic party, a matter which never seems to have entered into the minds of those responsible for the revision and issue of the Articles, as the following point proves beyond all question.

3. The most striking feature is the increased emphasis placed on the anti-Roman character of the Articles in view of the fact that the Articles of 1553 were supposed to represent the high-water mark of Protestantism. This strengthening of the Articles of 1563 in a Protestant direction is particularly noteworthy. Such an intensification of the anti-Roman features at a time when it is alleged by some that Elizabeth was doing her utmost to conciliate Rome is a clear proof that nothing of the kind was intended by the changes made by the Queen and Parker. A reference to the following Articles, and a comparison of their wording with that of 1553 will amply illustrate the position.

Article VI.—Of the Sufficiency of the Holy Scriptures for Salvation. The addition of the reference to the Apocrypha with the distinction made between that and the Canonical Books.

Article XXII.—Of Purgatory. " Doctrine of School authors " changed to " Romish doctrine."

Article XXV.—Of the Sacraments. The wording about speaking in a tongue understood of the people made much stronger.

Article XXX.—Of Both Kinds. Addition of the Article.

Article XXXII.—Of the Marriage of Priests. Made much stronger.

Article XXXIV.—Of the Traditions of the Church. Addition of a new paragraph claiming authority for National Churches.

Article XXXVII.—Of the Civil Magistrates. Addition of a sentence denying jurisdiction of the Bishop of Rome in England.

Facts like these amply suffice to show that conciliation of Roman Catholics was entirely outside the purpose of the Church and the Queen.

---

[1] "Cranmer, his great predecessor, whom he valued so highly, that he 'would as much rejoice to win' some of the lost writings of that prelate as he 'would to restore an old chancel to reparation'" (Hardwick, *ut supra*, p. 117 f.).

Hardwick (*ut supra*, p. 138) seems to suggest that this change was really against the Swiss School, but Dimock (*Papers on the Eucharistic Presence*, p. 657) proves beyond all question the harmony of Parker's views with those of (not Zwingli but) Calvin, and this is tantamount to saying that he agreed with Cranmer (Dimock, p. 639).

[2] Dimock, *op. cit.*, p. 667.

The policy of Elizabeth was not to win Rome, but to unite all Protestants in support of her position. It was this that led to the omission of Article XXIX, and to acts like the insertion of the Ornaments Rubric.[1] But even so, it is a mistake to suppose that the Queen's own view of the Lord's Supper was Lutheran, for there are proofs of her sympathy with the Swiss or Reformed view.[2] An additional testimony is afforded by the *Reformatio Legum*.[3] Another witness, speaking of the Articles, says they

" expressed the doctrine of the Reformed or Calvinist as distinguished from the Evangelical or Lutheran form of Protestant doctrine, and the distinction lay mainly in the views which the respective Confessions of the two Churches held about the Presence of Christ in the Sacrament of the Holy Supper."[4]

And referring to the Queen's action in regard to Articles XX and XXVIII, he remarks :—

" The Queen's action was probably due to political reasons. It was important in international politics for a Protestant Queen not yet securely seated on her throne to shelter herself under the shield which a profession of Lutheranism would give."[5]

THE THIRTY-NINE ARTICLES OF 1571

Literature.—Cardwell, *Synodalia*, pp. 73-107; Lamb, *Historical Account of the Thirty-nine Articles*, pp. 24-40.

It is a natural question why the Articles should have needed attention again after the short period of eight or nine years. The explanation is found in the attitude of Queen Elizabeth. Although the Articles of 1563 were promulgated by Convocation, authorised by the Queen herself, and printed and published by her own printer, they were not presented to Parliament. Elizabeth apparently refused to allow this, though pressed by Convocation and Parliament to do so.[6] The result

[1] The Black Rubric is sometimes used as a further proof of this policy, but the Black Rubric was not "omitted," because it never formed any part of the liturgy of 1552. The revival of 5 and 6 of Edward VI could not therefore include this Royal Declaration, while the Acts giving to Royal Declarations the force of law had meantime been repealed. See Dimock's pamphlet on the subject, and Tomlinson, *Prayer Book, Articles and Homilies*, Ch. XI.

[2] Dimock, *Vox Liturgiæ Anglicanæ*, pp. vi., vii.-xii., 60–63; *Papers on the Eucharistic Presence*, pp. 567–570.

[3] See p. xlviii.; Dimock, *Vox Liturgiæ Anglicanæ*, p. xv., quotes Cardwell, that the *Reformatio Legum* represented "the state and condition of the Church of England in the reign of Queen Elizabeth, when the Reformation may be said to have been completed" (*Synodalia*, pp. x., xi.).

[4] Lindsay, *History of the Reformation*, p. 411.   [5] Lindsay, *ut supra*, p. 414.

[6] "Her Majesty considered it an encroachment upon her Prerogative of Supreme Head of the Church" (Lamb, *ut supra*, p. 24).

was that for four years after 1563 the Articles do not seem to have been
circulated, or appealed to, though they were enforced as far as they could
be by the ecclesiastical authority of the Episcopate.[1] The delay seems
to have been due to political circumstances. All the efforts of Parliament to obtain clerical subscription to the Articles were blocked by the
Queen. Her policy at that time was one of religious toleration, and
this " non-committal " attitude served her purpose, for as long as the
clergy were not required to subscribe to the Articles, the Queen could
appear free to deal with Rome, or to negotiate with the Lutherans, while
subscription would mean a definite committal to one side. But though
the delay was regrettable and in some respects serious, yet the influence
of the Bishops, all of whom were Protestant, tended to keep matters
fairly straight. In 1570, however, the Queen yielded to the pressure of
Parliament. It is usually thought that the primary cause of this sudden,
remarkable, and complete change was the Papal excommunication of
Elizabeth,[2] yet even when the House of Commons took action against
this aggression of Rome, and also prepared a Bill requiring clerical subscription to the Articles, the Queen opposed it until on the fourth time
of reading by the Commons she gave way,[3] and a Bill was passed
requiring clerical subscription. During this struggle between the
Queen and Parliament, Convocation had been engaged in the
revision of the Articles of 1563. This work was due mainly to
Jewel, Bishop of Salisbury, though partly also to Archbishop Parker.
Jewel prefixed " de " to the Latin titles and " of " to the English,
and added the names to the list of Books of the Apocrypha in
Article VI. Article XXIX was inserted, and accepted by the Queen,
while the first clause of Article XX was accepted by Convocation.
Article X was changed to " working with " instead of " working
in," and Article XXVII added " or new birth " to " regeneration."
The only change of importance was the reinsertion of Article
XXIX, and this was profoundly significant of the Church doctrine on
the Holy Communion.[4]

The Articles were submitted to Convocation, passed, and then became
law. For the first time clerical subscription was required. They were

[1] Hardwick, *History of the Articles of Religion*, p. 143.
[2] "The Papal Bull of excommunication was delayed until 1570, when its publication
could harm no one but Elizabeth's own Romanist subjects, and the dangerous period
was tided over safely. When it came at last, the Queen was not anathematised in terms
which could apply to Lutherans, but because she personally acknowledged and observed
'the impious constitutions and atrocious mysteries of Calvin,' and had commanded
that they should be observed by her subjects. Then, when the need for politic suppression was past, Article XXIX was published, and the *Thirty-nine Articles* became
the recognised doctrinal standard of the Church of England (1571)." (Lindsay, *History
of the Reformation*, p. 415.)
[3] "This seems to have been the first successful resistance made by the constitutional
party in the House of Commons to that arbitrary authority in Church matters, which
Henry VIII first assumed, and to preserve which his daughter Elizabeth was peculiarly
anxious" (Lamb, *ut supra*, p. 25, Note c).
[4] The details of the history will be given under the Article itself.

d

issued in Latin and English, and both are equally "authentic,"[1] one often throwing light on the other.[2]

Since 1571 no change has taken place in the Articles, and as we review the period from 1536 onwards, especially the three last stages from 1553, we see that they are the result of years of controversies, and their wording shows what English theology really was. Their statements must always be taken in the light of the circumstances which brought them forth.

NOTE ON THE "REFORMATIO LEGUM ECCLESIASTICARUM"

Literature.—Cardwell, *Reformatio Legum Ecclesiasticarum*, Preface; Maclear and Williams, *Introduction to the Articles of the Church of England*, New Edition, p. 455; Hardwick, *History of the Articles of Religion*, p. 86 ff.; Gibson, *The Thirty-nine Articles*, p. 28 f.

The abolition of Roman Catholic jurisdiction made it necessary to consider the question of the Canon Law and to frame a body of Ecclesiastical Law, especially as a counter-influence to the action of the Council of Trent. In 1544 Cranmer began the work of selection and adaptation, and a Committee was appointed to assist him, including Bishop Goodrich, Dr. (afterwards Bishop) Cox of Ely, Peter Martyr, and Dr. Rowland Taylor. But the King's death prevented the ratification by Parliament, and for some reasons this result must be regarded as particularly welcome.[3] A copy fell into the hands of Archbishop Parker, who edited it, and did not merely reproduce Cranmer's text.[4] In 1571 it was published with his consent, but was not accepted by the Queen and Parliament. It is valuable for comparison, and for the elucidation

[1] Dr. Stephens in his speech in the Bennett Case (p. 76), denies that the Latin version is in a legal sense "equally authoritative," and the "littlebok" enacted by 13 Elizabeth was certainly the *English* version.

[2] "The Articles of our Church were at the same time prepared both in Latin and English; so that both are equally authentical" (Burnet, *Articles*, p. xxi.).

"As to the Articles, English and Latin, I may just observe, for the sake of such readers as are less acquainted with these things—*First*, That the Articles were passed, recorded, and ratified in the year 1562, and *in Latin only*. *Secondly*, That those Latin Articles were revised and corrected by the Convocation of 1571. *Thirdly*, That an authentic English translation was then made of the Latin Articles by the same Convocation, and the Latin and English adjusted as nearly as possible. *Fourthly*, That the Articles thus perfected *in both languages* were published the same year, and by the royal authority. *Fifthly*, Subscription was required the same year to the English Articles, called the Articles of 1562, by the famous Act of the 13th of Elizabeth.

"These things considered, I might justly say, with Bishop Burnet, that the Latin and English are both *equally authentical*. Thus much, however, I may certainly infer, that if in any places the English version be ambiguous, where the Latin original is clear and determinate, the Latin ought to fix the more doubtful sense of the other (as also *vice versa*), it being evident that the Convocation, Queen, and Parliament, intended the same sense in both" (Waterland, "Supplement to the Case of Arian Subscription Considered," *Works*, Vol. II, p. 316; quoted in Hardwick, p. 156).

[3] "It was as well, for the book enacted death penalties for various heresies, which would have made it a cruel weapon in the hands of a persecuting government" (Lindsay, *ut supra*, p. 364).

[4] See *Church Intelligencer*, April 1909, pp. 60–63.

of the mind of Cranmer and Parker. As such, it has a definite bearing on the Articles, throwing light on their meaning and purpose. It is incorrect to call it a draft, or explanation of the Articles, because its character and contents show it to be a code of Reformed Canon Law which was never legally adopted. But on subjects of which the Articles treat it is well worth comparison. Thus one section is on " The Catholic Faith and the Trinity," another on " Heresies," and another on " Sacraments." In considering the Articles on these subjects the *Reformatio Legum* will naturally be used for illustration and comparison.

INTERPRETATION AND OBLIGATION OF THE ARTICLES

AT this stage it is necessary to notice the question of Puritan objections to the Articles.[1] It is important to observe that these objections were almost wholly concerned with points of Calvinism, for on other subjects the differences were quite insignificant.[2] On the subject of Calvinism there is the greatest need of care, for nothing is more apt to be misunderstood and misconceived. It may mean so much or so little.

All the Reformers were moderate Calvinists, or Augustinians, Melanchthon as well as Calvin himself.[3] And the opposite view associated with Arminius never had any real footing in the Church of England until the time and through the influence of Laud.[4] " In the sixteenth century Predestination was universally accepted,"[5] and it was only

[1] Hardwick, *ut supra*, Ch. X.
[2] "As regards the early Puritans, it must be remembered that there was a well-understood agreement between them and their opponents on matters of doctrine. The questions in controversy were questions, not of doctrine, but of order and discipline and ceremonies" (Dimock, *Vox Liturgiæ Anglicanæ*, p. xx). Dimock adds that the only exception to this was the observance of the Lord's Day, which was the first doctrinal disagreement.
[3] "It is a striking fact that the Protestant theology of the sixteenth century both began and ended in strict theories of Predestination. . . . The severe doctrine of Calvin on the subject of Predestination is notorious; but it should be remembered that the teaching of Melanchthon in the first edition of his work was not less severe" (Wace, *Principles of the Reformation*, p. 129).
"No impartial person, competently acquainted with the history of the Reformation, and the works of the earlier Protestant divines, at home and abroad, even to the close of Elizabeth's reign, will deny that the doctrines of Calvin on redemption and the natural state of fallen man are in all essential points the same as those of Luther, Zwinglius, and the first Reformers collectively" (Coleridge, *Aids to Reflection*, quoted Wace, *ut supra*, p. 140). (See the entire section, Wace, *ut supra*, pp. 129-153.)
[4] "Before his time there was a general consent among our divines; for, as Bishop Carleton observes, though disputes arose between the Bishops and the Puritans with respect to Church government, they perfectly agreed in doctrine. Anti-Calvinists have indeed endeavoured to force the Article to speak their own sentiments; yet they must confess, that they would not have expressed them in those words; and a sufficient refutation of their statement is the fact, that Rogers, the first expositor of the Articles, and Chaplain to Archbishop Bancroft, to whom he dedicated his work, maintains that it conveys a contrary meaning" (Macbride, *Lectures on the Articles*, p. 30 f.).
[5] Sargeaunt, *Journal of Theological Studies*, Vol. XII, p. 428.

later that Calvinism underwent further developments. For the balance of our Article XVII we should be rightly grateful, but of its essential Calvinistic doctrine no one who knows the history can have any doubt.[1]

A further illustration of the essentially Calvinistic view of the Articles is found in the action of King James I in sending three Anglican representatives to the Synod of Dort, when Calvinistic doctrine was unanimously endorsed, and in 1625, a few years after that Synod, a sermon preached at Cambridge, by Dr. Ward, gave striking evidence of the universal acceptance of Augustinian views from the opening of the Reformation,[2] while Bishop Hall, one of the three representatives at Dort, bore testimony in the same direction.[3] The ineffectual attempts of the Puritans in 1604 to get the Lambeth Articles included in our Formularies is another reason for gratitude, and one that makes the positive Scriptural doctrine of the Articles stand out all the more clearly.

HISTORY OF SUBSCRIPTION

Literature.—Hardwick, *History of the Articles of Religion*, Ch. XI; Gibson, *The Thirty-nine Articles*, p. 57; Kidd, *The Thirty-nine Articles*, p. 52; Tyrrell Green, *The Thirty-nine Articles and the Age of the Reformation*, p. 17; *The Tutorial Prayer Book*, p. 544.

Subscription to the Articles was thought necessary to secure uniformity of doctrine among teachers of the Reformed Faith, and it was enjoined

[1] "It is absurd, with some Anglican writers, to deny the Calvinism of the Articles on this subject; but for Calvinistic influence and example they would not have discussed the subject at all. . . . It is unhistorical to deny the Calvinism of the English Articles, as distinct from the English Service Book to which they were added, merely because they do not, with *later* Calvinistic Confessions, endeavour to carry out the broad principles of election and grace to their narrowest ultimate conclusions. Anglican Puritanism might not be able to appeal for authority and vindication to the Prayer Book in its entirety, but to the Edwardine Articles it could legitimately look as to the rock whence in England it was hewn. These Articles are not developed, much less exaggerated, Calvinism. They are not Calvinistic in any partisan sense. But with Calvinistic doctrine, as already formulated, they are in unmistakable sympathy" (Curtis, *ut supra*, pp. 176, 177).

The joint letter of Parker and Grindal to Sir William Cecil is a proof of the value set on the Geneva Bible (*Correspondence of Parker*, p. 261). The influence of Calvin in Elizabeth's reign and the high estimation in which he and his writings were held may be seen in Hardwick (*History of the Articles*, Ch. 7). Hooker's testimony is well known (*Eccl. Pol.*, Preface II, 1). But perhaps the strongest evidence of the hold which Calvin's teaching had obtained in the Universities is the testimony of Bishop Sanderson, and this is all the more significant as the Bishop did not admire Calvin's theology (Wordsworth, *Eccles. Biog.*, IV, p. 416). As Sanderson is referring to 1603, when the Arminian Movement had already greatly influenced English theologians, the testimony to Calvin's *Institutes* is particularly remarkable (cf. Carter, *The English Church and the Reformation*, pp. 143–145, for further references).

[2] "This also I can truly add, for a conclusion, that the Universal Church hath always adhered to St. Austin, ever since his time till now. The Church of England also, from the beginning of the Reformation and this our famous University, with all those from thence till now who have with us enjoyed the Divinity Chair, if we except one foreign Frenchman (Peter Baro), have likewise constantly adhered to him" (Macbride, *ut supra*, p. 31).

[3] "I shall live and die in the suffrage of the reverend Synod, and do confidently avow, that those other opinions cannot stand with the doctrines of the Church of England" (Macbride, *ut supra*, p. 33).

on the clergy as early as 1553, but the death of the King prevented its enforcement. No further action was taken until 1571, when, as we have seen, an Act of Parliament required all clergy to assent to all the Articles concerning Faith and Sacraments. It is interesting to notice that the subscription enforced referred to the Articles of 1563. There seems to have been a certain verbal ambiguity in this order, and some have thought that Parliament intended it to apply only to those Articles concerning Doctrine and Sacraments, and not to those on Discipline.[1] But the Act says he shall "subscribe to *all* the articles of religion which only concern the confession of the true Christian faith and the doctrine of the sacraments, comprised in a book imprinted" and requires him to read publicly the "Said Articles." So that it could not be intended that he might skip and omit to read any of the Articles which in his judgment are not doctrinal. Thus the wider interpretation naturally prevailed, and subscription was required to all the Articles. The controversy, however, appears to have led to a good deal of laxity, though Archbishop Whitgift, in 1583, tried to improve matters by proposing a form of subscription from every clergyman, requiring among other things:

"That he alloweth the Book of the Articles of Religion agreed upon by the archbishops and bishops of both provinces, and the whole clergy in the Convocation holden at London in the year of our Lord 1562, and set forth by Her

---

[1] Cardwell's note is as follows:
"This view of the matter certainly receives support from the parliamentary history of the time (D'Ewes' *Journal*, p. 239. *Docum. Ann.*, Vol. I, p. 411), and is also confirmed by the proceedings of the Convocation in 1575, the first year of the primacy of Archbishop Grindal, where the limitation of the statute is distinctly quoted, and applied to all cases of subscription to the Articles (Wilk., *Conc.*, Vol. IV, p. 284). But it is clear that the statute was otherwise interpreted by Sir E. Coke (*Inst.*, Part IV, p. 323); and as the Queen and her Commissioners would not suffer any reserve or qualification, a different practice certainly prevailed in the administration of the Church. From the year 1584, when Archbishop Whitgift issued his orders for subscription to the three Articles, which were afterwards confirmed by King James in the canons of 1603, it appears that no exception or limitation was permitted. In the last Act of Uniformity (13 and 14 Car. II, c. 4) there is no trace of any such distinction being allowed between articles of doctrine and discipline" (Cardwell, *Synodalia*, Vol. I, pp. 61–62). Hardwick (*ut supra*, pp. 227–229), also discusses the question and says the idea of a limitation was due to "those who were in search of pretexts for their nonconformity." But Whitgift and Rogers both contended that "all and every of the Articles therein contained, being in number nine and thirty" were the subject of the subscription. Rogers adds: "no more, no fewer" (Preface, p. 24). It should be noted that the "Convocation of 1575" merely quotes the *ipsissima verba* of the statute. Then, too, lawyers, who are the fit expounders of statutes, with one consent have interpreted the 13 Elizabeth in the sense of a full subscription. The so-called disciplinary articles are the Church of England's doctrine relating to matters of discipline, and the words of the Act cover the whole. The reference in Cardwell to D'Ewes is really irrelevant, for at the p. 239 cited, Wentworth tells us that the Archbishop had asked him: "Why we did put out of the book the articles for the Homilies, consecrating of bishops, and suchlike?" But Wentworth was compelled to see these very Articles enacted with all the rest and made statutory law. This is a refutation of his entire claim. On the Puritan contention all these articles ought to have been expunged as not binding on the clergy, but the articles were imposed to "avoid diversities of opinion, and establish consent touching true religion," and the "diversities" of their day were *not* doctrinal, but disciplinary and ecclesiastical.

Majesty's authority, and that he believeth all the articles therein contained to be agreeable to the Word of God."[1]

Not much was done until the Canons of 1604, when Canon V censured the impugners of the Articles, and Canon XXXVI required all Articles to be accepted *ex animo* at Ordination and Institution :—

CANON XXXVI

" *Subscription to be required of such as are to be made ministers.*"
"No person shall hereafter be received into the ministry, nor either by institution or collation admitted to any ecclesiastical living, nor suffered to preach, to catechise, or to be a lecturer or reader of divinity, in either university, or in any cathedral, or collegiate church, city, or market town, parish church, chapel, or in any other place in this realm, except he be licensed either by the archbishop, or by the bishop of the diocese where he is to be placed, under their hands and seals, or by one of the two universities under their seal likewise ; and except he shall first subscribe to these three articles following, in such manner and sort as we have here appointed :—
" I.—That the King's Majesty, under God, is the only supreme governor of this realm, and of all other his Highness's dominions and countries, as well in all spiritual or ecclesiastical things or causes, as temporal ; and that no foreign prince, person, prelate, state, or potentate hath, or ought to have, any jurisdiction, power, superiority, preeminence, or authority, ecclesiastical or spiritual, within His Majesty's said realms, dominions, and countries.
" II.—That the Book of Common Prayer, and of ordering of Bishops, Priests, and Deacons, containeth in it nothing contrary to the Word of God, and that it may lawfully so be used ; and that he himself will use the form in the said Book prescribed, in public prayer, and administration of the sacraments, and none other.
"III.—That he alloweth the Book of Articles of Religion agreed upon by the archbishops and bishops of both Provinces, and by the whole clergy in the Convocation holden at London in the year of our Lord God 1562 ; and that he acknowledgeth all and every the Articles therein contained, being in number nine and thirty, besides the ratification, to be agreeable to the Word of God.
" To these three Articles, whosoever will subscribe he shall, for the avoiding of all ambiguities, subscribe in this order and form of words, setting down both his Christian and surname, viz. :—
" *I, N. N., do willingly and* ex animo *subscribe to these three Articles above mentioned, and to all things that are contained in them.*
"And if any bishop shall ordain, admit, or license any, as is aforesaid, except he first have subscribed in manner and form as here we have appointed, he shall be suspended from giving of orders and licences to preach for the space of twelve months. But if either of the universities shall offend therein, we leave them to the danger of the law, and His Majesty's censure."[2]

But this strictness did not continue in the years that followed, and it was only at the Restoration that greater efforts were made to insist on

[1] Strype's *Whitgift*, Bk. III, Ch. III.   [2] Cardwell, *Synodalia*, Vol. I, p. 267.

proper and full subscription according to this Canon. While the Act of Uniformity demanded assent to the Prayer Book it did not deal with the Articles. But the Act recognises 13 Elizabeth as " in force," and its 17th Section extends the operation of the Act to an additional set of persons, while the 31st Section transfers the reference of Article XXXVI to the Ordinal of 1662.[1]

The attempt in 1689 to bring about comprehension proved unsuccessful, and the usual practice was to combine the terms of subscription required by the Act of Elizabeth and Canon XXXVI with the following form :—

" I, *A.B.*, do willingly and from my heart subscribe to the Thirty-nine Articles of Religion of the United Church of England and Ireland, and to the three Articles in the Thirty-sixth Canon, and to all things therein contained."

The effort made in the eighteenth century to obtain relief from subscription, associated with the name of Archdeacon Blackburne, was too definitely Arian to command assent, and it was therefore summarily rejected.

In 1865 the Formula of subscription was altered by the assent being made much more general, the form being :—

" I, *A.B.*, do solemnly make the following declaration : I assent to the Thirty-nine Articles of Religion, and to the Book of Common Prayer, and of ordering of Bishops, Priests, and Deacons ; I believe the doctrine of the [United] Church of England [and Ireland], as therein set forth, to be agreeable to the Word of God : and in public prayer and administration of the Sacraments, I will use the form in the said book prescribed, and none other, except so far as shall be ordered by lawful authority."[2]

The Act requires that a clergyman on being instituted to a living, or on his first Sunday, " publicly and openly in the presence of his congregation read the whole Thirty-nine Articles of Religion, and immediately after reading them make the Declaration of assent to them." While they were not to be understood in any non-natural sense, there was to be no narrow interpretation, and the intention of the Act was certainly to grant relief. It is, of course, well known that subscription is only required of the clergy, and that from the laity it is not demanded as a term of Communion. The only lay subscription was that required at Oxford and Cambridge, which was abolished in 1871, except so far as Degrees in Divinity were concerned.

THE ROYAL DECLARATION

The Calvinistic controversy continued unabated during the reign of James I, when, as we have seen, the deputation to the Synod of Dort,

---

[1] Tomlinson, *Prayer Book, Articles, and Homilies*, Ch. XII.
[2] The words in brackets were, of course, disused after the Irish Church was disestablished in 1869.

1618, was the most important feature. On the accession of Charles I in 1625 he found the Church much agitated by factions and controversy, and issued a Proclamation forbidding the clergy to introduce principles which were not clearly those of the Church. In 1628 he ordered Archbishop Laud to reprint the Articles and to prefix a Declaration that no one was to wrest them, but to take them in their literal and grammatical sense. This project was not submitted to Convocation, but was issued on the King's authority alone. As Parliament at once replied against the King the Declaration did not acquire any legal force.

PURPOSE OF THE ARTICLES

It is sometimes said that the Articles are ambiguous and were intended as a compromise, and that therefore any clear, definite statement of Church doctrine is impossible and not to be expected. But this does not agree with the facts of the case. Cranmer's object in promulgating the Articles was clearly expressed in his letter to John a Lasco, 1548 :—

" We are desirous of setting forth in our churches the true doctrine of God, *and have no wish to adapt it to all tastes and to trifle with ambiguities*, but, laying aside all carnal and prudential motives, to transmit to posterity a true and explicit form of doctrine agreeable to the rule of the sacred writings."[1]

The words used in 1563 are evidence of the same intention : " For the avoiding of the diversities of opinions, and for the stablishing of consent touching true religion."[2] The same intention is seen by the requirement of clerical subscription, for the purpose was obviously to obtain consent to a recognised statement of doctrine.[3]

That the Articles were intended to be the legal and authorised statement and test of Church of England doctrine on all subjects treated in them is quite clear from all that we know of their origin, history, and purpose. From the first they were regarded as affording the supreme test of Churchmanship, and from this standpoint there is nothing to compare with them. In order that this may be quite clear, it seems necessary to state as fully as possible what subscriptions and declarations have been required and made since the time the Articles were first promulgated.[4]

1. The Act of 13 Elizabeth, 1571, required a declaration of assent,

[1] *Original Letters*, Vol. I, p. 17.   [2] Tyrrell Green, *ut supra*, p. 14.
[3] "One fact is plain, viz., that the Articles thus drawn up, subscribed, and authorised, have ever since been signed and assented to by all the clergy of the Church, and until very lately by every graduate of both Universities; and have hence an authority far beyond that of any single convocation or parliament, viz. the unanimous and solemn assent of all the bishops and clergy of the Church, and of the two Universities for well-nigh three hundred years" (Harold Browne, *Exposition of the Thirty-nine Articles*, p. 10).
[4] These materials are taken in substance from Dean Goode's pamphlet, *A Defence of the Thirty-nine Articles* (Hatchard & Son, 1848).

and a subscription to the Articles expressive of " unfeigned assent " and against the maintenance or affirmation of any doctrine " directly contrary or repugnant."

2. Canon XXXVI of 1603-1604, as already seen, states that the Articles are " agreeable to the Word of God," and that every clergyman must subscribe " *ex animo* " to them.

3. The Act of Uniformity, 1662, is virtually to the same effect, as already observed.

4. The title of the Articles is " for the avoiding of the diversities of opinions and for the stablishing of consent touching true religion."

5. The Canons of 1571, though not legally binding, enable us to see the mind of the Bishops and the Crown. Preachers are to subscribe to the Articles, and promise to maintain and defend " that doctrine which is contained in them as most agreeable to the verity of God's Word."

6. A Canon of the Provincial Synod, held in London, 1575, issued with royal sanction and authority, speaks of the profession of the doctrines expressed in the Articles, and all ministers are to render an account of their faith " agreeable and consonant to the said Articles, and shall first subscribe to the said Articles."

7. Canons drawn up in 1584 and again in 1597 have similar directions, requiring a statement of faith " according to the Articles of Religion."

8. Canon XXXIV, of 1603-1604, makes the same demand on all applicants for Holy Orders.

9. The Royal Declaration prefixed to the Articles by Charles I in 1628 speaks of the Articles containing " the true doctrine of the Church of England," and prohibits " the least difference from the said Articles."

10. The statute law of the realm as seen in the Act of 1571, already briefly mentioned, speaks very definitely about those who maintain or affirm " any doctrine directly contrary or repugnant to any of the said Articles," while no one is to be admitted as a minister unless he professes " the doctrine expressed in the said Articles."

11. In 1566 Archbishop Parker drew up a document containing a petition of the Bishops to the Queen to obtain a Bill " concerning uniformity in doctrine and confirmation of certain Articles." This consent and unity of doctrine is said to be necessary to quiet and safety, and that great distraction and dissension existed " for want of a plain certainty of Articles of Doctrine by law to be declared."

12. In 1721 the Crown issued directions for unity and purity of faith, requiring the clergy not to preach any other doctrines than " what are contained in the Holy Scriptures and agreeable to the three Creeds and the Thirty-nine Articles of Religion."

13. Thomas Rogers, Chaplain to Archbishop Bancroft, published an Exposition of the Articles in 1607, in which the Articles are constantly spoken of as " the doctrine of our Church," and that by them " there is now a uniformity likewise of doctrine by authority established." Further, he teaches that the doctrine of our Church is to be judged by the Articles.

To the same effect testimonies can be adduced from representative men like Burnet, Hall, Stillingfleet, and Beveridge.

14. The Act of 28 and 29 Victoria requires everyone instituted to a living to read the whole of the Thirty-nine Articles and to declare his assent to them. And this is all the more remarkable that while, up to the year 1865 a clergyman was required to read over the whole Morning and Evening Service as well, the latter was dispensed with, the requirement to read the Articles was retained.

From all these facts and documents the conclusion ought to be obvious, that the Articles pledge their subscribers to certain definite doctrines, and that for the Church of England the Articles are an adequate safeguard of orthodoxy. It is clear, therefore, that subscription to the Articles is to be regarded as a definite adoption of their doctrines and something very much more than the negative position of restraint within their limits.[1] Hardwick, following earlier writers, suggests the desirableness of the following rules or Canons of interpretation as both reasonable and suitable to the situation:

" *First*, to weigh the history of the Reformation movement in the midst of which the Articles had been produced.

Secondly, to read them in this light, approximating as far as possible to the particular point of view which had been occupied by all the leading compilers.

Thirdly, to interpret the language of the formulary in its plain and grammatical sense (*i.e.* the sense which it had borne in the Edwardine and Elizabethan periods of the Church), bestowing on it ' the just and favourable construction, which ought to be allowed to all human writings, especially such as are set forth by authority.'

Fourthly, where the language of the Articles is vague, or where (as might have been expected from their history) we meet with a comparative *silence* in respect of any theological topic, to ascertain the fuller doctrine of the Church of England on that point, by reference to her other symbolical writings—the Prayer Book, the Ordinal, the Homilies, and the Canons.

Fifthly, where these sources have been tried without arriving at *explicit* knowledge as to the intention of any Article, to acquiesce in the deductions which ' the catholic doctors and ancient bishops' have expressly gathered on that point from Holy Scripture; in accordance with the recommendation of the Canon of 1571 in which subscription to the present Articles had been enjoined upon the clergy."[2]

While making every allowance, therefore, for the fact that these Articles exhibit marks of the circumstances which gave them birth, and on this account cannot be regarded as a full and systematic statement of Anglican theology, yet on the subjects with which they deal their character

[1] "Although the latter view has been occasionally advanced by writers of the highest reputation and ability, the former seems to be consistent with the nature and intention of the Articles as well as with the principle embodied by the Church of England in the Canons of 1571" (Hardwick, *ut supra*, p. 222).

[2] Hardwick, *ut supra*, p. 224.

and purpose are easily understood when the above facts are weighed, and the use made of them for the last three centuries considered. The Articles represent one of the most remarkable theological documents ever seen. They were the result of two generations of controversy. Parties were face to face, and every word was weighed. The Scholastic theology had been working itself out and the result was seen in the Reformation. The actual words show what their theology was, and bear clear testimony to the meanings of Roman and Reformed doctrines. The Articles can only be understood in the light of their history, and when thus considered they are as weighty as any formula in existence.[1]

INTERPRETATION OF THE ARTICLES

It is sometimes urged that the Articles being incomplete are to be interpreted in the light of " Catholic principles." This means that they are to be distinguished rigidly from the Protestant Confessions of the sixteenth century in spite of their evident connection with and imitations of them. On this view our Articles are held to condemn extreme mediaevalism, but not the recognised doctrines of the Church of Rome, and it is said that our Church occupies a middle position between two extremes, being neither Roman nor Puritan, but " Catholic." It is, of course, correct to say that truth is often found between two extremes (*in medio tutissimus ibis*), and that in many respects the Church of England stands for a *via media*, but this is very different from saying that our Church is " midway " between Roman Catholicism and Protestantism. On the contrary, no Roman Catholic could do anything but admit that our Articles are essentially Protestant. Further, our Formularies on many vital points are fundamentally at one with Continental Protestantism. The history of our Articles has already shown their close association with the Confessions of Augsburg and Wurtemberg. And it must never be forgotten that

" there are only two systems of Dogmatic Theology, coherent in structure and capable of scientific exposition, the Romish and the Protestant ; these words being understood not in the popular sense, but of the principles of the respective systems, as they are found stated in the public Confessions of Faith, and elaborated in the works of the principal theologians, on either side since the Reformation."[2]

It is well known that the experiment of a *via media* theology was made by Newman in connection with Tract 90. But it soon proved

[1] "The Articles, if viewed under one aspect, were *pacificatory*; they strove by silence, or at least by general statements, to divert and calm the speculations of the English clergy on mysterious and scholastic questions which remain unsolved in Holy Scripture, and transcend the present limits of the human understanding. On the other hand those Articles were meant to be *denunciatory*; plain and positive errors were unsparingly rebuked. Criteria had been provided, so that advocates alike of Romanism and Anabaptism, Papist and fanatic, Puritan and Zwinglian, 'sacramentary,' were all excluded from the office of public teachers in the Church of England" (Hardwick, *ut supra*, p. 159).
[2] Litton, *Introduction to Dogmatic Theology*, Second Edition, p. xviii.

to be utterly impossible, and " the golden mean, in its actual application, was found to involve as many difficulties as either extreme."[1]   Indeed, the fact that Newman himself was compelled to set it on one side and join the Roman Church is the strongest possible testimony to the essential Protestantism of the Anglican Formularies.   In view, therefore, of these statements it is impossible to avoid drawing the conclusion in regard to Newman of one of the ablest thinkers of the last century :—

" A writer may be pardoned who accepts the judgment of so great a master, and ventures to think that nothing in Dogmatic Theology that will satisfy the demands of consecutive thinkers is likely to be produced except on the lines either of genuine Romanism or of genuine Protestantism."[2]

It is a simple matter of fact that no trace can be found of any such idea as that represented by the phrase " Catholic principles."   The plain grammatical sense of the Articles in the light of Holy Scripture is the Anglican position, and the appeal to Scripture shows what is our ultimate authority.   The Church, and even the Creeds, are subject to Holy Scripture (Articles VI, VIII, XX).[3]

[1] Litton, *ut supra*, p. xviii.   [2] Litton, *ut supra*, p. xix.
[3] Three recent testimonies to this are to the point:
"Is it not then entirely inconsistent with this principle of our Church to say, as is constantly said by many among us, that the Prayer Book and Articles were to be read and interpreted in the light of the belief and practice of the Catholic Church? Her principle demands, on the contrary, that our formularies, and more particularly our Articles, should be interpreted in the light of Holy Scripture, rather than in that of mediæval theology" (Wace, *Principles of the Reformation*, p. 248).
"Is it quite accurate to say that the appeal of the English Church is to the Scriptures and the primitive fathers? I should have thought that the sixth Article was sufficiently conclusive. 'Holy Scripture containeth all things necessary to salvation.' Nothing is to be received which is not read therein nor to be proved thereby. The English Church, as it seems to me, claims to rest upon the rock of the Bible, and the Bible only, as exclusively as any body of Protestants in Christendom" (Simpson, *The Thing Signified*, p. 13).
"It may be convenient to assert that a particular statement in the Articles is 'patient' of a certain interpretation, but it is obviously important to know whether that interpretation is consistent with the sense in which, and the purpose for which, it was originally set forth" (Tait, *Lecture Outlines on the Thirty-nine Articles*, p. 8).

ANALYSIS OF THE ARTICLES

IT has already been shown that the Articles do not present a complete system of doctrine because they were largely due to the historical circumstances which called them forth. If they had been intended as a complete, systematic statement of Christian doctrine the logical place of Articles VI-VIII would have been first instead of as at present. But the fundamental doctrines of Articles I-V were doubtless put in the foreground in order to show the vital agreement of Reformation doctrine with that of the mediæval and primitive Church on the realities of Christian Theism. But there is more fulness and completeness of teaching than many are inclined to believe. The main omission is in connection with Eschatology, and on this, the History of the Forty-two Articles is interesting and perhaps significant. The Articles, as they stand, are best divided as follows :—

I.—THE SUBSTANCE OF FAITH (Articles I-V).

    1. The Holy Trinity.
  2-4. The Son of God.
      (a) The Word or Son of God, which was made very Man.
      (b) The going down of Christ into Hell.
      (c) The Resurrection of Christ.
    5. The Holy Ghost.

II.—THE RULE OF FAITH (Articles VI-VIII).

    6. The Sufficiency of the Holy Scriptures for Salvation.
    7. The Old Testament.
    8. The Three Creeds.

III.—THE LIFE OF FAITH (Articles IX-XVIII). *Personal Religion.*

A.—ITS COMMENCEMENT (Articles IX-XIV). Doctrines connected with Justification.
    9. Original or Birth-sin.
  10. Free-will.
  11. The Justification of Man.
  12. Good Works.
  13. Works before Justification.
  14. Works of Supererogation.

B.—Its Course (Articles XV-XVIII). Doctrines connected with Sanctification.

    15. Christ alone without Sin.
    16. Sin after Baptism.
    17. Predestination and Election.
    18. Obtaining eternal Salvation only by the Name of Christ.

IV.—The Household of Faith (Articles XIX-XXXIX). *Corporate Religion.*

A.—The Church (Articles XIX-XXII).

    19. The Church.
    20. The Authority of the Church.
    21. The Authority of General Councils.
    22. Purgatory.

B.—The Ministry (Articles XXIII, XXIV).

    23. Ministering in the Congregation.
    24. Speaking in the Congregation in such a Tongue as the people understandeth.

C.—The Sacraments (Articles XXV-XXXI).

    25. The Sacraments.
    26. The Unworthiness of the Ministers, which hinders not the effect of the Sacrament.
    27. Baptism.
    28. The Lord's Supper.
    29. The Wicked which eat not the Body of Christ in the use of the Lord's Supper.
    30. Both Kinds.
    31. The one Oblation of Christ finished upon the Cross.

D.—Church Discipline (Articles XXXII-XXXVI).

    32. The Marriage of Priests.
    33. Excommunicate Persons, how they are to be avoided.
    34. The Traditions of the Church.
    35. The Homilies.
    36. Consecration of Bishops and Ministers.

E.—Church and State (Articles XXXVII-XXXIX).

    37. The Civil Magistrates.
    38. Christian men's Goods, which are not common.
    39. A Christian man's Oath.

The scope of the Articles covers the twofold ground of (1) Divine Revelation: its fact and evidences; (2) Human Response: its method and consequences.

The contents of Divine Revelation may perhaps be stated thus—

1. The Doctrine of God. Theology. God in His Being, Character, and Relationships.

2. The Doctrine of Man. Anthropology. Before and after the Fall.

3. The Doctrine of Christ. Christology. His Person, Nature, and Work.

4. The Doctrine of Redemption. Soteriology. Its need, nature, means, and effects.

5. The Doctrine of the Spirit. Pneumatology. The Spirit in the Old Testament, the New Testament, the Christian Church.

6. The Doctrine of the Church. Ecclesiology. The Church, the Ministry, and the Sacraments.

7. The Doctrine of the Future. Eschatology. Death, Life, Heaven, Hell.[1]

It will be seen that with the exception of the last section the Articles have something to say on all essential points, and in regard to Eschatology, the Church has probably been wise in omitting the controverted subjects stated in Articles XXXIX, XL, XLI, and XLII of 1553, and limiting the teaching of the Church to the brief but plain statements of the three Creeds.

---

[1] Another outline, which may be compared with the above, will be found in *Outlines of Theological Study*, compiled and published with the approval of the Committee of the Conference upon the Training of Candidates for Holy Orders, pp. 29–32 (London: George Bell & Sons). The entire pamphlet is one of great value for all students.

I. THE SUBSTANCE OF FAITH

ARTICLES I–V

1. THE HOLY TRINITY.

2–4. THE SON OF GOD.

    (*a*) THE WORD OR SON OF GOD, WHICH WAS MADE VERY MAN.

    (*b*) THE GOING DOWN OF CHRIST INTO HELL.

    (*c*) THE RESURRECTION OF CHRIST.

5. THE HOLY GHOST.

A

ARTICLE I

Of Faith in the Holy Trinity.	*De Fide in Sacrosanctam Trinitatem.*
There is but one living and true God, everlasting, without body, parts, or passions; of infinite power, wisdom, and goodness; the Maker and Preserver of all things both visible and invisible. And in unity of this Godhead, there be three Persons, of one substance, power, and eternity; the Father, the Son, and the Holy Ghost.	Unus est vivus et verus Deus, æternus, incorporeus, impartibilis, impassibilis; immensæ potentiæ, sapientiæ, ac bonitatis; Creator et Conservator omnium, tum visibilium, tum invisibilium. Et in unitate hujus divinæ naturæ, tres sunt Personæ, ejusdem essentiæ, potentiæ, ac æternitatis; Pater, Filius, et Spiritus Sanctus.

IMPORTANT EQUIVALENTS.

Without body	= *incorporeus.*
Without parts	= *impartibilis.*
Without passions	= *impassibilis.*
Infinite	= *immensæ.*
Of this Godhead	= *hujus divinæ naturæ.*
Of one substance	= *ejusdem essentiæ.*

It was essential to put this subject in the forefront to show the fundamental beliefs of the Reformers as against Rome, and also as against extremists on the Protestant side, some of whom had gone so far as to deny the doctrine of the Trinity.

The Article, which dates from 1553, is drawn mainly from the First Article of the Confession of Augsburg, 1530, and the Thirteenth Article of the Concordat of 1538. It can also be illustrated by the *Reformatio Legum*, where the same language is seen.[1] The main truths of the Article are two: (1) the Unity of the Godhead; (2) the Trinity in the Godhead, the former being the necessary foundation and presupposition of the latter. But in the course of the statement there are several aspects of truth connected with the Deity which call for attention.

I.—THE EXISTENCE OF GOD

" There is . . . God." This is the general theistic position on which all religion rests, and as the Article starts here, it seems necessary to discuss briefly the grounds of Theism. The word " God," according to Skeat,

---

[1] "De Deo.—Ecclesiæ magno consensu apud nos docent decretum Nicenæ Synodi de unitate essentiæ, et de tribus personis, verum et sine ulla dubitatione credendum esse. Videlicet, quod sit una essentia divina, quæ appellatur et est Deus æternus, incorporeus, impartibilis, immensa potentia, sapientia, bonitate, Creator et Conservator omnium rerum visibilium et invisibilium, et tamen tres sint personæ ejusdem essentiæ potentiæ, et coæternæ, Pater, Filius, et Spiritus Sanctus; et nomine personæ utuntur ea significatione qui usi sunt in hac causa scriptores ecclesiastici, ut significet non partem aut qualitatem in alio, sed quod proprie subsistit" (Gibson, *The Thirty-nine Articles*, p. 90).

comes from the Indo-Germanic " *Ghu*," " to worship." It does not mean, as often formerly suggested, " good." The Article treats belief in God in two parts, dealing first with that which is common to all theistic religions, and then stating that which is distinctive of Christianity. Theism is, of course, not peculiar to Christianity, and definitions of God differ. Although for convenience the order of the Article is followed it is not necessary to think that Theism rests on two separate and distinct foundations, natural and supernatural, for our highest authority for God is Revelation, not Nature (Rom. i. 20). Following Scripture, the Article does not argue or prove, but assumes the existence of God. " There is . . . God." " In the beginning God created the heaven and the earth " (Gen. i. 1). " But without faith it is impossible to please Him : for he that cometh to God must believe that He is, and that He is a rewarder of them that diligently seek Him " (Heb. xi. 6). Our aim, therefore, is not so much to prove as to explain what the existence of God is and involves. Scripture recognises a natural knowledge of God (Rom. i. 19).

What is the origin of the idea of God ? There are two general explanations. By some the idea of God as a Supreme Being is regarded, in technical language, as " an intuition of the moral reason." St. Paul seems to have recognised in the mind an innate perception of God (Acts xvii. 28). This means that the belief in a Personal God is born in every man, not as a perfect and complete idea, but as involving a capacity for belief when the idea is presented. If this is so, it is one of the primary intuitions of human nature. It is certainly a mistake to suppose that we derive the idea of God from the Bible, for races that have never heard of the Bible possess a definite belief in a Supreme Being. The Bible reveals God's character and His purpose for man, and thus gives us a true idea of the Divine Being, but the emphasis is on the truth rather than on the mere fact. In the same way it is equally incorrect to say that we obtain the idea of God from reason, for reason is not in this respect originative.[1] By reflection we can obtain a fuller conception of God, but the reason itself is not the source of the conception. By those who hold that our idea of God is intuitive the conception of God is analysed into three elements : first, a consciousness of power in God which leads to a feeling of our dependence on Him ; second, a consciousness of His perfection which leads to a realisation of our obligation to Him ; third, a consciousness of His Personality which leads to a sense of worship of Him.

Others object to the idea of God as intuitive, and say that it is the result of the reason instinctively recognising Truth, Beauty, and Good-

---

[1] "We do not reach the idea of God as the final and irrefragable result of a long chain of syllogistic reasoning. Neither do we find God vindicated to the intellect as the crown of a slow and patient induction from data given to us in consciousness. No doubt the apprehension of God is an intellectual act, but it is an intellectual act that is saturated with emotion" (Miller, *Problem of Theology*, p. 15 f.; see also Note B., p. 306).

ness, and that these coalesce in the thought of one Reality. On this view these three elements afford an argument for Theism.[1]

But however it comes, natural religion means the idea of God formed by men independently of Revelation, and one thing is quite clear, the belief is universal. This is usually termed the *Consensus Gentium*, and is a fact which has to be explained, since "a primitive Revelation presupposes a Revealer: an innate idea presupposes an Author."[2] It shows that religion is not illusive, but real, and that the universe is spiritual.[3]

This universal belief in the existence of God is confirmed by arguments suggested by the world without and man's nature within, and it is necessary to enquire as to these proofs of the existence of God. While we may rightly deny the possibility of finding God by reason only, the proofs usually adduced are valuable and, indeed, essential for the knowledge of the Divine Nature and for the vindication of the convictions otherwise obtained.[4] There are two ways of procedure. Some maintain that it is possible to prove the existence of God on *a priori* grounds. By reasoning from the nature of things it is urged that we may deduce the proof of God's existence. This was attempted in the eighteenth century by Dr. Samuel Clarke, and called by him "A Demonstration of the Being and Attributes of God." In the nineteenth century the same method was seen in "The Argument *a priori* for the Being and Attributes of the Living God," by W. H. Gillespie,[5] who was dissatisfied with Dr. Clarke's work. By means of a series of propositions it is argued that "there is a Being of Infinity, of Expansion, and Duration"; and that this Being is a Spirit, All-Knowing, the Creator and Governor of all things. But it may be questioned whether this metaphysical method will satisfy many minds. It is an attempt to demonstrate a First Cause by showing that however far back we go every effect must have a first adequate cause, and that the mind must at last come to an existence without a cause, an uncaused cause. But it is at once better and certainly easier to proceed along the other, the *a posteriori* road. The questions of natural religion are facts and must be dealt with inductively and by the same processes we apply to all other realms of knowledge. This does not mean that the results of the *a priori* method are barren, for once the existence of God has been established on *a posteriori* grounds we are inevitably led to

---

[1] Everett, *Theism and the Christian Faith* (Unitarian and Hegelian).

[2] Litton, *Introduction to Dogmatic Theology*, Second Edition, p. 61; see also Strong, *Manual of Theology*, p. 33; Miller, *Topics of the Times*, "The Idea of God," pp. 10, 23.

[3] Peake, *Christianity: Its Nature and Truth*, Ch. IV.

[4] "It is very doubtful whether a single individual has ever found God as the sequence of a syllogistic process. To-day the agnostic points out hopeless flaws in the argument, and the vast majority of intellectual believers ground their faith on a totally different basis. But though we cease to hold these arguments as demonstrations of God's existence they are still essential elements in enriching our knowledge of God. Rightly apprehended, they have an all-important place in the communion of the soul with God, and in strengthening those tendrils of faith with which the human spirit grasps the Divine" (Miller, *ut supra*, p. 16 f.).

[5] T. & T. Clark, 1906.

attribute to Him the conceptions of Infinity, Eternity, and Spirituality which the *a priori* method emphasises.

We have already seen that Scripture never attempts to prove God's existence, but always assumes and affirms it (Psa. xix. 1). It may be questioned whether the existence of God is really capable of direct proof, for there seems no line of evidence absolutely conclusive to the mind of man. This fact has been said to show that belief in God is not like a mathematical axiom, self-evident. But since demonstration is impossible, for then there would be no room for faith, so the non-existence of God is equally impossible of demonstration. Many of life's essential elements are of this character, and the true position is that of Butler: "Probability is the very guide of life." This probability admits of degrees from the lowest possibility to the highest moral certainty, the latter reaching to the strongest kind of proof.

It is important to note the reason why it is said that we can have no demonstrable proofs for the existence of God. This is not due to the fact that belief in God is unreasonable, but because the fact to be proved is in the very nature of the case so great as not to admit of strict demonstration. To demonstrate God would require some greater truth or truths by which to prove our point. Indeed, it may be said without any question that the existence of a God of reason and love is so certain and fundamental a fact that it actually has to be assumed in all our thought and life. So that it is a fact which cannot be proved because it is the foundation of all proof, the postulate without which we should have to give up the possibility of rational thought. Hence, this position really gives in a way the deepest proof that we could possibly have, and that, in spite of the fact that strict mathematical demonstration is impossible.

The truth is, as we shall see in the course of our consideration, that it is impossible to distinguish between the existence and the character of God. The two ideas are inextricably bound up together, so that as we ponder what are often called the proofs of God's existence we are all the while giving attention to the necessary elements of the Divine character. While, therefore, there are no direct proofs of the Divine existence, there are several indirect proofs involving evidence which points to it as the essential basis of all other existence. These proofs are not all of the same value, but they call for separate attention, and also combine to produce cumulative force.

1. The Ontological Proof.—By this is meant that a subjective conception in man implies an objective existence apart from man. It is sometimes expressed by saying that the thought of God is latent in the mind, but is not produced by the mind. Man "claims to interpret the nature outside him on the analogy of his own."[1] The unity he imposes on nature is modelled on his knowledge of himself. We have an idea of an independent perfect Being, and when the thought of this comes to us we inevitably think of Him as existing, and as necessarily existing. It

[1] Strong, *ut supra*, p. 25.

must be admitted, however, that many scholars regard this proof as of only small value. Thus, Dean Strong says it is an assumed claim which cannot be proved, and an ideal which cannot be realised.[1] On this view the argument seems rather to assume God's existence while proving His perfection. But it is still possible to use it as a way of stating the fact that belief in God's existence is a necessity of the practical reason.[2] And as Orr says :—

" It would be strange if an argument which has wielded such power over some of the strongest intellects were utterly baseless. . . . Kant himself has given the impulse to a new development of it, which shows more clearly than ever that it is not baseless, but is really the deepest and most comprehensive of all arguments."[3]

2. The Cosmological Proof.—This means that every effect must have its adequate cause. Antecedents and consequents are insufficient because they only imply succession. Sequences of events are not merely chronological. It is true that night follows day, but not as effect following cause. Yet there is a cause both to day and night. The universe is an effect because it had a beginning (Gen. i. 1), and its only adequate cause is the First Cause, God. Everything, therefore, in existence must have had a cause to produce it. The world exists and must have had a cause, and as God is the only adequate Cause, God exists. This means that the mind intuitively perceives a cause from what is visible (Rom. i. 20). Matter must have been created. Motion must have had an impetus. Life must have had a Life-giver. The argument has been stated thus : (1) The process of development in the universe, or in any part of it, had a beginning ; (2) this requires a cause ; (3) this cause was not physical ; (4) the only non-physical cause is will or mind ; (5) these imply a personal being.[4] According to Huxley, Causality is the first great act of faith on the part of a man of science.[5]

Another recent statement of the same position is worthy of mention : (1) every phenomenon must have a cause adequate to produce it ; (2) the universe must have a cause ; (3) whatever is intelligible bears witness to a cause that is intelligent ; (4) the universe, being intelligible, proclaims its cause to be intelligent ; (5) in all phenomena controlled by human agency, regularity and uniformity are the evidences of design and intention ; (6) the universe, being full of regularities and uniformities, demands for its explanation a purposive causative agency ; (7) human personality is constituted by the attributes of consciousness, intelligence,

---

[1] Strong, *ut supra*, p. 27; see also Litton, *ut supra*, p. 59 f.
[2] Litton, *ut supra*, p. 60.
[3] Orr, *Christian View of God and the World*, Tenth Edition, p. 103 f.
"I cannot but maintain, therefore, that the ontological argument, in the kernel and essence of it, is a sound one, and that in it the existence of God is really seen to be the first, the most certain, and the most indisputable of all truths" (Orr, *ut supra*, p. 106).
[4] A. D. Kelly, *Rational Necessity of Theism*, pp. 142–149
[5] A. D. Kelly, *ut supra*, pp. 50, 156.

and purposive will; (8) the same attributes would constitute personality in the cause of the universe, which is, in effect, the contention of Theism.[1]

By some it is urged that apart from Scripture it cannot be proved that the universe had a beginning, but the argument now stated is valid and strong for the probability and reasonableness of the Divine existence as the only adequate cause.[2]

3. The Teleological Proof.—This is better known as " the argument from design." There are evidences of design in nature, *e.g.* the adaptation of means to end imply a designer, a personal, purposive cause. The gills of a fish in relation to water, the wings of a bird to air, the teeth of animals to tearing, the hand of man to work, the solar system with its fixed orbits, unchanging speeds and distances calculated according to mathematical law—all these things, and many more besides, suggest the presence of mind and purpose in the universe. In his *Natural Theology*, Paley used the illustration of a watch, which could not make itself, the mechanism presupposing a watchmaker, and although the form of the argument may have changed since his day the fact remains the same, that the world as a whole shows evidence of design, that it could not make itself, but must have had a Maker, that Maker being God.

Objection is sometimes raised to this argument, because as it rests on finite data it is urged that it cannot prove God's infinity or eternity. But it is at least an argument for the rationality of the universe. While it may not be possible, following Paley, to argue design from particular details, yet viewing the universe as a whole the argument is as valid as ever.[3] " Man expects to find the world a coherent whole."[4] This is the necessary basis of all thought and experience, for in the use of the various avenues of life man naturally and rightly expects to find all the facts harmonise.[5] The very word *uni*verse implies mind.

4. The Anthropological Proof.—This means an argument from man to God, from the human nature to the Divine. Man's mental,

---

[1] Warschauer, *The Atheist's Dilemma*, p. 22 f.

[2] "This common-sense Theism, however roughly defined, has elements of truth in it. No sophistry will prevail on us to throw it away. It is held that the great Greek philosopher, Aristotle, in his doctrine of a first cause of motion outside the universe, stated a cosmological proof for the being of God" (Mackintosh, *A First Primer of Apologetics*, p. 35). See also Orr, *ut supra*, p. 95.

[3] "The Design argument is the expression of a deeply-rooted and reasonable conviction that a world existing apart from purpose is not a rational world at all, that is, it is not a world which answers to the demand of our reason. As stated in its traditional form it lacks convincingness. But if we turn our minds from adaptations manifested in a particular organism to the fact of the universe as a whole—to the fact that the universe is a Cosmos not a Chaos, the old argument regains its old force" (A. D. Kelly, *ut supra*, p. 155).

[4] Strong, *ut supra*, p. 20.

[5] "Man has five senses. Each one of these admits him into a different world. The world of sight is not the same as the world of sound, or the world of sound as the world of smell. But man's capacity to live and utilise his experience depends upon his being able at will to translate the reports of one sense into terms of another, and to feel himself certain of the truthfulness of his results" (Strong, *ut supra*, p. 21).

moral, and spiritual natures demand God as their Creator. The existence of human free will implies a greater Will. The fact of conscience with its emphasis on law involves a Law-giver. When man says, " I ought," he means, " I owe it," and herein lies one of the essential distinctions between man and the lower animals. Man's conscience can be trained to the highest degree, but it is impossible to train that which does not exist, and the lower animals can only be compelled to certain actions by a sense of fear, never by a consciousness of right and wrong. The fact of personality in man is also an argument for the existence of God, since it is impossible to conceive that man's personality is the only or highest in existence. Personality is the supreme element in the universe, as Huxley himself admitted in one of the latest of his writings.[1] All this tends to show that mind cannot come from matter, or spirit from flesh, or conscience from anything purely physical, and for this reason a Being possessing both mind and spirit must have made man. This Being was God, Who therefore exists.

Further, man is impressed by the three ideas of Truth, Goodness, and Beauty, and these point to the character of God in Whom they are fully realised. Some thinkers have rested their view of God on one or other of these alone. Plato laid stress on the beautiful, Spinoza on unity, Kant on morality. But the whole man demands attention. The idea of truth argues for unity, and this in turn involves the eternity, omnipresence, and omnipotence of God. The idea of goodness argues for the character of God as love. The idea of beauty implies the glory of God, as seen in the manifestations of the Divine nature and work. According to the law stamped on all life, like begets like, flower begetting flower, animal begetting animal, man begetting man. And so we believe God " created man in His own image " (Gen. i. 26, 27).[2]

Here, again, because man is finite it may not be possible to argue God's Infinity, but it certainly postulates Personality. There are four great facts in nature : Thought, Forethought, Law, and Life, and these demand respectively a Thinker, a Provider, a Law-giver, and a Life-giver. We must beware of the fallacy of personifying Nature and Law, which are expressive only of method, not of source.

It is sometimes said that the doctrine of Evolution has destroyed the cosmological, and especially the teleological, proofs of the Divine existence, that the Darwinian doctrine of Natural Selection is not concerned with ends, but results, and for this intelligence is not required. But this position involves much that is open to question and calls for serious consideration. It is sometimes thought that the Christian Church has been needlessly suspicious of Evolution and far too slow in applying it to religion. But it should never be forgotten that Evolution entered the

---

[1] "I cannot conceive how the phenomena of consciousness as such, and apart from the physical processes *by which they are called into existence*, are to be brought within bounds of physical science" (Quoted in A. D. Kelly, *ut supra*, p. 29).
[2] Orr, *ut supra*, "God as Religious Postulate." Appendix to Lecture III, p. 112.

world originally, not simply as a theory of science, but as an ally of a philosophy of materialism which, if true, would have banished Christianity, and, indeed, all spiritual religion from the earth. It was hardly to be expected, therefore, that the Church could give a welcome to a theory which entered in connection with such associations. Then again, time has shown that the Darwinian theory is not necessarily to be identified with the general doctrine of Evolution. It has been pointed out by several writers that there are factors of which Darwin took little or no account, and these factors have led to a decided modification of the original theory of Natural Selection. [1]

There is scarcely anything more important than a clear understanding of what Evolution means. The term is commonly used in a very indefinite way. It may mean little or it may mean much. There are three main divisions commonly included in the word "Evolution"; the sub-organic, the organic, and the super-organic. The first refers to the development of matter without life, and is generally applied to the formation of the solar or stellar systems from some more crude conditions of matter. Organic Evolution is the name for a process of derivation or development for the forms of life, vegetable and animal, that have existed, or now exist in the world. Super-organic Evolution refers to the same process in non-material spheres. But even in connection with organic Evolution there is a very wide divergence of opinion as to the use of the term. It is applied also to ordinary growth, and also to gradual, progressive development made without interference from without, but by the inherent potentiality of some primordial germ up to all the varied forms of life on the globe. Yet again, Evolution may be regarded as either causal or modal, as the cause of all life or as only the mode by which a Personal Creator has brought about the diversity which now exists. In other words, Evolution may be regarded as atheistic or as theistic. Now there can be no doubt that if Evolution is considered to be causal it is entirely opposed to all theistic conceptions. But the causality of Evolution is very far from being proved; indeed, it is entirely opposed to all that is known of science. Evolution within certain limits is a fact, but it has not yet been proved to be of universal application. There are physical gaps, to say nothing of mental and moral chasms. By means of a good deal of vagueness and inaccuracy of thought, men frequently speak of the uniformity of nature, but they forget that man is included in nature, and man's life is very far from uniform by reason of his possession of will. So that while we may rightly accept Evolution as a working hypothesis, and within certain limits an undoubted truth, yet this is wholly different from regarding it as the full explanation of all things

[1] Henslow, *Present-Day Rationalism critically Examined*; Orr, *God's Image in Man*; Otto, *Naturalism and Religion*. It is also obvious that Natural Selection cannot apply to the inorganic world which is dead, and yet the geological strata, comprising over a hundred zones, are without exception advantageous to man. This is a clear proof of the force of the Teleological argument in the inorganic realm.

in the universe.[1] If, however, we regard Evolution as modal it is not only not anti-theistic, but in many respects gives a far deeper, richer and fuller conception of the Divine working than the older theories. It is only opposed to Theism if regarded as causal and materialistic. Testimonies to this can be found in the writings of scientific men like Huxley, Ray Lankester, and others.[2] The best thought of to-day tends more and more to agree with the opinion expressed by Sir Oliver Lodge, that "the existence of a great World-soul is the best explanation of things as they are."[3]

The place and value of these proofs vary with different writers, though there is a general agreement that they do not amount to a demonstration of the existence of God. But in their place and for their purpose they are as valuable as ever.[4] The main point of importance to remember is that these proofs are hardly capable apart from Revelation of assuring us of a Personal God, with the attributes associated with Him.[5] One thing is absolutely certain, that it is only by Revelation we attain to fellowship with God as a Personal Redeemer.[6] And it is for this reason

[1] "We may otherwise make too much of the effect of the discovery of the principle of 'natural selection.' It is very doubtful whether this principle will be found able to bear all the burden which some would place upon it. . . . It is by no means plain that current theories of 'evolution' have so disposed of the Argument for Design in every possible form as is sometimes hastily assumed" (Webb, *Problems in the Relations of God and Man*, p. 161).

[2] "There is a good deal of talk and not a little lamentation about the so-called religious difficulties which physical science has created. In theological science, as a matter of fact, it has created none. Not a solitary problem presents itself to the philosophical theist at the present day which has not existed from the time that philosophers began to think out the logical grounds and the logical consequences of Theism. . . . The doctrine of Evolution is neither theistic nor anti-theistic. It simply has no more to do with Theism than the first book of Euclid has" (Quoted in A. D. Kelly, *ut supra*, p. 37).

[3] For the general subject of Evolution and the Christian Religion see, in addition to the works quoted or referred to above: Stokes, *Gifford Lectures*, Second Series, Lecture X; McCosh, *The Religious Aspect of Evolution;* Gurnhill, *Some Thoughts of God*, Chs. VII, VIII; Gant, *Modern Natural Theology*, Ch. I; Kennedy, *Natural Theology and Modern Thought*, Ch. III; Salmon, *Evolution and Other Papers*, Ch. I; Fairhurst, *Organic Evolution Considered*; Orr, *God's Image in Man*, s.v. Evolution.

[4] "Considered as proofs, in the ordinary sense of the word, they are open to the objections which have been frequently urged against them; but viewed as an analysis of the unconscious or implicit logic of religion, as tracing the steps of the process by which the human spirit rises to the knowledge of God, and finds therein the fulfilment of its own highest nature, these proofs possess great value" (Caird, *Introduction to Philosophy of Religion*, p. 133). See also Litton, *ut supra*, p. 62 ff.; Webb, *ut supra*, pp. 154–188; Orr, *ut supra*, p. 94.

[5] "The old theistic proofs have their value. Yet it is doubtful how far, apart from revelation, reason can make us sure of a personal God; and it is certain that only revelation can do what is of vital importance for us—introduce us to God's friendship. Moreover, Kant seems to strike the right note at least in this respect, when he tells us that we are concerned to be certain of God, of immortality, and of free will. The Christian knowledge of God (whatever previous elements it may take up into itself) is the knowledge of God in Christ as our Friend and our Saviour. Where do we see God acting a Father's part? Where does He directly manifest Himself as a Person, personally interested in the welfare of beings who seem so often the sport of Nature's laws? How can we obtain permanent, lasting assurance of His favour? There is only one answer" (Mackintosh, *A First Primer of Apologetics*, p. 38 f.).

[6] "But no one of these methods conducts a man to a true knowledge of the nature of God so long as he is ignorant of the revealed testimonies which Christianity awakens around us and in us" (Martensen, *Christian Dogmatics*, p. 74).

that modern thought tends increasingly in the direction of Revelation for the main support of the theistic position. While ready to give reason its due and to allow it its proper place, there still remains the consideration that for the character of God we need the knowledge that Revelation alone can provide. The main objection taken to the usual proofs, as now set out, is not their error so much as their inadequacy :—

" The God whom they prove may be God, but He is not the Father of our Lord Jesus Christ."[1]

This tendency of recent thought to regard natural religion as secondary and to make the Christian Revelation our primary ground for Theism is undoubtedly important and needs careful consideration. It is urged that while belief in Christ presupposes natural theology, yet the latter is difficult because it tends to become metaphysical and philosophical,[2] so that our true method is not so much to reach through God to Christ as through Christ to God. But, nevertheless, we must not deny natural theology by undue emphasis on belief in God through Christ. To natural theology we may rightly look for indications of the existence of God, though as inevitably we turn to Christianity for the marks of the Divine character. The Nature of God in the abstract may be inferred from natural theology, but His personal character as Love comes from Christ. For this reason we must therefore give attention to the next line of proof.

5. The Christological Proof.—The Incarnation of Christ, which for the present we assume to be true, corresponds with the foregoing considerations and demands a belief in God. God can only be adequately known in Christ, and any speculations about God which stop short of Christ's revelation are necessarily inadequate. The bearing of this on the theistic controversy is important, for all objections proceed on the fallacy of excluding from consideration our Lord's life and teachings and endeavour to place our knowledge of God on a natural basis. Now though we do not now *prove* Christ's words to be a revelation of God, we have a right to say that no philosophy is scientific which fails to notice the testimony of Christ as, in any case, the greatest human experience on the subject. No testimony ought to be excluded from notice, and we hold that God was revealed in Christ because nature alone was insufficient to reveal Him in the character and attitude essential for human life, as good and gracious.

[1] W. Adams Brown, *Christian Theology in Outline*, p. 125. See also Mullins, *The Christian Religion in its Doctrinal Expression*.
[2] "Sanctioned by usage as it is, the distinction which the epithet connotes is open to question; Natural Religion, like the social contract, exists for thought rather than in things. . . . No one ever held or taught it: it is an abstraction or residuum left behind by concrete religions when the rest of the conception has been thought away. The evidences of religion are historical and psychological; religion is part both of civilization and of the furniture of the mind. But the isolation of such notions as God, freedom, and immortality is formal; the proofs, however irrefutable, do not convince" (Review of Mr. A. J. Balfour's "Theism and Humanism" in *The Nation*, 2nd October 1915).

The New Testament claims that Christ revealed God, and this proof consists of several elements: (1) The character of Christ; (2) the fulfilment of prophecy; (3) the elements of the supernatural and miraculous; (4) the character, claim, and power of the Bible; (5) the existence and growth of the Christian Church; (6) the progress and power of Christianity in the world; (7) the moral miracle of personal and corporate regeneration and renovation. These matters are necessarily left for detailed consideration and proof, and are mentioned here simply as parts of the Christological proof of the existence and character of God. They require nothing short of a Divine presence and power to account for them. Thus this Christological conception confirms our belief in a First Cause, a Personality, and a Moral Governor of the universe, as set forth in the previous considerations.

As we review these five lines of argument we observe that their force lies in their combination. As each thread of a rope may be easily broken while separated, though the rope as a whole may be unbreakable, so it may be said that each of these proofs taken alone may be inconclusive, but when all five are united they are conclusive of the Personal existence of God. Nor are we concerned with the essential difference between theology and other sciences in regard to nature and method. While no science proves its own first principles, but must derive them from elsewhere or assume them, theology uses the fact of the existence of God both as premiss and conclusion.[1] So that if we grant belief in the existence of a Personal God the value of these proofs may be stated as follows: The Ontological argument proves God's Perfection; the Cosmological argument proves God's Causality; the Teleological argument proves God's Intelligence; the Anthropological argument proves God's Personality; the Christological argument proves God's Character as Love.

It is also important to remember that belief in God always contains a moral element and cannot be limited to that which is merely intellectual.[2] It is for this reason that the various proofs associated with natural theology cannot originate the idea of God in one who does not possess it. The idea must first of all be postulated, and then the proofs become powerful and cumulative.[3] While, therefore, we must not undervalue natural theology,[4] yet to Christians the argument from nature is rather the confirmation of our belief in God than the foundation of it. Christian

---

[1] Strong, *ut supra*, p. 2 f.
  "To take a parallel case, the evidence for the existence of our own personality is of the same character as the evidence for the existence of God. It appears both as conclusion and as premiss. To prove the existence of my own personality, I must assume it. . . . The evidence we allege in proof of the fact proves also that the investigation is reasonable only when the fact is assumed—that is, that the existence of God is the hinge upon which the whole process turns" (Strong, *ut supra*, p. 3).
[2] Strong, *ut supra*, p. 7 f.
[3] Miller, *Topics of the Times*, "The Idea of God," pp. 6–11.
[4] "A thoroughgoing denial of natural theology has usually proved a help to religious scepticism rather than to the assertion of revelation" (Mackintosh, *ut supra*, p. 33).

Theism is not merely natural theology in the light of Christ's teaching, or even Christ added to the God of natural theology; it is Theism embodied in and expressed by Christ, so that in Him we see Who and what God is and are thereby satisfied (John xiv. 8). Thus "Theism needs Revelation to complete it."[1]

It may be well to point out at this stage that the position of this Article is a testimony to the fact that the doctrine of God is fundamental for all else, settling everything. As this is, so will be our idea of Religion, Christ, the Bible, Man, Sin, and Revelation. It is the regulative idea and covers the whole of life.

II.—THE NATURE OF GOD

Heresy compelled the Church to provide a closer definition than would have otherwise been necessary, and to this is due the difference of tone between Scripture and philosophical theology. Nevertheless, we believe that all is implicit in Scripture and that the statements, abstract though they be, are only the explicit expression of what is implied and contained therein. There are five aspects of the Nature of God stated in the Article.

1. His Unity.—"There is one . . . God." This is much more than anything merely numerical; it is essential. Plurality is impossible (Deut. vi. 4; Isa. xli. 4; xliv. 6; xlviii. 12). The mind demands a First Cause, and the word "universe" points in the same direction, though it does not for a moment mean that the universe is God. God is the Infinite Being Who includes all in Himself. As such, He is our highest conception and loftiest principle, and there can be no other. This does not mean the "Infinite and Absolute" that "leaves room for no other and can brook none," but it does mean that whatever plurality of beings there are in the universe there is One Who is "highest of all."[2]

2. His Life.—"There is one living . . . God." The word is *vivus*, not *vivens*. God is life and its source. Scripture lays much stress on the "Living God," especially as against idolatry (Josh. iii. 10; Psa. xlii. 2; Jer. x. 10; Dan. vi. 26; Matt. xvi. 16; John vi. 57; Acts xiv. 15; Rom. ix. 26; Heb. iii. 12; Rev. vii. 2).

3. His Truth.—"There is one living and true God." The word is *verus*, not *verax* (*true*, not *truthful*), and answers to ἀληθινός rather than ἀληθής. But the two words are found in Scripture descriptive of God as "true." The latter means faithful, as against falsity (Tit. i. 2); the former means substantial, genuine, as against unreality (John xvii. 3).

4. His Eternity.—"There is one living and true God, everlasting." This, too, is a necessity in a First Cause, and is accordingly emphasised in Scripture (Rom. i. 20; 1 Tim. i. 17). It means a Being with no limitation of space and time. As He is not limited in space, so He is

---

[1] Orr, *God's Image in Man*, pp. 77–79, 111.
[2] Ward, *The Realm of Ends*, p. 443 and p. 436.

not limited in time. This statement should be carefully compared with the Creed, which emphasises the Almightiness of God.[1]

5. His Spirituality.—" Without body, parts, or passions."

(*a*) " Without body," *incorporeus*; that is, without limitation of power and space (John iv. 24). Yet, as we shall see, God's Infinity is always to be regarded as personal.

(*b*) " Without parts," *impartibilis*; that is, incapable as a Spirit of being represented in bodily shape, and without change, without imperfection, indivisible, and with no possibility of conflict.

(*c*) " Without passions," *impassibilis*; that is, incapable of being subjected with anything by an agent stronger than Himself (*sub-fero*). This simply denies His impotence and imperfection. But it is essential to distinguish it from the voluntary suffering endured by God on account of sin. As everyone that loves suffers, so God must suffer by reason of His unrequited love to man. This, however, is a self-limitation of God associated with the Divine Self-sacrifice. So that when the Article speaks of God as " without passions " it is manifestly unfair to say that it denies to God any moral character.[2]

Objection is sometimes raised to the Biblical conception of God as anthropomorphic, but the objection is not sound because we must use human language, and the conceptions of man and personality are the highest possible to us. It is obviously better to use anthropomorphic expressions than zoo-morphic or cosmo-morphic, and when we attribute to God emotions and sensibilities we mean to free Him from all the imperfections attaching to the human conceptions of these elements. In revealing Himself God has to descend to our capacities, and use language which can be understood. But this can never fully reveal Him since that which is finite could never explain the Infinite. So that God must necessarily speak of Himself as a Man, for so only could we comprehend anything about Him. Hence, both as to Person and actions, everything is spoken of after the manner of men. But all these are only figures of speech, by which alone we can obtain an idea of the reality. Any objection to such anthropomorphism only has force so far as man's thoughts of God are unworthy and untrue.[3]

III.—THE ATTRIBUTES OF GOD

By an attribute is to be understood " any conception which is necessary

---

[1] Westcott, *The Historic Faith*, p. 36 f.

[2] For the truth in the Patripassian heresy, see Fairbairn, *Christ in Modern Theology*, p. 483 f.; and for a fine treatment of the sense in which God is capable of suffering, see Bushnell, *The New Life*, Sermon XVII. See also Platt, *Immanence and Christian Thought*, pp. 414–418.

[3] "The God of religion and therefore of religious doctrine is always conceived anthropopathically or anthropomorphically; an abstract idea, such as that of the absolute, can never occupy the place of a religious conception of God; therefore the idea of personality, which is never entirely free from figure, is absolutely indispensable" (De la Saussaye, *Manual of the Science of Religion*, p. 230). See also Kennedy, *ut supra*, p. 260 ff.; Strong, *ut supra*, p. 39; Platt, *Immanence and Christian Thought*, p. 219.

to the explicit idea of God; any distinctive conception which cannot be resolved into any other."[1] The Article describes God as " of infinite power, wisdom, and goodness."

1. " Infinite power " (*immensæ potentiæ*).—This, which may be called physical, means power adequate to all possible requirements. There is no sphere higher than His (Psa. cxxxv. 6; Rev. i. 8). By this idea of omnipotence we are not to think of anything that is contradictory of any other Divine attribute, or as ruling out the conception of self-limitation such as is involved in the creation and redemption of man. The Latin, "*immensæ*," referring to infinity, may be compared with the similar phrase in the Athanasian Creed, " *Immensus Pater.*"

2. " Infinite wisdom " (*immensæ sapientiæ*).—This is the intellectual aspect expressed by the word " omniscience." It implies that nothing can escape the Divine knowledge (Psa. cxxxix. 2, 3, 6; cxlv. 7). He is " the only wise God " (1 Tim. i. 17).

3. " Infinite goodness " (*immensæ bonitatis*).—This is the ethical attribute and emphasises the Divine benevolence and beneficence.

It is, of course, in the moral attributes of God that natural religion is most defective. The Old Testament revelation is mainly concerned with the Holiness of God (Isa. vi. 3),[2] and the New Testament with the Divine Love (1 John iv. 8). So we may say that the characteristic revelation of God in the Bible is that of Holy Love.[3] The reason why the statement of the Divine character is incomplete is probably due to the fact that the main object of the Article is to affirm the doctrine of the Trinity. For this reason it names no other moral attribute than goodness. At this point it is therefore fitting to introduce the special teaching of St. John in reference to the Divine character :—

(a) God is Spirit (John iv. 24). This refers to God in Himself, and perhaps may be spoken of as the metaphysical aspect.

(b) God is Light (1 John i. 5). This refers to God mainly in relation to creation, and may perhaps be described as the moral aspect.

(c) God is Love (1 John iv. 8, 16).—This refers to God in relation to man and redemption, and may be regarded as His personal aspect.

Of these, the first speaks of God as He is in Himself; the second seems to refer largely to inanimate beings; while the third is concerned with creatures capable of making a response. It is essential to take care that in our conception of God physical and metaphysical elements are not permitted to predominate over the ethical elements, lest belief in a Divine Incarnation becomes difficult and almost impossible. It has often been pointed out that in the New Testament God is not defined as " Being," or " Infinity," or as " Substance," but by predicates that involve ethical ideas and ideals, Spirit, Light, and Love, ideals that appeal to the intellect, the will, and the heart, and all pointing to the possibility of God Himself

[1] H. B. Smith, *Systematic Theology*, p. 12; see also W. Adams Brown, *ut supra*, p. 100 ff.
[2] George Adam Smith, *Isaiah*, Vol. II.
[3] See Forsyth, *The Holy Father and the Living Christ*, passim.

becoming incarnate in human nature. And, as we shall see, Divine Revelation tells us that He has actually entered into human life in the Person of Jesus Christ in Whom all the fulness of the Godhead permanently dwells.

IV.—THE MANIFESTATION OF GOD IN NATURE

The Creeds connect creation with the existence of God, and the Article naturally follows the same line.[1] "The Maker, and Preserver of all things both visible and invisible."

1. "The Maker of all things."—This implies the simple but obvious truth that matter is not eternal. To use modern phraseology, it teaches that God is Transcendent.

2. "The Preserver of all things."—This means that God has not left the world He has created. It teaches what may be called the Immanence of God. If man is above the world, much more is God, and it may be said without any hesitation that there never has been a religion worthy of the name which did not believe that its God was above the world. Christianity, in particular, has always taught the Immanence of God.[2] While emphasising the Transcendence in association with the Divine Personality, Christian theology in all ages has always taken account of the presence of God in the world and in human life. But there is an un-Christian view of Immanence as well, which is rightly described as Pantheism. Christianity is neither deistic in the sense of making the Divine Transcendence absolutely remote from life, nor pantheistic in the sense of absorbing God in His Creation; on the contrary, it teaches the essential truth of both positions. If Immanence is over-pressed God becomes limited within creation and incapable of exceptional action.

Reviewing the statement of the Article, so far, we observe its clear implications against Atheism, Materialism, Polytheism, Pantheism, Deism, and Agnosticism, all these being in one way or another opposed by the teaching of the Article. In regard to the last point, it may be specially noted that facts compel us to predicate a knowledge of God, for it is impossible for the mind to remain in suspense.[3] In the same way the Article clearly opposes Dualism and Monism. The former teaches that there are two first principles, the latter the converse, that there is only one principle, thereby making God the Author of evil.

The various human conceptions of Deity have always lain between the two extremes of infinite impersonal power, as in Pantheism, and a Finite

---

[1] Litton, *ut supra*, p. 95.

[2] Illingworth, *Divine Immanence*; Platt, *Immanence and Christian Thought*.

[3] Agnosticism assumes a double incompetence—the incompetence not only of man to know God, but of God to make Himself known. But the denial of competence is the negation of Deity, and it is impossible to assert the non-existence of God; for before one can say that the world is without a God, he that makes this great denial must first have become thoroughly conversant with the whole world" (Miller, *Topics of the Times*, "The Idea of God," p. 13).

B

Person, as implied in Polytheism. Polytheism must involve finiteness of person, because only one God can be infinite, and personality is not strictly allowed by Pantheism. Of course, the problem is how to reconcile the thought of absoluteness and infinity with personality, since personality is assumed to imply limitation. But when we speak of the Infinite we do not intend thereby an impersonal substance, but One Who is a Person.[1] Our conception of God must be found between the two extremes. We must find room for the infinity of Pantheism while rejecting its impersonality, and we must find room for the personality of Polytheism while rejecting its finiteness. Pantheism, because it is almost always and wholly speculative and philosophical, never has been, never can be the religion of the masses of people. On the other hand, Polytheism is equally impossible because of its association with a crude and impure Theism.[2] The conception of Personality is central and fundamental, and no religion is possible unless God is regarded as at once Transcendent and Personal. This idea of the Personality of God has to be faced in every system of Philosophy, and is the determining factor of success or failure. Polytheism is therefore impossible and Monotheism is essential, and one of the greatest needs is a right conception of the One God as righteous. It is doubtless difficult to harmonise Personality and Immanence, but this is mainly due to the fact that the mind is apt to hold too material a conception of Immanence. Instead of conceiving of it as some extended or diffused matter or substance, we ought to regard it as the sustaining will of God active in every part of the universe.[3] "God is where He acts." In this sense the Immanence of God is merely His dynamic presence in every part of creation, together with the denial of the independence of the universe at any point. The doctrine is a welcome and salutary recognition of the fact that God is necessary to the world at all points, and it is intended to bring home to men the conviction that the only power in the universe is finally the power of God Himself. When this is understood there need be no insuperable difficulty in harmonising the ideas of Immanence and Personality. There is great danger in speaking of God as the Absolute, as though this meant independence of all relations. This is not our ordinary

[1] "'Infinite' (and the same is true of 'absolute') is an adjective, not a substantive. When used as a noun, preceded by the definite article, it signifies, not a being, but an abstraction. When it stands as a predicate, it means that the subject, be it space, time, or some quality of a being, is without limit" (Fisher, *The Grounds of Theistic and Christian Belief*, p. 69).
"Even when religion and philosophy both agree to speak of God as 'the Infinite,' for the one it is an adjective for the other a substantive" (Aubrey Moore, *Lux Mundi*, p. 65. Tenth Edition).
[2] "So far is Monotheism from having been evolved out of an original Polytheism, that Polytheism is rather a diseased outcome, through the influence of language, of an original Monotheism, which, amid all the forests of myths and rabble rout of divinities, may distinctly be traced at every stage of their existence in one and all of the ethnic religions of which history has preserved a record" (Miller, *Topics of the Times*, "The Idea of God," p. 32).
[3] Platt, *ut supra*, p. 205.

use of the term when applied to "absolute monarchy," etc., for it only means that God is not to be limited by anything or anyone outside Himself. The term is virtually synonymous with infinite, though emphasising the independence rather than the greatness of God. But in any case Personality is essential and indispensable so long as we are careful to remove from the idea of Divine Personality all our conceptions of change and development. We must hold His essential attributes of Omnipotence and Omniscience together with the perfection of His moral character. However difficult it may be for us to conceive of it, He is the "Absolute Person," and in this term we unite the two extreme conceptions of the Supreme Being.

Divine Personality seems to call for particular emphasis at present because of certain current scientific conceptions of the universe which, by reason of the evolutionary idea, tend in the direction either of Deism or Pantheism. Nature and Evolution are apt to shut God from sight, but, as we have already seen, Evolution is nothing but modal, and Nature is not personal, and we must therefore not allow them to be associated with anything materialistic or non-theistic.

So that the Divine attributes are Omnipotence, Omniscience, Transcendence, and Immanence, the last-named being perhaps somewhat more than the old Omnipresence.[1] The Divine character includes Truth, Holiness, Faithfulness, Wisdom, and Benevolence.

Reviewing our consideration thus far, we have arrived at a view of God which predicates Unity, Rationality, Morality, and Personality. But it is perhaps necessary to say again that we must not think our Christian Faith rests on Nature together with Scripture; on the contrary, our full view of God rests solely on Christ's Revelation :—

"The Christian doctrine of God is a Theism enriched by what was given historically in and through Jesus Christ."[2]

The problem of the Divine existence and character is complicated by the fact of sin. The difficulty is undoubtedly serious, and men frequently express their inability to believe in a Loving Father Who could create man and involve him in such sorrows as the human race knows in sin and suffering. It may be said at once that the problem of evil is incomprehensible in full, and it is hardly possible to think that human limitations will ever permit of our fully understanding it during earthly life.[3] But there are certain considerations which help to relieve some of the pressure with which this forces itself on the thought of mankind. Whatever may have been the origin, and whatever is the present power of evil, it cannot be said to defeat the purpose of God with regard to moral and spiritual progress. On the contrary, there is ample proof that God actually overrules the power of evil for the purpose of accomplishing His own designs. Further, sin is only temporary, and as it had a beginning,

[1] Platt, *ut supra*, p. 71.   [2] Paterson, *The Rule of Faith*, p. 205.
[3] Litton, *ut supra*, pp. 87–95.

so it is to be believed that it will have an end, since the permanent presence of wrong seems incompatible with a universe created by a perfectly good God. A consciousness of a fundamental distinction between right and wrong is rooted in the very idea of things, and man's conscience testifies to the fact that sin is a violation of the Divine law and therefore repugnant to God's character. Then, too, it is quite impossible to contemplate the fact of sin without the fact of redemption. Whatever we may say in regard to the Divine permission of sin there can be no doubt about the Divine provision of redemption, which more than meets the effects of human wrongdoing. There were only two possible ways in which man could have been created; either as a machine, compelled to do always and only what is right, or as a moral being, with the risk of wrongdoing through the power of choice. So that objection to God because of sin is really an objection to our very creation, which is obviously futile. Whether we like it or not, we have been created with all the solemnity of responsibility for character and action, and in the midst of our circumstances of probation God has, we believe, provided a remedy for the wreck wrought by sin, and the vital question now is not how, or why, sin has been permitted to come into the world, but how we are to get rid of it by redemption, and why we should not accept God's perfect deliverance. As succeeding Articles will show, there has been a Revelation of Redeeming Grace provided for men in Jesus Christ, and all the ravages caused by sin are more than met and healed by the wondrous provision made by God for salvation.

The moment we come to the conclusion that God is personal the question arises whether He is interested in us, and whether He can communicate with us. Still more, the enquiry is made whether He has actually done so. The answer is found in God's Revelation in Christ, which is the subject of the next section of the Article.

V.—THE REVELATION OF GOD IN CHRIST

Christianity agrees so far with natural theology, but adds its own specific view of God, the Trinity. This is the distinctive doctrine of Christian Theism.[1] Its basis is the Unity of God, for the Trinity is essentially Monotheistic. While it is true that the Trinity in Scripture is almost always concerned with Redemption, this aspect of Revelation is necessarily based upon an essential Trinity.[2] This distinction between

---

[1] "It was, therefore, with a sound instinct that the Christian Church, in the first period of its history, devoted its thinking mainly to the elucidation and consolidation of its knowledge of God. It was a task which entailed centuries of controversy, for the problem was a difficult and complicated one. The hard problem for theology was to combine the doctrine of an ethical monotheism, which it took over from the Old Testament, with the new matter that was given in the mediatorial work and the Divine Sonship of Christ, and in the economy of the Holy Spirit" (Paterson, *ut supra*, p. 203).

[2] "A trinity of Revelation is a misrepresentation if there is not behind it a trinity of reality" (Dormer, quoted in O. A. Curtis, *The Christian Faith*, p. 484).

a Trinity of Revelation and a Trinity of Reality is sometimes expressed by the words " Trinity " and " Tri-unity."[1]

1. The Doctrine Stated.[2]—By the Trinity we mean the specific and unique Christian idea of the Godhead, and we must always understand by it both the doctrine of Trinity in Unity and the Unity in Trinity, for the Trinity should suggest the Unity quite as much as the threefoldness of the Deity. But the specific Christian thought of God is that of a Spirit in the unity of whose Being is revealed a distinction of Persons whom we call Father, Son, and Holy Spirit; the God from Whom, through Whom, and by Whom all things come—the Father as the primal Source, the Son as the Redemptive Mediator, and the Holy Spirit as the personal Applier of life and grace. The Christian idea of the Trinity may be summed up in the words of the Athanasian Creed: " The Father is God, the Son is God, and the Holy Ghost is God. And yet there are not three Gods, but one God. The Godhead of the Father, and of the Son, and of the Holy Ghost is all one, the Glory equal, the Majesty co-eternal. And in this Trinity none is afore or after other; none is greater or less than another, but the whole three Persons are co-eternal together and co-equal."

2. The Doctrine Approached.—It is sometimes asked why we are not given a definite statement that there are three Persons in the Godhead. One reason for the absence of any such categorical teaching is probably to be found in the fact that the earliest hearers of the Gospel were Jews, and that any such pronouncement might (and probably would) have seemed a contradiction of their own truth of the unity of the Godhead. Consequently, instead of giving an intellectual statement of doctrine, which might have led to theological and philosophic discussion, and ended only in more intense opposition to Christianity, the Apostles preached Jesus of Nazareth as a personal Redeemer from sin, and urged on every one the acceptance of Him. Then, in due course, would come the inevitable process of thought and meditation upon this personal experience, which would in turn lead to the inference that Jesus, from Whom, and in Whom, these experiences were being enjoyed, must be more than man, must be none other than Divine, for " Who can forgive sins but God only ? " Through such a personal impression and inference based on experience, a distinction in the Godhead would at once be realised. Then, in the course of their Christian life, and through fuller instruction, the personal knowledge and experience of the Holy Spirit would be added, and once again a similar inference would in due course follow, making another distinction in their thought of the Godhead. The intellectual conception and expression of these distinctions probably concerned only comparatively few of the early believers, but, nevertheless, all of them had in their lives a definite experience which could only

[1] So W. N. Clarke, *An Outline of Christian Theology*, and *The Christian Doctrine of God*.
[2] This is taken in substance from the article "TRINITY," by the author, in Hastings' one-volume *Bible Dictionary*.

have been from above, and which no difficulty of intellectual correlation or of theological co-ordination with former teachings could invalidate and destroy.

3. The Doctrine Derived.—The doctrine of the Trinity is thus an expansion of the doctrine of the Incarnation, and emerges out of the personal claim of our Lord, as seen in the New Testament. In the Gospels we note that our Lord's method of revealing Himself to His disciples was by means of personal impression. His character, teaching, and claim formed the centre of everything, and His one object was, as it were, to stamp Himself on His disciples, knowing that in the light of fuller experience His true nature and relations would become clear to them. We see the culmination of this impression in the confession, " My Lord and my God " (John xx. 28). Then in the Acts of the Apostles we find St. Peter preaching to Jews, and emphasising two associated truths: (1) the Sonship and Messiahship of Jesus, as proved by the Resurrection; and (2) the consequent relation of the hearers to Him as to a Saviour and Master. The emphasis is laid on the personal experience of forgiveness and grace, without any attempt to state our Lord's position in relation to God. Indeed, the references to Jesus Christ as the " Servant (wrongly rendered in A.V. ' Son ') of God " in Acts iii. 13, 26 and iv. 27, seem to show that the Christian thought regarding our Lord was still immature so far as there was any purely intellectual consideration of it. It is worthy of note that this phrase, which is doubtless the New Testament counterpart of Isaiah's teaching on the " Servant of the Lord," is not found in the New Testament later than these earlier chapters of the Acts. Yet in the preaching of St. Peter the claim made for Jesus of Nazareth as the Source of healing (iii. 6, 16), the Prince of life (iii. 15), the Head Stone of the corner (iv. 11), and the one and only way of Salvation (iv. 12), was an unmistakable assumption of the position and power of the Godhead.

In the same way the doctrine of the Godhead of the Holy Spirit arises directly out of our Lord's revelation. Once grant a real personal distinction between the Father and the Son and it is not difficult to believe it also of the Spirit, as revealed by the Son.[1] As long as Christ was present on earth there was no room and no need for the specific work of the Holy Spirit, but as Christ was departing from the world He revealed a doctrine which clearly associated the Holy Spirit with Himself and the Father in a new and unique way (John xiv. 16, 17, 26; xv. 26; xvi. 7-15). Arising immediately out of this, and consonant with it, is the place given to the Holy Spirit in the Book of the Acts. From chap. v,

[1] "The doctrines of the Incarnation and the Trinity seemed to me most absurd in my agnostic days. But now, as a *pure* agnostic, I see in them no rational difficulty at all. As to the Trinity, the plurality of persons is naturally implied in the companion doctrine of the Incarnation. So that at best there is here but one difficulty, since, duality being postulated in the doctrine of the Incarnation, there is no further difficulty for pure agnosticism in the doctrine of plurality" (Romanes, *Thoughts on Religion*, pp. 174, 175).

where lying against the Holy Ghost is equivalent to lying against God (v. 3, 4, 9), we see throughout the Book the essential Deity of the Holy Spirit in the work attributed to Him of superintending and controlling the life of the Apostolic Church (ii. 4; viii. 29; x. 19; xiii. 2, 4; xvi. 6; xx. 28).

Then in the Epistles we find references to our Lord Jesus and to the Holy Spirit which imply quite unmistakably the functions of Godhead. In the opening salutations Christ is associated with God as the Source of grace and peace (1 Thess. i. 1 f.; 1 Peter i. 2), and in the closing benedictions as the Divine Source of Blessing (Rom. xv. 30; 2 Thess. iii. 16, 18). In the doctrinal statements He is referred to in practical relation to us and to our spiritual life in terms that can be predicated of God only, and in the revelations concerning things to come He is stated to be about to occupy a position which can refer to God only. In like manner, the correlation of the Holy Spirit with the Father and the Son in matters essentially Divine is clear (1 Cor. ii. 4-6; 2 Cor. xiii. 14; 1 Pet. i. 2).[1] It is the function of the Spirit to make redemptive history live again before the gaze of faith.

In all these assertions and implications of the Godhead of Jesus Christ, it is to be noted very carefully that St. Paul has not the faintest idea of

---

[1] "It is natural to think of the doctrine of the Trinity as a later growth. So, in one sense, it is. It is not complete until we come to the enlarged form of the Nicene Creed and the Council of Chalcedon, in A.D. 451. But all that is essential in the doctrine—the main lines—were already laid down when St. Paul wrote his first two groups of Epistles, in the years 52, 53, and 57-58. In the very earliest of all his extant letters, St. Paul solemnly addresses the Thessalonian Christians as being 'in the fellowship of God the Father and the Lord Jesus Christ,' placing the two names in the closest juxtaposition, and giving to them an equal weight of authority. And from the date of his second Epistle to the same Church onwards, he invokes 'grace and peace' also 'from God the Father and the Lord Jesus Christ,' making them the one conjoint source of Divine blessing.

"And if it is urged that this is but the first stage in the history of the doctrine, we have only to turn to the Second Epistle to the Corinthians, written, in any case within a year or two of A.D. 57, and we have there the familiar benediction at the end of the Epistle, in which the Name of the Holy Spirit is associated on equal terms with that of God the Father and God the Son; while in the body of the Epistle, as in two almost contemporary Epistles—1 Corinthians xii. and Romans viii.—the doctrine of the Holy Spirit has already received a considerable development. I say a development, but only in the sense that the doctrine comes to us as a new one. St. Paul himself does not teach it as if he were teaching something in itself wholly new. He assumes it as already substantially understood and known. Does not this cast back a light upon, and does not it supply an extraordinary confirmation of, what the Gospel tells of the promise of the Comforter, and what the Acts tells us of the fulfilment of that promise? When we are brought so near in time to our Lord's own ministry upon the earth, can we help referring this rapid growth of a doctrine, which seems to us so difficult, to intimations directly received from Him? But, indeed, the greatest difficulty in the doctrine of the Trinity was already over, and the foundation-stone of the doctrine was already laid, the moment that it was distinctly realised that there was walking upon the earth One, Who was God as well as Man. If the Son of God was really there, and if there was, nevertheless, a Godhead in the heavens, then, in the language of men, we must needs say that there were two Persons in the Godhead; and if two, then it was a comparatively easy step to say that there were three. The doctrine of the Trinity is only one of the necessary sequels of the doctrine of the Incarnation" (Sanday, Church Congress, 1894).

contradicting his Jewish Monotheism. Though he and others thus proclaimed the Godhead of Christ, it is of great moment to remember that Christianity was never accused of Polytheism. The New Testament doctrine of God is essentially a form of Monotheism, and stands in no relation to Polytheism. There can be no doubt that, however and whenever the Trinitarian idea was formulated, it arose in immediate connection with the Monotheism of Judæa; and the Apostles, Jews though they were, in stating so unmistakably the Godhead of Jesus Christ, are never once conscious of teaching anything inconsistent with their most cherished ideas about the unity of God.

4. The Doctrine Confirmed.—When we have approached the doctrine by means of the personal experience of redemption, we are prepared to give full consideration to the two lines of teaching found in the New Testament. (a) One line of teaching insists on the unity of the Godhead (1 Cor. viii. 4; Jas. ii. 19); and (b) the other reveals distinctions within the Godhead (Matt. iii. 16, 17; xxviii. 19; 2 Cor. xiii. 14). We see clearly that (1) the Father is God (Matt. xi. 25; Rom. xv. 6; Eph. iv. 6); (2) the Son is God (John i. 1, 18; xx. 28; Acts xx. 28; Rom. ix. 5; Heb. i. 8; Col. ii. 9; Phil. ii. 6; 2 Peter i. 1); (3) the Holy Spirit is God (Acts v. 3, 4; 1 Cor. ii. 10, 11; Eph. ii. 22); (4) the Father, Son, and Holy Spirit are distinct from one another, sending and being sent, honouring and being honoured. The Father honours the Son, the Son honours the Father, and the Holy Spirit honours the Son (John xv. 26; xvi. 13, 14; xvii. 1, 8, 18, 23). (5) Nevertheless, whatever relations of subordination there may be between the Persons in working out redemption, the Three are alike regarded as God. The doctrine of the Trinity is the correlation, embodiment, and synthesis of the teaching of these passages. In the Unity of the Godhead there is a Trinity of Persons working out Redemption. God the Father is the Creator and Ruler of man and the Provider of redemption through His love (John iii. 16). God the Son is the Redeemer, Who became man for the purpose of our redemption. God the Holy Spirit is the " Executive of the Godhead," the " Vicar of Christ," Who applies to each believing soul the benefits of redemption. We see this very clearly in Heb. x. 7-17, where the Father wills, the Son works, and the Spirit witnesses. The elements of the plan of redemption thus find their root, foundation, and spring in the nature of the Godhead; and the obvious reason why these distinctions which we express by the terms " Person " and " Trinity " were not revealed earlier than New Testament times is that not until then was redemption accomplished.

5. The Doctrine Supported.—When all this is granted and so far settled, we may find a second line of teaching to support the foregoing in the revelation of God as Love. Following the suggestion of St. Augustine, most modern theologians have rightly seen in this a safe ground for our belief. It transcends, and perhaps renders unnecessary, all arguments drawn from human and natural analogies of the doctrine.

" God is Love " means, as someone has well said, " God as the infinite
home of all moral emotions, the fullest, and most highly differentiated
life." Love must imply relationships, and as He is eternally perfect in
Himself, He can realise Himself as Love only through relationships
within His own Being. We may go so far as to say that this is the only
way of obtaining a living thought about God. Belief in Theism postulates a self-existent God, and yet it is impossible to think of a God without
relationships. These relationships must be eternal and prior to His
temporal relationships to the universe of His own creation. He must
have relationships eternally adequate and worthy, and when once we
realise that love must have an object in God as well as in ourselves, we
have the germ of that distinction in the Godhead which is theologically
known as the Trinity.[1]

6. The Doctrine Anticipated.—At this stage, and only here, we
may seek another support for the doctrine. In the light of the facts of
the New Testament we cannot refrain from asking whether there may
not have been some adumbrations of it in the Old Testament. As the
doctrine arises directly out of the facts of the New Testament, we do
not look for any full discovery of it in the Old Testament. We must
not expect too much, because, as Israel's function was to emphasise the
unity of God (Deut. vi. 4), any premature revelation might have been
disastrous. But if the doctrine be true, we might expect that Christian
Jews, at any rate, would seek for some anticipation of it in the Old
Testament. We believe we find it there. (a) The use of the plural
" Elohim," with the singular verb, " bara," is at least noteworthy, and
seems to call for some recognition, especially as the same grammatical
solecism is found used by St. Paul (1 Thess. iii. 11, Greek). Then, too,
the use of the plurals " us " (Gen. i. 26), " our " (iii. 22), " us " (xi. 7),
seems to indicate some self-converse in God. It is not satisfactory to
refer this to angels because they were not associated with God in creation.
Whatever may be the meaning of this usage, it seems, at any rate, to
imply that Hebrew Monotheism was an intensely living reality.[2] (b) The
references to the " Angel of Jehovah " prepare the way for the Christian
doctrine of a distinction in the Godhead (Gen. xviii. 2, 16; xvii. 22
with xix. 1; Josh. v. 13-15 with vi. 2; Jud. xiii. 8-21; Zech. xiii. 7).
(c) Allusions to the " Spirit of Jehovah " form another line of Old
Testament teaching. In Genesis i. 2 the Spirit is an energy only, but in
subsequent books an agent (Isa. xl. 13; xlviii. 16; lix. 19; lxiii. 10 f.).
(d) The personification of Divine Wisdom is also to be observed, for the
connection between the personification of Wisdom in Prov. viii, the
Logos of John i. 1-18, and the " wisdom " of 1 Cor. i. 24 can hardly
be accidental. (e) There are also other hints, such as the Triplicity of

---

[1] Paterson, *ut supra*, p. 220 f. See an able presentation of this doctrine of a "Social
Trinity" in "Monotheism and the Doctrine of the Trinity," by A. T. Burbridge, *London
Quarterly Review*.

[2] Ottley, *The Incarnation*, p. 183 f.

the Divine Names (Numb. vi. 24-27; Psa. xxix. 3-5; Isa. vi. 1-3), which, while they may not be pressed, cannot be overlooked. Hints are all that were to be expected until the fulness of time should have come. The special work of Israel was to guard God's transcendence and omnipresence; it was for Christianity to develop the doctrine of the Godhead into the fulness, depth, and richness that we find in the revelation of the Incarnate Son of God.

7. The Doctrine Justified.—It is sometimes urged by opponents of the orthodox faith that the doctrine of the Trinity cannot be defended on rational grounds, and has to be received simply upon the authority of revelation. But it should be noticed that the element of mystery in this doctrine is really due to the fact that it is a doctrine of God rather than a doctrine of the Tri-unity of God. From the very nature of the case we can only know God in part and cannot possibly grasp the infinite reality with our finite powers. If, therefore, our doctrine of God, apart from the Trinity, is to be set aside because of its element of mystery, then nothing but agnosticism is possible. So that while fully admitting the mystery associated with the doctrine of the Trinity it is important to remember that this mystery is not exclusively associated with the conception of God as Three in One. And although the knowledge of God as Triune comes to us through revelation, yet we believe that having thus received the knowledge it can be justified on perfectly rational grounds. Before attempting to state this it is necessary to point out that there can be no *a priori* objection to the doctrine since we can know God only as He reveals Himself. The facts alone must settle His character, and on this basis alone we are prepared to justify the position.

(*a*) The Facts of Scripture.—The doctrine of the Trinity is entirely without any trace of Hellenic or mythological influence. It is derivable solely from the record of Scripture concerning the Person and claim of Christ.[1] The doctrine is an expansion, extension, and necessary sequel of the doctrine of the Incarnation. " If the Incarnation, in the Christian sense, be true, the doctrine of the Holy Trinity is true also. For there is no break between them; they are parts of one and the same truth."[2] The doctrine of the Trinity is thus no independent speculation, or intellectual figment, but is historically traceable to the facts of Christ's consciousness and claim. Christ's revelation of Himself implies and unfolds mutual relations between Himself and God which are unique, and in the course and issue of His revelation He reveals a doctrine of the Holy Spirit that demands co-ordination with that of the Father and the Son.

(*b*) The Facts of Christian Experience.—It is simple truth to state

---

[1] "If in Scripture the nature of the Holy Spirit is left mysterious and undefined, only some strong impulse and necessity of Christian thought could ever have driven either Christian thinkers to formulate, or the Christian Church to accept, a doctrine so difficult as the personality of the Spirit and the Triune nature of God" (Lendrum, *An Outline of Christian Truth*, p. 71).

[2] Strong, *ut supra*, p. 142.

that Christians of all periods of history claim to have personal direct fellowship with Christ. This claim must be accounted for. It is only possible by predicating the Deity of our Lord, for such fellowship would be impossible with One Who is not a God.[1]

(c) The Facts of History.—Compared with other religions, Christianity makes God a reality in a way in which no other system does. The doctrine of the Trinity has several theological and philosophical advantages over the Unitarian conception of God, but especially is this so in reference to the relation of God to the world. There are two conceivable relations —as Transcendent (in Mohammedanism), or as Immanent (in Buddhism). The first alone means Deism, the second alone Pantheism. But the Christian idea of God is of One Who is at once Transcendent and Immanent.[2] It is, therefore, the true protection of a living Theism, which otherwise oscillates uncertainly between these two extremes of Deism and Pantheism, either of which is false to it. It is only in Christianity that the Semitic conception of God as Transcendent and the Aryan conception as Immanent are united, blended, correlated, balanced, and preserved. One of the most striking illustrations of this is found in the speech of St. Paul at Athens, when he, a Semite, was addressing Aryans. First of all he presented his Gospel to them on its Semitic side, God being declared to be Judge, King, Creator, and God of Righteousness. But there was a further message to this Aryan audience, providing the answer to their yearnings for fellowship with the Divine. "He is not far from each one of us, for in Him we live, and move, and have our being." So the truth the Semites saw and the truth the Aryans saw are harmonised in the Gospel, and the two truths run through the whole teaching of the New Testament. On the surface they may seem contradictory, and during the centuries of Christian history one has obtained the upper hand at times, the other at others. In the Puritan age and the Deistic period which arose after it, the Semitic conception dominated thought. Then came the pantheistic tendency of the Aryan rebellion against the Semitic conception, and this tendency has been found in the philosophical thought of German writers, and in devout circles in Mysticism. But whenever this tendency spends its force there is an inevitable reaction

---

[1] "As to the Trinity, I do understand you. You first taught me that the doctrine was a live thing, and not a mere formula to be swallowed by the undigesting reason; and from the time that I learnt from you that a Father meant a real Father, a Son a real Son, a Holy Spirit a real Spirit, who was really good and holy, *I have been able to draw all sorts of practical lessons from it in the pulpit, and ground all my morality and a great deal of my natural philosophy upon it, and shall do so more*" (Kingsley, *Letters and Memories of His Life*, 1877).

[2] "It was to maintain this double relation that Philo conceived of the Logos as a middle term between God and the creation and the Neo-Platonists distinguished between God, the νους, and the soul of the world. When a middle term is wanting we have either, as in the later Judaism and Mohammedanism, an abstract and immobile Monotheism, or, in recoil from this, a losing of God in the world in Pantheism. In the Christian doctrine of the triune Son we have the necessary safeguards against both these errors, and at the same time the link between God and the world supplied which speculation vainly strove to find" (Orr, *The Christian View of God and the World*, p. 276).

towards Semitic modes of thought. Deity is never a bare unity, but always a fulness of life and love. Fatherhood and sonship are archetypes of human relationships, and the escape from all reactions and extremes is found in Jesus Christ, in Whom, as Pascal says, "all contradictions are reconciled." Some time ago a Jewish Rabbi, speaking at a meeting of Christian ministers, said that "the Jews have a higher, clearer vision of God because they are able to see Him without the garment of flesh which seems so necessary to Christians. Christians have not yet grown up; they need illustrations, and Christ is their picture of God." To this the answer is obvious. "No man hath seen God at any time." And that the modern Jew has a higher conception of God is amply disproved by the spiritual sterility that has overtaken the race, a sterility which is true of every Unitarian conception. There are men, both Jews and Gentiles, who have remarkable powers in art, in music, in finance, and in other natural abilities, whose mental powers are of the highest, and yet in moral force they are decidedly lower and their conception of God has been tried and found wanting. The one thing lacking in their vision of God is that reality which is so characteristic of the Christian conception.[1]

(d) The Facts of Reason.—It is simple truth to say that if Jesus be not God, Christians are idolaters, for they worship One Who is not God. There is no other alternative. But when once the truth of the doctrine of the Trinity is regarded as arising out of Christ's claim to Godhead as Divine Redeemer, reason soon finds its warrant for the doctrine. Every theist wants to believe in a self-existent Deity, and yet it is impossible to conceive of One Who has no relationships. This is the only way of obtaining a living thought of God. Philosophy is always faced with the question whether matter or spirit is the ground of things, and a conception is needed which will include the incomprehensibility of Agnosticism, the immanence of Pantheism, the transcendence of Deism, and the personality of Theism. It is only Christianity that does this. Thus while the doctrine of the Trinity comes to us by revelation and not by nature, it is seen to have points of contact with thought and reason.[2]

[1] "Every Church which has departed from this Faith has *ipso facto* sealed its own death-warrant. It is beyond question that those Churches, and congregations, in England and in Ireland which, in the eighteenth century, let go the doctrine of the Trinity, faded away and disappeared" (Cooper, *Religion and the Modern Mind*, "The Doctrine of the Holy and Undivided Trinity," p. 145).
[2] "It started in the concrete with the baptismal formula . . . emanating from Jesus Christ. And throughout the history of its dogmatic formulation, we are confronted with this fact. It was regarded as a revelation by the men who shaped its intellectual expression; and it was only in the process . . . of that expression, that its congruity with human psychology came out, that psychology in fact being distinctly developed in the effort to give it utterance. . . . They did not accommodate Christian religion to their philosophy, but philosophy to their Christian religion. It appeals first to elemental humanity in the hearts of unsophisticated men; far removed from Alexandria or Athens; yet the very words in which it does so, turn out, upon analysis, to involve a view of personality which the world had not attained, but which, once stated, is seen to be profoundly, philosophically true" (Illingworth, *Personality Human and Divine*, p. 212 f.).

And it is a perfectly rational belief when it is not misinterpreted. While necessarily it transcends reason it does not contradict it, and any contradiction is due not to the doctrine, but to our misunderstanding of it.[1] And so we do not hesitate to affirm that if the Trinitarian view is omitted, nothing characteristic is left in the Christian conception of God.

These considerations may perhaps be brought to a close by a reference to certain analogies which, as they are not proofs, do not carry us far, though they are useful as illustrations. Everywhere in nature unity co-exists with plurality, unity in plurality being a distinctive mark of all organic life. The only perfect concord of music is a trinity,[2] consisting of the fundamental note with its third and fifth which proceed from it and form the complete chord, known as the Perfect Triad. From this chord all other harmonies are built, and the moment we add any other note we get what is technically known as a discord, a chord which requires resolution, which leaves the ear unsatisfied, and which must invariably be resolved on to the concord of the Perfect Triad before the musical sentence can be satisfactorily finished. Then, too, there are three instruments of progress : Religion, Science, and Art. And according to recent science the universe is triune, consisting of Ether as invisible substance, Matter as visible fact, and Energy as consisting of the forces of heat, light, sound, and electricity. The rays of light are also threefold. There are heat rays which are felt but not seen ; light rays which are seen and not felt, and actinic rays which are known only by the effects of their chemical action (as in photography), being neither seen nor felt. So also is it with vapour, which we have invisible in the air, visible in the form of water, and experienced in its effects. Nor may we overlook the analogy of human personality in Thought, Feeling, and Will, and the human constitution as consisting of Spirit, Soul, and Body. It is impossible to avoid noticing the co-existence of the unity of the soul with its plurality of faculties. Even Kant, when adducing his moral argument for Theism, recognised three postulates, God, Freewill, Immortality. Reference has already been made to the singular threefoldness in Scripture (Numb. vi. 24-26; Isa. vi. 3). The value of analogy is to suggest that numerals are found elsewhere than in theology.

To sum up : the doctrine of the Holy Trinity is evidently and eminently one for faith. The title of the Article suggests this, " Of Faith in the Holy Trinity," and the Collect for Trinity Sunday points

[1] "The result seems to be that the New Testament, besides revealing the œconomical Trinity, or the Trinity as related to the Church and operative *ad extra*, furnishes a revelation of the same Trinity as it exists intrinsically, and is operative *ad intra*, and teaches that apart from all manifestations of God in creation or in redemption, He is, in Himself, not an abstract Monas, but a Trinity of immanent relations expressed under the terms, Father, Son, and Holy Spirit; that is, that in the Godhead there exist energies which terminate in itself " (Litton, *ut supra*, p. 103).

See also Illingworth, *ut supra*, p. 73 f.; *The Doctrine of the Trinity*, pp. 144, 254; Orr, *The Christian View of God and the World*, Lecture VII.

[2] "It is curious how the number three starts up to meet us unsought and unexpected" (Mackintosh, *ut supra*, p. 38).

in the same direction, " Keep us steadfast in this faith." It is a doctrine for the apprehension of faith, not for the comprehension of reason, and its truth is really independent of all that technical terminology which necessarily came at a much later time.

In the sub-apostolic Church the outstanding feature is Christian experience, not theological technicality. While the doctrine of the Trinity is clearly implied, yet it is rather spiritually apprehended than intellectually expressed. Towards the end of the second century more formal language was used in the τρίας of Theophilus of Antioch and the *Trinitas* of Tertullian. But here again it was heresy that compelled closer definition, and the terms *Person* and *Substance* became used. Heresies as to the Person of Christ necessitated emphasis on His Deity and His distinctness from the Father, and so came *substantia* in Tertullian to emphasise the essential oneness with the Father. Greek writers used οὐσία and ὑπόστασις. In opposition to this came the Sabellians, who taught that the Trinity were temporary distinctions only, simple manifestations of the one Divine essence. It was this that compelled the Church to use the word " Person." The general impression left on the reader is that the doctrine was a matter of spiritual apprehension during the first three centuries, though this became the foundation of that mental apprehension and expression which first found authoritative utterance in the Council of Nicæa. What, then, was the doctrine of Nicæa in regard to the Trinity ?

1. The word " Trinity " does not occur, nor even the word " Person " in the Nicene Creed.

2. In the Creed, as then promulgated, the only reference to the Holy Spirit was " The Lord, the Life-giver." It is clear that the Council of Nicæa desired to keep as closely as possible to the spiritual apprehension of the Trinity, but its inadequacy is seen in the way in which the doctrine is stated, partly as a spiritual reality and partly as a mental concept. Thus οὐσία is used for " substance," though in the anathemas ὑπόστασις is found as an equivalent.

3. But this position was not tenable for long, since it was essential to show not only the relation of the Father and the Son, but also the relation of the Holy Spirit to both. While Nicæa used ὁμοούσιος in reference to the oneness of the Son to the Father, Athanasius does not employ it in regard to the Holy Spirit. But the use of terms like " substance " and " Person " led to great discussion, and the result was that πρόσωπον was disused, as implying a mere aspect and not an essential distinction. Then οὐσία became applied to the Divine Nature, and ὑπόστασις was employed to indicate the distinctions in the οὐσία. The outcome was the formula μία οὐσία ἐν τρισὶν ὑποστάσεσιν.

---

[1] Bethune-Baker, *An Introduction to the Early History of Christian Doctrine*, pp. 139–147.

4. But this made a difficulty in the West, where *substantia* was equivalent to *essentia*, and as the Latin could not possibly say *tres substantiæ*, the terminology became fixed as *una substantia, tres personæ*.

5. The term " Person " is also sometimes objected to. Like all human language, it is liable to be accused of inadequacy and even positive error. It certainly must not be pressed too far, or it will lead to Tritheism. While we use the term to denote distinctions in the Godhead, we do not imply distinctions which amount to separateness, but distinctions which are associated with essential mutual co-inherence or inclusiveness. We intend by the term " Person " to express those real distinctions of Father, Son, and Holy Spirit which are found amid the oneness of the Godhead, distinctions which are no mere temporary manifestations of Deity, but essential and permanent elements within the Divine unity.

While, therefore, we are compelled to use terms like " substance " and " Person," we are not to think of them as identical with what we understand as human substance or personality. The terms are not explanatory, but only approximately correct, as must necessarily be the case with any attempt to define the Nature of God. As already noted, it is a profound spiritual satisfaction to remember that the truth and experience of the Trinity is not dependent upon theological terminology, though it is obviously essential for us to have the most correct terms available.

ARTICLE II

Of the Word or Son of God which was made very man.	*De Verbo, sive Filio Dei, qui verus homo factus est.*
The Son, which is the Word of the Father, begotten from everlasting of the Father, the very and eternal God, and of one substance with the Father, took man's nature in the womb of the Blessed Virgin, of her substance: so that two whole and perfect natures, that is to say, the Godhead and Manhood, were joined together in one Person, never to be divided, whereof is one Christ, very God and very Man, who truly suffered, was crucified, dead and buried, to reconcile His Father to us, and to be a sacrifice, not only for original guilt, but also for all actual sins of men.	Filius qui est Verbum Patris, ab æterno a Patre genitus, verus et æternus Deus, ac Patri consubstantialis, in utero beatæ Virginis ex illius substantia naturam humanam assumpsit: ita ut duæ naturæ, divina et humana, integre atque perfecte in unitate personæ, fuerint inseparabiliter conjunctæ: ex quibus est unus Christus, verus Deus et verus homo: qui vere passus est, crucifixus, mortuus et sepultus, ut Patrem nobis reconciliaret, essetque hostia non tantum pro culpa originis, verum etiam pro omnibus actualibus hominum peccatis.

IMPORTANT EQUIVALENTS.

Of one substance with the Father	=	*ac Patri consubstantialis.*
Man's nature	=	*naturam humanam.*
Of her substance	=	*ex illius substantia.*
So that two whole and perfect natures, that is to say, the Godhead and Manhood, were joined together in one Person, never to be divided.	=	*ita ut duæ naturæ, divina et humana, integre atque perfecte in unitate personæ, fuerint inseparabiliter conjunctæ.*
Very	=	*verus.*
Sacrifice	=	*hostia.*
Original guilt	=	*culpa originis.*

It is appropriate that after the Article on the Christian Doctrine of the Trinity we should be led to consider that doctrine on which the Trinity mainly rests, the Doctrine of the Person of Christ. So that the Article is a corollary of Article I since the doctrine herein stated is at once the complement, presupposition and exposition of Trinitarian doctrine.[1] This, too, was placed in the forefront of the Reformation to show the essential unity of the Reformed with the mediæval Faith, and also because of the denials of the doctrine of the Incarnation seen at an early period of the Reformation movement.[2]

---

[1] "The dogma of the Trinity is closely bound up with the dogma of the Person of Christ. The former is concerned with the inner life of the eternal Godhead, and the place therein of the only-begotten Son; while the latter deals with the mode of the existence of the Son as incarnate, and this both in His estate of humiliation and exaltation. The doctrine of the Person of Christ is at once a presupposition and a consequence of the doctrine of the Trinity" (Paterson, *The Rule of Faith*, p. 224).

[2] Hardwick, *History of the Articles of Religion*, pp. 89, 90; Boultbee, *The Theology of the Church of England*, p. 15.

The Article is derived from the Third Article of the Confession of Augsburg. Its title in 1553 was *Verbum Dei verum hominem esse Factum*, "That the Word or Son of God was made a very Man." The phrase descriptive of our Lord's eternal generation and consubstantiality, "Begotten from everlasting of the Father, the very and eternal God, and of one substance with the Father" was inserted in 1563 from the Confession of Wurtemberg. There were other verbal but insignificant changes in 1563 and 1571. Comparison should also be made with the statement in the *Reformatio Legum*.[1]

The problem then, as now, was how to reconcile and harmonise the two natures in the one Person of Christ. How was the union to be conceived and expressed? The Article naturally follows the orthodox interpretation of Christology, derived from the formula of Chalcedon.[2] We must, therefore, look first at this as it is, and then enquire as to any modern variations. The earliest commentator on the Articles, Rogers, sets forth four propositions as covering the teaching: (1) Christ is very God; (2) Christ is very Man; (3) Christ is God and Man in one Person; (4) Christ is the Saviour of Mankind.

I.—THE DIVINE NATURE OF CHRIST

Although this is involved in the teaching of Article I it is necessarily repeated here.

1. The title, "Son."—The term "Son" is used in several connections in regard to the earthly life of Christ, meaning thereby His Sonship by the Incarnation, *e.g.* Luke i. 35; John i. 34; Rom. i. 4; Heb. i. 2-5.[3] But here the word is, of course, to be referred to our Lord's personal relationship with the Father.[4] No two titles are more frequently used in the Fourth Gospel than "Father" and "Son," and these are corre-

---

[1] "Credatur etiam, cum venisset plenitudo temporis, Filium qui est Verbum Patris, in utero beatæ virginis Mariæ, ex ipsius carnis substantia, naturam humanam assumpsisse, ita ut duæ naturæ, divina et humana, integre atque perfecte in unitate Personæ, fuerint inseparabiliter conjunctæ; ex quibus unus est Christus, verus Deus et verus homo: qui vere passus est, crucifixus, mortuus et sepultus, descendit ad inferos ac tertia die resurrexit, nobisque per suum sanguinem reconciliavit Patrem, sese hostiam offerens illi, non solum pro culpa originis, verum etiam pro omnibus peccatis quæ homines propria voluntate adjecerunt" (*De Summa Trin.*, c. 3).

[2] "We teach men to confess one and the same Son, our Lord Jesus Christ, the same perfect in Godhead and also perfect in Manhood, truly God and truly Man, of a reasonable soul and body; consubstantial with the Father according to the Godhead, and consubstantial with us according to the Manhood, in all things like us without sin . . . in these latter days, for us and for our salvation, born of the Virgin Mary, the Mother of God, according to the Manhood, one and the same Christ, Son, Lord, only begotten, to be acknowledged in two natures, inconfusedly, unchangeably, indivisibly, inseparably, the distinction of natures being by no means taken away by the union, but rather the property of each nature being preserved, and concurring in one Person and one subsistence, not parted or divided into two persons, but one and the same Son, and only-begotten, God the Word, the Lord Jesus Christ" (Schaff, *Creeds of Christendom*, Vol. II, p. 62 ff.).

[3] Pearson, *On the Creed*, Article II, Ch. III.

[4] Note the Greek (ἴδιος) of John v. 18 and Rom. viii. 32. See also Matt. xi. 27 (Greek).

C

latives, for as God was eternally Father, so Christ was eternally Son.
It is a serious error to limit our Lord's Sonship to the Incarnation even
while we hold to His eternity as the Word.   Doubtless the term " begotten " seems to imply an event in time, but care is needed in the use of
human language to express transcendental truths.   The New Testament
is clear that Christ's full title as " Son of God " is part of His Divinity,
and is not to be limited to the Incarnation.   This is the force of such
phrases as, " The Son of His love "; " God sent forth His Son ";
" Sent His Son to be the propitiation."   These and similar passages
clearly imply a Sonship prior to the Incarnation, and point back to
eternity.   Then, too, the word " Son " in Scripture often means something more and other than mere descent, e.g. " Sons of Thunder ";
" Son of Consolation "; " Sons of Disobedience."[1]   May not " Son of
God " in its fuller meaning be used without any reference to the Incarnation ?   If it be said that μονογενής implies " begetting," it is noteworthy that the Hebrew term, found nine times, is translated μονογενής
by the Septuagint, with the meaning, " Darling," or " Beloved " (Gen.
xxii. 2, 12; Jer. vi. 26; Amos viii. 10; Zech. xii. 10).   This is the
thought in Luke vii. 12; viii. 42; ix. 38.   May it not be so with Christ
as well (John i. 14, 18; iii. 16, 18; 1 John iv. 9) ?   It is, of course,
true that the ordinary meaning of πρωτότοκος, " firstborn," is that of
a first child (see Matt. i. 25; Luke ii. 7).   But in Heb. xii. 23 it has a
spiritual meaning, implying dignity and privilege, so that it is impossible
to limit it to the Incarnation (cf. Rom. viii. 29; Col. i. 15, 18; Heb.
i. 6; Rev. i. 5).   Further, we can see this view of the meaning of " Son
of God " by contrast with the term, " Son of Man," which is used
eighty times in the New Testament, and all except three by Christ
Himself.   The fundamental idea seems to be the impersonation of
humanity.

    The title, " Son of God," is found in three forms in the Greek, some-
times with the article before each of the two words, sometimes with the
article before " God " only, sometimes the article is omitted altogether.
It seems impossible to think that there is not some distinction intended
by these different usages.   In the first of the three, at least, it must be a
title of Deity, and it is found in this form twenty-five times (cf. Matt.
xvi. 16; Rev. ii. 18).   In these words the Sanhedrin adjured Jesus
Christ to declare Himself, and on His acceptance of the title He was
condemned (Matt. xxvi. 63; Luke xxii. 70; John xix. 7).   It was not
a claim to Messiahship, but to Deity (John viii. 58, 59; John x. 31,
33).   So at the close of His ministry the disciples confessed not what He
became at Bethlehem, but what He had been from eternity (John xvi. 30).

    2. The title, " Word."—This is found in two places (John i. 1, 14;
Rev. xix. 13).   Two questions are usually asked in regard to it: (1)
Whence it was; (2) What it means.   Opinions differ as to whether the

---

[1] The distinction between "children" (τέκνα) and "sons" (υἱοί) is frequently
ignored by the English Versions. See Rom. viii. 14-17.

Apostle John was influenced by Philo in his use of this word, but there is now a general opinion that whether derived from this source or not the meaning is fundamentally different. There seems to be no doubt that as used by St. John the term is intended to express One who is a personal revelation of God, who is also essentially one with God Himself. The eternity and the identity with the Father are both implied and understood in it.[1]

These two terms, " Son " and " Word " are complementary. The former guards the personality and emphasises the distinctness of the Son from the Father, though by itself it might easily suggest an essential subordination as of a Son to a Father. The latter guards the identity and emphasises equality with the Father, though by itself it might easily suggest impersonality. When, however, the two are taken together we have at once the doctrine of a Son Who is distinct from the Father and of a Personal Word who is one with the Father. As Son, He is the impersonation of the character and attributes of God; as Word, He is the perfect expression of the mind of God. Both connote essential Deity. Thus the two together express the two sides of the truth concerning our Lord's Divine nature.

3. " Begotten from everlasting of the Father."—This is an attempt to express in human language the two aspects of our Lord's relation to the Father. For this it is essential to distinguish between priority of order and superiority of nature. " Begotten " calls attention to priority in order of the Father to the Son; "from everlasting " calls attention to the Son's co-existence with the Father. Thus the phrase teaches us that we must not regard this " begetting " as an event of time, or else there would have been a time when the Father was not Father, and the Son was not Son. It is an eternal relation or fact of the Divine nature. It is only so that the truth can be safeguarded and the various passages of Scripture harmonised. If it be urged that " begotten " implies inferiority, the following phrase must be at once associated with it, "from everlasting." There is a constant and yet an inevitable danger in the use of human terms to express Divine realities. Thus, it has been pointed out that we may say:—

Mary was the Mother of our Lord.

Our Lord was God.

Therefore, Mary was the Mother of God.

Our premisses are absolutely correct; our logic perfectly flawless, and yet we know that the conclusion is strictly untrue, since there is another thought implied (our Lord's humanity) which finds no place in

---

[1] "The conception of the Logos as taken over in the Johannine Theology was undoubtedly enriched by the notion of a personal life and of personal relations to the Father; and it cannot be supposed that the Catholic theologians fell back from the Apostolic testimony on the position of Philo, and regarded the Logos as a mere impersonal link between God and the world" (Paterson, *ut supra*, p. 219).

For further consideration of the contrasts between St. John's doctrine of the Logos and other ideas of the "Word," see Alexander's *Leading Ideas of the Gospels*, p. 185.

the syllogism. So, in the same way, our use of the word " begotten "
must always be safeguarded by the association of " from everlasting."[1]

4. " The very and eternal God, and of one substance with the Father."
—This naturally follows from the foregoing statement :—

" The logic of the position seemed to be : Christ is known to be God, and if
now God, He must have been God eternally. If not God eternally He is not
God even now."[2]

Arianism rendered it necessary to speak of Christ as " the very and
eternal God," " the One Who is absolutely, genuinely God," " Deity,"
according to Article I. The term, " Of one substance with the Father,"
is the great word of the Nicene Creed, which formed the battle-ground
of controversy. It was rejected by the Arians, but insisted upon by
Athanasius as the only way of expressing the truth of the essential Deity
of the Son. The Arians were ready to place our Lord at any point above
manhood so long as He was kept lower than Deity, but this only predicated a Being neither man nor God, who was unknown and really
unthinkable. It was this more than anything else that led to the Nicene
Fathers insisting upon the proper Deity of the Son and the truth that He
was not merely " like the Father " (ὁμοιούσιος), but without any
qualification identical with the Father (ὁμοούσιος).[3] Although there
was a natural hesitation about using it because it had been employed in a
different connection before, yet circumstances made it necessary to use
it to express the oneness of essence with the Father, and this was an
entirely new meaning to the term and altogether different from former
interpretations. There was no thought of addition to Scripture, but
only the explanation of that which was implied and involved in the
Scripture teaching concerning Christ. The truth safeguarded by this
word is seen in such passages as Matt. xi. 27; John i. 1; iii. 13; v.
19, 20; viii. 54; xvii. 10; Phil. ii. 6 (Greek; see Lightfoot); Col.
ii. 9).

[1] "Many times, and even in recent years, we have been told that this eternal generation,
or begetting, of the Son of God is empty verbiage, a sort of theological rhetoric,
incapable of conception by the human mind. I entirely fail to respond to the objection;
and I fail to comprehend how any thinking man, familiar with the struggle over the
Athanasian contention, can ever have even the slightest difficulty in clearly grasping
the meaning of Athanasius. . . . I will dare to affirm that this eternal generation of the
Son is not only conceivable, it is also one of the most fruitful conceptions in all Christian
thinking. It helps us to understand all those sayings of Christ where, at one stroke,
He insists upon both His equality with the Father and His dependence upon the Father,
for these sayings reach widely beyond our Saviour's temporary condition of humiliation"
(O. A. Curtis, *The Christian Faith*, p. 228).
[2] Paterson, *ut supra*, p. 209.
[3] "Upon this term *substance* a surprising amount of learned research has been expended
with a small amount of philosophical insight. The instant meaning of the word is of
little concern, for it was nothing but a weapon, and an accidental weapon at that, to
protect an underlying and extremely important idea, namely, that the Father and the
Son are what they are by means of one and the same organism; that they are, therefore,
structurally necessary to each other, so that neither can exist at all without the other"
(O. A. Curtis, *ut supra*, p. 227).

THE DEITY OF CHRIST

Two great truths occupied the attention of the early Church in regard to the Lord Jesus Christ: the fact and the method of the Incarnation. The problem in regard to the former was as to how Christ could be both Divine and human. At first the Ebionites went to one extreme and denied His Deity. Then the Docetæ went to the other and denied His humanity. Then later came Arianism, which denied both and made Christ a sort of *tertium quid*. Docetism, which taught the illusory appearance of the Deity, had but few followers, but Ebionism was more prevalent, and in the Monarchianism of Paul of Samosata it assumed a refined form similar to the Humanitarianism of modern days. Socinianism and Arianism show the same fundamental tendency.[1]

The prolonged discussions argue powerfully for assuming the reality of the union between God and man in Christ. The notion of a real Incarnation does not appear to have been inherited from Judaism or Hellenism, but was indigenous to Christianity itself, and the idea took firm hold of the entire Church, including the keenest minds. This belief in a real union between God and man arises inevitably out of the claim and character of Christ as depicted in the Gospels. It is impossible to deny the New Testament picture of our Lord's unique relation to God,[2] and the significance of His claim to authority cannot be exaggerated in its relation to Christology.[3]

Modern solutions of the union between God and man in Christ call for attention. One is that of the essential oneness of Divinity and Humanity, so that we may speak of the humanity of God and the Divinity of man, thereby making the union credible. But this is too easy for the solution of the problem, and is merely poetical or rhetorical. If Divinity and Humanity are identical terms, then we can dispense with one of them. This would solve the problem by denying its existence. Another suggestion is that the union between Christ and God, and therefore between God and man, is moral and not metaphysical. But this only amounts to moral likeness, not essential union. The fact is that Humanitarianism under any form cannot provide a satisfactory explanation of the Incarnation. It is helpless before the problems. The New Testament has to be accounted for. Christ is unique. If there was no real Incarnation we have no real knowledge of God in relation to man's life, especially in regard to sin and deliverance from it, except so far as the (by itself) imperfect revelation of the Old Testament is concerned. Unitarianism is a failure, because it cannot bear the stress of the doctrine of the Divine Fatherhood.[4] If the Incarnation be denied Christianity

[1] Paterson, *ut supra*, pp. 209, 213.
[2] The evidence can be seen in Whitelaw, *How is the Divinity of Christ depicted in the Gospels?*; Parkin, *The New Testament Portrait of Jesus*; Holdsworth, *The Christ of the Gospels*; Hoyt, *The Lord's Teaching concerning His own Person.*
[3] Streatfield, *The Self-Interpretation of Jesus Christ: The Incarnation*; Johnston Ross, *The Universality of Jesus*; Griffith Thomas, *Christianity is Christ*, with Bibliography.
[4] Gwatkin, *The Knowledge of God*, Vol. II, p. 298.

cannot long survive. Besides, the truth is that of God becoming Man rather than of man becoming God. No mere Immanence will suffice, and certainly no apotheosis.[1]

It must never be forgotten that there is vital, essential, and intimate connection between our Lord's Deity and His work of redemption. It is not merely that one man is made unique, but it is a case of God coming to the world in human form, " for us men and for our salvation."

" The Incarnation may be inexplicable as a psychological or ontological problem ; but it satisfies the yearnings of those who are seeking after God and His righteousness."[2]

It is this that has made the Church so persistent in her determination to be satisfied with nothing less than the real and complete Deity of Christ. " A Saviour not quite God is a bridge broken at the farther side."[3]

Herein lay the vital problem raised by Arianism at Nicaea, and it is imperative that the bearings of the conflict should be thoroughly known. It is a very shallow and superficial view that regards that great battle as merely metaphysical and intended for doctrinal accuracy. In reality it was something infinitely more important, because reaching deep down to the needs of human life. Christian men were conscious of salvation from sin associated with Jesus Christ. For generations they had inherited the primitive interpretation of the connection between His work of redemption and His unique Person, and the real spiritual experience of Apostolic and sub-Apostolic times was potent at that period and could not be set aside. They worshipped Christ as God, and recognised that His redemption was nothing short of a Divine work, while instead of this Arianism offered them One Who, after all, was only a creature of God. It is the consciousness of this remarkable but significant fact that leads the truest thinkers to believe that the victory of Arianism would have swept Christianity entirely away. It was with no desire to indulge in mere metaphysics that Athanasius insisted upon the doctrine of the Homoousios, but because of the real subtilty of Arianism. Up to that time ordinary practical experience had sufficed, but now it was proving inadequate, and so the Church was compelled to insist upon the truth of Jesus Christ being " Very God of very God, Begotten, not made, Being of one substance with the Father."

It has often been pointed out that to-day's peril lies in Agnosticism in Christology. Ritschlianism teaches that Christ has the value of God for us, but will not allow any discussion of His fundamental relation to God. And yet if Jesus Christ has for man the value of God He must in some way or other be Divine and not simply human. No creature could

---

[1] Warfield, *Princeton Theological Review*, Vol. IX, p. 689.
[2] Mead, *Irenic Theology*, p. 257.
[3] Bishop Moule, Preface to Sir Robert Anderson's *The Lord from Heaven*.

remain a creature and still act for God and on behalf of man beyond the range of finite power and experience. It is therefore essential to have a Christology that answers to the facts of Christian experience, since life, not philosophy, is at stake. Agnosticism in Christology inevitably tends to empty the work of Christ of its redemptive power. If Christ be a creature, however great, there is no redemption, because there is no real point of contact between the sinner and the Holy God. Our Christology must be adequate to the facts of redemptive experience. In connection with certain recent discussions it has been pointed out[1] that the importance of Christ made flesh lies in its bearings on Christ made sin, since this is the true proof and reason of the Incarnation. No mere Immanence will suffice for redemption, for while Immanence overcomes the Deistic position it cannot touch the Unitarian, since many Unitarians hold the Immanence of God in nature. Then, too, Immanence alone is defective in regard to guilt and grace. It " antiquates the Reformation, and every tendency is to be discredited that does that." Redemption must, therefore, be preserved and not lost in evolution. " Immanence gives us a lapse, but not sin, a relative Saviour, not an eternal one." Herein, therefore, lies the vital question of the Deity of Christ, since no salvation can possibly come to us except by means of miracle, and miracle implies the ultimate power of the spiritual to control the material. Amid all the changes and chances of this mortal life, amid all the principles of science and the revelations of law, the heart demands salvation; salvation is only possible by Divine grace, and grace can only come through a Divinely human Saviour. It will be seen from this that the very nature of Christianity is at stake, and all that Christianity means in regard to salvation from sin.

II.—THE INCARNATION OF CHRIST

The Article continues to employ terms inherited from the controversies of the first five centuries, and it will be well to consider the results before becoming acquainted with the details of the process by which they were arrived at.

1. The Human Nature.—" Took Man's nature in the womb of the blessed Virgin, of her substance." This teaches the reality of the human nature of Christ which is so clear in the New Testament. The method of His entrance upon human life shows that He did not assume an adult personality, or else there would have been two persons, the Divine and the Human. Human nature was necessary for the redemption of mankind, and this beyond all else is the reason why our Lord assumed it.

2. The two Natures.—" So that two whole and perfect Natures;

---

[1] This section is greatly indebted to a paper by Principal Forsyth, written during the "New Theology" controversy. The latest and in some respects the best argument in favour of an agnosticism in Christology will be found in Loof's *What is the Truth about Jesus Christ?* But there could not be adduced a better testimony to the uniqueness of our Lord's Personality as stated in the traditional Christology.

that is to say, the Godhead and Manhood." The phraseology is very important, and both the Divine and the Human Natures are described as " whole and perfect," that is, possessing all the properties perfect in each. According to the orthodox Christology settled at the Council of Chalcedon, it was Human Nature, not a Human Person that the Son of God took into union with Himself. By Human Nature is to be understood all those qualities which the race has in common. By a Human Person is meant a separate individual possessing the distinctive power known as personality. Adam did not transmit his personality, which is incommunicable, but his nature, so that personality can be distinguished from nature. Human nature is organised on a new personality in each individual. There is no concrete humanity, but there are concrete persons.

3. The One Person.—" Were joined together in one Person, never to be divided." This is a further statement of the result of the Incarnation as it affected the Man Christ Jesus as depicted in the Gospels. The union of the two natures in one Person is sometimes called the Hypostatic Union; that is, two natures in one, ὑπόστασις. In the New Testament there is a clear unity of consciousness throughout, and it is often quite impossible to distinguish between the human and Divine elements. It is, of course, a great mystery how two natures can be joined together in one Person, never to be divided, and the distinction between nature and Person must not be unduly pressed. Our knowledge of personality, as of psychology in general, is only small, and it is impossible to fathom the mystery of the union of two natures in one personality. We must emphasise the Divine Nature, the Human Nature, and the Divine Personality, without expecting to solve the problem of their correlation. The consideration of our Lord's life on earth tends to make some people lose sight of the Divine in the human, and the result is often a merely humanitarian Christ. On the other hand, a consideration of the glorified Lord tends to make some lose sight of the human in the Divine, and the outcome is often a craving for some Mediator between the Divine Lord and ourselves. Our safety will always be found in emphasising and balancing both aspects, the Divine and the human. However difficult it may be to conceive of it, our Lord's Human Nature was somehow or other taken up into the Personality of the Word, and the three differences between His Humanity and ours: (a) no human Father; (b) no human Person; (c) no sin; do not touch the integrity and perfection of His Human Nature.[1]

. 4. The One Christ.—" Whereof is one Christ, very God, and very Man." Here, again, the Article endeavours to state what is clearly seen in the New Testament, a unity of consciousness in the one life of Jesus Christ, and yet while one Christ, He is very God and very Man. Theology sometimes speaks of this as *communicatio idiomatum*, that is, the conjunction of natures is so close that we can attribute to the one

[1] Bruce, *The Humiliation of Christ*, p. 169.

Person what is really only appropriate to one of the two natures. Thus, we read of " the blood of God " (Acts xx. 28); " The Son of Man which is in heaven " (John iii. 13); " Crucified the Lord of glory " (1 Cor. ii. 8).[1] This statement is simply an effort to express what is found in Scripture; the reality of Christ's Humanity, the reality of His Divinity, and withal the unity of His Personality.

" We can discern in the separate moments of the doctrine a religious justification or necessity, while the synthesis in which they are united is difficult and even bewildering. The constituent elements of the doctrine were the truths which remained after the exclusion of the apparently impossible positions."[2]

These four statements may be said to sum up the Christology of Chalcedon, which substantially completed the orthodox Christology of the ancient Church, and this is now the common heritage of Greek, Latin, and Evangelical Christendom, except that Protestantism naturally reserves the right of searching afresh into the profound mystery of the Christ of the New Testament. It should never be forgotten that Christ is of necessity infinitely more than any human formula. This is true even of human personality, and much more is it true of the Divine. Statements such as those of the Creeds and this Article are intended to guide and guard our thought, enabling us to form clear conceptions and indicating limits within which our thoughts may move in safety. The decision of Chalcedon cannot be said to preclude discussion, but only to indicate the lines on which it is thought a true statement of Christology will be made. Chalcedon has been rightly described as a lighthouse to show the channel between the reefs of Nestorian Dyophysitism and Eutychian Monophysitism. We may sum up the leading ideas of Chalcedon as follows :—

1. The true Incarnation of the Divine Logos.
2. The distinction between Nature and Person.
3. The result of the Incarnation as the God Man, Jesus Christ.
4. The duality of the Natures.
5. The unity of the Person.
6. The work of Christ as based upon His Person.
7. The relative impersonality of the human nature of Christ.

On this subject four heresies are particularly notable and call for study by all who wish to know the process by which the early Church came to its conclusion concerning the Deity and Incarnation of our Lord.

(a) Arianism, 325, which denied the true Godhead of Christ.

(b) Apollinarianism, 360, which denied the perfect Manhood of Christ.

(c) Nestorianism, 431, which denied the unity of the Person of Christ.

(d) Eutychianism, 451, which denied the distinction of the natures of Christ.

[1] Hooker, *Ecclesiastical Polity*, Bk. V, Ch. 53, Section 4.
[2] Paterson, *ut supra*, p. 227.

Against these four errors the Church, as represented at Chalcedon, emphasised four watchwords. In opposition to Arianism, Christ was declared to be " truly " God ($\dot{a}\lambda\eta\theta\hat{\omega}s$); in opposition to Apollinarianism, Christ was declared to be " perfectly " Man ($\tau\epsilon\lambda\epsilon\dot{\iota}\omega s$); in opposition to Nestorianism, Christ's Person was declared to be " indivisibly " one ($\dot{a}\delta\iota\alpha\iota\rho\dot{\epsilon}\tau\omega s$); in opposition to Eutychianism, the two Natures of Christ were declared to be " unconfusedly " distinct ($\dot{a}\sigma\upsilon\gamma\chi\dot{\upsilon}\tau\omega s$).

HISTORY OF CHRISTOLOGY

Although the Article states the Chalcedonian Christology, it may be well to keep in mind the three periods of Christology indicated by Dorner. (1) Up to Chalcedon the Church insisted on Christ as being very God and very Man. (2) From Chalcedon to 1900 the Church approached, but did not solve, the union of Natures. Before the Reformation the tendency was to lay too great stress on the Divinity and to exclude the true view of His Humanity. Since the Reformation the tendency has been to lay too great stress on the Humanity and to exclude the true view of His Divinity. (3) Since 1900 thinkers have been attempting to realise the unity of Christ's personal consciousness as seen in the New Testament, and to harmonise this with the clear distinction of Natures, Human and Divine. It will be seen that the Church has been mainly concerned with the adjustment of the dual aspects of the Nature of Christ. This in various forms occupied attention from the third to the seventh century, and is still a subject of controversy. Apart from Rationalism, pure and simple, which makes Jesus Christ nothing but Man, controversy has not been so much directed to the fact of an Incarnation as to how it is to be conceived and explained. Even Chalcedon which, as we have seen, taught the doctrine of the two Natures in the one Person, did not settle the question, as the subsequent Monothelite controversy shows. Moreover, modern thought is widely dissatisfied with the Chalcedon formula because it is considered unreal and impossible on psychological grounds. The Chalcedon doctrine has been particularly criticised during recent years as unsatisfactory.[1] It is said to be untrue to the Gospel picture of Christ, because it is too abstract and because it severs the unity of that picture of Him, destroying the single consciousness of the Gospels and giving us " two abstractions instead of one reality, two impotent halves in place of one living whole."[2] Then, too, its doctrine of " impersonal humanity " is said to be unthinkable because unreal and untrue to experience.[3] The result is said to be a dilemma,

[1] Dykes, *Expository Times*, Vol. XVII, pp. 7, 55, 103, 151; Garvie, *Expository Times*, Vol. XXIII, pp. 353, 414, 448, 505, 548; Mackintosh, *The Person of Christ*, pp. 209-215, and 383 ff.

[2] Mackintosh, *ut supra*, p. 295.

[3] Mackintosh quotes Dean Strong, *Manual of Theology*, Second Edition, p. 130, in regard to what is usually called "an impersonal humanity," that "it suggests a kind of abstract idea of man lying untenanted, and adopted by a Divine Person, and it is obvious that it opens the door to scholasticism of an unduly technical sort" (*ut supra*, p. 386).

" the Scylla of a duplex personality and the Charybdis of an impersonal manhood."[1] On this view genuine faith in Christ is not to be identified with adherence to this Christological formula,[2] and the call comes to reconsider the position and to interpret the data, because it is essential to have a Christology.

There have been five general ways of explaining the method of the Incarnation.

1. The doctrine of the *communicatio idiomatum*.—This means, as we have seen, the interpenetration of the human nature by the Divine, each nature communicating to the other its properties because of the oneness of the Personality. This doctrine is associated with John of Damascus, in whose hands it means the permeation of the human and Divine. But, of course, it has the obvious reservations that the human cannot permeate the Divine and the humanity cannot contain the Divinity, so that the *communicatio* is one-sided, and as the Logos imparts to the human intellect perfect knowledge, and to the human will Divine Omnipotence, the very attributes essential to humanity are really denied to Christ. In reality this doctrine is a deification of humanity, the Manhood being regarded as the organ through which the Logos manifests Himself. But any real condescension of the Logos is excluded and the humanity is virtually absorbed. This doctrine was fully developed in after times by the Lutheran Church in connection with the Ubiquitarian hypothesis of the Lord's Supper, which, however, our Church has definitely rejected. The doctrine has been very severely criticised, and Gibbon speaks contemptuously of it as " the deepest and darkest corner of the whole theological abyss." In the same way modern writers reject it as impossible as a way of explaining the relationship of the Divine and Human in Christ.[3] It is, however, only fair to say that it was never intended to mean any change in the Divine Nature such as would reduce it to the limits of mere humanity, nor does it mean any exaltation of the Human such as would make it entirely different. All that was meant was that the two Natures were so united that the experiences which came from their union was one thing, and not two independent lines of activity. Its aim was to preserve the great and necessary truth that the redemption wrought by Christ was in some way dependent on His Person as the Son of God.

2. Gradual Incarnation.—This is a view which starts with the two Natures, and by gradual growth from embryonic and infantile unconsciousness arrives at a conscious personality which culminates after the Resurrection. This view is associated with the great name of Dorner, but it cannot be said to solve the problem, for the union of two Natures without as yet a personality is still a question. What is a Nature which has no knowledge, love, and will? In ordinary men it is possible to distinguish between the nature, which is the whole constitution, and the

---

[1] Mackintosh, *ut supra*, p. 296.   [2] Mackintosh, *ut supra*, p. 298 f.
[3] Mackintosh, *ut supra*, p. 241 f.

person, which is the self-consciousness alone.   But in Christ the matter is different because He had a human soul and will as well as a body.

3.   The Kenosis.—This means the self-emptying of the Logos.   It is based on Phil. ii. 5-8, and is said to involve in some way the laying aside of Divine attributes.   The theory takes various forms,[1] but in spite of the great names, the profound abilities, and, indeed, the genuine aim of those who advocate it, it may be questioned whether any such Kenosis is possible.   Laying aside the use of attributes is one thing, but laying aside the attributes themselves is quite another.   Jesus Christ had a Divine Nature and a Divine experience, but it was the latter not the former that He gave up, and instead took a human experience.   It was therefore impossible for Him to achieve Manhood by renouncing His Deity, since after He became Man He still had Divine attributes.   It was the non-use that constituted the Kenosis.   These attributes did not appear, and by a constant act of will He voluntarily laid aside equality with God in order to assume human nature.   The true interpretation of the passage on which so much is based is that our Lord did not, because He could not, surrender His essential form of being ($\mu o \rho \phi \acute{\eta}$).[2]   This doctrine of the Kenosis is really an attempt to explain the Humanity at the expense of the Deity, and notwithstanding all that has been urged in its favour it really fails, and thought to-day is tending more and more away from it. It has well been pointed out that a century engaged in "the Quest of the Historic Jesus" would have been unnecessary if the Kenotic theory is true.   It is admittedly only true

"provided we are to give weight to the religious considerations which demand the pre-existence of the Son of God, and also to give weight to the evidence of the evangelists who reported to us all that is known of Jesus Christ."[3]

But this is to admit that there is no real Kenosis, since such a theory does not "give weight to the evidence of the evangelists."

4.   One recent attempt to solve the problem is a blend of the second and third views stated above.   It starts from the Christ of History, and from Him as Redeemer, not merely as Teacher.[4]   His manhood was real, individual, and full, and yet He was a personal manifestation of God in human form.[5]   His Incarnation and pre-existence are facts, and there was a self-emptying, though this emphasises principle rather than method.[6]   Keeping close to the facts, we may say :—

"We are faced by a Divine self-reduction which entailed obedience, temptation, and death.   So that religion has a vast stake in the *kenosis* as a fact, whatever the difficulties as to its method may be.   No human life of God is possible without a prior self-adjustment of deity."[7]

[1] See Bruce, *ut supra*, Ch. IV.
[2] Gifford, *The Incarnation*, clearly shows that ὑπάρχων in Phil. ii. 6 must mean permanent subsistence during His incarnate life, as well as pre-existence, according to Lightfoot's interpretation.
[3] Paterson, *ut supra*, p. 232.
[4] Mackintosh, *ut supra*, p. 306 ff.; 321 ff.
[5] Mackintosh, *ut supra*, p. 407 ff.
[6] Mackintosh, *ut supra*, p. 466.
[7] Mackintosh, *ut supra*, p. 470.

This is interpreted to mean a self-abnegation of Deity by which Jesus Christ came to live a life "wholly restrained within the bounds of humanity."[1] In this view no attempt is made to state the theory of the relations between the Divine and Human in Christ, and there is no reference to the ".Word," or "Son," apart from the Incarnation, since we know nothing of it. It is represented that only by contracting His Divine fulness within earthly limits could the redeeming Lord draw nigh to man, and so it is said that in Jesus Christ—

"There is realised on earth the human life of God, and it is a life whose chiefest glory consists in a voluntary descent from depth to depth of our experience. It is the personal presence of God in One who is neither omniscient nor ubiquitous nor almighty—as God *per se* must be—but is perfect Love and Holiness and Freedom in terms of perfect humanity."[2]

According to this criticism the defect of Chalcedon is that it leaves no room for growth in the Person of Christ, that growth referred to the Manhood only. But it is said that the Divine element was also gradually developed, that as the work of Christ was a process, so the Person must also grow. Not that He became Divine in the sense of deification, but that there was a development of what was originally Divine and Human.[3] So that side by side with this view of a Kenosis there is the corresponding doctrine of a Plerosis, or the self-fulfilment of God in Christ.[4]

It will be seen that this view endeavours to harmonise the thought of a Kenosis with a gradual development of the Personality, according to Dorner's view. But it is open to serious objection, and, indeed, its author allows that the problem "contains, and is created by, two imperfectly known factors."[5] It is difficult to know what is meant by "a human life of God "; a life "unequivocally human."[6] The theory seems to demand an unthinkable metamorphosis of God into a man. It does not seem to satisfy the conditions of the Gospels, which represent Jesus Christ as at once human and Divine, and it is because this theory fails to satisfy all the conditions required that it has to be set aside as virtually amounting to little, if any, more than the ordinary Kenotic theories.[7]

5. The sub-liminal consciousness Theory.—One more modern view needs attention because it has been presented by Dr. Sanday. He is unable to accept the Chalcedon doctrine of the two Natures, and in order to have a Christ who in His earthly manifestation was strictly human, he suggests that the Deity underlay the Humanity, as the sub-conscious element in man underlies his consciousness, that as the place of all Divine action upon the soul is the sub-liminal consciousness, so the proper seat of Deity in the Incarnate Christ is found there also. But this, as several

---

[1] Mackintosh, *ut supra*, p. 479.   [2] Mackintosh, *ut supra*, p. 486.
[3] Mackintosh, *ut supra*, p. 498 f.
[4] Mackintosh, *ut supra*, p. 504 f.; Forsyth, *The Person and Place of Jesus Christ*.
[5] Mackintosh, *ut supra*, p. 499.   [6] Mackintosh, *ut supra*, pp. 469, 470.
[7] For an acute criticism of Mackintosh see the *Princeton Theological Review*, Vol. XI, p. 141 ff., by Dr. B. B. Warfield.

writers have pointed out, does not meet the difficulty, still less solve the
problem, for it really makes Christ to possess one Nature, so that in
endeavouring to do justice to the Humanity of Christ Dr. Sanday's view
fails to do justice to His Deity, and instead of deriving his interpretation
from the New Testament picture of the Divine-Human Christ, this
theory really reduces our Lord to a purely human Christ, in whom God
dwelt in fuller measure than He dwells in all men. The theory has been
subjected to very acute and severe criticism, and although it is deserving
of the greatest possible consideration, coming from the source it does, it
hardly seems likely to be more satisfactory than other theories in solving
the problem of the Incarnation.[1]

It would seem as though, after all, we shall have to be content with
the general line of the Chalcedon formula. Not that it explains the
mystery, but that it lays down the limits outside which we cannot go
without sacrificing the essential truth of the New Testament and Christianity. What is required is a theory that will do justice both to the
Deity and the Humanity, as they are both depicted in the Gospels, and
it is the virtue and value of the Chalcedon view that it satisfies this
requirement while all modern Christologies seem to fail at one point or
another.[2] The objections to the Chalcedon view are obvious and have
often been ably stated, and yet in spite of all recent criticisms no better
explanation seems to be possible.[3]

Although in connection with Chalcedon the term " impersonal
humanity " is used and charged against that decision, yet the proper idea
is not that the human nature exists impersonally, but that it is taken up
into the Personality of the Logos.[4] The reality of the facts does not stand

[1] For criticisms see Mackintosh, *ut supra*, p. 487 ff.; Garvie, *Expository Times*, Vol.
XXIV, pp. 305, 373; Warfield, *Princeton Theological Review*, Vol. IX, pp. 166, 686;
Mullins, *The Christian Religion*, p. 199 f.

[2] "It ought by now to be clearly understood that no resting-place can be found in
a half-way house between Socinianism and orthodoxy. We cannot have a Christ purely
Divine in essence and purely human in manifestation. And what on this ground can
be made of the exalted Christ? Does He remain after His ascension to heaven the purely
human being He was on earth? Or does He, on ascending where He was before,
recover the pure deity from which He was reduced that He might enter humanity?
In the one case we have no Divine Christ, in the other no human Jesus, to-day: and
the Christian heart can consent to give up neither" (Warfield, *Princeton Theological
Review*, Vol. XI, p. 155).

[3] An illustration of this is shown in the simple fact that in September 1912 (*Expository
Times*) Dr. Garvie strongly objected to the use of the term "Person" for the distinctive
doctrine of the Trinity. In January 1913 he had come to favour the use of it.

[4] "The doctrine of the Two Natures does not suppose that there ever existed or ever
could exist an impersonal human nature, and never dreamed of attributing any kind
of reality to any human nature apart from 'the unifying Ego.' . . . No one ever
imagined a 'human nature' which was or could be 'unconscious and impersonal.'
The conjunction of a human nature with a divine nature in one conscious and personal
subject no doubt presents an insoluble problem to thought. But this is just the mystery
of incarnation, without which there is no incarnation; for when we say incarnation
we say Two Natures—or can there really be an incarnation without a somewhat which
becomes incarnate and a somewhat in which it becomes incarnate"? (Warfield, *ut
supra*, p. 151).

"The stone of stumbling here is ever again 'the impersonality of Jesus' human

or fall with our ability to explain all the difficulties. It is worth while to remember that heresy sometimes has sufficient vitality in it to be of spiritual blessing to men,[1] so that we can distinguish between the individual and his system, and even show that while a Humanitarian may be a Christian, Humanitarianism is not Christianity. But it is also true, looking at the entire Christian history, that heresies have one after another proved themselves incapable of bearing the full weight of human need, especially of redemption and all that it involves. There is no need to fetter research so long as all the facts are kept in view. To put it on the lowest ground, the orthodox doctrines of the Trinity and the Person of Christ are " the least unsatisfactory of the attempts that have been made to state the truth."[2] Meanwhile, we say that " the Father is God, Christ is God, the Holy Spirit is God, and yet that they are not three, but one God." This has been the only safe and satisfying foundation of that salvation from sin which is the deepest need of the soul.[3]

THE VIRGIN BIRTH

This subject has been one of great controversy during recent years, and it is not surprising, since it has a very definite bearing on the Christological problem. It is impossible to do more than indicate the proper

nature.' The grievance is always repeated: the Christological dogma no doubt teaches that the Logos assumed a complete human nature, but this is really not the fact. If the humanity of Christ was perfect, it should have possessed also personality. It is the intention that no other alternative should be left but this—either an incomplete human nature, or a complete human nature, but then also a human person. And if you take the latter, then you come to the absurdity, that two persons are joined together. But the fault of this reasoning lurks in this—that the nature of personality as such is sought in self-consciousness and in free self-determination, as the principle that forms the person; or rather that personality is conceived as a product of the process of self-consciousness and self-determination. This view cannot be right. An hypostasis or person is a substance which exists as a whole and for itself. An hypostasis is nothing else but the Aristotelian πρώτη οὐσία, the *prima substantia*, the in and for itself existing individual substance. A nature—divine or human—cannot be actual in its abstract generality, but only in a determinate hypostasis. But the nature can readily belong to a plurality of hypostases. And just so a plurality of natures can belong to one hypostasis. In the case of the church dogma this must be kept in view. There can be a complete human nature, without its existing in a human person, provided that it exists in another higher person, that is, here, in the Logos. No doubt if the human nature had been without any personality, the objection would be just. But when we speak of the *enhypostasia* of the human nature of Christ, we mean by it only that this nature does not exist in a human person. And we recognise at the same time its enhypostasisation in the Logos. It was thus then the Person of the Son which thought and acted in the human nature and had the disposition of all its gifts and powers. I do not suppose, of course, that by this the union of the two natures in the unity of the person is made conceivable for our finite understanding. No, it remains a mystery. But no absurdity. And by what I have said the charge of absurdity only is met. The human nature was perfect, just because it existed in the Person of the Son" (Honig, quoted in the *Princeton Theological Review*, Vol. X, p. 337).

[1] Paterson, *ut supra*, p. 233.
[2] Paterson, *ut supra*, p. 235.
[3] For a complete statement and criticism of modern Christologies, together with a view similar to the above conclusion, see La Touche, *The Person of Christ in Modern Thought*.

line of approach, leaving the thorough discussion to special works on the subject.[1]

1. The first thing to do is to take the life of Christ and study His sinlessness and uniqueness. How are these to be accounted for apart from some Divine intervention that made them possible ?

2. Then we should proceed to the Apostolic interpretation of Christ. To the Apostles Jesus Christ stood in an unique relation to God, and of this, the simplest expression is found in the idea of His pre-existence (1 Cor. viii. 6; Col. i. 15 ff.; 2 Cor. viii. 9; Phil. ii. 6).[2]

3. At this point the narratives in the Gospels may be studied. They are very early manifestations, but give no evidence of being inventions, or of having come from earlier sources, or of being of composite character.

4. One of the surest proofs of primitive belief on this subject is the opposition to it and denials from the time of Cerinthus. These disputes have to be explained.

5. Then comes the enquiry as to how Jesus Christ can be accounted for ? If He is unique in history, must He not also be so in origin ? Every effect must have its adequate cause, and it is only by the Virgin Birth that we can account for the unique earthly life of Jesus Christ. The miracle of the Incarnation is thus fitly expressed in the miraculous entrance, and harmonises with the miraculous departure in the Resurrection.

6. It is believed that a new start was then made, by means of which the eternal Son of God entered into humanity : as the second Adam, the Lord from heaven, did not come by ordinary generation. The first Adam had failed, and a new race was necessary, of which Jesus Christ was the new Head. This necessitated a fresh creation, and the Virgin Birth meant this (Luke i. 35).

7. The decision will depend almost wholly upon our view of the miraculous in general. The Virgin Birth is not impossible unless all miracles are impossible, but if on *a priori* grounds we believe that no miracle has ever occurred, then the Virgin Birth necessarily falls to the ground. Yet if we believe that Jesus rose from the dead we shall avoid greater difficulties by accepting the miraculous birth. Thus opinion will depend upon the conception we form of His Person.

8. It is perfectly true that the Virgin Birth had no place in the preaching and teaching of the Apostolic days, and this is only natural and to be expected because the Virgin Birth is no necessary proof of Deity, but only of a Divine Personage. While the rejection of the Virgin Birth would certainly undermine faith, yet its acceptance is quite compatible with the rejection of the Deity of Christ. The truth of His Sonship, as implied in the Virgin Birth, is merged into the profounder truth of His greater

---

[1] Orr, *The Virgin-Birth of Christ*; Knowling, "The Birth of Christ"; Hastings' *Dictionary of Christ and the Gospels*; Box, "The Virgin Birth"; Mackintosh, *The Person of Christ*, p. 527 ff.; Simpson, *Fact and Faith*, p. 24 ff.; Griffith Thomas, *Christianity is Christ*, Ch. XII.

[2] Denney, *Studies in Theology*, p. 250 f.

Sonship which is proved by the Resurrection (Rom. i. 4). St. Peter's confession at Cæsarea Philippi was not due to the Virgin Birth, because "flesh and blood" could easily have revealed this fact to him.

9. Denials of the Virgin Birth proceed from the assertion that a sinless character is possible without a Virgin Birth, or without even ordinary paternity. But the real question is not a sinless character, but a sinless personality. Character is always an attainment, while personality is an endowment.

10. In reality the difficulty is one that Christianity has always had to face, and the force of the objections can easily be perceived. Yet the Gospel has never been destroyed by this weight, and although historical scholarship may still be able to say something in regard to the documents and the historical side, yet in the future, as in the past, the problem will naturally be solved in the light of the complete impression formed of the life of Jesus Christ. We do well to emphasise the almost insuperable difficulties of the mythical theory by asking how the idea of the Virgin Birth arose, if it was not based on fact, and how the narratives could have obtained such appearance of trustworthiness unless they were historical. But the fundamental question is, that Christ being such as He was, and coming into this world for the purpose of redemption, it cannot be regarded as either unnatural or incredible that His life should have begun in this way. The ultimate decision will assuredly lie in the realm of effects. If we believe that the world is only imperfect and not sinful we shall be content with an ethical and human Christ. But if there is such a thing as human sin we shall be compelled to fall back upon a miraculous Christ, who was "conceived by the Holy Ghost, born of the Virgin Mary."

III.—THE DEATH OF CHRIST

It is natural that the Article should proceed to state the true idea of the work of Christ in close association with His Person, and the view here taken is in strict harmony with what was taught at and from Chalcedon.

1. The Fact of Christ's Death.—"Who truly suffered."—The emphasis on the reality of the sufferings was doubtless due to the reappearance of Docetic teaching in the sixteenth century, whereby our Lord's sufferings were regarded as apparent only. Since then Swedenborg taught a very similar doctrine. The true interpretation is that the Person Who suffered is the Son of God, but the Nature in which He suffered is the human nature. We are not saved by the work apart from the Person, but by the Person through the work. The Person gives efficacy to the work. This is the meaning of Hooker's phrase, "The infinite worth of the Son of God," and it was this beyond all else that led to the strong insistence in the early Church on the Deity of our Lord, and the real union of God and man in the Incarnation. This, too, as we have seen, is at the heart of the doctrine of the *communicatio idiomatum*,

D

the prevailing thought being that no one could atone who was not at once perfectly Divine and perfectly human.

2. The Form of Christ's Death.—" Was crucified, dead, and buried."
—This reference to the death by crucifixion and the act of burial is in exact agreement with the statement of the Creeds, and, indeed, is intended to express the same truths.

3. The Purpose of Christ's Death.—" To reconcile His Father to us, and to be a sacrifice."—The wording of the Article is sometimes criticised because it is said that reconciliation in the New Testament seems to suggest the manward side only. " Be ye reconciled to God." This is true, but it presupposes an already existing reconciliation of God to man by the Death of Christ. We shall see later when we study more closely the doctrine of the Atonement that the statement of the Article is intended to express a real and profound Bible truth. Only on one point might the Article be a little more exact. Reconciliation in the New Testament is associated with *God*, not with the *Father*, the judicial rather than the paternal relations are involved. Reconciliation is concerned with the Father as God, not with God as Father. In this respect the wording of the Article might have been kept closer to the New Testament, but apart from this verbal inadequacy the truth implied is undoubted and important.

4. The Scope of Christ's Death.—" Not only for original guilt, but also for all actual sins of men."[1]—The phrase, " original guilt," apparently means the same as " original sin " in Article IX. At any rate, there is no other statement in the Anglican formularies which seems to distinguish between " original sin " and " original guilt." The Article is thus intended to cover all forms of moral evil, whether those associated with the sin of Adam, or those due to man's personal action. The Bible clearly distinguishes between " sin " and " sins," the root and the fruit, the principle and the practice, and the Article teaches that our Lord's Atonement covers both of these.

These statements of the Article when taken in connection with similar expressions in Articles XV and XXXI give the Anglican doctrine of the Atonement, but it is necessary to pay much closer attention to the subject by reason of its prominence in the New Testament, in the history of Christian thought, and in various theological discussions to-day.

THE DOCTRINE OF THE ATONEMENT

No one can question the centrality of the Cross in the New Testament. It is admittedly the heart of Christianity.

---

[1] The words : " Not only for original guilt, but also for all actual sins of men," are inserted by the Reformers in their Confession with a deliberate and important purpose, in order to state, in the most comprehensive manner, that, in the words of our Prayer of Consecration, our Lord, 'by His one oblation of Himself once offered, made a full, perfect, and sufficient sacrifice, oblation, and satisfaction, for the sins of the whole world.' Nothing more can be required by the divine justice in satisfaction for sin, in addition to that one perfect and sufficient sacrifice of Christ" (Wace, *Principles of the Reformation*, p. 49 f.).

" The centre of gravity in the New Testament. . . . Not Bethlehem, but Calvary is the focus of revelation."[1]

It is obvious that the New Testament connects our salvation with the Death of Christ; indeed, from the standpoint of apologetics Christianity is the only religion with a Cross. Yet few doctrines have given rise to greater differences of opinion. Ever since the days of St. Paul the Cross has been to some people a " stumbling-block," and to others " foolishness." But, meanwhile, Christians continue to say and sing : " In the Cross of Christ I glory." It is essential, therefore, that we should do our utmost to discover, first of all, what the Bible says about the Death of Christ, and then to get behind this and endeavour to find out what it means.

Before looking at the subject in detail it will be well to consider the meaning of the word " Atonement," and the history of it is the best clue to its use in theology. It was not originally a religious term, and apparently its admission in a theological sense dates from the latter part of the seventeenth century. The Christian idea of the word is thus much more comprehensive than its original scope, and it is in this that the danger of its misuse lies by those who are unable to accept the profound Biblical doctrine which it represents. As early as the thirteenth century there existed in English an adverbial expression, *at-one*, meaning " agreed." This phrase was related to the numeral adjective, *one*, then pronounced as we now pronounce *own*. From this came the verb, *to atone*; and at a somewhat earlier date the substantive, *atonement*, the mediæval form of which was the simple noun, " onement " (pronounced as "own-ment") About the same time *atonemaker* was introduced as an Anglo-Saxon equivalent for " mediator." From examples that can be adduced it is clear that the thought conveyed was simply that of reconciliation. Then at a later date theologically the word came to mean the revealed way of reconciliation with God through the mediation of His Son—a far more extensive idea.[2] In the Authorised Version the term

---

[1] Denney, *The Death of Christ*, p. 324 f.
[2] (1) *Atone*, adv., "agreed" (opp. at odds, atwin).
Chaucer, speaking of the patient Griselda in his *Clerk's Tale*, says:
"If gentlemen, or other of that contree
  Were wroth, she wolde bringen them *aton*,
  So wise and ripe wordes hadde she."
Again elsewhere:
"After discord they accorded. . . .
  'Sir,' saiden they, 'we ben *aton*.' "—*Romaunt of the Rose*.
It occurs in this sense in our older versions of the Bible: "After this was God *atone* with the land " (2 Sam. xxi. 14; Coverdale, 1535).
"We pray you that ye be *atone* with God" (2 Cor. v. 20; Geneva Version).
(2) *At-one-ment*. Hence sprang the word *atonement*, in the sense of "reconciliation."
"What *atonement* is there between light and darkness?" (Philpot, 1554).
"God hath given to us the office to preach the *atonement*" (2 Cor. v. 18).—Tyndale, 1526.
"As a perfect sign of your *atonement* with me, you wish me joy."—Massinger, 1632.
"He was desirous to procure atonement between them and make them good friends (*cura reconciliandi eos in gratiam*)."—Philemon Holland, trans. of Livy (i. 50), 1600.

atonement is used of the Levitical sacrifices to translate the Hebrew, *kippurim* (lit. " cover "), and in one passage of the New Testament (A.V.) in the sense of *reconciliation*, to represent the Greek καταλλαγή (Rom. v. 11). It is, therefore, essential to discover whether the use of the term is intended to represent the Biblical idea of vicarious satisfaction, or merely to designate some thought of reconciliation with God apart from " the blood of the Cross." Between these two conceptions there is an impassable gulf, and it is necessary to know precisely what we are to understand by the term.

I.—THE NEW TESTAMENT REVELATION

It is best to start here and to make the approach along three lines.

1. In General.—We must first observe the prominence given to the Death of Christ in the New Testament.

(*a*) In the Gospels attention should be called to the space devoted to the events of the last week of our Lord's life. Thus taking an ordinary English Bible, St. Matthew has one-third devoted to this week, St. Mark over one-third, St. Luke one-fourth, and St. John five-twelfths, or nearly one-half. There must be something in this proportion, or rather disproportion, in view of the fragmentariness of the remainder of the record connected with the three years of our Lord's ministry.

(*b*) In the Epistles the prominence is almost equally clear. Thus St. Paul speaks of the Death as " delivered first of all " (1 Cor. xv. 3), while the teaching in such doctrinal Epistles as Romans, Galatians, Ephesians, Colossians, and 1 Peter is permeated with the truth of the Death of Christ.

(*c*) In the Apocalypse the central figure almost from first to last is " a Lamb as it had been slain " (Rev. i. 18 ; Rev. v. 6, 12 ; xii. 11 ; xiii. 8).

2. In Particular.—A careful survey of the words and phrases associated with the Death of Christ is needed at this stage.

(*a*) There are six terms calling for attention : Sacrifice ; Offering ; Ransom ; Redemption ; Propitiation ; Reconciliation. (1) Sacrifice, θυσία (1 Cor. v. 7 ; Eph. v. 2 ; Heb. x. 12). What is its root-idea ? According to Robertson Smith[1] it is communion with the Deity, but a more recent authority, who adduces proofs of his contention from life among the Bedouin, maintains that expiation is the primary conception.[2]

(3) *Atonemaker, i.e.* Reconciler.
"There is but one Mediator. By tha understand *Atonemaker*, Peacemaker."—Tyndale, 1533.
(4) *To atone* (i) prop., to reconcile.
"I was glad I did *atone* my countryman and you."—Shakespeare, *Cymbeline*, 1611.
"I would do much to *atone* them."—*Ibid., Othello*, 1604.
(ii) Later, to appease, satisfy for.
"Mankind thought that the principal thing required of them in religion was to *atone* and pacify the Divine power."—Owen, *Pneumatologia*, iv, I, 1674.
"The murderer fell, and blood *atoned* for blood."—Pope.
[1] *The Religion of the Semites.*   [2] S. I. Curtiss, *Primitive Semitic Religion To-day.*

The latter seems to be decidedly truer to the Biblical conception than the former, and although nothing is actually said about the original meaning of sacrifice, as seen in the earliest records, yet in the light of all that follows in the New Testament, it would seem as though Abel's sacrifice were best understood as implying sin and redemption in the light of previously given revelation. Certainly the statement that " By faith Abel offered " (Heb. xi. 4) seems to imply a prior revelation to which his faith could attend and respond. (2) Offering, προσφορά (Heb. x. 10, 14). The word is familiar from the LXX rendering of corresponding Hebrew terms. (3) Ransom, λύτρον (Matt. xx. 28; 1 Tim. ii. 6). Scripture is silent as to Whom the ransom is paid, and only emphasises the worth of that which was thereby given (cf. Rev. v. 9; Gal. iii. 13). (4) Redemption, ἀπολύτρωσις (Eph. i. 7; Col. i. 14). The original seems to mean " to loose by a price," while the English, following the Latin, means, " to buy back," " to re-purchase" (cf. λυτροῦν, 1 Pet. i. 18). The thought appears to be the removal of bondage and thraldom. (5) Propitiation, ἱλασμός, and ἱλάσκεσθαι (Rom. iii. 25; 1 John ii. 2; iv. 10). No word calls for more careful consideration. In propitiation there must be a subject and an object, one who propitiates and one who is propitiated. It is obvious that God cannot thus propitiate man, while man, himself unaided, is unable to propitiate God. The thought of the word is the removal of God's judicial displeasure and the taking away of an obstacle to fellowship, the removal being accomplished by God Himself. This is clearly the idea of the word in the publican's prayer, " God be propitious to me the sinner " (Luke xviii. 13).[1] (6) Reconciliation, καταλλαγή (Rom. v. 10; 2 Cor. v. 18; Eph. ii. 16-18). This refers to the adjustment of differences by the removal of enmity and separation. There is practical unanimity among scholars that reconciliation in St. Paul means a change of relation on God's part towards man, something done by God for man, which has modified what would otherwise have been His attitude to the sinner. Thus, reconciliation is much more than a change of feeling on man's part towards God, and must imply first of all a change of relation in God towards man. It is this that the Article was intended to express by the phrase, " To reconcile His Father to us." If it should be said that such a change in God is unthinkable, it may be answered that even in forgiveness, if we are to understand it aright, there must be some change of attitude, for God cannot possibly be in the same attitude before as after forgiveness.

(b) There are three phrases that need to be studied. " Made sin for us " (2 Cor. v. 21); He died " the just for the unjust " (1 Pet. iii. 18);

---

[1] As a confirmation of this interpretation, it may be pointed out that the Greek Papyri are perfectly clear that the meaning of propitiation was that of an offended God, who needed to be appeased. When this conception is purified of its heathen associations the principle seems obvious that propitiation is something offered by God on man's behalf to God for the purpose of removing judicial displeasure and hindrances to fellowship.

" Made a curse for us " (Gal. iii. 13). The true and complete meaning of these words must be insisted on.

(c) There are also four prepositions requiring attention : περί, " with reference to "; ὑπέρ,[1] " on behalf of "; διά, " on account of "; . ἀντί, " instead of " (Matt. xx. 28; 1 Tim. ii. 6).[2]

3. Not least of all, consideration must be given to the Biblical doctrine of sin, its nature and effects, and the Divine attitude towards it.

(a) The words used for sin are important, especially ἁμαρτία, " failure," " coming short "; παράβασις, " transgression "; παράπτωμα, " falling aside."

(b) The consequences of sin are also clearly taught. They seem to be mainly two. A debt (objective), which requires payment, and a disease (subjective), which requires cure.

(c) The term " Wrath of God," ὀργὴ θεοῦ (Rom. i. 18) must have some meaning, and it seems best to interpret it of God's judicial displeasure against sin. " This abominable thing that I hate " (Jer. xliv. 4).

(d) The meaning of Forgiveness, ἄφεσις, " the sending away " of sin.

II.—THE OLD TESTAMENT ANTICIPATION

1. The New Testament points back to the Old, and sacrificial terms of the former find illumination in the ritual of the Old Testament. It must never be forgotten that nearly all the great terms of the New Testament are stated without any explanation, and apart from the Old Testament through the Septuagint they would be unintelligible.[3]

2. The Old Testament sacrifices call for interpretation, for whatever view we hold of the Old Testament they must have had some spiritual meaning. As we contemplate the sacrifices of Genesis, the sacrifice of the Passover, and the various Levitical offerings, they are evidently intended to embody some spiritual reality and to set forth some profound truths.

3. There are several words and phrases in the Old Testament connected with the Atonement, especially a word like *kaphar*, to cover.

III.—THE PRAYER BOOK EXPLANATION

We proceed to enquire what use the Prayer Book and Articles make of the Biblical teaching.

---

[1] Sometimes ὑπέρ has a clear substitutionary meaning (John xi. 50).

[2] There are two other words not found in the New Testament which are useful for expressing aspects of the Atonement: (1) Expiation, *i.e.* "cancelling by sacrifice" (cf. 2 Cor. v. 21); (2) Satisfaction, *i.e.* " restitution for broken law."

[3] "It stands to reason that to describe the ceremonialism of Judaism, for example, apart from the cardinal doctrines of Christianity is like writing a history of the acorn and saying nothing of the oak to which it grows; it stands to reason that the theologian who defines the Christian doctrine of the Atonement without reference to the expiatory features of Mosaism might as wisely undertake a philosophical biography and ignore the entire story of childhood and the early display of hereditary tendency" (Cave, *The Scriptural Doctrine of Sacrifice*, Preface).

1. The Creeds state the fact of the Atonement rather than any theory. They are historical, not theological, and yet even here we are reminded of the uniqueness of the Death of Christ, in that it was " for us men and for our salvation."

2. In the Collects and Communion Office the devotional aspect of the Atonement is naturally emphasised, but we are reminded of Him " Who made there by His one oblation of Himself once offered, a full, perfect, and sufficient sacrifice, oblation, and satisfaction, for the sins of the whole world."

3. In the Articles the subject is dealt with from the doctrinal standpoint, and in particular Articles II, III, XV, XXVIII, and XXXI give the Anglican view of the Atonement. Special attention should be given to all the phrases as they are set forth in these doctrinal pronouncements. In addition to the statement of the Article now under consideration, we have the following : " Christ died for us " (Article III); " He came to be the Lamb without spot, Who by sacrifice of Himself once made, should take away the sins of the world " (Article XV); " our Redemption by Christ's Death " (Article XXVIII); " the offering of Christ once made, is that perfect redemption, propitiation, and satisfaction, for all the sins of the whole world, both original and actual ; and there is none other satisfaction for sin, but that alone " (Article XXXI).

IV.—THE THEOLOGICAL INTERPRETATION

When the subject of the Atonement is considered from the historical standpoint the three eras of Athanasius, Anselm, and the Reformation naturally call for special attention.[1] Athanasius laid great stress on the moral and spiritual renovation, which resulted from the Incarnation of the Son of God in connection with His Death on the Cross. Anselm laid emphasis on the profound truth of the satisfaction offered to God as caused by the outrage of sin. The Reformation naturally dealt with this subject in connection with its emphasis on the work of Christ and the direct application of redemption to the individual soul.[2]

Leaving, however, the historical development of this doctrine, it seems essential to consider it in the light of modern thought, which follows two main lines, subjective and objective. These are the two classes into which all theories of the Atonement can be divided.

[1] For the history, see Cave, *The Scripture Doctrine of Sacrifice*; Crawford, *The Doctrine of the Atonement*; Orr, *The Progress of Dogma*; Mozley, *The Doctrine of the Atonement*.

[2] Most modern writers criticise with great severity the early idea of a ransom being paid to Satan. It would be well, however, if while rightly criticising and rejecting this view care were taken to disentangle the truth from the error, and to endeavour to discover the profound reality intended by the conception. It may fairly be argued that the great minds who occupied themselves with this thought were not wholly ignorant of some of the modern implications. A book that endeavours to do justice to this thought, while rightly indicating the error associated with it, is Dimock's *The Death of Christ*.

A.—*Subjective*

This is concerned with the Atonement as directed towards man, and from this standpoint the work of Christ is to be understood as a revelation of Divine Love to elicit our repentance. In Ritschl the Atonement is a test of fidelity to God; with Bushnell it is expressive of God's sympathy; in Maurice and Robertson it is indicative of the surrender of Christ; in McLeod Campbell and Moberly the Atonement is regarded as vicarious penitence. Thus, in one way or another, the Atonement is a revelation of truth and of the Divine character as Love, which is intended to overcome the fears of the sinner, to assure him of God's friendship, and thereby to incite him to rise to a true life.

All this is, of course, so far accurate and helpful, but in itself it is inadequate and therefore unsatisfactory as a full explanation of the Atonement. The illustration has been given of a man throwing himself into the water from a pier to prove his love, but the mere effect of throwing himself into the water without accomplishing a rescue does not seem to be sufficient. The man who rescues another who is drowning at once proves his love and saves the lost. It may also be pointed out that this theory fails to deal with the reality of sin and to justify forgiveness, since evil is passed over and not brought to an end. When a man has gone headlong into sin for years and then sees the horror of it and changes his life, there is still the stain of sin, its effects upon his character, and its results on others. Then, too, the general weakness of this theory is that there is nothing in it to show how those are affected who are unconscious and cannot respond. There are many on whom such a revelation of Divine love cannot possibly make any impression or elicit any response, such as infants, the insane, and the heathen. Are these to be unsaved because they remain consciously uninfluenced?

Of these various interpretations of the moral theory, that of McLeod Campbell and Moberly is at present most prevalent, and it has received additional support through the Essay in *Foundations*, by Mr. W. H. Moberly, who therein presented afresh his father's view. It would seem, however, as though the criticism of this interpretation is convincing. Thus, the Archbishop of Armagh, Dr. D'Arcy, has asked how penitence can be vicarious any more than punishment, especially since penitence cannot atone for past sin?[1] Nor does it explain why the quality of penitence should culminate in the act of death. Then, too, it gives no account of the New Testament imagery of Ransom, Propitiation, Redemption, nor does it explain how the soul is enabled to break the power of sin. Dr. Armitage Robinson is of opinion that the use made by this theory of the word " penitence " is at once unreal and unfamiliar.[2]

---

[1] D'Arcy, *Christianity and the Supernatural*, p. 80.

[2] "Does not *penitence*, we are bound to ask, involve as an indispensable element, *self-blame*, and not merely the sense of shame? Must not its language be, 'We have sinned . . . of our own fault'? Love's self-identification with the sinner may go as far as the sense of shame, on the ground of physical relationship (as of mother and

To the same effect are the criticisms of Dr. Denney, who holds that to express the Atonement as penitence is really unthinkable.[1] Indeed, it may be said without much question that such a theory changes the entire meaning of the word " penitence," and involves an utter contradiction.[2] When Dr. Moberly's book first appeared a similar criticism was made.[3] Not least of all, this view cannot find any real foundation in the passages of the New Testament dealing with the Atonement.[4]

B.—*Objective*

This is concerned with the Atonement as directed towards God, and the work of Christ is to be understood as a revelation of Divine righteousness and grace to convict and convert. On this view the Atonement includes three great truths.

1. The Manifestation of Divine Character.—The Death of Christ is a demonstration of God's righteousness, God's holiness, God's love. Very few modern books give any true consideration to a crucial passage like Rom. iii. 21-26, where the Cross is shown to be the revelation and vindication of righteousness. Pardon, according to the New Testament, is based on justice as well as mercy.[5]

child) or of deeply affectionate friendship. It may go as far as self-blame without losing touch with reality, if it is conscious that further effort on its part might have prevented the shameful issue. But can self-blame be genuine where *ex hypothesi* there has been no responsibility for the sin?" (*Journal of Theological Studies*, January 1913).

[1] "No rhapsodies about love, and no dialectical juggling, will ever make this anything but a contradiction in terms. It is a thoroughly false way of describing a familiar fact, which has, no doubt, its significance for the Atonement, though it does not exhaust it. . . . resolved the Atonement into 'a perfect lesson in humanity to the judgment of God on the sin of man'; a response to God which has in it 'all the elements of a perfect repentance—a perfect sorrow—a perfect contrition—all excepting the personal consciousness of sin.' The exception, it may be said, destroys the theory" (*British Weekly*).

[2] "The theory—unless the whole meaning of the word penitence is altered—is a contradiction in terms. An infinite repentance is performed to avert an infinite penitence. The repentance is for human sin. The repentance is by Him who knew no sin. The guilt is incurred by the human race, and the availing repentance takes place in the guiltless Jesus. How can this be? What element of penitence can enter into the mind of One who did no sin, neither was guile found in His mouth? One of the most extraordinary passages in theology is that of Mcleod Campbell, when he says that our Lord's mind had 'all the elements of a perfect repentance in humanity, for all the sin of man—a perfect sorrow—a perfect contrition—all the elements of such a repentance, and that in absolute perfection—all excepting the personal consciousness of sin.' Need we point out that the exception is the very essence of the whole? Where there is no personal consciousness of sin, penitence is impossible. Contrition is the sign of an inner change from evil to good. How can such a change take place in the Eternal Son?" (*Church Family Newspaper*).

[3] H. G. Grey, Introduction to Dimock, *The Death of Christ* (Second Edition); Clow, *The Cross in Christian Experience* (p. 319): "Moberly calls the Incarnation the crucial doctrine. Mark how he gives his case away even in his adjective."

[4] The most recent searching and conclusive criticism of this view, while preserving all its truly valuable features, is "The Vicarious Penitence of Christ," by Dr. H. R. Mackintosh in *The Expositor*, Eighth Series, Vol. XI, p. 81 (February 1916).

[5] One of the most useful books discussing the legal aspects of the Atonement is *Law and the Cross*, by Dr. C. F. Creighton. The value of the book is largely due to the fact that it consists of Addresses to Lawyers, Students, and Professors, at College and Law Schools (Eaton & Mains, New York).

2. The Vindication of Divine Law.—Is not Christ's Death in some way " penal " ? Retribution is in the very constitution of the universe, and on this view God in Christ bears the " penalty." And yet it has been well pointed out that the transference is not of guilt, or of moral turpitude, but simply of legal liability.[1] It is surely in this sense that the Death of Jesus Christ is " vicarious "; otherwise what meaning can be attached to that term ? If we are not to be allowed to speak of vicarious punishment, why may we speak of vicarious suffering ? What is the precise meaning and value of " vicarious " ?

3. The Foundation of Divine Pardon.—It is sometimes urged that as human forgiveness does not need an atonement, God's pardon should be regarded as equally independent of any such sacrifice as is now being considered. But this is to overlook the essential feature of all forgiveness, which means that the one who pardons really accepts the results of the wrong done to him in order that he may exempt the other from any punishment. Thus, as it has been well illustrated, when a man cancels a debt, he, of necessity, loses the amount, and if he pardons an insult or a blow, he accepts in his own person the injury done in either case. So that human pardon may be said to cancel at its own expense any wrong done, and this principle of the innocent suffering for the guilty is the fundamental truth of the Atonement. It is, therefore, urged with great force that every act of forgiveness is really an Act of Atonement, and thus human forgiveness, so far from obviating the necessity of Divine Atonement, really illuminates, vindicates and necessitates the Divine pardon, for " forgiveness is mercy which has first satisfied the principle of justice." It is on this ground we hold that Christ's Death made it possible for God to forgive sin. What His justice demanded His love provided. This fact of the Death of Jesus Christ as the foundation of pardon is unchallengeable in the New Testament. Repentance cannot undo the past ; it can only affect the future, and any religion which does not begin with deliverance can never be a success as a discipline. Christ spoke of and dealt with the fact of deformity as well as of growth. " That we being delivered . . . might serve."[2]

The value of this view is that it keeps close to the New Testament and gives a satisfying explanation of such words as Redemption, Propitiation, Reconciliation, Substitution, Representation, Identification, Satisfaction. It appeals not only to the heart, but also to the conscience, and is based at once on absolute righteousness and on the power of Divine grace to undo sin. This is also in harmony with the deepest needs of human nature.

Thus, the Atonement means that God in the Person of His Eternal Son took upon Himself in vicarious death the sin of the whole world. The offer of mercy is made to everyone, since there is no sinner for

[1] Bruce, *The Humiliation of Christ*, p. 316.
[2] In various forms this is the essential view of Dale, Denney, Forsyth, and Simpson.

whom Christ did not die, and every sin, past, present, and future, is regarded as laid on and borne by Him.[1]

1. The true idea of the Atonement is wide and inclusive, and danger lies in limiting it to one explanation. We need at least the four ideas of the representation of the sinner before God: the substitution of the Saviour for the sinner; the identification of the sinner with his Saviour; and the revelation of God in Christ to the sinner. Thus, if only the objective view is accepted as fundamental, there is no reason whatever why all that is true in the subjective theories should not also be accepted as the natural sequel and consequence. As Priest, Christ is our Representative, but as Sacrifice He is of necessity our Substitute.[2] If, therefore, as Birks points out, sin were only debt, substitution would be all that was necessary, while if sin were only disease, no atonement but only healing would be required.

" A Creed in which there is no substitution and a Creed in which there is nothing but substitution depart equally on opposite sides from the truth of God."[3]

Three aspects of truth should always be included in the true view of the Atonement: (*a*) The removal of sin by expiation; (*b*) the removal of enmity by means of the moral and spiritual dynamic of the indwelling Christ; (*c*) the provision and guarantee of fellowship with Christ by means of our oneness with Him. Then, too, the word " for," by reason of its ambiguity, necessarily includes several aspects. (1) It means Representation. This can be illustrated by the position of a Member of Parliament, or an advocate in a court of law. David may be said to have represented Israel in his fight with Goliath (1 Sam. 17), while we read of the elders representing the people (Lev. iv. 15), and princes standing for the entire nation (Josh. ix. 11). (2) It means Exact Substitution. This is the literal idea of the term " vicarious," and may be illustrated by the well-known instance of a substitute in military service. Scripture has similar instances of exact substitution, as the ram for Isaac (Gen. xxii. 13); Judah for Benjamin (Gen. xliv. 33); the Levites for the first-born (Numb. iii. 12); David for Absalom (2 Sam. xviii. 33); and Paul for Onesimus (Philem. v. 17). (3) It means Equivalent Substitution. This is to be distinguished from identical or exact substitution, for as it has been illustrated, a man who rescues another from drowning does not substitute himself by being drowned instead, but does what the

[1] "This, then, is the New Testament doctrine of Atonement, that He whose office it had ever been to reveal the mind of the Father, and who had assumed human form, having passed through this mortal life without sin, and being, therefore, non-amenable to any penalty decreed upon transgression, had voluntarily submitted to that curse of death, with all its mystery of meaning, including the sense of the Divine withdrawal, which He had Himself announced and that submission rendered the forgiveness of sins possible to man" (Cave, *ut supra*, p. 324).

[2] Bruce, *ut supra*, p. 307.   [3] T. R. Birks, *Difficulties of Belief*, pp. 176, 179.

other is incapable of doing. This is the meaning of the ransom (Lev. xxv. 47-49), and is illustrated by the payment made for Richard Cœur de Lion in Austria. It is the second of these two ideas of substitution that applies to the Atoning Sacrifice of Christ, and it is obvious that everything depends upon the power of the substitute and the adequacy of his work. No man could accomplish this task ; it must be done by someone who is capable of rescuing the whole of humanity, because he himself is more than man.[1]

2. No theory can be satisfactory which does not include and account fully for three factors.

(a) The adequate exegesis of the New Testament teaching both Godward and manward. The true doctrine will never be realised unless it is approached first from the Godward side, as in the New Testament. Every theory must start here or else it will inevitably go wrong. "God was in Christ reconciling the world to Himself." The key is found in Rom. iii. 25, in which the Divine propitiation is shown to vindicate the Divine righteousness. It is this that warrants the bold and yet true statement that the Atonement was offered by God to God.[2] This is the only feeling that satisfies men who are oppressed with sin. Repentance never suffices. There is always some demand for satisfaction and restitution. Man's inner sense of rectitude requires that vindication of the Divine law of righteousness be made. Man inevitably feels that God must necessarily demand from Himself that which He requires of man, the vindication of His own righteousness, and the supreme value of the Cross of Christ is that it at once vindicates God's righteousness, and assures of Divine pardon. It is scarcely possible to exaggerate the importance of insisting upon the fullest, clearest interpretation of all the New Testament passages dealing with the Atonement.[3]

(b) The proper interpretation of the Old Testament sacrificial system. Our familiarity with the New Testament tends to make us forget that sacrificial terms and phrases are stated without explanation, and for these it is essential to go back to the Old Testament.

" The institutions of the Old Testament are to a large extent a dictionary in which I learn the true sense of the language of the New."[4]

(c) The full meaning of Christian Experience.—There can be no

[1] For a fuller treatment of these various aspects see Girdlestone, *The Faith of the Centuries*, pp. 200–202.
[2] By Forsyth. See his books, *passim*.
[3] "There have been conspicuous examples of essays and even treatises on the Atonement standing in no discoverable relation to the New Testament" (Denney, *The Death of Christ*, Preface).
"One may, or may not accept the teaching of the New Testament, but it is at any rate due to intellectual honesty to recognise what that teaching is" (Law, *The Tests of Life*, p. 163).
"We must find a theory that will harmonise with everything that comes under New Testament authority" (Creighton, *Law and the Cross*, p. 25).
[4] Dale, *Jewish Temple and Christian Church*, p. 146.

doubt that one of the great essentials is a working theory adequate for the experience of ordinary men and women. In all ages the truth that " Jesus died for me " has adequately met and perfectly satisfied the conscience of the sinner, and it will always remain the test of a satisfying doctrine of the Atonement that it meets the demand for peace with God and assures the conscience burdened with sin and guilt.[1] The idea of substitution has given such unfailing comfort that it cannot be regarded as ethically wrong.[2] It is, of course, impossible to explain it fully, and no one really believes that the Death of Jesus Christ was demanded by the anger of God. On the contrary, God gave Jesus Christ because before He gave He loved the world. We cannot help speaking in terms of earthly justice by referring to penalties and satisfaction, but we know that the righteousness of God is not contradictory of, but in full harmony with, His love. Yet Jesus Christ died, the just for the unjust, shedding His blood for the remission of sin, and when conscience is aroused in a man the only antidote to despair is the Cross.[3] To those to whom the use of the word " satisfaction " is objectionable it may be said that so long as the truth enshrined in it is emphasised the word itself counts for very little. " If the disuse of a word would reconcile thoughtful men to the truth intended to be conveyed, one might easily forget it."[4] All

[1] "This, therefore, must be the test of a satisfactory doctrine of atonement still, viz. its power to sustain the consciousness of peace with God under the heaviest strain which can be put upon it from the sense of guilt, and of the condition which guilt entails" (Orr, *The Progress of Dogma*, p. 235).

"Explain it how you will, it yet remains true, and while human nature continues what it is it will always remain true, that no religion will satisfy the heart of man which does not turn upon the presentation of an offering for sin" (Simpson, *Christus Crucifixus*, p. 207).

[2] "Even if the doctrine of penal substitution be regarded as only one among several possible theories, we cannot but appreciate the intensity of the moral earnestness which it presupposed, and also its singular adaptation to meet a deep religious need. It has been criticised as unethical; but it may be doubted if a more splendid tribute was ever paid to the dignity and the claims of the moral law than in the conception that sin is so awful an evil and so shameful a scandal, and that it so entirely merits the extremity of punishment, that it was impossible for God to forgive it in the exercise of a paternal indulgence—that, on the contrary, mercy could only come into play when the appalling guilt had been expiated in the death of the Son of God, who was also the representative of mankind. Regarded merely as a measure of the conception formed of the heinousness of sin, it has no parallel in point of moral earnestness in the speculative thinking of the schools. It is no less obvious that it met an intellectual need of the religious life. We feel more sure of the Divine mercy if we think that we perceive the grounds on which God acted, and by which He was enabled to act, in the dispensation of mercy. The believing soul feels more sure that God forgives for Christ's sake. . . . There is no theory which is so intelligible as the theory of penal substitution; and there is no religious message which has brought the same peace and solace to those who have realised the sinfulness of sin, and the menace of the retributive forces of the Divine government, as the conception that the penalty due to sin was borne by the crucified Saviour, and that the guilty may be covered by the robe of His imputed righteousness" (Paterson, *The Rule of Faith*, p. 285 f.).

[3] A striking testimony to this fact of experience, that a man's conscience when awakened cannot accept God's love without atonement, will be found in Falconer, *The Unfinished Symphony*, telling of a conversation with the late Professor Pfleiderer, who asked for an actual instance. On one being given, Pfleiderer replied: "If a doctrine really meets a deep human need it must be true" (pp. 243-245).

[4] Bruce, *ut supra*, p. 316.

that is desired is that the conscience and heart of a man convicted of sin shall find perfect rest and peace, and apparently this is impossible apart from the acceptance of a Saviour Whose death was at once a vindication of righteousness and a guarantee of pardon. " We cannot in any theology which is duly ethicised dispense with the word ' satisfaction.' "[1]

3. In view of the difficulties connected with this subject some suggestions may fitly be made.

(a) There are scientific difficulties. With the evolutionary theory of man's origin and nature there seems to be no room for sin, and therefore there can be no room for the Atonement. It is sometimes said that there is no trace of a Fall in nature, and this is, of course, true of physical nature, and it is not to be expected. But what about moral nature ? What of the sense of guilt and responsibility ? Surely this is a fact in the moral universe. In a recent work,[2] the author argues that evolution has really emphasised the need of atonement, but he is careful to insist upon the fact that the doctrine of evolution does not admit of any outsider entering in, so that a theory of substitution which seems to require the entrance of such an outsider is rejected. Such a view seems to come under the condemnation already expressed, that " there have been conspicuous examples of essays, and even treatises on the Atonement standing in no discoverable relation to the New Testament." If, as one critic[3] of this book remarked, human thought is moving in the direction of identification rather than simple substitution, yet since, as he proceeds to say, such identification may undoubtedly involve some form or degree of substitution, the theory of the book will certainly be destroyed. It seems impossible, on any fair statement of the theory of evolution, and on any proper exegesis of the New Testament view of sin and atonement, to explain the Atonement by evolution. Evolution cannot give an ethical basis for a theory of sin, and therefore all definitions of sin furnished by it are at the least defective. Sin concerns the relation of man to God, involving separation from God, and this can never be explained adequately in terms of evolution. It is no case merely of being hindered in upward progress, but, what is much more serious, the consciousness of being alienated from God through sin, for which we are responsible.

Then, too, from a scientific standpoint man's littleness is used as an argument against the thought of the Son of God coming down to redeem him. It is suggested that for such a speck in the universe it would be unworthy and unthinkable of God so to act, but in reply to this it may be at once said that even in nature the value of things is not judged by their size, and for this reason it is impossible to argue fairly from man's relative insignificance in the universe. This would apply equally to the conception of any revelation of God quite apart from the thought of Atone-

---

[1] Forsyth, *The Cruciality of the Cross*, p. 214.
[2] Stuart McDowall, *Evolution of Atonement*, with Preface by Bishop H. E. Ryle, Dean of Westminster.
[3] Dr. Hastings in *Expository Times*.

ment. On every ground, therefore, we maintain the New Testament position, and notwithstanding all scientific theories which seem to run counter to it we must continue to teach the great realities of sin and redemption.

(b) There are theological difficulties. For many years past there has been in certain quarters a tendency to preach mainly about the Incarnation. But this is not the Gospel. In the New Testament the heart of Christianity is found in the grace of Christ, and recent theological thought has been bringing us back to a truer perspective in which we are enabled to see much more clearly than before the centrality of Calvary.[1]

It is also sometimes argued that there is no real reason for the Atonement, since God can hardly be different from man, who is willing to forgive on simple repentance. But we have already seen the essential identity of Divine and human forgiveness, and it may also be answered that the relations between man and man have vital differences compared with those between God and man. In the latter there are governmental as well as personal aspects, and the fact that righteousness is in the very constitution of the universe seems to suggest the impossibility of God overlooking sin, especially with its many and terrible consequences, on the profession of repentance, however genuine.[2]

(c) There are also moral difficulties. The offence of the Cross has not yet ceased, and it is either a "stumbling-block" or "foolishness" to many to-day. It is possible to preach the Incarnation in such a way as to exalt human nature. It is possible to proclaim the Trinity in a way to interest, and even please, reason. But the preaching of the Cross tends to humble and even humiliate human nature, because it requires submission to a crucified Saviour. And yet it is the Cross which is the Christian Gospel. If it be said that God is Love, and therefore will deal gently with sinners; if it be said that God is merciful, and therefore will show mercy to the wandering; if it be said that God is Father, and therefore will be pitiful to His erring children—the answer is that the facts are true, but the inferences are wrong, because this is not the Gospel. It leaves out Christ. God is Love; God is merciful; God is Father, but not apart from Christ. "Herein is love, not that we loved God, but that He loved us, and sent His Son to be the propitiation for our sins" (1 John iv. 10).

---

[1] It is the supreme merit of Denney, Forsyth, and Simpson that they are recalling thought to the right direction. And the recent little volume by Mozley confirms this general line and justifies what the author said a few years ago:
"It cannot be said too often that the Cross, not the manger, Calvary, not Bethlehem, is the heart of the New Testament. In England the influence of Dr. Westcott, from Cambridge, and of the Anglo-Catholic successors of the Tractarians, from Oxford, combined, has tended in the opposite direction. In the writer's judgment it is a perilous course to throw the doctrine of propitiatory atonement to the wolves of Rationalism, while yet believing that the Incarnation can be preserved in its integrity; and it is a course against which the New Testament, as he reads it, stands opposed" (Mozley, Review in *Record*).

[2] Mabie, *Under the Redeeming Ægis, passim.*

Further, this attitude leaves out sin, and yet it is only when we see sin in the light of the Cross that we ever get adequate views of its reality and enormity.   If God's forgiveness can be declared and bestowed apart from the Atonement, we cannot explain Christ's death at all.   Sin is a momentous fact, and Fatherhood is not the only attitude of God to us. He is a Law-giver, Judge, and Ruler, and cannot be indifferent to sin. These elements are all included in the Divine Fatherhood, which is always moral and righteous.   The only adjectives used by Jesus Christ of the Father were " holy " and " righteous " (John xvii. 11, 25).   And so it is essential to emphasise the Cross.   We must not proclaim the Cross without Christ, the work without the Person ; nor must we proclaim Christ without the Cross, the Person without the work ; we must not proclaim the substitutionary work without its practical bearing ; nor must we proclaim the practical side without the vicarious element.   The New Testament teaches the two sides, the objective reality of the vicarious sacrifice and the subjective power in the life of the believer.   Christ saves, sanctifies, satisfies.[1]

[1] "There is little doubt that the sympathetic tendency is the more popular to-day, and to press salvation in a real sense is to be accused of a reactionary bias to theology. But a God who is merely or mainly sympathetic is not the Christian God.   The Father of an infinite benediction is not the Father of an Infinite Grace" (Forsyth, *ut supra*, p. 58).

"If we spoke less about God's love and more about His holiness, more about His judgment, we should say much more when we did speak of His love. . . . It is round this sanctuary that the great camp is set and the great battle really waged.   Questions about immanence may concern philosophers, and questions about miracles may agitate physicists.   But the great dividing issue for the soul is neither the Bethlehem cradle, nor the empty grave, nor the Bible, nor the social question.   For the Church at least (however it may be with individuals), it is the question of a redeeming atonement.   It is here that the evangelical issue lies" (Forsyth, *ut supra*, p. 73).

ARTICLE III

Of the going down of Christ into Hell.	*De Decensu Christi ad Inferos.*

As Christ died for us, and was buried, so also it is to be believed that He went down into hell.	Quemadmodum Christus pro nobis mortuus est, et sepultus, ita est etiam credendus ad inferos descendisse.

IMPORTANT EQUIVALENT.

Into hell   =   *ad inferos.*

HISTORY

THIS Article was derived from the Augsburg Confession in which the statement was incorporated with the Article, *De Filio Dei.* It is natural to enquire why the subject should be so prominent as to have one Article devoted to it. This is probably due to the fact that the Article in its present form is the remainder of the Article of 1553, which had a reference to the spirits in prison (1 Pet. iii. 19). This was omitted in 1563. The actual wording of the original portion was as follows: " *Nam corpus usque ad resurrectionem in sepulchro jacuit, Spiritus ab illo emissus, cum spiritibus qui in carcere sive in inferno detinebantur, fuit, illisque prædicavit: quemadmodum testatur Petri locus* " ("For the body lay in the sepulchre until the resurrection: but His Ghost departing from Him, was with the ghosts that were in prison, or in hell, and did preach to the same: as the place of St. Peter doth testify "). These words were written by Cranmer, and actually signed by the Royal Chaplains, but at the last moment they were omitted before the publication of the Articles. In 1553 there was some acute controversy on the subject, and it is probable that this was the cause of the omission of the latter part of the Article in 1563.[1] Between 1553 and 1563 there was evidently a tendency to a greater moderation of statement on questions connected with the future, and it is impossible to dissociate this omission from the entire omission of the Eschatological Articles, XLI and XLII of 1553. Yet even after 1563 the subject continued to be discussed, for in 1597 Bishop Bilson maintained that Christ descended to the lowest hell, there to triumph over Satan in his own dominions.

---

[1] Micronius wrote to Bullinger from London, 20th May 1550: "They are disputing about the descent of Christ into hell" (*Original Letters*, Vol. II, p. 561). The Bishop of Exeter also alludes to the same subject: "There have been in my Diocese great invectives between the preachers one against the other" (Strype, *Annals*, I, p. 348). (*See* Hardwick, *History of the Articles of Religion*, pp. 98, 137).

E

I.—THE MEANING OF THE WORD "HELL"

It is important to pay special attention to the various words associated with this subject. The Latin equivalent for "into hell" is *ad inferos*, "to those below," *inferi* being the Latin equivalent of ἐν-έροι, ἐν-έρα(γῆ), meaning "subterranean." The English word "hell" is derived from the Anglo-Saxon *hellan*, "to cover," meaning the "unseen" or "covered" place. It is thus the exact equivalent of Hades, ᾅδης. Unfortunately, however, the word is now used with two different meanings.

1. The Greek Hades corresponds to the Sheol of the Old Testament. It is translated "hell," as meaning the place of punishment, twelve times in the New Testament, and "hell," as meaning the place of departed spirits without any reference to personal character, eleven times. It thus seems to be a general term for the unseen world. It includes the souls of the righteous as well as of the wicked, though these are separated by "a great gulf fixed" (1 Sam. xxviii. 19; Luke xvi. 23, 26). In the Old Testament Hades is placed in antithesis with heaven: "It is as high as heaven; what canst thou do? deeper than hell: what canst thou know"? (Job xi. 8). It may or may not be significant that the entrance to one is always a going down, the other always a going up. To ascend to Sheol or to descend to heaven is never mentioned in Scripture. Then, too, Hades is never spoken of as the permanent abode of the righteous. Rather it is a place of gloom, out of which they are in constant expectation of a translation into the brightness of heaven (Psa. xlix. 15; xvi. 10). And it is significant that after Christ's triumphal resurrection Hades seems to fade out of the believer's horizon, and is not used to describe the place for the soul of a believer after the death of Christ.

2. Gehenna.—Quite literally this was the Valley of Hinnom, where malefactors and offal were cast, and from its perpetual fires it became the synonym for everlasting punishment (Josh. xv. 8; 2 Kings xxiii. 10; Jer. vii. 31). The word is easily identified by English readers of the New Testament, since it is invariably associated with fire, or judgment (Matt. v. 22; x. 28; Jas. iii. 6). It occurs twelve times. Gehenna seems to be the abode reserved for the ungodly after the final judgment.

3. Tartarus.—This is found only once, and as a verb (2 Pet. ii. 4). It seems to answer to the "deep" or "abyss" (Luke viii. 31; Rev. ix. 11), and to indicate the place of detention for fallen angels and wicked spirits until their final doom.

4. Paradise.—The word means literally "a pleasure park," and is found only three times in the New Testament (Luke xxiii. 43; 2 Cor. xii. 4; Rev. ii. 7). A corresponding word occurs three times in the Old Testament in a secular sense, meaning a "grove" or "forest" (Neh. ii. 8; Eccl. ii. 5; Song Sol. iv. 13).

Various passages of Scripture have been used in this connection.

1. Luke xxiii. 43.—The malefactor asked for future blessing and received assurance of immediate happiness. This is the first time that Paradise is mentioned in the Bible in a religious connection. But it is not at all clear that we are justified in using this passage in support of our Lord's descent into Hades. Certainly the passage was never used in early days in this connection, and it is probably best to distinguish clearly between Hades and paradise. A man in the "third heaven" or "paradise" could hardly be in Hades at the same time, and it would seem in every way best to identify paradise with heaven (Rev. ii. 7). There does not seem to be any real warrant for supposing that the Jews regarded paradise as a part of Hades.[1]

2. Acts ii. 27-31.—*See* Psalm xvi. 10.—This is the only clear passage on the subject, and it will be noticed that it simply states the fact without giving any idea as to the meaning or purpose.

3. Eph. iv. 9.—There are two views of this passage, some interpreting it of our Lord's descent to earth in the Incarnation, and others of a descent into the unseen world. The passage is a quotation from Psa. lxviii. 18, and the captives to whom the Apostle alludes seem more natural as inhabitants of the unseen world. The quotation refers to some gracious act, and is in close connection with a passage referring to gifts of ministry.

4. 1 Pet. iii. 18–iv. 6.—This passage is sometimes used to support the belief in the fact of our Lord's descent into Hades, and its continuance as the Epistle for Easter Eve is thought to confirm this view. But as the passage was deliberately omitted from this Article in 1563, it is obvious that we have no right to use it here or in connection with the similar statement in the Creed. We are bound by the fact of a descent, and not by any particular interpretation of it. Before this omission the descent into Hades could only have been accepted by those who took this view of the present passage. But now we are certainly free, if necessary, from any obligation to interpret it in this way.[2]

Opinions have widely differed in regard to the purpose of our Lord's descent into the unseen world. The earliest commentator on the Articles, Rogers, has only a brief note expressive of the variety of interpretations :—

[1] Muller, *The Christian Doctrine of Sin*, Bk. IV, Ch. II, Section 6; Dorner, *System of Christian Doctrine*, Section 153 (English Edition): "Paradise indeed is certainly not Hades"; Salmond, Article, "Paradise" in Hastings' *Dictionary of the Bible*: "It is not clear that the lower Paradise was ever conceived to be in the underworld, or that the happy side of Hades was called by that name."
[2] If it is permissible to argue elsewhere from omissions, as is frequently done in connection with prayers for the dead in Article XXII, it is certainly allowable to use similar arguments here.

" That Christ went down into hell all sound Christians, both in former days and now living, do acknowledge ; howbeit in the interpretation of the Article there is not that consent as were to be wished."[1]

The fact of the descent is clear from Acts ii. 25-31, and the main difference of opinion in regard to its purpose largely turns upon the sense given to the word " hell."

1. Some, like Calvin, regard the meaning as implying that the soul of Christ went to the place of punishment, and that there He suffered " the dreadful torments of a person condemned and irretrievably lost."[2] This would be for the purpose of being our Saviour, that He might drink of the cup of Divine wrath against sin to the very dregs, and thereby become more perfectly the sinner's substitute, but when the word " hell " is properly interpreted of " Hades " and not of " Gehenna," this view, though prompted by a true desire to express completely our Lord's redemptive work, is at once and necessarily set aside.   Yet it is interesting to notice that this view was held in general by Bishop Beveridge.[3]

2. Others identify the descent with the burial, considering the phrase equivalent to the former one, " He was buried."   There is some reason to think that this was the view held by Rufinus of Aquileia, in connection with whom the Article is found in the Creed.   But whether this was so or not, the Article cannot possibly have this meaning, since it clearly distinguishes between the burial and the descent.   Further, there seems no doubt that the Hebrew " Sheol " ought never to be translated " grave," for it appears invariably to mean the unseen world as distinct from both heaven and hell (considered as the place of final punishment).

3. It has also been interpreted to mean the descent into hell, properly so called, considered as a place of punishment, for the purpose of triumphing over Satan and his powers in their own dominions, Col. ii. 15 being quoted in support of this view.   But this is, at any rate, an inadequate, if not an inaccurate, interpretation of the passage, and it is difficult to see why our Lord should have done more than He had already accomplished on the Cross.

" Why should He descend to hell to triumph there over them over whom He had already triumphed on the Cross ?   Why should He go to lead captive those whom He was to captivate when He ascended into heaven ? "[4]

4. The best, and indeed the only, possible interpretation is that the doctrine results from our Lord's oneness with us at this, as at every other point.   This would seem to be the real meaning of its place in the Creed, and therefore in the Article.   Our Lord is considered to have satisfied every condition of manhood " for us and for our salvation."   He was born, He grew, He lived, He died, His body was buried, His Spirit went

---

[1] *The Catholic Doctrine of the Church of England*, p. 60.
[2] Calvin, *Inst.*, Bk. II, Ch. XVI, Section 10.
[3] *On the Articles*, pp. 126-137.   [4] Pearson, *On the Creed*.

into the unseen world to await resurrection, He was raised, and He ascended. Thus, both the Creed and Article emphasise the fact, and thereby testify to the reality of His work on our behalf.

" As it stands it completes our conception of the Lord's Death. To our minds death is the separation of body and soul. According to this conception Christ in dying shared to the full our lot. His Body was laid in the tomb. His Soul passed into that state on which we conceive that our souls shall enter. He has won for God and hallowed every condition of human existence. We cannot be where He has not been. He bore our nature as living : He bore our nature as dead."[1]

IV.—THE HISTORY OF THE DOCTRINE

1. The clause, " He descended into hell," is not found in an Eastern Creed, and, indeed, the first Creed of any kind which contains it is apparently an Arian Creed, accepted at Ariminum, 359, a Latin Creed known to us through the Greek version in Socrates' *Ecclesiastical History*. The wording is interesting : " Was crucified, and died, and descended into hell, and disposed of the matters there ; at sight of Whom the door-keepers of Hades did tremble." The suggestion has been made that the clause may have been inserted in this Creed " the more effectually to blind the eyes of the orthodox."[2] But it was not until about 400 that the Article is found in a Baptismal Creed in connection with the Church of Aquileia. Rufinus says that at that time the clause was not in the Creed of the Roman Church. So that we have this curious combination : in the Nicene Creed there is the statement of the burial, not the descent ; in the Athanasian the descent, not the burial ; in the Apostles' Creed there are both. It was only gradually accepted, and then mainly through the writings of St. Augustine. In the seventh century occurs probably for the first time the form, *descendit ad inferos*, and after this the two forms are found. In the Protestant Episcopal Church of the United States the phrase is optional, and a rubric states the interpretation to be : " He descended into the place of departed spirits."

2. The fact of the descent, although not found in a Creed until the fifth century, was, nevertheless, used definitely in connection with the heresy of Apollinarius. It afforded clear proof that our Lord possessed a human soul, since this alone could have descended into the unseen world. It is therefore curious that this article should occur in an Arian Creed before it appeared in an orthodox one, and it is for this reason that the suggestion has been made that the Arian profession was intended to distract attention from the error of the real question between them and the Church in regard to our Lord's essential deity.

3. It is, however, most noteworthy that much earlier than these credal statements a belief in a descent into Hades was widely adopted.

---

[1] Westcott, *The Historic Faith*, p. 76 f.
[2] Heurtley, *Harmonia Symbolica*, p. 134.

It was already developed in the second and third centuries, and, indeed, the belief may be regarded as unanimous, though there was great difference of opinion as to its meaning and purpose.[1]

4. But it is important to notice that notwithstanding this widespread and detailed reference to the descent into hell, there does not seem to have been any thought of a purgatory, or of a fresh opportunity for those who had left the earth without the acceptance of Christ.[2]

V.—THE DESCENT INTO HELL AND THE INTERMEDIATE STATE

Much attention has been called of late to the doctrine of an intermediate state between death and judgment, and although this doctrine is not based on the Article or the Creed, it seems necessary to consider it. While, as we have seen, the Church no longer binds us to associate 1 Pet. iii. 19 with this doctrine, yet because the passage is found as the Epistle for Easter Eve it is often said that usage still indicates the Church interpretation of that passage. There can be no doubt that this was the general view of the Reformers, as seen in contemporary documents.[3] It will be noticed, however, that these passages for the most part state only the fact that our Lord's Spirit descended into the unseen world. It is well known that the passage is one of very great difficulty, and it is natural to enquire what Christ did in those regions of death. Looking at the passage as a whole (1 Pet. iii. 18–iv. 6) there seem to be two important and distinct parts of His work. He made a proclamation to the imprisoned antediluvian souls (iii. 18-21), and He liberated those spirits of the righteous, who through fear of death had all their lifetime been subject to bondage (iv. 1-6). In regard to the former of these acts there are grave differences of opinion as to the identity of " the spirits in prison." The word " prison," which has evil associations, should be noted, and it is also significant that the word " spirit " is never used elsewhere to describe human beings. Then, too, the word " preached " is not the usual term for the Gospel, but indicates the proclamation of a herald. It would seem, therefore, that our Lord proclaimed His victory to " the spirits in prison," and, as the context indicates, thereby proved

---

[1] Moule, *Outlines of Christian Doctrine*, p. 96; Gibson, *The Thirty-nine Articles,* p. 175 f.

[2] Moule, *ut supra,* p. 97.

[3] "Then He truly died, and was truly buried, that by His most sweet sacrifice He might pacify His Father's wrath against mankind, and subdue him by His death who had the authority of death, which was the Devil; forasmuch not only the living but the dead, were they in hell or elsewhere, they all felt the power and force of His death, to whom lying in prison (as Peter saith), Christ preached, though dead in body yet re-lived in spirit" (Catechism of 1554).

"Christum ut corpore in terræ viscera, ita, anima a corpore separata, ad inferos descendisse; simulque etiam mortis suæ virtutem, atque, efficacitatem ad mortuos atque inferos adeo ipsos ita penetrasse, ut et incredulorum animæ acerbissimam iustissimamque infidelitatis suæ damnationem, ipseque inferorum princeps Satanas, tyrannidis suæ, et tenebrarum potestatem omnem debilitatam, fractam atque ruina collapsam esse persentiret: contra vero mortui Christo dum vixerunt fidentes, redemptionis suæ opus iam peractum esse, eiusque vim atque virtutem cum suauissima certissimaque consolatione, intelligerent atque perciperent" (Nowell's *Catechism,* 1570).

His supreme authority (ver. 22). But the other commission seems to be quite different. The saints who died before the Incarnation were "prisoners of hope." They were "gathered to their people" (Gen. xxv. 8), but there does not seem to have been any immediate outlook after death except that which was obscure and depressing. But the death and descent of Christ into Hades wrought a great change for those Old Testament worthies, and no longer do we hear of the abode of the spirits as "down," but as "up," or "away." Such passages seem to indicate the fact that great changes were wrought through the finished redemption of our Lord, that the Sheol of the Old Covenant was emptied of the saints of the former dispensation, and that on our Lord's ascension He carried them with Him in triumph (Heb. xi. 40). And then they seem to be described as "the spirits of just men made perfect" (Heb. xii. 18, 23); that is, those old Hebrew Christians were now "made perfect," and that with them the New Testament Christians ("the Church") were "brought near." Is it not possible that the widespread belief in the early Church that our Lord had released the pious souls of the Old Testament saints in Hades and carried them with Him to heaven expressed a great truth? Of course, the extravagant stories added by men's imaginations tended to identify Scriptural truth with human fables, and in the controversies of the sixteenth century it seems pretty clear that the dread of the Roman Catholic doctrine of purgatory led our Reformers to refrain from giving more thorough attention than they did to the Scriptural doctrine of the descent of Christ into Hades rather than admit any teaching which seemed to favour the *Limbus Patrum* of the Church of Rome. They either ignored the truth of our Lord's having effected any change, or else they allowed themselves to indulge in interpretations which are now seen to be impossible. But we must neither fall into the error of exalting Hades into heaven, nor into the modern danger of reducing heaven to Hades.[1]

It seems necessary to observe that this view of our Lord's having translated the souls of the Old Testament saints by His death is not to be regarded as in any way providing an argument for another opportunity of salvation, or for the doctrines associated with future probation after this life. On the contrary, the passages are to be interpreted strictly in accordance with their context, without drawing from them any doctrine that is not fairly warranted, and in any case, it may be well to bear in mind the solemn words of a great modern writer, and to be content with them :—

"It carries light into the tomb. But more than this we dare not say confidently on a mystery where our thought fails and Scripture is silent. The stirring

---

[1] I am greatly indebted for the above interpretation to two pamphlets, *The Gospel in Hades*, by the Rev. R. W. Harden (Dublin, Combridge & Co.), and *Hades or Heaven?* by the same author (Dublin, William McGee), where a fuller discussion of the various passages can be seen. For a statement of other interpretations of the passage in St. Peter's Epistle reference may be made to the present author's *The Apostle Peter* (pp. 210–222).

pictures which early Christian fancy drew of Christ's entry into the prison-house of death to proclaim His victory and lead away the ancient saints as partners of His triumph; or again, to announce the Gospel to those who had not heard it, rest on too precarious a foundation to claim general acceptance. We are sure that the fruits of Christ's work are made available for every man : we are sure that He crowned every act of faith in patriarch or king or prophet or saint with perfect joy; but how and when we know not, and, as far as appears, we have no faculty for knowing. Meanwhile, we cling to the truth which our Creed teaches us. To the old world, to Jew and Gentile alike—and it is a fact too often forgotten —'the Under World,' 'Sheol' the place of spirits, was a place of dreary gloom, of conscious and oppressive feebleness. Even this natural fear of the heart Christ has lightened. There is nothing in the fact of death, nothing in the consequences of death, which Christ has not endured for us : *He was buried, He descended into Hades*, the place of spirits."[1]

[1] Westcott, *ut supra*, p. 77 f.

"There is an extraordinarily strong tradition among the Fathers that Christ descended to the patriarchs and prophets of the Old Dispensation, and preached to them, and bettered their condition. There is no other passage of Holy Scripture from which such a tradition can have originated; and it would therefore seem that the Fathers took it that those mentioned by St. Peter were but specimens, so to speak, of a class—of those, that is, who had lived and died under the Old Covenant. It *may* be so. But this is all that can be said. Where Scripture is silent such an inference must be more or less precarious, and though the opinion may appear a probable one, it can only be held (if at all) as a 'pious opinion,' which cannot be pressed upon any as a part of the faith. In any case, it would be rash in the extreme to infer from this passage the possibility of an extension of the day of grace, or an opportunity of repentance beyond the grave, for Christians, whose case is wholly different. It cannot be said that the apostle's words afford the slightest grounds for expecting a second offer of salvation to any of those who have slighted or misused God's revelation made 'in His Son '" (Gibson, *ut supra*, p. 174).

See also Martensen, *Christian Dogmatics*, pp. 316–318; Litton, *Introduction to Dogmatic Theology* (Second Edition), p. 196; C. H. H. Wright, *The Intermediate State*.

ARTICLE IV

Of the Resurrection of Christ.	De Resurrectione Christi.
Christ did truly rise again from death, and took again His body, with flesh, bones, and all things appertaining to the perfection of man's nature; wherewith He ascended into heaven, and there sitteth until He return to judge all men at the last day.	Christus vere a mortuis resurrexit, suumque corpus cum carne, ossibus, omnibusque ad integritatem humanæ naturæ pertinentibus, recepit; cum quibus in cœlum ascendit, ibique residet, quoad extremo die, ad judicandos homines reversurus sit.

IMPORTANT EQUIVALENTS.

From death   =   *a mortuis.*
To the perfection of man's nature   =   *ad integritatem humanæ naturæ.*

THE Article is virtually the same now as it was in 1553, but there is nothing corresponding to it in the Confession of Augsburg, or the Articles of the Concordat of 1538. It is the natural sequel of the preceding Articles on the Person and Work of Christ. Its purpose was evidently to emphasise the truth of the Resurrection and the reality of our Lord's humanity in the face of primitive and subsequent denials. The Docetism of the early Gnostics had been revived in the sixteenth century, and some taught that the flesh of Christ had not been real, and is now so deified as to have lost all real humanity.[1] On this account it was felt essential to emphasise the real and actual physical resurrection[2] which would show that our Lord did not lay aside His humanity when He arose from the grave and ascended into heaven.

But as with previous Articles, so with this, there is no doubt that the Reformers wished to emphasise their agreement with the fundamental teaching of the universal Church concerning our Lord's Resurrection. Then, too, there seems to have been a special reference to certain eucharistic views associated with the ubiquity of our Lord's humanity, which this Article would indirectly but effectively meet and controvert.[3]

I.—THE TEACHING OF THE ARTICLE

As the Article contains several separate and yet connected truths, it seems best first to analyse it as a whole, and then to consider more in detail the chief doctrines taught and implied.

[1] Hardwick, *History of the Articles of Religion*, p. 99.
[2] See *Reformatio Legum Ecclesiasticarum, De Hæresibus*, c. 5, *De duabus naturis Christi.* This sentence of it is particularly important, though the entire section should be consulted: *Quidam verbum in carnis naturam conversum asserunt, quam, quamprimum a morte in cœlum fuit recepta, rursus volunt in naturam divinam reversam et absorptam esse.*
[3] See also on Article XXIX.

73

1. The Fact of the Resurrection.—" Christ did truly rise again from death."—The emphasis is plainly on the reality of the physical resurrection.

2. The identity of the risen body.—" And took again His body."—This is a further proof of actual resurrection which necessarily involves identity with the past.

3. The difference between the risen body and that which was buried.—" With flesh, bones, and all things appertaining to the perfection of man's nature."—The omission of " blood " may possibly refer to the essential difference between the body buried and that which was raised. The Article, following Scripture, speaks of " flesh and bones," and this phrase contrasted with St. Paul's words about " flesh and blood " being unable to enter the Kingdom of God, may suggest that while the resurrection body was not constituted on a natural basis through blood, yet that it possessed " all things appertaining to the perfection of man's nature." Thus, the true description of the Resurrection seems to be that it was an objective reality, and yet not merely a physical resuscitation. It was the same, yet different; different, yet the same.

4. The Ascension.—" Wherewith He ascended into heaven."—The Latin is significant, *cum quibus*, *i.e.* with all the parts of His physical nature herein specified. Thus, following Scripture, the Article makes no distinction between the Resurrection and the Ascension as actual facts.

5. The Session.—" And there sitteth."—This is a virtual repetition of the statement of the Creed, as based upon New Testament teaching.

6. The Return.—" Until He return."—Another reference to that which is so prominent in the New Testament, the Second Advent of our Lord.

7. The Judgment.—" To judge all men at the last day."—Again, following the Creed, the statement is quite general in regard to the purpose for which Christ returns.

II.—THE PLACE OF THE RESURRECTION IN THE NEW TESTAMENT

The statements of the Article with reference to the Resurrection of Christ require the consideration of what Holy Scripture teaches concerning this event, and in order that we may more fully realise its spiritual meaning and practical use it is essential to look at the position it occupies in the record of the New Testament.

1. It was predicted by Christ Himself.—At first He used only vague terms (John ii. 19).—Later on He spoke plainly, and whenever He mentioned His death He added a reference to the Resurrection (Matt. xvi. 21). These statements are numerous and form an integral part of the teaching of Christ concerning Himself (Matt. xii. 38-40; xvi. 21; xvii. 23; xx. 19; xxvii. 63; Mark viii. 31; ix. 31; x. 34; xiv. 58; Luke ix. 22; xviii. 33; John ii. 19-21).

2. The record of the appearances after the Resurrection.—In all four

Gospels the appearances of Christ are clear and prominent. There were
two sets of appearances, one in Jerusalem and the other in Galilee. The
detailed accounts of these appearances, especially when contrasted with
the comparative fragmentariness of the story of Christ's earthly life up
to Palm Sunday are undoubtedly significant.

3. The Resurrection was prominent in the preaching of the Apostles.
On every occasion when they were faced with unbelievers, both Jews
and Gentiles, the main theme of their testimony was " Jesus and the
Resurrection " (Acts iv. 2). The choice of the new Apostle was asso-
ciated with testimony to the Resurrection (Acts i. 22); the sermons of
St. Peter made the Resurrection prominent (Acts ii. 32; iv. 10; x. 40).
In the same way, St. Paul was first of all convinced of the Resurrection
(Acts ix. 5), and then proclaimed it everywhere (Acts xiii. 30; xvii. 31;
xxvi. 8, 23; 1 Cor. xv. 1-4). It is impossible to ignore the prominence
of this subject in Apostolic preaching.

4. The Resurrection is shown to be a spiritual force in the life of
Christians (Rom. i. 4; iv. 25; vi. 9-11; Eph. i. 19, 20; 1 Pet. i. 21).

5. It is also set forth as the guarantee of hope in a future life (1 Cor.
xv. 20-23; 1 Thess. iv. 14; 1 Pet. i. 3, 4).

III.—THE PROOFS OF THE RESURRECTION[1]

As the Resurrection has always been regarded as vital to Christianity,
it is not surprising that opponents have concentrated their attacks on it.
There are several converging lines of evidence.

1. The first proof is the life of Jesus Christ Himself. Whether in
ordinary experience or in fiction there is a disappointment when a life
which commences well finishes badly. With Jesus Christ a perfect life
ends in a shameful death, and it is impossible to regard this as a fitting
close. The Gospels give the Resurrection as the completion of the
picture of Christ. There is no doubt that He anticipated His own
Resurrection, and His veracity is at stake if He did not rise. Thus, the
Resurrection is that of no ordinary man, but of One whose character had
been unique, and for whose shameful death no proper explanation was
conceivable.[2] In view, therefore, of His perfect truthfulness, any denial
of His assurance of resurrection is impossible.[3] Then, too, if death closed
a life so remarkable, we are faced with the insoluble mystery of the
permanent triumph of wrong over right;[4] so that the Resurrection
cannot be isolated from what preceded it, and the true solution of the
problem is to be found in that estimate which " most entirely fits in with
the totality of the facts."[5]

[1] The substance of this section is taken from an article by the author in the *International
Standard Bible Encyclopædia*. See also his *Christianity is Christ*, Ch. VII. For other works
on the Resurrection see p. 528.
[2] Denney, *Jesus and the Gospel*, p. 122 f.
[3] C. H. Robinson, *Studies in the Resurrection*, p. 30.
[4] C. H. Robinson, *ut supra*, p. 36.
[5] Orr, *The Resurrection of Jesus*, p. 14.

2. Another line of proof is the fact of the empty grave and the disappearance of the body. The details of the record as to Christ's death and burial are not now seriously challenged, and yet on the third morning the tomb was empty and the body had disappeared. There are only two alternatives. His body must have been taken out of the grave by human hands or else by superhuman power. The human hands would have been those of His friends or His foes. Even if the former had wished to do so they could hardly have accomplished their desire in the face of the obstacles. If the latter had contemplated the removal it may be questioned whether they would have seriously considered it, since this would have been the most likely thing to spread the report of His Resurrection. As St. Chrysostom said, " If the body had been stolen, they could not have stolen it naked, because of the delay in stripping it of the burial clothes and the trouble caused by the drugs adhering to it."[1] Besides, the position of the grave clothes proves the impossibility of the theft of the body.[2] Then, too, it is impossible to account for the failure of the Jews to disprove the Resurrection, since it was not more than seven weeks after the Resurrection that St. Peter preached the fact that Jesus Christ had been raised. If the Jews could have produced the dead body it would have silenced the Apostle for ever. " The silence of the Jews is as significant as the speech of the Christians."[3] Thus, the fact of the empty tomb with the disappearance of the body remains a problem to be faced. It is now admitted that the evidence for the empty tomb is adequate, and that it was part of the primitive belief;[4] and it is important to realise the force of this admission because it is a testimony to St. Paul's use of the term " third day," and to the Christian observance of the first day of the week. And yet it is often argued that the belief in the empty tomb is impossible, and some interpret the idea of resurrection to mean the revival of Christ's spiritual influence on the disciples. It is thought that the essential value of the Resurrection can be preserved even while surrendering belief in His bodily rising from the grave.[5] But how is it possible to believe in the Resurrection while regarding the foundation of this belief as an error ? The disciples, finding the tomb empty, believed that He had risen, and the belief can hardly be true if the foundation is false. Besides, the various forms of the Vision theory are now regarded as inadequate, since they involve the change of almost every statement in the Gospel and the invention of new conditions of which the Gospels know nothing.[6] Why should the disciples have had this abundant experience of visions, and why should these have been strictly limited to a very brief period, and then suddenly come to an end ? They knew of the apparition of a spirit, like Samuel's, and had witnessed the resuscitation of a body, like

---

[1] Quoted in Day, *Evidence for the Resurrection*, p. 35.
[2] See Greek of John xx. 6, 7; Cf. xi. 44; Grimley, *Temple of Humanity*, pp. 69, 70; Latham, *The Risen Master*; *Expository Times*, Vol. XIII, p. 293 f.; XIV, p. 510.
[3] Fairbairn, *Studies in the Life of Christ*, p. 357.
[4] Streeter, *Foundations*, pp. 134, 154.
[5] Orr, *ut supra*, p. 23.   [6] *Orr, ut supra*, p. 222.

that of Lazarus, but they had never experienced or imagined the fact of a spiritual body, the novel combination of body and spirit. It is, therefore, impossible to accept the theory of a real spiritual manifestation of the risen Christ, for no telepathic communication is equivalent to the idea of resurrection. Psychical research in any case does not answer to the conditions of the physical resurrection recorded in the New Testament. " The survival of the soul is not resurrection." " Whoever heard of a spirit being buried " ?[1] Even though it is said that faith is not bound up with holding a particular view of the relation of Christ's present glory to the body that was once in Joseph's tomb, yet faith must ultimately rest on fact, and it is difficult to see how Christian belief can be " agnostic " with regard to the facts which are so prominent in the New Testament, and which form a vital part of the Apostolic witness. The attempt to set faith and historical evidence in opposition is unsatisfactory, and there is a growing feeling that it is impossible to believe in the Easter message without believing in the Easter facts. When once the evidence for the empty tomb is allowed to be adequate, the impossibility of any other explanation is at once seen. The evidence must be accounted for and adequately explained. It is becoming more and more evident that various theories cannot account for the records in the Gospels or for the place and power of those Gospels in all ages of the Church. The force of the evidence is clearly seen by the explanations suggested by some modern writers.[2] Not one of them is tenable without doing violence to the Gospel story and without putting forth new theories which are both improbable and without any historical or literary evidence.

Others suggest that the Resurrection was a real objective appearance without implying physical reanimation, that " the Resurrection of Christ was an objective reality, but was not a physical resuscitation."[3] But difficulty arises as to the meaning of the term re-surrection. If it means a *return* from the dead, a rising *again (re)*, must there not have been some identity between that which was put in the tomb and the " objective reality " which appeared to the disciples ? Wherein lies the essential difference between an objective vision and an objective appearance ? If the testimony of the Apostles to the empty tomb is believed, why may not their evidence to the actual Resurrection be also accepted. It is, of course, clear that the Resurrection body was not exactly the same as when it was put in the tomb, but it is also clear that there was definite identity as well as definite dissimilarity, and both elements must be explained. We are, therefore, brought back to a consideration of the facts recorded in the Gospels, and must demand an explanation which will take all of them into consideration and do no violence to any part of the evidence. To predicate a new Resurrection body in which Jesus

---

[1] Orr, *ut supra*, p. 229.

[2] Those of Oscar Holtzmann, K. Lake, and A. Meyer can be seen in Orr, *The Resurrection of Jesus*, Ch. VIII, and that of Reville in C. H. Robinson, *Studies in the Resurrection of Christ*, p. 69. See also article by Streeter, in *Foundations*.

[3] C. H. Robinson, *ut supra*, p. 12.

Christ appeared to His disciples does not explain how in three days' time the body which had been placed in the tomb was disposed of. The theory seems to demand a new miracle of its own.[1]

3. The next line of proof is the transformation of the disciples, due to the Resurrection. Through their Master's death they had lost all hope, and yet this returned three days afterwards. When the message of the Resurrection first came they were incredulous, but when once they became assured of it they never doubted again. This astonishing change in so short a time has to be explained. Legendary growth was impossible in so brief a period, and the psychological fact of this marvellous change demands a full explanation. The disciples were prepared to believe in the appearance of a spirit, but never seem to have contemplated the possibility of a resurrection (Mark xvi. 11). Men do not imagine what they do not believe, and the women's intention to embalm a corpse shows that they did not expect His Resurrection. Besides, hallucination involving five hundred people at once and repeated several times is unthinkable.

4. The next line of proof is the existence of the primitive Church. It is now admitted that the early community of Christians came into existence as the result of a belief in the Resurrection of Christ.[2] Two facts stand out: (1) the Society was gathered together by preaching; (2) the theme of the preaching was the Resurrection of Christ. The evidence of the early chapters of Acts is unmistakable, and it is impossible to allege that the primitive Church did not know its own history, and that legends quickly grew up and were eagerly received. Any modern Church could readily give an account of its history for the past fifty years or more.[3] There was nothing vague about the testimony of the early Church. " As the Church is too holy for a foundation of rottenness, so she is too real for a foundation of mist."[4]

5. One witness in the Apostolic Church calls for special attention, the Apostle Paul. He possessed the three essentials of a true witness: intelligence, candour, and disinterestedness. His conversion and work stand out clearly in regard to his evidence for the Resurrection.[5] In view, therefore, of St. Paul's personal testimony to his own conversion, and to his interviews with those who had seen Christ on earth, with the prominence given to the Resurrection in his teaching, we may rightly arguet hat he stands out beyond all question as a witness to the Resur-

---

[1] Kennett, *Interpreter*, Vol. V, p. 271.
[2] "There is no doubt that the Church of the Apostles believed in the resurrection of their Lord" (Burkitt, *The Gospel History and Its Transmission*, p. 74).
[3] Orr, *ut supra*, p. 144.
[4] Archbishop Alexander, *The Great Question*, p. 10.
[5] "He affirms that within five years of the crucifixion of Jesus he was taught that 'Christ died for our sins according to the Scriptures; and that He was buried, and that He rose again the third day according to the Scriptures'" (Kennett, *ut supra*, p. 267).
"That within a very few years of the time of the crucifixion of Jesus, the evidence for the Resurrection of Jesus was, in the mind of at least one man of education, absolutely irrefutable" (Kennett, *ut supra*, p. 267).

rection. His twenty-five years of service were based upon the sudden change wrought at his conversion, and if his conversion was true, Jesus Christ rose from the dead, for everything the Apostle was and did he attributed to the sight of the risen Christ.[1]

6. The next line of proof is the record in the Gospels of the appearances of the risen Christ, and in view of the dates when the Gospels were written this should be considered in the order now stated. The Resurrection was believed in by the Church for a number of years before the Gospels were written, and it is therefore impossible for these records to be our primary evidence. We must get behind them if we are to appreciate the force of the testimony, and it is for this reason that, following the proper logical order, we reserve to the last our consideration of these appearances. The point is one of great importance.[2] Whatever theory may be held as to the origin and relation of the Gospels, the appearances can be safely and thoroughly examined. There are two sets of appearances, one in Jerusalem and the other in Galilee, and their number and the amplitude and weight of their testimony call for careful estimation. Books dealing specifically with the Resurrection examine each appearance minutely, but this is impossible under the conditions of this work, though it may be remarked that no one can read the story of the walk to Emmaus (Luke xxiv), or the visit of St. Peter and St. John to the tomb (John xx) without observing the striking marks of reality in the accounts.[3] The difficulties connected with the number and order of the appearances are probably due mainly to the summary character of the story, and do not invalidate the uniform testimony to the two facts: (1) the empty grave; (2) the appearances of Christ on the third day.[4] The very difficulties in the Gospels are a testimony to a conviction of the truth of the narratives on the part of the Christian Church through the ages. The records have been fearlessly left as they are because of the facts they embody. If there had been no difficulties artificiality could have been charged against the records, and the fact that we possess these two sets of appearances is really an argument in

---

[1] It is well known how that Lord Lyttelton and his friend Gilbert West left Oxford University at the close of one academic year, each determining to give attention respectively during the Long Vacation to the conversion of St. Paul and the Resurrection of Jesus Christ, in order to prove the baselessness of both. They met again in the autumn and compared experiences. Lord Lyttelton had become convinced of the truth of St. Paul's conversion, and Gilbert West of the Resurrection of Jesus Christ.

[2] Denney, *ut supra*, p. 111.

[3] "It carries with it, as great literary critics have pointed out, the deepest inward evidences of its own literal truthfulness. For it so narrates the intercourse of 'a risen God' with commonplace men as to set natural and supernatural side by side in perfect harmony. And to do this has always been the difficulty, the despair of imagination. The alternative has been put reasonably thus: St. Luke was either a greater poet, a more creative genius than Shakespeare, or—he did not create the record. He had an advantage over Shakespeare. The ghost in Hamlet was the effort of laborious imagination. The risen Christ on the road was a fact supreme, and the Evangelists did but tell it as it was" (Bishop Moule, *Meditations for the Church's Year*, p. 108).
See also Orr, *ut supra*, p. 176 f.

[4] Orr, *ut supra*, p. 212.

favour of their credibility, since one set only might have been rejected for lack of support.

When we examine all these converging lines of evidence it seems impossible to escape from the problem of a physical miracle, and this is the *prima facie* view of the evidence afforded. It is this question of the miraculous that is at the root of much modern disbelief in the Resurrection. The scientific doctrine of the uniformity and continuity of nature leads to the conclusion that miracles are impossible. We are either not allowed to believe, or else we are told that we are not required to believe, in the reanimation of a dead body. If this view is taken, " there is no need, really, for investigation of evidence; the question is decided before the evidence is looked at."[1] But this position proves too much, since it would rule out all Divine interventions which might be called miraculous. On this view it would be impossible to account for the Person of Christ at all. " A sinless Personality would be a miracle in time." Those who hold a theistic view of the world cannot accept any *a priori* view that miracles are impossible. The Resurrection, therefore, means the presence of miracle, and " there is no evading the issue with which this confronts us."[2]

Of recent years attempts have been made to account for the Resurrection by means of ideas derived from Babylonian and other Eastern sources. It is argued that Mythology provides the key, and that not only analogy, but derivation is to be found in it. But there is nothing worthy of the name of historical proof afforded, and the idea is often quite arbitrary and prejudiced by the attitude to the supernatural. There is literally no link of connection between these Oriental cults and the Christian belief in the Resurrection.

And so we return to a consideration of the various lines of proof. Taken singly, they are strong; taken together, the argument is cumulative and almost irresistible. Every fact must have its adequate cause, and the only proper explanation of Christianity to-day is the Resurrection of Christ.

IV.—THE THEOLOGY OF THE RESURRECTION

The Resurrection is not only a fact; it is a force, and its theology is so important as to call for special attention. Indeed, the prominence given in the New Testament to teaching connected with it affords a strong confirmation of the fact itself, for it seems incredible that such varied and important truths should not rest on historical fact. The doctrine may be briefly summarised.

1. Evidential.—The Resurrection is the proof of the atoning character of Christ and of His Deity and Divine exaltation (Rom. i. 4). It is shown in the New Testament to be the vindication of His character and the justification of what He had said concerning Himself and His Divine

[1] Orr, *ut supra*, pp. 44, 46; C. H. Robinson, *ut supra*, Ch. II.
[2] Orr, *ut supra*, p. 53.

mission. In this connection it is particularly significant to notice the emphasis placed on the fact that the Resurrection was the act of God rather than of Christ Himself. After the actual Resurrection there does not appear to be a single text which attributes the Resurrection to Christ Himself. Even those passages which are doubtful in the English are quite clear in the Greek, teaching that He *was raised* from the dead (Acts ii. 32; Rom. iv. 24, 25; 1 Cor. vi. 14; 1 Thess. i. 10). This emphasis on the act of God the Father is a striking testimony to His approval of the life and work of Jesus Christ.

2. Evangelistic.—The primitive Gospel included testimony to the Resurrection as one of its characteristic features, thereby affording to the hearers the assurance of Divine redemption. It sealed the Atonement and bore testimony to its adequacy and certainty for men's salvation (Rom. iv. 25; 1 Cor. xv. 1-4).

3. Redemptive.—The Resurrection is shown to be the guarantee of the believer's justification, that on his acceptance of the message of the Gospel there is the absolute assurance of acceptance with God (1 Pet. i. 21).

4. Spiritual.—The Resurrection of Christ is regarded as the source and standard of the holiness of the believer. Every aspect of the Christian life from beginning to end is somehow associated therewith (Rom. vi).

5. Eschatological.—The Resurrection is the guarantee and model of the believer's resurrection (1 Cor. xv). As the bodies of the saints arose (Matt. xxvii. 52), so ours are to be quickened (Rom. viii. 11), and made like Christ's glorified body (Phil. iii. 21), thereby becoming spiritual bodies (1 Cor. xv. 44), that is, bodies ruled by their spirits and yet continuing to be bodies. Thus, the Resurrection of Christ guarantees our resurrection (1 Thess. iv. 14). He completed a human experience which prepared Him to be the Saviour of the world, the Head of the Church, and provided Him with a Resurrection body which was the type of ours. It is, of course, impossible to speak definitely about the believer's resurrection body, but the example of our Lord's Resurrection body is the best, indeed the only, illustration we possess. All that we may say is that it will be a body and yet spiritual; spiritual and yet a body. There will be identity and continuity with whatever differences of which at present we know, and perhaps can know, nothing.[1]

V.—THE ASCENSION AND SESSION

1. The Ascension.—The New Testament regards the Ascension with its complementary truths of the session and intercession of Christ as the culmination of His redemptive work. Our Lord Himself said to His disciples : " It is expedient for you that I go away," and in this " expediency " there is something which has been very largely neglected by the Church. It is doubtless due to the fact that Ascension Day is a

---

[1] *See* Westcott, *The Gospel of the Resurrection*; Milligan, *The Resurrection*.

F

weekday festival, instead of a Sunday one, that its observance has been very insignificant compared with that of Easter Day, and yet perhaps this is not the entire explanation of the comparative neglect of the festival of the Ascension and its profound meaning. In the fourth Gospel there are at least twelve clear references to it (*e.g.* i. 51 ; iii. 13 ; vi. 62 ; xiii. 3 ; xvii. 11 ; and especially chaps. xiv-xvi). In the Epistle to the Hebrews no reference to the Resurrection is found, except in the concluding doxology, while the Ascension is the main spiritual truth. Then, too, we see what it meant to our Lord Himself in St. Luke ix. 51 and Acts ii. 33. It was at the Ascension that our Lord entered upon His work as Priest and King, and this is why the doctrinal position of the Epistle to the Hebrews centres in the fact of the Ascension in relation to our Lord's priesthood.

But it also meant much to the disciples as well, for the " expediency " applied to them as well as to our Lord. (*a*) It brought a deeper peace. Christ's Ascension was the culmination of His earthly life and work, and gave purpose and reason to all the rest. While the removal of the guilt of sin was associated with His death, and the destruction of the power of sin with His Resurrection, the removal of the separation caused by sin was associated with His Ascension, and herein lies the force of the Apostle's word : " It is Christ that died, yea rather, that is risen again, *who is even* at the right hand of God " (Rom. viii. 34), so in the assurance that " He Himself is the propitiation for our sins " (1 John ii. 2) the conscience and heart find rest. Christ's righteousness has been accepted, His position is assured, and now access is possible to all believers. (*b*) It elicited a stronger faith. There was a great work to be done, and one that needed much confidence and boldness. Only the thought of a victorious Master could make victorious disciples. As long as His life was incomplete, or one of suffering only, their life would lack inspiration. But the Ascension was the pledge of a victorious result (Heb. iv. 14), and the disciples were therefore to " hold fast their confession," for whatever struggle they might have it was certain to end in victory (2 Tim. ii. 12). (*c*) It led into a larger work. During the earthly life of Christ His work was local only, but after He had been received into heaven He could not be limited to Judæa or Galilee. The word was, " Go ye into all the world," and in the Ascension of their Master the disciples would be elevated above narrowness and pettiness as they contemplated the purpose of world-wide evangelisation. (*d*) It gave a clearer hope. They doubtless had the usual Jewish ideas of salvation, but it was their Master's presence in heaven that made it real to them. At once human and Divine He had told them that He was going to prepare a place for them (John xiv. 2, 3). He went there as Forerunner and Pledge, and told them to rejoice because He was going to the Father (John xiv. 28). His word for them was an inspiration, " Because I live ye shall live also." (*e*) It provided a greater power. On earth their Master was necessarily limited and circumscribed, but at the right hand of God authority and power were His, and the disciples could therefore depend upon His presence and grace in all the work which He was sending them to do (Mark xvi. 20). This was the meaning of His own word, " Greater works than these shall he do; because I go unto My Father " (John xiv. 12), and so when the Comforter came they were enabled to accomplish tasks which even the Lord on earth was unable to do. His presence and power led to the accomplishment of spiritual results of marvellous extent and influence (John vii. 37-39; xvi. 7; Acts ii. 33; Eph. iv. 8). Thus, the Ascension was to the disciples at once a cause of joy (Luke xxiv. 52; John xiv. 28), the secret of fellowship (John xvi. 16; xx. 17), and the standard of life (Col. iii. 1 f.).

2. The Session.—Following the act of ascension the New Testament has not a little to say of our Lord's present life in heaven. Most Lives of Christ written of recent years commence with Bethlehem and end with the Ascension. But the New Testament commences earlier and continues later. It is with the glorified life of Christ above that the Article deals, and it is important to observe with some detail the Scripture teaching. He is seated on the right hand of God (Col. iii. 1; Heb. i. 3; viii. 1; x. 12). He bestowed the gift of the Holy Spirit on the Day of Pentecost (Acts ii. 4). He added disciples to the Church (Acts ii. 47). He worked with the disciples as they went forth preaching the Gospel (Mark xvi. 20). He healed the impotent man (Acts iii. 16). He stood to receive the first martyr (Acts vii. 56). He appeared to Saul of Tarsus (Acts ix. 5). He makes intercession for His people (Rom. viii. 34; Heb. vii. 25). He is able to succour the tempted (Heb. ii. 18). He is able to sympathise (Heb. iv. 15). He is able to save to the uttermost (Heb. vii. 25). He lives for ever (Heb. vii. 24; Rev. i. 18). He is our Great High Priest (Heb. vii. 26; viii. 1; x. 21). He possesses an intransmissible or inviolable priesthood (Heb. vii. 24). He appears in the presence of God for us (Heb. ix. 24). He is our Advocate with the Father (1 John ii. 1). He is waiting until all opposition to Him is overcome (Heb. x. 13). This includes all the teaching of the New Testament concerning our Lord's life above. It is important to keep strictly to this, because of a current view found in certain quarters that He is now offering Himself before the Father. Many years ago a number of clergymen declared their belief in these terms: " We believe that in heaven Christ our Great High Priest ever offers Himself before the Eternal Father."[1] And some recent works teach the same doctrine. But it is impossible to reconcile this with what is found in the New Testament. All our Lord's offering is there regarded as in the past in connection with the Cross (Heb. vii. 27; ix. 14). The offering is said to have been " once for all " (Heb. x. 10); and He is seated at God's right hand (Heb. i. 3; viii. 1; x. 12). There was no *altar* in the Holy of Holies, the symbol of heaven (Heb. ix. 3-5; and the Lamb in the midst of the throne in the Revelation is not offering Himself (Rev. v. 6; vii. 17). In a word, there is not a trace to be found of Christ's presence above

[1] Correspondence between the Rev. W. B. Marriott and Canon T. T. Carter, p. 3.

being a perpetual presentation before God of His sacrifice. The Greek verb " offer " in the phrase, " somewhat to offer " (Heb. viii. 3) is in the aorist tense, implying something completed, and, like all other references in the New Testament, it looks back on Calvary.[1] One great authority, Bishop Westcott, shows that our Lord's present work is that of applying the fruits of His completed Atonement, and that " we have no authority to go beyond " the teaching of Hebrews in this connection. Further, no trace of this doctrine can be found in the Prayer Book. If Christ were offering Himself or His sacrifice in heaven it would be so important a truth that it ought to occupy a position of definite prominence in the teaching of our Church. But on opening the Prayer Book we find no trace whatever of it.[2] If, therefore, a doctrine is taught which cannot be found either in the New Testament or in the Prayer Book it is certainly no part of Anglican teaching.

A somewhat different yet closely connected doctrine is sometimes taught by saying that our Lord is pleading His sacrifice above, as though pleading were not fundamentally different from offering. The two must never be identified or confused. It is, of course, true that our Lord is present in heaven because of the sacrifice He offered on Calvary, and obviously His intercession is founded on the fact of His complete atoning work. But the New Testament, significantly as it would seem, never associates His intercession with the pleading of His sacrifice, and some of the best scholarship is entirely opposed to this view that our Lord is now engaged in pleading His sacrifice. Thus, Bishop Westcott :—

" The modern conception of Christ pleading in Heaven His Passion, ' offering His blood ' on behalf of man, has no foundation in this Epistle. His glorified humanity is the eternal pledge of the absolute efficacy of His accomplished work. He pleads, as older writers truly expressed the thought, by His presence on His Father's throne. Meanwhile, men on earth in union with Him enjoy continually through His blood what was before the privilege of one man on one day in the year."[3]

[1] See Dimock's treatment in *Our One Priest on High* (pp. 14–16), with the striking quotations from three masters of New Testament scholarship, Marriott, Westcott, and Gifford.

[2] "Echo may answer 'where'? It is the only sound in reply. There is a dead silence—no voice, or any to answer. . . . We look at our time-honoured creeds—it is not there. We turn to the grand anthem, which has come down to us from remote antiquity—the 'Te Deum'; not a word. We examine our Eucharistic Service—it is not there. We find a proper Preface for the day of our Lord's Ascension into heaven—it is not there. In the obsecrations of our Litany we find mention of all the prominent points in our blessed Lord's work for our salvation, but no word of any offering of sacrifice in heaven. We look at the Articles of Religion. It certainly is not there" (Adapted and abbreviated from Dimock, *The Christian Doctrine of Sacerdotium*, p. 13 f.).

[3] Hebrews, p. 230.

"The words, 'Still . . . His prevailing death He pleads' have no apostolic warrant, and cannot even be reconciled with apostolic doctrine. . . . So far as the Atonement in relation to God is spoken of in any terms of time, the Bible seems to me to teach us to think of it as lying entirely in the past—a thing done 'once for all'" (*Life and Letters of F. J. A. Hort*, Vol. II, p. 213).

It need hardly be said that the words connected with the Holy Communion, " Do this " ; " Remembrance " ; " Shew," tell us nothing of our Lord's present life in heaven.[1]

So that our Lord is not offering Himself to the Father, or pleading His sacrifice, or representing, or even re-presenting His sacrifice, but He is appearing in God's presence on our behalf; interceding there by His presence and on the basis of His completed redemption on the Cross; sympathising; succouring, and saving the sinful; giving the Holy Spirit; governing and guiding the Church; waiting till He shall appear again.

We are therefore to "lift up our hearts." It is significant that the Epistle to the Hebrews describes the crowning point or pith of the Epistle as " An High Priest who is set down " (chap. viii. 1). When the High Priest had presented the blood on the Day of Atonement his work was complete, and if we could imagine him able to remain there in the presence of God, it would be on the basis of that completed offering, and not on his continuing to offer, or present anything. Besides, as there was no altar in the Holy of Holies, so there could not be any sacrificial offering. Christ is not now at, or on an altar, or at a mercy seat, but on the throne. His presence there on our behalf, as our representative, includes everything.

Dr. Swete agrees with Bishop Westcott in holding that our Lord's presence in heaven is His intercession :—

" The Intercession of the Ascended Christ is not a prayer but a life. The New Testament does not represent Him as an *orante* standing ever before the Father, and with outstretched arms, like the figures in the mosaics of the Catacombs, and with strong crying and tears pleading our cause in the presence of a reluctant God ; but as a throned Priest-King, asking what He will from a Father Who always hears and grants His request. Our Lord's life in Heaven is His prayer."[2]

We can well be content with the thought that He is there, and that His presence with the Father is the secret of our peace, the assurance of our access, and the guarantee of our permanent relation with God. It is just at this point that one essential difference between type and antitype is noticed. The High Priest went into the Holy of Holies *with* blood, but with regard to Christ's entrance into heaven there is a significant alteration in the phrase. He is said to have gone there " *through* His own blood " ; His access is based on the act of Calvary (Heb. ix. 12). It is in the priesthood of Christ that Christians realise the difference between spiritual immaturity and spiritual maturity (Heb. vi. 1 ; x. 1), and it is the purpose of the Epistle to the Hebrews to emphasise this truth above all others. Christianity is " the religion of free access to God," and in proportion as we realise this privilege of drawing near and keeping near, we shall find in the attitude of *Sursum corda*, " Lift up

---

[1] Plummer, " St. Luke," *International Critical Commentary*, p. 497 f.; Gore, *The Body of Christ* (First Edition), p. 315; W. B. Marriott, *Memorials*, p. 206.
[2] Swete, *The Ascended Christ*, p. 95.

your hearts," one of the essential features of a strong, vigorous, growing, joyous, Christian life.[1]

There is one other matter that seems to call for attention connected with our Lord's session in heaven. When controversies arose in regard to the presence of Christ in the Eucharist, some writers used language concerning the glorified body of our Lord which seemed to suggest that after His ascension His human nature became deified, and almost, if not quite, lost the attributes of humanity. It is this that has led to the enquiry: Can we think of our ascended Lord as present everywhere as Man? There can be no doubt whatever that the Article was intended to oppose this opinion, and a strong confirmation of this is seen by a comparison of the words of the Article with the rubric at the end of the Communion Service.[2] The subject was thus clearly before the compilers of our Articles.[3] The Article teaches unequivocally the local presence of Christ's humanity in heaven, since He " took again His body . . . wherewith He ascended into heaven, and there sitteth," etc. So that in regard to His humanity we may rightly speak of the Real Absence of Christ, just as we may also equally speak of the Real Presence in and through the Holy Spirit. But while this is so, we are not for a moment to suppose that " the Two Natures " are in any way separated from each other even though, as in the record of our Lord's earthly life, the union and correlation are beyond our comprehension. Hooker has endeavoured to state the truth, though it must be confessed that even he is unable to shed much, if any, light on it. While on the one hand he holds it " a most infallible truth that Christ as Man is not everywhere present," he adds that " in some sense He is everywhere present even as Man," and he speaks of this universal presence as " after a sort," since wherever the Word is the Manhood is united with it. According to Hooker, therefore, there is a sort of presence of the Manhood by conjunction, a presence of co-operation and a presence of force and efficacy.[4] There is really no danger of Nestorianism or Eutychianism if we carefully adhere to the

---

[1] The last few sentences are based on and taken from the author's article, "Priest," in Hastings' *Dictionary of Christ and the Gospels.*

"Our faith has to lift up its head and thank God that our Great High Priest is no longer sacrificing for sin; that, having by one offering perfected for ever them that are sanctified, He now lives and reigns, sitting in His majesty, throned in His glory, holy, harmless, undefiled, and separate from sinners, and made higher than the heavens, with power before which every knee must bow, giving victory to His saints, whom He loves to the end, able also to save to the uttermost all that come unto God by Him, seeing He ever liveth to make intercession for them" (Dimock, *Our One Priest on High,* p. 78).

[2] "No adoration is intended, or ought to be done, either unto the Sacramental Bread or Wine there bodily received, or unto any Corporal Presence of Christ's natural Flesh and Blood. For the Sacramental Bread and Wine remain still in their very natural substances, and therefore may not be adored (for that were Idolatry, to be abhorred of all faithful Christians); and the natural Body and Blood of our Saviour Christ are in heaven and not here; it being against the truth of Christ's natural Body to be at one time in more places than one."

[3] See also *Reformatio Legum, De Hæresibus,* c. 5.

[4] Hooker, *Eccl. Pol.,* Bk. V., Ch. LIV, Section 7.

plain teaching of Scripture as interpreted by the Article, that our Lord is absent as Man and yet present as God. The difficulty is almost wholly due to an erroneous conception of our Lord's glorified humanity as associated with the Holy Communion, but Scripture, with our Prayer Book following it, clearly limits the thought of our Lord's death, and not His glorified state, to the Holy Communion, where, as Cranmer says, we are concerned with the body *ut in cruce non in coelo.*

The Article follows the Creed in stating briefly yet plainly the expectation of our Lord's coming again.

1. The Coming.—The return of the Lord Jesus Christ is not a mere doctrine to be discussed, nor a matter for intellectual study alone. Its prominence in the New Testament shows the great importance of the truth, for it is referred to over three hundred times, and it may almost be said that no other doctrine is mentioned so frequently or emphasised so strongly.[1] Just before our Lord died He told His disciples that He would come again (John xiv. 3), and when He ascended, two heavenly messengers appeared to the Apostles corroborating the Master's words by saying that He would come back in like manner as they had seen Him go (Acts i. 11). Thenceforward this Coming was to be the "blessed hope" of His people until His glorious appearing (Tit. ii. 13). It is, therefore, important to distinguish clearly and constantly between our death and the coming of the Lord. The two are always contrasted. Death comes to all, Christian and heathen, but the Lord's appearance is to apply to Christians alone. Christ Himself clearly distinguished between death and His Coming (John xxi. 23). The Creed, following the New Testament, is also quite clear as to the future and personal coming of Christ. While there is a sense in which Christ came in and by the Holy Spirit at Pentecost, and while, moreover, He still comes to dwell in His people by the same Spirit, yet these are never to be identified with His future coming, for those who had received the Spirit were still to wait for Him from heaven (1 Thess. i. 8-10). Thus, the Coming is the climax and culmination of His work of redemption, when the Body of Christ, the Church, will be completed, and the Lord will usher in that Kingdom which will eventually result in God being all in all (Eph. i. 14; Rom. viii. 19-23; 1 Cor. xv. 23-28).

2. The Judgment.—The Article states in general terms the purpose of our Lord's Coming as that of judgment "at the last day." But the New Testament has much more detail than this, and judgment is only a part

---

[1] Baptism is mentioned nineteen times in seven Epistles, and in fourteen out of twenty-one is not alluded to. The Lord's Supper is only referred to three or four times in the entire New Testament, and in twenty out of twenty-one Epistles there is no mention of it. The Lord's Coming is referred to in one verse out of every thirteen in the New Testament, and in the Epistles alone in one verse out of ten. This proportion is surely of importance, for if frequency of mention is any criterion there is scarcely any other truth of equal interest and value.

of His work.   In the familiar words, " Lo, He comes, with clouds descending," we have what may be called the second part of His Coming, the coming to judgment, according to the Creed.   But before that the New Testament seems to teach a coming for His people, and a taking of them away before He returns to the earth for judgment.   Of all the Scriptures which treat of the first part of the Coming there is none more explicit than 1 Thess. iv. 13-18.   And while on details students of Scripture may differ, it may be said that there is universal belief in regard to the general lines of teaching expressive of the purpose of our Lord's coming again.   Among other objects for which He is coming again are : (1) the taking to Himself of His redeemed disciples, including the resurrection of those who have died and the transformation of those who will be alive at His Coming.   (2) To reward His servants after their life of grace on earth.   (3) To usher in peace and rule this world now in rebellion.   (4) To gather together Israel and to place them in their own land.   (5) To execute judgment on the rejecters of His grace.   (6) To swallow up death in victory.   (7) To bind Satan and to usher in Eternity.   It is, therefore, usual to distinguish between Christ coming *for* His people and *with* His people, the latter being that which is specifically referred to in the Creed and the Article.   But whatever may be our view of detail we must not allow anything to interfere with our firm belief in the fact of the coming. In the light of St. Paul's inclusion of this in the Gospel preached at Thessalonica (2 Thess. ii. 5), the outcome can only be spiritual loss if the coming of Christ is ignored or set aside.   There is no truth that so purifies and exalts the Christian life, none that so inspires the worker with earnestness and the discouraged and perplexed with hope.   On the institution of the Lord's Supper reference was made by Christ to His coming again, and no one can enter fully into the meaning of the Holy Communion without looking forward to the Coming as well as backward to the Cross.   Salvation includes spirit, soul, and body, and this threefold completeness will only be realised in and through " that blessed hope, the glorious appearing of our Great God and Saviour."

   The reference to judgment is of particular value in the light of all the mysteries connected with the presence of sin and suffering.   Scripture clearly teaches that Christ the present Saviour is to be the future Judge (John v. 22, 27 ; Acts xvii. 31 ; Rom. ii. 16), and in this judgment, marked, as it will be, by absolute impartiality and complete knowledge, man will find the perfect vindication of God and an explanation of all that is now mysterious and inexplicable.   The craving for judgment which is forced upon us by our reason and conscience will find its perfect realisation in the action of Him to whom all judgment has been committed.[1]

SUMMARY OF ARTICLES II-IV

   Following the line of the Apostles' Creed, these three Articles bring

[1] Maclear and Williams, *Introduction to the Articles of the Church of England*, p. 86, Note 2.

before us our Lord's Person and work as Redeemer in a series of connected acts and facts which are to be factors and forces in our life. It will be well to summarise these truths for the sake of completeness.

1. The Divine Sonship in which He is " equal to the Father, as touching His Godhead "; " Jesus Christ His only Son our Lord " (Apostles' Creed); " the only-begotten Son of God, Begotten of His Father before all worlds, God of God, Light of Light, Very God of very God, Begotten, not made, Being of one substance with the Father; By whom all things were made " (Nicene Creed).

2. The Incarnation by which the Son of God became Son of Man. " Conceived by the Holy Ghost, Born of the Virgin Mary " (Apostles' Creed); " And was incarnate by the Holy Ghost of the Virgin Mary, And was made man " (Nicene Creed).

3. The Death by which He made an atonement for sin. " Suffered under Pontius Pilate, Was crucified " (Apostles' Creed); " And was crucified also for us under Pontius Pilate. He suffered " (Nicene Creed).

4. The Burial and Descent into Hell by which He realised in completeness our human experiences. " Dead and buried " (Apostles' Creed); " And was buried " (Nicene Creed).

5. The Resurrection in which He was victorious over Sin, Satan, and Death. " The third day He rose again from the dead " (Apostles' Creed); " And the third day He rose again according to the Scriptures " (Nicene Creed).

6. The Ascension and Session by which He was crowned as Priest, Intercessor, and Lord, bestowing grace and building up His Church. " He ascended into heaven, And sitteth on the right hand of God the Father Almighty " (Apostles' Creed); " And ascended into heaven, And sitteth on the right hand of the Father " (Nicene Creed).

7. The Return, when He will receive His people, judge the world, and usher in eternal righteousness. " From thence He shall come to judge the quick and the dead " (Apostles' Creed); " And He shall come again with glory to judge both the quick and the dead : Whose kingdom shall have no end " (Nicene Creed).

ARTICLE V[1]

Of the Holy Ghost.	*De Spiritu Sancto.*
The Holy Ghost, proceeding from the Father and the Son, is of one substance, majesty, and glory, with the Father and the Son, very and eternal God.	Spiritus Sanctus, a Patre et Filio procedens, ejusdem est cum Patre et Filio essentiæ, majestatis, et gloriæ, verus ac æternus Deus.

IMPORTANT EQUIVALENTS.

Of one substance   =   *ejusdem essentiæ.*
Very   =   *verus.*

THERE was nothing corresponding to this Article in the Forty-two Articles of 1553, and there was none in the Confession of Augsburg. It was derived entirely from the Confession of Wurtemberg, presented to the Council of Trent, 1552, and was introduced here in 1563. The purpose was doubtless to give greater completeness of presentation of doctrine, but there seems to have been a necessity for the statement of the truth against certain denials of the time. The Section, *De Hæresibus*, of the *Reformatio Legum*, contains frequent reference to, and denunciation of the various forms of, misbelief which existed at the time,[2] and Article I of the Concordat of 1538 condemned those who represented the Holy Spirit as impersonal.

The only virtual change was "substance" for "essence" in the English of 1571, the Latin remaining unchanged.

I.—THE TEACHING OF THE ARTICLE

The Article elaborates the statement of Article I in regard to the Holy Spirit, and thereby follows naturally from the statements of Articles II, III, and IV respecting our Lord. Before looking in detail at the theological topics embraced in the Article it will be useful to analyse it as a whole.

1. The Fact of the Holy Spirit; "The Holy Ghost."

---

[1] The various aspects of this subject are more fully treated in the author's *The Holy Spirit of God*, of which the treatment here is an abbreviation. Reference may also be made to the bibliography in that work, special attention being called to the books by Dr. Swete, Bishop Moule, Professor Denio, Dr. Smeaton, and Dr. Davison.

[2] "Quomodo vero hæc putida membra sunt ab Ecclesiæ corpore segreganda, quæ de Christo capite tam perverse sentiunt, sic illorum etiam est execrabilis impudentia, qui cum Macedonio contra Spiritum Sanctum conspiraverunt, illum pro Deo non agnoscentes" (*Reformatio Legum, De Hæresibus*, c. 6).

2. The Procession of the Holy Spirit; " Proceeding from the Father and the Son."

3. The Equality of the Holy Spirit with the Father and the Son; " Of one substance, majesty, and glory, with the Father and the Son."

4. The Godhead of the Holy Spirit; " Very and eternal God."

It will be seen that the Article follows closely the statements of the Nicene Creed in harmony with the Church doctrine of Chalcedon.

II.—THE SCRIPTURE DOCTRINE OF THE HOLY SPIRIT

1. This is clearly a Bible doctrine and cannot be derived from any other source. It is essentially a truth of revelation. Naturally the subject is not so prominent in the Old Testament as in the New, but it is referred to in about half of the thirty-nine books, and the idea of the Spirit in Genesis is regarded as quite familiar, just as it is in St. Matt. i.

2. The doctrine of the Holy Spirit in the Old Testament calls for attention, first of all, and it is noteworthy that the New Testament identifies the Holy Spirit with the Spirit of God in the Old Testament, thereby showing that there is no difference between them. Indeed, the New Testament conception of the Spirit is very largely only intelligible when read in the light of the teaching of the Old Testament. There are three main lines of teaching in the Old Testament in regard to the Holy Spirit: (a) the cosmical, or world-relation of the Spirit of God. The Spirit associated with creation and human life as a whole; (b) the redemptive relation of the Spirit. The connection of the Spirit with Israel; (c) The personal relation of the Spirit. This is concerned with the spiritual life of individuals. It is often asked whether there are indications of development in the Old Testament of the doctrine of the Spirit of God. In the earlier books the Spirit is certainly depicted as a Divine energy, but in the later there seems to be something like an approximation to the doctrine of the Spirit as a Personal Being (Isa. xlviii. 16; lxiii. 9, 10; Zech. iv. 6). Perhaps, in general, the Spirit in the Old Testament is a Divine Agent rather than a distinct Personality. God is regarded as at work by His Spirit. One strong confirmation of the truth that the doctrine of the Spirit is a Bible doctrine is the fact that for all practical purposes the period of the Apocrypha from Malachi to Matthew contributed nothing to it. It is only when we come to New Testament times that we are enabled to see the real implications of the Old Testament in the fuller light and richer experience of the days of Christ.

3. The New Testament is very full of the subject of the Holy Spirit, and it is found in every book, except three short and personal ones. It emerges naturally and clearly from the revelation of Jesus Christ. When we look at it in the light of the New Testament we notice three main divisions :—

(a) The character and teaching of Christ. In the Synoptic Gospels we have the Holy Spirit in relation to Christ Himself at each stage of

His earthly manifestation. Then there is the teaching of Christ, the general idea being that of the Holy Spirit as a Divine power, promised to the disciples for the fulfilment of the Divine purpose of redemption. The Fourth Gospel is much fuller and more thoroughly developed, though it is particularly noteworthy that here, as in the Synoptic Gospels, there is a clear assumption of familiarity with the Holy Spirit (John i. 32 ff.). But there is a distinct development of teaching in the Fourth Gospel, where the Spirit is personal, and closely associated at all points with the redemption of Christ. Perhaps the most important feature in this Gospel is the use of the new term " Paraclete," which is found in connection with the detailed teaching of chaps. xiv-xvi. The general idea of the Johannine teaching is that the departure of Christ was to issue in the gift of the Holy Spirit, as the special bestowal of the new covenant for the purpose of perpetuating Christ's spiritual presence and effecting His redemptive work. Thus, the Holy Spirit would at once be a revelation of truth, a bestowal of life, and an equipment for service.

(b) From the Gospels it is natural to pass to the Acts of the Apostles as expressing the first thirty years of the Church's life and work, and the prominence given there to the Holy Spirit is very remarkable. There are at least seventy references, and on this account the book has been well called " The Acts of the Holy Spirit." This emphasis is really a testimony to the prominence of the Divine over the human element, and starting from the Day of Pentecost we see that the Spirit of God is at work, and, indeed, in supreme authority in every part of the early Church. His Person, His gifts, and His work are everywhere, and the book is dominated throughout by the Spirit, because the life of the Church was controlled by His Divine presence and power.

(c) The teaching of the Epistles will naturally follow, and in this St. Paul's work is of the very first importance. A remarkable fulness is seen in his writings and the teaching touches every part of his message. The usual fourfold grouping of his Epistles reveals references to the Spirit in a variety of ways, and both in regard to the work and the nature of the Spirit St. Paul has very much to say. The Holy Spirit is closely related to God (Rom. viii. 9); is regarded as possessing personal activities (Eph. iv. 30); and is intimately bound up with Christ (Rom. viii. 9). The activity of Christ as the Redeemer and Head of the Church is regarded as continued by the Holy Spirit, and yet with all this intimacy of association they are never absolutely identified. A careful study of St. Paul's teaching will support the view of a well-known writer that " the Apostle's entire thinking stands under the influence of his estimate of the Spirit."[1] Other parts of the New Testament are slight and insignificant in comparison with the writings of St. Paul and St. John.

4. The summary of the teaching of the Bible on the subject of the Holy Spirit suggests the following lines:—(a) A close and essential relation of the Spirit to Christ; (b) the Holy Spirit as " the Executive of the

[1] Quoted in *The Holy Spirit of God*, p. 37.

Godhead " in and for the Christian Church; (c) the Deity of the Spirit (Matt. xxviii. 19; 2 Cor. xiii. 14); (d) the Personality of the Spirit.

It will be seen from a study of the New Testament that the distinctions in the Godhead are always closely connected with Divine operations rather than with the Divine nature. While there is nothing approaching the metaphysical Trinity of later days, the association of the Father, the Son, and the Holy Spirit with Divine operations is a clear implication of essential Deity. The fundamental conceptions are the same throughout the whole of the New Testament, and there is no development of the doctrine of the Spirit through Ebionism to Orthodoxy.

III.—THE HISTORY OF THE DOCTRINE

1. The Ante-Nicene Period.—Sub-Apostolic Christianity was marked by experience rather than by reflection. And yet immaturity of thought does not indicate error of experience, for the Spirit of God is never regarded as a creature. It was heresy that compelled the Church to pay closer attention to the intellectual statements of the doctrine of the Spirit, and in particular Montanism led to a careful discrimination and thorough statement of the truth. But the strongest confirmation of the doctrine in this non-reflective period is seen in the devotional life of the Church. Experience is often the best witness to what is doctrinally implicit, and the evidence we possess of the life of the Church in these days bears unqualified testimony to the reality of the Divine Spirit. Not only have we the earliest form of the Apostles' Creed from this date, but Doxologies, and other hymns of praise, the Ordinance of Baptism, and the Invocation of the Holy Spirit in connection with the Lord's Supper. All bear witness to what the Church believed concerning the Holy Spirit.

2. From Nicæa to Chalcedon.—This non-reflective period concerning the Spirit could not continue in the light of the controversies of the time, and when the Deity of the Son had been established in opposition to Arianism, thought necessarily turned in the direction of the Deity of the Holy Spirit. The Nicene Creed closed with a simple statement of belief: " And in the Holy Spirit." But if the Son was consubstantial with the Father, and therefore Divine, the Personality and Deity of the Spirit would naturally be inferred, even though not as yet specifically stated. The question gradually arose after the Nicene Council, and controversy was due to those who were unable to accept the Deity of the Holy Spirit. They were described by Athanasius as " enemies of the Spirit," and afterwards designated Pneumatomachi. They were led by Macedonius, Bishop of Constantinople, and it was the acuteness of the controversy that led to the summoning of the Second General Council at Constantinople, 381. The result was the promulgation of a Creed which made some important additions to the declaration of belief in the Holy Ghost.

" The Lord, the Life-Giver, that proceeds from the Father, that with Father and Son is together worshipped and together glorified."

But it is noteworthy that the term Homoousios (ὁμοούσιος) was avoided in expressing the Spirit's oneness with the Father and the Son, nor was He even called God, though the terms in which His work was described cannot be predicated of any human being. Thus, the question of the Deity of the Spirit was settled as the Deity of the Son had been settled at Nicæa fifty years before. But the subject was still discussed and developed both in the East and in the West, and in 451 the Council of Chalcedon confirmed the decisions of Nicæa and Constantinople, stating that the clauses added in 381 were only intended to make the Nicene doctrine more explicit against those who had endeavoured to deny the Deity of the Spirit. The Council endorsed both Creeds and incorporated them in the " Definitio " of Chalcedon.

3. Chalcedon to the Reformation.—The doctrine of the Deity of the Spirit being fully established, there still remained the question of His relation to the Father and the Son. The term " Generation " was used to describe the relation of the Son to the Father, and the term " Procession " was employed to denote that of the Spirit. But the question was whether this eternal " Procession " or " Forthcoming " was from the Son as well as from the Father. The problem was Western, not Eastern, and the attitude indicates a difference which is explained by the conditions of the two Churches. The Eastern was confronted with those who tended to regard the Spirit as inferior to the Son, and in order to protect the full Deity of the Spirit it was regarded as essential to represent Him as proceeding solely from the Father as the Fountain (πηγή) of the Godhead. The Western Church, on the other hand, starting with the essential unity of the Son and the Father, desired to protect the truth that the Spirit is as much the Spirit of the Son as He is of the Father. Otherwise there could be no equality. It was this that led the West to express its truth by saying that the Spirit " proceeded " from the Father and the Son. It was the great influence of St. Augustine that led the West to endorse this twofold " Procession," and it became part of Western doctrine by incorporation into the Creed at the Council of Toledo in Spain, 589. At Toledo the authority of the first Four Councils was acknowledged, and the Creeds of Nicæa and Constantinople rehearsed, and it is curious that in this rehearsal the Synod imagined that the Latin Creed represented the Greek original. It is thus a matter of discussion how the words " And the Son " came into the Creed. Some have thought this was due to a marginal gloss. Dr. Burn adduces evidence to prove that the Council never added the words at all, that they are due to a blunder of a copyist of the Toledo text of the Constantinopolitan Creed.[1] The interpolation did not cause suspicion, but was repeated in several Synods as the orthodox doctrine, so that we have the remarkable

[1] Burn, The Nicene Creed, p. 40.

fact of the Council professing to keep the text of the Creed pure, and yet laying stress on the Spirit's " Procession " from the Son. It is probable that increasing error was rendering further dogmatic definition necessary. " The Toledan Fathers were only drawing out what seemed to them latent in the Creed."[1] It is essential to distinguish between the doctrine itself and its insertion in the Creed. However and whenever it was inserted, the addition was unwarranted, because it was without proper ecumenical authority, and it was some time before the addition became part of the Roman version of the Constantinopolitan Creed. The Western doctrine is thought to have come to England from Augustine of Canterbury, and during the Middle Ages little or nothing occurred of importance in connection with the doctrine of the Holy Spirit.

Thus, three things were settled in the Western Church: the Deity of the Son at Nicæa, and the Deity of the Spirit at Constantinople, and the Procession of the Spirit from the Father and the Son in the Western Creed. Up to the time of the Reformation, Christian thought had been concerned too little with the Person of the Holy Spirit, but the Reformation marks an epoch in the history of the doctrine by its emphasis on His work in the individual and in the Church. Further reference to the history up to the present day does not seem to be called for in connection with this Article; it must suffice to say that the problems which arose at the time of the Reformation may be said to extend to the present time.[2]

IV.—THE DOCTRINE OF THE HOLY SPIRIT

The teaching of the Nicene Creed in regard to the Spirit is as follows: " I believe in the Holy Ghost, The Lord and Giver of life, Who proceedeth from the Father and the Son, Who with the Father and the Son together is worshipped and glorified." This statement involves the three doctrines in the Article: Personality, Deity, and Procession.

1. The Personality of the Spirit.—The use of the term " Person " in relation to the Godhead is, of course, difficult, because it expresses something essentially different from our modern view of personality. Instead of meaning the fact of separate individuality, Personality in God is intended to convey an idea of an inner distinction which exists in the unity of the Divine Nature. The facts of Scripture demand from us an acknowledgment of the unity of the Godhead and at the same time those interior distinctions between Father, Son, and Spirit which we can only express by our word " Person." While, therefore, it is true that the term is used to-day in connection with human life in a way that is quite different from its use in connection with the Godhead, it is also true that no other term has yet been found adequate to express the essential distinctions in the Godhead. The Holy Spirit is a Person because He works by personal activities on persons, and the facts of Scripture require this belief. Further, the consciousness of the Church has always borne

---

[1] Burn, *ut supra*, p. 41.   [2] *The Holy Spirit of God*, Chs. XIII-XVI.

witness in the same direction. Personal working needs continuity of action, and a clear conception of the Personality of the Holy Spirit is essential to His vital relation to the individual Christian and to the Church.

2. The Deity of the Spirit.—The Deity is a necessary consequence of His Personality, for that which is attributed to the latter involves the former. Here, again, belief is based on the facts and implications of Scripture, for the allusions to the Holy Spirit cannot be predicated of anyone but God Himself. As we have seen, there is not the same clearness and fulness of revelation in the New Testament in reference to the Deity of the Spirit, yet it clearly arises out of the Scripture revelation and cannot possibly be expressed in any other way without doing violence to the facts of the case. The Holy Spirit is at once the personal life of God and the " Executive of the Godhead " in relation to man, and however difficult may be the conception of the Holy Spirit within the Godhead it can never be disregarded without spiritual loss.

3. We have already seen something of the history of the doctrine of the Procession of the Holy Spirit from the Father and from the Son, and it is important to obtain a true idea of the meaning of the Western Church in expressing and insisting on this doctrine. On the one side the Spirit is associated with the Father as sent, given, and proceeding (Matt. x. 20; John xiv. 16, 26; xv. 26). On the other hand, He is associated with the Son, being called the Spirit of Christ (Rom. viii. 9); described as sent by the Son from the Father (John xv. 26); bestowed by the Son on the Apostles (John xx. 22; Acts ii. 33); and called the Spirit of Jesus (Acts xvi. 7, R.V.). (See also Gal. iv. 6; Phil. i. 19; 1 Pet. i. 11.) So that, in the statement of the Creed, the Spirit proceeds from the Father and the Son, there was no intention of denying the one *principium* in the Father, but only a general assertion that the essence which the Father eternally communicates to the Spirit is also the essence of the Son, and that the Son shares, and is involved in the act and process of communication. The Eastern Church regards the Procession from the Son as temporal only through the Mission, and suspects our Western view of a tendency towards Sabellianism. It would seem as though no reunion were possible without some change of doctrine; at any rate the Eastern Church does not regard the difference as merely verbal. On the other hand, if the West dropped the *Filioque*, it might be thought to deny or question the Consubstantiality of the Son with the Father.[1]

---

[1] An authority on the Eastern Church, Mr. W. J. Birkbeck, writing to the *Guardian*, 28th January 1910, described what he called the chief of the many theological objections which the Easterns have to the insertion of the *Filioque*:

"It is not so much that it puts something fresh into the Creed which has no Ecumenical sanction, but that its insertion cuts out something which was there before—namely, the μοναρχία in the Godhead. That the Fathers of Constantinople I. intended to emphasise this doctrine seems quite plain from their alterations of the παρὰ τοῦ πατρὸς, John xv. 26 into the ἐκ τοῦ πατρὸς ἐκπορευόμενον of the Creed. This is the reason that in ordinary parlance Russian theologians speak of the Western form nine times out

One question of supreme importance has been raised during recent years : Is the doctrine of the Procession from the Son really justified, and does it represent a vital difference ? Several authorities are of opinion that it is this addition which has given to the West its admitted spiritual superiority over the East.[1] One writer goes so far as to say that the denial of the Procession from the Son has done much to fossilise the Greek Church. It is undoubtedly true that no Western theologian ever wished to do anything more than to associate in the closest possible way the Holy Spirit with the Son of God, and in so doing it would seem as though this was keeping quite close to the characteristic New Testament conception of the Holy Spirit as the Spirit of Christ, the Spirit of Jesus. And so we may say that " without the Holy Spirit we have practically no Christ," and without Christ we have practically no Holy Spirit.

V.—THE PLACE OF THE DOCTRINE OF THE HOLY SPIRIT IN CHRISTIANITY

It will be evident from the foregoing that the Holy Spirit occupies a vital and essential place in the Christian system.

1. In Relation to the Godhead.—The full New Testament idea of God is that of Father, Son, and Holy Spirit. It is impossible to question the fact that the New Testament affords clear proofs of such distinctions within the unity as can only be adequately expressed by the Christian doctrine of the Trinity. And as Christ is *within* the Godhead it is impossible for the Spirit to be *without*, since this would imply an inferiority of the Spirit which is contradicted by the facts of Scripture and spiritual experience.

In the same way the doctrine of the Holy Spirit in the New Testament is inextricably bound up with the revelation of Christ. It is not in His absolute Being, but as the Spirit of Christ that He is revealed in the New Testament (Acts xvi. 7, R.V.). The language in St. Paul's Epistles about the indwelling of Christ and of the Spirit is practically identical (2 Cor. iii. 17 ; Gal. iv. 6), and yet with this practical identity there is an equally clear distinction. Christ and the Spirit are different, yet the same; the same, yet different. Redemption comes from the Father, through the Son, by the Spirit. Christ is the Divine Saviour, and the Spirit is the Spirit of Christ, and in this association we have the spiritual and experimental foundations of the Trinity. But however difficult it may be to express the difference between Christ and the Spirit, regarded as in the Being of God Himself, no difficulty must allow us to ignore the clear teaching of the New Testament and the personal testi-

of ten not as 'the interpolated symbol,' but as 'the mutilated symbol' (*iskazhenny sy mvol*; Miklosich in his *Slavonic Roots* gives εὐνουχιάζειν as the first meaning of this verb). By adding the word *Filioque* the Latins not only added to the Creed, but cut out from it what the Greeks look upon as a vital truth. Our theologians ought at least to realise this before they press for the restoration of the Creed to its original form; they will then be able to do so with much better effect."

[1] *The Holy Spirit of God*, pp. 145, 146.

G

mony of Christian consciousness. There is a close and intimate connection, and yet Christ and the Spirit are never absolutely identical. The Spirit is at once the Spirit of God and the Spirit of Christ, and we believe that God can only become known to us in the Historic Jesus, Who is mediated to us by the Holy Spirit.

2. In Relation to Holy Scripture.—The Nicene Creed expresses a profound truth when it associates the Holy Spirit with the Old Testament, " Who spake by the prophets." It involves the important question of a Divine revelation which we believe has been given in the Person of Jesus Christ. Holy Scripture as the embodiment of that revelation comes to us from God through the Spirit, and both in the Old Testament and in the New the Spirit is clearly associated with the written record of the Divine revelation (Acts i. 16; 2 Tim. iii. 16; Heb. iii. 7; 2 Pet. i. 21). On any showing inspiration implies a specific and unique work of the Holy Spirit in giving to the Church the written embodiment of the Divine religion of redemption, and it is this uniqueness that gives Scripture its supreme authority as the work of the Holy Spirit of God.

3. In Relation to the Individual.—The Holy Spirit is described in the Nicene Creed as the " Life-Giver," and this includes everything essential in His relation to the individual Christian. Without that Spirit no man can be regarded as a Christian (Rom. viii. 9; 1 Cor. xii. 3), and it is the peculiar work of the Holy Spirit to reveal Christ to man, and thereby to link the Jesus of history with the Christ of experience. The great needs of the soul : conversion, communion, and character, are all made possible by the Holy Spirit, and His action covers the entire life of the believer from first to last. The Spirit uses the truth of God to reveal Christ to the soul, and then every means of grace is associated with the Holy Spirit as " the Spirit of Christ." In whatever way we contemplate individual life we see the need of the presence of the Spirit of God.

4. In Relation to the Church.—It is not without point that the expression of belief in the Holy Ghost in the Creeds is immediately followed by the confession of our faith in the existence of the Church. This close connection suggests the truth of the relation of the Holy Spirit to the body of Christian people. The New Testament teaches that the Spirit constituted the Church on the Day of Pentecost (Acts ii; 1 Cor. xii. 13), and thereupon the Spirit abides in the Christian community, builds it up, governs it, unifies it, and provides in every way for its needs. There is no part of the Christian Church, its life, work, power and progress, which is not in some way influenced by the Holy Spirit.

5. In Relation to Christianity.—The Holy Spirit is the guarantee of the best, and, indeed the only, satisfactory apologetic Gospel. Mohammedanism and Buddhism have their ideas, their sacred books, and even their founders, but it is only in Christianity that God is made real to

men.   In many respects the Holy Spirit is the ultimate fact in Christianity, for no other religious system has anything corresponding to this truth. The Divine revelation given historically in the Person of Christ is made real to the soul by the Holy Spirit, and this is a characteristic mark in Christianity, since only therein is religion realised as a matter of personal communion with the Deity.   So that the Holy Spirit is the unique element of Christianity, and His presence constitutes the only "dynamic" by means of which Christianity can be recommended and vindicated to the world.   Whether we think of the individual or the community, the presence and power of the Holy Spirit are absolutely essential for life and progress.   The deepest needs of humanity can never be solved by philosophy, scholarship, or criticism.   The supreme need to-day is for that personal discipleship to Christ which is alone made available by the Holy Spirit.   Everything in the Old Testament points forward to the Coming of the Spirit, and everything in the New Testament emphasises His presence in the Christian community.   It is this that makes the Article so important and the truth it enshrines of the most vital necessity in every aspect of life to-day.

II. THE RULE OF FAITH

ARTICLES VI–VIII

6. The Sufficiency of the Holy Scriptures for Salvation.

7. The Old Testament.

8. The Three Creeds.

THE subject of the Rule of Faith should obviously be considered before discussing particular doctrines included in the Faith. It is only natural and right to think of the depository of Faith before we attempt to elicit the various aspects of teaching found therein. And so the doctrines discussed in the first five Articles are derivable only from Scripture, the fount of essential Christian truth, which is the subject of the next Article. From another standpoint it may be possible to regard the present as the logical order, that is, if we think of the doctrines of the Godhead as in general a Revelation, and then proceed to consider the seat and sphere wherein that Revelation is manifested and declared.[1] But in view of the fact that the Articles are concerned with the substance of specific Christian doctrine the present arrangement is not appropriate to logical order. For symmetry and proportion we naturally ascertain the depository of our Faith before we examine the contents. It is also interesting to observe that the Helvetic Confessions and the Westminster Confession, together with the Irish Articles of 1615, put an Article on Scripture in the first place.[2] Our order is doubtless due to the fact that the Reformers were desirous of exhibiting the common Faith of Christendom before dwelling upon the differences between us and Rome, of which the question of the Rule of Faith is one of the chief. Everything depends upon the point of view. In a sense we say first of all, " I believe in God," before we bear our testimony to the Scripture as the Word of God. But inas-

---

[1] This aspect of the subject is taken by Maclear, who quotes Salmon's *Introduction to the New Testament*, p. 1:—

"For after settling that there is a Revelation, the question follows, How is that Revelation to be made known to us ? What are the Books that record it ? In other words, What is the Canon of Scripture ? "

[2] "Et in hac Scriptura sancta habet universalis Christi ecclesia plenissime exposita quæcunque pertinent, cum ad salvificam fidem, tum ad vitam Deo placentem, recte informandam. Quo nomine distincte a Deo præceptum est, ne ei aliquid vel addatur vel detrahatur" (*Second Helvetic Confession*, Article I).

much as our faith in God in this sense is only concerned with the conviction of His existence, and of a revelation from Him, the true spiritual order is, " I believe God has spoken through His word," and then, " I examine that Word to see Who and what God is, and what He has said and done."

ARTICLE VI

<table>
<tr>
<td>Of the sufficiency of the Holy Scriptures for salvation.</td>
<td>De divinis Scripturis, quod sufficiant ad Salutem.</td>
</tr>
<tr>
<td>

Holy Scripture containeth all things necessary to salvation: so that whatsoever is not read therein, nor may be proved thereby, is not to be required of any man, that it should be believed as an article of the Faith, or be thought requisite or necessary to salvation. In the name of the holy Scripture we do understand those Canonical Books of the Old and New Testament, of whose authority was never any doubt in the Church.

</td>
<td>

Scriptura sacra continet omnia quæ ad salutem sunt necessaria, ita ut quicquid in ea nec legitur, neque inde probari potest, non sit a quoquam exigendum, ut tanquam articulus fidei credatur, aut ad salutis necessitatem requiri putetur. Sacræ Scripturæ nomine, eos Canonicos libros veteris et novi Testamenti intelligimus, de quorum auctoritate in Ecclesia nunquam dubitatum est.

</td>
</tr>
</table>

<table>
<tr>
<td>Of the Names and Number of the Canonical Books.</td>
<td>De Nominibus et Numero Librorum sacræ Canonicæ Scripturæ veteris Testamenti.</td>
</tr>
<tr>
<td>

Genesis.
Exodus.
Leviticus.
Numbers.
Deuteronomy.
Joshua.
Judges.
Ruth.
The First Book of Samuel.
The Second Book of Samuel.
The First Book of Kings.
The Second Book of Kings.
The First Book of Chronicles.
The Second Book of Chronicles.
The First Book of Esdras.
The Second Book of Esdras.
The Book of Esther.
The Book of Job.
The Psalms.
The Proverbs.
Ecclesiastes, or Preacher.
Cantica, or Songs of Solomon.
Four Prophets the Greater.
Twelve Prophets the Less.

</td>
<td>

Genesis.
Exodus.
Leviticus.
Numeri.
Deuteronomia.
Josuæ.
Judicum.
Ruth.
Prior Liber Samuelis.
Secundus Liber Samuelis.
Prior Liber Regum.
Secundus Liber Regum.
Prior Liber Paralipom.
Secundus Liber Paralipom.
Primus Liber Esdræ.
Secundus Liber Esdræ.
Liber Hester.
Liber Job.
Psalmi.
Proverbia.
Ecclesiastes, vel Concionator.
Cantica Solomonis.
IV Prophetæ Majores.
XII Prophetæ Minores.

</td>
</tr>
</table>

<table>
<tr>
<td>

And the other books (as Hierome saith) the Church doth read for example of life, and instruction of manners; but yet doth it not apply them to establish any doctrine. Such are these following:

The Third Book of Esdras.
The Fourth Book of Esdras.
The Book of Tobias.

</td>
<td>

Alios autem libros (ut ait Hieronimus) legit quidem Ecclesia, ad exempla vitæ, et formandos mores; illos tamen ad dogmata confirmanda non adhibet: ut sunt:

Tertius Liber Esdræ.
Quartus Liber Esdræ.
Liber Tobiæ.

</td>
</tr>
</table>

The Book of Judith.	Liber Judith.
The rest of the Book of Esther.	Reliquum Libri Hester.
The Book of Wisdom.	Liber Sapientiæ.
Jesus the Son of Sirach.	Liber Jesu filii Sirach.
Baruch the Prophet.	Baruch Propheta.
The Song of the Three Children.	Canticum Trium Puerorum.
The Story of Susanna.	Historia Susannæ.
Of Bel and the Dragon.	De Bel et Dracone.
The Prayer of Manasses.	Oratio Manassis.
The First Book of Maccabees.	Prior Liber Machabeorum.
The Second Book of Maccabees.	Secundus Liber Machabeorum.

All the books of the New Testament, as they are commonly received, we do receive and account them for Canonical.

Novi Testamenti omnes libros (ut vulgo recepti sunt) recipimus, et habemus pro Canonicis.

IMPORTANT EQUIVALENTS.

Of the sufficiency of the holy Scriptures for salvation.	=	*De divinis Scripturis, quod sufficiant ad salutem.*
Or be thought requisite or necessary to salvation	=	*aut ad salutis necessitatem requiri putetur.*
Of the names and number of the Canonical Books	=	*De nominibus et numero librorum sacræ Canonicæ Scripturæ.*
For example of life and instruction of manners	=	*ad exempla vitæ, et formandos mores.*
To establish any doctrine	=	*ad dogmata confirmanda.*

THIS Article was the Fifth of the Forty-two Articles of 1553, when its title was *Divinæ Scripturæ doctrina sufficit ad salutem* ("The doctrine of Holy Scripture is sufficient to salvation "). The Article asserted the sufficiency of Scripture, but did not enumerate or define the Canonical books. It read as follows:—

" Holy Scripture containeth all things necessary to Salvation : So that whatsoever is neither read therein, nor may be proved thereby, although it be sometime received of the faithful, as Godly, and profitable for an order and comeliness : Yet no man ought to be constrained to believe it, as an article of faith, or repute it requisite to the necessity of Salvation."

In 1563 the clause " Although it be sometime received of the faithful, as Godly, and profitable for an order and comeliness " was omitted, because the Article deals with questions of faith, not of order, the latter being discussed in Articles XX and XXXIV.

The clause which defines the Canonical books was derived from the Confession of Wurtemberg, and was inserted in 1563. This also contained a list of the Canonical books and also of the Apocrypha. In 1571 the catalogue of the Apocrypha was completed by the addition of the names of several books.

The language of the first paragraph of the Article may be compared with a similar statement in the *Reformatio Legum*, in which after a list of the Canonical books it is said:—

" Hæc igitur generatim est sancta Scriptura, qua omnia creditu ad salutem necessaria, plene et perfecte contineri credimus, usque adeo ut quicquid in ea non legitur nec reperitur, nec denique ex eadem aut consequitur, aut convincitur, a nemine sit exigendum ut tanquam articulus fidei credatur."[1]

The object of the Article is to state the position of our Church in regard to Scripture, both in opposition to Rome and also to the extreme wing of the Protestants of the sixteenth century. It effectually meets the errors rife on both sides. On the one hand it states the true position against the Roman view of the Rule of Faith ; on the other it opposes the opinion of those who were so concerned with the illumination of the Holy Spirit in the hearts of believers that they despised the thought of religious teaching in books.[2] The true Anglican position, following that of essential Protestantism, is careful to emphasise the written Word as against any dominion of ecclesiastical institution, or of subjective impressions of even genuine religious experiences.[3] But there does not seem much doubt that the Article is mainly directed against the fundamental error of Rome which had been stated by the Council of Trent several years before.[4]

I.—THE CANON OF HOLY SCRIPTURE

The second sentence of the Article logically comes first by showing what Scripture is before considering its position and the use made of it.

[1] *De Summa Trinitate et Fide Catholica*, c. 9.

[2] Hardwick, *History of the Articles of Religion*, pp. 99, 373.

[3] "In quo genere teterrimi illi sunt (itaque a nobis primum nominabuntur) qui sacras Scripturas ad infirmorum tantum hominum debilitatem ablegant et detrudunt, sibi sic ipsi interim præfidentes, ut earum authoritate se teneri non putent, sed peculiarem quendam spiritum jactant, a quo sibi omnia suppeditari aiunt, quæcunque docent et faciunt" (*Reformatio Legum, De Hæresibus*, c. 3).

[4] "The sacred, holy, œcumenical, and general Synod of Trent, lawfully assembled in the Holy Ghost . . . clearly seeing that this truth and discipline (of the Gospel of Christ) are contained in the written books and in the unwritten traditions, which, received by the Apostles from the mouth of Christ Himself, or from the Apostles themselves, the Holy Ghost dictating, have come down even unto us, transmitted, as it were from hand to hand; (the Synod) following the example of the Orthodox Fathers, receives and venerates with an equal affection of piety and reverence, all the books both of the Old and of the New Testament—seeing that one God is the Author of both—and also the said traditions, as well those appertaining to Faith as to Morals, as having been dictated either by Christ's own word of mouth, or by the Holy Ghost, and preserved in the Catholic Church by a continuous succession. And it has thought meet that a list of the Sacred Books be inserted in this decree, lest a doubt may arise in anyone's mind which are the Books that are received by this Synod, they are set down here below: of the Old Testament: the five books of Moses—Josue, Judges, Ruth, four books of Kings, two of Paralipomenon (Chronicles), the first book of Esdras, and the second which is called Nehemias; Tobias, Judith, Esther, Job, the Davidical Psalter consisting of 150 Psalms ; the Proverbs, Ecclesiastes, the Canticle of Canticles, Wisdom, Ecclesiasticus, Isaias, Jeremias with Baruch; Ezechiel, Daniel; the twelve Minor Prophets . . . two books of Maccabees, the first and the second. Of the New Testament: (this Canon is the same as the Protestant). But if anyone will not receive the said books entire with all their parts as they have been used to be read in the Catholic Church, and as they are contained in the old Latin Vulgate Edition; and knowingly and deliberately contemn the traditions aforesaid: let him be anathema" (*Conc. Trident., Sessio Quarta, Decret. de Canon. Script.*, Waterworth's Translation, pp. 18, 19. London, 1848).

The attitude of the Church is one of reverence for a volume consisting of sixty-six books; thirty-nine in the Old Testament and twenty-seven in the New; by many authors, and of very varied nature. The former part is the Bible of the Jews, setting forth the Jewish religion in its historical development and different aspects covering centuries of time. The Church inherited belief in the sacredness and authority of the Old Testament from our Lord and His Apostles. The New Testament sets forth the Christian religion in various aspects, covering some sixty years, or two generations. In contrast with the Koran, which is alleged to have come from Mohammed, none of the books of the New Testament are by the Founder of the Christian religion. The Church had the Old Testament from the first, even in Gentile Christianity, and then gradually the books of the New Testament were added. Canonicity is the fact, and canonising is the method of recognising these writings as possessed of Divine authority.[1]

1. The word " Canon " comes from κανών,[2] and is akin to קָנֶה, κάννα (reed).—The words " cane " and " canon " are cognate terms. The word had active and passive senses. A thing which is employed as a measure is first measured, and only then used to measure other things. The passive meaning, anything measured, e.g. a measured racecourse at Olympia, in turn becomes a measure, and the word means a straight road or rule used for measurement: 2 Cor. x. 3-16 (passive); Gal. vi. 16 (active). Then the word came to mean any list of things for reference, e.g. at Alexandria a list of classical writers was called κανών, and Eusebius calls chronological tables κανόνες χρονικοί (This is the meaning of the technical word " Canon " in relation to Scripture.) The Canon of Scripture is used first of all in a *passive* sense, meaning that which is measured off, or separated from others, and then it is employed in an *active* sense, meaning that which measures or tests others. Thus Scripture is (1) that which is measured or defined by the rule of the Church, and (2) that which, being measured, becomes thereby the rule of the Church for other cases. The Bible contained the recognised list of books which have been measured by a certain rule or standard of measurement and have thereby become measures of other books. The word is first used in the Christian Church by a poet, Amphilochius, 380, ὁ κανὼν τῶν θεοπνεύστων γραφῶν. But Origen had spoken of " canonised books " or books put on the list. Afterwards Jerome and Augustine, 400, used the word quite technically.[3]

2. What, then, is the rule of the Church by which a book is measured, or defined as canonical ?—The Article describes a Canonical Book as one " of whose authority was never any doubt in the Church." The

---

[1] For the history of each separate book reference should be made to the Commentaries and Introductions. For the New Testament as a whole Salmon's *Introduction* is the most important.

[2] *See* Westcott, *Canon of the New Testament*, Appendix A.

[3] Jerome's *Prol. Galeatus*; and Augustine, *De Civitate Dei*, 18, 38; Jerome saying of Tobias and Ruth, "*non sunt in canone.*"

reference is to authority, not to authorship. The statement is usually regarded as a difficulty, since it cannot apply to all the books and all the Churches, for the Reformers knew well the early doubts about some of the books. It is probable that as the doubts were dead by the sixteenth century the reference is to the Church as a whole as distinct from individual Churches. The matter was originally settled mainly by public reading and general usage. The first three centuries never pronounced on the subject except by the testimony of individual and representative writers. No corporate evidence was possible. But when it became available and necessary it was soon seen that there was no real doubt as to our books. The first corporate witness dates from the Council of Laodicea, 364, where the testimony is clear, and when once the whole Church was able to bear its testimony the words of the Article are seen to be justified.

3. The grounds of Canonicity need consideration.—Why were certain books received and certain rejected ? The fundamental reason is the conviction that certain books came from men who were divinely inspired to reveal and convey God's will : Prophets in the Old Testament and Apostles in the New. Prophets were the recognised expounders of God's will, and their writings were regarded as immediately authoritative. The best illustration is found in Jeremiah xxxvi., where the Prophet's words were recognised as possessing authority at once. Each book had this authority by reason of its prophetic source, and thence gradually came the collection into one volume, so that the Old Testament represents those books which Israel accepted on proper evidence as the Divine standard of faith and practice, because they were either written or put forth by prophetic men. It was not the decision of the people that caused the collection, but the collection was due to their acceptance by the people. The authority came from God through the prophets, and the recognition by the people was the effect of the Canonicity. The action of the people was the weighing of evidence, and the outcome was testimony rather than judgment.

In the same way the books of the New Testament were regarded as possessing Apostolic origin. This may have been either by authorship or sanction, but there is no doubt that the primary standard of verification and acceptance was the belief that the books came from Apostolic men, either Apostles themselves or their associates. So that the ground of Canonicity was not merely the age, or the truth, or the helpfulness of these books, but, beneath these characteristics, because they came from uniquely qualified instruments of God's will. All other tests were subsidiary and confirmatory. It is, therefore, important and essential to distinguish between the ground of Canonicity and the ground of the conviction of Canonicity. The latter is quite separate from the former, and is subjective, while the former is rational, objective, and leaves man no excuse.

4. The character of Canonicity.—It is particularly important to

notice what Canonicity really implies and involves. It created a book not a revelation. Canonicity is analogous to codification, which implies the existence of laws already as separate books. The authority of each book of the Bible would have been the same even if there had been no collection and codification. So that the authority is not that of a book, but of a revelation; the revelation did not come to exist because of the Canonicity, but the Canonicity because of the revelation, and the Bible, as we have seen, is regarded as a revelation, because it is held to be the embodiment of the historic manifestation of the Redeemer and His truth.[1] It has been well said that the Bible is not an authorised collection of books, but a collection of authorised books. It is essential to remember that the quality which determines acceptance of a book is its possession of a Divine revelation. So that Canonicity did not raise a book to the position of Scripture, but recognised that it was already Scripture. Canonisation was a decision based on testimony, and the canonising process was the recognition of an existing fact. It is, of course, true that the process of canonisation implies accumulative authority, and adds immensely to the strength of the position as representing the witness of the entire Church, but it must never be forgotten that the authority of each separate book was in it from the first.

5. The History of the Old Testament Canon.—Although of necessity there was no complete history of the Canon in the Old Testament itself, yet there are indications of a growth which need to be considered. While there is no record of the canonisation of any book or collection, there is a frequent recognition of books as authoritative. Provision was evidently made for writing, preserving, and teaching. There are indications all through of gradual growth and accretion. Among the passages the following may be adduced: Exod. xxiv. 4-7; Deut. xxxi. 9-13; 24-26 (Cf. 2 Kings xxiii. 2); Josh. i. 8; xxiv. 26; 1 Sam. x. 25; Deut. xvii. 18 f. (Cf. Psa. xix; cxix, "testimony"); Prov. xxv. 1 (Cf. history by prophets); Isa. xxxiv. 16; Isa. viii. 19, 20; Jer. xxxvi. 4; xlv. 1; Dan. ix. 2; Zech. vii. 12. Proofs are forthcoming that in all periods this law was imposed and taught: Josh. xi. 15; Jud. iii. 4; 1 Kings ii. 3; 2 Kings xiv. 6; 2 Chron. xxx. 16; Dan. ix. 11; Ezra iii. 2; Neh. x. 28. All this shows the gradual growth and progress, and the deposit of Sacred Books in the Sanctuary, a custom which is in harmony with the practice of other nations.[2]

6. The History of the New Testament Canon.—The idea of a New Testament was natural from the analogy of the Old. The Divine authority of the Old Testament is clear from the New ("oracles," Rom. iii. 2), and this influenced the early Church. The Christian community, therefore, did not need to create the idea of a Canon, for it was there already, and in due course the books of the New Testament

[1] Fairbairn, The Place of Christ in Modern Theology, pp. 500-508.
[2] For fuller details of the history and progress, see W. H. Green, The Canon of the Old Testament.

were regarded as authoritative, because they revealed Christ by the Divine Spirit, through inspired men. As the Church did not grow up by natural law, but was founded by Christ, and authoritative teachers were sent forth by Him carrying with them a body of Divine Scriptures, the Church was never without its Bible or Canon, for wherever they went they imposed on the Churches they founded the Old Testament as the code of laws. Christ was the authority, side by side with the Old Testament, and Christ was declared first by the words of the Apostles, and later by their writings (Acts xx. 35). This immediate placing of the new books among the Scriptures was inevitable, and gradually the books became known to the whole Church through the separate testimony of individuals and communities. At the outset, Christ with the Old Testament was the authority for Christians, and this authority was necessarily oral at first, but it is almost certain that the words of Christ were put into writing very early.[1] As the words of Christ were considered holy from the first, it was easy and natural to reverence a report as truly as the living voice, and thus no distinction was made between the spoken and written words of Apostles.[2] Then came letters of Apostles to particular Churches or individuals, and these would obviously be treasured and read at gatherings side by side with the Old Testament. This public reading was the first step in the process whereby we got our New Testament. Then came interchange with other Churches as the second step. At first the Church seems to have been unconscious of the goal, and it was only later that the process was deliberate. The Church had a New Testament Canon long before it had the conception of it, the fact before the idea. The reception of an Apostolic letter would at once separate it from all else as an authoritative guide, and this would be the canonisation of a single book. While particular circumstances helped forward and accelerated the process, these cannot wholly account for it. Heresy and schism doubtless hastened the completion of the Canon, but the New Testament was inevitable in any case. Oral tradition was soon found to be inadequate, especially as heretics claimed their own tradition. To the earliest Churches Scripture was not a closed, but an increasing Canon, one of gradual growth, like the Old Testament, and this would be so as long as there were living men specially " moved by the Holy Ghost." And so at the end of the process it was not felt to be anything novel or strange, but the whole Church confirmed what had long been familiar in individual Churches. The formal recognition of the entire New Testament was exactly the same as that of separate books used by particular Churches and individuals, and the Church declarations were not the primary investment with authority, but only the record and registration of an authority long existing. There is no evidence whatever of a gradual heightening of the estimate of books originally received on a lower level and at the

---

[1] Sir W. M. Ramsay considers that parts of our First Gospel were written before the death of Christ: *Luke the Physician*, p. 87.
[2] Sanday, *Inspiration*, p. 366.

commencement tentatively accounted Scripture. On the contrary, the evidence is conclusive of estimation and attachment from the beginning. As book after book came from the Apostolic circle it was received as Scripture and added to the old collection, until the books were numerous enough to be regarded as a separate section of Scriptures.

All through, the question was, which were Christian writings, so that they might be used for life and worship. The answer was that only the writings that could be regarded as of Apostolic sanction were to be included, all others being, therefore, ruled out. And so Christianity was soon seen to be a book religion like the Jewish, for in no other way could the purity of tradition about Christ be preserved. The Canon was part of a general movement of the Church during the last thirty years of the second century, when there was (1) a gradual collection of separate books to form the New Testament; (2) a gradual organising of the Christian Church against its foes; (3) a gradual expression of belief as a deposit from the Apostles. Thus, Scripture, the Christian Church, and the Christian Creeds were a threefold testimony to essential Christianity, and while everything on the surface seemed natural, incidental, and even occasional, a Divine power was really at work from the first giving the Church its authoritative books. The Church was spiritually guided as to the Canon, which has been well called " the slow miracle of history." But this does not mean that the New Testament, the Ministry and the Creeds are of equal authority; it only refers to the human and historical side of the process of collecting the authorised books into a volume. While the Canon (as a volume) is the work of the whole Church, the separate authority of each book is *not*, and in this latter sense the New Testament is *not* the product of the Church. And the witness of the Church to Episcopacy is very different from, because far less assured, universal and primitive than, the witness to the books of the New Testament and the truths of the Creed. These date from the first century, whereas Episcopacy confessedly is much later. Nothing is more fallacious, as we shall see, than the idea that the New Testament is the product of the Church. The Canon is, but the separate books are not.

It is impossible to give anything like an adequate account of the process in these pages,[1] but the germs during the first century seem to call for notice. The claim to Divine authority is evident; Apostolic preaching was regarded as in the Holy Spirit (1 Pet. i. 11), and even words were held to come from the Divine source (1 Cor. ii. 13). Apostolic commands carried Divine authority (1 Thess. iv. 2), and these were found in writing (2 Thess. ii. 15), and obedience to them was demanded (2 Thess. iii. 14). The acceptance of this was regarded as a test of

[1] Reference may be made to Westcott, *The Canon of the New Testament*; Sanday, *Inspiration*; Lightfoot, *Essays on Supernatural Religion*; Charteris, *Canonicity*; Sanday, *The Gospels in the Second Century*; Gregory, *Text and Canon of the New Testament*; Souter, *Canon and Text of the New Testament*.

spiritual life (1 Cor. xiv. 37). It was inevitable that writings making such claims should be given equal authority, because possessing equal quality with the Old Testament.[1] And they were therefore read at worship, a practice required by the Apostles (1 Thess. v. 27; Col. iv. 16; Rev. i. 2), and interchanged between Churches (Col. iv. 16). Something like mutual attestation also seems to be found; thus, Hebrews, 1 Peter, and James appear to use St. Paul's Epistles; 1 Tim. v. 18 quotes Luke x. 7 as "the Scripture" ($\dot{\eta}$ $\gamma\rho\alpha\phi\dot{\eta}$); 2 Peter iii. 16 refers to St. Paul's Epistles as "among the other writings" (Scriptures). After this the line of such quotations is unbroken.[2]

The process of canonisation may be outlined as follows:—

1. A.D. 50-100: composing, writing.
2. A.D. 100-200: collecting, gathering.
3. A.D. 200-300: comparing, sifting.
4. A.D. 300-400: completing, recognising.

Without entering upon the detailed history in the second century it may be noted that suddenly, about 170, we find the New Testament practically complete, with a hesitation about seven of our books, and four other books as a sort of New Testament Apocrypha. Evidently there was a process of collecting going on very rapidly, and more interest was felt in getting hold of possible Scriptures than of sifting them. Through the absence of accurate knowledge some temporary mistakes were made, but though a section of the Church may not yet have been satisfied of the apostolicity of certain books, and though doubts may have arisen afterwards in sections of the Church as to the apostolicity of others, yet in no case was it more than a minority of the Church which was slow in receiving, or which came afterwards to doubt the credentials of any of the books now received, and in every case the principle on which a book was accepted, or doubts against it laid aside, was the historical tradition of apostolicity. After the second century no one ever really attempted to put forth new documents as Apostolic and authoritative, or to amend them. The content of Scripture was substantially made up, and henceforward differences were not so much on Scripture as on the interpretation. It is particularly striking that hitherto no Councils, Synods, or Decrees had been connected with the Canon. These had absolutely no influence in making the Canon, but only in registering it after it was made. This is particularly important because of the modern tendency to think the Canon was due to the arbitrary arrangement of Church leaders. The movement for the Canon was inevitable and vital, neither artificial nor superficial. It was due to the great mass of Christian people who from their spiritual life provided testimony to the separate

---

[1] St. Paul "is evidently as sure as any of the Old Testament prophets was ever sure that the message which he delivered was no invention of his own . . . but that he was merely an instrument in the hands of God" (Sanday, *Inspiration*, p. 332).

[2] Revelation: "The strongest language found in the older Scriptures he uses and applies to his own book," Ch. i. 3; x. 7; xxii. 6, 7, 9, etc. (Sanday, *ut supra*, p. 375).

books which led to the collection of a complete Canon. Unconscious at first, the movement was ever tending towards the goal. In the third century a great process of sifting went on. The Church was cautious and conservative, while heretics were free in dealing with books. The fourth century naturally addressed itself to the task of obtaining testimony from all parts of the Church to the New Testament books in use, in order thereby to show clearly what was the authoritative Canon. The greatest writer of this period was Eusebius of Cæsarea, who gives a list of New Testament books in three classes :—

> (a) Class 1.—His New Testament; books accepted: "Homolo-goumena" (ὁμολογούμενα). Hebrews is probably included in Paul's Epistles, and Revelation is accepted "with hesitation."
>
> (b) Class 2.—Books spoken against or disputed: "Antilegomena" (ἀντιλεγόμενα). "But yet read by the majority," viz. James, 2 Peter, 2 and 3 John, Jude.
>
> (c) Class 3.—Books rejected: "Notha" (νόθα). Regarded as spurious. A number like Hermas, Barnabas, etc., and "with hesitation," Revelation.

The rejection of certain books was due to the fact that they were not accepted by the Churches of his day. Soon catalogues of the accepted New Testament appeared, and the Church received into their New Testament all the books historically evinced to them as given by Apostles to Churches as the code of law. We must not mistake the historical evidences of slow circulation to authentication over a widely-extended Church for the evidences of slowness of canonisation by the authority or test of the Church itself.

The Middle Ages accepted implicitly the Canon thus stamped, and notwithstanding the discussion at the Reformation, especially in connection with Luther, the matter rested until the end of the eighteenth century, when in the general movement of criticism the Canon was inevitably included in discussion. Westcott says that the evidence for the authenticity of the New Testament is "more complete, more varied, more continuous than can be brought forward for any other book."[1] And Sanday, speaking of the importance of early Christian literature, says that the Church has not discarded "one single work which after generations . . . have found cause to look back upon with regret."[2] The re-opening of the question to-day and the thorough examination of the historical materials is not likely to alter the New Testament, and certainly cannot deny, or even minimise its significance in the history of Christianity. It may be confidently said that no critical conclusion will alter, even by one book, our New Testament, which has been rightly described as "the fixed magnitude." One thing especially should count in this connection. Westcott says, "No one can read it as a whole without

---

[1] *The Canon of the New Testament*, p. 503.   [2] Sanday, *ut supra*, p. 27.

gaining a conviction of its unity, not less real because it cannot be expressed or transferred."[1]

In studying the history of the Canon four questions must be asked and carefully distinguished :—

1. When was the New Testament Canon completed? That is, when was the last authoritative book given to any Church by an Apostle?

2. When did any one Church acquire a completed Canon? (This is a matter for historical investigation.)

3. When did the completed Canon obtain universal circulation and acceptance?

4. On what ground and evidence did Churches with incomplete New Testament accept the remaining books when they were made known to them?

II.—THE LIMITS OF THE CANON OF HOLY SCRIPTURE

After giving a list of the names and number of the Canonical books the Article refers to " other books," which it is said that the Church reads for instruction and example, but does not use to establish any doctrine. These are all concerned with Old Testament times, and are generally spoken of as the Apocrypha. This term, however, is inaccurate. The word ἀπόκρυφος originally had two meanings : (a) esoteric teaching, and (b) that which shunned the light because it was afraid. But these books were on the contrary (a) read publicly to all, and (b) are not spurious. A better term would be Ecclesiastical Books. They are sometimes called Deutero-Canonical. It is, therefore, important to be quite clear in regard to the distinction between the Canonical and non-Canonical books. The Jewish Old Testament of to-day is identical with our own, and the same fact can be traced back to the first century. A Tract in the Talmud, of second century date, bears witness to this, and in particular the testimony of Josephus is quite clear. He was born A.D. 37, and as a man of learning and information his testimony is of the first importance. The fact that he endeavours to harmonise the Bible of his day with the twenty-two letters of the Hebrew alphabet is an illustration of what he held to be the Jewish Bible.[2] There is no trace of any difference on this point among themselves. Alexandrian Jews would naturally avoid any breach with their Palestinian brethren, and the Prologue to Ecclesiasticus shows what was believed in Egypt among Greek-speaking Jews. Although Philo, A.D. 41, is not so clear, no list of his being available, yet there is not much doubt about his agreement with the rest.

---

[1] *The Canon of the New Testament*, p. 502.
[2] "We have not tens of thousands of books discordant and conflicting, but only twenty-two, containing the record of all time, which have been justly believed. . . . From Artaxerxes [Artaxerxes Longimanus, 465–425] everything . . . is not deemed worthy of like credit because exact succession of prophets has ceased. . . . No one has dared to add, or take from, or alter anything."

H

And yet the " other books " referred to in the Article are found in the Septuagint, not in the Hebrew, and the question at once arises whether they were part of the Canon.   Unfortunately the origin of the Septuagint is obscure both in regard to date and authorship, and, to add to the difficulty, all our present Septuagint MSS. are Christian in origin.   It seems more probable that these books were regarded as an appendix, especially as the Alexandrian and Palestinian Canon agreed.   It is thought by some that the question of the Old Testament Canon was only settled at the Synod of Jamnia, A.D. 90.   But the question then discussed was not so much as to admission as to continuance and possible exclusion. There does not seem to be any proof of an unsettled Canon, but only of action against a Canon already decided.   An open Canon at that date would be altogether against the plain testimony of Josephus.[1]   The witness of the New Testament is clear, even though no list of books is available.   Negatively, we may note that our Lord never charged the Jews with mutilation, or corruption, or addition, but only with making Scripture void, and, positively, it may be noted that although the use of the Septuagint is seen as the familiar version, not one quotation appears from the Apocrypha.   There are reminiscences, but no authoritative quotations.

The following are the main reasons why the distinction made in the Article is maintained :

1. These books of the Apocrypha were never included in the Jewish Canon.

2. They are never quoted in the New Testament.

3. They were never confused by men like Origen and Jerome, who knew Hebrew.

4. They are not found in the earliest extant catalogue, Melito of Sardis, 171.

5. They are not found in the earliest Syriac version, Peschitto.

6. In Justin Martyr's dialogue against Trypho the Jew, no mention is made of any difference between them as to the Canon.

7. In Origen's catalogue the Canonical Old Testament is found, not the Apocrypha.

8. Tertullian gives the books of the Old Testament as twenty-four, which agrees with the Talmudic number.

9. In the fourth century full testimonies are found to this distinction both in East and West, e.g. Athanasius, Cyril of Jerusalem, Epiphanius, Jerome, Hilary of Poictiers.

10. St. Augustine associates the Apocrypha with the Old Testament, and his confusion was pretty certainly due to his ignorance of Hebrew, though even he shows that the Old Testament was regarded as of higher rank.[2]   But it is through his influence that these books are now included in the Roman Catholic Canon.

---

[1] Green, *Canon of the Old Testament*, Ch. VI, especially, p. 78.
[2] *De Civitate Dei*, Bk. XVII, last chapter.

11. In the following centuries, from the sixth to the sixteenth, Augustine's confusion is rejected " by a continuous succession of the more learned Fathers," who follow Jerome and distinguish clearly between the Canonical and the Apocryphal books.[1]

12. Even in the Septuagint they are found as an appendix, and not with the rest of the Old Testament. So that it was not their authority which led to their insertion, but the insertion which led to their being regarded as authoritative.

13. Internal evidence also condemns them. Thus Tobit and Judith have doctrinal, chronological, historical, and geographical errors. The books make no claim to Divine inspiration, and several clearly disown any such feature.

The question is important as between us and the Roman Catholic Church, because by the Council of Trent, 1546, seven of the books were placed in the Old Testament Canon, while in 1692 the books were included in the Canon of Scripture by the Eastern Church. But, as already seen, this action is without any justification from history, or the contents of the books, which contain many clear proofs of mere human origin, and that they are not to be regarded as part of Holy Scripture. This is one of the fundamental points of difference between the Church of England and the Church of Rome on the subject of the Rule of Faith.

And so we return to the statement of the Article, following St. Jerome, that we use the books for information about the period from Malachi to Matthew, and also for guidance in regard to life, but we do not accept them as Divinely authoritative for doctrine.[2] Our usage may be summed up as follows :—

" (a) The *Benedicite* from the Apocrypha is appointed as a Canticle for use at Morning Prayer.

(b) *Lessons* are appointed from the Apocrypha at Morning and Evening Prayer. See the Prayer Book Calendar, October 27th–November 18th, Holy Innocents' Day, and the feasts of St. Luke and All Saints.[3]

(c) Two of the *Offertory Sentences* in the Communion Service are taken from the Book of Tobit.

(d) In the *Homilies* the Apocrypha is very often quoted, and is even spoken of as the Word of God."[4]

III.—THE CHARACTER OF HOLY SCRIPTURE [5]

The Article refers to the Bible as the record or embodiment of a

---

[1] Smith's *Bible Dictionary*, pp. 255–259; see also article, "Canon of Old Testament," by Moller in Murray's *Illustrated Bible Dictionary*.

[2] "Sicut ergo Judith et Tobiæ, et Machabæorum legit quidem Ecclesia, sed eos inter canonicas Scripturas non recipit; sic et hæc duo volumina legat ad ædificationem plebis, non ad auctoritatem ecclesiasticorum dogmatum confirmandam" (Preface to the Books of Solomon).

[3] The Revised Lectionary of 1922 has added many more lessons from the Apocrypha.

[4] Tyrrell Green, *The Thirty-nine Articles and the Age of the Reformation*, p. 52.

[5] Several of the topics of this Article are treated more fully in the author's *The Holy Spirit of God*, Chs. XX, XXVI–XXIX.

Divine revelation which, as such, is meant to be authoritative for life. Revelation is the unfolding of the character of God, the supernatural communication from God to man of truth which the human mind unaided could not discover, and of grace for life which human power alone could not provide. This revelation of the will of God for man may be oral or written, but for our present purpose it is to be understood of a written communication. And it is taught by the Articles, here and elsewhere, that this unfolding is found supremely in Holy Scripture.[1] The possibility of revelation is obvious from the character and power of God, whilst its probability is equally clear from the conception of God as One who having made man, would desire to communicate with him. When, therefore, we accept a Divine revelation as both possible and probable it is not difficult to accept its credibility.

1. The need of such an Authoritative Revelation is universally admitted. Authority is essential in every aspect of life and in every branch of knowledge, and when we apply the question to religion we see that man, even as man, and still more man as a sinner, requires an authoritative revelation to guide him in the way of life. Whatever may be said of the light of nature, it is impossible to doubt the necessity of the further and fuller light of revelation (Psa. xix.; Acts xiv. 17; Rom. i. 17-20, 32; ii. 15; Eph. iii. 9). The only light on such subjects as the character of God, the possibility of deliverance from sin, and the assurance of a future life comes from Divine revelation, while the ignorance and helplessness of man in his natural state called for the light and grace of Divine revelation.

2. The Source of this Authority must necessarily reside in God Himself. He is the Fount of truth and grace, and authority can only be found in the revelation of God. This revelation is personal, both in God as Source and in man as the object, and the personal expression of it was the Lord Jesus Christ.

3. But at this point the question arises, where is this personal revelation embodied or recorded, and how may it become available for man? God is invisible, and in order that a personal Divine revelation may influence human life it must be available somewhere. If God has revealed Himself to man in Christ, it ought to be possible to find and use the revelation. There are only three possible answers to this question.

Some say that human reason is the seat of authority. But while reason is both valuable and necessary as one of the means of distinguishing the claims of authority it is quite another thing to claim for it the seat of authority itself, especially as it is only one of several human faculties, and as it has been affected by sin. Reason is rightly regarded as a channel, but

---

[1] For proofs that Holy Scripture is a Divine revelation references must be made to the usual books on Christian Evidences, where the apologetic aspect of the subject is necessarily treated. Of these perhaps special attention should be given to the chapters in Fishers' *Grounds of Theistic and Christian Belief*, and Henry Roger's *The Supernatural Origin of the Bible*.

not a source. It weighs and appropriates the data offered to it, but does not create them.

Others say that the Church is the seat of authority, but, leaving for the present the full consideration of this question, it may be asked where such a Church is to be found, since the Church in the fullest, truest meaning of the term, " the blessed company of all faithful people," is itself the product of Divine revelation, having come into existence by accepting God's revelation in Christ. Since, then, the Church is thus the result of revelation it is difficult, if not impossible, to think of it as the seat of authority, for this would mean that the Church embodies its Creator.

The only other answer is that given by the Article, that the seat of authority is found in the Word of God recorded in the Bible. This means that Holy Scripture preserves for us God's revelation in the purest available form. Christianity is based on the Person of Christ, and our supreme need is the clearest and completest form of His revelation of Himself. Our great requirement is that the vehicle of transmission, whatever it may be, shall be certain and assuring, and we believe that this certitude is guaranteed in Holy Scripture as in no other way. Written language seems best to serve the Divine purpose, having the marks of durability, catholicity, and purity, and the testimony of the entire community of Christians through the ages corresponds to the teaching of the Article that in Holy Scripture God has revealed Himself. He might have made direct and oral communications to every person, but to this method there are many serious objections. It would have to be repeated as many times as there are persons, and it would so open the way for imposture that there would be no means of detecting those who were guilty of fraud. On the other hand, a written communication, properly accredited and given once for all, has decided advantages in its certainty, permanence, and universal availability.

4. This Divine authority of Holy Scripture as the embodiment of a Divine revelation is based on a belief in the unique inspiration of the writings, for both in the Old Testament and also in the New there are marks and claims of a position in regard to God's will that can only be described as unique (Acts i. 16 ; Heb. iii. 7 ; 2 Tim. iii. 16 ; 2 Pet. i. 21). Whether we describe it as inspiration or not, there is an element in Scripture which makes it stand out from all else in literature and history, and by this we mean a special influence differing both in degree and also in kind from the ordinary spiritual influence of the Holy Spirit. It is a communication of Divine truth for human life, and it is that which makes the Bible, and the New Testament in particular, fundamental for Christianity. It has been well described as " not the first stage of the evolution, but the last phase of the revelationary fact and deed."[1] When the New Testament is compared, or rather contrasted, with the literature of the second century, we are enabled to see this unique activity of the Holy Spirit as the Spirit of inspiration, for the most valuable and beautiful

[1] Forsyth, *The Person and Place of Jesus Christ*, p. 152.

of later works cannot compare with what is found in the New Testament. Writers of various schools testify to this remarkable difference, and from this we argue that the Holy Spirit in the New Testament was the Spirit of inspiration, while later He was the Spirit of illumination. It is thus that the revelation in Scripture gives it its uniqueness. The revelation is the proof of inspiration, and the inspiration in turn guarantees the revelation. Nor is this truth set aside by the emphasis placed in recent years on the "human element" in the Bible. In the details scholars have discerned traces of the idiosyncrasies of various writers, and this is not surprising, for it is patent everywhere. But there is a serious danger in this kind of examination, because a man may so concentrate on details as to miss the meaning and purpose of the whole book. This is perhaps one of the perils of a good deal of modern investigation of the Bible. Inspiration means such an union of the Divine and human elements that the result is guaranteed to us as the thought of God for the life of man. The Holy Spirit so used the faculties of the writers that without any supersession, but working through them, the Divine truth was given to, through, and for man, and when we accept the book as a record of the Divine revelation it will be found that it is not the "human element" that impresses, but the Divine element. God is realised as speaking through its pages and revealing truth to the soul. By all means let us discover all that we can about the "human element," but let us never forget that it is not the human but the Divine element that constitutes the Bible, the Word of God. It is fallacious, and indeed, impossible to attempt to separate and distinguish the Divine and the human elements. The true idea is not the Divine *and* the human, but the Divine *through* the human. When this is realised the Bible speaks with Divine and convincing authority.[1]

The proof of this position may be briefly stated without encroaching unduly on the province of apologetics. The authority and inspiration of Holy Scripture are evident from the objective and subjective phenomena associated with it. The objective history of the Bible, especially in the element of prophecy in the Old Testament, the record of the unique people of Israel, and the picture of Christ, all stamp it as Divine, while

---

[1] For the theory of Inspiration, see the author's *The Holy Spirit of God*, pp. 155–158, and Additional Note. It is sometimes said that the Church of England nowhere lays down any theory of inspiration. This is doubtless true, and the explanation is that the question of inspiration was not a matter of dispute in the sixteenth century. This question is not formally mentioned simply because it is presupposed. Our Church was not then engaged in establishing the authority of Scripture or in basing that authority on Divine inspiration. These things were not questioned, and being universally admitted were taken for granted. What the Church was then doing was asserting that these Divinely inspired Scriptures, "of whose authority was never any doubt in the Church," were the sole and exclusive authority for the consciences of men as the Articles of Faith, or as necessary to salvation. In view of these circumstances it is simply impossible to argue that the inspiration of Scripture was left an open question, when every reference to Scripture shows that the compilers of the Articles based their teaching on the claim that Scripture alone should be regarded as an authority. A suggestion of this is found in the reference in Article XXII, "God's Word Written."

the experiences of the people of God in response to this objective revelation support the contention that it comes from God. The words of Coleridge that the Bible " finds " us more thoroughly than any other book are often quoted, but unless this effect is understood to arise out of the supernatural revelation objectively contained in the Scripture it is, of course, inadequate. Indeed, it has been well pointed out, it is inadequate on other grounds, because the teaching of our Lord does very much more than " find " us, for it creates and transforms the life of everyone that receives it.[1]

Thus, the Bible stands apart from all other books on the threefold ground : (1) that it embodies a supernatural revelation ; (2) that because of this it possesses a unity of structure and purpose ; (3) that it reveals and produces spiritual qualities which can only be explained by direct inspiration. It is sometimes said that the Bible *is* the Word of God, while at other times it is said that the Bible *contains* the Word of God. These are both true, if held together, though either alone is liable to misapprehension. If we only say the Bible *is* the Word of God we are in danger of forgetting that it contains the words of men also, many of which are not true in themselves, though the record that they were spoken is true and reliable. If, on the other hand, we limit our belief to the phrase, the Bible *contains* the Word of God, there is the opposite danger of not knowing which is God's word and which is man's, an entirely impossible position. The Bible *is* the Word of God in the sense that it conveys to us an accurate record of everything God intended man to know and learn in connection with His will. The Bible *contains* the Word of God in the sense that in it is enshrined the Word of God which is revealed to us for our redemption.

Thus, there is no contradiction between these two expressions. From different standpoints they are both true, each balances the other, and both together should be held clearly and firmly. The one thing which can never be removed from the Bible is its character as a continuous, complete, and coherent revelation of the mind and will of God for redemption, and when we accept the revelation embodied in Scripture we are led to understand more thoroughly than ever what Scripture is, its place and power. Faith in the revelation leads to faith in the Scriptures, and the character of the Bible, as expressed in this Article and as used elsewhere in the Church of England, may be summed up in the following statements :

" 1. Assuming a true revelation to be given us by God, could such a revelation be preserved without a pure Scripture ?

[1] "We may say in Coleridge's phrase that we believe the teaching of Jesus, or acknowledge its (or His) authority because it 'finds' us more deeply than anything else; but any Christian will admit that 'find' is an inadequate expression. The teaching of Jesus does not simply find, it evokes or creates the personality by which it is acknowledged. We are born again by the words of eternal life which came from His lips, and it is the new man so born to whom His Word is known in all its power" (Denney, Article, "Authority of Christ," *Dictionary of Christ and the Gospels*).

2. Granting Christ to be the culmination of Divine revelation, what could we know of Jesus without a faithful Scripture ?

3. Assuming the Church to be an institution of Christ, what could we know of the foundation, laws, sacraments, doctrine of the Church without an authoritative Scripture ?

4. Assuming that the Church has a mission to the world, how could the Church carry on the propagation of the gospel and the evangelisation of the world without a trustworthy Scripture ?

5. Assuming the end of salvation to be holiness, and growth in knowledge and grace in the believer, how could spiritual life be perceived, described, and Christian character be built up without an inspired Scripture ? "[1]

IV.—THE SUFFICIENCY OF HOLY SCRIPTURE

1. In stating that Holy Scripture contains everything necessary for salvation the Article emphasises one of the fundamental principles of the Reformation, because the Mediæval Church had taught and practised the view that Scripture was not " sufficient," but had to be supplemented and interpreted by the traditions which the Church possesses and has preserved from the beginning. The question of the place of Scripture was therefore vital in the sixteenth century, and it is not surprising that it is emphasised here and elsewhere with such clearness and force. Without any hesitation or qualification our Church teaches that Holy Scripture contains all that is necessary for " salvation." The Bible is a book of and for redemption. It is not primarily a collection of literature, though it is full of literature, nor is it scientific in character or purpose, though it contains not a little science. It is not even merely a book of history, though it is probably true that the substance of more than half of it is in the form of history. It is a spiritual book intended for man's salvation. This statement can be further interpreted and illustrated by the words of the Ordination Service when men are commissioned to the work of the priesthood :—

" *The Bishop.*—Are you persuaded that the holy Scriptures contain sufficiently all Doctrine required of necessity for eternal salvation, through faith in Jesus Christ ? and are you determined, out of the said Scriptures to instruct the people committed to your charge, and to teach nothing, as required of necessity to eternal salvation, but that which you shall be persuaded may be concluded and proved by the Scripture ?

Answer.—I am so persuaded, and have so determined by God's grace."

2. The reason for this position is that Scripture presents the written record of the revelation of God in Christ in its purest form. Christianity is built on Christ, and our supreme requirement is the clearest and purest form of that revelation. The books of the New Testament being products of the Apostolic age give this, but at a later date it would have been impossible, because the writings would not have come from men in special and unique association with Jesus Christ.

---

[1] Orr, "The Church and the Holy Scriptures." An Address.

(1) Our first reason for regarding Scripture as sufficient is found in the claim of Scripture itself. The Old Testament could not claim finality for itself as a whole because of its gradual growth from separate authors, but we can see throughout the process the claim of the prophets to authority and inspiration (Deut. viii. 15-20; 2 Sam. xxiii. 1, 2; Isa. ix. 8; Jer. ii. 1; Ezek. i. 1), and the New Testament sets its seal retrospectively on the sufficiency and finality of the Old Testament. Thus, our Lord's relation to the Old Testament is seen in His quotations, prefaced by, " It is written "; " Have ye not read ? " He also used the facts of the Old Testament (*e.g.* John v. 39), and He referred to the three divisions of the Old Testament Canon (Luke xxiv. 27-44). Then the Apostles held the same views of the Old Testament, St. Paul referring to the authority of the writings (2 Tim. iii. 16, 17), and St. Peter to the inspiration of the writers (2 Pet. i. 21). This is the uniform view of the Old Testament in the New (Matt. xxii. 29; Acts xvii. 11; Rom. xv. 4). In the same way the New Testament could not claim sufficiency or finality for itself for the same reason of gradual growth, for, of course, Rev. xxii. 18, 19 and John xx. 30, 31 refer to these two books alone. Yet it is impossible to avoid noticing our Lord's emphasis on His words (John xvii. 12; xviii. 9, 37). Then, too, St. Paul makes a claim to inspiration (1 Cor. xiv. 37; 1 Thess. iv. 2-8), and there seems to be a mutual attestation of various authors (Acts i. 1 and Luke i. 1-4; 2 Pet. iii. 15, 16; Luke x. 7 and 1 Tim. v. 18; Cf. Deut. xxv. 4). One passage in particular is very striking as showing signs of portions of Gospel already known, either orally or in writing. In 1 Cor. ix. 9-14 we have the exact order of thought found also in 1 Tim. v. 18. St. Jude is able to speak of the faith " once for all delivered " (ver. 3), while special emphasis is laid upon the finality of God's revelation in His Son in contrast with the fragmentary revelation of older days (Heb. i. 1, 2). We may consider, too, the remarkable significance given by our Lord to the words of Scripture (John x. 34 with Psalm lxxxii. 6; John xv. 25 with Psa. xxxv. 19). Again, the opening of the Epistles conveys the same idea (Gal. i. 1; 2 Cor. i. 1; Col. i. 1; 1 Pet. i. 1; 2 Pet. i. 1; 1 John i. 5), and also the substance of the Epistles (1 Thess. iv. 1, 2; v. 27; 2 Thess. ii. 15; iii. 14). All this shows an implicit claim to sufficiency and finality; indeed, it is assumed in the whole matter and manner of the New Testament. A father is not in the habit of frequently reminding his children of his position and authority; the very nature and tone of his commands will lead them to realise and acknowledge his relationship of authority, and this much more effectually than by means of any verbal assertion.

(2) The testimony of Church history is wholly in the same direction. This position of our Church on the sufficiency of Scripture can be supported by writings extending from the earliest ages of the Church. The value of this testimony lies in the fact that the Fathers in bearing witness to the sufficiency of Holy Scripture constitute one of the strongest

supports of the view held by our Church. And it is hardly too much to say that these authorities are practically unanimous as to the sufficiency of Holy Scripture as our Rule of Faith :—

" The ancient Church did faithfully and continually recur to this pattern, and faithfully recognised the limitation of its function. It is evident how constant is the effect of the scriptural pattern, on which they are mainly occupied in commenting, in moulding and restraining the teaching of Origen and Chrysostom and Augustine. The appeal to Scripture is explicit and constant. These fathers knew that they existed simply to maintain a once-given teaching, and that the justification of any dogma was simply the necessity for guarding the faith, once for all, delivered and recorded. There can be no doubt of their point of view."[1]

It is not without point that at the Council of Chalcedon the Gospels occupied a place in the middle of the assembly.

(3) Then, too, every heresy in the early ages claimed to be based on Holy Scripture, and in particular the Gnostics asserted that they had their own Canon and interpretation.

(4) Further, certain books that were reverenced in the early Church died out, like the Epistle of Barnabas, the Didache, the Epistle of Clement of Rome, and the Shepherd of Hermas.

(5) The ancient Liturgies are saturated with Scripture, and the most severe attacks of opponents were invariably directed against Scripture.

(6) Indeed, the whole record of the Church tells the same story, and if there is one fact plainer than another in Christian history it is that Christ does not fully reveal Himself independently of knowledge and study of the Bible as the Word of God. Whenever Scripture has been neglected the reality of Christ's presence and grace has been obscured, and as often as men have come back to the Bible our Lord has again become real among His people. As a body of divinely authoritative writings the books of the Bible were accepted by the post-Apostolic age, and Church history is full of examples of the use of these writings as the sufficient authority on the matters of which they speak.

(7) The spiritual and practical value of Holy Scripture is another reason for believing in its sufficiency as a Rule of Faith. Although the Bible is comparatively small it is, nevertheless, so full that nothing can be required for the spiritual life that is not found there. Then, too, in spite of all that may be said to the contrary, Scripture is clear in regard to the guidance required for man's spiritual life. It is also remarkable for its definiteness. There is never any real doubt as to its meaning on vital issues, for it contains an answer to every essential question concerning Redemption, Holiness, and Immortality. Such titles as " The Word of God," " The Gospel of Christ," " The Law of the Lord " indicate this sufficiency. Indeed, we may speak of the very existence of

[1] Gore, *The Body of Christ*, pp. 222, 223. Detailed testimonies can be seen in Maclear, *Introduction to the Articles of the Church of England*, p. 104 f., and, as he says, "Such quotations might be greatly multiplied."

the Bible as one of the most convincing proofs of the truth of the Article, for obviously any written account is intended to supply a trustworthy record. Even the accessibility of the Bible can be adduced in support of its sufficiency. It is a book easily obtained, quickly read, and admittedly adequate to every conceivable circumstance, and to the soul that receives it it affords its own convincing proofs. To the soul that receives its message the Bible gives implicit satisfaction and thereby proves its own adequacy.[1]

V.—THE SUPREMACY OF HOLY SCRIPTURE

From the sufficiency the Article naturally proceeds to state the supremacy of Scripture: "So that whatsoever is not read therein, nor may be proved thereby, is not to be required of any man, that it should be believed as an article of the Faith, or be thought requisite or necessary to salvation." This is borne out by the emphasis placed on Scripture in other Articles. Thus, the three Creeds are to be received and believed "because they may be proved by most certain warrants of Holy Scripture." Points of doctrine are constantly based on passages of Scripture (see Articles IX, XIV, XV, XVII, XVIII). The doctrine of the Church is also tested by and made subject to the Word of God (see Articles XIX, XX, XXI). Certain doctrines are condemned because they are repugnant to Holy Scripture (Article XXII). In the Sacramental Articles in addition to actual quotation of the words of Scripture there is a constant appeal to Holy Writ (Article XXVIII). Questions of Church order and discipline are discussed in the light of Scripture (Articles XXXII, XXXIV); and even in questions dealing with the relations of Church and State we find the same principle laid down (Articles XXXVII, XXXIX). Thus eighteen out of the Thirty-nine Articles make definite reference to Holy Scripture, some of them more than once, while there are verbal quotations from and references to "Christ's ordinance and commandment." The Old Testament has an Article to itself. Nothing could well be clearer than this emphasis on the supremacy of Holy Scripture.

If it is asked why this is and must be so, the answer is that which has already been given, because Scripture embodies the revelation of God to the world as the Source of authority. The revelation of the Person of Christ is found in Holy Scripture in its clearest, fullest, and purest form. Since Christ is the Source of our religious knowledge the condition of our knowing Him centuries after His historical appearance is that we must know about Him, and for this perpetuation and transmission we must have an objective body of historical testimony. The supremacy of the Bible is due to the fact that it gives this, for the great outstanding fact of history is the supernatural figure of Christ, who is enshrined for

---

[1] "Unto a Christian man there can be nothing either more necessary or profitable than the knowledge of Holy Scripture, forasmuch as *in it* is contained God's true *word*, setting forth His glory, and also man's duty. And there is no truth or doctrine necessary for our justification and everlasting salvation, but that is or may be drawn out of *that* fountain and well of Truth" (First *Homily*).

us in the written word. We adhere to the Bible ultimately on this ground alone, for it is the presence of Christ in the Bible that gives it its uniqueness as our supreme authority in religion.

This supremacy of the Bible has several applications which call for special consideration.

1. Holy Scripture is supreme over Reason. There is a great tendency to find the seat of authority within man himself, as though the consent of the mind is the foundation of all certitude. Now while reason is both valuable and necessary as one of the means of distinguishing the claims of authority, and also as a recipient of the truth of revelation, it is altogether different to claim for it the seat of authority itself. We are, of course, prepared to insist upon the importance of reason as the only faculty for judging anything, as Butler showed long ago, for no authority can be legitimate which subverts or stultifies reason, and the right of verification is the bounden duty of every man. But if there is such a thing as reality independent of our mind, it is obvious that human consent cannot be the foundation of truth, for certitude is only the result of the acceptance and experience of a reality outside ourselves. To regard reason as autonomous is to deny the existence of objective reality. Reason does not create, it only weighs, and then accepts or rejects what is offered. The true idea of authority is that which is not against reason, but in accordance with it. We therefore hold, following the Article, that the supreme authority is the Divine revelation in Christ embodied in the Bible. We believe that in this way the vehicle of transmission is certain for *litera scripta manet*, and that this could not be so with any mere human faculty. Revelation does not dishonour reason, but honours it by appealing to it with evidence, for to the spiritual, enlightened mind the Scriptures make a constant appeal. Reason has the vital duty to perform of judging of man's need of Divine revelation and then of examining the credentials of revelation. Then when the credentials are examined, reason necessarily yields to the superior authority of Divine revelation and finds in it the principle and law of life. The modern tendency to fix the seat of authority within is liable to the error of pure subjectivity unless it is safeguarded by the consciousness of a true objective element in knowledge. The idea that " objective " and " external " are identical is incorrect, for since the ultimate authority is Christ Himself we can see at once that while Christ is dwelling in us He is not thereby identical with us. He is the Divine revelation mediated through Holy Scripture, and applied by the Holy Spirit at once objective and subjective, external and internal. It is perhaps necessary to repeat that as the Lord Jesus Christ is our supreme authority we accept the Bible because it enshrines His Divine revelation in the best available form. All that we desire is the highest knowledge of Christ, and this we hold to be found in Scripture, and while we constantly emphasise the importance and necessity of reason in its work of testing the proofs of revelation, it is equally essential that reason should yield to those proofs when it has proved them satisfactory.

2. Holy Scripture is also supreme over the Church. This was the fundamental principle laid down at the Reformation, as the whole history testified. Holy Scripture was regarded as the warrant for everything essential in Church life and progress. Indeed, the Church itself is the product of Divine revelation by the acceptance of the Word of God proclaimed through inspired Apostles. The Christian community, whether regarded as universal, or consisting of national Churches, has its rightful place of authority, but it is certainly not co-ordinate with Scripture, as the Articles plainly teach (Articles XX, XXI, XXXIV).[1]

But it is sometimes said that as the Church existed many years before the New Testament was written the Church must necessarily be supreme. This conclusion, however, does not necessarily follow. To be anterior does not of necessity mean to be superior. To be before does not always mean to be above. Besides, it is not quite correct to say that the Apostolic Church had no Bible, because the Old Testament was constantly used and appealed to in Jewish and Gentile Churches, and St. Paul could say, with the simple addition of faith in Christ Jesus, these Old Testament Scriptures were "able to make wise unto salvation" (2 Tim. iii. 15),[2] and we can see the position of the Old Testament from our Lord's appeal to it, and the use made of it in the Apostolic Church (cf. Acts xvii. 11). But quite apart from this the argument that because the Church was before Scripture therefore it is above Scripture calls for further attention. It is quite true that the Church existed before the written word of the New Testament, but first of all there was the spoken word through Christ and His Apostles. On the Day of Pentecost the Word of God was proclaimed, and on the acceptance of that Word the Church came into existence, being formed by the Word of God. Every similar proclamation of the Gospel led to the same results, and communities of Christians came into existence based on the acceptance by faith of a Divine revelation. As long as the Apostles' teaching was available nothing more was required, but as time went on it was necessary to embody the Apostolic message in a permanent form. Thenceforward to all ages the written Word became equivalent to the spoken Word as the seat of authority. The fact is the same throughout; the form alone was changed.[3] Thus,

---

[1] Litton, *Introduction to Dogmatic Theology* (Second Edition), p. 27; Wace, *Principles of the Reformation*, p. 236 ff.

[2] "It is sometimes said, and an important truth lies concealed under the phrase, that the Church existed before the Bible. But a Christian of the earliest days, if you had used such words to him, would have stared at you in undisguised amazement. He would have explained to you that in the Law and the Prophets and the Psalms the Christian possessed all the Scriptures he could want, for they all spoke of Christ" (Turner, *The Journal of Theological Studies*, October 1908, p. 14).

[3] "In the history of the world the unwritten Word of God must of course be before the Church. For what is a Church (in the wider sense of the word) but a group of believers in God's Word? And before the Word is spoken, how can there be believers in it? 'Faith cometh by hearing, and hearing by the Word of God.' Therefore the Word of God must be before faith. It is only of the Bible, or written volume of God's oracles, assuredly not of God's spoken Word, that we assert it to have been brought into existence later than the Church" (Goulburn, *Holy Catholic Church*; quoted in *Four Foundation Truths*, p. 13).

the Apostles were the seat of authority at the first, and they have continued so to this day, the only difference being between their spoken and
written word. The Word created the Church, not the Church the
Word.[1] The same thing is seen to-day in the Mission Field, where a
Church exists in most places through the Word spoken long before the
written Word can be given. The Rule of Faith is the conveyance of a
Divine Authority to man, and the Bible as a Rule of Faith must have
existed in the minds of Christ and His Apostles long before it was or
could be committed to writing. As such, it preceded and conditioned the
origin and life of the Church. The relation of the Church to the Word is,
in the words of Article XX, " a witness and a keeper " ; a witness
to what Scripture is, and a keeper of that Scripture for the people of God.[2]
But this is very different from being the maker of Scripture, for the
Church, as such, is not the author of Holy Writ.[3] Thus, the Word
first spoken and then written is at once the foundation and guarantee of
the Church. The witness of the primitive Christian community is
valuable, because of its nearness to Apostolic times, but if it should be said
that we are therefore bound to receive what the Church says, we reply
that on the one hand we do not receive Scripture on account of the
Roman Catholic Church, and on the other that the Church in the
present consideration is universal, and its work is only ministerial, not
supremely and finally authoritative. But this is simply the position and
work of a witness to an already existing revelation. The function of the
Church is exactly parallel to that of the Jewish Church in relation to the
Old Testament. The Prophets were the messengers and mouthpieces
of Divine revelation and delivered their writings to the Jews, who thereupon preserved them, and thenceforward bore their testimony to the
authority of the Divine revelation embodied therein. In the same way
the Christian Church received the New Testament writings from the
Lord Jesus Christ through His Apostles and Prophets, and now the
function of the Church is to witness to this fact and to keep these writings
for use by Christian people.[4] We therefore apply the touchstone of

---

[1] "Our authority is not the Church of the first century, but the Apostles who were
its authority. The Church does not rest on its inchoate stage (which would poise it
on its apex) but on its eternal foundation—a Christ who, in His apostolic Self-Revelation,
is the same deep Redeemer always" (Forsyth, *The Principle of Authority*, p. 96).

"We have a variety of opinions and sections in the first *Church*, but I am speaking
of the *representative apostles*, and of the New Testament as their register and index. The
Church of the ages was not founded by the Church of the first century, but by the
apostles as the organs of Christ. We are in the apostolic succession rather than in the
ecclesiastic. It is not the first Church that is canonical for us Protestants, but the
apostolic New Testament" (Forsyth, *ut supra*, p. 142; see also pp. 146–155).

[2] See also on Article XX.

[3] "The Church from her dear Master
  Received the gift Divine"—(*Bishop Walsham How*).

[4] "The books of the Bible were given *to* the Church more than *by* it, and they
descended on it rather than rose from it. The Canon of the Bible rose from the Church,
but not its contents. The Bible and the Church were collateral products of the
Gospel" (Forsyth, *The Person and Place of Jesus Christ*, p. 140).

"The New Testament is not the first stage of the evolution, but the last phase of

continuity and ask two questions : Has the Church preserved Scripture aright ? Has it properly interpreted Scripture ? But the former does not involve the latter. There is no desire to detract from the place of the Church as testifying and teaching;[1] on the contrary we are prepared to give every possible weight to the testimony of the Church as of real importance in its proper place, but for every reason we refuse to co-ordinate the Church with Scripture as our authority for the Christian religion.[2] This position of the supremacy of Holy Scripture above the Church is fundamental to the Church of England, and represents one part of what has been called " a line of deep cleavage "[3] between us and Rome.

3. This question of the Bible and the Church has a special application to what is known as Church Tradition. The Church of Rome puts tradition, that is, Church beliefs, customs and usages, on a level with Scripture as the Rule of Faith, and this constitutes a fundamental difference between the two Churches, as Bellarmine, one of the ablest Roman controversialists, allows. While granting that Scripture is a Rule of Faith, according to Rome it is not a complete, but only a partial Rule, and therefore there are some things not found in it. This subject was considered at the Council of Trent in 1546, and the decree was well known to the compilers of this Article. It is as follows :—

" The sacred and holy Œcumenical and General Synod of Trent . . . keeping this always in view that, errors being removed, the purity itself of the Gospel should be preserved in the Church, which (gospel) before promised through the prophets in the Holy Scriptures, our Lord Jesus Christ, the Son of God, first promulgated with His own mouth and then commanded to be preached by His apostles to every creature, as the fountain both of every saving truth and also of the discipline of morals ; and perceiving that this truth and discipline is contained in the written books and in the unwritten traditions which, received by the

---

the revelationary fact and deed. . . . The Creeds are not parallel to the Church, but the Bible is. They are products of the Church. The Bible is not. It is a parallel product of the Spirit who produced the Church. They are two products of one Spirit; the one is not the product of the other. The Bible was not produced by the Church, and yet the Church was there before the Bible. Both were there collaterally from the Spirit" (Forsyth, *op. cit.*, p. 152).

"If He died to make a Church that Church should continue to be made by some permanent thing from Himself, either by a continuous Apostolate supernaturally secured in the *charisma veritatis*, as Rome claims, or by a book which should be the real successor of the Apostles, with a real authority on the vital matters of truth and faith. But we discard the supernatural pope for the supernatural book" (Forsyth, *op. cit.*, p. 171).

[1] "By experience we all know that the first outward motive leading men so to esteem of the Scripture is the authority of God's Church" (Hooker, *Eccl. Pol.*, Bk. III, Ch. VIII, Section 14).

[2] "All communities of Christians agree in this, that the Divine Rule is contained in Holy Scripture. They differ as to the authority of an *Ecclesia Docens*. Necessarily there must be something analogous to the latter, even in the smallest sect. The danger lies in the direction of substituting an *independent* for an *interpretative* authority. Undoubtedly this danger, always insidious, is contemplated here. The intention is not to dispense with an *Ecclesia Docens*, but to indicate its proper function and to insist upon its responsibility for fulfilling the same" (Maclear and Williams, *ut supra*, p. 99).

[3] *Report of the Royal Commission on Discipline*, 1906, Vol. IV, p. 53.

apostles from the mouth of Christ Himself, or from the apostles themselves, the Holy Ghost dictating, have come down even to us, transmitted, as it were, from hand to hand ; (the Synod) following the example of the orthodox Fathers, receives and venerates, with equal affection of piety and reverence, all the books both of the Old and also of the New Testament—seeing that one God is the author of both—as also the said traditions, both those appertaining to faith as well as those appertaining to morals, as having been dictated either by Christ's own word of mouth, or by the Holy Ghost, and preserved by a continuous succession in the Catholic Church."[1]

This position calls for careful consideration. The word " tradition " has a great variety of meanings. (1) Sometimes it refers to a usage in worship (1 Cor. xi. 2); (2) at other times it means a doctrine (Matt. xv. 3; 2 Thess. ii. 15). In the latter case doctrinal traditions may be those that are not found in Holy Scripture or those that are recorded there. No one objects to all tradition, for we constantly use rites and ceremonies which are not found in Holy Scripture, though they are in proper accord with it. What our Church rejects is any doctrinal tradition which has no warrant in Scripture. Thus, all through the ages the doctrines of our Lord's Deity, Incarnation, and Atonement have been handed down, and we accept them. But, on the other hand, there are distinctive doctrines of Rome, such as Transubstantiation, Purgatory, Mariolatry, which we do not accept because we hold that they are not Apostolic, for it is a matter of supreme importance to know whether a tradition is really Apostolic, since only that which can be proved to originate with our Lord and His immediate followers can rightly be regarded as possessing Divine sanction, and there is not the slightest proof that any of the distinctive doctrines of the Church of Rome are derivable from that source.[2]

The words of the Apostle are sometimes used to support this view of the co-ordination of tradition with Scripture : " Hold the traditions which ye have been taught, whether by word, or our epistle " (2 Thess. ii. 15). But the question is not what St. Paul taught in his day, but whether at the present time we can distinguish between oral and written traditions of Christianity. No one questions for a moment that St. Paul's oral instructions were obligatory on his converts, but it is altogether different to believe that the oral tradition claimed to-day by Rome corresponds with this apostolic teaching. The supreme question is whether there are not fundamental Divine truths which are not found in the New Testament. The same thing is true in regard to the Apostle's exhortation to Timothy, to " guard the deposit " (1 Tim. vi. 20 ; 2 Tim. i. 12-14). St. Paul assuredly taught certain doctrines to Timothy by word of mouth, but again the question arises whether there are any

---

[1] *Conc. Trident., Sessio Quarta, Decret. de Canon. Script.*
[2] "Whether the Apostles taught more or otherwise than what is recorded in the Canonical Scriptures, no Church or individual is now in a position to adduce a syllable thereof with certainty" (Litton, *ut supra*, p. 37).

doctrines to be believed to-day which are not contained in the written Word.

But it is sometimes urged that there are certain doctrines which are taught to-day, not because of Scripture, but by reason of Church custom, special reference being made to the observance of the Lord's Day, as to which, it is said that we reverence it because of the tradition of the universal Church. But the argument is more plausible than real, for, in the first place, the principle of one rest day in seven is fundamental in Scripture and is not merely Jewish, while the change from the seventh day to the first is entirely suitable to the circumstances of our Lord's Resurrection. The strongest argument for setting apart one day out of seven for the worship of God is neither Jewish precedent nor Christian practice, for the authority of the Lord's Day is essentially Scriptural, and the usage of the Church is in reality only a witness to an observance which finds its supreme warrant in Holy Scripture. We value all proper appeal to Church tradition, believing that it has its place and power, but this is very different from co-ordinating it with Scripture. The natural tendency in such a case is to reverse the order and to make Scripture subject to tradition, so that while in theory tradition is equal to Scripture in practice it becomes paramount. The moral authority of the universal Church is weighty, and no individual Christian can lightly reject it. But, after all, this is only the work of a witness to an ultimate and original authority, and in making the Bible supreme in things essential we are only doing that which is at once natural and necessary.[1] Tradition is of great value in the interpretation of Scripture, and no one would wish to under-rate its importance.

" It is one thing to use tradition as a help towards arriving at the true sense of Scripture, and quite another thing to make it a source of Christian doctrine."[2]

Tradition is also of value for rites and customs, and all such ecclesiastical matters, so far as they are in harmony with the principles of the Word of God, the Anglican Church heartily accepts.[3] But this is altogether different from regarding Church tradition as our supreme authority in matters of doctrine and practice.

" This risks making the *Ecclesia Docens* independent instead of interpretative, as though Scripture were not the *sole* source of Catholic truth, and as though an Article of the Faith might rest on Church teaching alone as a sufficient basis in itself. Such were a departure from the primitive conception of the authority of Scripture."[4]

---

[1] Bishop Gore said at the Bristol Church Congress, 1903: "The Word of God in the Bible is the only final testing ground of doctrine."
[2] Gibson, *The Thirty-nine Articles*, p. 238.
[3] *See* Article XXXIV; *see* Bishop Kaye's *Tertullian*, pp. 299–304; quoted in Gibson, *ut supra*, pp. 246–248.
[4] Maclear and Williams, *ut supra*, p. 104.

I

This position of the supreme authority of the Bible over tradition is the assertion of the historic basis of Christianity. Sabatier truly says :—

"It is a historic law that every tradition not fixed in writing changes in the process of development."[1]

Bishop Gore shows the truth of this in connection with the history of the Jews, and points out the application of this fallacy to those in authority in the Christian Church. They ought to have been more thoroughly on their guard against anything that would tend to detract from the constant appeal to Scripture as the supreme authority. In regard to the Mediæval Church, Dr. Gore's words are important and significant :—

"The specific appeal to the Scriptures of the New Testament to verify or correct current tendencies is gone. . . . The safeguard has vanished."[2]

There is perhaps nothing more certain in history than the untrustworthiness of tradition without some historic and literary safeguard.[3] It is also curious that in every religion, true or false, men have tended to be wise above that which is written. The people of the book have not been contented with it. Jews, Mohammedans, as well as Roman Catholics, have their traditions, and not seldom these are found to subvert the written authority. Our Lord's words about the Jews in this respect are of special importance, and the threefold charge made in the Gospels is particularly noticeable. The Pharisees first of all held tradition (Mark vii. 3); the result was that they laid aside the Divine command to hold tradition (ver. 8), with the outcome of rejecting God's Word in order to keep their own traditions (ver. 9).

Thus, insecurity of tradition constitutes the supremacy of the Bible the charter of spiritual freedom. It is a great mistake to think that the function of the Church is to settle definitely every question of difficulty as it arises, for no trace can be found of any such view, either in Scripture, or in the Creeds, or in the early Church history. Nothing would have been easier than for the Church to summon a Council and settle all disputes by a majority, but no such action was ever taken; on the contrary, we know that after the Council of Nicæa the struggle went on for many years before the decisions of that Assembly were universally

[1] Sabatier, *The Religions of Authority and the Religion of the Spirit*, p. 40.
[2] Gore, *The Body of Christ*, p. 220.
[3] "Tradition is utterly unsafe. The Roman Catholic doctrine of tradition is the concrete proof of the assertion. Unwritten tradition is always coloured and transformed by the medium through which it passes. An unwritten Gospel would be subject to all the fluctuations of the spiritual life of man and most likely to gravitate downward from the spiritual to the carnal and formal. Institutions may symbolize or embody truth, but without a written standard they always tend to become external means of grace, or sacraments. They are ladders on which we may climb up or down. Without a corrective it is usually down" (Mullins, *Freedom and Authority in Religion*, p. 349).

accepted. The great authority of the first Four General Councils is acknowledged, and their doctrinal standards are our heritage to-day. But even their decisions were accepted only because they commended themselves to the entire Church as in accordance with Divine revelation. It was this subsequent endorsement by the whole Christian world and not the mere decision of a Council which constituted the real test of universality.[1] But while we cannot for a moment co-ordinate tradition with Scripture, we are ready to appeal to the former whenever possible and necessary. The testimony of the primitive Church is invaluable in many respects, but there is a wide difference between the Roman Catholic and Protestant appeals to tradition :—

"Tradition is either an exposition of apostolic doctrine, or an addition to it. If an exposition, how is it to be shown that the Reformation branch of the Church was wrong. If an addition, what becomes of the claim for the apostolicity of all Catholic doctrine ? "[2]

It is this fundamental difference that enables us to see the right and wrong view of appeal to the beliefs and customs of the Church.[3] It is always a satisfaction to obtain the consensus of Church opinion, but its use is only that of historical evidence, and not something which settles the matter apart from proper consideration.

When this is clearly understood it removes all objections to what is called " private judgment." It is easy to introduce confusion by contrasting and opposing Church authority and private judgment. But there is no such contradiction. What is called private judgment is the decision of the whole nature of man, judgment, conscience, and will, in his desire to know and follow the truth. He does not thereby separate himself from, or set himself above the corporate Christian consciousness, so far as he can discover that, but while he welcomes and weighs truth from every side he feels that Scripture is the supreme and final authority for life.[4] Authority is always based on the possession of superior know-

---

[1] *See* on Article XXI.

[2] Forsyth, *The Principle of Authority*, p. 359, Note.

[3] "Romanists appeal to the Church in her organized and official capacity. Protestants appeal to the individuals who compose the Church, and appeal to them, not for their official *sanction*, but for *information* upon a simple question of fact. Romanists appeal to the Church as a judge whose decision is final. Protestants appeal to her 'members as credible witnesses. Romanists appeal to her for an authoritative decision upon a question which they are unable or indisposed to examine for themselves. Protestants appeal to her members for evidence, which they weigh as they would any other evidence. According to the Romish view, the Church collects the evidence, passes upon it, and declares her judgment in the premises, from which judgment there is no appeal. According to the Protestant view, the persons who compose the Church may collect the testimony and perpetuate it from generation to generation, but each individual may and should pass upon it for himself" (McPheeters, "Objections to Apostolic Authorship or Sanction as the Ultimate Test of Canonicity," *Presbyterian and Reformed Review*, Vol. VI, p. 42).

[4] "As a matter of fact, the unlimited right of private judgment is not a fruit or the Reformation but of the Renaissance and of the Revolution with their wild individualism. It is Socinian and rationalist, it is not Protestant. The Reformation certainly made

ledge, and no true Christian can have any objection to the authority that comes from any individual or corporate body which actually possesses more and better information than himself. All that his duty to Christ requires is that the information derived from others should be examined, compared, and tested by Holy Scripture as the supreme and final authority in all matters of faith and practice, and when this is done there will be little or no practical difficulty in arriving at a proper decision.

This position is abundantly justified on every ground. Our Lord Himself appealed to the Scriptures as the touchstone of truth. Our personality has been created in a relationship of direct responsibility to God. The Christian religion teaches beyond all else that the soul is in direct personal relationship to God, while welcoming all possible light through human channels in helping us to decide for ourselves. Then, too, this position has ever been productive of the finest characters and the noblest examples of individual and corporate Christian life. It is also at least noteworthy that all the great systems of religion have their sacred books, as though a book were absolutely necessary to a religion. So that the ultimate court of appeal must be the spiritual, enlightened judgment of the individual Christian with reference to any and every matter of conscience. This is the absolute right of the individual, whether like the Protestant he exercises it continually from the Bible, or whether like the Roman Catholic he exercises it once for all in deciding to submit himself to what he believes to be an infallible guide. But the final decision must be made by the spiritually illuminated Christian consciousness, guided by the Word of God, advised by every possible channel of knowledge available, and led by the Holy Spirit of God.

VI.—THE PRACTICAL USE OF HOLY SCRIPTURE

The use of Holy Scripture as sufficient and supreme in all essential matters can be applied in various ways.

1. We use it against a Rationalism which is not content without demanding a reason for everything. But, as we have already seen, reason is only one faculty, while religion speaks to all. In the light of what has been said about the duty of verification of revelation by reason, it is obvious that to set up reason as supreme would be to insist upon a false or at least an inadequate and partial criterion. Christ is our authority, and to the spiritual enlightened reason Christ makes His constant appeal.

2. We use it against what is called Mysticism, which in various

religion personal, but it did not make it individualist. The Reformation, if it destroyed the hierarchy of the Church, did not destroy the hierarchy of competency, spiritual or intellectual. In a political democracy we speak of one vote, one value; but in the intellectual and spiritual region all opinions are not of equal worth; nor have they all an equal right to attention. What the Reformation said was that the layman with his Bible in his hand had at his side the same Holy Spirit as the minister. Each had the testimony of the Spirit as the supreme religious Expositor of Scripture" (Forsyth, *ut supra*, p. 320).

forms tends to emphasise the inner light as against, or additional to, the written Word. This is a modern danger of real force and seriousness, and it is essential to remember that the Holy Spirit speaks through and according to the Word of God and never contrary to it.[1]

3. We use it against Scepticism. The Bible is a comparatively small book, and yet all that is necessary is found therein. This is a tremendous claim and the question is whether it is justified. The answer is obvious : the Bible has moulded literature, coloured civilisation, affected philosophy, and transformed individuals and races.

4. We use it against an extreme Protestantism or Puritanism. In the sixteenth century men of this type taught that everything is in Scripture, and that nothing else was to be valued in Church life. But the Bible is a book of principles, not of rules, and presupposes natural law, social law, and civic law.[2] As spiritual life is varied it can and must express itself in various ways. So long as individual and Church life is true to the principles of Scripture all outside authority is to be welcomed. Scripture as sufficient and supreme is intended to emphasise things essential as distinct from things beneficial.

5. We use it against Roman Catholicism, which exalts the Church and Church tradition to the place which our Church gives to Holy Scripture. When once the Rule of Faith is settled, all else is really detail. Apart from the Bible as supreme, it is easy to appeal to Church authority and tradition. In the position of the Article, as laid down at the Reformation and maintained ever since, we find the safeguard of purity and the best guarantee of progress because we possess in Scripture the complete requirement of God for Christian faith and life.

[1] See *The Holy Spirit of God*, Ch. XXVIII.   [2] Hooker, *Eccl. Pol.*, Bk. I.

ARTICLE VII

Of the Old Testament.

The Old Testament is not contrary to the New: for both in the Old and New Testament everlasting life is offered to Mankind by Christ, who is the only Mediator between God and Man, being both God and Man. Wherefore they are not to be heard, which feign that the old Fathers did look only for transitory promises. Although the Law given from God by Moses, as touching Ceremonies and Rites, do not bind Christian men, nor the Civil precepts thereof ought of necessity to be received in any commonwealth; yet notwithstanding, no Christian man whatsoever is free from the obedience of the Commandments which are called Moral.

De Veteri Testamento.

Testamentum vetus novo contrarium non est: quandoquidem tam in veteri, quam in novo, per Christum, qui unicus est mediator Dei et hominum, Deus et homo, æterna vita humano generi est proposita. Quare male sentiunt, qui veteres tantum in promissiones temporarias sperasse confingunt. Quanquam lex a Deo data per Mosen, quoad cæremonias et ritus, Christianos non astringat, neque civilia ejus præcepta in aliqua republica necessario recipi debeant, nihilominus tamen ab obedientia mandatorum, quæ Moralia vocantur, nullus quantumvis Christianus est solutus.

IMPORTANT EQUIVALENTS.

Who is the only Mediator	= *qui unicus est Mediator.*
Wherefore they are not to be heard	= *Quare male sentiunt.*[1]
For transitory promises.	= *in promissiones temporarias.*
No Christian man whatsoever	= *nullus quantumvis Christianus.*[2]
Free from obedience.	= *ab obedientia solutus.*

THIS is a corollary to and application of Article VI in regard to the Old Testament and, as such, it constitutes part of the teaching of the Church on the Rule of Faith. In the Forty-two Articles of 1553 there were two Articles, the sixth and the nineteenth, each dealing with aspects of the Old Testament, and in 1563 they were brought together to form this Article because of their kindred topics. The first half of this Article (to the word " promises ") formed the sixth Article of 1553, with the title, *Vetus Testamentum non est rejiciendum* (" The Old Testament is not to be rejected "). But that Article began thus : *Testamentum Vetus, quasi Novo contrarium sit, non est repudiandum, sed retinendum* (" The Old Testament is not to be put away, as though it were contrary to the New ; but to be kept still "). The second half of the present Article formed the nineteenth of 1553, with the title, *Omnes obligantur ad moralia legis præcepta servanda* (" All men are bound to keep the moral commandments of the law "). That Article began thus : *Lex a Deo per*

---

[1] In the XLII, *"Non sunt audiendi,"* and hence the English.
[2] Translated in Article XIX of the XLII, "No man (be he never so perfect a Christian)."

Mosen, licet quo ad Cæremonias et Ritus. But only the first clause of it was incorporated in 1563 to make our seventh Article. The remainder of Article XIX of 1553 was as follows : *Quare illi non sunt audiendi, qui sacras literas tantum infirmis datas esse perhibent, et Spiritum perpetuo jactant, a quo sibi quæ prædicant suggeri asserunt, quanquam cum sacris literis apertissime pugnent* (" Wherefore they are not to be hearkened unto, who affirm that Holy Scripture is given only to the weak, and do boast themselves continually of the Spirit, of whom (they say) they have learned such things as they teach, although the same be most evidently repugnant to the Holy Scripture "). This was probably omitted because the difficulty had ceased by the time of Queen Elizabeth.

The Article is plainly directed against erroneous views rife at the time of the Reformation, and perhaps there are also echoes of similar errors in the early Church. We know the Gnostics held that the Old Testament is opposed to the New. Extreme Protestants in the sixteenth century insisted that the ceremonial law was binding,[1] while from another standpoint the Anabaptists taught that Christians were free from the law.[2] Then, again, there were those who held that internal illumination was sufficient without the written Word.[3] These are referred to in the sentence of Article XIX of 1553, omitted in 1563.

I.—THE ESSENTIAL UNITY OF THE OLD AND NEW TESTAMENTS[4]

1. The Article states that the Old Testament " is not contrary to the New." There is, of course, no question of exact spiritual equality, which has never really been held. The two Testaments are united in all essential features of a progressive revelation without exalting the Old to the spiritual level of the New, and the essential principle is taught by our Lord and His Apostles (Matt. v. 17 f. ; John v. 39).

[1] "De iis, qui vetus Testamentum aut totum rejiciunt, aut totum exigunt. Deinde quomodo priscis temporibus Marcionitarum sordes, Valentinianorum et Manichæorum fluxerunt, et aliæ similes earum multæ fæces, a quibus vetus Testamentum ut absurdum malumque, et cum novo dissidens, repudiabatur, sic multi nostris temporibus inveniuntur, inter quos Anibaptistæ præcipue sunt collocandi, ad quos si quis vetus Testamentum alleget, illud pro abrogato jam et obsoleto penitus habent, omnia quæ in illo posita sunt ad prisca majorum nostrorum tempora referentes. Itaque nihil eorum ad nos statunt pervenire debere. Aliorum autem contrarius est, sed ejusdem impietatis error, qui usque adeo vetus ad Testamentum adhærescunt, ut ad circumcisionem et a Mose quondam institutas ceremonias necessario nos revocent" (*Reformatio Legum, De Hæresibus*, c. 4).
[2] "Here I note only one thing, which is the temerity, ignorance, and blasphemy of certain phantastical heads, which hold that the prophets do write only to the people of the Old Testament, and that their doctrine did pertain only to their time; and would seclude all the Fathers that lived under the law from the hope of eternal salvation. And here is also a note to be gathered against them which utterly reject the Old Testament, as a book nothing necessary to the Christians which live under the Gospel" (Alley's *Poore Man's Librarie*, II, 97; quoted in Hardwick, *On the Articles*, p. 395).
[3] Hardwick, *History of the Articles of Religion*, p. 99 f., and Notes, p. 374.
[4] For the topics of this Article see Litton, *Introduction to Dogmatic Theology* (Second Edition), pp. 44-48.

2. The ground of this unity is stated to be the revelation of Jesus Christ as the Messiah. "Both in the Old and New Testament ever-lasting life is offered to Mankind by Christ, who is the only Mediator between God and Man." It is because Christ is the subject of both Testaments as the Divine Mediator that we can speak of the vital unity between them (Acts x. 43; Rom. iii. 21; Gal. iii. 24).

A careful study of the Old Testament will reveal three lines of spiritual teaching. (a) It is a book of unfulfilled prophecies. From the beginning to the end (Gen. iii. 15 to Mal. iv. 1), while there are prophecies of a temporal and temporary nature which find their fulfilment, the bulk of the announcements refer to the Messiah, and the Old Testament closes with the spirit of expectation. (b) It is also a book of unexplained ceremonies. On almost every page there are references to sacrifices and offerings, and yet there is comparatively little explanation of the meaning of these elements of worship. When the entire organisation of Levitical sacrifices, rites, and ceremonies comes into view the necessity of their explanation becomes more acute, and yet the book closes with little or no real elucidation. (c) It is also a book of unsatisfied longings. From the opening pages to the close there is the frequent expression of desire for God and satisfaction on the part of man. The heart cries out for the Living God and for the blessings God has promised, and though there is great there is no perfect satisfaction, for notwithstanding all the references to the King and the Kingdom, and to God in relation to the spiritual life, as recorded in the Psalms, the book closes in incompleteness (Heb. vii. 19). These are the three threads running through it, and they enable us to understand that the Old Testament is almost entirely con-cerned with the Divine preparation for the redemption of the world; the preparation of the Messiah for the people, and of the people for the Messiah. It is only when we turn to the New Testament that we find the explanation of all this incompleteness. On the very first page we have the keynote, "That it might be fulfilled," and we are soon able to realise that (a) Jesus Christ the Prophet fulfils (in His life) the prophecies; (b) Jesus Christ the Priest explains (in His death) the ceremonies; and (c) Jesus Christ the King satisfies (in His resurrection) the longings. And so "Jesus, my Prophet, Priest, and King" is the key of the lock, the perfect explanation of the Old Testament and the justification of all its spiritual teaching. Thus, the Article is strictly correct in emphasising the unity and pointing to the ground of this oneness between the two Testaments (Luke xxiv. 27).

II.—THE SPIRITUALITY OF THE OLD TESTAMENT

The Article goes on to state that the Old Testament is not concerned with transitory matters alone. "Wherefore they are not to be heard, which feign that the old Fathers did look only for transitory promises." The outlook of the Old Testament is quite evidently concerned with an expectation beyond the present life, and emphasises a reality apart from things visible, and yet in the face of this clear statement it is natural to enquire why the Old Testament lays such emphasis on the present, the visible and the temporal.   The answer may be found in connection with God's purposes with Israel, which were mainly concerned with temporal and national life in preparation for the Divine revelation for the world. Israel was to be God's depository of redemption, and, as such, it was to be expected that the work of preparation would be specially prominent, as the people were trained for their position in relation to other nations and to the whole world.   So that it is not surprising that there is comparatively little in the Old Testament with reference to the future life. But the future life is clearly there ; and, indeed, is involved in the very relation of the Jew to God.   The fact of fellowship between the Israelitish believer and God necessarily implied an everlasting relationship. It never seemed to enter into the consciousness of the godly Jew that this relationship with God was capable of coming to an end.   In spite of all the changes and chances of this mortal life he felt that his union and communion with God would last for ever.   It is this more than anything else that constitutes the real testimony of the Old Testament to a life beyond the grave (Psa. xvi. 11; lxxiii. 24; cf. John viii. 56; Heb. xi.). Our Lord's reference to God as the God of Abraham, Isaac, and Jacob, and therefore the God of the living, not of the dead, indicates at once the fact of the future life and its obscurity in Old Testament times.   To the same effect are the words of the Apostle when literally rendered : " Our Saviour Jesus Christ who . . . hath illuminated life and immortality through the Gospel " (2 Tim. i. 10).[1]

III.—THE TEMPORARY ELEMENTS OF THE OLD TESTAMENT

The Article proceeds to state with great care that notwithstanding this unity and spirituality there are features in the Old Testament that are not of obligation among Christian men to-day.   " The Law given from God by Moses, as touching Ceremonies and Rites, do not bind Christian men, nor the Civil precepts thereof ought of necessity to be received in any commonwealth."   In this statement we have suggested some of the characteristics of the Old Testament which, while necessary and important for the Jews in their relation to God, are no longer of force for the Christian Church.   Although the Article limits its attention to ceremonial and civil laws there is much more in the Old Testament which is now outside the life of Christian people, and the following may perhaps be regarded as a summary of those elements which are purely temporary and not of permanent binding force:

1. The Ceremonial Law.—The whole of the Levitical institutions of priesthood and sacrifice are obviously no longer binding, since they were

---

[1] For a fuller discussion see Salmond, *The Christian Doctrine of Immortality*, and A. B. Davidson, *Old Testament Theology*.

all fulfilled in the Lord Jesus Christ (Col. ii. 17; Heb. IX. 11; x. 1, 11, 12).

2. The Civil Precepts.—The identity of Church and State among the Jews, and the entire arrangement necessary for the preparation of Israel as the medium of God's revelation are all things of the past, and now it is impossible to insist upon the civil precepts being " of necessity received in any commonwealth."

3. The Theocracy.—The direct government by God was intended for Israel's life as the channel of God's religion of redemption, but even with Israel a pure theocracy proved to be too high and spiritual, and a theocratic monarch was introduced. It goes without saying that no such theocracy is possible to-day in connection with the Christian Church, or any Christian nation.

4. The Legal Spirit and Coercive Attitude.—The Old Testament had for its keynote, " Do, and thou shalt live," and we know from the New Testament that the keynote of the Gospel is " Live in order to do." The whole tendency of the Jewish life was works, and a spirit of coercion is implied in " Thou shalt " and " Thou shalt not." All these features are necessarily removed from the spirit of the New Testament, and form part of the temporary elements to which the Article refers. It is note-worthy how strikingly true to modern thought on the Old Testament this emphasis on the temporary features is, and a consideration of it will keep us from the two extremes of regarding the Old Testament as entirely on a level with the New and from the opposite standpoint of dispensing with it altogether. While there are temporary features there are also, as we shall see, other features that are of lasting force and obligation.

IV.—THE PERMANENT ELEMENTS OF THE OLD TESTAMENT

The Article in stating the obligation of the Christian man to the moral law suggests a topic which is much larger than this precise refer-ence, because there are elements in the Old Testament equally perma-nent, and therefore equally binding. It will be worth while to consider these.

1. The Doctrine of God.—This is of permanent value, because it is not superseded by that of the New Testament. We are not to understand the revelation of Scripture concerning God as somewhat like the early and later stages of a science, the latter perhaps contradicting and super-seding the former. But rather should it be considered as the progressive record of one continuous and increasing revelation. Our Lord and His Apostles do not in any way represent the Old Testament view of God as set aside; on the contrary, that doctrine is taken for granted, while it is naturally revised and completed. Even the manner of communication from God in its twofold characteristic of solemnity and sublimity cannot be said to be superseded by the New Testament. It has been rightly said

that the characteristic feature of the Godhead in the Old Testament is Holiness, and that in the New, Love, so that the complete revelation of the character of God is Holy Love.[1] The following special features of the Old Testament doctrine of God should be noted.

(*a*) The Existence of God.—The Semitic idea of God as transcendent, which is found in the Old Testament, is a great safeguard against Pantheism.

(*b*) The Personality of God.—As already noted, there is no need to be afraid of Anthropomorphism, which is the highest conception of Deity possible to us.

(*c*) The Uniqueness of God.—The prophets never tire of emphasising the truth that Jehovah alone is the one true God (Isa. xliv. 8).

(*d*) The Relation of God to man.—In various forms the Old Testament teaches from the beginning to the end that God and man are capable of fellowship, and that as it was originally, so it is the Divine intention consequent upon sin, that man should be restored to this true relation.

(*e*) The Revelation of God to man.—This is a fact in the Old Testament which is at the foundation of everything in the New Testament. Christ takes for granted this prior revelation and builds upon it (Matt. v. 21; Heb. i. 1, 2).

(*f*) The Character of God.—The Old Testament revelation is of God as essentially righteous both in regard to present and future. There will be a judgment based upon this eternal righteousness.

2. The Experience of Holy Men.—It is significant that there is no Psalter in the New Testament, that being almost the only part of the Old Testament writings without a counterpart in the New. Perhaps the reason for this is that the experience of believing people is essentially the same in all ages, implying and involving personal union with God. There is nothing more striking than the Christian use of such Psalms as the 16th, the 23rd, and the 103rd, as expressive of the highest Christian feelings to-day.

3. The Symbolical Teaching.—Although, as we have seen, all the offerings and types found their complete fulfilment in our Lord Jesus Christ, yet their principles abide, and the various characters, institutions, and events have a permanent value for instruction. They are written " for our admonition " (1 Cor. x. 11).

4. The Moral Lessons of History.—The Old Testament stories are not merely beautiful, but true. God is behind them, and the people of Israel were only instruments in carrying out His purpose. It is for this reason that St. Paul emphasises the importance of the Old Testament, as " written for our learning " (Rom. xv. 4).

5. The Moral Law.—This is the specific feature mentioned in the

[1] Hegel, quoted by Edward Caird, *Philosophy of Religion*, Vol. I, p. 185, speaks of Judaism as the religion of sublimity as contrasted with the Greek religion of beauty. Cf. Butcher, Harvard Lectures, I.

Article. "No Christian man whatsoever is free from the obedience of the Commandments which are called Moral." It is sometimes believed that the Reformation led to Antinomianism, but this was emphatically not the case in regard to those who were truly representative of that great movement. The moral law was clearly understood to convince of sin (Rom. iii. 20; iv. 15; v. 20; vii. 7-13). But with equal clearness it was taught that the law could not give judicial standing. It was, to use St. Paul's words, "the schoolmaster" to lead to Christ (Gal. iv. 24). But when the penitent and believing sinner became united to Christ he realised that he was "under law to Christ" (1 Cor. ix. 21), and the Ten Commandments were soon seen to embody and emphasise permanent principles long anterior to Judaism. While, therefore, the law could not justify, the believer fully recognised and accepted the place of the law as part of his attitude of loyal response to Christ (Eph. vi. 1 f.). In this connection the ethics of the Old Testament call for notice, because they are not really utilitarian. They emphasise the absolute majesty of the moral law, and while the Old Testament does not hesitate to indicate the present value of obedience to God, yet it is impossible to say that morality and utility are synonymous and identical terms. Then, too, the Old Testament doctrine of sin contains a principle of permanent validity because it teaches that sin is an offence against God, and not a mere infirmity of nature, or a misfortune, but a positive vice and crime. Consequently the prohibition of sin in plain terms means a great deal, especially as it is always rooted in the eternal principles of righteousness and law

6. The Element of Prophecy.—Whether we think of that part of the Old Testament which is fulfilled, or of the much larger section dealing with the Messiah, the prophetic parts are of vital value and are as capable of inspiring with hope to-day as they ever were.

All this teaches that we must avoid the two extremes: the one of ignoring the Old Testament altogether, the other of regarding it as of equal value with the New Testament. The former was the error of Marcion, who thought he was able to save the New Testament by throwing away the Old, thinking that the Old Testament was morally defective by reason of its severity. But it should always be borne in mind that if God is to be thought of at all as directing history and being the Judge of mankind, righteousness must be predicated of Him, whether in the Old Testament or out of it. The key to the solution of the problem is in the principle of progressive revelation, and every element of moral inferiority in the Old Testament is to be judged by it. While we are not to be guided to-day by many of the examples of the Old Testament, it is equally true that in so far as what was said and done at the time was due to the revelation of God, that revelation was perfect at that time, whatever additional truth came afterwards for newer needs. We have thus to distinguish carefully between the dispensational truth and the permanent truth in the Old Testament; that is, between those elements intended solely for immediate needs and those which are of eternal validity. To put it in another way, it is essential to remember the difference between what is written *to* us and *for* us. All Scripture was written " for our learning," but not all was written to us directly, much of it being addressed to the Jews primarily and often exclusively, and therefore only intended for us to-day by way of application. Thus, the first Commandment is of permanent value and force, but the introductory words, giving the motive for it (Exod. xx. 2) are no longer applicable, except by means of a process of spiritualising. This principle of the progress of doctrine is vital to all true understanding of the Old Testament, for thereby it is at once seen that development does not mean contrariety.[1]

The other error of regarding the Old Testament as equal to the New will be safeguarded by considering the one as supplementary to the other. It is simple truth that the New Testament could not stand alone, and the various doctrines found therein are seen to be the supplement and complement of what is recorded in the Old Testament. In the Old, God is revealed in history; in the New, in connection with individual redemption. In the Old, God's unity is emphasised; in the New, the Divine Trinity. So that there is profound truth in Beaconsfield's striking paradox that Christianity is incomprehensible without Judaism, and the authenticity of the Second Testament depends on its congruity with the First.[2]

V.—THE PROBLEM OF THE OLD TESTAMENT TO-DAY

The term " Old Testament Criticism " is often heard to-day, and it is at once important and inevitable, for no one can use the Bible without being a " critic "; that is, one who exercises his judgment. There is nothing unlawful in criticism; indeed, it is absolutely essential. Another term is also very familiar, " Higher Criticism," and this, too, calls for special attention. As Lower Criticism is concerned with the text of the Bible and involves the study and comparison of manuscripts and versions, so Higher Criticism investigates the origin, structure and contents of Scripture, being concerned with the historical setting and study of the books in the light of the times when they were presumably written. There is, however, a tendency to think that our view of the Old Testament has to be materially different from that of our forefathers, and it is sometimes thought that Higher Criticism is so technical as to be possible only for scholars and that ordinary Christians have nothing else

[1] A valuable pamphlet on this subject is *Progressive Revelation: Its Power on Old Testament Morality* (The Bible League, London).
[2] "It stands to reason, that to describe the ceremonial of Judaism, for example, apart from the cardinal doctrines of Christianity, is like writing a history of the acorn and saying nothing of the oak to which it grows; it stands to reason that the theologian who defines the Christian doctrine of the Atonement without reference to the expiatory features of Mosaism, might as wisely undertake a philosophical biography and ignore the entire story of childhood, and the early display of hereditary tendencies" (Cave, *The Scriptural Doctrine of Sacrifice*, Preface, p. 7).

to do but accept the decisions of scholarship.   But this is not the case, since ordinary Christians are dependent on scholars for two things only : a true text and a true translation, and when these are obtained every Christian has a right and a duty to test all things for himself.   It is admitted by leading scholars themselves that ordinary Christians can decide the outstanding problems from a careful study of the English Bible alone.   It is, therefore, important to understand in general what is involved in the modern critical discussions of the Old Testament.   It is true and fair to say that the simple but all-important issue is the historical trustworthiness of the Old Testament as it has come down to us to-day.

   1. The Critical Problem.—This is both literary and historical.   (a) There are three crucial points in the literary aspect.   (1) The question of documents.—It is generally admitted that the Pentateuch, and to a great extent the rest of the Old Testament, is composed of different strata, but it is quite another question whether the dissection favoured by modern criticism can be proved to be true.   (2) The date of Deuteronomy.— It is allowed on every hand that this is the key to the critical position. Criticism says that it was not written by Moses, but discovered in the time of Josiah (2 Kings xxii.), having been composed perhaps a century or so before.   It is perfectly true that if this critical position is correct the ordinary view collapses.   The book is either substantially Mosaic, or else it is not.   This is a definite and direct issue on which the two schools are absolutely at variance.   (3) The date of those parts of Exodus and Leviticus which are connected with a Tabernacle worship, now tech- nically known as the Priests' Code.   Do these date from the time of Moses or from the age of Ezra ?   These elements are practically inclusive of the vital literary issues.

   (b) There are also three crucial points in the historical aspect.   (1) Are the prophets before the law, or may we still use the old term, " the law and the prophets " ?   (2) Does the Theocracy as depicted in the Pentateuch date from the time of Moses, or was it not an actual fact before the Babylonian Exile ?   (3) Was Israel's religion of Monotheism in its purity a late evolution or an early revelation ?   It will be at once seen that there is a close connection between these two aspects, and it does not seem possible to separate them.   Modern criticism, however, argues that they can be distinguished, while extreme criticism, which is decidedly more logical, says this is impossible.   The difficulty is that extreme criti- cism, as represented by some of the leading scholars like Kuenen and Wellhausen, approaches the Old Testament with purely naturalistic and rationalistic presuppositions, and on the basis of these dissects the docu- ments.   It is difficult to see how conclusions can be accepted when super- natural premisses are denied.   Even moderate criticism is constantly arguing about Israel's religion, based on the literary grounds of dissection. So that it seems impossible to say that the problem is literary and not historical, since on the basis of the literary dissection historical conclusions are drawn. Even admitting to the full literary strata and different authors, this is no argument for placing the earliest documents as late as the ninth century B.C. So that the real problem facing us to-day is the trustworthiness of the Old Testament, both as a historical record and as a spiritual revelation.

2. The Reaction.—There does not seem much doubt that during the last few years the whole question has been reopened, and matters that were thought to be settled beyond all doubt are being discussed as fully as ever. In Germany and in England there are leading scholars who have raised the whole question connected with the critical theory, both in regard to its documents and to its presupposition of evolution as accounting for Israel's religion. Archæology is bearing its testimony in favour of the historical accuracy of the Old Testament, and new schools of criticism are rising in which the whole critical hypothesis is subjected to a severe and destructive criticism. It is being allowed by an increasing number of scholars that the fundamental principles on which the modern criticism of the Old Testament has proceeded are no longer tenable.

3. The Claim of the Old Testament.—Meanwhile, it is important to remind ourselves of the actual facts of the case. The Old Testament, with its thirty-nine books of varied kinds and dates, offers an immense field for study, in which questions arise that cannot possibly be settled without careful critical consideration. But the book, as it now stands, is marked by three elements, each of which must be faced and explained. (a) The Old Testament professes to be the record of a supernatural, continuous revelation to mankind in general, and then to Israel. This, whether right or wrong, is quite obvious, and calls for a proper explanation. The real question is whether the Old Testament view of religion is the result of a Divine revelation or of a human evolution. There is no doubt that the Old Testament itself founds everything on a belief in a Divine intervention with "Thus saith the Lord" as its keynote. (b) The presence of this revelation gives to the book a remarkable unity, which in spite of its variety is patent to all careful readers; indeed, the presence of these two elements of variety and unity is one of the most striking features of the book. Starting from the earliest period of the human race, the Old Testament proceeds through the patriarchal period to the Mosaic age, and the time of the Monarchy, and at each point there is a development and yet a unity of conception which links later books with the former in the one profound thought of an expected Deliverer, the Messiah. (c) The revelation and its unity are proved by the claim to inspiration found in the Old Testament. Whether we think of the earlier portions, or follow the story down through the ages, observing annals, poetry, prophecy, the supreme thought at every point is the presence of an all-pervading power that stamps these books as spiritually vital and ethically efficacious for human life. It is this threefold claim to a Divine revelation, a Divine unity, and a Divine inspiration that

stands out quite obviously in the Old Testament and compels attention and demands explanation.

4. How, then, may ordinary students of the Bible test the various critical hypotheses of the present day ? The following are suggested as some of the ways by which an examination can be made and conclusions derived.

(*a*) A careful consideration of the historical fact of the Jewish nation. Modern criticism compels a complete reconstruction of the national life, as recorded in the Old Testament, and as there is nothing whatever in Jewish history to support this reconstruction the question at issue becomes a very vital one.[1]

(*b*) The evidence of Archæology. Very few can discuss questions of Hebrew philology, but the evidence of archæology is available for, and tangible by all. During the last sixty years a vast number of discoveries have been made in Egypt, Palestine, and Assyria, and not one of these has gone to support the critical position. Not only so, but a number of leading archæologists, formerly critics, have abandoned that view and now oppose it.

(*c*) The necessity of spiritual work. No one doubts the blessing of the Spirit of God on those who hold the conservative view. The seal of the Christian Church is on the books as they are, and the lessons have been brought home to us in their present form, so that any doctrine of the Bible for spiritual men must bear the stamp of the Holy Spirit as the Spirit of Truth. The conservative view has been abundantly blessed in all ages, but it can hardly be said that the critical view has had this seal.

(*d*) The witness of our Lord and His Apostles. This does not mean the invocation of the authority of Christ to close all questions, but simply the adducing of the witness of the Old Testament in support of the contentions of historical scholarship. The witness of Christ and His Apostles is clearly in harmony with the Jewish and the Church's view of the Bible, and the only question between our Lord and His opponents was as to the interpretation of that Scripture, the authority of which both sides accepted.

(*e*) The testimony of spiritual experience. There is that in the Bible which defies dissection and analysis because it transcends all historical and literary severances. The Bible is foremost a spiritual book, brought home to the heart by the Holy Spirit, and it is here that much criticism entirely fails us. Truth requires verification by the spiritual man, and when the Word of God is allowed to be our " critic " (Heb. iv. 12) it soon reveals its true character to the thoughtful, open-minded, spiritual follower of Christ.

---

[1] "The critical hypothesis, as it at present stands, assumes that the Jewish national consciousness was deliberately and successfully falsified, and that what the Jews have always believed to be the beginning of their religious life was really the end of it. I believe that this is both incredible and impossible" (Dean Wace, Paper read at the Victoria Institute, June 1913).

The matter is thus vital and is not merely literary, but historical, theological, and spiritual. This does not mean that there are no difficulties in the old view, but it does imply that the new view does not remove them. Nor is there any real standing-ground between the conservative and rationalistic positions, for if the modern critical view is correct, not only is the conservative position wrong, but Jewish history, Church history, and experience during the centuries, and even the New Testament are all wrong. Is it possible that the tradition of centuries is essentially erroneous ? The deepest interests are also involved, for it is proving impossible to stop short with the Old Testament, and the same scholars are now engaged on a dissection of the New Testament, which tends to give a picture of Jesus Christ our Lord scarcely discernible from a naturalistic and Unitarian position. So that what is required is a threefold criticism : a Lower Criticism, dealing with words and sentences under the guidance of grammar and dictionary; a Higher Criticism, which gets behind the text and endeavours to discover all that is possible of times, circumstances, conditions of various books ; and not least of all what may be called a Highest Criticism, which is based on spiritual sympathy, insight, and experience. This last is often possessed by humble, true-hearted souls, who do not know anything of literary, critical, and historical problems, but who do appreciate the religious and spiritual aspects of the Old Testament, and whose sincere judgment calls for respectful consideration before any merely intellectual conclusions can be regarded as entirely satisfactory. " The musical know what is music."

We may rest perfectly satisfied that no criticism of the Old Testament will ever be accepted by the Christian Church as a whole, which does not fully satisfy the following conditions :—

1. It must admit in all its assumptions, and take fully into consideration, the supernatural element which differentiates the Bible from all other books.

2. It must be in keeping with the enlightened spiritual experience of the saints of God in all ages, and make an effectual appeal to the piety and spiritual perception of those who know by personal experience the power of the Holy Ghost.

3. It must be historically in line with the general tradition of Jewish history and the unique position of the Hebrew nation through the centuries.

4. It must be in unison with that Apostolic conception of the authority and inspiration of the Old Testament, which is so manifest in the New Testament.

5. Above all, it must be in accordance with the universal belief of the Christian Church in our Lord's infallibility as a Teacher, and as " the Word made Flesh."

It is not too much to affirm that when modern Higher Criticism can satisfy these requirements, it will not merely be accepted, but will command the universal, loyal, and even enthusiastic adhesion of all Christians.

K

ARTICLE VIII

Of the Three Creeds.	*De Tribus Symbolis.*
The Three Creeds, *Nicene* Creed, *Athanasius's* Creed, and that which is commonly called the *Apostles'* Creed, ought thoroughly to be received and believed: for they may be proved by most certain warrants of Holy Scripture.	Symbola tria, *Nicænum, Athanasii,* et quod vulgo *Apostolorum* appellatur, omnino recipienda sunt et credenda: nam firmissimis Scripturarum testimoniis probari possunt.

IMPORTANT EQUIVALENTS.

Creeds   = *Symbola.*
Of Holy Scripture = *Scripturarum.*

THIS Article comes from the Forty-two Articles of 1553, and has remained virtually unaltered except that the words *et credenda* " and believed," were added in 1563, the other changes being merely verbal. It is a special application of Article VI in regard to the Rule of Faith, and no doubt it was placed here to show the adherence of the Church of England to the old faith of England.[1] At the same time it expresses a view which is fundamental to the position taken by the Reformers, showing clearly why they received the Creeds, that it was not on the authority of the Church, but because of the truth emphasised in Article VI, the supremacy of Holy Scripture.[2] The language of the *Reformatio Legum Ecclesiasticarum* should also be noted.

" Et quoniam omnia ferme, quæ ad fidem spectant Catholicam, tum quoad beatissimam Trinitatem, tum quoad mysteria nostræ redemptionis, tribus Symbolis, hoc est, Apostolico, Niceno, et Athanasii, breviter continentur ; idcirco ista tria Symbola, ut fidei nostræ compendia quædam, recipimus et amplectimur, quod firmissimis divinarum et canonicarum scripturarum testimoniis facile probari possint."[3]

I.—THE CREEDS

The word " Creed " comes from the Latin *credo*, with which both the Apostles' and the Nicene Creed commence. The Athanasian Creed does not begin in this way because it was not originally a personal confession, but a declaratory and expository statement of the true belief.

1. The Latin equivalent for " Creed " is *Symbolum*, σύμβολον. The

---

[1] Hardwick, *History of the Articles of Religion*, p. 44.
[2] Litton, *Introduction to Dogmatic Theology* (Second Edition), p. 41.
[3] *De Summa Trinitate et Fide Catholica*, c. 5.

suggestion that the word was *symbolé*, συμβολή, meaning a collection, the Creed being the work of the Apostles, one sentence to each man, is manifestly incorrect both etymologically and historically, for *symbolé*, συμβολή, was never used for the Creed. The word almost certainly meant "watchword," or "badge," referring to the oath or password required before an initiation. The best illustration of the term is the Early Church custom of repeating the Creed to the Catechumen orally on the eve of baptism, which was called *Traditio symboli*, and then requiring the repetition of it before the actual baptism, which was called *Redditio symboli*.

2. The number is three, and the order of enumeration is of some interest. The Nicene Creed probably comes first because it was used at Holy Communion; the Athanasian comes next perhaps because it was used daily at Prime; while the Apostles' is mentioned last because connected with ordinary use. And yet in the Articles of 1536 and in the *Reformatio Legum* the order is Apostles', Nicene, Athanasian.

3. The names of the Creeds are, of course, those by which they are usually known, for "as the Apostles' Creed was not composed by the Apostles, and the Nicene Creed is not the Creed of Nicæa, so the Athanasian Creed is not the work of Athanasius."[1] To the same effect are the words of Burnet: "None of them are named with any exactness."[2]

II.—THE ACCEPTANCE OF THE CREEDS

The wording of the Article is important. These confessions of our faith "ought thoroughly to be received and believed." The Latin equivalent of "thoroughly" is *omnino*, "altogether," emphasising very much more than mere intellectual credence. While the form of the Creeds is not strictly Scriptural and Apostolic, the contents are considered to be so, and on this account they call for thoroughness of acceptance. It is important to see from this where the Church of England stands in regard to the fundamental truths expressed in these formularies. Nothing could be clearer than this statement in committing the Church of England to a thorough belief in the verities set forth in the Creeds.

III.—THE GROUND OF ACCEPTANCE OF THE CREEDS

This thorough reception and belief is based upon agreement with Scripture. "For they may be proved by most certain warrants of Holy Scripture." It is not therefore the universality of their usage, though that is important, or their antiquity, which is equally noteworthy, but their Scripturalness. This is the basis of their acceptance in the Church, and the Article thereby subordinates the Creed to the principle laid down in Article VI. Creeds are no exception to this requirement of the sufficiency, supremacy, and finality of Holy Scripture.

[1] Gibson, *The Thirty-nine Articles*, p. 329.   [2] Burnet, *On the Articles*, p. 126.

IV.—THE HISTORY OF THE CREEDS[1]

The original germ would seem to have been a simple confession of faith in our Lord Jesus Christ (Matt. xvi. 16; Acts viii. 37), but the present form of the Creed is evidently an amplification of the baptismal formula (Matt. xxviii. 19, 20). This order of reference to the Persons of the Trinity is the framework of all later Creeds, and we may perhaps see some justification for this method in certain statements of the Apostle Paul (1 Cor. viii. 6; 1 Tim. iii. 16).

1. The Apostles' Creed.—This, though latest in its present form, is the earliest in substance. In origin it is a Western Creed, and the substance of it can be traced back to the Roman Church about the middle of the second century. In the Church of Aquileia, 400, such a Creed was in use, and it is here that the phrase, " He descended into hell," is first found. The present form is Gallican, dating about 750. It would seem that the Creed represents a gradual expansion of the baptismal formula.

2. The Nicene Creed.—The history of this Creed is, of course, associated with the Arian controversy, and at the Nicene Council, 325, the Creed which was taken as the basis of discussion was a document associated with Eusebius of Cæsarea. As the outcome of the discussions this Eusebian Creed became the basis of the Council's statement, with the significant and crucial addition of the word Homoousios, to safeguard the Deity of our Lord against Arianism. In reality a new Creed, founded on that of Cæsarea, was issued by the Council. This ended with the words, " And in the Holy Ghost."

But this literal Nicene Creed is not the one which we now use as Nicene, for certain important enlargements took place after the Nicene Council. Between Nicæa, 325, and Constantinople, 381, controversy became rife in regard to the Deity of the Holy Ghost, and the Creed, as we have it (apart from the *Filioque* clause), seems to have been based upon the local Creed of the Church of Jerusalem. It is first met with in a work of Epiphanius, Bishop of Salamis, 373, or 374, and is also found in some lectures of Cyril of Jerusalem. Dr. Hort has paid special attention to this interesting question, and his conclusion, as now stated, is thus described by a well-known authority, " The proof that he there offered has been accepted by practically all scholars as final, and need never be laboured through at length again."[2] But Bishop Gibson does not accept this view without certain material qualifications.[3]

How this local Creed of Jerusalem became the Creed of the Ecumenical Council of Constantinople is not clearly known, but it is thought

---

[1] It is unnecessary to state in detail the various points and stages of the history of these documents. Three modern works are ample for this purpose. Bishop Gibson, *The Three Creeds* (Oxford Library of Practical Theology); Dr. A. E. Burn, *The Apostles' Creed, The Nicene Creed, The Athanasian Creed* (three volumes, Oxford Church Text Books); C. H. Turner, *The History and Use of Creeds and Anathemas in the Early Centuries of the Church*. Earlier works are Maclear, *Introduction to the Creeds*; Swete, *The Apostles' Creed*; Lias, *The Nicene Creed*. A fuller bibliography is given in Gibson, *ut supra*, p. 316.
[2] C. H. Turner, *ut supra*, p. 41.   [3] Gibson, *ut supra*, pp. 169–174.

that Cyril of Jerusalem, one of the leading Bishops there present, laid his Creed before the Council and it was received as an orthodox document. At any rate, at Chalcedon, in 451, it was received as the Creed of Constantinople, following immediately on the Creed of Nicæa. The addition of the *Filioque* clause is usually associated with the Council of Toledo, 589.[1] Although, therefore, the Creed is not strictly Nicene in the sense that it was drawn up at that Council, yet it may be rightly described by this name because " it contains the great formula which was then inserted in the Creed, and it guards and maintains the faith that was then defined against Arianism.[2] Three matters connected with the English translation are usually noted.

(*a*) " By Whom all things were made."—The original clearly shows that the Son, not the Father, is referred to as the Agent of creation. " Through Whom all things were made " (John i. 3, 8).

(*b*) " The Lord and Giver of Life."—Attempts are sometimes made to express accurately the original idea, which is " The Lord and the Life-giver," referring to the Deity of the Holy Spirit in a way that the present English version cannot do. The new Canadian Prayer Book has a comma after Lord.

(*c*) " One Catholick and Apostolick Church."—It has often been a matter of surprise that there is no English equivalent to the word " Holy," and if, as is often thought, the omission was originally due to a printer's mistake, the question naturally arises why it has never been corrected. There seems no doubt whatever that the word " Holy " ought to be read in order that we may understand the four essential marks of the true Church as " One Holy Catholic and Apostolic."

3. The Athanasian Creed.—The history and authorship of this document are matters of great controversy, because it is neither a Creed, nor does it come from Athanasius as the author. Waterland argues very ably for the authorship of Hilary of Arles, 429, and there does not seem much doubt that it was due to some author of the fifth century. Not many years ago a prevalent view was that it consists of two separate parts which were brought together in the present form of the Creed in the eighth century.[3] But this is now universally rejected, and more recent authorities tend to return to an approximation to Waterland's view, at least of the date. It is thought that while verse 34 excludes Eutychianism, yet because that heresy is not formally condemned the Creed must be before 451. Ommanney argues that it probably arose in South Gaul in the fifth or sixth century. It was clearly influenced by the writings of St. Augustine. Bishop Dowden does not think that any evidence yet produced enables us with confidence to assign the authorship to any known writer, though he is strongly in favour of some time in the fifth century for its date.[4]

[1] But see Burn, *ut supra*.   [2] Gibson, *ut supra*, p. 115.
[3] In Swainson's and Lumby's works on the Creeds.
[4] Bishop Dowden, *Further Studies in the Prayer Book*, pp. 132-134.

Its use as a Creed is peculiar to the Church of England, and was probably due to the desire of our Reformers to emphasise the importance of instruction and the necessity of an intelligent, clear, full faith.   Up to that time the Creed had been used as a Canticle.   Since then it has become definitely a confession of faith.   It should be remembered that it is intended for those who already possess the actual faith.[1]   The first verse refers to the necessity of holding the faith, meaning thereby to retain what we possess, not to obtain what we have not.   It is not, therefore, for the heathen or those outside the Church, but for the Church's own members, to safeguard them against error, to prevent them letting go what they have.   As there is a tendency to deflect from the true standard the Creed is a test, a safeguard, like the plumbline or the spirit-level.   And so it does not pass any judgment on man, or individuals, but is a declaration of the whole counsel of God on the matters concerned. It has two parts, dealing respectively with the Christian doctrine of God and the Christian doctrine of the Person of Christ, emphasising the importance of revelation and redemption.   It means that we must have right thoughts of God and Christ, especially since in Christ alone God is a reality and power in human life.   Mohammedanism separates Him completely from men.   Buddhism loses Him entirely in the world. Paganism of every sort has no contact of God with men, no mediation, no salvation, no grace, no love.   It is, therefore, essential and important to have true ideas of God, and so it is unfair to speak of the Creed as teaching salvation by correct opinions.   Indeed, it refers to our giving account of our own works, though opinion always governs conduct.   The Creed is to be regarded as an amplification of Scripture, and we only receive it because it can be proved thereby.

It is urged that the clauses about condemnation are really no stronger than those found in the New Testament (Mark xvi. 16; John iii. 36; xii. 48), so that what Scripture means the Creed means.   At the same time, it is necessary to distinguish between the acceptance of the doctrines of the Creed and the use of the document itself in public services as a Creed.   There are many who accept the former while thinking the latter inexpedient.   They feel it better to avoid putting on the lips of a general congregation highly technical words and solemn assertions which can only be properly understood in the light of their original purpose and after due interpretation.   It is noteworthy that the Church has never

[1] "These condemnatory expressions are only to be understood to relate to those who, having the means of instruction offered to them, have rejected them, and have stifled their own convictions, holding the truth in unrighteousness, and choosing darkness rather than light: upon such as do thus reject this great article of the Christian doctrine, concerning one God and Three Persons, Father, Son, and Holy Ghost, and that other concerning the Incarnation of Christ, by which God and man was so united as to make one person, together with the other doctrines that follow these, are those anathemas denounced; not so as if it were hereby meant, that every man who does not believe this in every tittle must certainly perish, unless he has been furnished with sufficient means of conviction, and that he has rejected them, and hardened himself against them" (Burnet, *On the Articles*, p. 127).

included anathemas in any formulary of public worship, so that our present use of the Athanasian Creed has been rightly described as " a definite and far-reaching change from what had previously been the case."[1] It is also observable that Bishop Dowden is of opinion that " there is nothing essential to the faith in the retention of the minatory clauses."[2] Further, it is well known that the American Church has omitted the use of this Creed altogether, while the Church of Ireland, though retaining it in its place in the Prayer Book, has, by omission of the rubric, dispensed with its use in public service.[3] The Canadian Church has also made its use optional.

V.—THE USE OF CREEDS

1. The Place of the Creeds in our Church needs brief notice. The Apostles' Creed is used daily at Morning and Evening Prayer, in the Baptismal Services, and in the Visitation of the Sick. The Nicene Creed is used at Holy Communion; and the Athanasian Creed is appointed for thirteen times in the course of the Christian Year, when it is ordered to be used instead of the Apostles' Creed, and is especially associated with the Festivals of Christmas, Easter, Ascension Day, Whitsunday, and Trinity Sunday.

2. The Character of Creeds.—It is usual to distinguish between Creeds in the East and in the West. The East seems to emphasise ideas, while the West lays stress on facts, and although these are two different aspects of the same Christian verity, yet perhaps the usage indicates something of an essential distinction between the two sections of the Christian Church. The East was always primarily philosophical and theological, while the West was mainly practical. It is thought that these features are best seen respectively in the Nicene and Apostles' Creeds, while perhaps it may be added that the Athanasian Creed partakes of both features.[4]

3. The Value of Creeds.—Creeds are useful as conditions of fellowship, tests of orthodoxy, and a subsidiary Rule of Faith.[5] They were almost certainly a necessity when Christianity came in contact with the world of Greek thought, and yet their somewhat abstract and even philosophic statements did not involve any essential change of view from that found in Holy Scripture. The Creeds only state explicitly what is implicit in the New Testament. The change was simply one of emphasis,

---

[1] "The sense of the Spirit-bearing body, as true and real a thing as its more formal decisions, has always, it would seem, been clear in the end against the exaltation of anathemas into an integral and permanent part of the worship of the Christian people" (C. H. Turner, *ut supra*, p. 88).

[2] Dowden, *ut supra*, p. 127.

[3] For various views on the history, meaning, purpose, and liturgical use of the Athanasian Creed, see the valuable works by Dowden and Turner, already mentioned; and *Some Thoughts on the Athanasian Creed*, by Dean Armitage Robinson; and *The Athanasian Creed in the Twentieth Century*, by R. O. P. Taylor.

[4] Westcott, *The Historic Faith*, pp. 191–212.   [5] Litton, *ut supra*, p. 43.

necessitated very largely by heresy. It is often urged that the Creeds are unwarranted when viewed in the light of the simplicity of early Christian teaching, and it is asserted that they represent a corruption through the dogmatic strength of Greek philosophy. But this is not the case.

"The truth is just the reverse. The novel element in the compound was not philosophy, but the Gospel. The steps which led to the formulation of the doctrine of the Trinity are the steps by which the Christian spirit made for itself a home in the existing intellectual environment. However speculative in form, every one of them was due to a practical interest. . . . Putting ourselves back at the point of view of the men who made the decisions, and imagining ourselves faced with like questions, we should have been obliged to answer them in the same way."[1]

In the East the Creeds commenced with the plural, "We believe," while in the West the change was made to the singular, "I believe." It is often said that this expresses a fundamental difference between East and West in the fact that the latter laid greater stress upon individuality, though Dr. Burn believes that this does not represent any such vital difference, but simply the difference between conciliar and baptismal Creeds.[2]

4. The Danger of Creeds.—Of course, any such compendium of Christian truth has its peril, because it is so obviously incomplete. Rules of Faith derived from Scripture were never intended to express every element and aspect of the truth, and Creeds are not so much what we are to believe as what we do believe on the doctrines included. A Creed has been well described as a *norma crediti* rather than a *norma credendi*, a landmark, not a goal, a term of communion rather than a statement of truth in its entirety. When this is understood there need be no hesitation in the use of Creeds.

5. The Place of Creeds.—They are intended to lead up to personal reliance, and the intellectual statement of truth is only a guide to the simple yet perfect trust of the soul in God. This is clearly seen from the Church Catechism, which first of all sets out the Articles of Belief, and then leads up to the further question of personal "Belief in God." This is in strict harmony with the distinctions drawn in the New Testament between believing a fact (1 John v. 1), believing a person's word (John iv. 21), and trusting a person (John iii. 36). The same distinction is found in the Latin: *credo Deum esse ; credo Deo ; credo in Deum.*[3]

Note.—Versions of the Creeds in Greek, Latin, and English will be found in Turner's work, already cited; Harold Browne, *Exposition of the Thirty-nine Articles*, p. 288 ; and Westcott, *The Historic Faith*, p. 187.

---

[1] W. A. Brown, *Christian Theology in Outline*, pp. 143, 145.
[2] *The Apostles' Creed*, p. 4.
[3] For a fine treatment of this essential element see *The God We Trust*, by G. Johnston Ross. A series of lectures on the Apostles' Creed.

III. THE LIFE OF FAITH

ARTICLES IX–XVIII

PERSONAL RELIGION

A. ITS COMMENCEMENT (ARTICLES IX–XIV)

DOCTRINES CONNECTED WITH JUSTIFICATION

9. ORIGINAL OR BIRTH-SIN.

10. FREE-WILL.

11. THE JUSTIFICATION OF MAN.

12. GOOD WORKS.

13. WORKS BEFORE JUSTIFICATION.

14. WORKS OF SUPEREROGATION.

AT this point a long group of Articles commences, extending from IX to XVIII, wholly different from those preceding it, being concerned with personal religion, not with the verities or the Rule of Faith. The one topic is the application of truths to personal life. The group has also a historical significance, for it declares the Anglican position in relation to the great Continental sections of the Reformation movement, the Lutheran or German on the one side, and the Swiss and French on the other, first under Zwingli and then under Calvin. Of the first division the watchword was Justification by Faith; of the second, Predestination and Election. Our position, while insular, was not isolated, because insularity was impossible, since Continental thought necessarily affected ours and compelled us to define our position. This group may therefore be divided into two smaller groups. The first extends from IX to XIV, and is associated with Article XI on Justification. This, which forms a compact group, was of very great importance in the sixteenth century, because the Reformation was beyond all else an assertion of personal religion and of the attitude of the soul to God. The subjects of these Articles were in everyone's mouth, and the Council of Trent had to give as much care to them as we had to our Articles. It is significant that the first Article of the Augsburg Confession on the Holy Trinity was immediately followed by one on Original Sin. On this the Reformation primarily turned. The Reformers said, as Brad-wardine (1290-1349) Archbishop of Canterbury had said three centuries before, that the Roman Church was essentially Pelagian. In regard to purely controversial questions the prominence of this group is perhaps no longer important either inside or outside the Church, for outside the Church the battle is concerned with the first and second groups of Articles on first principles, while inside controversy has shifted to the fourth group on the Church and Sacraments. But while from the purely historical and theological standpoints the importance of this group has either passed away or become considerably less, yet spiritually and pastorally it is of permanent truth and value. The controversy is not and can never be extinct, for the principles are eternal.

The topics and relationships of these Articles should be noted. Articles IX and X deal with the actual condition of man in two respects : his original sin, carrying with it the need of atonement (Article IX); and his freedom of will, emphasising the need of grace (Article X). These are prefatory. Then comes Article XI on Justification, declaring what God does for us and how His work in Christ is received. The three following Articles show our fellow-working with God : Article XII declares our fellow-working as it ought to be, showing the value of works when put in their proper place ; Articles XIII and XIV show the perversion of works, the one seeking to make us independent of God, showing the worthlessness of works when put in the wrong place ; and the other, dealing with a view which was alleged to provide beyond God's requirements, is a link of connection between the two groups, having points of contact with Justification and Sanctification, showing that no Christian can attain to God's requirements. We can, therefore, see the coherence of this first group, though the second, while somewhat looser, is still in a measure coherent. They are not quite so compact, but may be associated with the Christian life, and in particular with Article XVII. Article XV shows that no Christian can fully attain to God's requirements ; Article XVI that none need despair of restoration should he fall ; Article XVI denies the possibility of a hell upon earth, as Article XV denied the possibility of a heaven upon earth ; and then Article XVII is the goal, of which the earlier Articles were the commencement. Article XVIII appropriately closes the group with a warning against that spirit of indifference which holds that true faith does not matter.

ARTICLE IX

Of Original or Birth Sin.

Original sin standeth not in the following of *Adam*, as the *Pelagians* do vainly talk;) but it is the fault and corruption of the nature of every man that naturally is engendered of the offspring of *Adam*: whereby man is very far gone from original righteousness, and is of his own nature inclined to evil, so that the flesh lusteth always contrary to the spirit; and therefore in every person born into this world, it deserveth God's wrath and damnation. And this infection of nature doth remain, yea, in them that are regenerated; whereby the lust of the flesh, called in the Greek *phronema sarkos*, which some do expound the wisdom, some sensuality, some the affection, some the desire, of the flesh, is not subject to the Law of God. And although there is no condemnation for them that believe and are baptized, yet the Apostle doth confess that concupiscence and lust hath of itself the nature of sin.

De Peccato Originali.

Peccatum originis non est, ut fabulantur Pelagiani, in imitatione Adami situm; sed est vitium et depravatio naturæ cujuslibet hominis ex Adamo naturaliter propagati; qua fit, ut ab originali justitia quam longissime distet, ad malum sua natura propendeat, et caro semper adversus spiritum concupiscat; unde in unoquoque nascentium, iram Dei atque damnationem meretur. Manet etiam in renatis hæc naturæ depravatio; qua fit, ut affectus carnis, Græce φρόνημα σαρκὸς, quod alii sapientiam, alii sensum, alii affectum, alii studium carnis interpretantur, legi Dei non subjiciatur. Et quanquam renatis et credentibus nulla propter Christum est condemnatio, peccati tamen in sese rationem habere concupiscentiam fatetur Apostolus.

IMPORTANT EQUIVALENTS.

Of Original (or Birth) Sin	= *De Peccato originali.*
Original sin	= *Peccatum originis.*
As the Pelagians do vainly talk	= *ut fabulantur Pelagiani.*
In the following of Adam	= *in imitatione Adami*[1]
Standeth not	= *non est situm.*
Fault and corruption of the nature	= *vitium et depravatio naturæ.*
Very far gone	= *quam longissime distet.*
In every person born into this world	= *in unoquoque nascentium.*
Regenerated	= *renatis.*
Infection of nature	= *naturæ depravatio.*
The lust of the flesh	= *affectus carnis.*
In them that are regenerated	= *in renatis.*
For them that are baptized	= *renatis.*
[Omitted]	= *propter Christum.*[2]
Concupiscence and lust	= *concupiscentiam.*
The nature of sin	= *peccati rationem.*

THE subject of Original Sin was at the forefront of the Reformation, and as the verbal alterations in the Article are very few it is clear that there was essential unity among the Reformers on this doctrine. It is thought

[1] The genitive of *Adamus, Adami*, m. 2. In Article X the word Adam is Latinised thus: *Adam, Adæ*, m. 1.
[2] For Christ's sake.

by some that the Article, which dates from 1553, is based on the corresponding one in the Confession of Augsburg from the Concordat of 1583.[1] But others think that the resemblance is only slight, and that it indicates little else than the general agreement among all Reformed Confessions.[2] It is also likely, or at least possible, that the Article is so worded as to state the true doctrine on the relation of baptism to original sin.[3]

In 1553, after the words " Pelagians do vainly talk " were *et hodie Anabaptistæ repetunt*, "and the Anabaptists to-day repeat." These words were omitted in 1563, probably because the error was not rife then, and also to leave the reference more general and avoid diverting attention from the Roman aspect. The Latin text is of particular importance in this Article.

" It is a link of connection with the scholastic phraseology of the Middle Ages, which must to some extent be understood by all who desire to appreciate the doctrinal position assumed by our Reformers. For they had been trained in the language, and now stood opposed to the system of the schoolmen."[4]

In addition to the important equivalents noted above the following points should be specially observed :—

(1) In 1553, " former righteousness which he had at creation " was altered in 1563 to the present phrase.

(2) In 1553 the word " baptized " was altered in 1563 to " regenerated."

(3) In 1553 *studium* was altered in 1563 to *studium carnis interpretantur*.

(4) *Nascentium*, " born," means at, not after birth (not *natorum*).

(5) *Renatis et credentibus*, " for them that believe and are baptized."

(6) " And lust," no equivalent in the Latin.

(7) *Peccatum originale* and *Peccatum originis* are equivalent terms.

I.—THE MEANING OF ORIGINAL SIN

Before considering in detail the teaching of the Article it is necessary to enquire into the nature of sin as moral evil. For this purpose we must seek to know what is the essential moral characteristic of man. What is it that constitutes him a moral agent ?

[1] Hardwick, *History of the Articles of Religion*, p. 62; Harold Browne, *Exposition of the Thirty-nine Articles*, p. 237.

[2] Gibson, *The Thirty-nine Articles*, p. 358; Boultbee, *The Theology of the Church of England*, p. 77.

[3] "In labe peccati ex ortu nostro contracta, quam vitium originis appellamus, primum quidem Pelagianorum, deinde etiam Anabaptistarum nobis vitandus et submovendus est error, quorum in eo consensus contra veritatem sacrarum Scripturarum est, quod peccatum originis in Adamo solo hæserit, et non ad posteros transierit, nec ullam afferat naturæ nostræ perversitatem, nisi quod ex Adami delicto propositum sit peccandi noxium exemplum, quod homines ad eandem pravitatem invitat imitandum et usurpandum" (*Reformatio Legum, De Hæresibus*, c. 7).

[4] Boultbee, *ut supra*, p. 76.

It is, first, his conscious relation to law, emphasis being placed on the consciousness, since, of course, all beings are subject to law. But man is sensible that in not acting up to it he is imperfect and guilty. Law applies to inanimate and also to animate natures, and it is in connection with the latter that man's moral attitude to God and his fellows is seen. But in proportion as man's spirit, soul and body form one being, the law has to deal both with inanimate nature and the ordinary animal nature. In regard to man law is concerned with his relation to the Law-giver, for law is the revelation of man being in contact with another and higher Will. This is the simplest form of the idea of God in the heart, and on this basis alone arises the duty of natural religion. Then, too, law concerns man's relations to his fellows and to the world around him, and it follows from this that the perfection of our own nature is blessedness, since there is such a thing as an ideal for our life as that which is dependent on our true relation to God and man. Law is either naturally discerned or supernaturally revealed, and the Apostle Paul insists upon both of these (Rom. i. 18; ii. 15).

But it is necessary to take another step. Men are not only conscious of law, but of responsibility to obey it, and this is the evidence of freedom of will which rests on the double basis of our own consciousness and the collective consciousness of man as seen in language (" you ought "), in institutions (laws), and in all religions.

Yet again, man not only has this consciousness, but also a conscience, a further and higher faculty, perpetually bearing witness to his obligation to use freedom in obedience to the law of his nature, whether declared by nature or revelation. Conscience has been called the " Categorical Imperative " (Kant). But this Imperative must be distinguished in two ways : sometimes it applies to the general principle of doing right; at others to the specific dictates or application of general principles of right and wrong. In determining this the co-ordinate faculties come into play, particularly the reason, and so this sense of duty is capable of indefinite enlargement.

Now these three facts are inherent in man's nature everywhere. They are antecedent to revelation and are recognised without its aid. They may be regarded as the basis of natural religion and ethics, and are the elements of man's normal state, as it ought to be.

But when we pass to man's condition, as it is, we come to the momentous question of moral evil, though here again we are not dependent on revelation for the fact of its existence. Nothing is so prevalent as this fact in all religions, for there is a universal consciousness, exemplified in history, confessed in literature, and experienced in life, that man is out of harmony with the law of his nature. The certainty and consciousness of this in man is a characteristic of him in relation to other animals, for of none else can it be said that they are out of harmony with the law of their nature.

It is striking that testimony is available to show that man acquiesces in the state he finds himself, and thus, original evil is acknowledged by all. When we say *evil* we do not mean in the full sense *sin*, for there are two aspects of evil to be distinguished, even though they cannot be separated. Evil may be either an unconscious or a conscious violation of law. Beings born corrupt, inheriting a certain taint and bias of will are partakers of evil which did not originate with the will. But another form originates with the act of the will itself, and then we have sin in the proper sense. Children are born with an evil nature in a state of what is called depravity, and when reason dawns they know something of right and wrong, though they only have a partial responsibility, but in course of time they become fully responsible for the sin of their own will. Adam was placed under law, and disobedience was sin. When a further law was given under Moses, disobedience again became sin and involved personal guilt, but with those who were not thus brought into contact with the law sin was not imputed or counted as guilt, though its consequences remained. So that evil has a double aspect, physical and personal. Physically, wrong-doing entails inevitable consequences; but, personally, it is not imputed as guilt so long as there is no clear revelation of law. But directly the law is recognised it is imputed. Human nature, as Butler points out, in its essential idea is a balanced constitution, and he shows that through sin every part is impaired. It is this that constitutes what the Article calls Original Sin.

The English word " sin " seems to be allied to the Latin *sons*, meaning " guilty," " sinful," and apparently the origin of the Latin term is " real," from the present participle of εἰμί, " I am." " Language regards the *guilty* man as the man *who it was* " (Curtius).[1] It is also worth while to distinguish between vice, crime, and sin. Vice is wrong-doing against our own nature; crime is wrong-doing against our fellows; sin is wrong-doing against God.

At this point it is necessary to observe the more important words found in Scripture for sin. The most frequent is ἁμαρτία, " error," " missing a mark." Others are παράβασις, " transgression," " crossing a boundary and παράπτωμα, " fall," " to drop by the wayside out of a proper path."

It is essential to distinguish between " sin " and " sins," between the principle and the practice, the root and the fruit. This distinction is seen in Rom. i. 19 to v. 11 (sins) and Rom. v. 12 to viii. 39 (sin), and also in 1 John i. 8, 10; John i. 29 with 1 John iii. 5. Original sin has to do with the former of these, the evil principle, the root within our nature.[2]

The phrase " original sin " is not found in Scripture, and is thought to have been due to St. Augustine in the fifth century. It is not the most accurate phrase to employ, especially because the Article speaks also of " original righteousness," and there cannot be two things " original." Perhaps a better term would be " inborn sinfulness," referring to that

---

[1] See Skeat, *Concise Etymological Dictionary*, s.v.
[2] Article, "Sin," Hastings' *Dictionary of the Bible*; Orr, *Sin as a Problem of To-day*.

principle of evil which has infected human nature by reason of the original connection of the race with Adam in contrast to actual sins which men themselves have committed. It is an endeavour to go behind the sinful acts and to explain the fact that all men possess that wrong element which the Bible calls sin.

The Article makes no reference to original guilt, and this is sometimes said to be due to the fact that guilt is personal, while sin is in the race. But it should not be overlooked that the phrase " original guilt " occurs in Article II, and something like this seems to be the truth of Holy Scripture. Indeed, a modern writer holds that the phrase " original guilt " balances the language of the Ninth Article, and represents much more nearly the dominant idea of the New Testament, and that guilt rather than sin " emphasises the fact that Christ's relation to sin in its social aspect is precisely the same as in its individual manifestations "[1] It is probably more correct to say that both guilt and sin are true, the former being imputed and the other imparted. Certainly the force of Rom. v. 12 (Greek) seems to indicate this. And if it should be said that the imputation of guilt is unreal and impossible, it may be shown to be met by the imputation of righteousness, which on any ground is part of our Lord's redemptive work on our behalf. There is, therefore, no injustice, or even unreality in speaking of original guilt, since it is met and more than met by the provision of Divine righteousness in Christ. If one is true so is the other. Adam's posterity stands just where he stood after the Fall. The " probation " of the race was at an end when its first parent fell. And now Christ, the last Adam, meets and more than meets the sin and guilt of the first Adam (Rom. v. 12-19; 1 Cor. xv. 22).

The Article first defines original sin negatively, as not consisting in copying Adam's example. " Original sin standeth not in the following of Adam."

Then it is defined positively as the defect and corruption of the nature. " But it is the fault and corruption of the nature " (*vitium et depravatio*). This inborn sinfulness is not only deviation, but deliberation; not mere absence of ethical vitality, but the positive presence of disease. As such, it is therefore unnatural in the sense that it was originally no part of human nature.[2]

Thus sin, while primarily a matter of the will, is very much more. No doubt in the strict sense of the word " sin " means " voluntary surrender to evil," but the fact goes very much deeper. It is " the propensity to evil in individuals which seems to be inexplicable from anything falling

---

[1] Simpson, *Fact and Faith*, pp. 107, 101.

[2] A striking testimony to this truth is seen in the words of Lord Morley, quoted by Dr. Simpson in *Fact and Faith* (p. 104), in which that statesman, writing an Introduction to a work of Emerson, criticises the American philosopher because he takes no account of "That horrid burden and impediment on the soul, which the Churches call sin, and which, by whatever name we call it, is a very real catastrophe in the moral nature of man" (p. 105).

within the individual's own life."[1]   It is this that the Article emphasises
as something far deeper than either act or volition.   It is the presence of a
moral disturbance in our nature, and concerns the dispositions and tendencies before the will begins to act.   The tendency is there antecedent
to our consciousness, and can rightly be called sinful.

" By Original Sin then seems to be meant the solicitations of the lower nature
conceived of proleptically as sin, because, as present in the nature of a rational
or moral being, they constitute the potentiality of the sin, which consists in such
a being's yielding to them, despite the consciousness that to do so is wrong."[2]

PELAGIANISM

The Article refers to the Pelagians, and it is essential to know a little
of what Pelagianism means.   During the first four centuries theological
controversies were concerned with the Nature of God and the Person of
Christ, and it was only after these questions were practically settled that
Christian thought became directed to the personal aspects of truth.   All
along, however, the results of the Fall and the necessity of grace had been
emphasised, but it was only in the fifth century that the subject of sin
came into prominence in connection with the heresy of Pelagius.   In
order to emphasise free-will he denied the ruin of the race and the necessity
of grace.   This was not only something novel, it was really opposed to
vital Christianity, and the struggle was soon seen to be one for the very
life of the Gospel.   The fundamental principle of Pelagianism is the
assumption of human ability to do all that righteousness requires, and thus
to provide not only its own salvation, but even its own moral and spiritual
perfection.[3]   From this general position the following results of the
teaching of Pelagius were soon seen :—

(1) Adam was created mortal and would have died if he had not
sinned.   Contrast " lest ye die " (Gen. ii. 17 ; iii. 3).

(2) The sin of Adam hurt only himself.

(3) Infants are, therefore, just as Adam was before his fall.

(4) Man is able to keep God's commandments if he will.

(5) And so, all men may be sinless if they choose, and many saints
even before Christ actually lived free from sin.

Thus, Pelagius denied the whole doctrine of inborn sinfulness, and
with it the belief that man needed supernatural help for the purpose of
obeying the Divine commands.   The tendency of Pelagianism was twofold : (a) to make sin a matter of isolated acts, and therefore entirely
separated from what preceded and followed.   But it is impossible to
ignore the continuity of life and to reduce man's nature to a number of
disconnected voluntary acts.   It is obvious that if sin is nothing more than

[1] Webb, *Problems in the Relations of God and Man*, p. 118.
[2] Webb, *ut supra*, p. 127.
[3] "This is the core of the whole theory; and all the other postulates not only depend
upon it, but arise out of it.   Both chronologically and logically this is the root of the
system" (Warfield, *Two Studies in the History of Doctrine*, p. 6).

the assertion of the will and the will remains intact after each act, the individual act of an individual man cannot possibly affect the acts of men as yet unborn.[1] (*b*) To disparage the need of Divine grace as a help to man's weakness through sin. It has been well described as the anthropological side of Arianism in separating man from God.

Although Pelagianism did not issue in any schism, and was perhaps a serious tendency rather than formally a distinct heresy, yet its consequences were absolutely vital to true Christianity.

" It is simply the Christianity of human nature, or that reconstruction of the Gospel scheme which approves itself to natural reason and superficial worldly observation ; hence its constant reappearance in the Church."[2]

It is true that the Pelagians spoke of grace, but they did not mean by it that supernatural provision in Christ which is intended to meet human sin. The universality of sin was, as our Article suggests, accounted for by Adam's example and the power of habit, and no corruption of nature even by the growth of habit was allowed.

The teaching of Pelagianism found its antagonist and conqueror in St. Augustine, for when this novel explanation of man's nature and needs was set forth, it compelled a reconsideration of the entire teaching of Christianity as to human nature and the work of our Lord Jesus Christ.[3]

ROMAN CATHOLIC DOCTRINE

Notwithstanding the efforts of St. Augustine, Pelagianism continued in the form of semi-Pelagianism, and seriously affected the thought of the Middle Ages, and the result was the full Roman Catholic doctrine seen in the sixteenth century. It was taught that original righteousness was not connatural with man, but a superadded gift which, when removed, leaves no detriment behind. The result was that original sin was regarded

---

[1] "Our life is all of a piece, and the most seemingly isolated actions have both their antecedents and their consequents. The will is not a mere form of choice, which remains unaffected by the actual choices which a man makes; it *is* affected by them; it gains contents, character, we might almost say nature, from them. If the atomic theory of sin were true—that it consisted only in separate actions—there could be no such thing in man as moral character, either bad or good; for such character is produced by the abiding and cumulative effect of precisely such actions" (Denney, *Studies in Theology*, p. 81).

Warfield (*ut supra*, p. 10) quotes from Matheson in illumination of the essential nature of Pelagianism:

"Dr. Matheson finely says (*Expositor*, I–IX, 21)—'There is the same difference between the Christian and Pagan idea of prayer as there is between the Christian and Pagan idea of sin. Paganism knows nothing of sin, it knows only sins: it has no conception of the principle of evil, it comprehends only a succession of sinful acts.' This is Pelagianism too."

[2] Litton, *Introduction to Dogmatic Theology* (Second Edition), p. 153.

[3] For the external history of the Pelagian controversy and of St. Augustine's part in it, see Warfield, *ut supra*, pp. 13–139; Bethune Baker, *Early History of Christian Doctrine* Ch. XVII; Bright, *Anti-Pelagian Treatises*.

L

as the loss of this original righteousness, and the effects of the Fall were simply corporeal, the difference being between a ship in a calm and the same ship in a storm through no fault of the ship. The Council of Trent differs from us in asserting that in Baptism all is removed which is sin, and that though concupiscence remains it is not sin, but is called so because it proceeds from and leads to sin.

REFORMATION DOCTRINE

This Roman doctrine with all its practical consequences led the Reformers to make definite and strong counter-statements. The Roman Catholic doctrine of " mere nature " was held to be a figment and inconceivable because against experience. Original righteousness was therefore held to be a change involving a corruption of nature. Deprivation must include " depravation." In opposition to Rome, we add that concupiscence is " of the nature of sin," meaning, as the Article teaches, an infection of nature which is essentially sinful. It has been well remarked, " How the Council could define a thing which is both the effect and the cause of sin not to be in itself sin, or sinful, is not easy to perceive."[1] Further, the question of this concupiscence in the unbaptised was not faced by the Council, which was " prudently silent on this point; for it is evident that a thing which is not sin in the baptised, and yet is common to them and the unbaptised, cannot be sin even in the latter."[2] It is well to remember that the New Testament deals with sin as a principle before it deals with sins as the aggregation of transgressions or omissions. Following the New Testament in this respect, the Reformers mainly emphasised the *depravatio* and its source.

The fact is that the Roman Catholic doctrine grew from Pelagianism and was essentially Pelagian in its features. There is no power in nature to enable man to do good, and his greatest need is the grace of God.

II.—THE EXTENT OF ORIGINAL SIN

" Of every man that naturally is ingendered of the offspring of Adam." This statement of the universality of sin has two implications of great importance connected with the word " naturally," for thereby Christ is excluded because He was ingendered, but not naturally, and the mother of our Lord is included because she was naturally ingendered.[3]

The Article clearly associates the inborn sinfulness of man to-day with the first transgression. There was something in Adam which rendered sin possible and which was influenced by an appeal from without. Adam had the liability to sin, but not the tendency. He was innocent, but not in the strict sense virtuous, and somehow or other the effect of sin upon his nature led to its propagation among his descendants.

When we seek to understand the cause of all this we naturally think

---

[1] Litton, *ut supra*, p. 164, Note 5.   [2] Litton, *ut supra*, p. 164.
[3] Litton, *ut supra*, pp. 149-151.

of the historic connection of man to-day with the first man, the head of the race, for inborn sinfulness in the individual is a testimony to the racial unity of mankind.　The Fall is a fact, account for it how we may, a case of arrested development, and the causal connection of sinfulness to-day with the primeval sin is clear, even though we may not know exactly what was the nature of the latter.　There are three elements in human life that together account for sin; heredity, environment, and freedom, and it is impossible to overlook any one of them.　Those who endeavour to explain sin merely as a matter of environment and of freedom fail at the vital point, which seems to imply hereditary tendencies.　There is still an inscrutable fact which compels attention and calls for explanation. There seems to be no doubt that St. Paul in his great passage in Rom. v. 12-21 derives inborn sinfulness from the Fall as recorded in the story in Genesis, and argues that the sin of Adam has affected all mankind with an inherited tendency to evil.　It is impossible to overlook the significance and vital importance of this passage, and no exegesis worthy of the name can avoid the implication of the Apostle's teaching that " by one man sin entered into the world."[1]　Nor is the force of this really affected by any theory of the precise character of the story in Genesis, for it is essential to distinguish between the fact of the Fall and its literary form.　Even though we may regard the story as pictorial, yet, nevertheless, figures of speech embody and even intensify the facts which they symbolise.[2]　To the same effect is the Apostle's teaching in 1 Corinthians, in which the twofold connection of Adam and Christ with humanity is clearly pointed out.　" As in Adam all die, even so in Christ shall all be made alive " (1 Cor. xv. 22).[3]

The Pelagian view of sin has found several modern advocates who, speaking of the Old Testament, say that there is no evidence that any connection between human sinfulness and Adam's transgression had as yet occurred at all to the human mind.[4]　But it has been well pointed out that the Old Testament bears ample proof of the universality of human sinfulness, e.g. Gen. vi. 12; Psa. xiv. 1; li. 5; Job xiv. 4; xv. 14; xxv. 4, and the belief in human descent from Adam who was made without sin and afterwards became sinful " at least suggests connection between the common descent and the common sinfulness of man as cause and effect."　Further, it has been shown that we are compelled to attempt to discover the sources of St. Paul's teaching, and if we regard these as arising outside the Old Testament it only puts the problem further back,

---

[1] "If you wish to know whether a man is a theologian, turn to his Greek Testament, and if it opens of its own accord to the fifth chapter of Romans, and you find the page worn and brown, you may safely set him down as a devotee of the sacred science" (Stearns, Present Day Theology, p. 321).

[2] Martensen, Dogmatics, p. 155; Sanday and Headlam, Romans, p. 146.

[3] Modern criticism admits that with the abandonment of the historical character of Genesis iii. we are left with "no account in the Bible of the origin of sin, thus excluding the subject from a strictly Biblical theology" (Orchard, Modern Theories of Sin, p. 24).

[4] So Tennant, Sources of the Doctrine of the Fall and Original Sin, and Origin and Propagation of Sin.

and compels the enquiry as to whence these writers who influenced St. Paul derived their teaching.[1] If, moreover, it be said that the doctrine of the Fall, found in Genesis and again in the teaching of St. Paul, is not found elsewhere in the Old Testament, the answer is that " the whole tenor of the Scriptural representation of man " points in the direction of sinfulness as due to its entrance at the beginning of the race, for " at no point in Scripture history does man appear as standing in right or normal relation with God."[2] So that the only conclusion that seems reasonable and possible is that " if a Fall were not narrated in the opening chapters of Genesis we should still have to postulate something of the kind to account for the Bible's own representation of the state of man."[3]

III.—THE RESULT OF ORIGINAL SIN

" Whereby man is very far gone from original righteousness, and is of his own nature inclined to evil, so that the flesh lusteth always contrary to the spirit."

The first effect of inborn sinfulness is stated negatively in the form of deprivation (*privatio*) ; " man is very far gone from original righteousness." The Latin equivalent is particularly noteworthy ; *quam longissime;* that is, " as far as possible," meaning thereby as far as he can, consistent with essential human nature. This is in entire harmony with the Scripture record of man's condition (Gen. vi. 5 ; viii. 21 ; Jer. xvii. 9 ; Rom. vii. 18 ; viii. 7). It is at this point that we may understand the meaning of St. Paul's words : " dead in trespasses and sins " (Eph. ii. 1). It seems impossible to limit this statement to the result of voluntary action, it must apply to something far deeper. The word " dead " when used metaphorically in the moral realm refers, of course, to moral inability, not moral insensibility. It means that man has been so thoroughly deprived of moral and spiritual power that he is incapable of doing the will of God.

" The doctrine of spiritual inability, as consequent upon the corruption of man's nature by sin, remains and will always remain to represent the great truth that there is *one* thing which man cannot do *alone*. He cannot bring his state into harmony with his nature."[4]

Then the positive aspect of inborn sinfulness is stated in the Article :
" Is of his own nature inclined to evil, so that the flesh lusteth always

---

[1] Eck, *Sin*, p. 14, Note.   [2] Orr, *God's Image in Man*, p. 198.
[3] Orr, *ut supra*, p. 201.
[4] Denney, *Studies in Theology*, p. 85 :
"It is a mistake, in all probability, in discussing this subject, to enter into metaphysical considerations at all; the question of man's inability to any spiritual good accompanying salvation is a question as to matter of fact, and is to be answered ultimately by an appeal to experience. When a man has been discovered, who has been able, *without Christ*, to reconcile himself to God, and to obtain dominion over the world and over sin, *then* the doctrine of inability, or of the bondage due to sin, may be denied; *then*, but *not till then*" (Denney, *ut supra*, p. 85).

contrary to the spirit." This is more than deprivation, for it implies the actual existence of an evil principle (*depravatio*). There is a constant conflict of flesh and spirit with an unholy dominance of the former. It is also noteworthy that this is said to be so " always." It is in entire harmony with this doctrinal statement that the devotional language of our Prayer Book has such phrases as, " There is no health in us "; " From whom all holy desires . . . do proceed "; " We have no power of ourselves to help ourselves "; " Can do no good thing without Thee." It is important to notice that in the Eastern Church the main emphasis was upon the aspect of deprivation (*privatio*), while in the West the emphasis was invariably upon the depravity (*depravatio*).

This necessitates a careful consideration of the phrases " total depravity " and " total corruption," because there is not a little confusion in regard to them. It is a case where usage fixes the meaning, because " total depravity " is not to be regarded as identical with " total corruption." The distinction between the two has well been stated, that " total depravity " means the condition of the nature in which the will refuses to obey the conscience in *everything*, while " total corruption " is the condition in which the will refuses to obey the conscience in *anything* and chooses evil in everything. It expresses the *extent*, not the *degree* of man's corruption. Thus, " total depravity " does not mean the absolute loss of every vestige of good, but that evil has affected every part of the nature and that nothing has remained untouched. The illustration has been used of a watch which may be of gold, and yet because it does not keep time it is of no use as a watch, notwithstanding the fact that it is made of gold. Or a cup of water with a few drops of poison is poisonous throughout, but not as poisonous as it could be. In like manner, " total depravity " does not for a moment mean that man has lost every vestige and trace of the Divine image in which he was made (Gen. ix. 6; 1 Cor. xi. 7; Jas. iii. 9). But it does mean that sin has so affected his nature that he cannot do anything that is good without the grace of God.[1]

So that it is altogether inadequate to speak of sin as merely human deprivation of God. The Biblical idea is much greater and deeper, involving separation from God though the separation is not the sin itself, but one of its consequences. Sin is defiance, revolt, and implies a deliberate, voluntary breaking away from the Divine will and a violation of

---

[1] "What it means is not that every individual is as bad as he can be, a statement so transparently absurd that it should hardly have been attributed to any one, but that the depravity which sin has produced in human nature extends to the whole of it. There is no part of man's nature which is unaffected by it. Man's nature is all of a piece, and that which affects it at all affects it altogether. When the conscience is violated by disobedience to the will of God, the moral understanding is darkened, and the will is enfeebled. We are not constructed in water-tight compartments, one of which might be ruined while the others remain intact; what touches us for harm, with a corrupting, depraving touch, at a single point, has effects throughout our nature none the less real that they may be for a time beneath consciousness" (Denney, *ut supra*, p. 83).

the Divine order. " Sin is lawlessness " (1 John iii. 4). Thus, sin at its deepest is the rejection of God and disobedience to His will. This involves a distortion of man's life, nature, and relationship with God, involving inability to do good and responsibility for what is evil. Sin is, therefore, much more than something merely negative and privative. Just as pain is a positive experience and not the mere absence of pleasure, so sin is both negative as the refusal to will what is good, and positive as implying the attitude of the will towards unrighteousness.

This view of sin is in harmony with universal experience. It is a fact to be accounted for. Man was created innocent, with no imperfection or flaw in the material, and it was God's purpose that he should develop from an innocent into a virtuous and perfect man. Modern science, not being concerned with moral realities, is unable to recognise anything abnormal in human development, and speaks only of the process of evolution, but the Bible and the Christian Church assume a very definite interruption of the process of development. Man's self-will has been exercised in opposition to the will of his Creator, and this constitutes the Fall, the marring of God's creative work and the thwarting of His Divine purpose. No one can say that the evolution of the human race has been normal in the moral sphere, for while on every other hand the universe indicates the presence of order and harmony, in human life there is just the opposite of disorder, lawlessness, and discord. It is, therefore, impossible to avoid connecting human sin to-day with the sin of our progenitors, for otherwise God would be made the author of evil. There is nothing more certain in the realm of physical science than the order of nature, and yet there is nothing more certain in the realm of morals than the presence of disobedience to law. Everything, therefore, in the Bible, in history, and experience testifies to the fact that man is not one who is merely imperfect and gradually making progress towards a state to which he has not yet attained, but that he has fallen from a primeval condition of innocence by reason of his self-will.

IV.—THE CONDEMNATION OF ORIGINAL SIN

" And therefore in every person born into this world, it deserveth God's wrath and damnation."

The wording of the English Article is very significant in its clear distinction between person and nature, between the sinner and his sin. " Every person born . . . it deserveth." This is sometimes charged with being philosophically incorrect, but it is certainly true spiritually, for while everyone is born into this world with the evil principle within derived and inherited, it is only as the individual asserts himself and does what is wrong that he is personally subject to the Divine condemnation.

" Is it not, in fact, the nature and not the person that is regarded in all such statements ? Sin may be considered abstractedly from the person in whom it resides : in its own nature it is ἀμαρτία, or a missing of the mark, and ἀνομία' or contrariety to the Divine Law. In whomsoever, therefore, it is found, even as a latent potentiality, it must *in itself* be an object of God's displeasure ; but it does not follow that the person must be so, still less that the sentence on sin will in such a case be actually inflicted. The *fomes*, or tendency, which if the infant lives will assuredly give birth to actual sin, cannot in God's sight be a thing indifferent ; but as it is only an objective guiltiness (to which the will has not consented, because the subject is incapable of will), it may be covered from God's sight by an objective atonement (not appropriated by an act of will) ; so that the infant himself, if he dies as an infant, is not, and never has been, an object of God's wrath."[1]

The word " deserveth " is also important, expressing the Divine justice and emphasising what sin is entitled to receive. It does not for a moment say that every case of inborn sinfulness actually receives the Divine judgment, but only refers to its essential nature in the sight of God. It is a profound truth that while Scripture does not hesitate to emphasise in the strongest way the actual fact of inborn sinfulness and its essential blameworthiness in the sight of God, yet on the other hand, " in no case does original sin, considered in and by itself, carry with it the penalty of eternal condemnation."[2]

Some little explanation of the phrase, " God's wrath and damnation " seems necessary. The New Testament statement, " the wrath of God " (ὀργὴ θεοῦ), always means His judicial displeasure against sin. There is, of course, nothing personal, arbitrary, and vindictive, but always and only that which is righteous in the Divine attitude towards that which is wrong. Sin, to use a Bible phrase, is " the abominable thing which God hates " (Jeremiah xliv. 4).

This reference to the Divine condemnation of inborn sinfulness is a definite reminder, as we have already seen, of man's conscious relations to law, and of his conscious responsibility to obey that law because of his possession of a conscience. Sin is the abuse of human freedom, and there is nothing more fundamental in the universe than the eternal distinction between right and wrong as it appears and appeals to man. No view of evolution can ever be allowed to destroy this basis of moral life. This at once introduces the question of guilt, for Scripture invariably associates sin and guilt. Whether we think of inborn sinfulness or personal transgression, sin is always regarded in Scripture as absolutely inexcusable and involving man in Divine condemnation.[3] By guilt is to be understood responsibility for sin and as a consequence the danger of God's righteous displeasure. Of course, as there are degrees of guilt in sin, so there will be degrees of punishment, but we are now concerned with the fact that

---

[1] Litton, *ut supra*, p. 162.   [2] Litton, *ut supra*, p. 163.

[3] "Sin in its broadest and most comprehensive sense is inexcusable, incurs the wrath of God, entails guilt and punishment, and therefore, whether original or actual, is equally ethical, equally personal. There is no warrant in Scripture for regarding it under any circumstances as a pathological condition" (Simpson, *ut supra*, p. 116).

the sinner whose conscience is awake invariably admits his responsibility and guilt. There is nothing more distinctive of human nature than the action of conscience in charging the soul with responsibility. This fact cannot possibly be explained away, for it is one of the fundamental realities in the universe. Nor is it merely the consciousness of actual disobedience, but the realisation of a spiritual state which is opposed to the will of God. The guilt of sin is invariably associated with the consciousness of a personal relation to God, and in that a consciousness of the breach of those relations. Whatever qualifications may be made, and however we may attempt to explain or even palliate sin, this consciousness of guilt remains. "The objective fact of evil is accompanied by the subjective side of moral condemnation."[1] This sense of guilt in man is thus an instinctive but very real confession that he has fallen, and as Coleridge has said, " A fall of some sort or other is the fundamental postulate of the moral history of man."[2]

This consideration of sin in the light of law is essential to a true understanding of the problem. Evil is a mystery in any case, but it would be absolutely inexplicable if God were supposed to place man under a law of development, which makes sin a necessity of his progress. This would altogether banish moral guilt. The animal impulses which we are to overcome are not sin in the lower creation, and it is impossible to identify sinful propensities with animal powers since in such a case there would be no moral responsibility. It must never be forgotten that human sins have no prototype in the lower creation. Thus, it would be impossible to speak of such things as pride and avarice among animals. Evolution fails to account for the present moral state of mankind,[3] and it is obviously incorrect to say with Matthew Arnold that sin is not a monster, but only an infirmity. It is impossible to assert that sin is merely a survival of the brute in man, for, as we have seen, its characteristic is moral, not physical. Besides, when we examine our own heart our conscience at once testifies to the fact of moral responsibility. Whence then has man this moral sense ? Nothing can rid him of it, and any denial really means the denial of life itself, to say nothing of Christianity.

Nor can we be satisfied to call sin inherited temperament, and still less is it to be explained simply by environment, for, if this were all, then it is obvious that, as we are often not responsible for our environment, we could not be responsible for our sin, and such a position is really indistinguish-

---

[1] See J. Scott Lidgett, *The Christian Religion*, p. 437 f.

[2] "This witness of the conscience is confirmed by everything we read in Scripture. A bad conscience is never treated there as a groundless fear of God; it is a reflection, all too feeble at the best, of God's awful judgment upon sin. A great mass of modern theology denies this. . . . But to make sin unreal is to make redemption unreal also; it is to cast the shadow of illusion over the whole extent of man's relations with God. There is nothing, I believe, which at the present time needs more to be insisted on, in theology and in gospel preaching, than the objectivity and reality of guilt" (Denney, *ut supra*, pp. 93, 94).

[3] Orr, *ut supra*, pp. 158, 209, 298.

able from the Pelagianism of old days, since Pelagius " never denied that our environment is a source of temptation."[1]

A familiar modern explanation of sin is that it is identical with selfishness, and here again we are conscious of inadequacy, for our life involves very much more than ourselves and our brothers. There are three circles of life : our relation to self ; to our fellows ; and to God. And when this is realised it is at once seen that sin and selfishness are not synonymous. Selfishness is, of course, one of the consequences and manifestations of sin, but it is not sin itself. Sin involves something far more than this. The New Testament definition of sin is not selfishness, but " lawlessness." Law is as real in the moral world as in the physical, and no definition of sin is adequate that does not regard it as a violation of the law of God, whether of conscience or Scripture. Without the conception of law there is no place for forgiveness, and, indeed, no need of it, for apart from law and responsibility to it the sinner is only in error and needs instruction alone. But we know that information is not redemption, and the deepest element that satisfies man is the Divine judgment on sin and deliverance from it. It must never be forgotten that our views of sin and salvation are related and inextricably bound up. As is the one, so will be the other.

We therefore hold that sin in its fullest sense is (a) an act ; (b) an attribute of the nature ; and (c) an attitude of the spirit. Scripture sometimes emphasises one and sometimes another of these. As such, sin is the corruption of the stock by race connection. The fact of propagated tendencies can hardly be denied, and this is a factor when the time of choice comes. Yet transmission and propagation do not lead to excuse or palliation. If it be said that this thought of the unity and solidarity of the race in sin and guilt is an impossible position, the reply is that there need be no difficulties in view of the fact that Christ died for the race. As sin has affected the whole of humanity, so the death of Christ meets and more than meets this universal fact. " Since by man came death by man came also the resurrection of the dead."[2]

MODERN THEORIES OF SIN

The various views held on this subject have been helpfully distinguished as follows :—[3]

[1] Simpson, *ut supra*, p. 120.

[2] As modern writers seem to think that this doctrine of inborn sinfulness can only be based on separate texts of Scripture, and that these texts do not warrant the exegesis often given to them, it is well to remember that the truth of original sin does not depend upon any isolated texts of Scripture, but on the whole trend and tendency of the Biblical revelation concerning man and redemption.

"The appearance of strength in Dr. Tennant's attack upon the biblical argument for the doctrine of original sin is chiefly due to his giving a negative turn to the proof-text method. He rests his case in this direction upon what the proof-texts do not prove, that is, when *separately considered*. He ought to have reckoned with the contention that catholic doctrine affords an explanation of all the relevant phenomena of revelation, *inductively considered*" (Hall, *Evolution and the Fall*, p. 140, Note).

[3] Orchard, *ut supra*.

(1) Theories which trace sin to the will of man (represented by Kant, Coleridge, and Muller).

(2) Theories which regard sin as a necessity (represented by Schelling, Weisse, and Hegel).

(3) Theories which seek to explain sin by confining it within the bounds of religion (represented by Schleiermacher and Ritschl).

(4) Theories which seek to explain sin from empirical observation (represented by Pfleiderer and Tennant).

The conclusion drawn by the author of the book now referred to is that most of these modern theories " tend to reduce largely the circle of human conduct to which sin in the strict sense can be applied, and to cast serious suspicion upon the alleged consciousness of guilt, in that they fail to confirm its judgment by the philosophical, religious, or empirical methods, at least in its depth and extent.[1]

Speaking of Dr. Tennant's theory, which is best known as the latest and ablest attempt in English theology to solve the problem, the same writer adds, " It is doubtful whether an empirical account really gives us an origin of sin at all."[2]   There is no doubt that the fact of guilt is the key to the position, and no explanation of sin which ignores this or sets it aside can be regarded as true, because with the guilt is associated the need and provision of an atonement, and the two may be said to stand or fall together.   It is, therefore, pretty certainly true that " on the basis of current anthropological theories we can never have anything but defective and inadequate views of sin."[3]   And anything defective and inadequate in this respect will assuredly bear upon the question of redemption, for superficiality in our consciousness of the nature and power of sin will tend not merely to a superficial statement of the Atonement of Christ, but to the destruction of the idea of atonement itself.[4]

Reviewing the entire subject, it is clear that human sinfulness consists on the one hand of an inborn tendency to evil, and on the other in the free choice of the individual man.   The fact of an inherited tendency to sin cannot well be denied, a propensity which, while it leads to actual guilt, is not in itself culpable.   But beyond this, voluntary choices which a person makes after the stage of moral responsibility are, of course, affected by the developed natural tendency, and it is impossible to conceive of conscious moral corruption which does not depend upon inherited tendencies.   It is this combination of the evil principle and the evil act that constitutes sin in its completeness, and at the same time provides the problem of human sinfulness.   Each attempt to solve the problem contains an important element of truth, and the subject is undoubtedly two-sided, according as man is considered either as a member of the race or as a distinct individual.   It is impossible to disregard either side, though in our endeavour to include both it is easy to conceive of difficulties and contradictions.   The prevailing tendency of modern thought is to ignore

[1] Orchard, *ut supra*, p. 102.   [2] Orchard, *ut supra*, p. 95.
[3] Orr, *ut supra*, p. 11.   [4] Orr, *ut supra*, p. 11.

the former element of inborn sinfulness, and to concentrate attention solely upon human acts. But no such partial view will suffice to meet all the facts of the case, and whatever difficulties and contradictions exist it is our duty to emphasise the facts on both sides, to adjust them to one another to the best of our ability, to recognise that there is an inscrutable element which at present is beyond our ken, and to believe that there will be an adjustment which will enable us to understand the awful fact of sin in God's universe. Meanwhile, it will be our safety to give attention to the conclusions stated by the great German writer, Julius Müller, in his Preface to *The Christian Doctrine of Sin.*

" That everything in Christianity is connected more or less directly with the great facts of Sin and Redemption, and that the plan of Redemption, which is the essence of Christianity, cannot be rightly understood until the doctrine of Sin be adequately recognised and established. Here, certainly, if anywhere, Christian theology must fight *pro aris et focis.*"

V.—THE PERMANENCE OF ORIGINAL SIN

The rest of the Article is concerned with teaching that this " infection of nature " remains in the regenerate, and that although there is no condemnation for them that believe and are baptised, yet that this infection of nature " hath of itself the nature of sin."

The Character of Original Sin.—It is here described as " infection of nature." It answers to the former phrase, " fault and corruption of the nature." It is further spoken of as " the lust of the flesh " and its Greek equivalent is given; φρόνημα σαρκὸς (Rom. viii. 6). The effort of the Article to interpret this term is particularly interesting : " Which some do expound the wisdom, some sensuality, some the affection, some the desire, of the flesh." It is probable that all these aspects are rightly included in the full meaning of the term, which suggests the general bent of the entire nature, thought, feeling, will. The principle of the idea is best understood from a reference to the passages where the word and its cognates are found : Matt. xvi. 23 (φρονεῖς, " thou savourest "); Rom. viii. 5 f. (φρόνημα τῆς σαρκὸς, the minding of the flesh); viii. 27 (φρόνημα τοῦ πνεύματος, the minding of the Spirit); xii. 16 (φρονοῦντες, mind); Phil. iii. 19 (φρονοῦντες, mind), Col. iii. 2 (φρονεῖτε, set your affection). It is further said, following the teaching of St. Paul, that this lust of the flesh is not subject to the law of God (Rom. viii. 7).

The Permanence of Original Sin.—" Doth remain, yea in them that are regenerated." It is clear that whatever happens in connection with regeneration this evil principle of sin remains. Nor is there any distinction between the " regenerated " and the " sanctified," as though it were possible for this " infection of nature " to be removed by some Divine act subsequent to regeneration. Any distinction of this kind may safely be said to have been altogether outside the view of the Reformers; indeed, it cannot be said to exist in reality, but is only used in certain quarters as a distinction by which it is attempted to justify a theory of the entire removal of the evil principle.

The Safeguard.—The Article clearly shows that no one will be condemned merely for the possession of inborn sinfulness. " There is no condemnation for them that believe and are baptized." The Latin equivalent here is particularly noteworthy : *renatis et credentibus nulla propter Christum est condemnatio.* Here the Article translates the Latin *renatis* (born again) by the English " baptized," and also omits to translate the Latin *propter Christum.* This use of *renatis* for " baptized " seems to show clearly that in the minds of the Reformers Baptism refers to birth, not life, to the introduction of an already living being into a new sphere, not the bestowal of the primal germ of life.

It is sometimes said that Baptism removes the " taint " of original sin. But at once the question arises, What is this " taint " ? It can only mean guilt or principle,[1] and if guilt is personal and cannot be said to exist in an unconscious child, there remains only the principle which, according to the Article, continues to exist in the regenerated. What, then, are we to understand by " taint " ? The question shows how necessary it is to be quite clear as to the meaning and fact of Baptism.[2]

The Sinfulness of Original Sin.—The closing words of the Article are that " the Apostle doth confess that concupiscence and lust hath of itself the nature of sin." *In sese rationem peccati.* It is sometimes said that this phrase does not really mean that concupiscence is essentially and inherently sinful, but only that " it leads to sin."[3] It is also urged that it is difficult to say exactly what the Article means on this point, and that its ambiguity was probably designed to emphasise the truth that while not in itself sinful, concupiscence is so closely connected with sin that if unchecked sin will be its result.[4] On this view a distinction is based between our Article and certain other Protestant formularies, which speak of concupiscence as " true and proper sin," and special attention is called to the proposal of the Westminster Assembly to substitute " is truly and properly sin " for the milder statement of our Article.[5] But there seems to be some confusion here, because the paragraph in the Article is concerned with what is " true and proper sin in the regenerate," since " concupiscence and lust " must, of necessity, mean the same as " this infection of nature." Either, therefore, it is sin or it is not, and it is noteworthy that the first Commentary on the Articles, by Rogers, dated 1587-1607,

---

[1] "In baptism the guilt is pardoned" (Gibson, *ut supra*, p. 374).

[2] The Church Catechism is sometimes understood to mean that Baptism makes us the children of grace: "A death unto sin, and a new birth unto righteousness: for being by nature born in sin, and the children of wrath, we are hereby made the children of grace." It should be noted, however, that the Latin version of Dean Durel, 1671, renders "hereby" by *hac ratione*, which can only refer to "a death unto sin and a new birth unto righteousness," rendered by Durel *mori peccato et denuo nasci justitiæ.* To the same effect is an old paraphrase of the Catechism, 1674. By contrast, Bright and Medd in their modern Latin version render "hereby" by *per Baptismum*, which is, of course, the *ex opere operato* view.

[3] Gibson, *ut supra*, p. 376.   [4] Gibson, *ut supra*, p. 376.   [5] Gibson, *ut supra*, p. 376.

clearly teaches that concupiscence is sin, and opposes those who teach otherwise.[1] There can be no doubt that our Article is clearly against the Council of Trent on this point, which declares that concupiscence is not of the nature of sin. In remission of sins there are two things: (a) guilt; (b) punishment, and in original sinfulness there are two elements: (a) penalty; (b) disposition. The sinful condition is twofold: negative in the absence of grace to maintain union with God; positive in the corruption of nature, and (throughout) the sinful characteristic. Nature and person in this connection are inseparable, because the nature involves the will, and the will is the most distinct personal characteristic and is disinclined to obey God. Remission affects the *person*, but not the *nature*. Men are forgiven personal punishments, but the *depravatio* and its effects remain and are still subject to such results as death. It is this positive habit and disposition which is concupiscence.

The important point of this statement is that it is directed towards the Roman Catholic theory of what is called sacramental justification. Whatever we may say about Baptism, if there still remains in our souls something that has " of itself the nature of sin " we must continually need the love and mercy of God to pardon our transgression, and His grace to overcome the power of inborn sinfulness. The distinction, therefore, which is made between that which " hath of itself the nature of sin " and that which is " sin " is really baseless, more particularly as the phrase, " nature of sin " comes directly from the Council of Trent, and is evidently intended to contradict the official Roman Catholic doctrine. In 1546 the Council said :—

" If any one denies, that through the grace of Jesus Christ which is conferred in Baptism, the guilt of original sin is remitted, or even asserts that all of that which hath the true and proper nature of sin (*peccati rationem habet*) is not taken away, but only cut down and not imputed, let him be accursed."

It is hardly possible to doubt that the statement of our Article, *peccati tamen in sese rationem habere*, was intended to be a definite reply to Rome. Rome's view is really a recurrence to the erroneous view of original righteousness, which regards concupiscence as a consequence of nature, both in the unregenerate and the regenerate. Further, it should be remembered that the same phrase occurs in Article XIII, where there is practically no doubt that the meaning is something essentially sinful.

This question of the permanence of original sin in the regenerate is important on two grounds: (a) in its opposition to all forms of what is called " sinless perfection "; (b) on the other hand, against any yielding to defeat and accepting it as inevitable. Something must be said on each of these two points.

(a) It is important to consider the relation of sin to our nature. The ultimate capacity in human nature is the capacity for feeling, for vivid

[1] Rogers, *On the Articles*, pp. 101–103.

impressions of pain and pleasure. These are called the primary sensibilities and have been disordered through sin, and are never entirely rectified in this life, though the Atonement covers their defect. Then come secondary sensibilities, leading to desires on the one hand and aversions on the other. It is at this point that Divine grace comes in. If the will does not consent there is no personal sin, but there is a disorder below the will which is sinful and needs to be dealt with. Personal responsibility is concerned only with that which the will determines. Atonement covers the rest, including incapacity and defect. It is also important to note the distinction between Adam and ourselves. He had the liability, but not the tendency to sin. We have both, and the tendency is what the Article calls the "corruption of the nature," "infection of nature," "concupiscence." The weakness of what is known as the Methodist doctrine of "Perfect Love" is that it teaches that grace meets all the needs of human nature in the sense of eradication. But it does not. Scripture continually distinguishes between sin and sins, between the root and fruit, but though the root remains, as stated by the Article, there is no need for it to bring forth fruit.

(b) But the presence of inborn sinfulness in the regenerate, while real and powerful, is no excuse, still less justification for sinning. The Apostle clearly teaches that the redemptive work of Christ was intended to render inert or inoperative the evil principle within (Rom. vi. 6, Greek). And thus we may say that while Scripture teaches something that is very near eradication, in order that we may not be satisfied with anything less than the highest type of Christian living, on the other hand, it as clearly teaches that the evil principle has not been removed. It loses its power over the believer, though the believer does not lose its presence. To the same effect is the Apostle's word : "Reckon ye yourselves to be dead indeed unto sin" (Rom. vi. 11). He thereby teaches that while we are to be dead to it, it is not dead to us. Sin is not dead, but we are to keep on reckoning ourselves to be dead to it. Such language would have been impossible if sin had been entirely removed. It is impossible to avoid noticing at this point the striking affinity between the Roman Catholic and Methodist doctrines of making sinfulness inhere in the will only.[1] Our Article, in harmony with the Protestant Confessions of the sixteenth century goes much deeper, and shows that sin has affected the nature long before the will commences to act.

The question is vital to many of the most practical and important aspects of living, for if we are wrong here we are liable to be wrong everywhere. Superficial views of sin inevitably tend towards superficial views of the redemptive work of Christ. We must, therefore, be on our guard against the two extremes : on the one hand we must insist that

---

[1] "Such are the difficulties in which the Council involved itself in its attempts to transfer the seat of sin from the affections to the outward manifestation, and yet to avoid coming into open collision with Scripture and Christian feeling" (Litton, *ut supra*, p. 170).

even in the regenerate the evil principle remains and will remain to the end of this life; on the other hand, we must be clear that this evil principle need not and ought not to produce evil results in practice, since the grace of God has been provided to meet and overcome it.[1]

---

[1] More will be said on this subject in connection with Articles XV and XVI.

ARTICLE X

Of Free Will.

De libero Arbitrio.

The condition of man after the fall of Adam is such, that he cannot turn and prepare himself, by his own natural strength and good works, to faith and calling upon God. Wherefore we have no power to do good works pleasant and acceptable to God, without the grace of God by Christ preventing us, that we may have a good will, and working with us, when we have that good will.

Ea est hominis post lapsum Adæ conditio, ut sese, naturalibus suis viribus et bonis operibus, ad fidem et invocationem Dei convertere ac præparare non possit. Quare absque gratia Dei, quæ per Christum est, nos præveniente ut velimus; et co-operante dum volumus, ad pietatis opera facienda, quæ Deo grata sunt et accepta, nihil valemus.

IMPORTANT EQUIVALENTS.

Of Adam	= *Adæ.*
By strength	= *viribus.*
By Christ	= *per Christum.*
That we may have a good will	= *ut velimus.*
When we have that good will	= *dum volumus.*
Good works	= *pietatis opera.*

THE title is not quite correct, and would be better as " The Limitations of Free Will," or " The Need of Grace." Free will is not mentioned at all, but only assumed, its limitations being the special subject of the Article. This is really a corollary of Article IX, an enlargement of that Article in regard to the " corruption of the nature." The first clause of the present Article was introduced in 1563 from the Wurtemberg Confession.[1] The latter clause is almost exactly from Augustine's work, *De Gratia et Libero Arbitrio.*[2] It would seem as though the teaching were directed against the extreme views of the Anabaptists on the subject of grace.[3] But it is more than likely that Archbishop Parker's object in prefixing the clause from the Confession of Wurtemberg was intended to deal with the theory of *Meritum de congruo*, which, however, is to be specially considered under Article XIII.

---

[1] "Quod autem nonnulli affirmant homini post lapsum tantam animi integritatem relictam, *ut possit sese naturalibus suis viribus et bonis operibus, ad fidem et invocationem Dei convertere ac præparare*, haud obscure pugnat cum vero Ecclesiæ Catholicæ consensu" (*De Peccato*).

[2] "We have no power to do good works without God working that we may have a good will, and co-operating when we have that good will."
"Sine illo vel operante ut velimus vel co-operante cum volumus, ad bonæ pietatis opera nihil valemus."

[3] "Similiter nobis contra illos progrediendum est, qui tantum in libero arbitrio roboris et nervorum ponunt, *eo solo sine alia speciali Christi gratia recte ab hominibus vivi posse constituant*" (*Reformatio Legum, De Hæresibus*, c. 7).

It will help to understand the entire situation if we analyse the Article first of all and see precisely what it teaches.

1. The Spiritual Helplessness of Man.—"The condition of man after the fall of Adam is such, that he cannot turn and prepare himself, by his own natural strength and good works, to faith, and calling upon God." The Roman doctrine of Original Sin as merely a state of deprivation would naturally lead to the view that man can co-operate with Divine grace in preparation for Justification. The right exercise of free will was regarded as giving man a claim to Divine help, and this, as we shall see, was the scholastic doctrine of "congruous merit." The view taken in the Article is that man is free, but powerless to do God's will.[1]

2. The Divine Provision against Human Helplessness.—"Wherefore we have no power to do good works pleasant and acceptable to God, without the grace of God by Christ." Here the Article emphasises the need of grace, and when it speaks of good works as "pleasant and acceptable," it obviously refers solely to those who, within the Christian revelation, are capable of considering the Divine requirements. All references to the heathen and any works of theirs are naturally ruled out in view of the historical circumstances that gave rise to the Article. The statement is concerned simply with an aspect of the spiritual life which was unduly and incorrectly emphasised in the Middle Ages.

3. The Primary Working of Divine Grace.—"The grace of God by Christ preventing us, that we may have a good will." The technical phrase implied here is "prevenient grace," and was possibly suggested by the Latin of Psalm lix. 10 : "The God of my mercy will pre-vent me." The truth is also seen in St. Paul's words : "It is God which worketh in you both to will and to do of His good pleasure" (Phil. ii. 13). The reason why grace is thus emphasised as necessary is "that we may have a good will," and the truth is found very frequently in Holy Scripture (John vi. 44 ; Acts xvi. 14).

4. The Continuous Working of Divine Grace.—"And working with us, when we have that good will." There was one slight alteration made in the English in 1571, when "working with us" was put for "working in us" as the equivalent of co-operante. The technical term for this is "co-operating grace," and again we may refer to Holy Scripture: "The Lord also working with them" (Mark xvi. 20). The need of this grace is equally clear, for whether we consider the beginning, or the course, or the end of the Christian life, our Lord's words are true:

[1] "And so likewise although there remain a certain freedom of will in those things which do pertain unto the desires and works of this present life (cf. Augsburg Confess., XVIII), yet to perform spiritual and heavenly things free will of itself is insufficient: and therefore the power of man's free will, being thus wounded and decayed, hath need of a physician to heal it, and an help to repair it; that it may receive light and strength whereby it may see, and have power to do those godly and spiritual things, which before the fall of Adam it was able and might have done" (*Necessary Doctrine and Erudition*, "Article of Free Will," pp. 360, 361).

M

" Apart from Me ye can do nothing " (John xv. 5); and St. Paul may
be said to have delighted in referring everything in his life to the grace of
God. " By the grace of God I am what I am " (1 Cor. xv. 10; Gal. ii.
20). Our Prayer Book has many similar references to this need of Divine
grace. Thus, at Daily Prayer we ask : " O God, make clean our hearts
within us." In the Collect for Easter Day : " As by Thy special grace
pre-venting us . . . so by Thy continual help." The Collect for the
Ninth Sunday after Trinity : " We, who cannot do anything that is
good without Thee." Collect for the Fourteenth Sunday after Trinity :
" Make us to love that which Thou dost command." Collect for the
Fifteenth Sunday after Trinity : " The frailty of man without Thee
cannot but fall." Collect for the Seventeenth Sunday after Trinity :
" Thy grace may always pre-vent and follow us." Collect for the
Nineteenth Sunday after Trinity : " Without Thee we are not able to
please Thee." Collect after Communion Office : " Pre-vent us . . .
with Thy most gracious favour, and further us with Thy continual help."
The Homilies teach the same truth.

" It is the Holy Ghost, and *no other thing*, that doth quicken the minds of men,
stirring up good and godly motions in their hearts, which are agreeable to the
will and commandment of God, such as otherwise of their own crooked and
perverse nature they *should never have*."
" As for the good works of the Spirit, the fruits of faith, charitable and godly
motions, if he have any at all in him, they proceed only of the Holy Ghost, who
is the *only* worker of our sanctification, and maketh us new men in Christ Jesus."[1]
" We are all become unclean, but we are not able to cleanse ourselves, nor to
make one another of us clean. We are by nature the children of God's wrath ;
but we are not able to make ourselves the children and inheritors of God's glory.
We are sheep that run astray, but we cannot of our own power come again to
the sheepfold, so great is our imperfection and weakness."[2]

II.—THE HISTORY

The question of the will was debated centuries before Christianity,
and the subject was forced on the Church and could no longer remain a
matter of mere philosophic discussion. A new element arose in connection with the Fall of man, and the problem was raised as to how far
that affected the will. The subject is not clearly set forth in the Apostolic
Fathers, mainly because there were no controversies to colour opinions,
though the freedom of the will is definitely taught by Justin Martyr.
Early heretics like the Gnostics were fatalists, but Origen emphasised
human freedom. The Pelagians insisted upon absolute freedom of will,
and Augustine was the first to face the problem fully. After him came
the Semi-Pelagians, who taught that man had free will sufficient to enable
him to turn to God, but not to persevere. The Semi-Pelagians taught

[1] Homily for Whitsunday.
[2] Homily on the Misery of Man. See also Third Homily for Rogation Week.

that so much good will remains as to wish to be healed, *velle sanari,
quærere medicum,* but later came the idea that even this *velle sanari* was
the result of a general action of grace on mankind, God's Spirit giving
the initial impulse.

In the Middle Ages there was a perpetual tendency towards Semi-
Pelagianism, due to the erroneous idea of original righteousness, for if
man is only deprived of superadded grace, the natural powers were capable
of good motions of themselves. But thought divided itself into two schools.
The Dominicans, as represented by Thomas Aquinas, 1274, were substantially Augustinian, and taught the need of grace before the will could
incline towards God. On the other hand, the Franciscans, represented
by Duns Scotus, 1308, taught entire freedom of will and were virtually
Pelagian. It was in this connection that the doctrine of grace *de congruo*
arose, which meant that man's endeavour to attain to godliness deserved
this congruous grace. They thought that some element of goodness was
to be attributed to man's unaided efforts towards the attainment of
holiness, and that in some way this effort merited the bestowal of Divine
grace. The Council of Trent was divided on the subject, though
generally through the Jesuits the Church of Rome tended towards the
Scotist view. It is well known that on these subjects the Roman view is
essentially Pelagian, or at least semi-Pelagian.

On the other hand, Luther and Calvin favoured the Thomist view,
and of course opposed the very idea of the doctrine of " congruous merit."
Our Article meets these points without entering into the subtleties of
controversy as to how far man's will has been affected by the Fall. It is
sometimes said that the second clause of our Article, dating from 1553,
was before the time when Calvin was known in England, and that
therefore it represents our own independent view. This is true, but it
is not the whole truth, since all our Reformers were what may be called
Augustinians. In 1553 this Article was followed by one " Of Grace,"
to oppose the fatalism of the Anabaptists. This was omitted in 1563,
probably because the error was no longer of serious importance, and also,
it has been suggested, to make it easier for strong Calvinists to accept the
Articles, since they believed in irresistible grace. During the Marian
persecution many English Divines were brought into contact on the
Continent with foreign Reformers, and afterwards came back strongly in
favour of more extreme Calvinistic views.

Later on came the controversy at the beginning of the seventeenth
century connected with the Dutch theologian, Arminius, who, by a
natural rebound from the extreme Calvinism of his time, took the Scotist
view. The result was the calling of the Synod of Dort, or Dordrecht, at
which the Arminians were excommunicated and definite Calvinistic views
were promulgated. After the Council of Trent the Church of Rome
continued to be divided on the subject, the Jesuits maintaining a Pelagian
view, while the followers of Jansenius, known as Jansenists, upheld the
Augustinian and Dominican position. At length the Jansenists were

condemned and the Jesuits gained the upper hand in the Church of Rome.[1]

III.—THE QUESTION STATED

There are few things on which clearness is more needed than on the subject of free will. For our present purpose it does not mean the absence of restraint from without, or perfect freedom of action, nor does it refer to the liberty of the believer, his freedom in Christ (Rom. viii. 2; Gal. v. 1). In the present connection it means the power of choice which enables a man to determine the course of his action. Man sees certain ends and chooses between them. Motives impel, but do not compel. The man selects what he desires, so that he is free to use his liberty aright, and the abuse of his freedom constitutes a sin. There are two functions of the will : (*a*) choice, and (*b*) volition. The former refers to selection, and by itself accomplishes nothing ; the latter refers to energy, by which the thing selected is accomplished. Human freedom belongs primarily to choice, because volition may be impracticable, yet even so choice has its limitations and loss. Freedom does not mean ability to choose anything at any time. Free will therefore means the freedom of the soul in choosing, enabling it to determine conscious action. The doctrine of the will as to the choosing is equivalent to the doctrine of the man. In this sense our freedom is real and the Fall has not affected it. We are conscious of it by our sense of responsibility. All denial of free will in this meaning must lead either to fatalism, which ends in materialism, or to an extreme mysticism, which involves such a contemplation of God as to leave for self a sort of Christian pantheism, or absorption into God. Fallen man has the faculty of will, as he has other faculties, and if he is free from external compulsion he must will what he pleases to do. But this does not prove that he has the power to do anything and everything that comes before him. Man's receptivity is real, but it needs to be purified and quickened by grace before it can fully discharge its functions. We have a capacity for redemption, but not the capability to redeem ourselves. It is not receptivity, but productivity that is needed. Freedom is thus opposed to servitude and implies the apprehension of various courses of action. It consists in choosing between possible alternative acts. Reason is, therefore, at the root of liberty, and as far as the reason discerns the good (or what is thought good) the will by nature chooses it. *Volo ergo sum*, " I will, therefore I am," is decidedly truer than *cogito ergo sum*, " I think, therefore I am." Freedom is thus an ultimate fact.

" Freedom is a point upon which we can allow no shuffling or juggling in argument. It is unique, but it is self-evident ; and every attempt to explain it away can be shown to involve a *petitio principii*."[2]

---

[1] For the history, of which the above is a brief outline, see Harold Browne, *Exposition of the Thirty-nine Articles*, pp. 252-264; the question will receive further attention under Article XVII.

[2] Illingworth, *Personality Human and Divine*, p. 107.

Our full freedom is limited to a few cases. There seem to be three main choices: (1) ultimate choice, the selection of an end which becomes permanent for life; (2) subordinate choice, the choice of means towards ends; (3) supreme choice, the choice of the highest ultimate, either God or self. Freedom is exerted mainly in regard to the first and third of these. To the first belongs character, which introduces the element of fixity into human life. It is in our character that our sins are rooted.

And yet will is not self-originating, but only chooses what it thinks is *good* and *possible*. It only reflects the το αὐτεξούσιον of the Creator, and it was in this respect that the Reformers felt led to deny freedom. Free will is a mode, not a source of action.[1] Behind the will is the nature, and as is the nature so is the will. Moral inability is thus due to the corruption of nature. Yet even so, on these motives, the will has certain powers of self-determination, and it is this that makes corruption possible. This corruption may be (1) the obscuration of the reasonable apprehension of good; (2) the succession of acts which tend to establish habit.

It is, of course, a great mystery how God knows and orders everything and yet leaves man free. These, however, are the two facts which need to be emphasised and kept ever in view even though they cannot be reconciled. Meanwhile, because of the provision of Christ there is no moral injustice, since Divine grace more than meets human weakness and inability.

Grace is perhaps the greatest word of the New Testament and of God's revelation in Christ, because it is the most truly expressive of God's character and attitude in relation to man. The root seems to mean " to give pleasure," and then it branches out comprehensively in two directions: one in relation to the Giver; the other in relation to the receiver of the pleasure. Grace is, first, a quality of *graciousness* in the Giver, and then, a quality of *gratitude* in the recipient, which in turn makes him *gracious* to those around.

But the idea has two distinct yet connected aspects even when applied only to God the Giver.

1. It expresses the Divine *attitude* to man as guilty and condemned. Grace means God's favour and good will towards us (Luke i. 30). So the Mother of our Lord is described as " permanently favoured " (" graced," Luke i. 28). This favour is manifested without any regard to merit; indeed, grace and merit are entire opposites. Grace is thus spontaneous (not prompted from outside); free (no conditions are required); generous (no stint is shown); and abiding (no cessation is experienced). It is also (as favour) opposed to " wrath," which means judicial displeasure against sin. Further, it must be distinguished from

---

[1] "Since the Fall, man is free to choose, and for that reason is accountable. . . . He is free to choose, in so far as no foreign will can irresistibly constrain him to will against his own will. He is not free, in so far as within his own personality the sin which has been allowed by himself rules and enslaves his will (Delitzsch, *Biblical Psychology*, p. 193).

mercy, even though mercy is one of the methods of its expression. Mercy is related to misery, and to those who are (negatively) non-deserving. Grace is related to redemption and to those who are (positively) un-deserving.

2. It then expresses the Divine *action* to man as needy and helpless. Grace means not merely favour, but also help ; not only benevolence, but also benefaction ; not simply feeling, but also force ; not solely good will, but also good work. It is Divine favour expressed in and proved by His gift ; attitude shown by action. Thus from *grace* comes *gift*, which invariably implies a gift of or by grace (Rom. v. 15 ; 1 Cor. iv. 6 ; Rom. xii. 6).

These two ideas are thus connected and united as Cause and Effect. They tell of God's Heart and God's Hand. Etymologically, therefore, Grace is a term that refers to the beautiful, which gives delight. Theolo-gically, it means God's favour as seen in His gift. Practically, it implies God's presence and redemptive power in human life. Blending all these aspects we may think of Grace as God's *spontaneous gift*, which causes *pleasure* and produces *blessing*. Hort defines grace as " free bounty," and, as such, it produces " joy and is the cause of actual power in daily living."

In relation to the will, grace implies (1) the illumination of the moral nature ; (2) a counteractive power against habit ; (3) new motives ; (4) by contact, healing, and strength. It is at this point that we may perhaps regret the omission of the Tenth Article of 1553, " Of Grace," which was omitted in 1563, as presumably not required. But it may be well, however, to quote it in order to see more definitely what grace does in relation to the human will.

Of Grace	*De Gratia*
The grace of Christ, or the Holy Ghost by Him given doth take away the stony heart, and giveth an heart of flesh. And although, those that have no will to good things, He maketh them to will, and those that would evil things, He maketh them not to will the same : yet nevertheless He enforceth not the will. And therefore no man when he sinneth can excuse himself, as not worthy to be blamed or condemned, by alleging that he sinned unwillingly or by compulsion.	Gratia Christi, seu Spiritus Sanctus qui per eundem datur, cor lapideum aufert, et dat cor carneum. Atque licet ex nolentibus quæ recta sunt volentes faciat, et ex volentibus prava, nolentes reddat, voluntati nihilominus violentiam nullam infert. Et nemo hac de causa cum peccaverit, seipsum excu-sare potest, quasi nolens aut coactus peccaverit, ut eam ob causam accusari non mereatur aut damnari.

The question of the relation of the human will to the Divine is one of great difficulty and profound mystery, but the following points seem to be fairly clear : (1) God at the beginning created man and endowed him with a will, so that although man acts as a " first cause " he is not one absolutely, for he is a first cause only in a secondary way. (2) God created man a holy being and with a will inclined to Him only. Then the weakness of a finite nature rendered man fallible, and under the influence of temptation Adam fell from his estate of holiness, sinfulness thus entering the world as the perversion of a life originally upright. (3) While Divine grace never compels souls, it frequently changes them for the better, for God creates man anew in righteousness. Such a transformation is altogether consistent with free agency, because it does not destroy, but only renews and thereby aids man's will.

This question of grace in relation to human life is of particular importance to-day, because from two separate quarters its need and power tend to be questioned and even denied. On the one hand, science tends to deny the possibility of grace. On the other, fiction either idealises human life or else leads men to despair by emphasising the impossibility of forgiveness. So that emphasis on grace is of special value against science with its teaching of a gradual evolution and improvement of human nature, and also against fiction, which idealises human nature and thereby denies the need of grace. In reality modern thought can find no fault with the teaching of this Article, since everything tends to show the continuity of individual life and to lay stress on the importance of heredity. The Article is of particular value in opposition to the really shallow conception that " a man can reform himself at any time if he will only make up his mind." To say this is to ignore some of the plainest facts of human experience, and in particular the real power of habit. The statement sometimes made that a child just entering upon a vague sense of right and wrong is able to stem the current of his innate impulses is not worthy of serious consideration. Everything tends to show that the doctrine of original sin has a solid foundation in the facts of human nature. There is in every human being a tendency to sin antecedent to the act of the conscious and mature man. It is at this point that Christianity comes in with its message of grace, and it is that the Article emphasises both in regard to what is called " pre-venient grace " and " co-operating grace." Whatever mystery there may be in theories and philosophies, when we approach the subject through personal experience we see abundant evidence of the truth of those statements, already quoted from our Collects, that " we have no power of ourselves to help ourselves," and for this reason " without Thee we are not able to please Thee."

ARTICLE XI

Of the Justification of Man.

We are accounted righteous before God, only for the merit of our Lord and Saviour Jesus Christ, by faith, and not for our own works or deservings. Wherefore, that we are justified by faith only is a most wholesome doctrine and very full of comfort, as more largely is expressed in the Homily of Justification.

De Hominis Justificatione.

Tantum propter meritum Domini ac Servatoris nostri Jesu Christi per fidem, non propter opera et merita nostra, justi coram Deo reputamur. Quare sola fide nos justificari, doctrina est saluberrima ac consolationis plenissima, ut in Homilia de Justificatione hominis fusius explicatur.

IMPORTANT EQUIVALENTS.

Only for the merit	= *Tantum propter meritum.*
By faith	= *per fidem.*
And not for our own works	= *non propter opera nostra.*
Or deservings	= *et merita.*
By faith only	= *sola fide.*
Of Justification	= *de Justificatione hominis.*

In the Forty-two Articles of 1553 this Article was as follows :—

Justification by only faith in Jesus Christ in that sense, as it is declared in the Homily of Justification, is a most certain and wholesome doctrine for Christian men.

Justificatio ex sola fide Jesu Christi eo sensu quo in Homelia de Justificatione explicatur, est certissima et saluberrima Christianorum doctrina.

But in 1563 the Article received its present form, and the alteration was a great advantage and improvement, for in 1553 it was necessary to study the Homily in order to learn what the Church of England meant by "Justification by faith only," while now we have a clear definition of the doctrine in the Article itself, the Homily being still referred to as providing a fuller expression of the same truth. It has sometimes been said that Archbishop Parker favoured mediæval views on Justification, but his devotion to Cranmer is a sufficient disproof of this, and, further, it is known that the Eleventh Article was drawn from the Wurtemberg Confession. The Augsburg Confession having defined the Evangelical faith, its teaching on Justification had been condemned by the Council of Trent in 1546-1547, and when the Council reassembled in 1551 the Protestant Princes presented Confessions of Faith reaffirming those points which the Council had condemned. The Wurtemberg Confession was one of these documents, and it is therefore not unnatural

that when our Articles were revised in 1563 they were thus definitely
and purposely brought into clearer verbal agreement with this Confession,
and at the same time shown to be in more thorough conflict with Rome
than before.

The question of Justification was the theological and spiritual foundation of the Reformation Movement; indeed, it lies at the very foundation of all Christian life and service, for only when this is settled can
there be any peace, power, and progress. The prominence given to it
at the Reformation is a striking testimony to its importance as the primary
question of the ages : " How should man be just with God ? " This
enquiry, found as far back as the Book of Job, is repeated throughout the
history of the Jews, expressed in heathen sacrifices, and implied in all
Oriental religions. The Bible alone gives the answer, and it was this
beyond all else that led to the definite and constant emphasis on the Bible
as the Rule of Faith at the time of the Reformation. Indeed, it may be
said that the whole movement of the sixteenth century was bound up
with the two great principles of the sufficiency and supremacy of the
Bible, and Justification by Faith in the completeness and finality of our
Lord's.work on the Cross. The first hint on the latter subject comes
in Genesis xv. 6; a little more light is afforded in Psalm xxxii.; still
more in Habakkuk ii. 4; while in Acts xiii. 38, 39; Galatians iii. ;
Romans iii. and iv., we have the full revelation of God's answer to man's
enquiry.

I.—THE MEANING OF JUSTIFICATION

Justification may be viewed from God's standpoint or from ours. In
the former case it means the Divine act and gift; in the latter the human
reception and result.

1. Justification is connected with our true relation to God. The
Article shows this by defining it as our being "accounted righteous
before God." Justification before men is only possible through good
works, to be dealt with in Article XII. So that in the primary sense
Justification is not concerned with our spiritual condition, but with
our spiritual relation, not with actual state, but with judicial position.
It is important to keep this in mind if confusion and difficulty are to
be avoided.

2. This true relation was lost by sin. Sin, as we have seen, is rebellion
against God's will and disobedience to His law, and as regards our true
relation to God there are three results of sin : (a) guilt; (b) condemnation; (c) separation. We see all these in the Garden of Eden as the direct
and immediate result of sin in connection with man's proper relation to
God.

3. Justification is the restoration of this true relation to God. It
includes (a) the removal of condemnation by the gift of forgiveness;
(b) the removal of guilt by the reckoning (or imputation) of righteousness;

(c) the removal of separation by the restoration to fellowship.[1] Justification thus means to treat as just, or righteous, to account righteous, to regard as righteous, to declare righteous, to pronounce righteous in the eyes of the law (Psa. li. 4; Prov. xvii. 15; Ezek. xvi. 51, 52; Matt. xi. 19; xii. 37; Luke vii. 35).[2]

4. Justification is, therefore, much more than pardon, and the two are clearly distinguished by St. Paul (Acts xiii. 38, 39). A criminal is pardoned, but is not regarded as righteous. But Justification is that act of God whereby He accepts and accounts us righteous, though in ourselves unrighteous. The Christian is not merely a pardoned criminal, but a righteous man. Forgiveness is an act and a succession of acts; Justification is an act issuing in an attitude. Forgiveness is repeated throughout the life; Justification is complete and never repeated. It relates to our spiritual position in the sight of God and covers the whole of our life, past, present, and future.[3] Forgiveness is only negative, the removal of condemnation; Justification is also positive, the removal of guilt and the bestowal of a perfect standing before God. In a word, Justification means reinstatement. Forgiveness is being stripped; Justification is being clothed. Day by day we approach God for forgiveness and grace on the footing of the relation of Justification that lasts throughout our life. In relation to the justified man, the believer, God is " faithful and righteous to forgive." Thus, Justification is the ground of our assurance, the reason why we know is because of what Christ has done for us and is to us.

5. Justification is also different from " making righteous," which is the usual interpretation of Sanctification. The two are inseparable in fact, but they are distinguishable in thought, and must be kept quite clear if we desire peace and blessing. Justification concerns our standing; Sanctification our state. The former affects our position; the latter

---

[1] It is at least a coincidence that St. Paul's three questions at the close of his great chapter in Romans deal with these three results of sin as seen in the story of the Fall: (a) "Who shall lay anything to the charge of God's elect" (ver. 33)? No guilt. (b) "Who is he that condemneth" (ver. 34)? No condemnation. (c) "Who shall separate us" (ver. 35)? No separation.

[2] It is often pointed out that Greek verbs in οω, are factitive if physical, like τυφλόω, to make blind, but are not factitive if moral, as ἀξιόω, to account worthy. Plummer, Luke, p. 208; Sanday and Headlam, Romans, pp. 28–31; Speakers' Commentary on 1 Cor. xi. 6.

"It is now generally acknowledged that the interpretation of this term, which was given by the mediævalists in the Reformation controversy, and which, though finding no support in the Anglican Articles and rejected by representative Anglican divines like Richard Hooker, has been revived by certain modern English theologians, as for instance Dr. Liddon, is inconsistent with Greek usage. The verb δικαιόω means 'to account righteous'; and no ingenuity will enable us to modify this interpretation. It does not mean 'to make righteous,' and all attempts to confuse it with sanctification must therefore be abandoned" (Simpson, Fact and Faith, p. 76).

See also Article "Justified," Dictionary of Christ and the Gospels.

[3] "The proportions of the Pauline theology abundantly prove that justification is no mere preliminary act in the progression 'justified, sanctified, glorified,' but that it covers the whole career of the Christian as the essential condition" (Simpson, ut supra, p. 85).

our condition. The first deals with relationship; the second with fellowship. And even though they are bestowed together we must never confuse them. The one is the foundation of peace, " Christ for us "; the other is the foundation of purity, " Christ in us." The one deals with acceptance; the other with attainment. Sanctification admits of degrees, we may be more or less sanctified; Justification has no degrees, but is complete, perfect, and eternal. " Justified from all things." Our Lord indicated this distinction (John xiii. 10) when He said, " He that has been bathed (Justification) needeth not, save to wash his feet (Sanctification)."[1]

ROMAN CATHOLIC DOCTRINE

At this point it is necessary to consider the Roman Catholic doctrine of Justification, more particularly as, owing to other prominent differences between us and Rome, it is apt to be overlooked that there is a fundamental difference between the two Churches on this subject as well. A brief reference to what happened at the Council of Trent will enable us to understand this difference. Dr. Lindsay describes the statement put forth at that Council as " a masterpiece of theological dexterity." This was doubtless due to the fact that there was not a little Evangelical doctrine in the Roman Church which had to be considered, and so much was this the case that at one time it had been thought possible to win over the Protestants. But that time, if it ever existed, had gone by, and the discussion in the Council revealed fundamental lines of difference. A small minority was ready to accept the Lutheran view of Justification by Faith alone, but the majority easily won the day on behalf of a view which was almost the exact opposite of the Lutheran doctrine. The definition adopted by the Council extends to sixteen chapters, and, as Lindsay says, " Almost every page includes grave ambiguities." At first there seems to be an agreement with Evangelical doctrine, but then a change commences, and " while some sentences seem to maintain the Evangelical ideas previously stated, room is distinctly made for Pelagian work-righteousness." The result was that Justification was no longer regarded as a change of position, but as the actual conversion of a sinner into a righteous man. Lindsay thus concludes :—

" It is scarcely necessary to pursue the definitions further. It is sufficient to say that the theologians of Trent do not seem to have the faintest idea of what the Reformers meant by faith, and never appear to see that there is such a thing as

---

[1] "The two are not the same, and they do not run into each other. When a bone is broken, it must be set before the process of healing can begin, and the setting is in order that the fragments may knit together and unite; but the setting and the healing are wholly distinct. Justification is the setting of the broken bone; it brings the soul into its true relation to God; it has sanctification for its object. Sanctification is the healing, a process wholly different and wholly distinct. Justification is God's work; sanctification is the united work of God and man" (Stearns, *Present Day Theology*, p. 474).

religious experience. . . . The result was that the Pope obtained what he wanted, a definition which made reconciliation with the Protestants impossible."[1]

For our present purpose we may quote one of the Canons of the Council, which teaches that "Justification consists not in the mere remission of sins, but in the sanctification and renewal of the inner man by the voluntary reception of God's grace and gifts."

The fact is that Rome teaches Forgiveness through Sanctification, while Scripture teaches Sanctification through Forgiveness. Rome confuses Justification and Sanctification, and says that the former is by the infusion of grace and includes both remission and renovation. But this is really to rob the soul of the objective ground of righteousness and confuses spiritual acceptance with spiritual attainments. Not only so, it tends to base Justification on our own merit. Justification in the Scriptural sense is independent of and anterior to the spiritual state or condition, which, however, necessarily follows.[2] It must, therefore, be evident that between the doctrine of Justification as taught in our Article and that inculcated by Rome, there is " a great gulf fixed," as indeed, our great theologian Hooker clearly teaches.

" Wherein, then, do we disagree ? We disagree about the nature of the very essence of the medicine whereby Christ cureth our disease ; about the manner of applying it ; about the number and the power of means which God requireth in us for the effectual applying thereof to our soul's comfort. . . . This is the mystery of the Man of sin. This maze the Church of Rome doth cause her followers to tread when they ask her the way of justification."[3]

It is of vital importance to keep clear this distinction between the doctrine of the two Churches because there is so much confusion to-day in regard to the basis and ground of our acceptance with God. Thus, a well-known preacher[4] published a volume of sermons entitled *The Life of Justification*, but it is only possible to accept this expression with careful qualifications and safeguards ; a more Scriptural idea would be " The Life of the Justified," or " The Life of Sanctification," since Justification is an act, not a process, and, as already pointed out, covers the whole of the Christian life from beginning to end. The confusion between the

---

[1] Lindsay, *History of the Reformation*, Vol. II, p. 580. See also pp. 576–580.
[2] "Protestants claim that justification is complete from the first. The father of the parable does not leave his prodigal son outside the house until he has shown his repentance by his works; but he goes forth to meet him, and falls upon his neck and kisses him, and has the best robe put on him, and a ring on his finger, and shoes on his feet, and kills for him the fatted calf. The sinner is not taken back into the Divine favour by degrees, cautiously and grudgingly, but he is restored to all his privileges as a child of God. This is the only way to make the work of sanctification, which immediately begins, complete. It is a work which can go forward only after the relation of fatherhood and sonship is fully re-established. It is only by such love that the sinner's love can be made perfect. 'We love Him because He first loved us' (1 John iv. 19)," (Stearns, *ut supra*, p. 447).
[3] Hooker, Sermon II, 5.   [4] Canon Body.

Anglican and Roman doctrines of Justification may perhaps be said to date from the time of the Tractarian Movement, when Newman's sermons took up a position scarcely recognisable from that of the Church of Rome.[1]

II.—THE FOUNDATION OF JUSTIFICATION

1. The Article teaches that we are accounted righteous before God " only for the merit of our Lord Jesus Christ." This, of course, refers to His atoning work by which He removed the alienation between God and the sinner, and brought about our reconciliation. As we have already seen, the New Testament doctrine of reconciliation implies a change of relationship and not a mere alteration of feeling on man's part.[2] This doctrine of Justification for the merit of our Lord is in harmony with St. Paul's words, " In Him all that believe are justified " (Acts xiii. 39). The ambiguity of the word " for " is entirely removed by a comparison of the Latin *propter*, " on account of."[3]

As already stated, the Article in its present form was due to Archbishop Parker's revision after the Confession of Wurtemberg, but there is one point of singular importance that should not be overlooked. In

---

[1] "In a most characteristic passage Cardinal Newman admits that δικαιόω means only to declare righteous, but adds that the divine declaration is *creative*. 'It is not like some idle sound, or a vague rumour coming at random and tending no whither; but it is "the *word* which goeth forth out of his mouth"; it has a sacramental power, being the instrument as well as the sign of his will. It never can "return unto him void, but It accomplishes that which he pleases, and prospers in the thing whereto he sends it." imputed righteousness is the coming in of actual righteousness. They whom God's sovereign voice pronounces just, forthwith become in their measure just.' How like Newman all this sounds; So original, so uplifting, and yet so empty of reality and so distant from Saint Paul! Through Newman's discussion one can seldom catch even the faintest and most flashing glimpse of the Apostle" (O. A. Curtis, *The Christian Faith*, p. 362).

For a fuller treatment of the various truths connected with Justification, see Paterson, *The Rule of Faith*, Index, s.v. Justification ; Wace, *The Principles of the Reformation*, pp. 50–64.

[2] "In Scripture, to reconcile one party *to* another means, to bring back the first party to the other's clemency, not to persuade the first party to lay aside prejudice against the other. 'Get reconciled to thy brother' (Matt. v. 24), means, 'Go to thy *offended* brother, and get his forgiveness.' 'Get reconciled to God' (2 Cor. v. 20), likewise means, 'Go to thy *offended* God and, in His own offered way, get His acceptance.' Reconciliation, studied in its Scriptural usage, is a word not in favour of a view which sees in the Atoning Sacrifice *primarily* an appeal to the heart of man to lay aside hard thoughts of God" (Moule, *Justification by Faith*, p. 29).

[3] "Christ took on Him the consequences of our sins—that is, He made our responsibilities, as sin had fixed them, His own. He did so when He went to the Cross—*i.e.* in His death. . . . All the responsibilities in which sin has involved us—responsibilities which are summed up in that death which is the wages of sin—have been taken by Christ upon Himself. The Apostle does not raise the question whether it is possible for one to assume the responsibilities of others in this way; he assumes (and the assumption, as we shall see, is common to all the New Testament writers) that the responsibilities of sinful men have been taken on Himself by the sinless Lamb of God. This is not a theorem he is prepared to defend; it is the gospel he has to preach. . . . Whoever says, 'He bare our sins' says substitution" (Denney, *The Death of Christ*, pp. 98, 99).

"There is no doubt about the word (ίλασμός). It means an offering that makes the face of God propitious" (Simpson, *ut supra*, p. 97).

the Wurtemberg Confession Jesus Christ is only spoken of as " Our
Lord," while our Article adds " and Saviour."   The significance of this
is that in opposition to the essentially legal view of Rome it was necessary
to institute the clearest possible contrast between the law and the Gospel
by declaring our Lord to be our Saviour.   This was an aspect frequently
and emphatically brought forward by the Reformers, especially in view
of the teaching of the Council of Trent that Jesus Christ was a Law-giver
and that the Gospel was the new " law."   It is therefore clear that the
introduction of these words, " and Saviour," were intended to emphasise
still further the difference between the Roman and Anglican views of
salvation.   Our Lord's perfect obedience even unto death, His payment of
the penalty due to our transgression, His spotless righteousness, the whole
merit of His Divine Person and atoning work, form the ground of our
justification.   The merit is reckoned to us, put to our account.   God
looks at us in Him, not only as pardoned, but as righteous.   " He who
knew no sin was made sin for us that we might become God's righteousness in Him " (2 Cor. v. 21).[1]   This is the great and satisfying doctrine
of the imputed righteousness of Christ which is clearly taught by the
Article as meritorious on our behalf.   It is sometimes argued that this
theory is not mentioned in the Article because of its association with what
is sometimes called " legal fiction."[2]   But in the light of the teaching of
the Article on our Lord's merit by which we are accounted righteous
before God, the doctrine of imputation is clear, and, indeed, has been
taught plainly, as we have just seen, by so representative a man as Hooker.[3]

2.   This reference to the merit of our Lord brings into greater contrast
the negative aspect emphasised in the Article, " and not for our own
works or deservings."   Here, again, the ambiguity of " for " is made
perfectly clear by *propter*, " on account of."   At this point another
significant change from the Wurtemberg Confession must be noted.   In
the German formulary the words are " on account of the merit of the
works of the law " (*meritum operum legis*), but in our Article this is
widened into " our own works and deservings " (*opera et merita nostra*).

[1] "Christ hath merited righteousness for as many as are found in Him. In Him
God findeth us if we be faithful, for by faith we are incorporated into Him . . . the
man which in himself is impious, full of iniquity, full of sin, him being found in Christ
through faith, and having his sin in hatred through repentance, him God beholdeth
with a gracious eye, putteth away his sin by not imputing it; taketh quite away the
punishment due thereunto by pardoning it, and accepteth him in Jesus Christ, as perfectly righteous as if he had fulfilled all that is commanded him in the law—shall I say
more perfectly righteous than if himself had fulfilled the whole law? I must take heed
what I say; but the Apostle saith (2 Cor. v. 21) 'God made Him which knew no sin,
to be sin for us, that we might be made the righteousness of God in Him.' Such we
are in the sight of God the Father as the very Son of God Himself . . . we care for
no knowledge in the world but this, that man hath sinned and God hath suffered; that
God hath made Himself the sin of men, and that men are made the righteousness of
God" (Hooker, Sermon II, 6).
[2] Gibson, *The Thirty-nine Articles*, p. 406.
[3] It is also curious that this very idea of the imputation of Christ's merit is vindicated
on another page by Bishop Gibson, who argues strongly in favour of the reality involved in what is called "a sort of legal fiction" (p. 396).

It seems clear that the intention was to make our Article more definitely anti-Roman in view of the teaching of the Council of Trent. Then, too, the word " deservings " is much wider than " works," and this would tend to exclude everything human from the ground of our Justification. It is also significant that in the Council of Trent we find these very words, " good works and deservings " (*bonis ipsorum operibus et meritis*). It is absolutely impossible for human works or merits to form the basis of Justification, for our obedience to law could not bring this about. God requires perfect obedience (Gal. iii. 10), and this man cannot render. Human nature has ever been attempting to establish its own righteousness, but failure has always been the result. The Jews of old (Rom. x. 3) and mankind to-day alike fail because of a twofold inability; inability to blot out the past, and inability to guarantee the present and future.[1] Justifying righteousness must be by a perfect obedience, and only One ever rendered this. Nothing could be clearer than the Article in regard to the absolute impossibility of human merit in connection with Justification.

III.—THE MEANS OF JUSTIFICATION

1. The merit of our Lord becomes ours " by faith." " Through Him all that believe are justified " (Acts xiii. 39). Here, again, the Latin distinction is clear and significant. We are justified *propter meritum Christi*, but *per fidem*. Faith is never associated with the ground of Justification, but only as its means or channel. And all the New Testament references to faith indicate this in the clearest possible way.[2] Trust implies dependence upon another and the consequent cessation of dependence upon ourselves. Faith is, therefore, the acknowledgment of our own inability and the admission of our need of another's ability. Faith links us to Christ and is the means of our appropriation of His merit. The full meaning of faith in the New Testament is trust. (1) The primary idea is belief in a fact (ὅτι, 1 John v. 1); (2) the next is belief in a person's word (μοι, John iv. 21); (3) but the fullest is trust in a person (εἰς, John iii. 16). Thus, faith in its complete sense includes the assent of the mind and the consent of the will, the credence of the intellect and the confidence of the heart. As such, it is best understood as trust, the attitude of one person to another.[3]

2. The reason why faith is emphasised is that it is the only possible answer to God's revelation. From the earliest days this has been so. The word of the Lord came to Abraham and he at once responded by simple trust (Gen. xv. 1-6). To the same effect are the various illus-

[1] "There is no man's case so dangerous as his whom Satan hath persuaded that his own righteousness shall present him pure and blameless in the sight of God" (Hooker, Sermon II, 7).
[2] In Romans iii. 25, διά, and the genitive case; Romans i. 17, ἐκ, and the genitive case; Romans iii. 28, the dative.
[3] For a thorough treatment see *Faith*, by Bishop Moule of Durham.

trations of faith in Hebrews xi., all implying response to a previous revelation. As between man and man the absence of faith is a barrier to communion, so it is in things spiritual. Faith in man answers to grace in God. Faith is the correlative of promise. Trust answers to truth; faith renounces self and emphasises God's free gift.[1] There is no merit in faith. It is self-assertion with a view to self-surrender. As Hooker has said, " God doth justify the believing man, yet not for the worthiness of his belief, but for His worthiness Who is believed."[2] We are not justified by belief in Christ, but by Christ in Whom we believe. Faith is nothing apart from its Object, and is only valuable as it leads us to Him who has wrought a perfect righteousness, and as it enables us to appropriate Him as the Lord our righteousness.[3]

The question of Baptism is often discussed in relation to faith, and it is sometimes argued that faith tends to make us dispense with Sacraments. But this is not the case. The Sacrament of Baptism is not a channel, which is the old *opus operatum* theory; it does not convey the germ of life, but only provides the sphere in which that germ may express itself and grow. The true idea of Baptism is, therefore, covenantal[4] as the seal of an already existing faith (Rom. iv. 11), and as such it has its necessary place, but it is not that of reception.

IV.—THE VALUE OF JUSTIFICATION

The Article speaks of the doctrine of Justification by Faith as " most wholesome, and very full of comfort," and this is not surprising because every real revival of spiritual life has been associated with it as the true explanation of how the Atonement is appropriated by sinful men.

1. Justification in Christ through faith is a necessity for spiritual health (" most wholesome "). The Council of Trent clearly taught the meritoriousness of Good Works.[5] But as long as this is emphasised there cannot possibly be that spiritual life which is found in the New Testa-

---

[1] "Faith is an activity of the whole soul, of the intellect, the sensibility, and the will. There is an intellectual element in it; in order to trust we must know the person whom we trust, and know something about him. This is where the assent to truth comes in, or rather begins to come in. Then there is an element of feeling in faith; we cannot stand in this relation to another person without experiencing certain emotions respecting him, such as love, reverence, admiration, or the like. Finally, there is an element of will in faith, and this is the distinctive element. This is what makes faith a moral activity. There is choice in it. We may exercise it or abstain from it. There is always in true faith, a laying of our will, to an extent greater or less, into the keeping of another will. These three elements are not always present in the same proportion. Now one is more prominent, now another. But always in its deepest essence faith is a matter of the will, of free choice" (Stearns, *ut supra*, p. 451).

[2] *Definition of Justification*, Ch. XXXIII.

[3] "Christian faith is the faith of a transaction. It is not the committing of one's thought in assent to any proposition, but the trusting of one's being to a *being*, there to be rested, kept, guided, moulded, governed, and possessed for ever. It gives you God, fills you with God in immediate, experimental knowledge, puts you in possession of all there is in Him, and allows you to be invested with His character itself" (*Life of Bushnell*, p. 192, *seq.*).

[4] See on Article XXVII.   [5] Session 6, Ch. XVI.

ment. Justification by faith is the foundation of spiritual peace. The soul looks backward, outward, upward, onward, and even inward, and is able to say with the Apostle, "justified from all things," and as a result of "being justified by faith, we have peace with God" (Rom. v. 1). When this is realised then all questions of human merit disappear, and the fabric of Roman Catholicism falls to the ground. This Justification is immediate, certain, complete, and abiding.[1] If it should be said that such a doctrine is Lutheran only, it may be at once replied that the teaching is ages earlier than Luther because it is the very warp and woof of the New Testament itself.[2]

Justification by faith is really the only answer to the moral perplexities of the doctrine of original sin. It vindicates God's righteousness while manifesting His mercy (Acts xvii. 30, R.V.; Rom. iii. 25, R.V.). Our deepest need is a right idea of the character of God with whom we have to do. How He can be just and yet justify the ungodly is insoluble apart from Jesus Christ. Jesus Christ is the proof of God's capacity to forgive while remaining just (Rom. iii. 26).[3] A sin-convicted soul demands at least as much righteous indignation of sin in God as it feels itself. This is seen in the Cross. It is characteristic of St. Paul's teaching in Romans that the Cross is the manifestation of God's righteousness rather than of His mercy (Rom. iii. 21-27).[4] In all this it will never be forgotten that faith is not the ground, but only the means of our Justification, and the strength or weakness of our trust will not affect the fact, but only the enjoyment of our Justification.

This doctrine is also the secret of spiritual liberty. All the Reformers felt and declared this, and it was with sure spiritual insight that Luther spoke of it as "the Article of a standing or falling Church"; indeed, we may go further and say with a modern writer that it is "the Article of a standing or falling soul." It removes the bondage of the soul, sets the

---

[1] Dr. Simpson quotes an interesting extract from the *Life of Dr. R. W. Dale*, referring to the life of Pusey:
"The absence of joy in his religious life was only the inevitable effect of his conception of God's method of saving man; in parting with the Lutheran truth concerning justification he parted with the springs of gladness" (*ut supra*, p. 155).

[2] "What other thing was capable of covering our sins than His righteousness? By what other One was it possible that we, the wicked and the ungodly, could be justified than by the only Son of God? O sweet exchange! O unsearchable operation! O benefits surpassing all expectation! that the wickedness of many should be hid in a single righteous One, and that the righteousness of One should justify many transgressors" (Epistle to Diognetus, c. 9, Clark's Ante-Nicene Library, Vol. I, p. 312).

[3] In *Present Day Theology*, by S. L. Wilson, two quotations are found which bear directly on this Article: "'Plato, Plato,' said Socrates, 'perhaps God can forgive deliberate sin, but I do not see how'" (p. 133). Dr. Shedd tells of a visit to St. Margaret's Church, Westminster, where he heard a sermon from a young clergyman on the Atonement. Among other striking and truthful utterances this was one: "The Atonement of Jesus Christ is the *hold* which the sinner has upon God." This sentence is the Gospel in a nutshell. By pleading the merits of Christ's oblation, the sinful creature, utterly powerless in himself, becomes almighty with God. For in so doing he brings an argument to bear upon the infinite justice and the infinite mercy which is omnipotent (p. 145).

[4] Simpson, *ut supra*, pp. 75, 77.

N

prisoner free, introduces him directly to God, and gives continual access to the Holiest. It therefore cuts at the root of all sacerdotal mediation as unnecessary and dangerous. As such, it is easy to understand the intense opposition shown to this doctrine on the part of the theologians of the Church of Rome.[1]

2. This doctrine is also a necessity for spiritual power (" very full of comfort "). It is the foundation of holiness. The soul is introduced into the presence of God, receives the Holy Spirit, realises the indwelling presence of Christ, and in these finds the secret and guarantee of purity of heart and life. It brings the soul into relation with God, so that from imputed righteousness comes imparted righteousness. It is this that keeps the doctrine from the charge of mere intellectual orthodoxy without spiritual vitality. So far from the doctrine putting a premium upon care-lessness, it is in reality one of the greatest safeguards of morality, because it is one of the springs of holiness. When St. Paul was charged with what is now called Antinomianism, he did not tone down his doctrine in the least, but declared it all the more fully as the very heart of the Gospel.[2]

It is also the secret of true spiritual service. The soul released from anxiety about itself is free to exercise concern about others. The heart is at leisure from itself to set forward the salvation of those around.[3] When Christian workers obtain a clear insight into this doctrine and yield the life to its power and influence it becomes the means of liberty to spiritual captives, and the secret of peace and blessing to hearts in spiritual darkness and fear.

From all this it is easy to see what the Article teaches, the intense and immense spiritual blessing of the doctrine, and there are signs that the truth is being realised afresh by many who have been " tied and bound by the chain of " a purely legal view of Christianity.[4] Certainly, if we

---

[1] "Nothing is more characteristic of Churches than their attitude to assurance, and the place they give it in their preaching and in their systems of doctrine. Speaking broadly, we may say that in the Romish Church it is regarded as essentially akin to presumption; in the Protestant Churches it is a privilege or a duty; but in the New Testament religion it is simply a fact. This explains the joy which, side by side with the sense of infinite obligation, is the characteristic note of Apostolic Christianity" (Denney, *ut supra*, p. 288).

[2] Simpson, *ut supra*, p. 134 f.

[3] "It is only in the assured peace of being 'joyfully ready' to meet the ultimate issues of life that the man's whole personality is liberated to serve the Lord in that beauty of holiness which is not marred by the painful efforts of a scrupulous self-consciousness" (Simpson, *ut supra*, p. 153).

[4] An able statement of this truth in modern form will be found in the *Church Missionary Review* for March 1910, in a paper by the Rev. H. G. Grey, of which the closing paragraph may be given: "Two or three years ago a student followed me home in the dark from our preaching-place in Lahore. On the way he said: 'I wish to ask you a question. You said just now in your preaching that according to Christianity a man can go to God by Jesus of Nazareth just as he is, before he has overcome his sins. Did you mean it?' I replied, 'Yes, if it were not so I should never be here myself.' 'Well,' he said, 'let me tell you about myself. I am a Mohammedan student at the Government College; and I often make resolutions to keep from sin, but I find that after a month or two I fall, and I pretty well despair of ever becoming better.

are to get back not merely to the joy, peace, liberty, and power of Reformation days, but still more to the primitive truth of the Christian life recorded in the New Testament, we must give the most definite prominence to this truth of Justification in Christ through faith.[1]

Roman Catholics say that the doctrine of Justification by Faith involves an inadequate estimate of sin and its consequences, and, therefore, implies a too easy apprehension of forgiveness. But the doctrine really arose out of the very opposite cause, namely, that at the Reformation Rome, by her teaching and practice, maintained a most inadequate and degraded sense of sin and its consequences, and the conscience of the Reformers revolted at the immorality of such teaching. Rome said that Justification by Faith was attended by a low estimate of penitence, and that it depreciated the office of the Church. But it really sprang from a deep sense of the need of penitence and grew to full distinctness under a desire to vindicate for the ministry and sacraments a real operative power. If we read the Theology of the pre-Reformation period we can see the levity, and then in the Reformation period the depth, of conviction of sin and the need of grace.

The theses of Luther commenced the subject by saying that our Lord wished our life to be one long penitence, and this obviously opposed the mediæval Indulgences. He said that the discipline of punishment for sin rested solely with God, and the Church could not dispense with it. He distinguished between *pœna* and *culpa*, punishment and guilt, a distinction which is always needed when personality is apt to be forgotten. Faith and forgiveness are essentially personal and imply a personal relation to God just as they do to man. Remission of guilt and remission of consequences are, of course, totally different.

But the notion being annihilated that the Church had power to remit punishment for sin, what do the ordinances do? Now while maintaining their office as means of grace, the controversy brought out their

But if what you say is true, it would give me courage and hope.' This led to many interesting talks with him, which I need not now detail. The point I would draw out is that both at home and abroad, both for Christians and non-Christians, the old fundamental truth of Justification by Faith—that God 'justifieth the ungodly' *freely*, in order to make him afterwards godly—is the attractive 'power of God unto salvation!'" (J. G. Simpson, *What is the Gospel?*, Ch. V). For other modern presentations see Falconer, *The Unfinished Symphony*, Chs. V, VI.

[1] "The doctrine of justification by faith is the reassertion, in theological language, of the truth put more simply by Jesus in His teaching concerning the childlike spirit. It describes the substitution of the attitude of personal trust which is characteristic of sonship for the legal relationship which is expressed in terms of good works, merit and reward. It has its psychological basis in the insight, won by Luther from a painful experience, that any attempt to earn or to deserve forgiveness by good works does but lead to deeper self-condemnation and distrust. Historically the way was prepared for it by the revival of Biblical scholarship, with its resulting rediscovery of the Pauline theology. From Paul Luther learned that the only sure way to find assurance and peace is to abandon all hope of self-righteousness, and to seek in personal commitment of the soul to God the spring of a higher life. Catholicism had recognized the legitimacy of this course in the case of exceptional individuals. Protestantism laid it down as the law of normal Christian living" (W. Adams Brown, *Christian Theology in Outline*, p. 313).

primary force as authorised witnesses from God to man to forgiveness and reconciliation. When man is struggling with a sense of guilt his supreme need is a comfort which comes from God with a positive authenticated assurance. It is, of course, true that assurance is conveyed by the Holy Spirit, but He has appointed the Church, the ministers and the ordinances to be His authorised witnesses to the soul for the forgiveness craved. So that we are not left alone to search, but God commands ministers to go and offer forgiveness.

The necessity of this doctrine thus arose out of these circumstances. The personal relation of God being obscured, the teaching of the later Middle Ages had exaggerated all forms of dread of consequences of sin hereafter. This is abundantly illustrated in Dante's great works. But when the real relation of God was brought out, and when it was proclaimed that God had reconciled man in Christ, the penitent sinner was enabled to grasp the promises of the Gospel with the result that heart and conscience were immediately and fully emancipated.

V.—THE CONFIRMATION OF JUSTIFICATION BY FAITH

1. The Article is unique in the fact that it refers to one of the Homilies for a fuller expression of the doctrine here stated : " As more largely is expressed in the Homily of Justification." The issue of the First Book of Homilies in 1547 is generally regarded as the first step towards doctrinal reformation. As long as Henry VIII lived any substantial doctrinal change in the direction of the Reformation was practically impossible, and even when the First Book of the Homilies was issued Roman doctrines and practices were still the religion of the nation as a whole. The Council of Trent had stated its position in regard to the Rule of Faith, Original Sin, Justification, and the Sacraments in relation to Justification in 1546-1547, and it is not without point to observe that the first three Homilies referred respectively to Holy Scripture, Sin and its Results, and the Salvation of Mankind, so that the First Book of Homilies may rightly be said to constitute the Anglican answer to Trent on the three great questions of the Rule of Faith, Original Sin, and Justification. It is, of course, frequently pointed out that there is no Homily with the exact title mentioned in the Article, " The Homily of Justification," but there can be no doubt that the reference is to what is known as " The Homily of Salvation." It is the Third Homily in the First Book, and is entitled " A Sermon of the Salvation of Mankind by only Christ our Saviour from sin and death Everlasting." This is immediately followed by " A short Declaration of the True and Lively Christian Faith," and " A Sermon of Good Works annexed unto Faith," both of which were apparently intended to be read in connection with that " Of the Salvation of Mankind " in order that the various points might be treated more fully. This Homily is known to have been peculiarly objectionable to the parties of the mediæval religion in England, because the battle of the

Reformation was already beginning when Gardiner opposed what he called " My Lord of Canterbury's Homily of Salvation." It is more than possible that the Homily originally written preceded the Council of Trent by five years.[1] If, on the other hand, it was not actually written till 1547, it may have been revised before publication to meet still more definitely the error of Rome promulgated at Trent. But this question of date is of very little significance, since in any case the Homily is fundamentally different from the teaching of the Church of Rome, and a careful comparison of the Tridentine definition with the wording of the Article shows that, as it has been well said, the rival Churches hit upon a closely similar language independently, with this difference, however, that Rome accepted, while the Church of England rejected the mediæval doctrine of Justification.

2. The precise authority of the Homily as a whole is frequently discussed. Bishop Harold Browne speaks of it as " a Homily which has unusual authority, as being virtually assented to by everyone who signs the Articles." [2] To the same effect, Boultbee says, " The Article so distinctly refers us to this Homily for a further explanation of the doctrine in question, that it becomes of almost equal authority with the Article itself.[3] In accordance with this view most works on the Articles quote freely from the Homily in illustration and confirmation of its teaching. Almost every point of the Homily is in direct opposition to the plainest teaching of Trent. Thus, instead of Divine grace making our works meritorious in the sight of God, the Homily ascribes all merit and glory to the Lamb of God Who is " best worthy to have it," adding that, " man cannot make himself righteous by his own works, neither in part nor in the whole."

A careful consideration of the Homily will show beyond all question (1) the emphatic teaching that faith alone has the office of justifying; (2) that while works are necessary, they are so not for the purpose of justifying, but as the fruits of Justification;[4] (3) that faith is no mere intellectual acceptance of truth but a personal trust in God's mercy and Christ's sacrifice.[5]

---

[1] Tomlinson, *Prayer Book, Articles, and Homilies*, p. 238.
[2] *Exposition of the Thirty-nine Articles*, p. 293.
[3] *The Theology of the Church of England*, p. 100; see also Tomlinson, *ut supra*, p. 232: "This Homily, it will be remembered, has an authority greater than any other, being especially referred to and incorporated in Article XI."
[4] "Faith does not shut out repentance, hope, love, dread, and the fear of God, to be joined with faith in every man that is justified; but it shutteth them out from the office of justifying."
[5] For those who are unable to read the Homily itself, reference may be made to Harold Browne, Gibson, and Boultbee, where full extracts are given. It is curious to notice in certain quarters the nervous dread apparently shown lest there should be any slight set upon good works, which, as we shall see in the next Article, was never done. All that was essential, as the Article and Homily show, was to exclude altogether the thought of good works from the province of justification. This caution is apparently as necessary to-day as ever, especially where there is a tendency somehow or other to reintroduce works wrought by grace as part of the element of justification.

One point remains for special notice, though it has been implied already and will call for further attention under the next Article. The doctrine of our Church is sometimes stated as " Justification by faith alone," though as this precise phrase does not occur in our formularies it is liable to misconstruction, and is often misrepresented both inside and outside our Church as " Solifidianism," as though it meant some purely intellectual acceptance of truth by which alone a man is justified. But in the first place, as we have seen, faith in the proper sense of the term is personal trust, and as this links on the soul to God in Christ we see at once that all that is intended by " faith only " is the avoidance of anything like works for the purpose of Justification. The quotation already made from the Homily suffices to show this, and in exact agreement with it are other statements :—

" Faith putteth us from itself, and remitteth or appointeth us unto Christ for to have only by Him remission of our sins or justification. So that our faith in Christ (as it were) saith unto us thus : It is not I that take away your sins, but it is Christ only, and to Him only I send you for that purpose, forsaking therein all your good virtues, words, thoughts and works, and only putting your trust in Christ."[1]

[1] Homily of Salvation. For further study of this subject, see Westcott, *St. Paul's Teaching on Justification*; Litton, *Introduction to Dogmatic Theology* (Second Edition), p. 264 ff. Articles on "Justification"; "Righteousness," *Protestant Dictionary*.

ARTICLE XII

Of Good Works.

Albeit that good works, which are the fruits of Faith, and follow after Justification, cannot put away our sins, and endure the severity of God's judgment; yet are they pleasing and acceptable to God in Christ, and do spring out necessarily of a true and lively Faith; insomuch that by them a lively Faith may be as evidently known as a tree discerned by the fruit.

De bonis Operibus.

Bona opera, quæ sunt fructus Fidei, et Justificatos sequuntur, quanquam peccata nostra expiare, et divini judicii severitatem ferre non possunt; Deo tamen grata sunt, et accepta in Christo, atque ex vera et viva fide necessario profluunt; ut plane ex illis æque fides viva cognosci possit, atque arbor ex fructu judicari.

IMPORTANT EQUIVALENTS.

Follow after justification	= *justificatos sequuntur.*
To put away	= *expiare.*
To endure the severity	= *severitatem ferre.*
Of God's judgment	= *Divini judicii.*
Acceptable to God in Christ	= *accepta in Christo.*
Out of a lively faith	= *ex viva fide.*
[May be] discerned	= *[possit] judicari.*

THIS and the next Article appropriately deal with the relation of works to Justification. Article XII shows their value when put in the right place; Article XIII shows their worthlessness when put in the wrong place. There was no Article corresponding to this in the Forty-two Articles of 1553, and it is thought that this was suggested by the Confession of Wurtemberg, and may have been intended against both Anabaptism and Rome. It is certain that there was no idea of opposing the teaching of Article XI, which was made so much clearer and more definitely anti-Roman in 1563, because there was an Article on Good Works in thorough harmony with this Article as early as the Confession of Augsburg, 1530, and Good Works is the subject of one of the Homilies of the First Book, dated 1547. The Article is the natural and necessary corollary of the teaching of Article XI on Justification by Faith.

I.—THE TEACHING OF THE ARTICLE

Before going into the subject in general it will be useful to look carefully at what the Article states concerning Good Works, for in the light of its teaching we shall be better able to appreciate the controversies connected with the subject.

1. The meaning of Good Works.—They are described as " the fruits of faith." The phrase " Good Works " corresponds to two distinct yet

199

connected terms in the Greek descriptive of the life of the Christian believer. Sometimes the reference is to works that are intrinsically good (ἀγαθά, Eph. ii. 10; cf. Phil. i. 6; 1 Tim. ii. 10). At other times the phrase refers to works which are also outwardly attractive (καλά, 1 Tim. iii. 1; v. 10; v. 25). So that the Christian is to produce in his life actions that are good in themselves and outwardly beautiful. Good works are in this respect contrasted with works that spring from law (Rom. ix. 32; Gal. ii. 16); unfruitful works of darkness (Eph. v. 11); dead works (Heb. vi. 1; ix. 14); evil works (1 John iii. 12).

2. The proper place of Good Works.—They " follow after Justification." Thus the Article briefly but clearly harmonises with the teaching of the preceding Article in regard to justification.

3. The imperfection of Good Works.—They " cannot put away our sins and endure the severity of God's judgment." Another emphasis on the Reformation doctrine, which was entirely opposed to the meritoriousness of works, and in this sense was in the strongest contrast with the teaching of the Council of Trent.

4. The Divine Regard for Good Works.—Although they are imperfect in the way the Article states, " yet are they pleasing and acceptable to God in Christ, and do spring out necessarily of a true and lively faith." It is thus seen that good works have their proper and essential place. When a man is " in Christ " and is exercising faith in Him, works necessarily and inevitably follow.

5. The relation of faith to Good Works.—" Insomuch that by them a lively faith may be as evidently known as a tree discerned by the fruit."

These statements of the Article give in outline form a true Scriptural view of the place and power of good works in the Christian life. There was no idea of stating a complete doctrine of Sanctification, but only of dealing with those points connected with the controversies of the sixteenth century in relation to excess or defect.[1]

II.—THE HISTORY OF THE ARTICLE [2]

Pelagianism and semi-Pelagianism necessarily involved the question of the value of good works. There was a tendency to semi-Pelagianism in the Greek Fathers, but it is difficult to quote accurately on this point, since the East was mainly speculative rather than moral, and was compelled to emphasise human freedom against Gnosticism. The question had not really been raised at that time, though speaking generally, the sense of sin and with it the consciousness of redemption and its expression in life cannot be found so deeply experienced and expressed in Eastern writers. It was St. Augustine who necessarily raised this question in all

[1] For the Christian doctrine of Sanctification see Moule, *Outlines of Christian Doctrine*, p. 190 ff.; Paterson, *The Rule of Faith*, Index, s.v. Sanctification; Hopkins, *The Law of Liberty in the Spiritual Life*; Walter Marshall, *The Gospel Mystery of Sanctification*; Macgregor, *The Holy Life and How to Live it*; Griffith Thomas, *The Catholic Faith*, p. 92 ff.; *Grace and Power*.
[2] See more fully, Moule, *ut supra*, p. 190.

its force and importance in his controversy with Pelagius, and his main position was that *gratia prævenit voluntatem*. Semi-Pelagianism, as we have seen,[1] maintained that some good will remained in man sufficient to wish to be healed, but more orthodox writers of the fifth century argued that even this " wish " was the result of Divine grace. It is not surprising that in the Middle Ages the tendency to semi-Pelagianism is found, because the leading writers were wrong on original sin, for if original sin meant only the deprivation of super-added grace, then man is necessarily capable of exercising primary good motions. Thomas Aquinas took substantially the Augustinian view and urged that God is the *primum movens*. On the other side, Duns Scotus took the semi-Pelagian view, and said : *Liberum arbitrium sic confitemur ut dicamus non semper indigere Dei auxilio tamen sine gratia non sufficit homini ad salutem.* This developed into the doctrine of man's capability of *bonum morale*, and of loving God *ex propriis viribus*. The Council of Trent was divided on this subject, but said : *Liberum arbitrium minime extinctum viribus licet attenuatum.* It was also virtually semi-Pelagian as to man's co-operation with Divine grace, and it anathematised those who denied merit to good works. This was the point at which the controversy became acute in the sixteenth century, and the whole question was raised in connection with man's Justification.

III.—THE QUESTION STATED

The Pauline doctrine of redemption clearly separates works from all part in Justification (Rom. iii. 27 ; iv. 1-5). This was one of the fundamental issues at stake between St. Paul and the Jews, and both Galatians and Romans were written almost entirely for the express purpose of repudiating all idea of works as having any share in man's Justification. On the other hand, the Apostle is equally clear as to works being the essential and necessary outcome of faith (Rom. vi. 18-22 ; viii. 4). Justification is a means to an end. It removes the penalty in order that by the grace of God the pollution and power of sin may also be met. And so the pardon, acceptance, and peace are intended to lead on to purity and progress. Following the Apostle, our Church makes it abundantly clear that works are in no sense included in or with faith as the condition of Justification, but spring from faith as the fruit of Justification. This is not only clear from the Article, but from the Homily on Good Works.

" Of this faith three things are specially to be noted. First, that this faith doth not lie dead in the heart, but is lively and fruitful in bringing forth good works. Second, that without it can no good works be done, that shall be acceptable and pleasant to God. Third, what manner of good works they be that this faith doth bring forth."[2]

---

[1] See above, Article X, pp. 178-9.   [2] *The Homilies.*

The way in which the third of these points is elaborated in the Article proves what our Church means by Good Works. After showing how the Jews set their own traditions as high as, or above God's commandments, the Homily goes on to speak of what happened in the sixteenth century to the same effect, including a number of superstitious beliefs and customs, and even pretence of fulfilment of the chief vows of religion, all of which is spoken of as " ungodly and counterfeit religion," and " other kinds of papistical superstitions and abuses." The Homily then closes with an earnest and forceful exhortation to keep God's commandments, emphasising the necessity of having " an assured faith in God," and then " for His sake love to all men." To the same effect is the teaching of the greatest of the Reformed theologians. Thus, Hooker says :—

" Wherefore, we acknowledge a dutiful necessity of doing well, but the meritorious dignity of well-doing we utterly renounce."[1]

" Christ came not to abrogate and to take away good works. . . . We ourselves do not teach Christ alone, excluding our own faith, unto justification ; Christ alone, excluding our own works, unto sanctification ; Christ alone, excluding the one or the other as unnecessary unto salvation . . . . because we teach that faith alone justifieth, we, by this speech, never meant to exclude either hope or charity from being always joined as inseparable mates with faith in the man that is justified ; or *works from being added as necessary duties, required at the hands of every justified man."* [2]

And the last reviser of the Articles, Bishop Jewel, emphasises the same salutary and essential doctrine :—

" Because we say that justification standeth only upon the free grace and mercy of God, the adversaries report that we forbid good works. This is God's holy will, that for our exercise, whatsoever we do or say, be it never so well, it shall be ill taken."

At this point it seems necessary to notice several modern attempts to distinguish between Lutheran and Anglican doctrine on Justification.[3] Thus, one writer says that Luther " reduced faith to the level of mere belief. He made it that on account of (*propter*) which, instead of that through (*per*) which, we are justified ; or, in other words, treated it as the meritorious cause, rather than the condition, of our justification."[4] To the same effect are statements that " the peculiar symbol of Lutheranism is that a man is justified when he believes himself to be justified."[5] The curious thing is that this view of Luther should be held in the face of the admission that he " dreaded anything that savoured of human

[1] Hooker, Sermon II, 30, 31.   [2] *Ibid.*
[3] B. J. Kidd, *The Thirty-nine Articles*, p. 137; Forbes, *Explanation of the Thirty-nine Articles*, pp. 171, 179.
[4] Kidd, *ut supra*, p. 137.
[5] Forbes, *ut supra*, p. 182; Gibson, *ut supra*, p. 389.

merit."[1] If, therefore, Luther held that faith is the meritorious cause of salvation and yet dreaded " anything savouring of human merit " he is not the vigorous, masculine common-sense thinker that he has been supposed to be. The fact is that these writers fail to realise that the doctrine of Justification by faith was the key to Luther's teaching, and the means of his redemption from spiritual bondage, and while he may at times have been led to express himself incautiously in regard to good works, no one in reality was more insistent upon the importance of works in their proper place than he was. It is almost unnecessary to illustrate this from any of his writings, but in view of the opposition raised to him on this point it seems essential to dwell upon the matter. Thus, he says :—

" By faith alone in Christ and not by the works of the law or love are we declared righteous. Not that we reject works or love, as the adversaries accuse us, but that we do not allow ourselves to be diverted from the state of the present case."[2]

It may be safely said that Luther never speaks of man as justified on account of the merit of our faith (*propter fidem*), for faith is never declared to be the meritorious cause of Justification, but only as the means whereby we are enabled to produce good works after Justification. It is noteworthy that in the Augsburg Confession the statement is made that men " are justified for the sake of Christ by faith," where the Latin exactly corresponds to our Eleventh Article with its distinction between *propter* and *per*. There are several other proofs confirming this position which go to show beyond all question that our Church is in entire harmony with Luther on Justification and good works ; indeed, we may say that Article XI has utilised the Lutheran distinction of *propter* and *per* as against the errors of Rome. The confusion about Luther's views of Justification and works is only possible when a view of Justification is held[3] which is virtually identical with that of Rome, against which Luther and our Article took their stand. There was no desire or intention on the part of Luther or our English Reformers to neglect good works, but only to put them in their proper place and to insist upon their being of the character and quality laid down. Those who have any doubt on the subject should give careful attention to the Homilies on Faith and Good Works, which, as already mentioned, accompany the Homily of Salvation.

This doctrine of Luther, as embodied in our Articles, was held practically by all leading Anglicans for over a century. Bishop Bull himself bears witness to this when he speaks of " the same error as Luther and

---

[1] Kidd, *ut supra*, p. 137.
[2] Luther on Galatians; see other extracts in Boultbee, *The Theology of the Church of England*, p. 97 f.
[3] Forbes, *ut supra*, pp. 171–179.

most of our divines after his time." But the Bishop in 1669 published a work endeavouring to show the harmony between St. Paul and St. James on Justification, and, followed by some modern writers,[1] distinguished between a first justification here in the present life and a second justification hereafter when we stand before the Throne of God. But neither Scripture nor the Articles give any ground for this distinction; indeed, it is only another way of bringing back the Roman confusion between Justification and Sanctification.[2]

A certain aspect of Bull's view has been revived in modern times in what is known as the "germ theory of Justification." This means that God sees in faith the germ of what we shall become, and therefore justifies us by anticipation.[3] But this view tends to divert attention from the truth of Christ's work for us as the objective ground of Justification independent of and anterior to His work in us which is the subjective result of the objective Justification.[4] It also tends to confuse, as Rome does, between judicial position and spiritual condition, between relationship and character, between attitude and experience. On this theory the imputation of righteousness is not in order to our acceptance, but is a contemplation and anticipation of the results of acceptance in us. Further, this view tends more and more to make faith the ground of righteousness, the very point which Luther and our Reformers opposed with all their strength.[5] The view is based upon a misconception of what the Apostle means. The sinner is not reckoned *as if* he was righteous, but because

---

[1] *e.g.* Forbes, *ut supra*, p. 175.

[2] "Justification, in the mind of St. Paul, is not only preliminary and tentative but ultimate and final, and that in relation to this verdict of God he is looking at the sinner, as we say, *sub specie æternitatis*, not in connection with his progressive development under the influence of the Spirit" (Simpson, *Fact and Faith*, p. 136. See also Boultbee, *ut supra*, pp. 108–119; Litton, *Introduction to Dogmatic Theology* (Second Edition), p. 289 ff.).

[3] "Justification by Anticipation" is the title of a pamphlet written by Bishop Gore when he was a member of the Oxford Mission to Calcutta, and was engaged in controversy with a missionary of the C.M.S., the late Rev. Henry Williams of Krishnagur. The pamphlet is now out of print, but the doctrine is identical with that found in the Bishop's work on *The Epistle to the Romans.* It is also held by Dr. Kidd (*ut supra,* p. 133), and from a different standpoint, by Archbishop Temple (*The Universality of Christ,* p. 106).

[4] "It is a fundamental misconception of Pauline theology to assert that final acquittal can only take place on the basis of a realised holiness. On the contrary, sanctification is part of the glory, which shall only be fully realised with the redemption of the body. It is part of the gift of God, the inheritance of the saints in light, an anticipation of that body which shall be, an earnest, a first-fruits of the Spirit. Any other teaching, as the Reformers of the sixteenth century clearly perceived, leads us back by a circuitous route to the bondage of dead works, and that in the more deceptive form of those 'voluntary works' which were roundly denounced by Hugh Latimer" (Simpson, *ut supra,* p. 87).

"That God looks at us not as we are but as we are tending to become is a formula which, while it throws a man back upon himself, only obscures the fulness of St. Paul's meaning" (Simpson, *ut supra,* p. 88).

"The transformation of character through the indwelling of the Spirit of Christ he describes quite differently as sanctification or holiness" (Simpson, *ut supra,* p. 89. See also p. 134 ff.).

[5] "To identify faith with incipient holiness is to convert faith into what the Reformers would have regarded as a work" (Simpson, *ut supra,* p. 143).

he is righteous in Christ.   It is impossible to make the preposition εἰς in Rom. iv. 3 equivalent to ἀντί or ὡς.   Then, too, the objection to the Pauline doctrine dealt with in Rom. vi. 1 shows the error of this germ theory, for on such a view the Apostle's doctrine would not have been open to question.[1]   The verb "to justify," δικαιόω, is to treat a man as one whose account is clear, and it is quite inaccurate to speak of this as a "legal fiction"; on the contrary, it is a spiritual fact from a judicial standpoint.[2]   The justification has to do with God as the Judge, and if we may use the legal illustration, the Judge on the Bench has to do with the question of innocence or guilt, not with the transformation of a prisoner's character.   When, therefore, God justifies us, He deals with us as the Judge, and although it is easy to speak of this action as "forensic," it is none the less expressive of an absolute spiritual fact.[3]

The question of the harmony between St. Paul and St. James is one of great importance, and must, of course, be studied in all discussions of Justification, but there is no real difficulty if the two situations are made perfectly clear.

(*a*) St. Paul in Rom. iv is dealing with Abraham as recorded in Gen. xv. 6 (cf. Gal. iii. 6), and in that story Abraham is regarded as a man "justified by faith."

(*b*) St. James in ch. ii is dealing with Abraham in regard to the story of Genesis xxii which happened twenty-five years afterwards.

(*c*) If, then, Abraham in Gen. xv was living by faith, his standing during those twenty-five years must have been in accordance therewith, and this we know was the case (Heb. xi. 8-19).

So that the two Apostles are dealing with different though related standpoints in the life of Abraham; the former referring to the instrument and the latter to the proof of Justification.   St. Paul is writing about non-Christians (Rom. iii. 28); St. James is writing about professing Christians (ch. ii. 24).   St. Paul uses Gen. xv to prove the necessity of faith; St. James uses Gen. xxii to prove the necessity of works.   St. Paul teaches that works must spring from faith; St. James teaches that faith must be proved by works.   St. Paul is thus dealing with the error of legalism; St. James with the error of Antinomianism.   St. Paul is warning against merit; St. James against a mere intellectual orthodoxy.

Like every truth of the New Testament, Justification has various

---

[1] "It would have been easy for him to explain that in the last resort there could be no righteousness which was not actual, if he had meant no more by his emphatic statements concerning imputation than to express a preliminary Divine healing which is content for the time being to view men as they are tending to become and to anticipate the final verdict on their perfected characters. But St. Paul never attempts any such explanation. His reply, whenever the obvious objections to his doctrine are placed before his readers, is always an indignant appeal to the primal moral instincts" (Simpson, *ut supra*, p. 135).

[2] It is this that makes the statement in Sanday and Headlam on *Romans* (p. 36), that "the Christian life is made to have its beginning in a fiction" gravely wrong, or at any rate seriously unfortunate. The imputation of Christ's righteousness to the believer through faith is not a fiction, but a blessed and eternal fact of the spiritual realm.

[3] Simpson, *ut supra*, p. 74; Orr, *Christian View of God and the World*, p. 464.

aspects. Thus, we are justified by God the Author (Rom. iv. 5); by grace the reason (Rom. iii. 24); by blood the ground (Rom. v. 9); by resurrection the acknowledgment (Rom. iv. 25); by faith the means (Rom. v. 1); by words the evidence (Matt. xii. 37); by works the fruit (Jas. ii. 24). It has been aptly said, and the words sum up the whole contention, that St. Paul and St. James are not two soldiers of different armies fighting each other, but two of the same army fighting back to back against enemies coming from different directions. All this gives point to the well-known words of Calvin, " It is faith alone which justifies, and yet the faith which justifies is not alone."

The importance of the relation of faith and good works is not so prominent to-day in regard to controversy, but it is probably as essentially vital as ever, because the teaching of the Church of Rome continues the same, and the Council of Trent said :—

"Whosoever shall affirm that the good works of a justified man are in such sense the gifts of God, that they are not *also his worthy merits*, or that he *being justified by his good works, which are wrought by him through the grace of God, and the merits of Jesus Christ*, of whom he is a living member, does not *really deserve* increase of grace, eternal life, the enjoyment of that eternal life *if* he dies in a state of grace, *and even an increase of glory*—let him be accursed."

In harmony with this Bellarmine says :—

" For the work of Christ hath not only deserved of God that we should obtain salvation, *but also that we should obtain it by our own merits*."
" The Catholic Church pursues a middle course, teaching that our *chief hope* and confidence must be placed in God, yet *some* also in our own merits."[1]

From these statements it is clear that the necessity of the teaching of the Articles is as great to-day as ever. Then, too, the mediæval distinction between *fides informis* and *fides formata* has always been held to be impossible. According to the teaching of the Middle Ages *fides informis* was a purely speculative faith involving intellectual thought, but including neither love nor holiness, while *fides formata* meant faith perfected by the love and good works which spring from it. It was this latter faith to which was attributed the office of justifying. On the one hand, Luther and the English Reformers never taught that the *fides informis* was the true Christian faith involving trust, and on the other, they as clearly denied that *fides formata* had any part whatever in Justification, though emphasising it as the fruit of faith. It is, therefore, altogether wrong to assume that the Lutheran teaching on Justification by Faith, which is identical with the Anglican, is antinomian in its tendency. This charge, though often repeated, is unfounded, as the Confession of Augsburg clearly shows. Similarly, Luther in his Commentary on Galatians, takes the same line, when he said, " When we are out of

[1] Quoted in Caley, *Justification*, p. 61.

the matter of Justification we cannot enough praise and extol these works which God has commanded, for who can enough commend the profit and fruit of only one work which a Christian does in and through faith ? "[1] There is nothing antinomian here. Faith and good works are exactly in the same relation to Justification as they are in the English Article. It is another point of similarity between the Lutheran and Anglican teaching that both have been accused of antinomianism, as may be seen from the defences made by Hooker and Jewel, but it is the bare truth to say that the centuries which have elapsed since the Confession of Augsburg have not shown that the moral standard of Protestant nations is lower than that of those which are not Protestant.

But if the matter is not so prominent or so important in the controversial sphere, yet spiritually it is essential to keep the true relation between faith and good works. It may help us to understand this if we bear in mind the twofold righteousness found in the New Testament.

1. God's Righteousness.—Romans is mainly taken up with the question, How God can be righteous and yet pardon the sinner. This righteousness of God is apart from all law-keeping (Rom. iii. 21), since it is not on the principle of human works that man can be made acceptable to God (Gal. ii. 21). Righteousness is based on the atoning work of Christ, and is intended for all without exception who are willing to receive Him by faith. And thus the work of Christ on the Cross gives God an eternal basis on which to declare a sinner righteous at and from the moment that he believes in the Lord Jesus Christ (Rom. iii. 21-26). This is our standing in righteousness before God.

2. The Believer's Righteousness.—Then comes the practical walk in righteousness of the man who believes, a subject clearly brought out in Rom. vi. These two aspects of righteousness, while distinct, always go together, so that while none are saved by their own practical righteousness, yet God has declared that those who have accepted the Lord Jesus Christ as their righteousness are to live " soberly, righteously, and godly." We see something of this in the records of faith in Heb. xi, where men are regarded as at once standing in righteousness and yet exhibiting practical righteousness in daily life. Scripture has much to say on this latter aspect. We are to " follow after righteousness " (1 Tim. vi. 11). It is the first of three things of which the Kingdom of God consists (Rom. xiv. 17). This practical righteousness is " the fruit of the light " (Eph. v. 9); Christ is the standard of it (1 John iii. 10); and if a man " doeth not righteousness " it proves that he is " not of God " (1 John iii. 10). This righteousness, therefore, is the uprightness of the Christian in his daily walk, his integrity in small matters as well as great. The truth of the Lord Jesus Christ as our righteousness before God (Article XI), and also as our practical righteousness in dwelling in us and producing good works (Article XII) is one that we have to keep at once distinct and united.

[1] On Galatians, iii. 22.

The same twofold aspect of truth is seen in the various references to Sanctification, and although, as we have seen, the Article does not deal with this subject in general, it is important to have clearly before us the New Testament revelation in order that we may see controversially and spiritually the true relation between faith and good works.

1. Sanctification is sometimes considered from the judicial standpoint. Just as Romans deals with righteousness from the standpoint of law, so Hebrews is concerned with the sanctuary and deals with defilement, not with guilt.   The same work of Christ on the Cross that puts away our sins sanctifies us perfectly and forever, thereby fitting us eternally for God's presence (Heb. x. 10).   Sanctification in the sense of judicial standing is, of course, absolutely independent of our feelings and actions. The moment we accept Christ for salvation He becomes not only our Righteousness, but our Sanctification (Acts xxvi. 18; Heb. x. 14), and it is for this reason that Christians can be described as "sanctified in Christ Jesus," even though some of them were living in sad defilement (1 Cor. i. 2).   It is noteworthy, too, that the Three Persons of the Trinity are all occupied in our sanctification: the Father (Heb. x. 10), the Son (Heb. x. 10), the Spirit (2 Thess. ii. 13).   So that the moment we are "begotten again" we are also sanctified judicially, set apart for God by the work of Christ, to be owned and used for the Divine glory.

2. Sanctification is also considered from the practical standpoint. Soon after entering into the peace and joy of God's favour the believer is conscious of the power of sin within him, since Justification still leaves the sinful nature open to the power of sin.   It is at this point that instruction is needed to show that not only was a work done for us on the Cross centuries ago, but that a work is being done in us now by the Holy Spirit, and at this point comes the life-long progressive Sanctification, or walking in purity and practical holiness, which follows necessarily from our judicial position in Christ.   This is the meaning of the well-known words of Hooker :—

"There is a glorifying righteousness of men in the world to come: and there is a justifying and a sanctifying righteousness here. *The righteousness wherewith we shall be clothed in the world to come is both perfect and inherent; that whereby here we are justified is perfect but not inherent; that whereby we are sanctified, inherent, but not perfect. . . .*[1] We have already shewed that there are two kinds of Christian righteousness: the one *without us*, which we have by imputation; the other *in us*, which consisteth of faith, hope, charity, and other Christian virtues. . . . God giveth us both the one justice and the other: the one by accepting us for righteous in Christ; the other by working Christian righteousness in us."[2]

This practical sanctification will show itself in holiness (1 Pet. i. 16) and obedience (2 Cor. x. 5).   And thus, whether we think of the past or the present, there is grace sufficient for us that we may be righteous in all

[1] Sermon II, 3.   [2] Sermon II, 21.

our ways, holy in all our life, and producing fruit which will show beyond all question that we possess true faith in Christ and are bringing glory to our Lord and Saviour.

There is one further consideration before the subject can be left. What is the best way of promoting Christian holiness and guaranteeing the true fruits of faith in our lives ? The supreme spiritual danger of the Christian life is that of legalism, for there is an inevitable tendency to assume that although Justification is by faith, Sanctification is somehow by struggle, that although the sinner is powerless in regard to salvation he is not so in the matter of holiness. The result of this view is frequently to cause trouble in the Christian life, making the believer feel that though he is unable to become justified apart from himself he cannot possibly be sanctified unless largely aided by his own efforts. But in reality there is one great principle of faith, covering the whole of the Christian life, which shows beyond all question that those who are fullest, freest, and frankest in their proclamation of Justification by faith are thereby enabled to show that Sanctification is likewise to be received in Christ by faith, and that there is one dominating principle throughout. We receive Christ Jesus by faith, and we are to walk in Him by the same principle (Col. ii. 6), and when this is fully realised and properly emphasised in relation both to Justification and Sanctification the outcome is liberty, joy, and practical holiness, which answer fully to the New Testament requirement of the Christian life.[1]

[1] "We come far short of our ministry if our hearts be not intently fixed upon the promotion of personal holiness in the lives of our people; we fail entirely in the effect of our ministry if our doctrine be not successful in securing it. But how is this blessed result to be secured? How shall we preach the way of a sinner's justification by faith, so as the most successfully to promote in him 'the sanctification of the spirit unto obedience'? I conceive, not by any *reserve* on the subject of Justification, exhibiting that doctrine only partially and fearfully in reduced terms and in a background position, as if afraid of the fulness in which the Scriptures declare it to all who read or hear them. Reserve here is reserve in preaching 'Christ and Him crucified.' Our grand message everywhere is, 'be it known unto you, men and brethren, that through this Man is preached unto you the forgiveness of sins, and by Him all that believe are justified from all things, from which they could not be justified by the law of Moses.' St. Paul waited not till men were well initiated into Christian mysteries before he unveiled the grand object of Atonement and Justification through the blood of Christ. No, the gospel plan of promoting sanctification is just the opposite of holding in obscurity any feature of the doctrine of Justification. It is simply to preach that doctrine most fully in all its principles and connections; in all its grace and all its works; in its utmost plainness and simplicity; so that whatever leads to it, whatever is contained in it, whether it be sin and condemnation as needing an imputed righteousness; the love of God as providing that righteousness in His only begotten Son; the blessed Redeemer as offering up Himself a sacrifice to obtain it; faith, as embracing it freely; hope, as resting upon it joyfully; the sacraments, as signing and sealing them effectually to those who duly receive them; a new heart, as the essential companion of loving faith; unreserved obedience, as the necessary expression of a new heart; obedience springing from the love of God in Christ, keeping its eye of faith for motive, strength, and acceptance upon the Cross, and embracing in its walk all departments of duty; all this, as coming legitimately within the embrace of the full preaching of Justification by faith, is the way to promote, through the effectual working of the Spirit of God upon the conscience and heart of the sinner, *his sanctification through the truth*" (McIlvaine, *Righteousness by Faith*).

o

ARTICLE XIII

Of Works before Justification.

Works done before the grace of Christ, and the inspiration of His Spirit, are not pleasant to God, forasmuch as they spring not of faith in Jesus Christ; neither do they make men meet to receive grace, or, as the School-authors say, deserve grace of congruity: yea, rather, for that they are not done as God hath willed and commanded them to be done, we doubt not but they have the nature of sin.

De Operibus ante Justificationem.

Opera quæ fiunt ante gratiam Christi, et Spiritus ejus afflatum, cum ex fide Jesu Christi non prodeant, minime Deo grata sunt; neque gratiam, ut multi vocant, de congruo merentur: immo cum non sint facta, ut Deus illa fieri voluit et præcepit, peccati rationem habere non dubitamus.

IMPORTANT EQUIVALENTS.

Inspiration	=	*afflatum.*
As the School-authors say	=	*ut multi vocant.*
Grace of congruity	=	*gratiam de congruo.*
Nature of sin	=	*peccati rationem.*

THIS is a natural corollary to the subject of the preceding Article and shows the worthlessness of works when they are put in the wrong place. The Article dates from 1553, and is probably original, for there is nothing corresponding to it elsewhere. The English " School-authors " has *Multi* as the Latin equivalent.

A good deal of discussion has been raised in connection with the title and the Article. The title speaks of " Works before Justification," while the Article refers to works done before the grace of Christ and the inspiration of His Spirit. It has been urged that there is a discrepancy between the title and the Article, but this hardly seems correct, since the subject of the Article is altogether different from such questions as are involved in the conviction of sin on the Day of Pentecost (Acts ii. 37), or the prayer of the awakened and really converted Saul (Acts ix. 11). Such workings of the Holy Spirit are never called by the term " Grace " in the New Testament. But what is still more important, the question discussed in the Article went by the name of the title at the Reformation, and especially at the Council of Trent. A contrast is made with the works referred to in the preceding Article. There, good works are mentioned as the fruit of faith ; here, works prior to Justification are in question. As, therefore, this Article refers to works which are clearly independent of Christ and His Spirit, there is no real discrepancy, and any thought of the Article contradicting the title is ruled out at once. Further, there are other titles, like those of Articles IV and X, which are not in strict harmony with the substance of the Articles themselves, and yet there is no fundamental difference involved. The earliest commentator on the Articles, Rogers, is a clear and convincing witness to what was intended by the compilers, showing that the Roman view of meritorious works as precedent to Justification are alone in view.[1]

I.—THE OUTLINE OF THE ARTICLE

1. A clear definition of works before Justification.—" Before the grace of Christ and the inspiration of His Spirit." There is, therefore, no reference whatever to the grace which moves the sinner towards Christ.

2. The Divine disapproval of works before Justification.—"Are not pleasant to God, forasmuch as they spring not of faith in Jesus Christ." An additional proof is afforded in this wording that the Article has reference to the thought of meritoriousness of works.

3. The spiritual powerlessness of works done before Justification.— " Neither do they make men meet to receive grace, or, as the School-authors say, deserve grace of congruity." An allusion to mediæval doctrine which will come under consideration in the history of the subject.[2]

4. The true nature of works done before Justification.—" Yea, rather, for that they are not done as God hath willed and commanded them to be done, we doubt not but they have the nature of sin."[3]

II.—THE HISTORICAL SETTING OF THE ARTICLE

The teaching of the Article is a necessary consequence of Articles IX to XII, and it was intended to oppose the *De Congruo* doctrine. According to the mediæval view, the Fall was the loss of a supernatural gift, *donum supernaturale*, and as this left man with faculties and abilities belonging to him by nature, the exercise of these powers formed the natural medium of transition to the grace of God, so that a proper exercise of them merited the grace of congruity, *de congruo*. Aquinas said that when the will is set in motion man disposes himself for further action and for the reception of habitual grace, and that in this is *meritum de congruo*. Then, when he has thus acquired the habitual grace to do good he thereby

---

[1] Rogers, *On the Thirty-nine Articles*, p. 125 ff.

[2] By "School-authors" the Article intends what is known as mediæval scholasticism, the effort to blend theology with philosophy in a great system. It is usually dated from the time of Charlemagne, through the monasteries founded by him, and since learning was at that time mainly limited to ecclesiastics it was only natural that human thought should express itself almost wholly in the realm of theology. Scholasticism rose from the ninth to the eleventh centuries and reached its climax in the twelfth and thirteenth. The leading names are Albertus Magnus, died 1280; Thomas Aquinas, died 1274; Duns Scotus, died 1308. Trench points out that while the Fathers were theologically productive, the Schoolmen simply endeavoured to vindicate and confirm what was ancient, and thereby to systematise in fullest possible detail the doctrine of the Church, at the same time vindicating its reason and showing its entire congruity with supernatural revelation (Trench, *Mediæval Church History*, Lecture XIV).

[3] The Latin has the same phrase, *peccati rationem*, as in Article IX.

obtains *meritum de condigno.* The Council of Trent speaks of works done before Justification as connected with *meritum de congruo,* and works after Justification as *de condigno.*[1] The merit of condignity is such that there is an absolute failure on the part of God if it is not recognised. The merit of congruity claims less, but the result is equally certain, since God must be conceived of as doing what is " congruous to His perfection to do." Although the Schoolmen allowed that neither before nor after the Fall man was capable in himself of meriting salvation, yet they maintained that in Paradise he could live free from sin, but to deserve everlasting life required grace. But, as we have seen, it was to the loss of the superadded gift and not to any depravity of his mind they ascribed the principal evil resulting from the Fall, a loss which by a proper exertion of his natural abilities they considered to be retrievable. It was from this that the objectionable doctrine of human sufficiency arose, which in the estimation of the Reformers tended to blot out the glory of the Gospel, and when applied to the conscience led to presumption. According to this idea the favour of God in this life was attainable by congruous personal merit, and His presence in the life to come by condign personal merit. But though we cannot, according to the Schoolmen, merit salvation itself without works of condignity, yet we can merit the means of attaining by works of congruity, the latter being introductory to the former. With such a view of man's powers it is not surprising that Melanchthon should have charged the Scholastics with teaching a doctrine that involved the superfluity of the influence of the Holy Spirit. The doctrine against which our Article is directed is thus expressed in a Note to the Rheims Testament (on Acts x. 2) :—

" Such works as are done before justification though they suffice not to salvation, yet be acceptable preparatives to the grace of justification, and such works preparative come of grace also, otherwise they could never deserve at God's hands of congruity, or any otherwise towards justification."

Now as the Ninth Article teaches that men are in a state of enmity to God, and that their propensities are such as lead into actual sin, and since from the Eleventh and Twelfth we learn that Christians are released from that enmity and are no longer under condemnation, it is abundantly clear that the Article is directed solely against those who conceived that they had the power so to dispose themselves for grace as to merit God's favour and bring about the commencement of their own salvation.[2] The Article

---

[1] The usual illustration of the distinction between these two views is that of a wealthy man with a servant, who does his work and receives wages *de condigno,* and then in old age, when unable to work he receives *de congruo.*

[2] As an illustration of an impossible way of interpreting the Article and of making it virtually identical with mediæval doctrine, the following extract from Forbes (*Explanation of the Thirty-nine Articles,* p. 208) may be given:

"Sufficient weight, in the consideration of this Article, has not been given to the fact that the only works excluded from merit *de congruo* by its terms are those done before the grace of Christ and the inspiration of the Spirit: consequently it does not prejudge

is thus part of the Reformation protest against any thought of man preparing the way for salvation by his own act. The Council of Trent, though avoiding the use of the terms *meritum de congruo* and *de condigno*, yet anathematises those who deny the value of works before Justification.[1]

III.—THE TEACHING OF THE ARTICLE

It is essential to note the special application of the Article. It refers solely to the question of Justification by works in the light of the Reformation controversies and the Protestant position against Rome. It was directed only against those who thought they could commence their own salvation. It is tantamount to saying that there is a universal necessity of the Atonement and the Holy Spirit. There is no reference whatever to heathen morality, unless that should be used as a title for Justification, nor is there any question of goodness on the part of those outside the Gospel (John i. 4, 9; Acts x. 2; xvii. 27 f.; Rom. i. 19 f.). So also works of charity by unbelievers are entirely out of the present question unless they should be done with a view to gaining favour with God. Revelation is for those to whom it comes. The negatives of the Article are doubtless sweeping, but it is probable that at the outset, as indeed to-day, people are more startled in this way than by the more positive and clear statement of the true place of good works, seen in the preceding Article. Actions may be good in themselves, but if they proceed from unworthy motives they cannot be regarded as praiseworthy. The matter, and yet not the manner, may be acceptable to God. It is motive that makes the man, and behind the act we have to enquire as to the reason why a man performs it. An action may be noble and yet out of proportion, just as characters entirely irreligious have not their true centre in God, and therefore are really a perversion of God's will. So that, although the term " grace of congruity " seems to imply a controversy altogether antiquated, yet the Article has a very definite bearing on some of the most vital ethical questions of to-day. There is a widespread opinion that all that is required is morality, and that a man's beliefs are of little or no effect.[2] Thus Matthew Arnold has spoken of conduct as " three-fourths of life."

the question whether other works, those which are the fruit of faith, do or do not dispose us in some way to justification, and *de congruo* (though not *de condigno*) merit the grace of justification."

Such a statement carries its own condemnation in the light of the Article when interpreted by mediæval and Tridentine doctrine.

[1] " Si quis dixerit opera omnia quæ ante justificationem fiunt, quacumque ratione facta sint, vere esse peccata, vel odium Dei mereri, aut quanto vehementius quis nititur se disponere ad gratiam, tanto eum gravius peccare: anathema sit."—Canon VII.

"Whosoever shall say that all the works which are done before justification, on whatsoever account they may be done, are truly sins, and deserve the hatred of God, or that the more vehemently a man tries to dispose himself for grace, the more grievously he sins, let him be anathema."

[2] This is seen in Pope's lines:
"For creeds and forms let senseless bigots fight,
His can't be wrong whose life is in the right."

But this entirely begs the question of the other one-fourth, which is obviously concerned with the foundation and motive-power. We might as well say that a building is three-fourths and the foundation only one-fourth of the entire structure; and yet obviously the former rests upon the latter. In spite, therefore, of any modern resentment against the assertion that actions done by irreligious men are " not pleasant in the sight of God," or are " after the nature of sin," it is essential to emphasise the absolute supremacy of motive. We must get beneath and behind actions and seek to discover the principle that dominates them. There is no thought of the confusion of virtue with vice, and there is no forget-fulness of degrees of sin and responsibility, but there must be a very strong insistence upon the essential difference in the Article between " works done before Justification " (Article XIII) and good works which " follow after Justification " (Article XII).[1]

[1] See Boultbee, *The Theology of the Church of England*, p. 122 f.; Macbride, *Lectures on the Articles*, p. 293 f.

ARTICLE XIV

Of Works of Supererogation.

Voluntary works besides, over and above, God's Commandments, which they call *Works of Supererogation*, cannot be taught without arrogancy and impiety; for by them men do declare, that they do not only render unto God as much as they are bound to do, but that they do more for His sake than of bounden duty is required; whereas Christ saith plainly, When ye have have done all that are commanded to you, say, We are unprofitable servants.

De Operibus Supererogationis.

Opera, quæ *Supererogationis* appellant, non possunt sine arrogantia et impietate prædicari; nam illis declarant homines, non tantum se Deo reddere quæ tenentur; sed plus in ejus gratiam facere quam deberent: cum aperte Christus dicat, Cum feceritis omnia quæcunque præcepta sunt vobis, dicite, Servi inutiles sumus.

IMPORTANT EQUIVALENTS.

Voluntary, besides, over and above God's commandments	= [No corresponding Latin.]
To be taught	= *prædicari.*
Than of bounden duty is required	= *quam deberent.*
Plainly	= *aperte.*

ARTICLES IX and X have a direct relation to the problems of Sin. Articles XI to XIII deal with various aspects of Justification. Articles XIV to XVI are concerned with aspects of Sanctification or Holiness. These last may be distinguished as follows :—

Article XIV teaches that no Christian can exceed God's requirements.

Article XV teaches that no Christian can attain to God's requirements.

Article XVI teaches that no Christian need despair of restoration after falling.

Article XIV dates from 1553, the only subsequent change being the word " impiety " for " iniquity." The phrase, " Voluntary . . . besides, over and above God's commandments " has no equivalent in the Latin.

I.—THE TEACHING OF THE ARTICLE

1. The technical term, Works of Supererogation.—The Latin, *rogare*, meant " to propose a law," answering to the modern phrase " to bring in a Bill." Then *erogare* meant to propose a law, or bring in a Bill, dealing with money matters, things concerned with the Treasury. From this came *supererogare*, meaning, " to pay out more than was necessary." And thus came the word *supererogatio*, which in eccle-

siastical matters meant doing more than God required. The vulgate of St. Luke x. 35 is *quodcumque supererogaveris.* Then arose the mediæval idea of " an excess of merit."

2. *The precise meaning of Works of Supererogation.*—In the light of what has been said of the term the Article in the English defines them as works that are " voluntary, besides, over and above God's commandments."

3. *The spiritual impossibility of Works of Supererogation.*—" Cannot be taught without arrogancy and impiety ; for by them men do declare that they do not only render unto God as much as they are bound to do, but that they do more for His sake, than of bounden duty is required." This statement suffices to show the entire impracticability of the conception.

4. *The demonstrated error of Works of Supererogation.*—" Whereas Christ saith plainly, When ye have done all that are commanded to you, say, We are unprofitable servants." Thus, again, the appeal is made to Scripture against erroneous doctrine.

II.—THE HISTORY OF THE DOCTRINE

In order to trace this peculiar idea to its source and follow its progress it is necessary to go back to the Decian Persecution of the third century, when there were not only splendid examples of martyrdom, but also cases of serious declension and apostasy. Under stress of persecution Christians lapsed, and when the Church had to face the question of their return to communion it was felt essential to insist upon discipline as a test. But in certain cases the lapsed endeavoured to obtain the help of prospective martyrs to intercede for them with a view to re-admission, and some of these confessors did not realise the danger of such appeals, for not being content with simple intercession they actually claimed the right to restore the lapsed to the Church by granting " Letters of Peace," or means of admission to Church fellowship without penitential discipline.[1] From this it is generally understood that the first form of " Indulgence " came, a remission of ecclesiastical penance. There was nothing essentially wrong thus far, but the experience became a kind of precedent, or was regarded as such by the mediæval Church, in reference to the subsequent system of Church Indulgences.

Side by side with this there sprang up in the Church a profound regard for virginity, based, as it was supposed, on the teaching of St. Paul in 1 Cor. vii. 25 ; " Concerning virgins I have no commandment of the Lord, but I give my advice." From this arose a distinction between " commandments " and " judgments," between that which is necessary and that which is advisable. Together with this the story of the rich young ruler was employed (Mark x. 22) for the purpose of obtaining a similar distinction between precepts of obedience and counsels of per-

---

[1] See Article, "Libelli," *Dictionary of Christian Antiquities.*

fection, between the ordinary and extraordinary, between the necessary
and the voluntary (though desirable). It was not difficult to take the
further step of teaching that by following the latter, the " counsels," a
Christian could do more than was really demanded by God, and from
this arose the thought of a special value or " merit " attaching to particular
aspects of life. Eventually the idea of works of supererogation developed,
being applied to works done in compliance with counsels. It must be
admitted, however, that this is one of the most extraordinary conceptions
that ever entered into the mind of man, though the system of Indulgences,
properly so-called, seems to date from the time of the Crusades at the
end of the twelfth century. But it soon became modified and embellished
in the next century, first by Alexander of Hales, and then by Albertus
Magnus, under the title of *thesaurus perfectorum supererogationis*. It was
taught that by virtue of the possession of the " keys " the Pope could
discharge the temporal penalties of sin here and the purgatorial penalties
hereafter. Aquinas completed the idea by saying that Indulgences
availed for the residuum of punishment after absolution, the reason being
that in the unity of the mystical Body of Christ many have supererero-
gated beyond the measure of their debt, and as there is an abundance of
these merits which exceed the punishment due, and as, moreover, the
saints wrought them not for any particular individual, they belong to the
whole Church and can be distributed by him who presides over it.

It will easily be seen that these ideas led to serious and grave abuses.
As long as Indulgence was limited to the remission of ecclesiastical discipline there was not very much moral harm, but the moment the conception of eternal penalties was introduced the danger became obvious,
and the door was opened to the gravest abuses. It is known that the
sale of Indulgences was the first step that led to the opposition of Luther
and the revolt in the sixteenth century. The Council of Trent only
touched upon the subject briefly and hurriedly, and did not pass any
direct decree upon it, but the Council acknowledges the power of granting
Indulgences and calls them *cœlestes ecclesiæ thesauros*. The Rheims New
Testament speaks quite plainly :—

"Holy saints may, in measure of other men's necessities and deservings, as
well allot unto them the supererogation of their spiritual works, as those that
abound in worldly goods may give alms of their superfluities to them that are in
necessity."

Pope Leo X speaks of the power to grant Indulgences from the superabundant merit of Christ and the saints for the living and the dead.
Cardinal Bellarmine says that there is an infinite treasure purchased by
the Blood of Christ which has not yet been applied to all. To this
" heap " Pope Clement VI said the merits of the Mother of God and
the saints add support. Thus, it will be seen that the highest authorities
of the Church of Rome teach this doctrine.[1]

[1] Boultbee, *The Theology of the Church of England*, p. 126.

III.—THE QUESTION STATED

That man can do more than his duty and even transfer superfluous merits to those who have fallen short of fulfilling required services is so astounding a view that on hearing it for the first time it seems incredible that it can be maintained, and yet, as we have seen, it is not only held by individuals, but is the avowed belief of the Roman Catholic Church, from which our Communion separated in the sixteenth century. It carries its own condemnation as introducing the principle of finance between God and man.[1]

The error is fundamentally due to the erroneous ideas prevalent in connection with the subjects of Articles IX to XII, and the proofs of those Articles are consequently the proofs of this. If we are justified by works we cannot be more than justified by them, and if our Christian life is so imperfect as to be only accepted through Christ it is obvious that we have no merit at our disposal. Further, since all men are sinners they would need more than all their merit for themselves. The whole question of human meritoriousness is set aside by our Articles, following the New Testament, for " if Christ's merits are infinite, how can finite additions increase them ? Infinity plus worlds is still only infinity."[2]   The Christian idea of our relation to God is that of reconciliation involving sonship, not slavery, and any thought of supererogation can only be due to a spirit of legalism which teaches that our duty to God can somehow be formulative. But if this were the case our duty would be always the same, since law is for all without reference to character and position, and it would follow that the duty could be discharged, for if it could be expressed we should be able to see whether we had discharged it or not. But inasmuch as no two of us are alike, duty necessarily varies, because it is relative and according to capacity. The case of the young ruler, which is so often used in this connection, shows that not every follower of Jesus Christ was required to sell all, and we know that the communism of the early Apostolic Church was voluntary. And yet to the young man our Lord's words came as a command and a duty. The duty towards God is love, and love grows with love, never asking, What must I do, but what may I, or what can I do ? Love cannot be restrained by law and always soars above it.

The truth is that the Roman Catholic idea of " counsels of perfection " has no warrant in Scripture, and, as taught in that Church, these counsels are nothing but distinctions of men. It is deplorable to think that Rome claims to discount venial sins and to have a substantial balance to the good. Scripture, on the other hand, says that the act is the expression of the

---

[1] "Tum et illorum arrogantia comprimenda est, et authoritate legum domanda, qui supererogationis opera quædam importaverunt, quibus existimant non solum cumulate Dei legibus, et explete satisfieri, sed aliquid etiam in illis amplius superesse quam Dei mandata postulent, unde et sibi mereri et aliis merita applicari possint" (*Reformatio Legum, De Hæresibus*, c. 8).

[2] Boultbee, *ut supra*, p. 127.

moral disposition and never can go higher than duty. What are called
" counsels of perfection " are really nothing more than the will of God
for individual men.   This is manifest in the very passages which are
adduced in support of the distinction between precepts and counsels
(Matt. xix. 16 ff. ; 1 Cor. vii. 7), since in each case the reference is to
that which was required of each as ordinary duty.[1] The distinctions
between men greater and less, extraordinary and ordinary, are due solely
to the gift of God, and have no human merit in them.   Certain men
did more because more had been given to them.   Under these circumstances the Article rightly speaks of works of supererogation as involving
" arrogancy and impiety " : " arrogancy," because out of harmony with
Christian humility ; " impiety " because so clearly against Holy Scripture,
as is proved by the reference to St. Luke xvii. 10.   God's standard is so
high that man cannot attain to it, much less go beyond it. Not only do
we never go beyond, but we never satisfy God's requirements. He calls for
love with all the heart (Mark xii. 30), for holiness like His own (1 Pet.
i. 15), and for a life in thought, word, and deed at the very highest point
(Jas. iii. 2 ; 1 John i. 8).   No wonder, then, that faced with God's
requirement the soul, even in New times with all the rich provision of
grace, can only say, in Old Testament language, " If thou, Lord,
shouldest mark iniquities, O Lord, who shall stand ? " (Psa. cxxx. 3).
From first to last, in everything connected with our thinking, speaking,
and doing, we need the infinite merit of our Lord and Saviour to meet
and cover our own utter demerit.   And as we are bought with a price,
it is plain that such people have no services to give away, nor is it possible
that anyone should do more good works than are commanded, when
nothing is a good work, but what is commanded, and only good because
commanded.   There would be no particular fault with the distinction
between precepts of obedience and counsels of perfection if only they were
kept free from anything like human merit, because there is no doubt
that some men are called to states and conditions of life to which other
men are not called.   But the danger lies in the precise way in which these
two aspects are distinguished, for, of course, everyone is bound to refrain
from what is sinful, and also to do to the utmost of his power everything
for which he has opportunity, since the whole of his life and all his
faculties belong to God.   It is, therefore, clear that every so-called
" counsel " respecting moral duty must of necessity be a command to
the man to whom it refers, and we know that " to him who knoweth
to do good and doeth it not, to him it is sin."
    Then, too, even supposing it were possible for us to go beyond our
plain duty, there would still be the question how we could transfer our
superabundant work or merit to another.   The possibility of such works

[1] Again Forbes fails to do justice to the Reformed position, and treats of "counsels
of perfection," "of which the main branches are poverty, chastity, and obedience" in
a way virtually identical with that of the Church of Rome. On this view it is difficult
to understand what the Article can possibly mean.

being made available for other people is obviously unthinkable, because it would destroy the very essence of the Gospel and introduce the element of human merit, when Christ alone is meritorious for salvation. It is also impossible to avoid noticing, as Boultbee remarks, that the very people who scoff at the imputation of Christ's righteousness as unreal accept something infinitely more unreal, namely, "the merits of one sinner applied to the redemption of another sinner, neither being in the least cognisant of the transaction."[1]

Merely to mention all these things is to show how far removed the Roman Catholic Church is on this subject from an understanding of the simplest principles of the Gospel of Christ. On the other hand, it is impossible to be too profoundly thankful for the clear insight into the fundamental realities of Christianity evinced by the teaching of the Article.

[1] Boultbee, *ut supra*, p. 127.

III. THE LIFE OF FAITH—*continued*

PERSONAL RELIGION

B. ITS COURSE (ARTICLES XV–XVIII).
DOCTRINES CONNECTED WITH SANCTIFICATION.

15. OF CHRIST ALONE WITHOUT SIN.

16. SIN AFTER BAPTISM.

17. PREDESTINATION AND ELECTION.

18. OBTAINING ETERNAL SALVATION ONLY BY THE NAME OF CHRIST.

ARTICLE XV

Of Christ alone without Sin.

Christ in the truth of our nature was made like unto us in all things, sin only except, from which He was clearly void, both in His flesh and in His spirit. He came to be the Lamb without spot, who, by sacrifice of Himself once made, should take way the sins of the world; and sin, as *Saint John* saith, was not in Him. But all we the rest, although baptized and born again in Christ, yet offend in many things; and if we say we have no sin, we deceive ourselves, and the truth is not in us.

De Christo, qui solus est sine peccato.

Christus, in nostræ naturæ veritate, per omnia similis factus est nobis, excepto peccato, a quo prorsus erat immunis, tum in carne, tum in spiritu. Venit ut agnus absque macula, qui mundi peccata per immolationem sui semel factam tolleret; et peccatum, ut inquit Johannes, in eo non erat. Sed nos reliqui, etiam baptizati et in Christo regenerati, in multis tamen offendimus omnes; et si dixerimus, quia peccatum non habemus, nos ipsos seducimus, et veritas in nobis non est.

IMPORTANT EQUIVALENTS.

Alone without sin	= *qui solus est sine peccato.*
Clearly void	= *prorsus immunis.*
He came to be the Lamb	= *venit ut agnus.*
Sacrifice	= *immolationem.*
Born again	= *regenerati* (See Article IX).
We deceive ourselves	= *nos ipsos seducimus.*

In contrast with Article XIV this teaches that a Christian, far from going beyond the Divine requirements, cannot even attain to absolute sinlessness. In 1553 the title of this Article was *Nemo præter Christum est sine peccato* ("No one is without sin but Christ alone"). Other changes were merely slight verbal differences. The most important equivalent is *prorsus immunis,* for " clearly void," that is, " entirely without sin."

I.—THE TEACHING OF THE ARTICLE

It will be useful to analyse the Article as it stands and notice carefully its teaching.

1. The true Humanity of Christ.—" Christ in the truth of our nature was made like unto us in all things." This is another statement of belief in the humanity of Christ in addition to what is seen in Article II.

2. The Sinlessness of Christ.—" Sin only except, from which He was clearly void, both in His flesh and in His spirit." This special point is derived directly from the New Testament.

3. The Sacrifice of Christ.—" He came to be the Lamb without spot, who, by sacrifice of Himself once made, should take away the sins of the world, and sin, as Saint John saith, was not in Him." The purpose of the coming of Christ is once again said to be human redemption.

4. The Sinfulness of all besides.—" But all we the rest, although baptized, and born again in Christ, yet offend in many things ; and if we say we have no sin, we deceive ourselves, and the truth is not in us." This is a similar statement to that found in Article IX, referring to the condition of man as one of imperfection and proneness to evil, so that no one should anticipate the judgment day.

II.—THE PURPOSE OF THE ARTICLE

1. From the title of the Article, especially in the light of the title in 1553, and also from the position of the Article in relation to the preceding, it is clear that the statement concerning Christ is secondary, and yet it should be carefully noted as one of four references in the Articles to the doctrine of the Atonement (Articles II, XV, XXVIII, XXXI). Sinlessness is shown to be needed for Atonement, though, of course, this does not mean that any sinless being could atone. There must be unity between God and man in order to a proper Atonement. This is the teaching of the Epistle to the Hebrews, where, in chap. i unity with God, and in chap. ii unity with man, are both emphasised. But assuming the Deity of our Lord, human sinlessness was essential for His work of redemption, and He was typified as the Lamb without blemish (Heb. vii. 26-28 ; 1 Pet. i. 19). Yet the sinlessness of Deity required for atonement does not detract from His real humanity. Although sinless, our Lord possessed all our human limitations, and so He could be tempted (Heb. iv. 15). He had human desires, but it was not the desires themselves, only the gratification of them, that would have been sinful. It is sometimes thought that sinlessness does not leave our Lord a genuinely human being, but although there is a mystery in the union of the Divine and human in Jesus Christ, it is essential to hold firmly to both aspects even though we may not see how they can reconcile. The Person of Christ is unique, and, as such, has an absolute value for man. The old problem concerning the sinlessness of Jesus Christ, whether *non posse peccare*, or *posse non peccare* be true, should certainly be answered by saying that *non posse peccare* is the correct view, since no Christian can possibly tolerate the thought that Jesus Christ might have sinned. And yet perhaps the solution of the problem may be found in the suggestion of a modern writer, that it may have been one of the elements of our Lord's human limitation that He was not aware of His immunity, and was therefore compelled to face all the reality and struggle of temptation.[1] When we read that " He suffered, being tempted," we know that the suffering was real. But the fact of His being unable to sin does not rob His example of reality, because though He was Divine, He was also complete as a man, and like us in all essential particulars. Further, the thought of human nature does not necessarily include sin, for the true ideal is a humanity triumphant over sin, and by the grace of God morally incapable of wrong. As it has been

---

[1] Forsyth, *The Person and Place of Jesus Christ*, p. 301.

often pointed out, Jesus would have been less than the Ideal Man if He had sinned, and also perhaps He would have been less than the Ideal Man if He had not possessed an incapacity, a *non posse*, which was at the same time a *posse non*. Further, there is nothing more striking in the Epistle to the Hebrews than the fact that our Lord's sympathy with us is associated with His sinlessness, that is to say, His oneness with us is based upon His unlikeness to us, and this is in exact accord with human experience. Men of conspicuous character influence and help their fellows, not by the various points of likeness, but by some special element of unlikeness as the secret of their power. In the same way Jesus Christ helps us, not because He is like us in regard to sinfulness, but because He is absolutely " separate from sinners," and therefore " able to save to the uttermost."[1]

2. There seems to be an indirect but clear reference to the Mother of our Lord, though authorities differ on this point. Gibson is strongly of opinion that the Article does not refer to this subject.[2] On the other hand, Hardwick and Harold Browne take the contrary view.[3] It is, at least, noteworthy that the earliest commentator on the Articles, Rogers, refers to the subject.[4] The topic was first definitely discussed by the Schoolmen, and in 1300 by Duns Scotus. Against him Aquinas and the Dominicans opposed it. At the Reformation the Church of Rome was equally divided, and there was a collision at Trent on the subject. The matter was referred to the Pope, who suggested a middle course, adding that original sin did not comprise the Virgin Mary, and that the Constitutions of Pope Sixtus IV were to be observed. These were neutral.[5]

---

[1] "The best doctor is the man whose knowledge, not whose experience of bodily ills, is the greatest. So a juror is the most capable of judging and knowing guilt if free himself from evil habits and qualified by excellence to administer justice. Not the smart juror who is guilty of crimes himself. Vice can never know itself and virtue, but virtue will in time acquire knowledge of itself and vice" (Plato, *Republic*, Bk. III).

"It is not necessary that He should have Himself succumbed . . . in order that He should know. . . . One knows the sin and the death which one has perfectly met and has perfectly overcome, better than if one had in the least been overcome by them " (Du Bose, *High Priesthood and Sacrifice*, p. 150).

"The problem was therefore to secure sympathy and yet to preserve sinlessness. The solution is found in temptation of the severest kind met by perfect resistance. And the keenest agony of temptation can be known only by one who remains sinless. Others are tried till they yield, and those who yield soonest suffer least. . . All our temptations He knew, feeling them not with our coarse and blunted perceptions, but with exquisite and fine-strung sensitiveness. . . . And sinlessness alone can truly estimate sin, for the very act of sinning disturbs the balance of the moral judgment" (Peake, *Century Bible*, on Hebrews iv. 14, 15).

"Sympathy does not depend on the experience of sin but on the experience of the strength of temptation to sin which only the sinless can know in its full intensity. He who falls yields before the last strain" (Westcott, *The Epistle to the Hebrews*, ii. 17, 18).

For further study on the temptation of Christ see Knight, *The Temptation of our Lord*; Forsyth, *ut supra*; Bruce, *The Humiliation of Christ*; Liddon, *The Divinity of our Lord*, Appendix).

[2] Gibson, *The Thirty-nine Articles*, p. 440.

[3] Hardwick, *History of the Articles of Religion*, pp. 101, 381; Harold Browne, *Exposition of the Thirty-nine Articles*, pp. 346-348.

[4] Rogers, *On the Articles*, p. 134.

[5] Boultbee, *The Theology of the Church of England*, p. 130 f.

P

Since the Reformation the doctrine has grown and developed, and was finally promulgated in 1854, though it is to be remembered that the Vatican Council of that date only authorised what had been believed for centuries. Although the subject was only first definitely considered in the fourteenth century, yet there were many ideas in regard to it floating about long before then. But St. Augustine refused to discuss it. The doctrine has had the usual Roman Catholic history, first speculation, then pious opinion, and at length defined dogma.[1] Our Church, while honouring the Mother of our Lord, has always kept true to the simplicity and sobriety of·New Testament teaching. There are two Red Letter Festivals in connection with the Virgin Mary : the Purification on February 2, and the Annunciation on March 25. But it is interesting to notice that the first title of the former is " The Presentation of Christ in the Temple," the latter and more familiar usage being described as " commonly called."[2] Further, it is impossible to avoid noticing that both Collects are entirely without reference to the Mother of our Lord. In the Calendar there are three Black Letter Days in which the name of the Virgin Mary occurs : July 2, September 8, December 8, while in the Collect for Christmas Day our Lord's birth is spoken of as from " a pure virgin," and in the Proper Preface for the Day a reference is made to our Lord being " very Man of the substance of the Virgin Mary His mother." From all this it will be seen that our Church is content with following the New Testament in regard to the Mother of our Lord, and there there is no suggestion that she was a woman into whose life sin had never entered. She is represented as a woman full of grace, tender of heart, and loyal to God, but marked by the ordinary limitation of spiritual understanding which comes from a sinful nature. Of course, the question is raised how if she were sinful her Son could be sinless, but the mystery of His Being is perfectly clear in the words of the angel referring to the Holy Spirit (Luke i. 35). Besides, if she were sinless, her parents would have been sinless, and so on before them. The fact that she spoke of God as her " Saviour " shows that, like the rest of the pious Israelites, she was looking for redemption in Israel, and when her Son's redemptive work was accomplished she was with the other disciples in the Upper Room to receive the fulness of the Spirit as the accomplished work of Jesus Christ.

[1] Again it is necessary to refer to the treatment of this subject by Bishop Forbes and the Rev. T. I. Ball. The former discusses the Mother of our Lord in a way almost identical with that of the Church of Rome (*Explanation of the Thirty-nine Articles*, pp. 224–226), while the latter says that "Catholic piety has loved to think that she who was full of grace when she conceived her God had also the privilege of an immaculate birth and an immaculate life" (*The Orthodox Doctrine of the Church of England*, p. 83). It need hardly be said that these views are in entire disharmony with the plain teaching of the Prayer Book and Articles.

[2] "Commonly called" seems to imply "erroneously called." Thus, in the Prayer Book of 1549, the Holy Communion Office had as sub-title, "commonly called the Mass." So in Article XXV, the "five commonly called Sacraments," and the Nativity is "commonly called" Christmas Day.

3. There is no doubt that the primary and immediate application of the Article is to Christians. The title of the Article of 1553 seems to support this view, " *No one but Christ* without Sin." The Anabaptists of the sixteenth century went into serious excesses on this point in their insistence upon what they believed to be a perfect visible Church. The sinfulness of human nature, as derived from the Fall, is too clearly seen in Scripture to be denied. But as it has been said that Baptism has placed us in a new state and that the declarations that " there is none that doeth good," and that " all are under sin," must not be applied to the regenerate, the view has arisen that the believer is not only justified, but fully sanctified, and that original sin has been obliterated. In Article IX the reference seems to be to sinfulness as the root, while the present Article appears to refer to acts of sin as the fruit, and it is important for several reasons to insist upon the permanence of the sinful nature in the regenerate and the possibility of that sinfulness bursting out into overt acts of sin at any time unless the proper conditions are fulfilled. This view of the sinfulness of all except the Lord Jesus Christ is based upon several grounds, each calling for careful attention.

(1) We have already observed the Scriptural distinction between sin and sins, between the principle and the practice. There is no doubt that this distinction is clearly made not only by St. Paul in Romans, but also by St. John in his Epistle (1 John i. 8, 10).

(2) The Epistles are addressed to Christians, and a spiritual conflict is implied throughout. Not only so, but the very people who are addressed as " saints " or " consecrated ones " are shown in the Epistles to possess an evil nature, which is liable at any time to commit sin. It is a serious spiritual mistake to make our consciousness the measure of our sinfulness.

(3) In the Old Testament there was a provision for sins of ignorance, and it seems natural to assume that there must be something corresponding to this in the Atoning Sacrifice of Christ. The language of the law is " though he wist it not, yet is he guilty " (Lev. v. 17), and for the same reason the sinner to-day needs Divine mercy and grace even though he sins ignorantly and in unbelief. The plea of " mistaken judgment " is also insufficient. Law is law, whether we are conscious of it or not, and there must be a provision in the sacrifice of our Lord for sins unwittingly committed.

(4) Then, too, if the evil nature is entirely removed a natural question arises, what further need there can be for Atonement. The sacrifice of Christ deals with sin and sin only, and if there is no longer any sin there is no longer need of Atonement.

(5) The reference of St. Paul in Romans vii is a testimony in the same direction, for just as in chap. iii he had shown the inability of self to justify self, so in chap. vii he is equally clear on the inability of self to sanctify self. This is owing to the presence and power of the evil principle within.

(6) What the Apostle calls the " flesh " is never removed in this life. The flesh is in us, though we are not to be in the flesh. This means that while the evil power is there there is no need for it to exercise its force, if only we are living in the power of the Holy Spirit (Rom. viii. 5-9).

(7) It is a great mistake to think that the absence of sin is everything. Far too much attention is given to what is called " sinless perfection " or " sinlessness." Yet this is only negative, and a positive Divine standard is required, that of loving with all the heart. This is particularly evident when we speak of the " sinlessness of Christ," for the idea is wholly inadequate since He was not merely without sin, but His entire life was filled with the definite will and purpose of God.[1] So in regard to the believer's life, the English word " perfect " has nothing whatever to do with sinlessness, but always means spiritual ripeness, moral maturity (Matt. v. 48, R.V.; Phil. iii. 12). It is also to be remembered that the word " sanctify " means to consecrate, separate, dedicate, and not to purify from sin (1 Thess. v. 23). The teaching of Scripture is quite clear in its distinction between sanctification and purification (John xvii. 17, 19; Eph. v. 26, Greek).

(8) It is in the light of these considerations that the words of the Baptismal Service are to be understood, when we pray that the one baptised may " utterly abolish the whole body of sin." The reference is to the great passage in Rom. vi. 6, and must be interpreted accordingly. Both in St. Paul and in the Prayer Book there is no question of the destruction or annihilation of the evil principle, but only of its powerlessness by virtue of the greater power of the Atoning Sacrifice of Christ applied by the Holy Spirit.

In view of these considerations the Article emphasises one of the most vital truths of Christian living, and whether we consider the subject from the standpoint of Scripture, or of Christian experience, it is only too true that " If we say that we have no sin, we deceive ourselves, and the truth is not in us."

[1] Forrest, *The Authority of Christ*, p. 12. See also the same author's *The Christ of History and Experience*, Lecture I.

ARTICLE XVI

Of Sin after Baptism.

Not every deadly sin willingly committed after Baptism is sin against the Holy Ghost, and unpardonable. Wherefore the grant of repentance is not to be denied to such as fall into sin after Baptism. After we have received the Holy Ghost, we may depart from grace given, and fall into sin; and by the grace of God we may arise again, and amend our lives. And therefore they are to be condemned which say, they can no more sin as long as they live here, or deny the place of forgiveness to such as truly repent.

De Peccato post Baptismum.

Non omne peccatum mortale post Baptismum voluntarie perpetratum est peccatum in Spiritum Sanctum, et irremissibile. Proinde lapsis a Baptismo in peccata locus pœnitentiæ non est negandus. Post acceptum Spiritum Sanctum possumus a gratia data recedere, atque peccare; denuoque per gratiam Dei resurgere, ac resipiscere. Ideoque illi damnandi sunt, qui se, quamdiu hic vivant, amplius non posse peccare affirmant, aut vere resipiscentibus veniæ locum denegant.

IMPORTANT EQUIVALENTS.

Deadly sin	= *peccatum mortale.*
After baptism	= *post baptismum.*
After baptism	= *a baptismo.*
Grant of repentance	= *locus pœnitentiæ.*
Amend our lives	= *resipiscere.*
To such as truly repent	= *resipiscentibus.*

As in Article XV, the question of human sinlessness was faced and denied, so here, the opposite view of hopeless sinfulness is considered and rejected. Thus the negative and positive extremes are denied by the Articles. It was an important matter to consider in the light of their early history and also of certain circumstances of the sixteenth century. If Christ alone was sinless, what about those who sinned after Baptism? In reply to this, as it has been suggestively said : Article XV denies the possibility of a heaven on earth, while Article XVI denies the possibility of a hell on earth.

There were two errors rife at the Reformation : (*a*) the revival of the old third century idea that great sins after Baptism could not be forgiven ; (*b*) on the other hand, some taught that it was absolutely impossible for the regenerate to sin. The Article deals with both errors. The prevalence of these errors may be seen from two sixteenth-century statements. In the *Reformatio Legum* we read :—

" Etiam illi de justificatis perverse sentiunt, qui credunt illos, postquam justi semel facti sunt, in peccatum non posse incidere, aut si forte quicquam eorum faciunt, quæ Dei legibus prohibentur, ea Deum pro peccatis non accipere. Quibus opinione contrarii, sed impietate pares sunt, qui quodcumque peccatum mortale, quod post baptismum a nobis susceptum voluntate nostra committitur, illud omne contra Spiritum Sanctum affirmant gestum esse et remitti non posse."[1]

In the Augsburg Confession we read :—

" Damnant Anabaptistas, qui negant semel justificatos posse amittere Spiritum Sanctum. . . . Damnantur et Novatiani qui nolebant absolvere lapsos post baptismum redeuntes ad pœnitentiam."[2]

This Article was the Fifteenth of 1553, but was followed at that time with the Sixteenth, which had for its title, *De Peccato in Spiritum Sanctum* (" Of sin against the Holy Ghost"). This was omitted in 1563, probably because of a desire to avoid a precise definition of the sin against the Holy Ghost.[3] In 1563 the title of the present Article was *De Lapsis post Baptismum*. The present title dates from 1571.

I.—THE PROBLEMS OF SIN AND PARDON

The Article teaches that wilful sin is not necessarily unpardonable. " Not every deadly sin willingly committed after Baptism is sin against the Holy Ghost, and unpardonable." We have seen under Article XV that every Christian sins, but the question arises whether there are not certain sins of so grievous a character as to put men beyond the reach of forgiveness. This raises the enquiry as to the meaning of the epithet " deadly." The phrase " deadly sin " both here and in the Litany means a sin distinct from ordinary wrongdoing, wilful rather than ignorant, serious rather than light. There is no allusion whatever to the Roman Catholic distinction between mortal and venial sins, since " venial " is never referred to in our formularies.[4] The Roman Catholic idea of mortal sin is a sin that tends to withdraw the soul from God and to kill it. Such is the sin of unbelief. By venial sin is understood that which is committed in the inferior path of discipline during temptation, though the heart is really right. But the essence of sin is in the spiritual condition of the sinner. All sin is deadly in that it tends towards death, but there are sins which because they are deliberately committed against light are

---

[1] *De Hæresibus* c. 9. [2] Article XII, 3.

[3] "It was, probably, a wise exercise of discretion in Elizabeth's divines to strike out this Article, and to abstain from an attempt to define authoritatively the sin against the Holy Ghost. At the same time we may note that the Anabaptist extravagances occupy much less space in the Thirty-nine than they did in the Forty-two Articles. Those sects had declined in the intervening ten years, or it had become manifest that their adherents were of less consequence than had been supposed" (Boultbee, *The Theology of the Church of England*, p. 136).

[4] "While retaining the phrase 'deadly sin' in our Litany and in Article XVI, the Reformers by no means intended to retain the false and dangerous system of which the distinction between Mortal and Venial sins formed a part. The absence of any mention of *venial sins* must be considered conclusive. But they did not deny that some sins were more heinous than others, or that such sins in certain cases demanded exceptional treatment" (Drury, *Confession and Absolution*, p. 210).

obviously more injurious to the soul. Any classification by acts is therefore radically wrong, and the usual distinction between " mortal " and
" venial " is impossible, because life is not lived by rule. The law of the
land rightly distinguishes between murder and other crimes, but sin
cannot be reduced to law, because law can take no cognisance of conditions and opportunities. Any distinction, therefore, must be in character
and degree, not in kind, of sin. The only question, therefore, that remains
is whether a man after becoming a Christian may so deliberately commit
sin as necessarily to involve himself in anything unpardonable. This the
Article plainly denies.

II.—THE PROBLEMS OF FALLING AND RESTORATION

The Article goes on to teach that although the regenerate may fall
into sin they can be restored. " Wherefore the grant of repentance is
not to be denied to such as fall into sin after Baptism." A curious misconception arose in the early Church in regard to Baptism, as though that
involved a state of Christian perfection. On this account it was often
delayed lest the baptised should fall from the presumed state of spiritual
perfection and be eternally lost. It was unfortunate that the Scriptural
idea of Baptism as the beginning of life, not the end, was forgotten or set
aside. Baptism invariably means the introduction of the soul into a new
sphere, and under the figure of " birth " implies the commencement,
not the culmination, of the Christian life. But with this wrong view
the early Church exacted long discipline for sins after Baptism, and outside
the Church the Montanists[1] and Novatians[2] insisted upon still harsher
measures, refusing to admit the lapsed to Holy Communion. These
views were revived at the Reformation by the Anabaptists, as the Augsburg Confession, Calvin, and Hooper, clearly show. But in opposition
to this severe line the Article teaches that " the grant of repentance is not
to be denied to such as fall into sin after Baptism." The phrase " grant
of repentance " in the Latin is *locus pœnitentiæ*, and in the English of the
Fifteenth Article of 1553 the phrase was " the place for penitents."
The allusion is to the passage referring to Esau (Heb. xii. 16, 17). But
it is important to notice the exact wording of the original and the Revised
Version. When it said, " He found no place of repentance," it does not
mean that he was unable to repent, but that he was unable to reverse his
father's decision; he could not get his father to change his mind. The
verse should read thus : " For ye know that afterwards, when he wished
to inherit the blessing he was rejected (for he found no place of repentance),
although he sought it (the blessing) earnestly with tears."

[1] Montanus, a native of Phrygia, 170, the founder of a schism which spread with
great rapidity, and captured Tertullian. The main ideas were some special views of
the Holy Spirit and the Second Coming of our Lord.
[2] Novatian, a schismatic Bishop, 250, a man of great ability and genuine character.
He considered the discipline of the Church too lax, and founded a party which lasted
for centuries.

III.—THE PROBLEMS OF SINLESSNESS AND REPENTANCE

There are two errors coming from different points dealt with in the Article. One is the possibility of sin after receiving the Holy Spirit, and the other is the possibility of restoration after sinning. " After we have received the Holy Ghost, we may depart from grace given, and fall into sin, and by the grace of God we may arise again, and amend our lives." The result is a twofold condemnation: (a) first, of those who say that Christians " can no more sin as long as they live here " ; and (b) then of those who " deny the place of forgiveness to such as truly repent."

(1) The former of these errors was rife in the sixteenth century and is not unknown to-day. When, however, an appeal is made to Scripture, there is no great doubt on the subject. St. Paul addresses Christians as " saints," and " elect," and " baptised," and yet he assumed their liability to heinous sin, and at the same time the possibility of their repentance and restoration. His treatment of the serious offender at Corinth (1 Cor. v. 1) is a proof of this, for while in the first Epistle St. Paul is very severe on the sin and the sinner and insists upon discipline, in the second Epistle, repentance having been shown, there is an equal concern for the man's restoration to fellowship. Later theology tended to claim sinlessness for the regenerate, or else if there was the presence of sinfulness it was a proof that regeneration was not real. The result was much the same as in the old error of sin after Baptism. The main passage which is used in this connection is 1 John iii. 9, " Whosoever is born of God doth not commit sin." But it will be seen that the reference is to those who are born of God, including everyone without distinction. Further, it refers to conduct, " doth not commit sin." The reference is not to nature, whether good or bad, but to the actual practice of sin, and when the passage is looked at in the light of its context and in relation to the rest of the Epistle and its teaching on sin and sins, there can be no doubt that the meaning is that one who is born of God will not habitually practise sin. The reason for this statement is the abiding possession of the Divine seed. The believer has the two natures within him ; the old nature, the evil principle referred to in Article IX, and the new nature, the gift of God in the new birth. In proportion, therefore, as he allows the higher nature to have sway he does not and cannot sin, but if for any reason he does not abide there, but allows the old nature to be predominant, he practises sin and thereby shows that so far he is not exercising his new life from God.

(2) The other error tends to hopelessness and despair, and for this reason alone needs to be rejected. Whatever may be the state of the believer we must insist that by the grace of God he may arise and amend his life. There are no passages in Scripture that really contradict this position. Reference is sometimes made to Hebrews vi. 4-6, but a careful consideration will show that it refers to wilful and final persistence in sin and not to mere backsliding. The use of the present tenses implies a

constant and deliberate continuance in sinning, and as long as this remains
it is, of course, impossible to renew such an one to repentance. But quite
apart from this view the verses following show that the condition implied
is purely problematical, and has no reference to ordinary backsliding and
repentance (Heb. vi. 9). Another passage adduced is Heb. x. 26-29,
but again it will be seen that the whole thought is that of scornful apostasy,
not ordinary wandering and backsliding. The three places in Hebrews
are closely united in connection with the danger of apostasy to which the
Hebrew Christians were liable. Thus in chap. ii they are warned
against drifting ; in chap. vi they are warned against sinning ; in chap. x
they are warned against scornful rejection. One other text is sometimes
used, referring to " sin unto death " (1 John v. 16). Whatever this
may mean there is no reference to any particular form of wrongdoing.
It is not " a " sin, but " sin," and is evidently something which refers to
Christian fellowship, for it refers to a brother committing the error. It
is more than likely that death here is purely physical, and that the wrong-
doing is analogous to those physical and temporal punishments to which
the Corinthian Christians were subject through their sins (1 Cor. xi. 30).
But whatever be the interpretation of the passage it does not in the least
contradict the statement of the Article that we may fall into sin and by
the grace of God arise and amend our lives.

There are three main views of the relation of the believer to inborn
sinfulness : (a) some hold that the evil principle is met by Suppression, by
keeping it down, and striving for victory over it. But this seems to
exaggerate the human side and tends to make the believer despair of
victory. (b) At the other extreme is the view known as Eradication,
which teaches that the evil principle is entirely removed. This is as
wrong in the direction of exaggeration as the former is in the direction of
inadequacy, and the Articles are quite clear in their opposition to it. (c)
The true view which meets all the conditions of the case is best described
as Counteraction. This means that the presence and power of evil
within are counteracted by the presence and greater power of the Holy
Spirit. So that evil though mighty is subjugated by the mightier force of
the Spirit of God. It is thus that we are to understand the entire teaching
of St. John's Epistle, especially those passages which on the one hand
show clearly that sin remains in the believer, and those on the other which
teach the possibility and reveal the secret of victory. Thus, when the
Apostle says, " My little children, I write unto you that ye sin not, and
if any man sin, we have an Advocate with the Father " (1 John ii. 21),
we see at once that while there is perfect provision against sinning, no
allowance is, or can be made for it. It is this combination of truths that
best explains the relation of the believer to sinfulness and sinning. There
must be no allowance whatever for sin, and any thought of the inevitable-
ness of sinful actions is to be regarded as absolutely intolerable. On the
other hand, the fact that the evil principle remains within necessitates the
Divine provision being made against its possible expression, and thus the

two sides of the truth are balanced and safeguarded. There is no need for us to sin, especially as we pray in the *Te Deum* : " Vouchsafe, O Lord, to keep us this day without sin " ; and in the Collect : " Grant that this day we fall into no sin, neither run into any kind of danger." But if by any possibility we should sin we can be restored and amend our lives, because of the Divine provision of the " Advocate with the Father, Jesus Christ the righteous." As it has been well put, " the equipment of a ship with life-belts is not a proof that it is intended the vessel shall be wrecked. The captain is not to wreck his ship, he seeks to avoid that ; but should disaster overtake him the provision is at hand." Once again, let it be thoroughly understood in the light of all the Articles, that there is no allowance for sinning, but the most perfect provision in case of it.[1]

THE SIN AGAINST THE HOLY GHOST

Although the Article on this subject, which was contained in the Forty-two of 1553, was struck out in 1563, it may be worth while considering the Article and its subject in view of the fact that our present Article refers to "sin against the Holy Ghost," which is regarded as " unpardonable." The following is the exact wording of the omitted Article :—

Blasphemy against the Holy Ghost	*Blasphemia in Spiritum Sanctum*
Blasphemy against the Holy Ghost is when a man of malice and stubbornness of mind, doth rail upon the truth of God's Word manifestly perceived, and being enemy thereunto persecuteth the same. And because such be guilty of God's curse, they entangle themselves with a most grievous, and heinous crime, whereupon this kind of sin is called and affirmed of the Lord, unpardonable.	Blasphemia in Spiritum Sanctum, est cum quis Verborum Dei manifeste perceptam veritatem, ex malitia et obfirmatione animi, convitiis insectatur, et hostiliter insequitur. Atque hujusmodi, quia maledicto, sunt obnoxii, gravissimo sese astringunt sceleri. Unde peccati hoc genus irremissible a Domino appellatur, et affirmatur.

The circumstances of our Lord's words were due to the cavil of the Pharisees that He was performing His miracles by the power of the devil, and the fact that the incident is in all three Evangelists seems to imply that the words made a deep impression. Our Lord clearly distinguishes between sin against Himself as the Son of Man, and sin against the Holy Ghost. The former would seem to apply to sins against His humanity, while the latter were sins against Deity itself. It will be remembered that the sin of open opposition and scorn in Hebrews is described as in relation

---

[1] One of the best helps to a true understanding of this important subject is a little work, *Tenses and Senses of Sin and Sinlessness as seen in the First Epistle of John*, by Graham (Pickering & Inglis, Glasgow).

to " the Son of God " (Heb. x. 29). It is clear from the context that the sin of which the Pharisees were in danger of being guilty (not that they had of necessity actually committed it) was the wilful shutting of their eyes against the light of truth, so that there is no reference to any particular kind or class of sin, but the attitude of the soul against knowledge, the determination not to see what the soul knows to be true. St. Augustine probably describes with correctness this sin as *perseverantia in nequitia et in malignitate cum desperatione indulgentiæ Dei*. This attitude would seem to accord with the "reprobate mind" mentioned by St. Paul (Rom. i. 28), that which does evil as evil, and because it is evil. If this is the true interpretation of the sin, then it is evident that wherever there is any desire to know whether the sin has been committed the desire itself is positive proof that the sin has not taken place. When we remember the words of the Lord's Prayer about forgiveness, the story of Simon Magus and the Apostle Peter's relation to him, and the restoration of St. Peter himself after his denial, we can see fresh illustrations of the truth of the Article concerning the restoring mercy and grace of God.[1]

N.B.—By some writers[2] the subject of final perseverance is considered in connection with this Article, but it is very doubtful whether this should be done. It should come under Article XVII, especially as our Reformers undoubtedly held the doctrine. There is some confusion as to the meaning of the phrase " indefectibility of grace," for in the sense of sinlessness or the absence of backsliding, no Calvinistic writer holds it. The belief in grace being indefectible is quite consistent with the view held by Calvinists that there may be sinning in the Christian life.

" The most extreme Calvinists would admit that the truly regenerate may and do fall into sin—but (they would add) not finally."[3]

The Puritans came later than the last revision of the Article, and therefore the controversy with them has no real bearing on the Article itself. It is also noteworthy that there is nothing of this subject in the earliest Commentary on the Articles, by Rogers, or the later and representative treatments by Burnet and Beveridge. The subject will therefore receive attention under the next Article.

---

[1] "Whereupon we do not without a just cause detest and abhor the damnable opinion of them which do most wickedly go about to persuade the simple and ignorant people, that, if we chance, after we be once come to God, and grafted in His Son Jesus Christ, to fall into some horrible sin, repentance shall be unprofitable to us, there is no more hope of reconciliation, or to be received again into the favour and mercy of God" (Homily of Repentance).

[2] Harold Browne and Kidd.

[3] Boultbee, *The Theology of the Church of England*, p. 135.

ARTICLE XVII

Of Predestination and Election.

De Prædestinatione et Electione.

Predestination to life is the everlasting purpose of God, whereby (before the foundations of the world were laid) He hath constantly decreed by His counsel, secret to us, to deliver from curse and damnation those whom He hath chosen in Christ out of mankind, and to bring them by Christ to everlasting salvation, as vessels made to honour. Wherefore they which be endued with so excellent a benefit of God be called according to God's purpose by His Spirit working in due season: they through grace obey the calling: they be justified freely: they be made sons of God by adoption: they be made like the image of His only-begotten Son Jesus Christ: they walk religiously in good works: and at length, by God's mercy, they attain to everlasting felicity.

As the godly consideration of Predestination and our Election in Christ is full of sweet, pleasant, and unspeakable comfort to godly persons, and such as feel in themselves the working of the Spirit of Christ, mortifying the works of the flesh and their earthly members, and drawing up their mind to high and heavenly things, as well because it doth greatly establish and confirm their faith of eternal Salvation to be enjoyed through Christ, as because it doth fervently kindle their love towards God: So for curious and carnal persons, lacking the Spirit of Christ, to have continually before their eyes the sentence of God's Predestination, is a most dangerous downfall, whereby the Devil doth thrust them either into desperation, or into wretchlessness of most unclean living, no less perilous than desperation.

Furthermore, we must receive God's promises in such wise, as they be generally set forth to us in Holy Scripture; and, in our doings, that Will of God is to be followed, which we have expressly declared unto us in the Word of God.

Prædestinatio ad vitam est æternum Dei propositum, quo ante jacta mundi fundamenta, suo consilio, nobis quidem occulto, constanter decrevit, eos quos in Christo elegit ex hominum genere, a maledicto et exitio liberare, atque (ut vasa in honorem efficta) per Christum, ad æternum salutem adducere. Unde qui tam præclaro Dei beneficio sunt donati, illi Spiritu ejus opportuno tempero operante, secundum propositum ejus vocantur, vocationi per gratiam parent, justificantur gratis, adoptantur in filios Dei, unigeniti ejus Jesu Christi imagini efficiuntur conformes, in bonis operibus sancte ambulant, et demum ex Dei misericordia pertingunt ad sempiternam felicitatem.

Quemadmodum Prædestinationis et Electionis nostræ in Christo pia consideratio, dulcis, suavis, et ineffabilis consolationis plena est vere piis, et his qui sentiunt in se vim Spiritus Christi, facta carnis et membra, quæ adhuc sunt super terram, mortificantem animumque ad cœlestia et superna rapientem; tum quia fidem nostram de æterna salute consequenda per Christum plurimum stabilit atque confirmat, tum quia amorem nostrum in Deum vehementer accendit : ita hominibus curiosis, carnalibus, et Spiritu Christi destitutis, ob oculos perpetuo versari Prædestinationis Dei sententiam, perniciosissimum est præcipitium, unde illos Diabolus protrudit vel in desperationem, vel in æque perniciosam impurissimæ vitæ securitatem.

Deinde, promissiones divinas sic amplecti oportet, ut nobis in sacris literis generaliter propositæ sunt; et Dei voluntas in nostris actionibus ea sequenda est, quam in verbo Dei habemus diserte revelatam.

IMPORTANT EQUIVALENTS.

Before the foundations of the earth = *ante jacta mundi fundamenta.* were laid

236

By His counsel, secret to us	=	*suo consilio, nobis quidem occulto.*
Endued	=	*donati.*
In due season	=	*opportuno tempore.*
They be made sons of God by adoption	=	*adoptantur in filios Dei.*
Religiously	=	*sancte.*
Working of the spirit	=	*vim Spiritus.*
Their earthly members	=	*membra quæ adhuc sunt super terram.*
Drawing up	=	*rapientem.*
Their faith	=	fidem *nostram.*
It doth establish	=	*stabilit.*
Their love	=	amorem *nostrum.*
Most dangerous downfall	=	*perniciosissimum præcipitium.*
Wretchlessness[1]	=	*securitatem.*
We must receive God's promises	=	*promissiones divinas amplecti oportet.*
Expressly declared	=	*diserte revelatam.*

At this point we reach the goal of which Articles IX to XI may be regarded as the starting-point. Looking back over these Articles it is possible to review the process step by step from Predestination to Glorification. This Article is concerned with the completed salvation, of which the various aspects and details have been brought before us in previous Articles. The predestinating love of God is thus the original ground of salvation, and the meaning and dangers of the doctrine are here noted.

The Article dates from 1553, and the fact that only slight verbal changes were made in 1563 and 1571 shows the essential unanimity among the Reformers on this important subject. This is all the more remarkable when it is remembered that the two aspects of the Continental Reformation Movement, Lutheran and Calvinistic, were in turn influential on English thought.

I.—THE TEACHING OF THE ARTICLE

This is by far the longest of the Articles, and in view of its importance at each point it is essential to look with the greatest care at what is actually taught before considering the subject in general.

A.—The Nature of Predestination.—What it is

1. The Fact.—The title uses two words, " Predestination " and " Election," and the former is also mentioned in the Article, together with the phrase implying the latter. There are three New Testament words, together with their various cognates, which call for special study : " Purpose," " Predestination," " Election." It is impossible to discuss them in full in these pages, but it seems essential to refer to the first, dealing with the Divine purpose, leaving the others to be considered in the light of the best exegetical commentaries available.[2]

---

[1] The English of the XLII has "rechlessness," *i.e.* recklessness.

[2] "The terms 'predestination,' 'election,' 'saints,' 'effectual calling,' represent the same fact under different aspects. Predestination (πρόθεσις) signifies the general intention of God to provide a plan of salvation, and has no direct reference to the

The following words of Dr. Denney fitly form the starting-point of study :—

" Πρόθεσις in this theological sense is a specially Pauline word. The purpose it describes is universal in its bearings, for it is the purpose of One who works all things according to the counsel of His will, Eph. i. 11 ; it is eternal, a πρόθεσις τῶν αἰώνων, Eph. iii. 11 ; it is God's ἰδία πρόθεσις, 2 Tim. i. 9, a purpose, the meaning, contents, and end of which find their explanation in God alone ; it is a purpose κατ'ἐκλογήν, i.e. the carrying of it out involves choice and discrimination between man and man, and between race and race ; and in spite of the side of mystery which belongs to such a conception, it is a perfectly intelligible purpose, for it is described as πρόθεσις ἣν ἐποίησεν ἐν Χριστῷ Ἰησοῦ, and what God means by Christ Jesus no one can doubt. God's eternal purpose, the purpose carried out κατ' ἐκλογὴν, yet embracing the universe, is clearly revealed in His Son."[1]

Arising out of this purpose is the Divine Predestination and Election, the latter of the words expressing the action taken by God consequent upon the purpose.[2]

2. The Limit. " Predestination to Life."—The Article strictly and significantly limits the reference to the predestination of the believer to life, and there is no reference to anything else. It is, of course, open to the charge of being illogical since it may be fairly said that " predestination to life " involves what is known as preterition, or leaving those who are not predestinated to themselves. But the Reformers evidently saw that mere logic was faulty in dealing with the Divine purpose, and for this reason they tended to keep themselves to the thought of God's attitude to the believer. This seems to be in strict agreement with the important distinction found in Scripture between the origination of good and evil. Thus, in speaking of " vessels of wrath " and " vessels of mercy " (Rom. ix. 22, 23), St. Paul makes a marked difference. Of the former he simply uses the passive participle, " fitted to destruction," while of the latter he uses the active voice of the verb, and the preparation is distinctly attributed to God as the originator, " which He had afore prepared unto glory." To the same effect is the distinction made by our Lord Himself between the sentence to be passed on those on His right hand and that on those on His left. To the former the words are : " Come, ye blessed of My Father " ; to the latter, it is simply, " Depart from Me, ye cursed," the omission to the latter being a mere indication that the curse was solely of themselves. Nor is it possible to overlook the departure from strict

individuals comprised in the plan. It is otherwise with foreknowledge (πρόγνωσις) and predetermination (προορισμός), the former of which implies distinct recognition of the individuals who should believe; the latter, the providential arrangements leading to that result. These expressions relate to the Divine acts before time" (Litton, *Introduction to Dogmatic Theology* (Second Edition), p. 348).

[1] *The Expositor's Greek Testament*, Romans, p. 661.
[2] See Vaughan; Sanday and Headlam; and Denney, on Rom. viii. 29; ix. 11. Also Ellicott; Armitage Robinson; and Westcott, on Eph. i. 4, 5.

parallelism in other words of that passage. "The kingdom prepared for you" is contrasted with "everlasting fire, prepared for the devil and his angels." Thus, the Article in limiting attention to predestination to life seems clearly to follow Scripture in ascribing to God the work of grace for the believer, and associating evil and the doom of evil with men themselves. The election of believers is invariably referred to "the good pleasure of God's will," but nothing else is mentioned in this connection (Eph. i. 5, 9; Phil. ii. 13; 2 Thess. i. 11). So that whatever may be urged on purely logical grounds it is in every way truest, safest, and best to keep Divine predestination where Scripture places it.[1]

3. The Foundation.—This predestination is associated with "the everlasting purpose of God." This is the Divine side, and shows that redemption is in pursuance of God's eternal purpose.[2]

4. The Object.—"Whereby (before the foundations of the world were laid) He hath constantly decreed by His counsel secret to us, to deliver from curse and damnation those whom He hath chosen in Christ out of mankind, and to bring them by Christ to everlasting salvation, as vessels made to honour." This statement of the Article shows what is to be understood by predestination to life. The word "constantly" means in the old English, and according to the Latin, "firmly," and the Divine decree based on the Divine counsel is to deliver from sin, to redeem out of mankind, and to bring such to everlasting salvation. Nothing could be clearer than this statement of the Divine purpose in salvation, and it is almost wholly expressed in the actual words of Scripture (Eph. i. 4, 5, 11; Rom. viii. 28, 29; ix. 11; 2 Thess. ii. 13; 2 Tim. i. 9; 1 Pet. i. 2-5; Rom. ix. 21).

B.—The Proof of Predestination.—What it Involves

1. The Description.—It is clear that the reference is to something involving genuine spiritual life and experience. "They which be endued with so excellent a benefit of God." Nothing short of such a spiritual idea will satisfy the statements made.

2. The Stages.—A sevenfold process is mentioned as the means whereby the Divine purpose is accomplished. "Called according to God's purpose by His Spirit working in due season, they through grace obey the calling: they be justified freely: they be made sons of God by adoption: they be made like the image of His only-begotten Son Jesus

---

[1] "We stand, in fact, in presence of one of those antinomies which we not unfrequently meet with in Scripture, and which appear insoluble to human reason. Pushed to its logical conclusion, the necessity, from the condition of fallen man, of a grace superior to common, or preparatory, grace, leads, in conjunction with the doctrine of predestination, to reprobation, at least in its milder form of 'preterition'; pushed to its logical conclusion, the Arminian doctrine, which acknowledges no grace, but what is common, leads to Pelagianism. We await a fuller measure of revelation for an adjustment of the two lines of thought" (Litton, *Introduction to Dogmatic Theology* (Second Edition, p. 254).

[2] Denney, on Romans viii. 28.

Christ: they walk religiously in good works, and at length, by God's mercy, they attain to everlasting felicity." It is particularly noteworthy that these statements reproduce almost exactly the language of St. Paul, for the various phrases can be matched from his Epistles. Only one point seems to demand attention, the meaning of the word " called." It is now generally understood that " calling " in St. Paul's writings never means mere "invitation"; it is always " effectual calling,"[1] that is to say, the " called " are those who are invited and who also accept the invitation. In the Gospels the " called " seem to be limited to those who are invited.

3. The Two Sides.—In strict and careful agreement with Scripture the Article emphasises both aspects, the Divine and the human, in salvation. Not only is there the calling, the working of the Spirit, the free justification, the adoption to sonship, and the attainment of everlasting felicity, but also on the other hand the obedience to the calling, the conformity to the image of Christ, and the religious walk in good works. Here, again, we see the remarkable agreement with St. Paul's language in Rom. viii. 28-30.[2]

C.—The Effect of Predestination.—What It Brings

1. For the godly this thought of predestination and election in Christ is " full of sweet, pleasant, and unspeakable comfort to godly persons, and such as feel in themselves the working of the Spirit of Christ, mortifying the works of the flesh, and their earthly members, and drawing up their mind to high and heavenly things." This emphasis on " sweet, pleasant, and unspeakable comfort " is important and significant in relation to the true New Testament idea of assurance, and the reason for the comfort is said to be two-fold. It confirms faith and kindles love. " As well because it doth greatly establish and confirm their faith of eternal salvation to be enjoyed through Christ, as because it doth fervently kindle their love towards God." Thus, again, we see that the Article is concerned with the realities of spiritual experience.

2. For the ungodly the opposite is said to be the result. They are described as " curious (that is, inquisitive) and carnal persons, lacking the Spirit of Christ," and for such people " to have continually before their eyes the sentence of God's predestination " is rightly said to be " a most

---

[1] Denney on Rom. viii. 28.

[2] "The eternal foreordination appears in time as 'calling,' of course as effectual calling: where salvation is contemplated as the work of God alone (as here) there can be no breakdown in its processes. The next stages are summarily indicated: ἐδικαίωσεν God in Jesus Christ forgave our sins, and accepted us as righteous in His sight; ungodly as we had been, He put us right with Himself. In that, everything else is included. The whole argument of Chs. VI–VIII has been that justification and the new life of holiness in the Spirit are inseparable experiences. Hence Paul can take one step to the end, write οὓς δὲ ἐδικαίωσεν, τούτους καὶ ἐδόξασε. Yet the tense in the last word is amazing. It is the most daring anticipation of faith that even the New Testament contains: the life is not to be taken out of it by the philosophical consideration that with God there is neither before nor after" (Denney, ut supra, p. 652).

dangerous downfall," the spiritual peril being two-fold; either it will lead to spiritual desperation, or else to recklessness[1] of unclean living.

D.—The Safeguard of Predestination.—What it Demands

After stating in frank terms the two-fold effect of predestination the Article appropriately closes by indicating the proper precautions to be taken in the study of the subject.

1. The Divine promises are to be received, " as they be generally set forth to us in Holy Scripture." By " generally " is probably to be understood the thought of the promises being applied to the whole *genus* of mankind, including both good and bad. It is opposed to *singulus* or *specialis*,[2] or it may be regarded as referring to the entire *genus* of the Divine promises. The use of the terms " General Confession "; " General Thanksgiving "; and the phrase " generally necessary to salvation " seems to illustrate the true idea of the passage, that we are to regard God's promises in their universal aspect and offer as seen in Holy Scripture.

2. Obedience to God's will is to be according to what is " expressly declared unto us in the Word of God." So that in both ways the promises and the will of God are not intended to obscure the fullest offer of salvation or lessen the obligation to obedience. It is another way of saying that " the secret things belong unto the Lord our God, but those things which are revealed belong unto us and to our children for ever, that we may do all the words of this law " (Deut. xxix. 29).[3]

II.—THE HISTORY OF THE SUBJECT

Predestination is part of the great problem of Divine and human personality, of determinism and liberty. It is, therefore, not peculiar to Christianity, for the Stoics were fatalists, and so to some extent were the Pharisees, while it is known that Mohammedans are strongly of this view. It was impossible for the Fathers to avoid referring to the subject, though its first systematic treatment is found in St. Augustine. To him predestination meant the Divine act, not because we were going to be holy, but in order that we might be holy. Further, reprobation was not to be understood as a Divine decree, but a simple leaving of the wicked to the consequences of their sin, for which the technical word is " preterition." This view of predestination is the endeavour to interpret St. Paul's words,

---

[1] The older spelling of wretchlessness was rechelessness, meaning "carelessness." The Latin equivalent is *securitas*.

[2] This interpretation may be illustrated from the following words of the *Reformatio Legum* :
"Quapropter omnes nobis admonendi sunt, ut in actionibus suscipiendis ad decreta prædestinationis se non referant, sed universam vitæ suæ rationem ad Dei leges accommodent; cum et promissiones bonis et minas malis, in sacris Scripturis generaliter propositas contemplentur" (*De Hæresibus*, c. 22).

[3] See Boultbee, *The Theology of the Church of England*, p. 140.

which are concerned with the salvation of man from the Divine stand-point.[1]

In the Middle Ages Thomas Aquinas followed Augustine, while Duns Scotus followed Pelagius. The Church of Rome was much divided at the Council of Trent, but negatived reprobation. The Jesuits were the strongest force in that Council, and their view was virtually Pelagian.[2]

It must never be forgotten that the Reformers taught predestination long before the time of Calvin.[3] The doctrine was the theological implication of the very heart of the Reformation; indeed, that movement was in a sense the product of the doctrine rather than the doctrine of it. Zwingli taught it even more clearly than Calvin, and Luther was as dogmatic as Calvin himself. It was Melanchthon, not Calvin, who first gave predestination a formal place in the Protestant system.[4] Bucer taught the doctrine to Calvin, so that it was not Calvin who ingrafted it into the Reformation theology. No doubt his logic and austerity gave clearness and force to the teaching, but its origin was much earlier, and this is a point never to be forgotten. St. Augustine was the true founder of the Reformation on its doctrinal side, and it was he who placed this doctrine in the heart of the Reformation consciousness.

It is important to understand why predestination should have been made so prominent at the Reformation. It was not because of any thought of the "elect" as distinct from other people, but because of the sovereignty, supremacy, and primacy of Divine grace in relation to human needs. The whole Reformation movement was subjective, spiritual, and practical, and did not concern itself with mere speculation, and it was on this account that the doctrine of predestination was realised as of vital and supreme importance.[5]

---

[1] "Thus regarded—whatever speculative difficulties may attend it—it is simply the expression of an experience which lies at the root of all genuine Christian consciousness, viz. that in this matter of personal salvation, the last word is always grace, not nature; that it is not *our* willing and running which has brought us into the kingdom of God but *His* mercy; that it is He who first enkindled in us the desire after Himself, who drew us to Himself, who bore with us in our waywardness and resistance of His Spirit, who step by step overcame that resistance, and brought us finally into the number of His children; and that all this was no *afterthought* to God, but an eternal counsel of His love which has now effectuated itself in our salvation. This is the *religious* interest in the doctrine of predestination which gives it its abiding value" (Orr, *The Progress of Dogma*, p. 152).

[2] Boultbee, *ut supra*, p. 151 f.

[3] "It is a striking fact that the Protestant theology of the sixteenth century both began and ended in strict theories of Predestination" (Wace, *Principles of the Reformation*, p. 129).

[4] "The most has been made of supposed differences between Luther and Melanchthon on the one hand, and Calvin on the other, in respect of this doctrine. But the Reformers of all countries were strong Augustinians, and, with some modifications, held the same general cast of doctrine on election" (Boultbee, *ut supra*, p. 144).
"The severe doctrine of Calvin on the subject of predestination is notorious; but it should be remembered that the teaching of Melanchthon in the first edition of his work was not less severe" (Wace, *ut supra*, p. 129).

[5] "It is important to observe that the purpose with which the idea of predestination is introduced is to afford some explanation of the helplessness of man's will, and of the hopelessness of his condition by nature. It is introduced, that is, for a practical

Under these circumstances it is not surprising that the English Reformers were all what is understood as " Calvinists "; and, indeed, until
the time of Archbishop Laud no other doctrine was known in the Anglican
Church.[1] During the early years of Queen Elizabeth, and following the
Revision of 1571, the Protestants who had returned from exile under
Mary had imbibed the more severely logical Calvinism of Geneva, and
were therefore dissatisfied with our Articles as inadequate. It was this
that led to the proposal to add the Lambeth Articles to the Thirty-nine,
a movement which has been rightly described as " the ill-omened attempt
to lay the yoke of ultra-Calvinism on the Church of England."[2] This
effort was prevented, though the controversy raged furiously during the
whole reign of Queen Elizabeth.[3] At the Hampton Court Conference
the Puritans naturally desired the addition of the Lambeth Articles, but
again their efforts were frustrated. But in 1619 at the Calvinistic Synod
of Dort the English Church was represented for a time by some dis-

purpose, and arises out of the contemplation of our moral and religious weakness"
(Wace, *ut supra*, p. 136; see also pp. 132, 134).

"In opposing the dead works of the Church's belief in those days, the seductive
arts of indulgences and the arbitrariness of the hierarchy, they found support in the
doctrine of the absolute religious helplessness of the natural man, in order that henceforward he may live solely by God's grace, inasmuch as they thought that man could
never be too much humbled and that too much honour could never be ascribed to the
Lord. In arguing thus, they had the courage like St. Augustine to deduce the consequence as well, viz. unqualified predestination" (Von Hase, *Handbook to the Controversy with Rome*, Vol. II, p. 19).

"The supreme issue was soteriological. How is fallen man forgiven, justified,
saved? How is the salvation purchased by the Redeemer appropriated and made
effectual in the experience of the individual soul? All other doctrine was ancillary,
whether it concerned the elective decree that must have preceded the sending of the
Son and the Spirit, or the Scriptures that disclosed the way, or the Sacraments that
sealed and sustained the gift, or the Church that cherished all the means and fostered
the experience" (W. A. Curtis, *History of Creeds and Confessions of Faith*, p. 409).

"It was a necessary and wholesome reaction against the papal doctrine of human
merit. It was considered as the backbone of the doctrines of free grace, and was death
to all pride and self-righteousness. It furnished an immovable basis in eternity for the
salvation in time, and the most solid comfort to the believer in seasons of despondency
and temptation. Hence we find it among all the Reformers. Luther in his tract on
The Slavery of the Human Will, which he never recalled, but regarded as one of his best
books, goes even further in this direction than Calvin ever did" (Edgar, *The Genius of
Protestantism*, p. 45; see also Ch. V).

"It must give a powerful support to the religious life when the mind combines the
doctrine of justification with a doctrine of election, and, believing that God has elected
particular objects of His mercy from the foundation of the world, draws the inference
that He apprehends them by an effectual calling, enables them by His Spirit to fulfil the
conditions of salvation, guarantees that they will persevere in the state of grace, and
promises that no power in earth or hell will pluck them out of His hand. This train
of reflection is undoubtedly Pauline, and was only amplified by Calvin" (Paterson,
The Rule of Faith, p. 306).

[1] "No impartial person, competently acquainted with the history of the Reformation
and the works of the earlier Protestant divines at home and abroad, even to the close
of Elizabeth's reign, will deny that the doctrines of Calvin on redemption, and the
natural state of fallen man, are in all essential points the same as those of Luther,
Zwinglius, and the first Reformers collectively" (Coleridge, *Aids to Reflection*, Aphor-
ism II, "On that which is indeed spiritual religion").

[2] Boultbee, *ut supra*, p. 141.

[3] For the Lambeth Articles, see Boultbee, *ut supra*, pp. 141, 152.

tinguished men who did their utmost to mediate between the two extremes. Although Calvinism gained the victory at Dort the influence of the other side was only checked for a time, for it extended widely, especially through the English-speaking world.   Nor is this surprising, since it expressed the rebound of the heart from the severe logic of the intellect, and because it met learning with feeling it gained adherents in several quarters.[1]   The Arminian reaction under Laud was followed by one in the opposite direction during the Commonwealth by means of the West-minster Assembly.[2]   Once again the opponents of Calvinism gained the day at the Restoration, 1660.   In the eighteenth century the Evangelical Revival was the occasion of a fresh outbreak of the controversy.   The Methodists, on the one hand, were definitely Arminian, while the Anglican Evangelicals were almost wholly Calvinistic.   Simeon was, perhaps, the best representative of the time in that he accepted both sides and refused to attempt any reconciliation, only opposing the thought of reprobation.[3]

III.—THE PROBLEM

The subject of the Article is connected both with religion and with philosophy, and is part of the effort to relate the Finite to the Infinite. We have seen in previous Articles that man cannot save himself, that redemption is God's work, and at once the question arises whether God gives grace sufficient for salvation to all men, or whether there is special grace for a chosen few.   It is quite clear from a study of the Bible that alongside of the universality of God's grace in Christ there is a particu-larism which has to be considered and taken into account, and the Article constitutes an endeavour to state this Scriptural particularism, to show its bearing on the universal purpose of Christ's redemption and the offer of opportunity to all men.

It is important to notice again the careful adherence of the Article to the very words of Scripture ; indeed, its summary is almost in the terms of Scripture, and on this account it is to be interpreted in the light of the New Testament.   Whatever difficulties exist are difficulties, not of the Article, but of Scripture.   Then, too, it is important to note the clear and careful definition of predestination as " to life."   There is no refer-ence to Reprobation or Preterition, neither of which is a part of the Church of England doctrine.

Predestination is assuredly a principle of Scripture.   There is an unequal gift of privileges bestowed on men, and the story of Abraham shows the use of one to bless the many.   It is this element of selection which is at the foundation of all the work of redemption, so that there is

---

[1] W. A. Curtis, *ut supra*, Index, s.v. Dort; Boultbee, *ut supra*, p. 153.
[2] W. A. Curtis, *ut supra*, Index s.v. Westminster Assembly, and Westminster Con-cession.
[3] For a brief sketch of the history, see Moule, *Outlines of Christian Doctrine*, pp. 36-56.

no question as to the fact of predestination and election, only as to the character of it. As the Old Testament proceeds the election broadens out into the choice of Israel for the purpose of blessing the world, and then everything becomes deepened and spiritualised in the New Testament. It is, therefore, important to endeavour to discover what predestination really means, and there are three general interpretations of the doctrine in relation to Christianity.

A.—Ecclesiastical

By this is understood election to privilege, to the means of grace, to opportunities of present salvation without necessarily involving eternal salvation as well. Now there is undoubted truth in this position, because some men are placed within the sphere of Christian influences while others are in very different surroundings. The fact that our country and Africa differ in regard to Christianity cannot be explained solely on historical grounds; there must be something behind it in the way of Divine decision and choice. But while all this is undoubtedly true, it is clear that Scripture goes far beyond it (Rom. viii. 28-30). The Article speaks of " everlasting salvation," which is something much more than ecclesiastical, so that all theories which contemplate a mere election must be set aside as inadequate.[1] It is in accordance with this view that recent endeavours have been made to show that election refers to race or Church to bear God's Name in the world.[2] But again, this is entirely inadequate to the full teaching of St. Paul (Rom. ix. 18; 22-24).

" It appears, then, that the theory of ecclesiastical election, though perfectly Scriptural, does not cover the *whole* teaching of Scripture on the subject; and that we must recognise that there is a further truth, if not definitely revealed, at least implied, in the passages just referred to."[3]

Whether we like it or not, whether we understand it or not, St. Paul certainly teaches a profound doctrine of predestination and election.

B.—Arminian

This view is so called from the Dutch theologian, Harmen, latinised Arminius, who died 1609. But, of course, the view was substantially held ages before, and in some respects may be identified with the Pelagian position. It is also the general view of the Methodist Church to-day. According to this interpretation God foresees who will accept Christ, and thereupon He predestinates them. He determines salvation for those whom He sees will persevere. God has an antecedent will to save all, but

---

[1] Harold Browne (*Exposition of the Thirty-nine Articles*) is quite impossible on this point, p. 414 ff.
[2] Bishop Gore, on Rom. ix.–xi.
[3] Gibson, *The Thirty-nine Articles*, p. 469. See also Sanday and Headlam, *Romans*, pp. 266, 347.

only a consequent will to save believers. Again, we see the undoubted truth in this position in its emphasis on human responsibility. But on the other hand, if it be logically pressed it makes Divine salvation depend ultimately on human action. The view only becomes possible by an undue pressing of the term " foreknow," but a careful examination of the passages where this occurs shows that it never means simple foresight, but foresight with approval. Further, the Bible is perfectly clear in regard to God's election of Israel, that it was wholly independent of anything foreseen in Israel's life and conduct. Thus, the Arminian view strictly is inconsistent with any true and full conception of Divine grace. Salvation cannot be a mere contingency, for if no one accepted it, then Christ would have died in vain. Then, too, the Article speaks of God's counsel " secret to us," and this implies action prior to and independent of our life. Election contingent on foresight is really not election at all, since the choice in such a case would be solely man's, and would leave no room for distinction due to a Divine foreordination. As men are constituted, God must take the initiative in bringing about salvation, and yet it is universal experience that many resist all reformatory in-fluences. At this point arises the problem of the inter-relations of Divine and human agencies. One thing is absolutely certain ; the sinner cannot renew himself and needs the regenerating grace of God. He has liberty to sin, but not to save himself. It is curious that some writers, as for example, Aristotle, Rothe, and Martensen, deny God's foreknowledge of things that depend on human volition. But how can God be limited by time and space ? Yet knowledge does not mean compulsion. Because He is God He knows, but we do not know, and thus there is no loss of responsibility and no compulsion. There can be no doubt therefore that Arminianism as a *complete* explanation is scripturally inadequate and philosophically impossible.[1] Indeed, it has been rightly said that between the Calvinistic and Arminian extremes there is no essential distinction, because in both the number of the elect is absolutely fixed, foreseen, and settled.[2]

C.—Calvinistic

The name of Calvin is simply used for convenience, because the view was held by St. Augustine a thousand years before. Speaking generally, this teaches that God in His mercy determines to save, and that from first to last salvation is of grace apart from human merits or works, though requiring human faith for reception and full realisation. There are varieties of Calvinism, according as the view of predestination is associated with a time before or after the Fall. The former is called *supra-lapsarianism*, and the latter *sub-lapsarianism*.

The truth contained in this position is undoubted, for beyond all other

---

[1] Gibson, *ut supra*, pp. 472–474.
[2] Lightfoot, *Text-Book of the Thirty-nine Articles*, p. 142.

interpretations it magnifies the grace of God, and yet if it be logically pressed it tends to make God everything and man nothing, and to teach that God selects some and leaves the others to the consequences of their sins. But the element of logic, which is apt to be overpressed, must not blind us to the profound realities underlying this general position. It was the view, as already seen, of all the Reformers,[1] English and Continental, and is also seen to be the position of the compilers of our Prayer Book, as they teach the child to regard itself as among " the elect people of God."[2]

It is the fashion to criticise Calvinism, but it must be confessed that very often the criticism is only the measure of the ignorance of what Calvinism really means.[3] The first commentator on the Articles, Rogers, is as severely Calvinistic as anyone could be, and speaks in the strongest terms of " the errors, and adversaries unto this truth."[4] It is, of course, inevitable that exaggeration of one truth invariably leads to a reaction in an opposite direction, and yet no one can question the remarkable power of what is known as Calvinism in the life of individuals and communities during the last three hundred years.[5]

[1] Burnet (*On the Articles*, p. 207 f.) admits that the Article seems to favour the Calvinistic position.

[2] "This was the doctrine understood under the name by all the great theologians of the Church—Augustine, Anselm, Thomas Aquinas, the Reformers, English and foreign (with some modifications), Bellarmine, Calvin, Luther himself—and we find it stated in our own Article on the subject. It is the doctrine, too, of our Catechism. The child presumed at baptism to be regenerate is supposed in this formulary never to have lost the gift or fallen from it; pious instruction and example having been made instrumental to carry on the work. He is regarded as a Christian child—a child of God really, and not merely ecclesiastically; a member of Christ by vital union as well as by incorporation in a visible Church. He declares that he is actually sanctified by the Holy Ghost, and he trusts he is one of the elect as being thus sanctified. This is the 'state of salvation' for being called to which he returns thanks, and which he prays he may continue in unto his life's end. Not, surely, a mere access to the means of grace, which may never be used, or a mere possibility of being saved, which may never be realised; but an actual saving participation in Christ and His work. It would be strange if prayer were made for grace to continue in the former undetermined state" (Litton, *ut supra*, p. 345).

[3] "I assert what I have before asserted, and by God's grace I will persist in the assertion to my dying day, that it is far from the truth that the Church of England is decidedly Arminian, and hostile to Calvinism. . . . If we would look for warm advocates of Church authority in general, and for able writers in defence of our own form of Church government in particular, such we shall find among those divines who were called in their day the Doctrinal Calvinists. . . . The Calvinists contradict not the avowed dogmata of the Church; nor has the Church in her dogmata explicitly condemned or contradicted them. Anyone may hold all the theological opinions of Calvin, hard and extravagant as some of them may seem, and yet be a sound member of the Church of England and Ireland" (Bishop Horsley, quoted in O'Donoghue, *On the Thirty-nine Articles*, p. 149).

[4] Rogers, *On the Thirty-nine Articles*, pp. 145–147.

[5] "We have only to look to our sister Church in Scotland in order to see that such a view exhibits a real side of human experience, and has worked out magnificent results" (Wace, *ut supra*, p. 150).

Simpson (*Fact and Faith*, p. 131), refers to a criticism by a High Churchman on what he had called "the still more hideous doctrine of predestination." After pointing out the unmistakable animus of the writer against the Reformation, Dr. Simpson proceeds as follows:

"As to predestination, Mr. Dearmer would doubtless call it hideous to declare that 'just as predestination is a part of Providence in respect to those who are ordained

D.—*Summary*

Reviewing these three attempts to solve the problem, it is easy to see the element of truth and also the element of error in each. The Ecclesiastical view is an attempt to escape the mystery of Divine choice, though the problem is just as real with nations and Churches as with individuals. It is impossible to avoid associating St. Paul's teaching with some Divine foreordination (Rom. ix). The Arminian interpretation is an attempt to square the doctrine with reason and freedom, but the problem still remains how to account for the fact that some natures are more wilful than others. It is impossible to remove the difficulty by basing predestination on foreknowledge, for in reality the problem remains as acute as before.

" The truth is, as has often been demonstrated, the difficulty returns here in as acute a form as ever. For the question immediately recurs, how a free act can ever be foreknown. A free act, in the sense of the objector, is one which springs solely from the will of the creature ; it has no cause beyond that will ; it rests with the agent alone to say what it shall be. This raises the difficulty of supposing it to be foreknown what an action shall be before the creature who alone is to determine what it shall be has so much as been brought into existence."[1]

The Calvinistic view is an attempt to fit everything into a logical system, but the problem remains, why, if God can regenerate every sinner, He does not do it ? One thing may be regarded as certain, that there is nothing arbitrary in the Divine action. We may not be able to understand the reasons, but notwithstanding this we may be sure that they are based upon wisdom, truth, and love. The three references to the Divine will are significant in this connection : first, we have " the good pleasure

to eternal life, so is reprobation a part of Providence in respect of those who fall from this end.' But these are the words of Thomas Aquinas, and Calvin says no more. If Aquinas says that this is without prejudice to free will, so, if we will only consent to study Calvin in his own *Institutes*, we shall find that he does also. I admit that, in spite of certain passages in Romans, the logic of which it is difficult to avoid, I prefer the silence of the Church of England with regard to reprobation. But it is not fair to saddle the Genevan Reformers with all the predestinarian extravagances, which, as those who recollect the conversation of the Lady of Lochleven with Dryfesdale in Scott's *Abbot* will know, are as shocking to them as to the most faithful sons of 'our mother.' Presbyterians are all Calvinistic, and their record, if not in social service, at any rate in the kindred work of missions, is second to none. The fact is that justification by faith and predestination are leading principles of the New Testament, and it is for us, not to disparage them, but to tone up our Social Gospel to the level of them" (p. 132).

"No one who is acquainted with the history of the Augustinian or Calvinistic theology, and knows how great an influence for good it has had upon the Church of Christ, will speak of the doctrine which has just been given merely in the language of disparagement. Calvinism has had one great and most praiseworthy object, to exalt God. It has aimed to bring men to the realisation of their utter dependence upon God for all things here and hereafter. Believers owe their faith not to themselves or anything in them, but to God alone, working through Christ and the Holy Spirit" (Stearns, *Present Day Theology*, p. 430).

[1] Orr, *ut supra*, p. 165.

of His will " which, however, does not imply anything arbitrary (Eph. i. 5); then comes " the mystery of His will," a fact of which we are perfectly aware (Eph. i. 9); but last of all we read of " the counsel of His own will " (Eph. i. 11), and we are sure that God does nothing without due consideration, and, as it were, taking counsel with Himself.[1] The Calvinistic view is doubtless open to the serious objection that it tends to make God's righteousness conflict with His love, by asserting the Divine sovereignty in too unqualified a way.   But, as it has been pointed out, there is no need of this conflict if we recall the fact that election in Scripture is intended, not for exclusion, but for wider blessing to others. God's choice of Abraham and other similar men in Old Testament times was for the purpose of making them spiritual blessings to others, and when this is realised in connection both with Israel and Christ we see that election does not mean exclusion, but inclusion as the means of world-wide blessing.[2]

It is not at all surprising that the idea of a Divine election should have been regarded as inconsistent with Divine justice in view of the fact that all men are alike guilty before God.   This has been met by saying that as " there would have been no injustice in the punishment of all guilty beings, there can be none in the punishment of some guilty beings out of the number."[3]   But this reference to justice alone has never seemed satisfactory, since it may be urged that God is able to deal with all in the same way in which He deals with the few.   As a consequence of this difficulty the suggestion has been made that the doctrine of election only involves the remainder of mankind " in a temporary lack of privilege and of spiritual attainment," and it is certainly curious that Calvinism has that in it which makes credible " the theory of a universal restoration."[4]   On this account it is urged in some quarters that future progress in theology will be found in " the enlistment of the idea of Divine sovereignty in the service of the idea of infinite love," and one writer goes so far as to say that " the word of eternal hope seems the latest message of the Reformed Theology."[5]   On this view that the restoration of all fallen creatures is the ultimate issue of redemption " it is obvious that election can only mean their earlier or later entrance into the Kingdom of God."[6]   This is the general view taken by Dr. Forsyth, who insists strongly upon the fact and importance of a preferential element in the grace of God.

" No doubt there is *preference*. That is in the Divine order of the world. God is responsible for it. That is His election, His predetermining choice. And it is impossible for us to reach the Divine reasons for the order of its action. Pre-destination of some kind is an absolute necessity for religion. But while relative predestination is a tolerable mystery absolute predestination is intolerable. And

[1] Orr, *ut supra*, p. 163.   [2] Orr, *ut supra*, p. 167.
[3] Paterson, *ut supra*, p. 311.   [4] Paterson, *ut supra*, p. 312.
[5] Hastie, quoted in Paterson, *ut supra*, p. 313.
[6] Litton, *ut supra*, p. 353.

the relief is that it is a case of priority, it is not monopoly. The chosen are but preferred, not excluded. The left are but postponed, not lost. . . . Love has a necessity of its own. It is preferential in its nature, but not exclusive. If love be the surest thing in the world, the ruling thing, no less sure and dominant, is the principle of election, as the mode of action of God's holy love."[1]

In opposition to this is the view set forth by Dr. Warfield, who thinks that such writers fail to realise with sufficient keenness what sin and its consequences mean, and reason as though salvation were merely a question of the power of God. It is, therefore, urged that the obstacle of justice is not realised, and that there is no reason whatever why we should fall back upon a doctrine·of universal salvation.

" The difficulty is, however, purely artificial, and is wholly due to the practical elimination of the element of justice from the conception of the Divine character. It is not difficult to understand why a just God does not save all sinners ; the difficulty is to understand how a just God saves any sinners. It is precisely this difficulty which Christianity meets, and if neither the difficulty is felt nor the manner in which Christianity meets it appreciated—then Christianity is not understood, and we have substituted for it in our thought of it something which is essentially different."[2]

In conclusion, we must, as Dr. Orr says, dismiss entirely all thought of arbitrariness and keep the Divine purpose in the closest possible connection with the history by means of which it is realised. The fundamental fact is that there is such a thing as Divine choice.

" The appearance of great men at particular junctures of history is not to be attributed to chance. The question is not simply how, a man of Abraham's or Moses' gifts and qualifications being given, God should use him as He did ; but rather, how a man of this mould came at that precise juncture to be there at all—broke out at that precise point in the genealogical tree."[3]

The only possible solution is that a Divine purpose has been at work, preparing the means for the accomplishment of its own ends. While, therefore, we endeavour to perceive and retain the essential truth which is contained in each of the views now set forth we must be content to emphasise the primary and fundamental reality of the Divine action in redemption, and wait until further light enables us to see more clearly the solution of the relation between the Divine and the human.[4]

IV.—THE TEACHING OF SCRIPTURE

As we review the history of this doctrine in the light of the New Testament it is clear that there is a predestination which is more than

---

[1] Forsyth, *The Principle of Authority*, p. 406 f. See the entire chapter and also Ch. XI.
[2] Warfield, *Princeton Theological Review*, Vol. XI, p. 702.
[3] Orr, *ut supra*, p. 169.   [4] See Orr, *ut supra*, p. 170.

ecclesiastical and temporal (Rom. viii. 28-30). Divine grace is seen to be the source, support, and crown of salvation. And yet Scripture is equally clear and emphatic on human freedom and responsibility. Both sides are to be emphasised without any attempt at reconciliation. We must not isolate either the Divine or the human side and consider one apart from the other. The various scriptural associations of predestination help us to appreciate its place and power.

(a) It is associated with God's foreknowledge (Rom. viii. 28; 1 Pet. i. 2). Foreknowledge is something between foresight and foreordination, knowledge with favour.

(b) It is associated with God's cheer and encouragement for believers in their trials (Rom. viii. 32-39).

(c) It is associated with God's purposes of service (Eph. ii. 10). God's chosen are choice men.

(d) It is associated with God's demands for holiness (Rom. viii. 29; Eph. i. 5; 2 Thess. ii. 13; 1 Pet. i. 2).

(e) It is associated with God's preservation and glorification of believers (Rom. viii. 30; Eph. i. 3-6).

These are invariably the fundamental ideas in theology, in Augustine, and at the Reformation.[1] Thus, the question in Scripture is invariably practical and never speculative. The two aspects are like parallel lines, and both must be held. As St. Bernard says in a well-known passage: "Take away free will and there will be nothing to save; take away grace and there will be nothing to save with."[2] So that we may say: (a) God elects to save; (b) God elects to save in one way (in Christ); (c) God elects to save one class (believers). The difficulty will not as a rule be felt in the practical life of the Christian, but only when the matter is viewed from the standpoint of philosophy and speculation. It is significant that the doctrinal position of Rom. iii comes before that of Rom. viii, and the spiritual apprehension and experience of the one is the best, indeed the only, preparation for the other.[3]

The action of God is mysterious in human affairs, and yet it is a fact in providence and history. Why was Seth chosen instead of Cain; Jacob instead of Esau; Ephraim instead of Manasseh; Isaac instead of Ishmael; Joseph instead of Reuben? How are we to account for the differences, say, between Britain and Turkey? It is, therefore, quite in keeping if a similar difficulty is found in religion. The problem would be far more acute apart from Christianity. So that

[1] "In proportion to the depth of men's moral and spiritual struggle, in proportion to the intensity with which they apprehend the height of the Divine righteousness and the Divine ideal, must there arise in them a sense of the utter feebleness of their own powers, of the weakness and servitude of their wills, and of their absolute dependence on Divine grace and the Divine will" (Wace, *ut supra*, p. 145).

[2] "Tolle liberum arbitrium et non erit quod salvetur; tolle Gratiam, non erit unde salvetur" (St. Bernard, *De Gratia et libero Arbitrio*).

[3] A pious negro was once asked by his godless master whether he thought that he (the master) was one of the elect, to which the old slave replied: "I have never heard of an election without a candidate."

metaphysically the Divine and human are opposed, and yet practically they are united.

The one thing to remember is that there is no favouritism with God and no injustice, nor is there any interference with the freedom of man or the universality of the offer of the Gospel to human faith. The certainty that things will happen so does not imply necessarily that they must happen. Predestination magnifies grace, free will honours responsibility. The two are complementary, like the two poles of a magnet. They are not antagonistic, but two sides of the one truth often found in the same book and in the same sentence ; *e.g.* John vi. 44 f. ; x. 27 f. ; Acts ii. 23 f. ; xiii. 46, 48 ; Phil. ii. 12, 13 ; 2 Tim. ii. 19 ; 2 Pet. i. 10, 11. Thus these aspects are like two threads of colour so closely woven as not to be detachable, and it is probable that we shall never get nearer than the words of the poet :—

> " Our wills are ours, we know not how,
> Our wills are ours, to make them Thine."[1]

The reference in the Article to the spiritual value of the doctrine of predestination to " godly persons " is borne out by all that is known of genuine Christianity in those who hold this truth. The consciousness of God's electing love has inspired men with courage amid danger, confidence in perplexity, and the absolute conviction that nothing can hinder the purpose of God, but that " all things work together for good." There is no doubt of the spiritual power of those who magnified the grace of God and realised that God was all in their life.[2]

[1] "Are not these truths hopelessly incompatible with each other? So it may seem at first sight; and if we escape the danger of denying the one in the supposed interests of the other, if we shrink from sacrificing God's sovereignty to man's free will, with Arminius, and from sacrificing man's freedom to God's sovereignty with Calvin, we can only express a wise ignorance by saying that to us they seem like parallel lines, which must meet at a point in eternity, far beyond our present range of view. We do know, however, that being both true, they cannot really contradict each other, and that in some manner which we cannot formulate, the Divine sovereignty must not merely be compatible with, but must even imply the freedom of created wills" (Liddon, *Some Elements of Religion*, p. 191).
See also Sanday and Headlam, *Romans*, p. 348.
"It is a growing conviction of students of Scripture and of philosophy that, on the subject before us, there is more than one hemisphere of truth. That which both the Calvinist and Arminian chiefly prized was truth, not error. What each contended against was the supposed implications of a proposition which was valued by his opponent from its relation to a set of implications of a very different sort. Each connected with his antagonist's thesis inferences which that antagonist repudiated" (Professor Fisher, *North American Review*, Vol. CXXXVIII, p. 303).
[2] "The practical effect of this doctrine has been to make strong Christians. The men who had come to believe that they were nothing and God everything, and yet that God was working in them and through them, could do their work in the world, since God gave it to them to do, without fear of men or the devil. The Protestants of Geneva, the Huguenots of France, the Covenanters of Scotland, the Puritans of the English Civil War, and our own Pilgrim Fathers, got the iron in their blood from their Calvinism" (Stearns, *ut supra*, p. 341).
"When Calvinistic thought has been in the ascendant it has been associated with an unusual manifestation of moral vision, enthusiasm, and strenuousness. On the other

The opposite of election is not reprobation, but non-election, and no human being has any evidence that he is not elected. The opposite of reprobation is probation, and we are reprobate just as long as we will not accept Christ. Election rests on God's good pleasure, but reprobation rests on His holiness, which leads Him to antagonise and loathe that which is unholy (Rom. i. 26, 29; 2 Cor. xiii. 5-7; 2 Tim. iii. 8; Tit. i. 16). It is because man's dispositions are odious that they are disapproved, and thus reprobation is founded not on the Divine sovereignty, but on Divine justice.[1]

We must, therefore, distinguish between the efficient and permissive decree of God. He does not stand in the same relation to good and to evil. Of good He is the source, but evil He hates and opposes, and therefore has no share in it.[2]

In view of all that has been said the term "final preservation" is better and more accurate than "final perseverance," for if it is asked whether men can fall away finally it is best to modify the enquiry and ask whether they will. If sin is viewed in the abstract it may be regarded as going on unchecked, but it is impossible to overlook the provision made by God: "Ye are not under law, but under grace" (Rom. vi. 14). So that while from the standpoint of strict logic men can fall away, from the standpoint of spiritual religion we believe that they will not, and it is for this reason that each child is taught in the Catechism to regard itself as "elect," and yet to use means. When we start from Divine sovereignty we cannot help believing in preservation, and it is only when we start from human freedom that we contemplate the possibility of falling from grace. In the former case salvation is God's purpose from first to last; in the latter it depends upon man's will. If, therefore, we believe in the sovereignty of God and in the primacy of grace it is difficult to believe that a true follower of Christ, who has been laid hold of by the grace of God, can ever be lost. But this does not mean that he is exempt from sinning. On the contrary, there must be constant and careful dis-

hand, the ethical results have not been most deeply impressive in those epochs which have magnified the autonomy and self-sufficiency of man as over against God, and which have mainly relied on the appeal to man to rally his moral powers and accomplish his own destiny" (Paterson, *ut supra*, p. 310).

"His system, passing like iron into the blood of the nations which received it, raised up in the French Huguenots, the English Puritans, the Scotch, the Dutch, the New Englanders, brave, free, God-fearing peoples. Abasing man before God, but exalting him again in the consciousness of a new-born liberty in Christ, teaching him his slavery through sin, yet restoring to him his freedom through grace, leading him to regard all things in the light of eternity, it contributed to form a grave, but very noble and elevated type of character, reared a race not afraid to lift up the head before kings" (Orr, *ut supra*, p. 291).

"In this lay the real strength of the Calvinistic creed, and of the Puritan character which it trained and developed. On the other hand, in systems where there is little or no sense of God's power carrying out His purposes with resistless force through His chosen instruments, there the character trained under them is likely to be deficient in fibre and tenacity of purpose. So Dean Milman has, in a striking passage, pointed out the weakness of Pelagianism: 'No Pelagian ever has, or ever will, work a religious revolution'"(Gibson, *ut supra*, p. 483).

[1] Forbes, *Analytical Commentary on Romans*, p. 431. [2] Stearns, *ut supra*, p. 434 f.

tinction between falling from grace and backsliding. A believer by
reason of the power of inborn sinfulness is only too apt to backslide, but
by the gracious faithfulness of God he will not fall entirely from grace.[1]
Since no one can read his own name in the Lamb's Book of Life the only
thing required is to be sure that a spiritual change has taken place, and
then to receive the Divine assurance in the heart and to walk humbly
with God.

It must, therefore, never be forgotten that the difficulty of the relation
between the Divine foreknowledge and human freewill is one that is
really independent of Christianity and is part of the very constitution of
creation. Election in religion is only a part of the wider truth of Providence (control) in the world. It is, therefore, not surprising that with
our present limitations of knowledge, it is impossible to solve it. And
yet, as in many other practical matters, we act on what we know to be
true and leave the theoretical reconciliation entirely on one side. We
know that no one will be saved without faith in our Lord Jesus, and that
no one will be condemned who does thus believe. We are also sure that
everyone is invited to believe in Christ, and we are equally aware, from
personal experience, that individuals in their freedom either accept or
reject God's offer. Not only so, but the believer, in reviewing his past,
recognises quite clearly that God was leading him step by step, and yet
at the same time leaving him perfectly free.

If it be said that God knows about us, the answer is that if He did not,
He would not be God, but a being of limited knowledge. But it must be
said with equal definiteness that God's knowledge of us does not affect our
decision, since we are invited to accept, and it is our duty to respond to
this invitation. The illustration has been used that if a man were on a
sinking vessel and were invited to enter a lifeboat, he would not decline
on the ground that God knew whether he was going to be saved or
drowned, and that, therefore, there was no use doing anything. Such an
one would use the available means and entrust himself to God, while
acting in accordance with the opportunity for securing safety.

It is, of course, true that God never created men to send them to hell,

---

[1] "A moment's consideration will show that election, in the sense in which it was
understood by most of the great theologians of former times, Romanist as well as
Protestant, viz. election to eternal life, involves the doctrine of perseverance. For
the elect in this sense are not merely those who have been favoured with external
privileges, and who *may* be saved if they do their duty, but those who shall finally be
saved; and none such can or will perish. To say then that the elect may not persevere
to the end is to say that they are not elect, except in a lower sense of the word. The
elect are those who do persevere, and those who do not are not of the elect. Further,
it is to be observed that the question is not about perseverance merely, but about *final*
perseverance, or perseverance up to the moment when, at death, we lose sight of the
persons concerned. It is possible, and generally admitted, that persons may persevere,
or seem to do so, for a time, and then draw back; but it is endurance to the end, until
the individual passes into the unseen world, that is intended in the Calvinistic controversy. . . . That our Church leans to this latter view seems implied in Article XVII:
'They are made sons of God by adoption, they walk religiously in good works, and
at length, by God's mercy, they attain to everlasting life.' No intimation is given that
they may possibly come short of this destination" (Litton, *ut supra*, pp. 337, 338).

but that they might glorify Him in their lives and enjoy the fellowship which He offers and makes possible in Christ. But, if men refuse to accept God's purpose and oppose His will for them, it is not God's doing, but their own that they thereby lose eternal fellowship with all that is good and pure and true. Thus, it cannot be rightly said that God condemns anyone in the sense of inflicting any arbitrary punishment; everyone who is lost condemns himself by his attitude to Christ and his salvation.

Thus, there will always be an element of mystery in the relation of two wills in the universe, Divine and human. Christian people undoubtedly revolt against any view implying that the majority of the human race are everlastingly lost and only a few saved. Nor will any refuge be found by those who know and follow Scripture in the thought of purgatorial or purifying fires, which cannot be found in the Bible. Yet again, no careful and honest reader of Scripture can believe for an instant that all human beings will be saved, for, if the Bible teaches anything distinctly, it clearly shows that there are those who, through their own deliberate choice, remain outside the circle of the saved.

But a careful study of Scripture will reveal certain truths which may help to place the doctrine of election in a truer light. There is no doubt that all men *may* be saved, if only they are willing to accept Him who died for all without exception. Further, He will most assuredly save all, except those who, having heard, persistently and finally refuse to accept Him. These, having exercised their freewill, must suffer the inevitable result of such choice. Thus Christ is not only the possible, but the real Saviour of sinners, subject only and always to the power of any sinner to exercise his freewill in rejecting salvation. There is no other way of salvation, and no other merit than the sacrificial death of Christ on Calvary.

But while all this is true, it should be carefully noted that the Bible does not separate men merely into two classes, the saved and the lost, for it seems to reveal not only one class of saved ones, but several classes or grades of the saved, and it is along this line that at least some relief to our intellectual perplexity may be found.

The highest salvation is clearly associated with what the New Testament describes as " the Body of Christ," or " the Lamb's wife," and the various references to the " elect " are to this community of " heirs of God and joint-heirs with Christ," who are said to have been " chosen before the foundation of the world." Yet the Bible clearly indicates that these are not the only ones saved. On the contrary, there are plain statements that, in addition to the body of Christians called " the Bride," there are other communities of human beings who are saved from everlasting destruction, and yet do not, and will never, form part of the " Body of Christ." This salvation is outside of and altogether secondary to the salvation of those chosen persons who collectively make up His spiritual Church. The following passages seem to indicate these grades:

1. There are peoples of the world over whom, according to Scripture, the members of the Church of God are to reign with Christ as kings and priests (1 Cor. vii. 2; Rev. xx. 4-6). It is surely impossible that these people over whom the saints are to reign are the lost.

2. Reference is made to " the nations " at Christ's coming to judgment, and as the Church or " Bride " will have been previously caught up to meet Him in the air, it is clear that those who are set on the right hand of the King and are described as blessed and invited to inherit the kingdom cannot possibly be either the " brethren " of Christ or the Church (Matt. xxv. 31-46).

3. Then we read of people raised at the last Resurrection, judged according to the deeds done in the body, and out of this number those whose names are found written in the Lamb's Book of Life (Rev. xx. 12-15; xxi. 27). Seeing that the members of the Church have long before been raised and glorified in the first Resurrection (Rev. xx. 4-6), who are these mentioned as in the Lamb's Book of Life long after the first Resurrection ?

4. In Heb. xii. 23 we read of " the spirits of just men made perfect " as a distinct class from " the general assembly and Church of the first-born." If there be a " Church of the first-born " who inherit the full blessing, is it not a fair inference that there are second-born ones who inherit a lesser blessing ?

5. When St. Paul writes that " all Israel shall be saved," we are again apparently concerned with a number of persons who are altogether outside the " Body of Christ."

6. The Heavenly City, the Bride, the Lamb's wife (Rev. xxi) is generally accepted as representing the glorified Church, and if this is so, who are " the nations " who walk in the light of the City, and who are " the kings of the earth " who bring their glory and honour into the City ? There must be some distinction between these and the members of the glorified Church.

A careful consideration of these passages seems to show that, while God made a selection of men to form His Church, yet the members of this collective body are not the only ones who are in some sense saved. And although the truth of Election belongs to the mysteries of God and will never be finally solved in the present life, the consciousness of these various grades of the saved will help us to realise that Scripture seems to imply that it is incorrect to think of the majority of the human race as lost and only the few saved.

The practical power of this truth of " predestination to life " is clearly emphasised in the Article, for it is, indeed, " full of sweet, pleasant, and unspeakable comfort to godly persons." The comfort is not merely selfish enjoyment, for even when conscious of temporal blessings which others do not possess there is no thought of selfishness, but a deeper consciousness of the love that provides them. In the same way the realisation that we are predestinated and elected to life is one of the mightiest in-

centives to true Christian living.   It humbles pride by putting God first;
it encourages faith by making God's grace real; it rebukes unbelief by
reminding us of God's foresight and provision; it elicits earnestness by
the consciousness of God's wonderful thought and love; and it emphasises holiness by the remembrance of what manner of persons we ought
to be who are the subjects of this Divine and glorious purpose.[1]

[1] "Dr. Hey, certainly no Calvinist, asks, Is not the doctrine of Predestination hurtful
to virtue? and thus answers it : No; virtue is in our Article presupposed, before men
are allowed to meddle with predestination: those who are to hope that God's purpose
will prove favourable to them, must 'walk *religiously in good works*'; those who may
meditate on the Christian dispensation as having been planned in the Divine counsels,
must not be *carnal* but *godly persons*. And even these, according to our notions, ought
only to dwell upon the decrees of God as *far* as will promote and strengthen their virtue.
Besides, these texts which mention predestination are also so linked (Eph. i. 4; ii. 10)
with the mention of virtue and holiness, that no ingenious man will take the former
and leave the latter. He sums up with this remark, One would do a great deal to suit .
weak brethren; but there is no sufficient reason why those who are *not* weak should
lose such sublime devotion; especially as those who are perplexed by meditating on
the benign purposes and plans of the Supreme Being, are under no sort of *obligation*
to dwell upon them" (Macbride, *Lectures on the Articles*, p. 339).
    See also Stearns, *ut supra*, p. 439.
    The doctrine of this Article may be studied in the following works: Moule, *Outlines
of Christian Doctrine*, pp. 36–56 ; Paterson, *The Rule of Faith*, pp. 302–314; Litton,
Introduction to *Dogmatic Theology* (Second Edition), p. 247 ff.; 337 ff.; Stearns, *Present
Day Theology*, Ch. XXIII; Martensen, *Christian Dogmatics*, pp. 362–382; Orr, *The
Progress of Dogma*, Index, s.v. Predestination; Adam, *Cardinal Elements of the Christian
Faith*, Index, s.v. Predestinarianism.

R

ARTICLE XVIII

Of obtaining eternal Salvation only by the Name of Christ.

De speranda æterna Salute tantum in Nomine Christi.

They also are to be had accursed that presume to say, That every man shall be saved by the law or sect which he professeth, so that he be diligent to frame his life according to that law and the light of nature. For Holy Scripture doth set out unto us only the name of Jesus Christ, whereby men must be saved.

Sunt et illi anathematizandi, qui dicere audent unumquemque in lege aut secta, quam profitetur, esse servandum, modo juxta illam et lumen naturæ accurate vixerit: cum sacræ literæ tantum Jesu Christi nomen prædicent, in quo salvos fieri homines oporteat.

IMPORTANT EQUIVALENTS.

Of obtaining[1]	= *De speranda.*
By the name	= *in nomine.*
To be had accursed	= *anathematizandi.*
By the law	= *in lege.*
Be diligent to frame his life	= *accurate vixerit.*
Set out	= *prædicent.*
For Holy Scripture	= *cum sacræ literæ.*
Be saved	= *salvos fieri.*

It is significant that a group of Articles dealing with individual salvation should close with an anathema against the latitudinarian spirit which holds that it does not matter what a man believes so long as his life is consistent and earnest. But if salvation is due to the Lord Jesus Christ, according to Article XVII, then it is obviously impossible to be indifferent to Him. The language is reminiscent of the *Reformatio Legum* :

" Horribilis est et immanis illorum audacia, qui contendunt in omni religione vel secta, quam homines professi fuerint, salutem illis esse sperandam, si tantum ad innocentiam et integritatem vitæ pro viribus enitantur juxta lumen quod illis prælucet a natura infusum. Authoritate vero sacrarum literarum confixæ sunt hujusmodi pestes. Solum enim et unicum ibi Jesu Christi nomen nobis commendatum est, ut omnis ex eo salus ad nos perveniat."[2]

There were evidently unbelievers at the time of the Reformation, against whom the teaching of this Article was directed.

A careful comparison of the English and Latin equivalents helps towards a true understanding of the real meaning of the Article. Thus, the title of the Latin is *De speranda æterna Salute,* concerning the hope of

---

[1] The English title of the XLII had "We must trust to obtain," the Latin "*Tantum in nomine Christi speranda est æterna salus* (We must hope to obtain eternal salvation only by the name of Christ)."

[2] *De Hæresibus,* c. 11.

eternal salvation, thereby suggesting the real purpose and destination of the Article. The word "accursed," Latin, *anathematizandi*, is interesting, because it is the only place in the Articles where such an anathema is pronounced. It refers to severance from Church privileges.

I.—THE ERROR CONDEMNED

The title of the Article both in Latin and in English shows that there is no reference whatever to the heathen, but only to those who are acquainted with the Christian religion. Luther is known to have held charitable views on the subject of the heathen, and our Reformers never seem to have stated positively their position. The "Name" of Christ has the same meaning as that which is found in the New Testament, referring to the revelation, or revealed character, so that again it is evident that the reference can only be to those who have heard of Him.[1] In regard to the heathen, the principles of Holy Scripture are clear (Acts x. 34 f.; Rom. ii. 14).

There is some difficulty in regard to the bearing of the word "also" in "They also are to be had accursed." Some think that it connects the teaching with that of Article XVI, where there is an expression of condemnation. Others, however, connect it closely with Article XVII, as teaching that salvation is only through Jesus Christ. Whatever may be the true interpretation the reference is clearly to something that was definite and not vague and general, an error which the Reformers had to face.

II.—THE TRUTH EMPHASISED

In opposition to the error condemned by the Article, the teaching of Holy Scripture is inculcated, that "only the Name of Jesus Christ" is set out unto us "whereby men must be saved." This truth is clearly the fundamental reality of the New Testament, and the Article evidently refers to the well-known statement of St. Peter: "Neither is there salvation in any other; for there is none other name under heaven given among men, whereby we must be saved" (Acts iv. 12). Even Cornelius, with all his moral advantages, needed Jesus Christ and His salvation (Acts x. 2-5), and in various other connections the same truth is taught. Indeed, it is only another way of saying that "Christianity is Christ," for it is only by means of the redemption provided by God in the Person of His Son that human salvation becomes possible (Mark xvi. 16; John iii. 36; 1 Cor. iii. 11; 1 Cor. xv. 1, 2; Gal. i. 8, 9).

To hold the view anathematised would be to despair of absolute truth. In human life two things are needed: (*a*) objective truth; (*b*) subjective

---

[1] "I hold it to be a most certain rule of interpreting Scripture that it never speaks *of* persons when there is a physical impossiblity of its speaking *to* them. . . . So the heathen, who died before the word was spoken, and in whose land it was never preached, are dead to the word; it concerns them not at all; but, the moment it can reach them, it is theirs, and for them." (Dr. Arnold's *Life and Correspondence*, Letter LXV).

sincerity in response to it. As we have already seen, conduct does depend on creed, and thought is the basis of action. In this sense, therefore, the Article may be regarded as the corollary of Article XVII. In the light of the New Testament emphasis on the Lord Jesus Christ it is absolutely impossible to say that a man may be indifferent to what he believes so long as he holds it sincerely. Such latitudinarianism implies that the Person and work of Jesus Christ do not matter. It is, however, essential to remember that the Article does not refer to errors innocently committed, but to those who evidently consider all doctrines of unimportance, and " presume to say, That every man shall be saved by the Law or Sect which he professeth," so long as he is sincere. Nothing is said about being saved " in the Law or Sect," and therefore the view condemned and the opposite view inculcated cannot refer to any but those who deliberately and wilfully set aside the manifest Christian teaching concerning our Lord Jesus Christ. Christianity is not to be regarded as a matter of indifference, and the strong language of the Article, " They also are to be had accursed," is thoroughly justifiable in the light of what Scripture teaches concerning the Person and work of our Lord Jesus Christ. Men may be saved *in* their own religion, though not *by* it, and it is the latter opinion alone which the Article condemns, because it would destroy vital Christianity. We hold that whoever is saved, Christ is the Saviour, since it is His sacrifice which makes redemption possible. But when a man knows what Christianity is, and faces its solemn and pressing claim for allegiance to Jesus Christ, and in the face of it rejects its message, the case is altogether different, and such an one may rightly be anathematised for presuming to set aside " the Name of Jesus Christ, whereby men must be saved."

REVIEW OF ARTICLES IX TO XVIII

Before proceeding to the Articles dealing with corporate religion it may be well to look back over the Ten Articles which concern the personal relation of the soul to God. It will be seen that they cover very fairly the main aspects of individual religion.

I.—SIN

Article IX.—Man's lost condition through sin.
Article X.—Man's inability to save himself.

II.—JUSTIFICATION

Article XI.—The Method.—Justification is in Christ by faith, not by works.
Article XII.—The Proof.—Good Works as the evidence of justification through faith in Christ.
Article XIII.—The Impossibility.—Man is unable to justify himself.

III.—SANCTIFICATION

Article XIV.—The impossibility of exceeding God's requirements in regard to daily life.

Article XV.—The impossibility of reaching God's requirements.

Article XVI.—The impossibility of despair after failure.

IV.—COMPLETE SALVATION

Article XVII.—The Ground.—God's predestinating and electing love and grace.

Article XVIII.—The Source.—The Lord Jesus Christ as the Divine Redeemer.

IV. THE HOUSEHOLD OF FAITH

ARTICLES XIX-XXXIX

CORPORATE RELIGION

A. THE CHURCH (ARTICLES XIX-XXII).

19. THE CHURCH.

20. THE AUTHORITY OF THE CHURCH.

21. THE AUTHORITY OF GENERAL COUNCILS.

22. PURGATORY.

ARTICLE XIX

Of the Church.	De Ecclesia.
The visible Church of Christ is a congregation of faithful men, in the which the pure word of God is preached, and the Sacraments be duly ministered according to Christ's ordinance in all those things that of necessity are requisite to the same.	Ecclesia Christi visibilis est cœtus fidelium, in quo verbum Dei purum prædicatur, et Sacramenta, quoad ea quæ necessario exigantur, juxta Christi institutum recte administrantur.
As the Church of Jerusalem, Alexandria, and Antioch, have erred; so also the Church of Rome hath erred, not only in their living and manner of Ceremonies, but also in matters of Faith.	Sicut erravit Ecclesia Hierosolymitana, Alexandrina, et Antiochena; ita et erravit Ecclesia Romana, non solum quoad agenda et cæremoniarum ritus, verum in his etiam quæ credenda sunt.

IMPORTANT EQUIVALENTS.

Of the Church	= *De Ecclesia.*
A congregation of faithful men	= *cœtus fidelium.*
Duly	= *recte.*
Are requisite to the same	= *exigantur.*
In their living	= *quoad agenda.*
In matters of faith	= *in his quæ credenda sunt.*

It was essential to define the doctrine of the Church as against Roman Catholicism, from which the English Church separated in the sixteenth century. And it is significant that amid all the controversies of the Reformation period this Article underwent no change. It was suggested by the Seventh Article of the Confession of Augsburg, as these words indicate :—

" Est autem ecclesia congregatio sanctorum, in qua evangelium recte docetur, et recte administrantur sacramenta."

It is identical with the Twentieth Article of 1553. Comparison must also be made with the *Reformatio Legum Ecclesiasticarum*, for the connection of thought and word is obvious. In the same way the Anglican doctrine of the Church can be seen in opposition to Romanism.[1] It is,

[1] "Etiam illorum insania legum vinculis est constringenda, qui Romanam Ecclesiam in hujusmodi petra fundatam esse existimant, ut nec erraverit, nec errare possit; cum et multi possint ejus errores ex superiore majorum memoria repeti, et etiam ex hac nostra proferri, partim in his quibus vita nostra debet informari, partim etiam in his quibus fides debet institui. Quapropter illorum etiam intolerabilis est error, qui totius Christiani orbis universam ecclesiam solius episcopi Romani principatu contineri volunt. Nos enim eam quæ cerni potest ecclesiam sic definimus ut omnium cœtus sit fidelium hominum, in quo Sacra Scriptura sincere docetur, et sacramenta (saltem his eorum partibus quæ necessariæ sunt) juxta Christi præscriptum administrantur" (*De Hæresibus*, c. 21, " De Romana Ecclesia, et potestate Romani pontificis").

moreover, noteworthy that the Homily for Whitsunday, dated 1563, and attributed to Bishop Jewel, takes a similar anti-Roman view. It was evidently essential on the part of the English Reformers to vindicate their action by showing what they believed to be the true doctrine of the Church in opposition to that of the Church of Rome.[1]

When Jesus Christ saves an individual and unites that one to Himself, a new relation is thereby constituted between that individual person and others similarly joined to the Lord. To this community the New Testament gives several titles, the word " Church " being the most important. The English word " Church " comes from κυριακή, " that which belongs to the Lord." In northern nations we find corresponding terms, as in Scotland, " Kirk "; in Germany, " Kirche "; and in Sweden, " Kyrkan," instead of the Greek " Ecclesia," which is found in the French " Église," and other Latin derivatives. There does not seem to be any certain explanation of this, though it may be that the use of the term " Church " instead of " Ecclesia " indicates an independence of Rome in these nations, their Christianity being, perhaps, derived from Greek or Asiatic sources. The word " Ecclesia," rendered " Church," is found in the New Testament 114 times, and means an " Assembly," people " called." Hort says that we cannot press the ἐκ to imply " called out " of a larger body.[2] He defines the " Ecclesia " in Greece as a free community gathered in council, citizens of a Greek city deliberating and deciding on their affairs. They were the free men only, not the slaves. This secular Greek use can be seen in Acts xix. 32, 39, 41. In Acts vii. 38 the word is associated with the Old Testament congregation, " the Church in the wilderness." In the LXX " Ecclesia " is the equivalent of the Hebrew for assembly (קָהָל).[3] In St. Matthew xviii. 17 we have the Jewish idea (cf. 1 Cor. v. 3-5), and in St. Matthew xvi. 18 the prospect and promise of the Christian Church. The word is found in all St. Paul's Epistles, except Titus and 2 Timothy, and also in Acts, James (ch. v. 14; cf. ii. 2, " synagogue "); Hebrews (ch. ii. 12; xii. 23); 3 John, and Revelation. But outside the Gospels the word Church stands for a decidedly Pauline idea, and has two standpoints : (a) actual, the Church here on earth at the present time; (b) ideal, the Church regarded as spiritual and heavenly (Eph. i. 22; iii. 10; Col. i. 18).

It should also be noted that the Church and the Kingdom are not identical. The Church is an institution, intended solely for the present, the Kingdom stretches to the future. We have only to substitute the word " Church " for " Kingdom " in the Lord's Prayer, " Thy Church come," to see the impossibility of identifying the two terms. While the relations overlap, we may speak of the Kingdom as the ultimate end, and the Church as one of the means towards its realisation.

[1] "The second part of the Sermon for Whitsunday."—The Homilies.
[2] Hort, The Christian Ecclesia, p. 5.
[3] Hort, The Christian Ecclesia, p. 3 f.; Trench, Synonyms of the New Testament, p. 3 f.

I.—THE FOUNDATION OF THE CHURCH

1. When did the Church begin ?—Strictly speaking, the Christian Church commenced when the two disciples of the Baptist left their old master for the new One (John i. 37), though for all practical purposes the Day of Pentecost may be regarded as the birthday of the Church, since it was on that day that the Church was spiritually created by the presence of the Holy Spirit. There was, of course, a Jewish Church or community of believers before, so that the idea was by no means novel.

2. How did the Church begin ?—In Acts i. 15 and ii. 4 we observe preaching on the part of Christ's witnesses. Then came the acceptance of the Apostolic word, followed by baptism, but between these two ministerial acts of preaching and baptism came the contact of the soul with God, by faith on the human side, and through the Holy Spirit on the Divine side. The order was (1) the preaching of Christ; (2) the acceptance of Christ; and then (3) Christ adding penitent believers to the Church. So that it is Christ who adds men to the Church, not the Church that adds them to Christ. The passage referring to the Day of Pentecost (Acts ii. 37-47) is the germ of all that is found elsewhere. Members of the Church are often *media* in relation to the knowledge and acceptance of Jesus Christ, but the proper order is : Christ; the individual; the Church : not Christ; the Church; the individual.

II.—THE PURPOSE OF THE CHURCH

1. Perhaps the primary idea of the Church was fellowship. It was the corporate and social outcome of individual relation to Christ. Christianity is social as well as personal. The very nature of Christ's salvation was to create a community. Paganism might show the beauty of the old humanity, but Christianity created a new. The Church is a society of sinners saved by Christ.

2. But fellowship will necessarily express itself in service. The possession of Christ will lead to witness and work, for the Church will inevitably endeavour to extend itself, while at the same time it builds up its own members. At this point is seen the importance of the Church to the individual. It is not without point that the Creed first expresses belief in the " Holy Catholic Church," and then follows immediately with a phrase in explanation and amplification of it, " the Communion of Saints." Individualistic Christianity is a contradiction in terms. While a man is justified solitarily and alone, he is sanctified in connection with others. Christian character needs the community for development, for it is only possible in fellowship with members of the Christian Church (Eph. iii. 18 ; vi. 18). There is no future for any Christianity that does not express itself through a community. Mysticism by itself is too vague and individualistic. While Christianity is mystical, it is much more. Mere individualism is equally impossible, for " unattached " Christians find no place in the Christianity of the New Testament. It is a great

mistake to associate individualism with what is sometimes regarded as
" ultra " spirituality, which is often opposed to organised Christianity.

III.—THE PROGRESS OF THE CHURCH

1. There is a threefold use of the term " Church " in the New
Testament. (*a*) Local : Christians in one place, *e.g.* Jerusalem ; (*b*)
General : the aggregate of Christians in various places at one time (1 Cor.
x. 32 ; xii. 28) ; (*c*) Universal : all real Christians, past, present, and future
(Eph. i. 22 ; iii. 10 ; Col. i. 18). This last should dominate all our
thinking and all other views of the Church.[1] Fellowship in the Gospel
means membership in the Church, though the Church does not consist
of Churches, but of individuals. Membership in the Church is not
mediated through membership in one local body, but comes by relation
to Christ. The Christian does not experience a process like naturalisation
if he moves to another place, for he is a member everywhere. Locality
or nationality is a mere accident. There is no isolation, since all believers
are one in Christ.

2. It is noteworthy that these three uses are found in the Prayer Book.
(*a*) The local Church of England : Preface to the Confirmation Office.
(*b*) The Church of one time : Article XX. (*c*) The Church Universal :
Collects for St. Simon's and St. Jude's Day, and All Saints' Day.

IV.—THE NATURE OF THE CHURCH

It is important to distinguish the Church from its officials. The
Church is " the blessed company of all faithful people," and Ordination
is to the ministry, not to the Church. Nor does the Church exist as an
abstract personality apart from the individuals who compose it. The
Church is, therefore, first an organism and only secondarily an organisation. There is no hint given in Scripture of any precise form of organisation in which the organism must necessarily express itself. The organism
gradually developed an organisation as needed. A spiritual body would
naturally express its life in outward forms, but in the New Testament
there is nothing elaborate or fixed, but only a few principles indicating
liberty and responsibility. Serious error has invariably been caused by
the idea that Christ was a Law-giver and the Gospel a new Law. There
is nothing in the New Testament to compare with the detailed instructions in Leviticus.

There are two aspects of the Church : visible and invisible. In
regard to the Church visible, the Article is clear about the fact, but the
question of the meaning of the fact at once arises. What are we to
understand by a " visible " Church ? The adjective cannot possibly be
regarded as otiose, and yet we are not to understand two disconnected
Churches, visible and invisible ; but rather, one Church viewed from

[1] Moule, Eph. i. 22. *Cambridge Bible for Schools.*

different standpoints, the one having regard to its spiritual nature, the other to its ecclesiastical organisation; either in reference to its Divine Head or to its earthly members; either from within (ἔσωθεν), or from without (ἔξωθεν). The Church as "invisible" means all Christians now, with all those who have formed the true Church and will hereafter make up the complete Church. This is, of course, known only to God. It does not mean in the literal sense a Church that is "invisible," but that what constitutes membership of the Church is invisible. Nowell's Catechism says, "The Church is the universal society of all the faithful whom God has predestinated from eternity to everlasting life."

These two aspects are necessarily connected, but they do not cover the same ground. There may be membership in the visible and not in the invisible Church, because visible Churches are only partial manifestations of the Body of Christ. But membership in the invisible Church will naturally express itself in membership in the visible Church. So that we can distinguish in thought between the visible and the invisible, while we cannot separate them, for since Christianity is at once spiritual and social, we need both aspects. In the Creed the essence of the Church is associated with faith, not with sight, and St. Paul teaches that the Church is inseparable in idea from Christ the Head (1 Cor. xii. 12), and yet their oneness is not nominal adhesion, but vital cohesion. Every member possesses Christ's life.[1] The term "Body" is never to be identified solely with the aggregate of Churches throughout the world. It always implies vital union with Christ and refers to all those who are spiritually one with Him.

The distinction, therefore, between the Church as visible and invisible is rather between the formal and the real. The latter is not to be confounded with any visible community or aggregate of such communities which may and do contain persons who are not joined to Christ by a living faith. As Christ's Redemption is Divine, spiritual, eternal, universal, so the idea of the Church naturally follows. The Church is much more than any actual community of Christians, and on this account faith is needed to perceive it as the Creed teaches. This distinction between visible and invisible is clearly made by Hooker in a well-known passage which calls for special attention :—

"That Church of Christ, which we properly term His body mystical, can be but one; neither can that one be sensibly discerned by any man, inasmuch as the parts thereof are some in heaven already with Christ, and the rest that are on earth (albeit, their natural persons be visible) we do not discern under this property whereby they are truly and infallibly of that body. . . . For lack of diligent observing the difference between the Church of God mystical and visible, the oversights are neither few nor light that have been committed."[2]

---

[1] Litton, *The Church of Christ* (First Edition), p. 149; Bartlet, *Evangelical Principles*, pp. 31-33; Maclear, *Introduction to the Creed*, p. 222.
[2] *Eccl. Pol.*, Bk. III, pp. 2, 9.

No one questions the fact of visibility. The only question is as to any precise form of visibility being of the *esse*. To use a phrase like " the historical Church founded by our Lord "[1] is really to beg the entire question, for everything turns upon the sense in which we may regard any Church as "historical," and as in connection with " our Lord." All attempts to identify the visible with the invisible will only lead to confusion and trouble, as in the past. Archbishop Benson has rightly spoken of " the noble, and alas, too fruitful error of arraying the visible Church in the attributes of the Church invisible."[2]

What, then, is the relation of the two ? It may be seen in the purpose of visible Churches to make Christ real in human lives. In Eph. i. 3-14 individuals, and in Eph. i. 15-23 the community, are treated by St. Paul. Behind the outward life is Divine grace, and only as grace is realised can the visible be realised and expressed in the invisible and spiritual. The Christian on earth is to correspond with the purpose of the Church in God's sight. The true Church, or Body of Christ, is thus invisible by reason of the vital union of its individual members with Christ, which is of necessity invisible. Of this God alone can tell. As such, the Church in its essence is an object of faith until the manifestation of the sons of God (Rom. viii. 19). Until then it is in its organic unity and corporate capacity invisible, although, of course, real, with the certainty of perfect visible expression hereafter. But so far as the present is concerned the existence of the Church as the Body of Christ becomes known and visible under the forms of congregations or Churches, which are one by virtue of their presumed, and, if true, their actual union with the one Body of Christ. If a man fulfils the conditions of this Article he is a member of the visible Church. If he is spiritually united to Christ he is also a member of the invisible Church. In the true Christian both aspects are joined, but in the mere professing Christian they are not, so that the Body of Christ is neither separate from nor identical with the sum total of visible Churches.

The difference of visibility and invisibility turns on the relative importance in which these two aspects are regarded. If, following the Church of Rome, visibility is made the primary antecedent, one result will follow. If, in harmony with the New Testament, visibility is made the consequent of the spiritual life within,[3] another and very different consequence will ensue. Rome makes this visibility to be of the essence of the Church, while Anglicanism, following the New Testament, makes invisible or spiritual union with Christ the vital and fundamental requirement. Even allowing that the terms " visible " and " invisible " represent controversial conditions of the sixteenth century, the truth expressed by them is valid, because the distinction is between a real and an apparent Church, between spiritual reality and outward manifestations. The

[1] Gibson, *The Thirty-nine Articles*, p. 500.
[2] "Cyprian," Preface.
[3] Litton, *Introduction to Dogmatic Theology*, p. 70.

point of the term "visible" is that the reality is not identical with, or simply expressed by, the outward manifestations. The New Testament idea of the Church is never indifferent to visibility or order, but it nevertheless puts the main stress on spiritual gift and grace and not on institutions and organisations.

V.—THE CHARACTERISTICS OF THE CHURCH

In technical language this point is usually discussed as the "Notes" of the Church. The fundamental question is, "*What* is a true Church?" This comes before, and is distinct from, "*Which* is the true Church?" We must get our definition before we can apply it.

1. The Church as Visible.—The Article describes rather than defines the visible Church, referring to signs, not to essence; to what the Church does rather than to what the Church is. "The visible Church of Christ is a congregation of faithful men, in the which the pure Word of God is preached, and the Sacraments be duly ministered according to Christ's ordinance in all those things that of necessity are requisite to the same." (*a*) The visible Church is a community. It is a congregation, not an aggregation, because it has a principle of unity and union with Christ as the centre. (*b*) The Church has a life. It is a congregation of "faithful men," that is, men of faith, believers in Jesus Christ. (*c*) The Church has a standard. "In the which the pure Word of God is preached." This allusion to "pure" had an evident reference to the Roman Catholic additions made to the Word of God in preaching and teaching. (*d*) The Church has an observance. In which "the Sacraments are duly ministered." It is not said what "duly" implies, since the New Testament gives no clear indication of the precise ministers required for the Sacraments. But it is more than likely that "duly" has a reference to the denial of the cup to the laity.

It is interesting to notice that the definition of the Church given by certain Roman Catholic divines is not essentially different from the above except in one point, which, however, to them is fundamental and dominates the whole position. It insists upon the Church being united to the Roman See.[1]

One other point of importance calls for attention. In the Homily for Whitsunday, which is attributed to Bishop Jewel, an additional "Note" or "mark" of the Church is given, "the right use of ecclesiastical discipline."[2] This characteristic is also added in the "Short Catechism" of

---

[1] "Nostra sententia est ecclesiam unam tantum esse, non duas, et illam unam et veram esse cœtum hominum ejusdem Christianæ fidei professione et eorundem sacramentorum communione colligatum, sub regimine legitimorum pastorum, *ac præcipue unius Christi in terris Vicarii Romani pontificis*" (*Controvers. General*, Tom. II, p. 108, Lib. III; *De Ecclesia*, c. 2).

[2] "The true Church is an universal congregation or fellowship of God's faithful and elect people, *built upon the foundation of the apostles and prophets, Jesus Christ Himself being the head corner-stone*. And it hath always three notes or marks whereby it is known: pure and sound doctrine, the sacraments ministered according to Christ's holy in-

1553, and is interpreted to mean all necessary discipline, even to the extent of excommunication of the wilfully disobedient.[1] But it may be questioned whether this is really an additional " note," and it is generally regarded as implied in the word " duly " in regard to the administration of the Sacraments. Yet it is particularly interesting to observe that there is no definition of what is to be understood by " duly," the assumption being that all the New Testament requirements are to be fulfilled.[2]

It is impossible to overlook the general terms of this statement of the Article. This was intentional. It comes from the Confession of Augsburg and remained unaltered throughout all the Reformation controversies. It is in entire harmony with corresponding Prayer Book terms. Thus in the prayer for " All Sorts and Conditions of Men " there is a petition for " all those who profess and call themselves Christians "; in the prayer for the Church Militant, " all they that do confess Thy Holy Name "; in the Litany, " Thy Holy Church Universal "; in the Bidding Prayer (Canon of 1604), " the whole congregation of Christ's people dispersed throughout the whole world." This last point recalls the Canon prescribing the Prayer and including the Church of Scotland, which was then Presbyterian, since Episcopacy proper did not exist there until 1610.

2. The Church as Visible is not Infallible.

Error is stated in the Article to be both possible and actual. " As the Church of Jerusalem, Alexandria, and Antioch, have erred; so also the Church of Rome hath erred, not only in their living and manner of Ceremonies, but also in matters of Faith." Three Eastern Churches are first mentioned: Jerusalem, Alexandria, and Antioch. It is sometimes wondered why Constantinople was not included; perhaps this is due to the fact that Alexandria and Antioch, two of the three Patriarchates

stitution, and the right use of ecclesiastical discipline. This description of the Church is agreeable both to the Scriptures of God and also to the doctrine of the ancient Fathers, so that none may justly find fault therewith" (The Second Part of the Sermon for Whitsunday.—The Homilies).

[1] *Liturgies of King Edward VI* (Parker Society, p. 513). Nowell's *Catechism,* 1570, teaches the same truth: "In the same Church if it be well ordered, there shall be seen to be observed a certain order and manner of government, and such a form of ecclesiastical discipline."

[2] The Latin of the word "duly" is *recte,* as also in Article XXVII. This must be carefully distinguished from *rite,* which is often rendered by the same English word (Articles XXV, XXVIII, XXXIV, XXXVI). The latter word *rite* means "with due outward order" (our English word "rite"). The former, *recte,* seems clearly to include inward dispositions as well. Bishop Gibson considers that the difference between the two words "is not very great," though "*rite*" includes a "wider reference to due ecclesiastical order" than "*recte*" does. On the other hand, Bishop Drury (*Confession and Absolution,* p. 269 f.), says that careful use is made of the words by the compilers of our Articles. "*Rite* has a limited reference and denotes the due attention to external rite and order. . . . *Recte* is a word of wider and fuller meaning, and embraces moral qualification as well. . . . Thus *recte* stands alone in the two places where it is used, while *rite* is, if need be, strengthened by such words as *digne* or *cum fide.*" On this view, according to Bishop Drury, proper discipline is included in *recte* which "includes both moral and ceremonial essentials." He adds that "In the other place where *recte* occurs he use is exactly parallel."

t

recognised by the Council of Nicæa, were given precedence after Jerusalem, though the Patriarchate of Constantinople was not recognised until the Second General Council.[1] These three, moreover, were supposed to have been founded by Apostles, a point that gives special force to the statement about their error. This was also the tradition connected with the Church of Rome. Very early a tendency showed itself to rest far too easily as a test of intellectual orthodoxy on conformity with Apostolic Sees.

The precise errors are not stated, probably because it was sufficient to express the fact, but Church history records several features and periods of error in Churches of the East.[2] Further, a description of the Eastern Church, and a reference to the " Orthodox Confession of the Catholic and Apostolic Eastern Church " will show that in several not unimportant particulars the Eastern Church holds doctrines contrary to the teaching of the Church of England. In the present day exception has been taken to the statement of our Article because it offers a hindrance to reunion with the Eastern Churches, but while the opinion here expressed may have been due to the situation of the sixteenth century it remains as part of our Articles, and as long as it remains it must necessarily be a factor in connection with any proposals for intercommunion.

There is no doubt, however, that the special point of the Article is the statement that the Church of Rome has erred, for this was obviously the important issue when the Article was drawn up. The errors of the Church of Rome can easily be seen from the statements of the Articles themselves. Thus, in its " living " can be proved by the celibacy of the clergy (Article XXXII); in its " manner of Ceremonies," the error of speaking to the congregation in an unknown tongue (Article XXIV) and the denial of the cup to the laity may be adduced (Article XXX); in regard to " matters of Faith," the errors are almost too numerous to mention, including the use of tradition (Article VI), the works of supererogation (Article XIV), purgatory (Article XXII), the seven Sacraments (Article XXV), Transubstantiation (Article XXVIII), and several more.[3]

But in the face of the plain statement of the Article it is necessary to meet the claim of the Church of Rome to be an infallible visible Church. What are the grounds of our opposition ?

---

[1] Boultbee, *The Theology of the Church of England*, p. 167.

[2] Gibson, *ut supra*, p. 507.

[3] According to the Homily for Whitsunday, Rome is not to be regarded as a Church, but the Article and representative writers, like Hooker, clearly take the opposite view. It is a Church, and yet one marked by grievous and fundamental errors. Hooker says:

"Even as the Apostle doth say of Israel that they are in one respect enemies, but in another beloved of God, in like sort with Rome we dare not communicate concerning sundry her gross and grievous abominations, yet touching those main parts of Christian truth wherein they constantly still persist, we gladly acknowledge them to be of the family of Jesus Christ" (*Eccl. Pol.*, Bk. III, Ch. I, p. 10). See Harold Browne, *ut supra*, pp. 455, 457; Gibson, *ut supra*, pp. 508, 510.

s

(1) There is nothing in Scripture to support this contention. The great Petrine passage (Matt. xvi. 13-19) refers to St. Peter personally without any proof or even hint of transmission. It is the confession of Christ as Messiah, Saviour, and Lord, and of Him appropriated by faith as the basis of the Church.[1] St. Peter's part was stewardship, as in Luke xii. 42. The Apostles were not given power as such, but only as representatives of the whole Church.[2] They were spiritual founders, but possessed no other official authority. Still more, there is no hint given of any power of delegation by, or from them.[3] They were uniquely blessed in things spiritual in relation to Christ, but with " no official grace." It is essential to distinguish between their authority for the Gospel and for organisation, a distinction overlooked by many writers.[4] It is the same with the other Apostles in the Acts, and also with St. Paul; Apostolic authority was spiritual and in relation to the Gospel and its terms. The passage in the First Gospel is best interpreted by Eph. ii. 20 and 1 Peter ii. 4-6. The Roman Catholic view would need three things to substantiate it : (a) that Peter was the head shepherd ; (b) that he had power to transmit his office and authority ; (c) that in Rome these true successors of Peter are to be found. It is also noteworthy that the keys given to Peter were of the Kingdom, which, as we have seen, is not identical with the Church.

(2) There is no analogy to this claim in nature and humanity. God does not provide infallibility for human life through any of His gifts of nature and providence.

(3) There is nothing in Christianity in favour of it and much against it. No Pope presided at a General Council, and it was only after a long period and under circumstances well known in history that the Roman authority was claimed and recognised.

(4) All the fruits, intellectual, social, civil, religious, and moral are against it. A comparison of the countries where the Roman Catholic Church has been in supreme authority is one of the strongest disproofs of the Roman claims.

One argument of Rome calls for special consideration, the theory of Development, associated with Cardinal Newman. It is urged that Roman Catholicism is the legitimate development of what is found in germ in the New Testament. But is this capable of proof ? What are we to say about the ages before the full development was reached ? Germs do not produce full-grown trees at once. Then, too, is Roman Catholicism a true development from within or an accretion from without ? Are the distinctive Roman Catholic doctrines legitimate developments of the New Testament ? When we consider such subjects as the place of the Mother of our Lord, or the sacerdotal character of the Christian ministry, or the doctrine of Transubstantiation, we naturally ask if these are found in

---

[1] Lindsay, The Church and Ministry in the Early Centuries.
[2] Hort, The Christian Ecclesia, p. 33.
[3] Hort, ut supra, p. 230 f.   [4] Bartlet, Evangelical Principles, p. 8 and Note.

germ in the New Testament, and no historical student or properly-equipped exegete would for a moment allow this to be the case. Development must always be according to type.[1] It is, therefore, impossible to beg the question by saying that we need infallibility, and therefore God will give it. This represents our own thought alone, and is no part of the true Christian position.[2]

But if the Roman Catholic view is impossible, can we accept the current view which is essentially that of Rome, apart from the Papacy? This assumes that Christ delegated His authority to all His Apostles, and not to St. Peter alone. At once the question has to be raised whether this authority was vested in the Apostles as individuals, or as a College? Was each capable of founding a Church, or could they only act together? This point is, as a rule, not faced by modern writers, though it is obviously vital to the issue. If each Apostle had distinct power, then there was the possibility of twelve Apostolic Churches. On the other hand, if the power was corporate the evidence for its existence has to be produced. Proofs have been asked in vain that the Apostles appointed the first Bishops in twelve Churches, and that when one Bishop died his successor was dependent on the remaining eleven, and not on his own body of presbyters.[3] The theory is, therefore, weakest where it ought to be strongest, namely, at the point when the Apostles provided for their immediate successors. This is a vital flaw and cannot be overcome by hypothesis. So gigantic a claim requires absolute evidence. The Roman Catholic view avoids these difficulties, and has the merit of clearness by concentrating authority in St. Peter. But the view now considered has no foundation in Scripture, or history, or logic. It must never be forgotten that the logical outcome of Cyprian's view of episcopacy, which is held by many in the present day, is the Papacy as the topstone, since episcopacy apart from the Papacy is only a form of government for the diocese and not for the whole Church, which thereby has no visible head.[4]

3. The Church as Invisible.—It is important to enquire as to the true marks of the Body of Christ. We must derive them from the thing itself. It is imperative to know what is essential. The way to proceed is to study with care the New Testament, especially the Epistle to the Ephesians, which contains the fullest teaching. Or else we can study the Lord Jesus Christ and our relation to Him. The four marks are, " I believe One Holy Catholic Apostolic Church," but we must take care not to use these to define any one Church. We must see what they mean before applying them to the Church, since they are only strictly applicable to the Body of Christ. Three of them, Unity, Sanctity, and Catholicity can easily be attributed, if necessary, to other societies.

[1] Further discussion of this point may be found in the author's *The Holy Spirit of God.*
[2] For all questions connected with the claims of Rome the student will give special attention to Salmon's *The Infallibility of the Church.*
[3] Goode, *The Divine Rule of Faith and Practice*, Vol. II, p. 252.
[4] Litton, *The Church of Christ* (First Edition), pp. 469–474.

(*a*) What is the meaning of Unity? (1) Not unanimity of opinion. This is clear from the New Testament itself. There was essential unity in the midst of much difference of opinion. (2) Not uniformity of usages. This was not part of the early Church, as the four families of Liturgies clearly show. (3) Not a unit of organisation. This has not existed since the first congregation in Jerusalem. There is no such unit in the East to-day, where there is a federation of several independent and self-governing Churches. There is no such unit in the Anglican Communion, the highest point being that of the province with each Bishop the equal of the rest. Even the Archbishop of Canterbury is only *primus inter pares*, and it is by courtesy alone that he has his position as leader. It is only in the Church of Rome that a unit of organisation, with the Papacy as the head, is found, and this is only possible by the exclusion of all Christians who are unwilling to submit to the Papacy. (4) True unity is that of spiritual life in Christ by the Holy Spirit. St. Paul taught two unities; one " of the Spirit," which is present (Eph. iv. 3), and one " of faith and knowledge," which can only be fully realised hereafter (Eph. iv. 13). The former we are to endeavour to keep; the other we are to attain to and reach in the future. To the same effect Christ distinguishes between the unity of the fold and the unity of the flock (John x. 16). An organised Church is not the flock, but only one fold, so that no one community can be the Church. The truth, therefore, is not that the Church is one, but that there is one Church. Unity in New Testament times and in the sub-Apostolic age was maintained by very simple methods: (1) by hospitality between the Churches; (2) by visits of the prophets; (3) by letters. There was no formal confederation.

Unity of spiritual life is possible amid great variety of visible organisations. St. Paul teaches the Scriptural idea of unity when he says, " We, being many, are one body in Christ, and every one members one of another " (Rom. xii. 5). This is a present fact, not a prospect. So also in Ephesians the Apostle teaches the truth in the same way as a fact, that the Church is the Body of Christ, without division, absolutely one in the Divine purpose, a fact which no divisions can alter. It is, therefore, impossible for any one Church so to excommunicate another as to sever that one, or any member of it from Christ. No part of the Church can exclude from the whole Church or from God. Men like Savonarola and Luther were excluded from a part, but not from the entire Church. Such an one is just as really a member of the Body of Christ as though no excommunication had been pronounced.[1]

(*b*) What is the meaning of Sanctity? The word " holy " means

---

[1] The unity of the Church is dealt with at considerable length by Westcott in *The Gospel of the Resurrection*. It is clear that he did not believe any external visible unity was essential for the vital unity of the Church. "The conception of unity based on historic and Divine succession in the religious centre of the world was proved to be no part of the true idea of the Church" (p. 217). "No external organization can supersede the original relation in which the society stands to its Founder" (p. 221). See pp. 216–230.

"consecrated," "that which belongs to God." Only as this is real can it be predicated of the visible Church, and hence it is strictly only attributable to the true Church. It is probably no part of the New Testament idea of holiness to include the modern conception of purity from evil (see John xvii. 19 ; Eph. v. 26, Greek). But if by any possibility "purity" is to be considered an essential mark of a Church, then some of the oldest Churches have it least.

(c) What is the meaning of Catholicity ? The original idea was that of universality, not particularity ; a Church embracing all times, all places, all Christians, all truth. To speak of one locality as the Catholic Church is a contradiction in terms. Catholicity is not merely universality in age, race, etc., which would be a consequence not a cause, but is due to the universal Christian life based on spiritual truth. It must include all who are united to Christ.[1]

(d) What is the meaning of Apostolicity ? There are only two tests : (1) continuous succession ; (2) primitive truth. The first is impossible, since there are gaps which cannot be covered by any knowledge we possess. Besides, by itself it would be no guarantee of genuine adherence to Apostolic truth and life. The second is verifiable, since we have the New Testament, which represents the Apostolic teaching. This is why we are able to speak of the Church as " built upon the foundation of the apostles and prophets."[2]

It will be seen from the foregoing that these four " notes " are strictly not visible but invisible, referring only to the true Church. The " notes " of the visible Church are virtually independent of spiritual condition, referring, as we have seen, to preaching of the Word and administration of the Sacraments. Yet as far as these four are true of visible Churches they are, of course, " notes " of them also.

The true idea is that " Where Christ is, there is the Church." If it be asked, Where is Christ ? The answer is, Where the Holy Spirit is. And if it be further asked, Where is the Holy Spirit ? The answer is, Where the fruit of the Spirit is found. Anglicanism, following the New Testament, does not attempt to say *who* are members of the Church, but only *where* the true visible Church is, and *what* are the requirements of true visible membership. The Church of Rome endeavours to specify members because it identifies the visible and the true Church. Anglican theology proper (apart from the Creed) as represented by this Article, does not really assign " notes " to the one true Church, but only to visible Churches, namely, the Word and Sacraments, because where these are there will be a part of Christ's Body, and yet it is only a part of the true Church so far as its members possess vital union with Christ. Hence the members of the Body of Christ are rightly to be sought for in the visible Churches, for the true Church at present can only manifest itself in the form of visible communities. If, therefore, the question is asked,

---

[1] See the author's *The Catholic Faith*, p. 340 ff.
[2] Collect for St. Simon and St. Jude's Day.   Eph. ii. 20.

Which is the Body of Christ ? it cannot be answered.   But if enquiry is made, Where is the Body of Christ ? it can be confidently said to exist wherever vital union with Christ is found.

Many problems are solved the moment the word " Church " is correctly defined, and the New Testament idea is that of an " Assembly," called a " Body," people who believe in Jesus as the Messiah (1 John v. 1), and confess Him as the Son of God (1 John iv. 15).   Several metaphors are found descriptive of the Church as that body of people which is vitally one with Christ.   (1) It is a Vine (John xv. 5); (2) a Flock (John x. 16); (3) a Temple (1 Pet. ii. 4); (4) a Bride (Eph. v. 27); (5) a Family (Rom. viii. 29); (6) a Body (Eph. i. 22); (7) a Spirit (1 Cor. vi. 17).   Thus the one fact which constitutes membership in the Church is spiritual union with Christ.   It is clear that only of the true Church, the Body of Christ, can the four " notes," so often attributed to visible Churches, be properly predicated.

The Church is One because it is united to Christ, and it is so, notwithstanding the impossibility of outward unity of earthly government. The Church is Holy because it is possessed by the Spirit of God.   The Church is Catholic because Christ is proclaimed everywhere and its life is independent of place or time.   The Church is Apostolic because it is true to the New Testament Apostolic teaching.   Thus every " note " is associated with Christ, and the One Holy Catholic Apostolic Church is neither a mere aggregate of visible Churches nor a simple invisible community of individuals.   It is none the less real because its life is in Christ and its character is spiritual.   The Church of the New Testament is that Body of Christ which consists of all the faithful in Him, and every separate community of such people is a true visible Church.

There are in reality only two views of the Church ; that represented by the New Testament, and that seen in Roman Catholicism.   There is no other essential difference, except that there are views of the Church which stop short of that of Rome and are thereby less logical.   In the New Testament conception Christianity determines the Church ; in the Roman Catholic, the Church determines Christianity.   It is either through Christ to the Church, or through the Church to Christ.   In Rome the Church makes the Christian, in the New Testament, the Christian the Church.   This does not set aside the place and work of the visible organised Churches, or of the individual Christian in making Christ known and giving people the opportunity of knowing and receiving Him.   But all this is the work of the individual Christian or of the Church, as a medium, not a mediator.   It is like an introduction at Court which, after its work is done, leaves the person face to face with the King. These are the only two possible views, and there is no common ground. If one is right the other is wrong, for there is no *via media*.   It is no use disproving Papal supremacy if we leave untouched the roots from which it sprang, and which would produce something essentially like it if the Roman form were abolished.

Our study of this important subject shows the absolute necessity of avoiding all exaggeration of " the Church." In particular, care must be taken in regard to any personification of the Church as " Holy Mother," or, in the words of Augustine, that " He shall not have God for his Father who will not have the Church for his Mother."[1] " High " views of the Church often mean low views of Christ, for there is an undoubted danger of placing the Church between the soul and Christ. The true Churchman is one who believes in the view of the Church taught by St. Paul in the Epistle to the Ephesians. This is the highest doctrine, and has the virtue of being absolutely Scriptural.[2]

On the other hand, we must be equally careful not to depreciate the Church, for this extreme is almost equally serious. Its life must be fostered. The truest Catholicity is limited only by New Testament principles, excluding none who love the Lord in sincerity. We shall never arrive at New Testament doctrine by the extreme of a low doctrine of the Church. There is nothing higher than the New Testament view taught by our Lord and His Apostles, and what is often called " High " Churchmanship is really a low view of the New Testament conception of the Church by reason of its essential narrowness, and in reality is due to a " high," but erroneous doctrine not of the Church, but of the ministry.

If we exalt Christ the Church finds her right place, but Church history more than once shows that together with what are called " High " views of the Church visible have usually been found low views of the Church spiritual and of Christ the Head of the Church. Where the Church tends to precede, there Christ tends to recede. If we bring forward the Church as the depository of grace, we tend to push back Christ as the Source of grace. But if we exalt Christ in the Godhead of His Person, the completeness of His sacrifice, the power of His resurrection, the perfection of His righteousness, the uniqueness of His priesthood; if we exalt the Holy Ghost as the direct Revealer of Christ to the soul, as the immediate and not mediated Source of grace to all believers, as the Divine

---

[1] "Such language is so natural, that we imperceptibly adopt it; but the accurate thinker will take care not to suffer himself to become the dupe of his imagination. Even divines of our own communion, not content with the simple term our Mother the Church, have incautiously followed out the notion, describing her, and sometimes without thinking of its consequences, as a tender parent devising ceremonies and composing religious services for the benefit of her children, who in return are expected to show her filial reverence and affectionate obedience, till the hearer is led unconsciously into a refined idolatry, which transfers in a degree to an abstraction of the mind the homage due alone to the Redeemer and the Sanctifier. Such may well be called the magic effect of a word; translate ecclesia not *church*, but *congregation*, and the spell is broken; and *hear the Church*, assumes quite a new meaning" (Macbride, *Lectures on the Articles*, p. 358).

[2] "If we ask what is the Church, the Canon will reply, 'The whole congregation of Christian people dispersed throughout the whole world.' This simple definition at once demolishes a fanciful, unscriptural, and pernicious theory. I may well call it pernicious, for it substitutes for personal union with a personal Saviour, union with this abstraction; derives spiritual life not immediately from the vine, but from its branches" (Macbride, *ut supra*, p. 358).

Illuminator of the Word to each disciple—then we shall obtain, and retain in its true position, the primitive and positive truth of the Church as that body of which Christ is the Head; in which the Spirit dwells as the present, continuous, and permanent life; to which all the promises of God are made; outside which no one can ever be saved; from which no believer can ever be excommunicated; against which the gates of Hades shall never prevail; in which God's power will be specially manifested; and through which His grace and glory will be shown to the spiritually wise throughout the ages of eternity.

ARTICLE XX

Of the Authority of the Church.

De Ecclesiæ Auctoritate.

The Church hath power to decree Rites or Ceremonies, and authority in Controversies of Faith; and yet it is not lawful for the Church to ordain any thing that is contrary to God's word written, neither may it so expound one place of Scripture that it be repugnant to another. Wherefore, although the Church be a witness and a keeper of Holy Writ, yet as it ought not to decree any thing against the same, so besides the same ought it not to enforce any thing to be believed for necessity of Salvation.

Habet Ecclesia Ritus sive Cæremonias statuendi jus, et in fidei controversiis auctoritatem; quamvis Ecclesiæ non licet quicquam instituere, quod verbo Dei scripto adversetur, nec unum Scripturæ locum sic exponere potest, ut alteri contradicat. Quare, licet Ecclesia sit divinorum librorum testis et conservatrix, attamen ut adversus eos nihil decernere, ita præter illos nihil credendum de necessitate salutis debet obtrudere.

IMPORTANT EQUIVALENTS.

Power	= *jus.*
Authority	= *auctoritas.*
To ordain	= *instituere.*
May it	= *potest.*
That it be repugnant to another	= *ut alteri contradicat.*
Witness and keeper	= *testis et conservatrix.*
Of Holy Writ	= *divinorum librorum.*
To decree	= *decernere.*
To enforce	= *obtrudere.*

AFTER the Nature of the Church (Article XIX) it is fitting to consider something of its work, and so Articles XX to XXII take up several aspects of Church Authority: (1) XX, the Fact and Limitations of Authority; (2) XXI, the Expression of Church Authority in General Councils; (3) XXII, Certain Doctrines set forth by Church Authority, but not Scriptural.

HISTORY

The wording of the Article, except the first clause, clearly suggests as its source the *Reformatio Legum*, but there is nothing corresponding to it in the Confession of Augsburg.[1]

The first clause has a special history of its own. It was not found in Parker's draft, 1562, or in the Articles as then accepted by Convocation,

[1] *De Summa Trinitate et Fide Catholica*, C. XI: "Quamobrem non licet ecclesiæ quicquam constituere, quod verbo Dei scripto adversetur, neque potest sic unum locum exponere ut alteri contradicat. Quanquam ergo divinorum librorum testis sit et custos et conservatrix Ecclesia, hæc tamen prerogativa ei minime concedi debet, ut contra hos libros vel quicquam decernat, vel absque horum librorum testimonio ullos fidei articulos condat, eosque populo Christiano credendos obtrudat" (Cardwell's Edition, p. 5).

but it was included when the authorised publication appeared in 1563, and its insertion was almost certainly due to the Queen.[1] Then it was accepted by Convocation in 1571. As it came from, or was suggested by the Confession of Wurtemberg, we may perhaps regard it as indicating a desire to include Lutherans, though it is also urged that it is an instance of the Queen's attempt to exercise her prerogatives as the Supreme Governor of the Church.[2] The following are the main points of the discussion for and againt the clause.[3]

AGAINST

1. Not in Parker's copy, 1562.
2. Not in the first English Version, 1563.
3. Not in the manuscript signed by the Bishops, 1571.

FOR

1. In the first Latin Version, 1563, as authorised by the Queen.
2. In the English Version, 1571.
3. In six English Versions, 1581-1628, and all later copies.
4. In a copy made for Archbishop Laud, 1631, by a notary, from the manuscript signed by the Queen, 1562.

It is suggested that Laud finding it in that edition had it inserted in authoritative copies and enforced it.[4] The question is now simply one of historical interest, since the authority of the clause is clear from 1571 onwards. It is probable that Parker and the Bishops thought the teaching on Rites and Ceremonies was found essentially in Article XXXIV, and that the reference to " Controversies of Faith " is substantially identical with the latter part of the Article.[5] The agreement of the language with that of the Confession of Wurtemberg can be seen from the following article *De Ecclesia* :—

" Credimus et confitemur . . . quod hæc Ecclesia habeat jus judicandi de omnibus doctrinis . . . quod hæc Ecclesia habeat jus interpretandæ Scripturæ. . . . Quare et Ecclesia sic habet auctoritatem judicandi de doctrinis, ut tamen

[1] "It is evident from several other instances of the exercise of this power, and more especially from a letter of remonstrance addressed to her by Archbishop Grindal at a subsequent period, that she looked upon her supremacy as totally independent, not only of temporal but also spiritual control" (Cardwell, *Synodalia*, p. 39).

[2] Lamb, *Historical Account of the Thirty-nine Articles*, p. 33 ff.

[3] The details as to the rival editions can be seen in Cardwell, *Synodalia*, p. 40 f.

[4] Lamb, *ut supra*, p. 35 f.

[5] "Of this clause one part is contained expressly in Article XXXIV, and the other by implication in the sequel of Article XX; and perhaps, the method, in which the latter and more important part was elsewhere stated, being indirect but yet conclusive, may explain the different conduct of the two parties as to the adoption or the omission of the clause. The Confession of Wurtemberg, from which the additions made by Archbishop Parker were generally taken, would certainly have suggested to him the introduction of such a clause, had he not been satisfied that there was in other passages a sufficient acknowledgment made respecting the authority of the Church" (Cardwell, *ut supra*, p. 41).

contineat se intra metas Sacræ Scripturæ, quæ est vox sponsi sui, a qua voce nulli, ne angelo quidem, fas est recedere."

I.—THE NATURE OF CHURCH AUTHORITY

Every Society, whether involuntary or voluntary, natural or created, has its rightful sphere of authority, and authority in general is threefold : (1) legislative, making laws ; (2) judicial, declaring laws ; (3) executive, enforcing laws. The Church can exercise all three functions subject to the proper limitations, as stated in the Article.

It is to be noted that the Article is an anticipation of Article XXXIV, where our Church, as a national body, claims for itself what it teaches here concerning the entire Church.

1. As to Ceremonial, the Church has full legal right, *jus*. " The Church hath power to decree Rites and Ceremonies." It is now impossible to distinguish between Rites and Ceremonies, though it is often suggested that " Rite " is associated with the word and " Ceremony " with the accompanying action.[1]

The Church, like every other Society, has, and must have, the right to enact laws of ceremonial observance. The New Testament is for the most part a book of principles rather than rules (1 Cor. xiv. 26, 40), but even there we occasionally find rules as well (1 Cor. xi. 14-16 ; xiv. 34). And during the centuries the Church, as a Christian Society, has exercised this legal right of " ordaining," or " changing," or " abolishing " Ceremonies (Article XXXIV). The decision of Nicæa in regard to Easter, the retention of the sign of the Cross in Baptism, the abolition of mediæval Ceremonies connected with Baptism and Ordination, and the definite and remarkable modification of our Confirmation Office are cases in point.

2. As to Faith, the Church has moral authority (*auctoritatis*). " The Church hath . . . authority in Controversies of Faith." The change of wording from power (*jus*) to authority (*auctoritatis*) is highly significant, and affords a striking instance of the balanced judgment of those responsible for the phrase. There is a great difference between Discipline and Doctrine ; as to the first, the Church has full legal power ; as to the second, only moral authority. This is curiously exemplified by the use of these words in Roman law, where the people had *jus*, while the Senate had *auctoritatis*. The Senate was a Council, the concentrated wisdom of the people, and what was done was by the initiative of the Senate, but in case of emergency nothing was done except by the will of the people. The Senate initiated, the people consummated. The distinction in things ecclesiastical and religious is important and vital. A Society can prevent a man from speaking or acting, but not from thinking. And so in regard to matters of belief, the Church does not possess absolute

---

[1] The etymology of *Ritus* is unknown, though it may be connected with ῥῆτα, "words." *Cærus* is an obsolete word equivalent to *Sanctus*.

power (*jus*), but only authority (*auctoritatis*). " The first gives power which cannot be innocently resisted, the second only weight or influence."[1] The influence of the Society of the Church on our thinking is truly weighty. The Creeds and Articles show this demand for assent to doctrine. But even here it is not concerned with all questions of Faith, but only with matters of difference, for the reference is to " *Controversies of Faith.*" Private judgment is not given up, but the individual is expected to weigh fully the mind of the Church in all matters of difference. We can see this from St. Paul's counsel and warning at Miletus (Acts xx. 30, 31), by his exhortation to the Thessalonian Christians to " prove all things " (1 Thess. v. 21), and by his emphasis on " sound " doctrine in the Pastoral Epistles. But while the witness of the Church to doctrine is valuable and weighty (Matt. xvi. 17 ff.; 1 Tim. iii. 15) not even an Apostle could force belief. " Not that we have dominion over your faith " (2 Cor. i. 24). It should be noticed that authority in Controversies of Faith is associated with the Church and not with the ministry. Our Prayer Book was formed by the whole body of Christians; the clergy in Convocation, and the laity in Parliament, and the Articles rest on exactly the same foundation.

The first clause is plainly directed against those Puritans, as they came to be called, who held that nothing was of force in Church life unless it could be proved from Scripture. Against so narrow and impossible a view of the function of Scripture, Hooker wrote his great work.[2] The second clause is directed with equal force against Rome, which tended to make the Church of supreme authority.[3]

II.—THE LIMITATIONS OF CHURCH AUTHORITY

1. As to Ceremonial, nothing is to be ordained contrary to Scripture. " It is not lawful for the Church to ordain anything that is contrary to God's Word written." The reference to " God's Word written " indicates a clear determination to rule out the view of the Church of Rome which supplements Scripture by tradition.[4] No Ritual or Ceremony can be allowed that is contrary to the Word of God. Thus if a

---

[1] Macbride, *Lectures on the Articles*, p. 360.
[2] *Eccl. Pol.*, especially Bk. I.
[3] Hardwick, *History of the Articles of Religion*, p. 103.
[4] With the wording of this Article the Creed of Pope Pius IV should be compared:
"Apostolic and ecclesiastical traditions, and the remaining observances and constitutions of the same Church I most firmly admit and embrace. I also admit Holy Scripture according to that sense which Holy Mother Church has held and does hold, to whom it belongs to judge of the true sense and interpretation of Holy Scripture; neither will I ever receive and interpret them otherwise than according to the unanimous consent of the Fathers."
The very wording of these statements is significant of the place Scripture holds in the Church of Rome, ecclesiastical traditions being mentioned first, and the words, " most firmly " being associated with the former and not the latter.

Church refused the cup to the laity, or forbade the celebration of the Holy Communion in the evening it would be distinctly *ultra vires* in view of the plain teaching of Holy Scripture.[1]

2. As to Faith, the Church must not teach anything that is contradictory of Scripture. " Neither may it so expound one place of Scripture, that it be repugnant to another." Christianity has a historic basis in the revelation of Christ, and it is the duty of the Church to testify to this and to decline membership to any who do not accept it. At the same time it is essential for the Church to guard against requiring more than this primitive revelation as a condition of Church membership. The principle that the Divine Word must not be added to (Deut. iv. 2 ; Rev. xxii. 18, 19) has a direct application to all questions of belief, for it would be fatal to the purity and fulness of Christian truth for the Church to teach or insist upon anything that could be proved to be contradictory of Scripture.[2] As an example at once of Church authority and its limitation, it has been suggested that while the Church would be perfectly within its right in instituting a Harvest Festival, it would not be justified in including in that Service an adoration of angels, because that would be clearly contradictory of Scripture.[3]

III.—THE RELATION OF THE CHURCH TO SCRIPTURE

At this point there is a special application of Article VI.

1. The position of the Church in relation to Scripture. " Although the Church be a witness and a keeper of Holy Writ." It is a witness (*testis*), bearing testimony to what is actually Holy Scripture. It is also a keeper (*conservatrix*), preserving Scripture as it is. It is important to notice the term used here ; the Church is a keeper (*conservatrix*), not a keeper-back (*reservatrix*). It is also important to observe that the Church is not the maker or the judge of Scripture. Its work in regard to Scripture is that of bearing witness to what Christian people have received and are preserving. And even if the Church should forget the circumstances of the origin of Scripture it is still possible to accept the fact. But it is important to beware of the fallacy lurking in the phrase, " The Church

[1] The above principle is considered solely in the light of the New Testament idea of the Church without any reference to Establishment. But in England the Church, as established, has inherited much of the old Canon Law, and has adopted it so far as it does not interfere with Statute Law. And as to judicial and executive functions, it has expressly laid down that the supreme authority is vested in the Crown over all causes as the judicial head, and over all persons as the executive head. But this is not so because of the person of the Sovereign, or the royal prerogative, but because the Sovereign is regarded as the representative of the Church as a whole, and especially of the lay element. See further in regard to the position and power of the Crown in Article XXXVII.

[2] It has been well pointed out how the Middle Ages failed here, as the Jewish Church had done before, in covering Scripture with Church traditions, thereby causing Scripture to be "merged in a miscellaneous mass of authorities" (Gore, *The Body of Christ*).

[3] Goulburn, quoted in Gibson, *ut supra*, p. 515; see also pp. 517–519.

gave us the Bible," for this is to confuse between the source and the medium.[1] The real truth is :—

> "The Church from her dear Master
> Received the gift Divine."

And since that day the Church has testified to and kept the Bible for the use of Christian people.[2]

2. The subordination of the Church to Scripture.

(*a*) No legislative decree is to be made against Scripture. "It ought not to decree anything against the same."

(*b*) No doctrinal requirement is to be demanded in addition to Scripture. "Besides the same ought it not to enforce anything to be believed for necessity of salvation."

This relation of subordination of the Church to Scripture was a special feature of the work of the Reformation. It is sometimes said that the movement was the result of a rediscovery of the Bible, and although the Bible was in existence and regarded as authoritative during the Middle Ages there is a sense in which the Reformation was associated with a new view of Holy Scripture. The Reformers approached it in a new spirit and introduced a fresh method of using it. It has often been pointed out that mediæval writers regarded the Bible as a kind of Divine Law Book, containing truths for human life, and as these truths were too difficult for ordinary men to discover, the authority of the Church was considered to be essential to any true apprehension of the teaching of Scripture. As a practical result this interposition of the Church really closed Holy Scripture to ordinary people, and it was in connection with this that the deepest work of the Reformation was done. All the Reformers believed that in Scripture God was still speaking to them and revealing Himself to their individual experience. So that the Bible was at once a doctrinal and a personal revelation of God, and, as such, it was something entirely different from what it had been in the Middle Ages. God was regarded as still speaking to men through the pages of His Word, and it was for this reason that the Reformers placed the Bible in the hands of ordinary people, and urged its use by everyone as the supreme

---

[1] It has been well and pointedly said that it would be just as true to say, "The baker's boy gave us the bread," or "the postman gave us the letter."

[2] "The books of the Bible were given *to* the Church, more than *by* it, and they descended on it rather than rose from it. The canon of the Bible rose from the Church, but not its contents. Bible and Church were collateral products of the Gospel" (Forsyth, *The Person and Place of Jesus Christ*, p. 140). See also pp. 152, 171.

"In the mere sense that the Church was in existence before the New Testament was written, this is, of course, a mere truism. But in any other than this mere chronological sense, the statement is not true. The men who wrote the New Testament were the men who made the Church; and the authors of the New Testament, representing the teaching of the New Testament, were thus anterior to the Church, and superior to it. The Old Testament existed before the birth of the Christian Church; and the New Testament existed in living form, in the persons of its authors, contemporaneously with the birth of the Church" (Wace, *Principles of the Reformation*, p. 248).

way of hearing the voice of God, and learning the way of salvation through Christ. It was this change of view that led people to regard the Reformation as the time when Scripture was virtually rediscovered, because the saving faith in God through His Word led to such personal and definite fellowship between the believer and his Saviour as involved an entirely new conception of Christianity as the religion of personal fellowship with God through Christ in His Word. The consciousness of this fact and force of Holy Scripture led the Reformers to subordinate the Church to Scripture, and to put the Word of God high above all else as the dominating authority for religion, whether individual or corporate.[1]

The Article, of course, implies the work of the Church as the expounder of Scripture, and while on the one hand it is important to keep this in mind and give it all the weight it deserves,[2] on the other it is essential to define with the greatest care what the Church is, and to distinguish between the actual exposition of the Church and the opinions of individual Christians, however great, good, and representative they may be. The Church, as a Church, has expounded exceedingly little, and has wisely left most to the individual judgment and conscience of Christian people.

A modern phrase of frequent use is " The Church to teach, the Bible to prove."[3] But this needs the greatest possible care. It is true, but it is not the whole truth, and the sharp antithesis is liable to be misleading. It would be equally true to say, " The Bible to teach, the Church to prove," and also " The Bible to teach, the Church to learn." The meaning of the New Testament word, " disciple," is a " learner," and in order to be perfectly true and accurate the phrase must of necessity imply that the Church receives and teaches only what is found in the Bible. Even an Apostle had his teaching examined and tested according to Scripture (Acts xvii. 11). All this shows the importance and absolute necessity of defining the three words, " Church," " teach," " prove."

(a) What is the Church that teaches ? Certainly it is not the ministry only, for teaching cannot be thus confined, though this seems to be implied as a rule when the phrase is used.

(b) How does the Church teach ? The phrase, *ecclesia docens*, needs to be properly understood and explained. Scripture shows that the Church, " the blessed company of all faithful people," is itself taught by Christ, and being taught it believes and obeys the truth. The words " hear the Church " (Matt. xviii. 17) refer to discipline, not to doctrine, and when we speak of *ecclesia docens*, we really mean testimony rather than instruction. The Church as a whole has exercised its functions in

---

[1] All this Reformation doctrine is ably stated in Lindsay, *The History of the Reformation*, Vol. I, pp. 453–467.
[2] Maclear and Williams, *Articles*, p. 99, *Re Ecclesia Docens*. See Hooker, *Eccl. Pol.*, Bk. III, Ch. VIII, Section 14, both quoted under Article VI.
[3] Said by Dr. Salmon to be due to Dr. Hawkins of Oriel College, Oxford.

regard to faith by means of (1) Creeds; (2) Liturgies; (3) Councils; (4) ordinary ministerial and other teaching; (5) ordinary individual testimony. It is striking how little the Church has done in the way of the interpretation of Creeds. In all Councils there was some judgment of the laity, and although the clergy no doubt had a large amount of power, it is a question whether it was given to them by reason of their position as such, or because they were leaders or experts. Certainly at the Council of Nicæa the moving spirits were not Bishops, but Arius and Athanasius, a priest and a deacon.

(c) What is meant by " to prove " ? To test by a standard, and therefore the teaching of the Church ought to be proved by the Bible because it is the Word of God.

It is at this point that the danger of the phrase may be seen. The Church may so teach as to usurp the office of proving, for the Church must not go to Scripture to support its preconceived ideas. Then, the Bible may be so used to prove as to exclude it from its office of teaching, and thereby the Church may virtually supersede the Bible, as is done in the Church of Rome, by requiring the interpretation of the Church, and by teaching what is not found in Scripture. The fact that we learn our first lessons from Christians, not from the Bible, is often used to imply the superiority of the Church. But we readily accept the fact while refusing to draw the inference. First in order does not necessarily mean first in importance. Human teaching is valuable and essential, but to be anterior is not necessarily to be superior to Scripture. As already seen under Article VI, priority is not the same as superiority. The mind of the Church of England may be seen from one of the Homilies, where the following statements occur :—

" In Holy Scripture is fully contained what we ought to do and what to eschew, what to believe, what to love, and what to look for at God's hands at length. . . . The humble man may search any truth boldly in the Scripture without any danger of error. And if he be ignorant he ought the more to read and to search Holy Scripture to bring him out of ignorance. . . . If we read once, twice, or thrice and understand not, let us not cease so, but still continue reading, praying, asking of others, and so by still knocking at last the door shall be opened. . . . And those things in the Scriptures that be plain to understand and necessary for salvation every man's duty is to learn them, to print them in memory and effectually to exercise them. And as for the dark mysteries, to be contented to be ignorant in them until such time as it shall please God to open those things unto him."

It is surely not without importance that the Homily does not give the slightest suggestion that the consent of the Fathers or the interpretation of the Church is required for a true understanding of Holy Scripture.

The peril of the phrase, " The Church to teach, the Bible to prove," lies in refusing to the Bible any teaching place and limiting it to the work of proving. This would relegate it to the position of a mere reference book with little practical influence.[1] The Bible is not to be kept back in this way, but ever placed in the most prominent position as our pure, perpetual, and perfect source of Divine truth.[2]

The two sides of the truth must therefore be emphasised, for the office of the Bible is to teach as well as to prove, and the office of the Church is to be taught first from the Bible before it can either teach or prove. The true idea is not " Hear what the Church saith to her children," but " Hear what the Spirit saith to the Churches."[3]

As we consider the teaching of the Article, especially when associated with the well-known attitude of the Reformation, we see that our ultimate authority is Holy Scripture (Articles VI, VIII, XX), and it is therefore impossible to accept the principle that we are to interpret the Prayer Book and Articles in the light of what is sometimes called " Catholic " teaching and tradition. The Church of England nowhere implies, still less teaches this, but refers us direct to Scripture for our warrant.[4] The position of the New Testament in the Church to-day is exactly analogous to that of the Old Testament in the Jewish Church. To them and to us have been committed the oracles of God (Rom. iii. 2), and it is impossible for the individual or the Church to go beyond the Word of the Lord (Numb. xxiv. 13; Isa. viii. 20).

IV.—THE RELATION OF THE CHURCH TO THE INDIVIDUAL

At this point arises the question of private judgment, and although the

---

[1] "The Bible is not to be kept in the background, as a document to be referred to for the proof of doctrines, as a witness is called into court for the purpose of some special piece of evidence. It must, on the contrary, be our constant teacher, the one perpetual source of our knowledge of Divine things, under the guidance of the Spirit who inspired it, and who is ever at hand to illuminate the hearts and minds of those who seek His aid in prayer, and who look up to Him as the guide of every Christian into all the truth" (Wace, *ut supra*, p. 250). See also Salmon, *The Infallibility of the Church*, Chs. VII–X (especially p. 125); Bernard, *The Word and the Sacraments*, Ch. VI.

[2] Even Dr. Hall, *Dogmatic Theology* (p. 68), says that the phrase would be more adequate if expanded into "The Church to define and teach, the Scripture to confirm and illustrate." But it would be equally true to say, "The Scripture to define and teach, the Church to confirm and illustrate." The fact is that these antitheses cannot stand without due safeguarding.

[3] The well-known words of Chillingworth: "The Bible, and the Bible only, is the religion of the Protestants," is described by Bishop Gibson (*ut supra*, p. 528) as a "rather foolish saying," because it is said to contradict the incident of the Ethiopian eunuch who needed Philip to explain the Scripture to him. But is there not some confusion here? Did not Chillingworth refer to source and not to medium when he spoke of "the Bible only"? His reference was to the Bible rather than to the Church or tradition, and not to the Bible as opposed to the ministry. And would not a layman in such a case equally represent, if necessary, the *Ecclesia docens*? This criticism is a striking illustration of how easy it is to use the word 'Church' when what is meant is the limited term 'ministry.' It would therefore seem that Chillingworth's phrase was justifiable.

[4] "Is it not then entirely inconsistent with this principle of our Church to say, as is constantly said by many among us, that the Prayer Book and Articles were to be read and interpreted in the light of the belief and practice of the Catholic Church? Her principle demands, on the contrary, that our formularies, and more particularly our Articles, should be interpreted in the light of Holy Scripture, rather than in that of mediæval theology" (Wace, *ut supra*, p. 248).

T

problem is only implied in the Article, it is of the utmost importance to consider what is the precise relation of the Church to the individual, and what attitude the individual Christian should adopt towards the Church in regard to any of its teaching. It is often asked whether the Church has ever gone beyond the limits set forth in this Article. If it has, how is the individual to know it, and what is to happen if this has been the case ? Now it is quite impossible to say that the Church has been infallible at any time, and *Athanasius contra mundum* may quite easily occur again.[1] It is also impossible to say that the individual must accept every judgment of the Church. Indeed, the very wording of the Article implies this, for the Church is only concerned with " Controversies of Faith," matters of difference of belief, and not with all questions that may come up for consideration. So that the last resort must always be to the enlightened private judgment of the individual. And this is equally true of the man who surrenders his judgment to an infallible Church as well as of the man who maintains his position as individually responsible to God for his faith. The former asserts his judgment on choosing the authority, even though it be only to yield it afterwards to that authority, while the latter retains the exercise of his judgment as the essential and vital principle of true Christian character and conduct. Nor is it accurate to describe this enlightened private judgment as solitary, thereby involving an undue individualism and a dangerous self-assertion. On the contrary, the individual judgment will naturally and rightly be checked by the consensus of the Church so far as he is able to discover it, and then be exercised with all the light available.[2] This position is in thorough harmony with the example of our Lord, it agrees entirely with our responsible individuality, and the relation to God which is given to every man, while it has been productive of the noblest characters in history. Let it be added that very seldom will there be any practical difficulty, since on the one hand the Church, as such, has pronounced so few decisions that may be regarded as binding on the entire community, and on the other hand the presence of the Spirit of God in the believer will enable him first to consider every possible avenue of information, and then to arrive at a judgment which will involve the devoted surrender of mind, heart, conscience, and will, to what is believed to be the truth of God. The true follower of Jesus Christ will always be ready and glad to give the utmost weight to the universal testimony of the Church in so far as this can be obtained, for no individual will lightly set aside such a united belief, but the last and final authority must be the Word of God illuminating and influencing the human life through the presence of the Holy Spirit.

[1] Gibson, *ut supra*, p. 525.
[2] The difference between a true and untrue use of Church tradition as a help to the formation of individual opinion is discussed in the author's *The Holy Spirit of God*.

ARTICLE XXI

Of the Authority of General Councils.

General Councils may not be gathered together without the commandment and will of Princes. And when they be gathered together—forasmuch as they be an assembly of men, whereof all be not governed with the Spirit and Word of God—they may err, and sometimes have erred, even in things pertaining unto God. Wherefore things ordained by them, as necessary to salvation, have neither strength nor authority, unless it may be declared that they be taken out of Holy Scripture.

De Auctoritate Conciliorum Generalium.

Generalia Concilia sine jussu et voluntate Principum congregari non possunt: et ubi convenerint—quia ex hominibus constant qui non omnes Spiritu et Verbo Dei reguntur—et errare possunt, et interdum errarunt, etiam in his quæ ad Deum pertinent. Ideoque quæ ab illis constituuntur, ut ad salutem necessaria, neque robur habent neque auctoritatem, nisi ostendi possint e sacris literis esse desumpta.

IMPORTANT EQUIVALENTS.

Be gathered together	= *congregari.*
When they be gathered together	= *ubi convenerint.*
Be an assembly of men	= *ex hominibus constant.*
Things ordained by them	= *quæ ab illis constituuntur.*
To salvation	= *ad salutem.*
Strength	= *robur.*
Unless it may be declared that they be taken out of Holy Scripture	= *nisi ostendi possint e sacris literis esse desumpta.*

THIS Article dates from 1553, with certain small verbal alterations. It is placed here because General Councils were one important way of expressing Church Authority, and thus the Article is one application of the principles laid down in Article XX. Since the Church has authority, we ask how it has been sought and its decisions declared, and we naturally turn to those General Councils where it has been expressed and exercised. The subject is also pretty certainly found here because the question was proposed at the Reformation in order to settle differences, and in 1545 Pope Paul VII summoned a Council, to which, however, the Reformers were not invited.

I.—THE FACT OF GENERAL COUNCILS

By " General " is meant " universal," or " ecumenical " (οἰκουμένη), in which the whole Church is represented. These General Councils are to be distinguished from National, Provincial, and Diocesan gatherings, the National consisting of the representatives of one nation only, the Provincial of one ecclesiastical province, the Diocesan of one diocese.

These are really Synods, of which there were several before the First General Council of Nicæa.[1]

Councils for consultation among those who belong to the same community are natural and reasonable. The Jews had theirs, and the first Christian Council in Acts xv. was an inevitable and obvious method of discussing an important question. But this first gathering has no real bearing on the present Article beyond the fact of a Council and the warrant for subsequent gatherings. After the Council at Jerusalem there does not seem to have been any similar meeting until the third century, when some local Councils met.

The number of General or Ecumenical Councils varies with different Churches. According to the Church of Rome there are eighteen, but most of these are purely Western and apply to Rome only without being in any strict sense "ecumenical." According to the Greek Church there are seven, while in the English Church special reference is made to the first six. Thus the Homily against peril of idolatry speaks of "these six Councils which were allowed and received of all men." But notwithstanding this the first four Councils have always been regarded as permanent in view of their importance on doctrinal grounds.

The following are the only General or Ecumenical Councils which can be said to have been acknowledged by the whole Church.

1. Nicæa, 325.—This was summoned by the Emperor Constantine and met to deal with the Arian heresy. It was composed wholly of Bishops of the Roman Empire who acknowledged Constantine as their Emperor. The Pope sent two Legates, but Hosius the Spanish Bishop presided.

2. Constantinople I, 381.—This was summoned by the Emperor Theodosius I to deal with the heretical views of Macedonius. It completed the doctrine of the Holy Trinity by its full declaration in regard to the Holy Spirit.

3. Ephesus, 431.—This was called by the Emperor Theodosius II to deal with the heresy of Nestorius. Cyril of Alexandria, the haughty opponent of Nestorius, presided, and the behaviour of the gathering was so deplorable that the Emperor dismissed it with a rebuke. But its decision on the double nature of our Lord has always been accepted by the universal Church.

4. Chalcedon, 451.—This was summoned by the Emperor Marcianus at the suggestion and request of Pope Leo the Great. It condemned the error of Eutyches, and completed the orthodox expression of the Trinitarian doctrine.

5. Constantinople II, 553.—This was summoned by the Emperor Justinian, and confirmed the decrees of Ephesus and Chalcedon, though otherwise it was not of great doctrinal importance. It is noteworthy

---

[1] "Synod" is derived from σύνοδος, from σύν, *together*, and ὁδός, "a path," "a journey." It means literally a "coming together."

that Pope Vigilius refused his assent to its decrees, although he was present, and he was banished until he acquiesced in them.

6. Constantinople III, 680.—This was summoned by the Emperor Constantine Pogonatus, and condemned the heresy known as Monothelitism. At this Council Pope Marcellus was condemned as a Monothelite.

While these six are the only Councils which have been universally acknowledged it is correct to distinguish between the first four and the last two. Of the former Gregory the Great was accustomed to say that "he reverenced them as he did the four Evangelists."[1]

7. Nicæa II, 787.—This was summoned by the Empress Irene, but was opposed at the time by the Germans, French, and British. It authorised the worship of images and of the Cross, and denounced punishment against those who maintained that God was the only object of adoration.

An eighth is sometimes referred to as "General," that of Constantinpole, 869, under Photius, but it is not accepted either by East or West.

Later Councils which were held in the West, and convened by Popes, can only be regarded as Councils of the Roman Church or Patriarchate. Four of them met in the Lateran Palace, 1123, 1139, 1170, 1215, and the last of them was the largest ever assembled, consisting of over 12,000 persons. It broke up in less than a month, having accepted the documents presented to it by Pope Innocent III, confirming Transubstantiation and Auricular Confession. Among them is the Canon compelling secular powers to extirpate heretics under the penalty of excommunication. The three Councils that followed, at Lyons, 1245 and 1274, and at Vienne, 1311, were mainly of a political character. Then followed a new and very different series. The first at Pisa in 1409 dealt mainly with papal rivalry. The Council of Constance, 1416, is notorious for its condemnation and burning, in spite of the Emperor's pledge of safe conduct, of John Huss and Jerome of Prague. It was this Council that ordered the remains of Wycliffe to be disinterred and thrown into the stream at Lutterworth. The Council of Basle followed, 1431, but was excommunicated by the Pope, who called a rival assembly at Florence, which effected a union of the Greek and Roman Churches for a very short time. A fifth Lateran Council, 1512, was only of temporary importance, and, indeed, all the preceding ones were eclipsed by the Council of Trent, which completes the number, and settled the official doctrine of the Roman Church.

II.—THE SUMMONING OF GENERAL COUNCILS

The English " may not " is illustrated by the Latin " cannot " (*non possunt*), referring to lawful assembly.[2]

---

[1] Quoted in Maclear and Williams, *Introduction to the Articles of the Church of England*, p. 257.

[2] *Nec potest*, Article XX; and *possunt*, Article XXXVII.

The statement that General Councils cannot be gathered together " without the commandment and will of Princes," has led to the enquiry why this feature was thought to be necessary.   It has been said by some that as the secular law did not allow Bishops to leave their own country and to go into other Dominions without the permission of their own Princes, the result was that without such permission no General Councils were possible.   But this is not the true explanation.   There seems to be no doubt that the requirement is due to the necessity of guaranteeing universality and a full representation, especially of the lay power.   Not only so, but it is clearly directed against any summoning of Councils by the Pope.   The Western Councils were invariably called by the Pope alone, and the Council of Trent consisted only of Bishops in union with Rome.[1]

The requirement is also doubtless made because, as a matter of historical fact, this was the method adopted in the earliest General Councils.   They originated with Constantine, and Emperors alone summoned them. The Popes had no power over the Councils in early ages, and even later they petitioned Emperors to gather them together.   Nor did the Popes preside at any of the earliest.   The letter of Pope Leo read at the Council of Chalcedon had deserved weight, but in no sense did it settle the doctrine.   The Pope's power rested on false Decretals of the ninth century, which were not denied because the forgery was not discovered until the fifteenth century during the Revival of Learning.   There were other Decretals forged in the same way, and they were all included in Gratian's Decretum.   In the thirteenth century a catena was presented to Pope Urban IV, and was accepted by Thomas Aquinas.

III.—THE FALLIBILITY OF GENERAL COUNCILS

1. This is first stated as a possibility : " They may err." This is doubtless due to the truth that no visible Church can be regarded as inerrant.

2. Then the fallibility is stated as actual.   The history of Councils is clear, and the stories are often saddening, even though, as in the case of Ephesus, the results have been universally accepted.[2]   The words of Gregory Nazianzen are often quoted.   They were included in a document of 1536, signed by Archbishop Cranmer and others in the name of Convocation :—

" If I must write the truth, I am disposed to avoid every assembly of bishops ; for of no synod have I seen a profitable end ; rather an addition to, than a diminution of, evils ; for the love of strife and the thirst for superiority are beyond the power of words to express."[3]

[1] Collier, *Eccl. Hist.*, VI, p. 332, represents Queen Elizabeth as replying to solicitations to send representatives to Trent: "It was not the Pope's, but the Emperor's privilege to call a Council."
[2] Salmon, *The Infallibility of the Church*, p. 274 ff.
[3] See Harold Browne, *Exposition of the Thirty-nine Articles*, p. 488; Boultbee, *The Theology of the Church of England*, p. 181.

3. The explanation of the fallibility is said to be because these assemblies consist of men " whereof all be not governed with the Spirit and Word of God." This frank statement of the unchristian character of General Councils is peculiarly significant, and is all the more striking because the *Reformatio Legum*, about the same time, bore strong testimony to the honour paid to the first four General Councils.[1]

IV.—THE SANCTION OF GENERAL COUNCILS

1. Holy Scripture is regarded as the supreme test of anything decreed by such Councils. This is in exact accord with the principle already laid down in Articles VI, VIII, and XX. It is also illustrated by actual fact in connection with the early Councils. Thus the Council of Carthage speaks of being " mindful of the Divine precepts and of the magisterial authority of the Divine Scriptures."[2] And at Chalcedon the Gospels were placed upon a throne in the midst of the assembly as a testimony to the Divine authority of God's Word.

2. Further, the Conciliar decrees must be capable of proof from Scripture. " Things ordained . . . Holy Scripture." Again the English phrase, " may be declared " is to be compared with the Latin *ostendi possint*. This shows that there must be no doubt whatever as to the power of proving the truth of the decisions of the Councils from the Word of God.[3]

In view of all these considerations when regarded in the light of the history of the past centuries and the circumstances to-day, it would seem as though there were scarcely any room for the superior, restraining power of a General Council, especially after the principles set forth in regard to National Churches in Articles XX and XXXIV. Then, too, no General Council has ever been representative, and its decisions have only been accepted because they were endorsed universally by the Church afterwards. This is the sole test of a General Council. No Council can be regarded as infallible at the time of its meeting. The test of its

---

[1] Magna cum reverentia amplectimur et suscipimus. Yet even these are to be accepted only because based on Scripture.
"Quibus tamen non aliter fidem nostram obligandam esse censemus, nisi quatenus ex Scripturis sanctis confirmari possint. . . . Itaque legantur concilia quidem cum honore atque Christiana reverentia, sed interim ad Scripturarum piam certam rectamque regulam examinentur" *De Summa Trinitate Et Fide Catholica*, c. 14 (Cardwell, *Reformatio Legum*, p. 6).

[2] Quoted in Forbes, *Explanation of the Thirty-nine Articles*, p. 296.

[3] "As to the strict notion of a General Council, there is great reason to believe that there was never any assembly to which it will be found to agree. And for the four General Councils, which this Church declares that she receives, they are received only because we are persuaded from the Scriptures that their decisions were made according to them. . . . These truths we find in the Scriptures, and, therefore, we believe them. We reverence those Councils for the sake of their doctrine; but do not believe the doctrine for the authority of the Councils. There appeared too much of human frailty in some of their other proceedings, to give us such an implicit submission to them, as to believe things only because they so decided them" (Burnet, *Exposition of the Thirty-nine Articles of the Church of England*, p. 254 f.).

truth is to be seen in the subsequent reception of its decisions by the entire Church. When such decisions are universally accepted we believe that the Council has been faithful to the mind of the Church and of Holy Scripture.[1] In the light of all these circumstances there can be very little doubt that a real General Council is entirely impossible.[2] And, indeed, it is not at all necessary, since the Church was able to live and make progress long before the time of Nicæa. As then, so now, it is not impossible, indeed, it is not very difficult to arrive at the true mind of the Church on all fundamental and essential questions.[3]

The relation of the Church of England to the earliest General Councils is a matter of historical interest, though perhaps not of any definite and binding importance. Our Church accepts indirectly the validity of some of the General Councils, and, as we have seen, the Reformers spoke reverently of the first four, which are virtually recognised in the Act of Queen Elizabeth,[4] though even this had a reference to the ultimate authority of Scripture. It was a proviso against the undue use of the royal prerogative, and refers only to doctrine and not to discipline.[5] But it is almost certain that this is not now in force. The High Commission was a Judicial Court, or Committee, appointed by the Queen in 1559 to investigate ecclesiastical cases, members being nominated by the Crown. There were disputes in the times of James I between the High Commission and the Common Law Courts as to the powers of the Commission. In 1611 Chief Justice Coke decided that it had no right to fine or imprison except for heresy or schism. Laud used the High Commission very freely, but it was abolished by the Long Parliament in 1640.

---

[1] "The ultimate decision as to the universally binding force of Conciliar Decrees, and thus as to the ecumenical character of the Council whose they are, rests with the educated instinct of the Church; it is a matter for the *consensus post* of Christendom; what is permanent and adequate *persists*, what is transitory and inadequate *passes away*" (Maclear and Williams, *ut supra*, p. 260 f.).

[2] "The ideal, no doubt, of the Christian Church is that the whole congregation of Christian people, dispersed throughout the whole world, should be so united in Christian charity, as to be able to bring their united wisdom and spiritual experience together in council, and thus to guide, under the influence of the Spirit of God, the belief and the practice of the various local Churches. But no such authority has existed since the time of the primitive authority already mentioned. No General Council can possibly be appealed to; and in the absence of such general authority, each Church must exercise its own authority, on its own responsibility" (Wace, *ut supra*, p. 245).

[3] "And after all, what is the true description of those Councils, which are so confidently called General? Look at the extent of Christ's universal Church, embracing as it does within its wide circuit the Christians of the whole world, and then tell us what we are to say of the greatest and fullest Council ever assembled in Christendom? Verily it is nothing better than a private meeting of Bishops, it is a mere provincial Synod. What though there be the assembling of Italy, and France, and Spain, and England, and Germany, and Denmark, and Scotland. Is it a General Council? Are its decrees to be registered as the consenting voice of the Church Catholic? Then where are Asia and Greece? Why are their Churches to be forgotten? But indeed the truth of the Gospel of Jesus Christ does not depend on Councils, or, as St. Paul writes, on man's judgment. Without Councils and against Councils, God is able to advance His kingdom" (Jewel's *Apology*).

[4] See 1 Eliz., c. I; Hardwick, *History of the Articles of Religion*, p. 388.

[5] Boultbee, *ut supra*, p. 180.

A new Court was established by James II in 1686, but was abolished by the Bill of Rights, 1689.

But, it may be asked, do we not believe in the presence of Christ in His Church ?   Assuredly we do, and we believe that the Church as a whole shall be " kept."   God's providence works in similar ways, over-ruling, while evil is permitted and good is in abeyance.   But this does not prevent us from believing that God reigns supreme, and so while the Church as a whole will be preserved from fundamental apostasy we are not to expect that it will ever be wholly free from error.   Infallible authority is much easier and simpler for those who do not wish to have the trouble of personal responsibility.   But the question is not what is easy, but what is true.   It is part of our moral probation here to face questions of difficulty, and individuals as well as Churches are assured of the adequate guidance of God.   " The meek will He guide in judgment; and the meek will He teach His way " (Psa. xxv. 9).

At this point it may be well to combine the teaching of Articles XX and XXI by noticing the principles laid down.

1. The Church has full legal right in regard to Ceremonial.

2. The Church has moral authority in all questions of difference of belief.

3. This two-fold authority is always subject to the Word of God.

4. General Councils must have lay and full representation.

5. They may err, and have erred, thereby showing that they are not infallible.

6. Holy Scripture is the supreme authority in settling essential questions.

7. Conciliar decisions must be proved to be in harmony with Holy Scripture.

ARTICLE XXII

Of Purgatory.	*De Purgatorio.*
The Romish Doctrine concerning purgatory, pardons, worshipping and adoration as well of images as of reliques, and also invocation of saints, is a fond thing vainly invented, and grounded upon no warranty of Scripture, but rather repugnant to the Word of God.	Doctrina Romanensium de purgatorio, de indulgentiis, de veneratione et adoratione tum imaginum tum reliquiarum, nec non de invocatione sanctorum, res est futilis, inaniter conficta, et nullis Scripturarum testimoniis innititur: immo verbo Dei contradicit.

IMPORTANT EQUIVALENTS.

Romish	= *Romanensium.*
Concerning pardons	= *de indulgentiis.*
Concerning worshipping	= *de veneratione.*
Is a fond thing, vainly invented	= *res est futilis, inaniter conficta.*
Upon no warranty	= *nullis testimoniis.*
[Is] repugnant	= *contradicit.*

THE place of this subject seems at first incorrect, but in reality it is quite appropriate because the Article deals with certain doctrines set forth by Church and Conciliar authority, which are here condemned as unscriptural. Thus they afford an example of the wrong use of that Church authority stated in Articles XX and XXI.

The title is incomplete compared with the contents, and this is probably due to the fact that the first subject, Purgatory, was regarded as the most important. It would seem as though the Article, while composed by the English Reformers, had been influenced by the Smalcaldic Article of 1537, which refers to these errors and speaks of them as " not grounded on Scripture," and as " most pernicious." In 1553, in the Latin *perniciose* was associated with *contradicit*, but this was omitted in 1563, probably as superfluous, because anything that contradicts God's Word stands self-condemned without the need of further description. Even, in 1553, the English had no equivalent for *perniciose*.

THE OPENING WORDS

One change made in 1563 calls for fuller attention. In 1553 the Article spoke of " the doctrine of the School authors," and this was changed in 1563 to " the Romish doctrine," with Latin *Romanensium*. Newman, in Tract XC, used this change to prove that the Article did not deny the primitive doctrine, but only the purely Roman teaching, especially as the Council of Trent did not promulgate its decrees on the subject of purgatory until December 1563, after the issue of the Article. Newman has been followed by several modern writers,[1] all taking the line that as the questions of purgatory and pardons were not discussed at Trent for many months after the publication of the Article the present statement cannot be interpreted to refer to the Tridentine doctrine, but simply designates " the extreme mediæval party." But in spite of this series of contentions many still hold that the Article means what it says, and refers to the current doctrine of the Roman Church. It is, of course, true that the Tridentine decrees were not promulgated until after the Article was issued, but it is often overlooked that the general and persistent teaching of the Roman Church was well known long before the decree was issued. Besides, our Articles were revised again in 1571, several years after Trent had finished its sittings. This Article in particular was the subject of verbal attention. Then, too, the Articles were once more promulgated by law in 1662.

The question may be said to have been settled beyond all reasonable doubt by the able discussion of the late Bishop of Salisbury, who argues with great force that " Romish " means " official Roman and Tridentine doctrine."[2] The use made of Hardwick by several writers[3] is easily shown to be inaccurate, and Hardwick's view can be seen in his statement that the object of the Article was to " condemn scholastic and Tridentine errors," while in another place he speaks of the significant change to " Romish," the " Tridentine Doctors having then made further progress in the building and consolidation of the Neo-Romish system."[4] Trent had really been sitting for seventeen years, though dormant for ten years, from 1552 to 1562, and its work must have been in view in 1563, especially as Roman Catholics in England and elsewhere held these views long before.[5] When, therefore, the decisions of the Council of Trent were promulgated it was easily seen that there was no essential difference between the authorised teaching and that which had been held in former days. The view that the Article refers to some extreme mediæval opinions[6] is clearly impossible, because apart from all this popular teaching it is not at all likely that our Reformers in 1563 would concern themselves with a party referred to forty years before. Besides, the doctrines here opposed are specifically Roman and not merely

---

[1] Forbes; Gibson; Darwell Stone; Kidd.

[2] Bishop Wordsworth, *The Invocation of Saints and the Twenty-second Article.*

[3] Gibson; Kidd; Tyrrell Green; Darwell Stone. Dr. Darwell Stone has since removed the reference to Hardwick as the result of the Bishop of Salisbury's criticisms.

[4] Hardwick, *History of the Articles of Religion,* pp. 389, 130. See also p. 84, and Note 1.

[5] Thus purgatory was promulgated at the Council of Florence, Indulgences by papal bulls, while the Veneration of Images and Invocation of Saints were in general practice. The received doctrine of the English Romanists at the time can be easily verified from Gardiner's *Articles,* issued as a test for heresy in 1555 (Cardwell, *Doc. Annals,* Vol. I, p. 164).

[6] B. J. Kidd, *On the Thirty-nine Articles,* p. 189.

extreme mediæval.[1] So that although the decrees were not promulgated until December 1563, the beliefs were already virtually sanctioned and could properly be described as " Romish." It has been pointed out that in the Articles of Smalcald these errors sprang out of the Mass, and the doctrines of the Mass were defined in September 1562, some months before the Articles of 1563, and the work of Trent was not intended to provide a new definition, but only a declaration of the existing doctrine as *de fide*, and that such doctrine should be thenceforward properly and universally held. In view of all these facts the change from " School authors " to " Romish " is perfectly intelligible and decidedly significant.[2]

ANALYSIS OF THE ARTICLE

As the Article is concerned with several different subjects it may be well to look at it as a whole before discussing its details.

I.—THE DOCTRINES OPPOSED

1. The Roman Catholic doctrine of Purgatory.
2. The Roman Catholic doctrine of Indulgences.
3. The Roman Catholic doctrine of the Worshipping and Adoration of Images.
4. The Roman Catholic doctrine of the Worshipping and Adoration of Relics.
5. The Roman Catholic doctrine of the Invocation of Saints.

II.—THE GROUNDS OF OPPOSITION

1. Their character.—" Fond "; Latin, *futilis*; silly, foolish, absurd.
2. Their origin.—" Vainly invented "; Latin, *inaniter conficta*; that is, falsely devised, founded on no substantial reason.
3. Their unscriptural character.—" Grounded upon no warranty of Scripture."
4. Their anti-scriptural character.—" But rather repugnant to the Word of God."

Language could not well be plainer, and the revision of 1563 is sufficient to show that Queen Elizabeth could hardly have been desirous of conciliating Roman Catholics while she permitted such a significant change in an anti-Roman direction. Further, the idea sometimes suggested that it was only the Roman and not the general practice which

---

[1] Tyrrell Green, who favours the view that the Article refers to current teaching rather than to Tridentine doctrine, nevertheless remarks that:
"The change of this expression to 'Romish doctrine' in the Elizabethan revision is significant; it was doubtless made because our Reformers were realising that the Church of Rome, at the Council of Trent, was adopting the teaching of the later Schoolmen as its own" (*The Thirty-nine Articles and the Age of the Reformation*, p. 147).

[2] This point and the general question are discussed fully in *Doctrina Romanensium De Invocatione Sanctorum*, by H. F. Stewart, with Introduction by Bishop Wordsworth of Salisbury.

was denounced is disproved by the simple fact that at that time the Roman doctrine was the only one in existence.

PURGATORY

The Roman Catholic doctrine of Purgatory, according to the Council of Trent, is that " There is a purgatory, and that souls there detained are helped by the suffrages of the faithful, especially by the acceptable sacrifice of the altar " (Session xxv). This doctrine arises out of the belief that after the pardon of eternal punishment there still remains " a guilt of temporal punishment to be paid for either in this world, or in the future in purgatory " (Session vi, Canon 30). In order that we may arrive at the proper attitude to the doctrine which the Article opposes it is necessary to study the steps by which it was reached, for although it is said to have been " vainly invented " it is important to give attention to its history. No system can stand long if it is wholly erroneous, and we must, therefore, not only study the fact, but also endeavour to find out the reason of the error, by examining its growth and development. It is well known, and, indeed, universally acknowledged that no doctrine of Purgatory was taught in the primitive Church. It is sometimes thought to have arisen gradually in two ways : (1) out of prayers for the dead ; (2) by reason of the difficulty of conceiving the possibility of a future judgment for the mass of nominal Christians. From these came at length the idea of an ordeal after death. Then it would appear that with the thought and desire already in the mind, Scripture was searched, though to do this after the notions are formed is a dangerous method. One passage was of great interest (1 Cor. iii. 15), because of its reference to fire, though the context might have been supposed to prove at once the thought of testing and judgment, not of purification.

But apart from (or, at least, in addition to) any Christian speculation, the idea of a future purgation seems to have come definitely into Christianity from without, for Plato had three divisions : the good, the bad, and the middle, the last being purged. Neo-Platonism developed this, and Origen seems to have derived his doctrine from this source, for though he believed in pre-existence he maintained a purgatory. The earliest Christian writers make no mention of Purgatory while writing fully on the future life.[1] The evidence of the catacombs is to the same effect, for while there are expressions of desire for prayers there is no trace at all of anything like the doctrine of Purgatory. It is said that the first hint is found in Tertullian,[2] but the idea does not seem to have

---

[1] Athenagoras, p. 177, on "The Resurrection" (Clark, *Ante-Nicene Christian Library*, pp. 423–456; Irenæus, Hippolytus, Novatian, and Cyprian (*op. cit.*, Vols. VIII, IX, XIII). Clement of Rome and Ignatius both definitely speak of the future without any allusion whatever to purgatory (*op cit.*, Vols. I and XXV).

[2] Clark, *Ante-Nicene Library*, Vol. XV, pp. 539–541; Vol. XVIII, pp. 17, 41. Apart from the references in Tertullian, the Acts of Perpetua, and a passage in Clement of Alexandria, Gibson remarks that: "It is thought that no passage can fairly be quoted as implying a belief in a purgatory between death and judgment till we come to the fourth century" (*The Thirty-nine Articles*, p. 544).

been endorsed until the time of Ambrose and Augustine. Yet even this was not a doctrine identical with the later teaching of Rome. Gregory the Great, 600, was the first eminent personage who propounded a purgatory between death and judgment for slight offences.[1] This belief was promoted by legends, and the Schoolmen of the Middle Ages discussed purgation. At length the Council of Florence, 1439, declared the fact, and this is the first Conciliar Church judgment, though the doctrine had long before been held and taught with serious practical results. Thus we have the three inevitable stages of (1) mere speculation; (2) common opinion; (3) enforced truth.

The attitude of the Greek Church on this subject is of particular interest. Although from early days the Eastern Church has observed the practice of prayers for the dead, this has never been connected with any doctrine of purgatory. The Greek delegates at the Council of Florence were prevailed upon by the Pope to accept the doctrine, but on their return home they retracted, and threw themselves on the mercy of their brethren at home who had been offended by their adhesion. The rival Council of Basle had disowned the doctrine in its own name and in the name of the Eastern Church, adding, that " it ought to be cast out of the Church," while Bishop Fisher, who suffered under Henry VIII, frankly confessed that Purgatory had been rarely, if at all, mentioned by ancient writers. It can, therefore, be proved beyond doubt, and, indeed, is owned by competent Roman Catholic writers, that no Council or Father for five centuries taught the doctrine.[2]

The Council of Trent included a belief in Purgatory as essential, but avoided definite statements on subjects whereon Roman Catholic divines differed. The fact was asserted, and it was said that souls were helped by prayers and sacraments. The Council seemed rather to take the doctrine for granted than to define it, but in the Catechism drawn up by order of the Council there is a reference to purgatorial fire. Cardinal Bellarmine defined it as a prison where souls are purged which were not wholly purified on earth.

It is necessary at this point to recall the clear and important distinction between the Roman Catholic doctrine of Purgatory and a general belief in spiritual progress in the intermediate state. The latter may be held apart from any thought of Purgatory, for the Roman doctrine is really part of a penal process, the payment of a debt which was not fully discharged on earth, a view based on the distinction between mortal and venial sins.[3] But to carry the penal consequences of sin into the next world is really to deny the fulness and completeness of Atonement and Justification. We have already seen that our sole ground of acceptance with God is the " one oblation " of our Lord Jesus Christ " once offered "

---

[1] "Sed tamen de quibusdam levibus culpis esse ante judicum purgatorius ignis credendus est. Sed tamen hoc de parvis minimisque peccatis fieri posse credendum est; sicut est assiduus otiosus sermo, immoderatus risus," etc. (*Dial.* IV, C. XXXIX).

[2] Macbride, *Lectures on the Articles*, p. 376.

[3] Litton, *Introduction to Dogmatic Theology* (Second Edition), p. 308 ff.

as " a full, perfect, and sufficient sacrifice, oblation, and satisfaction, for
the sins of the whole world." So that the Roman Catholic doctrine of
Purgatory as a satisfaction to God for part of the punishment due to sin
seriously detracts from the perfection of Calvary, and from the Justification that comes through the acceptance by faith of the Divine Atonement.
And this is no doubt the reason why the Church of Rome is so bitterly
hostile to the doctrine of Justification by Faith. Besides, what are we
to say of those who will die on the eve of Christ's coming, and of the
living at the time of His return ? There can be no Purgatory for them.
Further, Purgatory tends to rob the soul of peace, and to fill it with fear
of the future. Scripture shows clearly that those who are now with
Christ are entirely free from sin and sinning. The Burial Service is
quite clear on this point : " After they are delivered from the burden
of the flesh, are in joy and felicity."[1] Then, too, the doctrine of Purgatory lends itself to the sad and deplorable practice of Masses for the dead.
The Church of Rome admits that there is entire uncertainty as to
the future of the person and cannot guarantee what number of Masses are
necessary to take a soul out of Purgatory, yet the practice obtains for
offering Masses for the repose of the soul, relatives paying for these
exercises in the hope of at least relieving the sufferings of those who have
passed away.

The question of Prayers for the Dead, though it is believed that the
practice is not in accord with Scripture or with the Church of England
formularies,[2] need not, and should not be associated with the Roman
Catholic doctrine of Purgatory. As already observed, the Greek Church
prays for the dead without holding any doctrine of Purgatory, and even
Roman Catholic commemorations of the dead in the Mass are found
without any allusions to Purgatory. There are also prayers to the Virgin
Mary and others, who are certainly not in Purgatory. The serious
objection to the Roman position is that (1) it teaches the actual certainty
of such a place of Purgatory ; (2) it permits the wildest teaching on the
subject ; (3) and often associates with it the system of Indulgences.
Roman Catholic writers make little of Scripture on this subject, and when
once the question of prayers for the dead is separated from that of Purgatory the warrant for the latter falls entirely to the ground.[3] We therefore maintain the truth of the Article that the Roman doctrine of Purgatory is (a) " a fond thing," contradictory to reason, derogatory to the
perfect satisfaction of Christ's Atonement and opposed to the justice of
God ; (b) that it is " vainly invented," having been derived very largely

[1] Scripture nowhere warrants the view of a "second chance," but teaches that the
present life is final (2 Cor. v. 10). The New Testament references to the state of the
pious dead are entirely opposed to any idea of purification (John v. 24; Phil. i. 23;
2 Tim. iv. 8; Rev. xiv. 13).
[2] See Additional Note, "Prayers for the Dead," p. 508.
[3] Passages which seem to suggest a limitation of punishment cannot be utilised to
prove a purgatory, while 1 Cor. iii. 15 is absolutely outside the question. See also
Gibson, ut supra, p. 549.

from sources outside Christianity ; (c) that it is not Scriptural, nothing in the Word of God being found to support it ; (d) that it is " repugnant to the Word of God," being opposed to some of the fundamental principles of the Gospel of Christ.

As the Latin of the Article suggests, this reference to the system of In-dulgences, which is an essential part of the doctrine of the Church of Rome, is closely and vitally connected with that of Purgatory.[1] And yet the doctrine of Indulgences is very difficult to define, because the Council of Trent is vague and general on the subject. The Creed of Pope Pius IV claims that the power of indulgences was left by our Lord in the Church, and that the use is salutary. The Council of Trent practically says the same thing, but orders the suppression of abuses. What, then, is an indulgence ? We have already seen something of the distinction between mortal and venial sin, between sin that involves eternal punish-ment, and sin that is concerned with temporal punishment alone. The eternal and temporal punishment of sin committed before Baptism is remitted in that Sacrament. The eternal punishment of sin after Baptism is remitted in Absolution, but the temporal punishment due to sin after Baptism is not necessarily remitted in Absolution, and the result is that a man has still to suffer the temporal punishment of that which has been spiritually and eternally forgiven. This temporal punishment often takes the form of penances imposed by the priest, but as the punishments endured on earth do not always exhaust the temporal punishment required, the result is that Purgatory is provided for further temporal punishment, and indulgences are exercised by the Pope to relieve souls in Purgatory from part of this temporal punishment.

Here, again, it is necessary to consider the history which led up to the Mediæval and Roman practice. In the Decian persecution, those who lapsed through persecution were permitted to return to the fellowship of the Church if they obtained " Letters of Peace " (libelli pacis) from a martyr, and the Council of Nicæa, 325, allowed Bishops to excuse the severity of penal Canons as might be required. But in the twelfth century the Pope began to claim the right of dispensing what was then called the Thesaurus supererogationis.[2] Indulgences were the immediate cause of Luther's protest against Rome. His indignation was provoked by the Indulgences issued by Leo X to provide for the rebuilding of St. Peter's, Rome, in magnificent style.

Now church discipline is right and necessary, and we may even go

[1] Indulgentia was originally used of "gentleness," and then came to be employed as a legal term, meaning a remission of punishment or taxation. This seems to have been the source of the Christian usage of the term, meaning either the remission of sins, or the relief of ecclesiastical penalties (Gibson, ut supra, p. 555; Maclear and Williams, Introduction to the Articles of the Church of England, p. 269).
[2] See Article XIV.

so far as to say that there was nothing essentially wrong in money fines and computations, except that they were dangerous in giving an undue power to wealth. But when the power was extended beyond the grave the error became evident and serious. Although the Council of Trent, as we have seen, declared that the power was bestowed by Christ, and enjoined moderation in use, and forbade abuse, yet this has not been adhered to, and now popular teaching is almost as bad as it was in the sixteenth century. In Spain and elsewhere Indulgences flourish and are easily obtained at very small cost.[1] The four grounds of rejection of this Roman doctrine, already noted in connection with purgatory, need no discussion; they are only too self-evident.[2]

VENERATION OF RELICS AND IMAGES

Jewish Christianity abhorred everything of this kind, and in the earliest days of the Christian Church it was equally impossible. It only came in later, and both Clement of Alexandria and Origen are against even the making of images. The Council of Elvira, in Spain, 305, was against the use of pictures in church. At first, like the remains of Poly-carp after his martyrdom, these relics were only a memorial of the dead, but later on the belief sprang up that if prayer was offered before them there would be some special power in the petition. At length came a belief in their miracle-working power, and as the result pilgrimages were made to shrines. Now it is impossible to deny that in these practices some reverence is paid to the relic or image in itself. In the eighth century the Iconoclastic controversy arose, and the Council of Constantinople, 754, suppressed images, but the West, while permitting them, prohibited worship and rejected the decree of Constantinople. At the Council of Nicæa, 787, the decision of Constantinople was reversed, and "salutary honour" was ordered to be paid to images, though not the supreme honour due to God alone. Charlemagne, 794, and the Council of Frankfort, condemned this Council of Nicæa as against Scripture and the Fathers. Thus, in spite of powerful voices, like those of Epiphanius and Augustine, against the practice the fourth century concessions to heathenism bore fruit. The story of Martin of Tours is a striking illustration of the extent of the error. The Council of Trent is merely general on this point, and says that images are to be venerated and retained in churches, while relics are to be honoured and are profitable for invocation, yet that this must be so only in reference to the person represented. It is sometimes said that Roman Catholics worship God through

---

[1] Proof of this can be seen in *Romish Indulgences of To-day*, by Fulano; *Indulgences*, by Rev. R. G. S. King (Dublin: Church of Ireland Printing Co.); *Some Thoughts on Purgatory* (London: Irish Church Missions); *The Controversy Concerning the Spanish Bull of Composition* (London: C. J. Thynne).
[2] It is scarcely necessary to do more than refer to Bishop Lightfoot's criticism of the Romanist commentators, who endeavour to found on Col. i. 24 the doctrine of the merits of the Saints and Indulgences (Lightfoot, *Colossians*, p. 233).

U

the images, and do not for a moment worship the images themselves. But the heathen could say the same. Both in the past and in the present this is urged by the devotees of false religions. The Second Commandment is of permanent obligation, and St. Paul is quite clear as to the doctrine of worshipping God under the form of anything made by man's device (Acts xvii. 29). Nor is it quite accurate to say that no adoration is given to the images themselves, for both the Council of Trent and the Creed of Pope Pius IV speak of " due honour and meet veneration," while, of course, not defining what is to be understood by " due " and " meet." All this implies that inordinate craving for the visible, which is a prominent feature of natural and unspiritual religion, together with the characteristic inability of such natures to conceive of the invisible as real. Once again we may recall the plain words of the Article, and say that these practices are indeed " fond things, vainly invented, and grounded upon no warranty of Scripture, but rather repugnant to the Word of God."

THE INVOCATION OF SAINTS

This practice grew up side by side with the veneration of images, and nothing was known of it in the Church for at least three hundred years. It started with the words, *ora pro nobis*, but soon went beyond this request for their intercessions. As the New Testament says that angels are ministers, the idea was extended to the tutelage of saints, who came to be thought of as God's ministers for good. In the Old Testament there is, of course, no hint of anything of the kind, and if the Jews had no need, this is still more true of Christians. Not even the mediæval doctrine of the *Limbus Patrum* availed in opposition to the silence of the Old Testament. But not only is there no trace of the practice in primitive Christianity, there is much against it. The earliest writers urge in the strongest way that Christians should worship none but God. Justin Martyr said :—

" It becomes Christians to worship God only."[1]

Tertullian :—

" For the safety of the Emperor, we invoke God, eternal, true, and living God. . . . Nor can I pray to any other than to Him, from whom I am sure that I may obtain, because He alone can give it."[2]

While the early Christians had a genuine, living belief in the communion of saints they never contemplated the possibility of addressing departed saints in prayer. This would really involve giving to saints quasi-angelic power, and the extent of which this is capable of going may be seen in the practice of Mariolatry.

[1] *Apology*, I, p. 63.   [2] *Apology*, Cap. XXX.

The Council of Trent takes a moderate line on this subject, saying that the saints pray for us and that it is, therefore, useful to invoke them. Rome also distinguishes between *latria*, the worship to be paid to God only; *dulia*, the worship or reverence to be paid to saints and angels, and *hyperdulia*, the devotion paid to the Mother of our Lord. But no such distinction can be found either in Scripture or in the primitive Church, and certainly ordinary people never distinguish between higher and lower forms of worship. If saints and angels can be addressed, then they must in some way be regarded as superhuman and semi-divine. But such a practice cannot help interfering with the sole mediation of our Lord Jesus Christ. Several references in the New Testament clearly indicate the impossibility of the practice (Acts x. 25; xiv. 14; Rev. xix. 10). An appeal to saints and angels of necessity involves virtual idolatry, since it means the interposition of someone between God and ourselves. It was this that elicited St. Paul's severe condemnation (Col. ii. 18). While, therefore, it is right to recognise to the full the balance and moderation of the Tridentine decree on the subject of the Invocation of Saints, it is impossible to overlook the deplorable extent to which popular practice has always gone in past days and at present.[1] In view of what has been adduced it is hardly necessary even to quote again the words of the Article, that this practice is " a fond thing, vainly invented, and grounded upon no warranty of Scripture, but rather repugnant to the Word of God."

But the subject has obtained fuller consideration during recent years by being associated with what is called " Comprecation." It is said that while direct invocation of saints is not permissible, we may rightly appeal to God for the prayers of departed saints, and that this practice of Comprecation is not to be regarded as condemned by the Article.[2] The entire question of the true meaning of the Article on this point has been fully discussed by the (late) Bishop of Salisbury, in the booklet already mentioned.[3] As the Bishop points out, the real question is whether Comprecation was in the minds of those who were responsible for the Articles of 1563 and 1571.[4] Not only is there no trace in Scripture of any such Comprecation, but no early authorities in the Church can be adduced in support of it. The entire absence of Scripture teaching as to

---

[1] Among many other examples the following may be adduced: (1) From certain prayers which have received Papal sanction and are specially "indulgenced" we may take the following: "Leave me not, my Mother, in my own hands, or I am lost. Let me but cling to thee; save me, my hope; save me from hell." (2) Many passages can be quoted from Liguori's *Glories of Mary*, a book which has received the highest sanction in the Roman Catholic Church. "Often we shall be heard more quickly and be thus preserved, if we have recourse to Mary, and call upon her name, than we should be if we called upon the name of Jesus our Saviour. Many things are asked from God and are not granted; they are asked from Mary and are obtained. . . . Mary so loved the world, that she gave her only-begotten Son."

[2] B. J. Kidd, *On the Articles*, p. 199 ff.; Gibson, *ut supra*, p. 569 f.; Gayford, Article, "Invocation of Saints," *Prayer Book Dictionary*; Darwell Stone, *Invocation of Saints*.

[3] *The Invocation of Saints and the Twenty-second Article*. Second and Revised Edition with new Preface. See also Stewart, *ut supra*.

[4] *Ut supra*, p. 5.

what is the life of the departed saints makes the idea of very doubtful strength. Nor can it be regarded as spiritually healthy to associate the possibility of the mediation of saints with our direct approach to God.

A still more recent pronouncement pleading for Comprecation was made by the Bishop of London at the Southampton Church Congress, 1913, in which he associated the practice with our belief in the communion of saints. But it is well known that the primary interpretation of that Article in the Creed had no reference whatever to the practice of Comprecation,[1] and our knowledge of the life of the departed is far too slight to permit us to base any such serious and definite practice upon it. Bishop Wordsworth well points out that God has concealed from us much that we should like to know because it is better for us to be ignorant.

"Therefore, in framing theories about this communion of saints, we should take our ignorance to be His will, and adapt all our actions to that will."[2]

Then, too, there is the question of how we are to reconcile the statement of Article VIII which teaches that we receive the Creeds because they can be proved by Scripture, and the description of the Invocation of Saints in Article XXII as "a fond thing, vainly invented, and grounded upon no warranty of Scripture, but rather repugnant to the Word of God." It is surely impossible to think of Comprecation as being in any way included in a belief in the Communion of Saints in view of the plain statements of the latter Article. And if it should be admitted that Comprecation is not contemplated by Article XXII, then the practice obviously finds no warrant within the formularies, or in any other representative authority of the Church of England, to say nothing of the entire silence of Scripture.

We may go further, and raise the question whether Supplication is a part of the worship behind the veil. We know from Scripture that our Lord is interceding on behalf of His people, but the question whether intercession implies supplication is a matter of very serious hesitation. It would almost seem as though the idea of our Lord as a Suppliant involves an entirely unworthy conception of Him in the presence of the Father, and it is in every way truer to think of His intercession as satisfied by His presence above as "our Advocate with the Father." At any rate, two modern writers have suggested this idea in words that call for careful consideration :—

"The modern conception of Christ pleading in Heaven His Passion, 'offering His blood' on behalf of men, has no foundation in the Epistle. His glorified humanity is the eternal pledge of the absolute efficacy of His accomplished work. He pleads, as older writers truly expressed the thought, by His Presence on the Father's throne."[3]

"The intercession of the ascended Christ is not a prayer but a life. The New

[1] So, Swete, *The Apostles' Creed, in loc.*   [2] *Ut supra*, p. xii.
[3] Westcott, *The Epistle to the Hebrews* p. 230.

Testament does not represent Him as an *orante*, standing ever before the Father, and with outstretched arms, like the figure in the mosaics of the Catacombs, and with strong crying and tears pleading our cause in the presence of a reluctant God ; but as a throned Priest-King, asking what He will from a Father who always hears and grants His request. Our Lord's life in Heaven is His prayer."[1]

If, then, it is unnecessary for our Lord to pray for us, there is certainly no room for the supplication of others. But whether this is so or not, there is nothing in Scripture to afford any encouragement of the view that departed saints offer supplication on our behalf.

One other point seems to call for some notice in connection with this subject. Latimer's name is frequently used in support of the practice of the Invocation of Saints, by the quotation of some words of his preached in Bristol in 1533, in which he said that " By way of intercession saints in heaven may be mediators and pray for us." But it is unfair to quote statements made as early as 1533, without placing alongside of them his more fully developed views. Thus, in a sermon preached in 1552, after saying that we may learn much goodness from the shepherds who went to Bethlehem, he adds, " We may not make gods of them, or call upon them, as we have been taught in times past ; because God will be called upon, honoured, and worshipped alone." Still stronger language can be adduced, bearing the same date, in which prayer to the saints is described as " most abominable idolatry." It may be said without any question or qualification that there is no adequate ground for believing that the Reformers of the sixteenth century, after they had entered upon the full light of their position, ever advocated this practice, while there is no representative Reformed divine of post-Reformation days who is an advocate of it. Bishop Wordsworth's discussion of the various authors adduced is sufficient to show the essential weakness of any attempt to produce support for this practice in the Reformed English Church, and the conclusion drawn by the Bishop may be stated in his own words :—

" I am constrained to say that I have found the arguments in favour of the laxer interpretation of the Article even weaker than I had expected. They are, indeed, so weak that I have some hope that those who have hitherto used them will feel it necessary at least to shift their ground."[2]

And the Bishop adds that there cannot be any consistent advocacy of invocation in the face of the Article, which speaks of it as " futile " and " repugnant to the Word of God " :—

" As long as the Articles remain unaltered we clergy of the Church of England are bound to defer to them in our own sphere so far as not to contradict them on any point of principle in our teaching."[3]

The entire practice, whether of direct Invocation, or of mediate Comprecation, reveals an apparently inherent tendency in unspiritual and

[1] Swete, *The Ascended Christ*, p. 95.   [2] *Ut supra*, p. 5.   [3] *Ut supra*, p. 63.

human nature to fear the holiness of God, and by stopping short of it to seek the influence of an intermediary. But this is in reality what St. Paul describes as " voluntary humility," which is false to the very idea of true Christian life. When once the soul has entered into a personal experience of what is meant by " fellowship with the Father, and with His Son Jesus Christ," there can be no thought of any intermediary. It is, therefore, not untrue to say that at the basis of the practice of the Invocation of Saints is the " evil heart of unbelief," which, under the guise of humility and unwillingness to approach God, occupies itself with beings who are thought to have more power with God than those for whom Christ died.[1] In the face of the full, deep, rich teaching of Holy Scripture concerning the direct approach of the soul to God, and the numerous invitations to " draw near with full assurance of faith," anything short of this really amounts to practical distrust and disobedience.[2]

---

[1] In *Les Origines du Culte des Martyrs*, by Père Delahaye, S.J., it is shown that the Cultus of the Saints arose out of that of the Martyrs, that in the earliest times no such Cultus existed, that it was not, and could not be, intended to be taught in the doctrine of the Communion of Saints, that there is no real trace of the Cultus before Nicæa, and that the practice arose largely out of the half-converted heathenism introduced into Christianity at and after the time of Constantine. These and other points are frankly admitted by the Rev. F. W. Puller in the *English Church Review* for 1914. They support entirely the view maintained above that our Church knows nothing either of Invocation or Comprecation.

[2] For all the questions connected with this Article, reference should be made to Dearden, *Modern Romanism Examined*, pp. 195–221; 269 297.

IV. THE HOUSEHOLD OF FAITH—*continued*

CORPORATE RELIGION

B. THE MINISTRY (ARTICLES XXIII–XXIV)

23. MINISTERING IN THE CONGREGATION.

24. SPEAKING IN THE CONGREGATION IN SUCH A TONGUE AS THE PEOPLE UNDERSTANDETH.

ARTICLE XXIII

Of Ministering in the Congregation.	De Ministrando in Ecclesia.
It is not lawful for any man to take upon him the office of public preaching, or ministering the Sacraments in the Congregation, before he be lawfully called, and sent, to execute the same. And those we ought to judge lawfully called and sent, which be chosen and called to this work by men who have public authority given unto them in the Congregation, to call and send Ministers into the Lord's vineyard.	Non licet cuiquam sumere sibi munus publice prædicandi, aut administrandi Sacramenta in Ecclesia, nisi prius fuerit ad hæc obeunda legitime vocatus et missus. Atque illos legitime vocatos et missos existimare debemus, qui per homines, quibus potestas vocandi ministros, atque mittendi in vineam Domini, publice concessa est in Ecclesia, co-optati fuerint et adsciti in hoc opus.

IMPORTANT EQUIVALENTS.

In the Congregation	=	*in Ecclesia* (as in Article XIX).
Lawfully called	=	*legitime vocatos.*
To execute the same	=	*ad hæc obeunda.*
Be chosen	=	*co-optati fuerint.*
Public authority given	=	*potestas publice concessa.*
Called to this work	=	*adsciti in hoc opus.*

From the Church to the ministry is a natural step, as the ministry is that through which the Church mainly grows. The title of the Article dates from 1571. The corresponding Articles of 1553 and 1563 were " *Nemo in Ecclesia ministret nisi vocatus* (No man may minister in the congregation except he be called)." The term "congregation" is identical with its meaning in Articles XIX and XX, the body of Christ's followers.

The Article is derived partly from the Confession of Augsburg and partly from the Thirteen Articles of the Concordat, 1538.[1] On this account it is studiously broad, emphasising the principles common to all the Reformed communities, and it is, therefore, necessary to turn to Article XXXVI for the specific Church of England view of the ministry.

The Article was probably directed against the Anabaptists, who went to the extreme of denying the need of any public authority and recognition of ministry, urging that anyone could become a minister since Divine illumination was sufficient.[2]

---

[1] Hardwick, *History of the Articles of Religion*, p. 20.

[2] "Similis est illorum amentia, qui institutionem ministrorum ab Ecclesia disjungunt, negantes in certis locis certos doctores, pastores atque ministros collocari debere; nec admittunt legitimas vocationes, nec solemnem manuum impositionem, sed per omnes publice docendi potestatem divulgant, qui sacris literis utcunque sunt aspersi et Spiritum sibi vendicant; nec illos solum adhibent ad docendum, sed etiam ad moderandam Ecclesiam et distribuenda sacramenta; quæ sane universa cum scriptis Apostolorum manifeste pugnant" (*Reformatio Legum, De Hæresibus*, c. 16).

I.—THE FACT OF THE MINISTRY

It should be observed at the outset that the Article refers to ministry in the " congregation " or " church," and therefore has nothing to do with what may be called private or unofficial ministry for Christ.

That there is such a thing in the New Testament as ministry is obvious, and the only question is as to its character. Prior to the Day of Pentecost our Lord's teaching and action pointed in the direction of men rather than institutions, of character rather than organisation, and yet there was an inevitable association of men with Himself. Such illustrations as " salt " and " light," and such metaphors as " city," " flock," " kingdom," clearly imply unity in relation to Himself. But thus far no trace can be found of a definite constitution, everything being left to the Holy Spirit as the Guide into all truth.

Another point of great importance is that the modern distinction between clergy and laity is not found in the New Testament, since κλῆρος means " the people of God " (1 Pet. v. 3, Greek). Yet there is a clear distinction between special ministries within the Church and the general service of the whole Church; the differences in the New Testament are of gifts and functions, not of office and order.

1. The Source of Ministry.—Concentrating attention on the time following the Day of Pentecost we observe that ministry comes from a Divine gift (Eph. iv. 11, 12). Christians were first disciples (John i. 37), and then more specifically " ministers " (Mark iii. 14). All true ministry starts here.[1]

2. The Proof of Ministry.—This is found in a recognition of the Divine equipment to ministry on the part of the existing body of believers, just as we see it in connection with the seven who were recognised by the Christians at Jerusalem as men fitted for the work (Acts vi. 3). This, of course, involves spiritual perception on the part of the Church.

3. The Commission of Ministry.—This is seen in the appointment or ordination, by the existing ministry, of the divinely equipped and ecclesiastically recognised men. Again, an illustration is afforded in the story of the seven who were both selected by the Jewish Church and commissioned by the Apostles (Acts vi. 1-6). The same principle is observed elsewhere (Acts xiv. 23; Tit. i. 5). The words used in connection with this commission are χειροτονεῖν, and καθιστάναι. The original idea seems to have been a " show of hands," or a " lifting up of hands in benediction," and it was only a long time afterwards that the meaning of the words was changed from appointment to ordination in the technical sense.[2] It is clear that the laying on of hands, whatever it meant, was not by the Apostles alone (1 Tim. iv. 13, 14), and the true

---

[1] Nothing need be said in the present connection of the society of Jewish believers that existed before Christ came. We are concerned with the specific Christian Church and ministry.

[2] Smith's *Dictionary of Christian Antiquities*, Vol. II, p. 1501 f.; Article, "Ordination."

idea of the laying on of hands seems to be that of benediction, following the Old Testament analogy.[1] St. Augustine associates the action of the laying on of hands with prayer, and so does the Roman Catholic Church. It is noteworthy that Pope Leo XIII said that the laying on of hands has no significance in itself.[2]

So far we notice that the New Testament conception of ministry is first of all that of a gift, and only afterwards of an office. Spiritual qualification comes first and ecclesiastical commission follows. If the second is emphasised apart from the first the result will be spiritual disaster; if the first is emphasised without the second there will be ecclesiastical disorder. The normal idea of New Testament ministry is the exercise of the spiritual gift in the ecclesiastical office.

The Article takes up the ministry at the third point, emphasising the external call following the inward equipment. " It is not lawful for any man to take upon him the office of public preaching, or ministering the Sacraments in the congregation, before he be lawfully called, and sent to execute the same." The inward requirement is not mentioned here because it is necessarily assumed, and is therefore stated in the Ordinal, the ordination being the recognition of the inward call and qualification. The Article speaks of men being " called " and " sent " by those " who have public authority to call and send ministers into the Lord's vineyard." The Latin equivalents expressive of the power of commission are interesting and significant : *co-optati et adsciti*. The ordination is by men " co-opted " and " adopted " for this work. It is generally understood that the distinction between " called " and " sent " is between the general summons into the ministry, and the commission to exercise it in a particular place.

II.—THE PURPOSE OF THE MINISTRY

1. The Work of the Ministry is two-fold, Evangelisation and Edification (Eph. iv. 11, Greek). The New Testament is quite clear on this point. The minister, in the words of the Ordinal, is to " seek for Christ's

---

[1] "Another question which goes to the root of the matter is that as to the significance of the laying on of hands. It is, no doubt, a widespread idea that this denotes *transmission*—the transmission of a property possessed by one person to another. But it cannot really mean this. It is a common accompaniment of 'blessing'—*i.e.* of the invoking of blessing. It is God who blesses or bestows the gift; and it is in no way implied that the gift is previously possessed by him who invokes it. True, that 'the less is blessed of the greater'; but that does not mean that the greater *imparts* a blessing. When we come to think of this, it seems clear enough; and the inference suggested is one for which we may be thankful. It may save us from some mechanical and unworthy ways of conceiving historic continuity, which is just as real without them" (Sanday, *The Conception of Priesthood*, p. 167; cf. p. 56 f.).

"Highly probable that (as a matter of fact) laying on of hands was largely practised in the Ecclesiæ of the Apostolic Age as a rite introductory to ecclesiastical office. But as the New Testament tells us no more than what has been already mentioned, it can hardly be likely that any essential principle was held to be involved in it" (Hort, *The Christian Ecclesia*, p. 216).

[2] C. A. Scott, *Evangelical Doctrine Bible Truth*, p. 240.

sheep that are dispersed abroad, and for His children who are in the midst of this naughty world, that they may be saved through Christ for ever." This includes the winning and the watching of souls, the bringing them into the Kingdom, and the building of them up in their most holy faith. It is impossible to read the New Testament without seeing that the minister is beyond everything a preacher and a teacher of the Gospel. The various titles connected with the ministry show the paramount importance placed on the ministry of the Word.[1]

2. The New Testament is clear that government is no part of the purpose of the ministry. Even St. Paul said: "Not that we have dominion over your faith, but are helpers of your joy " (2 Cor. i. 24). While ministers are spoken of in terms of great respect, and obedience to them is urged (Heb. xiii. 7, 17), yet this never went as far as government of the Church by the ministry. This is not vested in the ministry alone, or in the people alone, but in both combined, in the Church as a whole. Following the New Testament precedent the laity, as we understand the term, have a voice in the selection of their clergy, but not in the actual ministerial commission. This idea of government of the Church by the whole Church is seen in the Synodical arrangements of the Episcopal Churches of the United States, Ireland, Canada, and Australia. It was the ideal, and also the actual, arrangement made at the Reformation for the English Church, when Convocation and Parliament represented the entire community of clergy and laity. It is the confusion connected with Establishment in England that now makes the realisation of this ideal impossible.

3. Nor is mediation any proper part of the purpose of the Christian ministry. The New Testament never uses the word " priest " to describe the minister. Indeed, in the singular number it is only found of Christ, and His Priesthood is said to be " undelegated " or " intransmissible " (Heb. vii. 24). When it is used of the Church it is always in the plural, " priests " (Rev. i. 6), or collectively, " priesthood " (1 Pet. ii. 5). The truth, therefore, is that Christianity *is*, not *has*, a priesthood. The silence of the New Testament on this point is a simple and yet significant fact. It is what Bishop Lightfoot calls " the eloquent silence of the Apostolic writings."[2] And if it be said that the question is not one of words, but of things, Bishop Lightfoot may again be quoted : " This is undeniable, but words express things, and the silence of the Apostles still requires an explanation."[3] Neither the name nor the thing is found in the New Testament idea of the Christian ministry, and the reason is that it is irreconcilable with the letter and spirit of Apostolic Christianity. In regard to the priesthood " Christianity stands apart from all the older religions," for it is " the characteristic distinction of Christianity " to have

---

[1] Thus, the minister is a "herald," an "evangelist," a "witness," an "ambassador," a "servant," a "shepherd," a "teacher." The various verbs used to express the work of the ministry point in the same direction: to "evangelise," to "announce," to "herald," to "reason," to "teach," to "testify."

[2] Lightfoot, *The Christian Ministry*, p. 3.   [3] Lightfoot, *ut supra*, p. 129.

no such provision.[1] Three things invariably go together; priest, altar, and sacrifice, and where there is no offering there is no need of an altar; where there is no altar there is no sacrifice; where there is no sacrifice there is no priest. As Hooker says: "Sacrifice is no part of the Christian ministry."[2] The New Testament is clear as to the absence of sacrifice, and in regard to the absence of an altar, Bishop Westcott points out that the term "altar" in Heb. xiii. 10 is inapplicable to the Lord's Table, and, indeed, incongruous. He remarks that any such application to a material object would have been impossible in the early days. To the same effect, Lightfoot points out that St. Paul had a special opportunity of using the word "altar" in connection with the Lord's Supper (1 Cor. x), but that he quite evidently avoided it.

It is sometimes said, however, that our Lord's words in St. John xx. 19-23 constituted the ministry a priesthood. First of all, it is now generally recognised that these words were spoken not to the ministry only, but to the whole Church as there represented.[3] Then the question arises as to whether in any case the words can possibly be made to mean a sacerdotal priesthood. There seems to be some confusion in such an interpretation. A priest is one who represents man to God (Heb. v. 1), just as a prophet is one who represents God to man (Exod. vii. 1). The passage is clearly to be understood of a messenger from God to man, and this is the function of a prophet, not a priest. So that to speak of priestly absolution is really a contradiction, since the Old Testament priest never absolved, and absolution as a message from God to man is the work of a prophet, not of a priest. The title of a modern book, *Ministerial Priesthood*,"[4] is therefore strictly a contradiction in terms, because a ministry is not necessarily a priesthood; indeed, the representative character of the Christian ministry is not a priesthood at all. It is a beautiful and ingenious theory that the Church, like Christ, is priestly, and that therefore its ministers are the organs of the Church's priesthood, but this is really illusive, because it contains the doctrine of a special and specialised priesthood which is subversive of the New Testament priesthood of believers. Lightfoot explains the silence of the New Testament by pointing out that as there were no more sacrifices there were no more priests. It is only too easy to fall into fallacy and confusion by noticing how a view of ministerial priesthood develops from simple representation into substitution.[5]

The only passage approaching the idea of priestliness in ministerial functions is found in St. Paul's words concerning his own ministry (Rom. xv. 16). But the passage is quite evidently metaphorical, with preaching as the function and the Gentiles as the offering. On any showing the passage has no connection whatever with a "priest" offering or sacrificing the Holy Eucharist.

---

[1] Lightfoot, *ut supra*, p. 3.   [2] See Dimock, *The Sacerdotium of Christ*, pp. 79–81.
[3] This was admitted by all members of the Fulham Round Table Conference, 1901.   [4] By Dr. Moberly.
[5] Falconer, *From Apostle to Priest*, p. 285; Dulles, *The True Church*, pp. 245-247.

We, therefore, return to the New Testament view of the ministry, and call renewed attention to the striking fact of its absolute silence as to any special order of priests. The evidence taken separately in its parts is striking, but as a whole it is cumulative and overwhelming.[1] There is no function of the Christian priesthood which cannot be exercised by every individual believer at all times. Differences of function in the ministry exist, but none in the priesthood. It is almost impossible to exaggerate the importance of this simple, striking, and significant silence of the New Testament, that priestly mediation is no part of the purpose of the Christian ministry.[2]

In view of the foregoing it is sometimes asked why the term " priest " should have been retained in the Prayer Book, especially as it is well known that the word " altar " has been omitted since the Prayer Book of 1552.[3] The question is one of history, and calls for the careful attention of all the pertinent facts of the case. The English word " priest " has to do duty for two quite different sets of ideas and terms; πρεσβύτερος, " elder " and ἱερεύς, " priest." Lightfoot points out that it is a significant fact that in those languages which have only one word to express the two

[1] Bishop Westcott is reported to have observed in some of his lectures at Cambridge that the avoidance of the familiar term, "priest," was the nearest approach he knew to verbal inspiration. Some would venture a step further and take it as the unmistakable example of the superintending control of the Holy Spirit in the composition of the Scriptures. Humanly speaking the chances of avoiding the use of the word "priest" were almost insuperable; indeed, we may almost say, that to refuse to explain it by the guidance of the Holy Spirit is to require for its explanation what is virtually a miracle of human thought, foresight, and pre-arrangement among several writers.

[2] Perhaps it may be thought necessary to give special attention to "We have an altar" in Heb. xiii. 10. The writer is a Jew, addressing Christian Jews in danger of apostasy. The theme is a contrast of the two dispensations, the Christians being regarded as "better" and "eternal" by reason of the non-repetition of sacrifices, priests, etc. Then the writer turns to the most important festival of the Jewish religion, the Day of Atonement, and shows the analogy between the sin offering and Christ. There is no emphasis on the "we," and the true interpretation must be: "We Jews have an altar at which the priests who serve the tabernacle are not permitted to eat." It is impossible to associate the Holy Communion with a passage whose main point is a reference to "eat not." But in any case it cannot refer to the Lord's Supper, because such an idea would be contrary to the fundamental principles for which the whole Epistle contends. Everything in Judaism is shown to be spiritually fulfilled in Christ, and a reference to an ecclesiastical ordinance would be subversive of the very truths already insisted on. The word "altar" is found fourteen times in the Gospels and Epistles referring to the Jewish temple, and seven in the Apocalypse referring to heaven. It is never once associated with the Holy Communion, and, as already noted, Westcott points out that such an use would have been impossible in New Testament times. Even Bishop Wordsworth, speaking of the terms "altar" and "priest" in the time of Tertullian, says: "Perhaps it would be impossible to find distinct earlier authority for either word" (The Ministry of Grace, p. 133).

[3] It is well known that the Prayer Book of 1549 retained the term "altar," but it was removed in 1552, and has never been reintroduced. The action of the Reforming Bishops was in exact accordance with this omission, for in the reign of Edward VI altars were removed and tables substituted (Bishop Ridley's Injunctions, 1550). Then under Mary, altars were restored, and under Elizabeth were once more removed and tables returned. See Injunctions of Parker and Grindal, and Canon 82 of 1603. The explanation is quite simple: an altar involved a sacrifice while a table implies a feast. An altar can be a table (Mal. i. 12), but a table can never be an altar. And anything that was placed on an altar for sacrifice was never afterwards removed for the purpose of being eaten.

ideas, this word etymologically represents the word " presbyter," and not *sacerdos* ; French, *prêtre* ; German, *priester* ; English, *priest* ; thus showing that the sacerdotal idea was imported, not original. The question at once arises, which of these two ideas was intended by the Prayer Book. It is a question of fact and must be tested by all the available information.

1. Significant changes were made in the Holy Communion Service of 1552, showing an entire absence of anything sacerdotal and sacrificial.

2. The Ordinal of 1662 is described as " The Form and Manner of Ordering of Bishops, Presbyters, and Deacons."[1] To the same effect are the words of Hooker : " Whether we call it a priesthood, a presbytership, or a ministry, it skilleth not."[2]

3. In harmony with this the Latin Version of the Prayer Book, by Dean Durel, 1670, a few years after 1662, an almost official production, renders the term by *presbyterus*.

4. The word " priest " is frequently interchanged with " minister," as may be seen from the rubric before and after the Absolution at Morning Prayer, after the Creed, and before and after the Consecration Prayer in Holy Communion.

5. Nor is it without point that priests are entirely omitted from the *Te Deum*, which Blunt, in his annotated edition of the Prayer Book, regards as an argument for the extreme antiquity of that Song of Praise.

6. In Article XXXII, while the title speaks of " The Marriage of Priests " (*Sacerdotum*), doubtless referring to the Roman Catholic custom of celibacy, the Article itself refers to the three Orders, and describes them as " Bishops, Presbyters, and Deacons."

7. It is scarcely possible to overlook the significance of the change of usage in the versicle from Psa. cxxxii. 16 from " Let Thy priests be clothed with righteousness " to " Endue Thy ministers with righteousness."

8. The Roman Catholic Church gives her " priests " power to " offer sacrifices." But this is entirely absent from our Ordination Service.[3]

In view of these considerations, together with the fact that there is nothing sacerdotal provided in the ministry of our Church, it seems clear that the word " priest " can only be equivalent to " presbyter," and, as

---

[1] Dr. Ince, a former Regius Professor of Divinity at Oxford, says that the term "priests" is but the English for "presbyters" writ small, "and substantially corresponds to the pastors and teachers of primitive times" (Sermon on *The Scriptural and Anglican View of the Functions of the Christian Ministry*, p. 11).

[2] *Eccl. Pol.*, V, Ch. LXXVII, Section 3.

[3] Dr. Ince points out that this "is not one of the powers . . . committed to the Anglican priest." He goes on to remark that our Reformers had been accustomed to the phraseology of the Sarum Ordinal, and that:

"It cannot have been without significance that no counterpart to these expressions is found in the Reformed Ordinal. Our Reformers must have held the view which Hooker unhesitatingly asserted that sacrifice is now no part of the Christian ministry" (Ince, *ut supra*, pp. 12, 13).

such, expresses the evangelistic and pastoral ministry associated with the Presbyterate in the New Testament.[1]

In spite of all this it is said that the use of St. John xx. 22, 23 in the Ordinal carries with it sacerdotal authority and functions.   Dr. Pusey was accustomed to say that the Confessional is built up on these words. But, as we have seen, it is now admitted with practical unanimity that these words were spoken to the whole Church, as there represented, and form St. John's account of the great commission found in all the Gospels. When we turn to the Book of Acts we find that this, and this alone, was the work done (chs. ii ; viii ; x ; xiii).   Further, private confession was unknown for centuries, and these very words were not in any Ordinal until the thirteenth century, and even then were no essential part of the words of ordination.   This makes Cranmer's deliberate retention of them, while rejecting other words and customs, all the more significant, because of their close adherence to Scripture as part of Christ's commission.   The Prayer Book " priest " is, therefore, " presbyter," and corresponds to the prophet declaring the will of God.   As already noticed, absolution is the work of the prophet, not of the priest.   Keble took a similar position to Pusey in saying that it is impossible to get on without confession, and it is on this ground that these words are associated with priesthood to-day.

But the action of our Church at the Reformation ought to be sufficient to show its mind.   First, there is the public confession in Daily Prayer and at Holy Communion ; then there is the provision for the special case of a burdened soul before Holy Communion, though the wording, as distinct from that of the Prayer Book of 1549, shows quite clearly that there was no intention of a detailed and regular confession of sins. The usage in the Visitation Office is on similar lines, for the clergyman prays for forgiveness, and (as based on St. Matt. xviii. 18) pronounces the absolution in regard to sins against the community.   The power was left to the Church, not to the Ministry.   The prayer for forgiveness significantly follows the pronouncement of the absolution.   All this is totally different from the teaching and practice of the Roman Church, which compels auricular confession as a practice flowing out of the Sacrament of Penance.   In the Church of Rome absolution is described by the word "*judicium*," while with us we have its equivalent in " *bene-ficium* " by the ministration of God's Word.

It is, therefore, impossible to uphold confession from St. John xx, for if it means absolution after auricular confession, it must of necessity be connected with a spiritual discernment which enables a man either to

---

[1] While this is undoubtedly the proper interpretation, it is quite open to believe with Hooker that the word "presbyter" is more suitable to the Gospel of Jesus Christ than "priest":

"What better title could there be given them than the reverend name of "presbyters" or fatherly guides? .The Holy Ghost throughout the body of the New Testament, making so much mention of them, doth not anywhere call them Priests" (*Eccl. Pol.*, Bk. V, Ch. LXXVIII).

" forgive " or " retain " sins. We know that the Apostles had spiritual
perception to see the condition of people like Ananias, Sapphira, and
Elymas, but no such discernment exists now. As the words are not
found in any Greek Ordinal to-day it is clear that they are not essential
to Holy Orders, and their meaning in our own Ordinal can be illustrated
from representative Churchmen like Whitgift, Becon, Hooker, and
Jewel. In modern days the testimonies of representative High Churchmen support the contention that auricular confession is no part of the
English Church, and is not warranted by anything in our Ordination
Service. [1]

It is quite impossible to suppose, because our Church has continued
these three Orders of ministry, that therefore of necessity there must be
the same sacerdotal functions as in the Middle Ages. We have Bishops,
Priests, and Deacons, but the Priests are *Presbyteri* not *Sacerdotes*. Bishop
Gore has admitted that sacerdotal terms are only found connected with
the ministry at the end of the second century. [2] And Bishop Morton in
his reply to Bellarmine very forcibly said that if the terms " priest,"
" sacrifice," and " altar " had been essential to the Christian ministry
they could not and would not have been concealed by the Apostles. [3]
This is a striking anticipation of the very argument emphasised by
Moberly's *Ministerial Priesthood*.

4. Returning to the study of the actual ministry, as seen in the New
Testament and the Prayer Book, it is essentially pastoral, never mediatorial,
but always concerned with the work of preaching, teaching, and guiding
the flock. The minister is a prophet from God to the people, and not a
sacrificing or mediating priest, either in the old Jewish or in the mediæval
meaning of the term. Such being the case, the ministry must never be
considered apart from the Church as a whole. While there is a general
service of the entire Church there is also a specific ministry for the purpose
of order and progress, but in all this the minister is a medium, not a
mediator ; a mouthpiece, not a substitute ; a leader, not a director. The
idea of the Church always determines the form of the ministry, for the
Church as a whole was prior to the ministry, and the minister was intended to serve the entire community. We must, therefore, take the
greatest possible care not to exalt the ministry above the community, for
no ministry can fulfil its mission if it claims to control the Church. The
New Testament exalts the Body of Christ, and no trace can be found
of any direct Divine determination of the precise development of the
ministry. Any isolation of the ministry, of whatever Order, is spiritually
harmful as tending to make them unrepresentative of the Church. The
ministry only exercises its functions in connection with the Church.

---

[1] Bishop Jayne, *Anglican Pronouncements*; Prebendary Meyrick, *Confession*; Bishop
Drury, *Confession and Absolution*, p. 347 ff.; Bishop Denton Thompson, *Confession*.
The first of these contains a number of testimonies, all proceeding from definite and
representative High Churchmen.
[2] Gore, *The Church and the Ministry*.
[3] Dimock, *The Christian Doctrine of Sacerdotium*, pp. 74–77.

x

III.—THE FORM OF THE MINISTRY

1. This was gradually developed as it was needed. At first there were Apostles only; then came Deacons (Acts vi.), Evangelists (Acts viii.), and Elders (Acts xi. 30). Everything was adapted to the needs of a growing body. This is further seen in the difference between the lists of ministries in 1 Cor. xii. 28 and Eph. iv. 11. The ministry is thereby shown to be one of gifts rather than of offices. With regard to the origin of elders, there is now a general agreement " that this is nothing else than the standing office of the Jewish synagogue transferred to the Christian Church."[1] There are no indications in the New Testament of any direct Divine guidance of the development of the ministry. The suggestion that this was the subject of our Lord's instructions during the Great Forty Days after His Resurrection is, of course, a mere hypothesis and is wholly unsupported by evidence. It is impossible to explain the origin of the organisation of the ministry or, indeed, anything else in this way.

2. In time, however, the ministry naturally settled down into two main forms, evangelistic and pastoral, with something like an oversight in connection with the position of St. James in Jerusalem (Acts xv.). But the pastoral ministry was concerned throughout with spiritual provision and organisation, and possessing nothing sacerdotal in its functions.

3. Yet the terms " Presbyter " and " Bishop " are always interchangeable in the New Testament (Acts xx. 17, 28; Phil. i. 1; 1 Tim. iii. 1), and the term " Apostle " is applied not only to the Twelve, but also to St. Paul, St. Barnabas, and others.

" The absence of any sharp boundary between the Twelve and the larger class who bore the same name involves the exclusive claim which is made for the Twelve in serious difficulties."[2]

Timothy and Titus evidently fulfilled temporary offices only, and are perhaps best regarded as Apostolic Delegates. At most they represent " a movable episcopate."[3] There is no evidence that the Twelve received a commission to govern the Church, and in any case the appointment of elders later on shows the association of these with the Apostles (Acts xv. 6; xxi. 18).

4. The New Testament teaches a threefold function of ministry, not three distinct offices. This is really all that can be derived from the New Testament as essential, as distinct from what may be regarded as advisable. The term " Bishop " was, therefore, first of all descriptive of a function not an office.[4] " The ἐπίσκοποι of the New Testament have officially nothing in common with our Bishops."[5]

---

[1] Sanday, *The Conception of Priesthood*, p. 59.		[2] Sanday, *ut supra*, p. 53.
[3] Lightfoot, *The Christian Ministry*; Gibson, *The Thirty-nine Articles*, p. 763 f.
[4] Sanday, *ut supra*, p. 61.
[5] Alford, *New Testament*, Vol. III, p. 321 (Third Edition).

5. There does not seem to be much doubt that the Christian ministry followed closely the analogy of the synagogue with its deacon, elder, and president. But whether this is so or not, there is no trace of any historical connection, or even ecclesiastical analogy between the Christian ministry and the Levitical priesthood. It is sometimes said that the priesthood offers an exact parallel, and is therefore typical of the ministry. But first of all there is no real parallel, because the High Priest was really only *primus inter pares*. Besides, the Levitical priesthood was typical of Christ, not of the ministry, and the New Testament teaches that this priesthood is entirely abolished because fulfilled in Him (Heb. viii. 8, 9 ; 2 Cor. iii. 6-16). Christ's work was to bring us to God, and everything in the Old Testament was fulfilled so completely in Him that there is no room and no need for more. The question is not whether the powers of the ministry come short of those of the Old Testament priesthood, but whether they include them. This is not only devoid of proof, but is absolutely opposed to the very genius of the Christian religion. The first definite connection of the Christian ministry with the Levitical priesthood is seen in Cyprian,[1] just as he is responsible for the first definite use of " altar " to describe the Holy Table.[2] When episcopacy is seen in Ignatius there is absolutely nothing sacerdotal in it.

IV.—THE PERPETUATION OF THE MINISTRY

Hitherto attention has been limited almost solely to the New Testament, but it is now essential to enquire how the ministry there defined and described can be guaranteed to-day. How has it been perpetuated through the ages ? In three ways :—

1. By the act of God in continuing to bestow the spiritual equipment of ministry. We see this in the first question in the Ordinal. " Do you trust that you are inwardly moved by the Holy Ghost to take upon you this Office and Ministration, to serve God for the promoting of His glory, and the edifying of His people ? "

2. By the attitude of the Church in continuing to recognise the spiritual gift of ministry. This, too, is provided for in the Ordinal, in the opportunity given to the people to object to the candidate, and also in the request for congregational prayer. This implies fellowship with God on the part of the Church, leading to spiritual perception.

3. By the action of the existing ministry in continuing to commission by Ordination, those who are seen to possess the Divine spiritual gift.

From this it will be seen that continuance of ministry is primarily inward, and evil inevitably arises if emphasis is placed on the outward first. Outward continuance alone is no guarantee of a proper ministry, as we see from the Jewish priesthood, where son followed father in direct line. Spiritual fitness must, therefore, be emphasised first, and only then outward continuance and continuity. The New Testament view of

[1] Lightfoot, *ut supra.*   [2] Westcott, *Hebrews*, p. 458.

the laying on of hands, as already seen, is benediction, and commission of authority, not transmission of power, and this meaning necessarily continues in the present use of the method.

Following Article VI, it is necessary to insist that everything absolutely required for ministry must be found in the New Testament. Bishop Gore admits that on two points the New Testament needs supplementing by the witness of the Church; the first being as to the exact division of ministerial functions, the second as to the exact form of the future ministry.[1] This clearly shows that if the New Testament is to be regarded, as the Bishop says elsewhere, as "the testing-ground of Christian doctrine," we cannot regard as absolutely binding anything that is not found there. Much else may be early, universal, and truly valuable, and yet not entirely essential. The Church of England emphasises the former of these truths by its insistence on the New Testament as fundamental, and signifies its adherence to the second by means of the historical continuity set forth in our Ordinal.

4. So far we have been concerned with the New Testament requirements of ministerial continuity, but it is necessary to proceed further and to give attention to the witness of the early Church. There is no proof in the New Testament of the Apostles appointing successors, so that what should be the strongest link in the chain is really the weakest, namely, the connection between the Apostles and their first successors.[2] This is vital to any theory of precise visible continuity, making the words of Archbishop Whately true, that not a single clergyman can prove his succession from the Apostles.[3] The words of our Lord, "As My Father hath sent Me, even so send I you" (John xx. 21), are obviously not conclusive, especially as the words were uttered in the presence of those who were not Apostles, and we know that the Twelve gave way to a wider body bearing this name. Only once in the Acts and once in the Epistles (1 Cor. xv. 5) do we read of the Twelve. So that there is a threefold failure if we insist on outward continuity by Apostolic transmission; failure to prove (a) that the Apostles had absolute authority; (b) that St. Paul ever transmitted his authority to others to rule absolutely; (c) that Timothy and Titus recognised it as their duty to transmit authority to others.

Then, again, the question is involved in the important problem as to how the Apostles exercised their authority. Did our Lord give His authority to the Twelve, or, as the Roman Church maintains, to Peter alone as supreme? The Roman claim is quite simple and easy if we accept the premiss, but if we believe that Peter did not receive any

[1] Gore, *The Church and the Ministry* (Fourth Edition), p. 246; see also his *Orders and Unity*, p. 83.
"It must be admitted that if the documents of the New Testament stood alone . . . we should feel that . . . the picture presented was confused, and that no decisive conclusion as to the form of the ministry could be reached."
[2] Harrison, *Whose are the Fathers?*, p. 39.
[3] Whately, *Apostolic Succession Considered* (New Edition), p. 94.

authority beyond that which was given to the other Apostles, the question at once arises whether this authority was vested in the Twelve as individuals, or as a College. If it be said that each Apostle could be the Head of an Apostolic Church, then there would be at least the possibility of twelve Apostolic Churches. If, however, the Twelve were only authorised to act as a collective body we still require the historical proof that they ever constituted themselves, or were constituted, into a body to ordain successors. This is a point which is not usually faced by the leading writers of to-day. Bishop Wordsworth holds that the Apostles were a College and had not separate authority.

There is abundant proof that the terms and offices of Bishops and Presbyters were interchanged until at least the time of Clement of Alexandria.[1] Primitive Christianity was undoubtedly congregational, each local Church being autonomous, though with a definite consciousness of real spiritual unity with other Churches under Christ the Head. Then came what may be called a Presbyterian form, and, lastly, an Episcopal. Wordsworth admits that in some parts, " especially at Rome and Alexandria, there were at first only two Orders "; the governing Order acting normally as a corporate body, or College.[2] The *Didache* is clearly congregational, the local Church being addressed. So also are the Canons of Hippolytus and the Apostolic Constitutions of the third century. Each local community was as yet unconnected by any permanent organisation with other Churches, though, nevertheless, all felt that they were one Church, the unity being spiritual, not ecclesiastical.[3]

Great use is made of Clement of Rome, and three recent writers (Moberly, Hamilton, and Puller) adduce him as a witness to a succession based upon Apostolic transmission. But Dr. Sanday is quite definite in his opinion that Clement is not hinting in any way at a transmission of powers.[4]

The witness of Ignatius is, of course, of great importance, but it is essential to be careful not to misconstrue it and to derive from it what it does not convey. The following points seem clear:—

(*a*) The fact of episcopacy in Asia Minor by the time of Ignatius, 120.

(*b*) And yet it is purely congregational. Ignatius is attacking separatists who disobeyed an existing order, and is not referring to other Churches which may have had another order. This congregational aspect is now admitted by scholars.[5] Ignatius bases episcopacy on two grounds: (1) Fitness. It is in harmony with the teaching of the Gospels, being regarded as analogous to Christ, while the Presbyters correspond to the Apostles. (2) Direct revelation to himself. " The Spirit said." This argument is often overlooked, for, of course, it proves too much to claim

[1] Gibson, *ut supra*, p. 741.
[2] Wordsworth, *ut supra*, pp. 125–136.
[3] Hort, *The Christian Ecclesia*, p. 168.
[4] Sanday, *ut supra*, p. 72; see also Henson, *Godly Union and Concord*, pp. 33–40.
[5] Sanday, *ut supra*; Gore, *The Church and Ministry*, pp. 94, 102; Thompson, *The Historic Episcopate*, p. 183.

direct Divine authority in this way.   Two important testimonies to the
real meaning of Ignatius may be adduced : (1) Lightfoot shows clearly
that there is nothing sacerdotal in the Ignatian episcopacy ; (2) Gwatkin
shows the true meaning of the urgency used by Ignatius.

" Time after time he insists, ' Obey the Bishop,' and presses it in every way he
can.   His urgency has not been exaggerated ; and, indeed, it hardly can be
exaggerated.   So much the more significant is the absence of the one decisive
argument which would have made all the rest superfluous.   With all his urgency,
he never says, Obey the Bishop as the Lord ordained, or as the Apostles gave
command.   Even if this is not always the first argument of a man who believes
it, he cannot get far without using it.   The continued silence of so earnest an
advocate as Ignatius is a plain confession that he knew of no such command :
and the ignorance of one who must have known the truth of the matter would
seem decisive that no such command was given."[1]

Thus, Ignatius, while proving the early evidence of a real episcopacy
in Asia Minor, gives no indication either of sacerdotalism, or even of
anything like the monarchical and diocesan episcopates.   The fact of
continuity is clear as a matter of history without any association with a
specific doctrine of what is now called Apostolic Succession.   Bishop
Wordsworth has the following conclusion as to the ministry.

" While the ministry had a primitive origin its development in orders proceeded
at an uneven rate.   There was a longer duration of the charismatic ministry in
some places than in others, as well as persistence as a reserve force latent in the
episcopacy.   There was a general tendency to monarchical episcopacy, but not
always in the same form or date."[2]

The fact that Presbyters and Bishops were one and the same is the ruling
factor in the early years of the second century.   According to Jerome
this was the case in the Apostles' time, and Jerome's position has never
been seriously assailed.   Then to prevent schism the usage gradually
grew up which made the chief care of the Church devolve upon one
person, who was called a Bishop or an Overseer.   This gradual development was partly natural and legitimate, and partly a declension from New
Testament standards.   (1) It indicated a lack of spirituality, as the consciousness of Christ's presence faded ; (2) It was due to political circumstances, the Church being largely fashioned on the State.   (3) It expressed
a natural tendency towards the present life and progress of the Church.
(4) It was largely the result of the personal character of particular men.
(5) It was also explicable by circumstances calling for unity.   Error
seems to have arisen by confusing between superintendency or overseer-
ship and a Bishop *jure divino*.   The fact of superintendency is no proof
of a superior order, and when the Fathers mentioned Bishops it only

---

[1] Gwatkin, *Early Church History*, Vol. I, p. 294.
[2] Wordsworth, *Ministry of Grace*, p. 7.

proves the fact of superintendence, not superiority of order. This is clear in Clement, Ignatius, Justin Martyr, and even Irenæus.

Reviewing the second century, we see the gradual and natural growth and differentiation of the ministry   There is no trace whatever of anything answering to an absolute and assured transmission of Divine powers from the Apostles. Continuity and commission are seen everywhere, but the ministry throughout is evangelistic and pastoral, and with practically nothing sacerdotal in it. It is not generally known how and when the sacerdotal idea became associated with the Christian ministry, but certainly the idea finds no warrant either in the New Testament or in the writers of the second century. Bishop Lightfoot remarks that " the progress of the sacerdotal view of the ministry is one of the most striking and important phenomena in the history of the Church."[1] But it is not until we come to Tertullian that we find any sacerdotal language, and even he is strong on the universal priesthood of all believers. Bishop Lightfoot traces what he calls " the gradual departure from the Apostolic teaching in the encroachment of the sacerdotal on the pastoral and ministerial view of the clergy "[2] until it culminated in Cyprian, to whom we owe the full, clear teaching which regards the ministry as essentially sacerdotal.

It is not necessary to follow the history of the ministry further than Cyprian, except to say that the sacerdotal idea gradually grew stronger until it dominated the entire Church and came to a climax in the West in the Papacy. It was in connection with the sacerdotal aspect of the ministry that the doctrines of Transubstantiation and Auricular Confession became imposed upon the Church.

V.—THE ANGLICAN VIEW OF THE MINISTRY

1. The first point of importance is found in a careful comparison of the Ordinal with the Roman Catholic *Pontificale*. Of seven particulars in the latter only one now remains; the words, " Receive ye the Holy Ghost," etc.[3] It is all the more striking that the Church of England alone retained these words, especially since it is now known that they are not to be found in any Ordinal before the thirteenth century. It would seem clear that they are to be interpreted by the words that immediately follow: " and be thou a faithful dispenser of the Word and Sacraments." Bishop Andrewes says that they refer to function and not to internal quality.[4] The fact that this Scriptural passage is retained in our Ordinal makes the rejection of the other six particulars all the more significant. The doctrinal meaning is thus quite clear. All Anglican Liturgies, Catechisms, Homilies, and writers bear witness to the removal of mediævalism, thereby causing " a doctrinal gulf " between the Church of Rome and ourselves. It is not surprising that Rome

[1] Lightfoot, *ut supra*.   [2] Lightfoot, *ut supra*.
[3] Dimock, Article, "Ordinal," *Protestant Dictionary*, p. 474.   [4] Dimock, *ut supra*.

rejects our Orders as invalid, because they must of necessity be null and void in the absence from the Ordinal of the distinctive features of the Roman priesthood. Nothing could be more definite or significant than the removal from our Ordinal of the gift of the sacramental vessels to the newly ordained, and the omission of the words said at the same time : " Take thou authority to offer sacrifices for the living and the dead."

2. We have already noted the omission of the term " altar," from the Anglican formularies, and the true meaning of the retention of the term " priest."

3. The studied breadth and generality of statement in the Articles concerning the ministry is recognised by all, and it is significant that amid the acute controversies of the Reformation period the terminology of these Articles was never modified. Bishop Gibson recognises the fact that these documents are remarkably silent on the question of episcopacy even when they might have been reasonably expected to shed some light.[1] This breadth of view is in entire harmony with the well-known attitude of Cranmer to non-episcopalian Reformers in his day, and the wording of the present Article, emphasising the need of an external call to the ministry, is couched in terms that would be accepted by all communities which possessed any ministry. Article XXXVI has the same general attitude, as is evident from the following admission :—

" Certainly all that the actual terms of the Article now under consideration bind us to is this : that Episcopacy is not in itself superstitious or ungodly. This amounts to no more than saying that it is an allowable form of Church government, and leaves the question open whether it is the only one. This question is not decided for us elsewhere in the Articles ; for even where we might have reasonably expected some light to be thrown upon it we are met with a remarkable silence. . . . The Articles, then, leave us without any real guidance on the question whether Episcopacy is to be regarded as necessary."[2]

On this several points of importance call for attention.

(1) Holy Scripture is associated with " ancient authors," and this, together with the expression, " Had in reverend estimation," indicates a very different attitude and tone from that of Article VI, which insists upon the supremacy of Scripture for all essential doctrine.[3]

(2) The opening sentence of the Preface comes from the pen of Cranmer, who was in constant fellowship with non-episcopalians, and this, together with the association of Scripture with " ancient authors," seems to show that while our Reformers naturally and rightly maintained

---

[1] Gibson, *ut supra*, p. 744.   [2] Gibson, *ut supra*, p. 744 f.

[3] " The sovereign position of the Holy Scriptures having been once established, the Reforming divines gladly appealed to antiquity. They did so with confidence. The support of antiquity enormously strengthened their position in the great controversy of the day. They appealed to antiquity against the usurpation of Papal authority; they appealed to antiquity against the corruptions of mediævalism" (Ryle, *On the Church of England*, p. 20).

the episcopacy which they themselves possessed, they did not by word or deed do anything to reflect on other Reformers or Churches, where for any reason episcopacy was impossible.

(3) The wording of the Preface is marked by extraordinary caution, for there is no definition of the Apostles, no reference to a distinct Order of Bishops as superior to Presbyters, no reference to any universal establishment of the three Orders from the Apostles' time, and entire silence as to the crucial point of the method of ordaining Bishops.

4. In harmony with all this the first rubric in the Ordering of Priests and Deacons is significant, for while a sermon is ordered, showing the necessity of Deacons and Presbyters in the Church, there is no such rubric ordering a sermon, stating the necessity of Bishops. This dates from 1662, and is the more significant when the facts are considered. The Ordinal of 1552 directed an " exhortation declaring . . . how necessary such orders (Bishops, Priests, and Deacons) are in the Church of Christ." This wording might fairly be thought to support the theory of the necessity of Bishops. But in the last revision this was removed and separate rubrics were inserted in the offices for the ordination of priests and deacons. And lest it should be thought that the omission of a corresponding rubric in the office for Bishops was an oversight, it may be pointed out that the Consecration Service does mention a sermon, but only as part of the Holy Communion Office.

5. It must never be forgotten that the act of Ordination confers authority to perform duties, not power. The word " ordain " in English is the translation of no less than twelve very different Greek words, all suggesting some kind of causation, appointment, or selection.[1] Since, therefore, spiritual power comes from God, it is clear that Ordination was intended only to give ministerial authority; that is, authority to use the gifts and powers, but certainly not by that act conferring them.

6. It is well known that Cranmer, the author of the first sentence and nearly the whole of the entire paragraph of the Preface, expressly maintained that Presbyters and Bishops were originally identical, and that the development that made them distinct and gave Bishops rule over Presbyters was of human origin. It is hardly likely, therefore, that he would intend by this statement an entirely different view of episcopacy.[2]

7. In the original Ordinal before 1662 there was no difference in the words for ordaining Bishops and Presbyters, and the same passages of

[1] Jacob, *Ecclesiastical Polity of the New Testament*, p. 116, and Note; Litton, *The Church of Christ* (First Edition), p. 565, Note; Dimock, *ut supra*, p. 474 f.

[2] In 1540 Henry VIII submitted to Commissioners appointed to draw up a statement of Christian Doctrine seventeen questions, of which the tenth was Whether Bishops or Priests were first; and if the Priests were first then the Priest made the Bishop. Answers came from both parties on the Commission, Cranmer's being that "the Bishops and Priests were at one time and were not two things, but were both one office in the time of Christ's religion." This was the belief of all parties in the Elizabethan Church down to 1589. Thus, Jewel writes to Harding, endorsing Jerome's words that "a Priest and a Bishop is all one thing," adding that before the working of evil in the Church " the Churches were governed by the common counsel of the Priests."

Scripture were used for both. It is particularly noteworthy that up to 1662 the well-known passages in St. John xx. and St. Matt. xxviii., which are now the stronghold of those who believe in an Apostolic Succession through Bishops, were used in the Ordinal for Priests.

8. When the distinction was made in 1662 in the two Services there was no difference in principle, but only of detail and arrangement, because Article XXXVI declares the first Ordinal sufficient, and those ordained by it validly ordained.

9. The question is not whether Bishops are a distinct class, but whether this is so because they are a superior Order by Divine right. Was the distinction of class made by Divine authority, or was it only an ecclesiastical arrangement by way of development?

10. In the Church of Rome Bishops and Priests were regarded as of the same Order for centuries before the Reformation, and even the Council of Trent refused to acknowledge the Divine right of Bishops. All that they were concerned with was the Hierarchy, with the Pope as the Head, so that what is now often claimed for Bishops in the Anglican Church is claimed for the Pope, a distinct and fundamental difference of Order.

11. It must never be forgotten that, as already noticed, ministry derives its sanction from the entire Church, of which it is regarded as the representative. This is the " most fundamental principle in the Anglican theory of Orders."[1]

12. In addition to, and illustrative of the principles laid down in the Articles and Ordinal, it is essential to consider the views and actions of those who were responsible for our formularies, and also those who may be regarded as proper representatives of the Church.

(1) It is well known that Cranmer endeavoured to effect a union with the non-episcopal Reformers, 1548-1552, and the Articles on the Church and Ministry are a standing testimony to his view. His association with a Lasco, Peter Martyr, and Martin Bucer confirm this position.

(2) The correspondence between our divines and those of the Swiss Churches in the time of Elizabeth indicates a fundamental unity of doctrinal view.

(3) The earliest books on the Articles, by Rogers and Burnet, plainly state the same fundamental agreement. Rogers, as the Chaplain of Bancroft, Archbishop of Canterbury, who himself saw and approved of the book, is particularly noteworthy.

(4) It is also well known that in 1570 an Act was passed, making it easy for men in Presbyterian Orders to hold livings in the English Church, and Travers, the companion of Hooker, when attacked for having only foreign Orders, took his stand upon this very Act.

(5) In 1580 the English Church authorities allowed a community of Huguenots to have a Service in Canterbury Cathedral, and this remains to the present day.

---

[1] Blunt, *Studies in Apostolic Christianity*, pp. 73-76.

(6) In 1585 the Bishop of London issued an order to his clergy to provide themselves with Bullinger's Decades, and to read a portion every week. The Convention of 1586 issued a similar order to the junior clergy.

(7) In 1603 the Canon ordering the Bidding Prayer included a reference to the Church of Scotland, which at the time was Presbyterian, not Episcopalian, since episcopacy was not introduced into Scotland until 1610.

(8) In 1619 King James I sent three representative men to the Calvinistic (Presbyterian) Synod of Dort.

(9) Laud was the first to question the validity of non-episcopal Orders, and was rebuked for so doing.

(10) Bishop Overall fully recognised Presbyterian Orders, and admitted a Presbyterian into the English Church.

(11) Casaubon, the intimate friend of Bishop Andrewes, received the Communion at the hands of that Prelate, though he himself was a foreign Protestant and unconfirmed. Mark Pattison in his *Life of Casaubon*, says : " Before the rise of the Laudian school the English Church and the Reformed Churches of the Continent mutually recognised each other as sisters."

(12) Bishop Cosin's words and actions are particularly noteworthy because he was so representative a High Churchman. When in exile in France he kept up a friendly intercourse with Protestant ministers. He advised his friends to communicate when on the Continent at the Reformed Church and not at the Roman altars, and in 1650 he wrote quite definitely to the effect that a minister ordained in the French Church would not be reordained when entering ours, all that would be required would be the subscription to the Articles.

(13) The testimonies of Archbishop Sancroft, 1688, various authorities in the eighteenth century, and Archbishop Howley in the nineteenth, all point in the same direction, while the earliest missionaries of the Society for the Propagation of the Gospel were only in Lutheran Orders.

(14) The doctrine of " No Bishop, no Church " did not come into the English Church as part of the heritage from the mediæval Church of Rome. It was not heard of for fifty years until after the time of Cranmer, and was due solely to the exigencies of controversy between Churchmen and Puritans in the closing days of Elizabeth's reign. The late Dr. Pocock, a well-known High Church historian, wrote that :—

" The belief in the Apostolical Succession in the Episcopate is not to be found in any of the writings of the Elizabethan Bishops."[1]

The well-known statement of Keble in his preface to Hooker takes exactly the same line, for he points out that :—

" The Elizabethan Bishops were content to show that government by Bishops

[1] *The Guardian*, 23rd November 1892.

is ancient and allowable ; they never ventured to urge its exclusive claims or to connect the succession with the validity of the Holy Sacraments. . . . Nearly up to the time when Hooker wrote, numbers had been admitted into the Ministry of the Church of England with no better than Presbyterian ordination."[1]

(15) This was the prevailing view in the Church of England down to the Oxford Movement, and the present isolation dates from that time.[2]

(16) Efforts have been made to show that the Church of England did not officially recognise non-episcopal ministries from the time of Elizabeth to 1662,[3] but this is only possible by ignoring the testimony of men like Bishop Hall, Fleetwood, Clarendon, Keble,[4] and Hallam. The last-named points out that the narrow view commenced with Bancroft, but it never became part of the recognised and official doctrine.[5]

(17) The simple question remains whether the leading Churchmen ever regarded foreign Orders as invalid. Of this there is not only no proof, but very much to the opposite effect. As Dr. Sanday has truly said :—

" It should be distinctly borne in mind that the more sweeping refusal to recognise the non-episcopal Reformed Churches is not, and can never be made, a doctrine of the Church of England. Too many of her most representative men have not shared in it. Hooker did not hold it ; Andrewes expressly disclaimed it ; Cosin freely communicated with the French Reformed Church during his exile. Indeed, it is not until the last half of the present century that more than a relatively small minority of English Churchmen have been committed to it."[6]

A full and long catena of authorities can be adduced in support of this position, and if representative men are of any account in a matter of this kind, the mind of the Church is revealed beyond all question.[7]

[1] Pp. 59, 76.
[2] Henson, The Relation of the Church to the Other Reformed Churches, pp. 11, 18, 39.
[3] Denney, The English Church and the Ministry of the Reformed Churches, p. 18 ff.
[4] Wilson, Episcopacy and Unity, p. 83.
[5] Hallam, Constitutional History, Vol. I, p. 389 f.
[6] Sanday, ut supra, p. 95.
[7] "It would be easy to form a catena of our divines from the time of Archbishop Whitgift and Hooker, who, while they maintain the desirability of episcopal ordination deny its necessity; and who would echo the sentiment of Bishop Cosin, 'Are all the Churches of Denmark, Sweden, Poland, Germany, France, Scotland, in all points of substance or circumstances disciplinated alike? Nay, they neither are nor can be; nor yet need be, since it cannot be proved that any set and particular form is recommended to us by the Word of God.' Bishop Hall writes: 'Blessed be God, there is no difference in any essential matter betwixt the Church of England and her sisters of the Reformation. Their public confessions and ours are sufficient conviction to the world of our full and absolute agreement. The only difference is in the form of outward administration, wherein also we are so far agreed, as that we all profess this form not to be essential to the being of a Church, though much importing the well or better-being of it according to our several apprehensions thereof, and that we do all retain a reverent and loving opinion of each other in our several ways, not seeing any reason why so poor a diversity should work any alienation of affection in us, one towards another'" (Macbride, Lectures on the Articles, p. 415). See also Bacon and Burnet, quoted by Macbride, ut supra, p. 415.
See Goode, Divine Rule of Faith and Practice, Vol. II, pp. 247–348; Wilson, ut supra, passim.

VI.—MODERN CONTROVERSIES

There are few subjects which give rise to greater differences of opinion to-day than the subject of the ministry, and yet it is only by careful consideration of various views that we can expect to arrive at the truth.

1. In the Anglican Church since the Tractarian Movement there have been two views in the Church of England.

(1) One of these insists upon ministerial succession through the episcopate as an eternal fact and as the only guarantee of grace. Popularly this view may be described in the words, "No Bishop, no Church." This conception was put forth by the leaders of the Tractarian Movement, and in one form or another is definitely held to-day.[1] Now it is a simple matter of historical fact that this view was not held in the Church of England before the Tractarian Movement by any representative Churchmen of importance.

(2) The other view accepts the historical fact of succession in the ministry, but refuses to make it of the *esse* of the Church and Sacraments. Hooker takes this line, and Caroline divines, who are supposed to represent a definite High Church attitude, are not essentially different. Even Laud writing against Fisher did not reject the validity of non-episcopal ordination. We have already seen that this is the line taken by the Elizabethan Bishops, and it is the view held in substance by some of the leading scholars of the English Church.[2]

It must be evident that these views are not complementary, but contradictory, and until our Church really settles which of the two is correct, it is not possible for us to speak with a clear and certain voice on the subject of the ministry. We have already seen that, according to representative admissions, the New Testament is not sufficient by itself without the witness of the primitive Church, and yet it would seem to be obvious from Article VI that anything which is not absolutely settled by the New Testament cannot be of the *esse* of the Church, however valuable and even essential it may be for proper administration and order.[3] It is surely significant that of the three Orders, that which has the least Scriptural warrant of all should be regarded as essential to the existence of the Church. Is there not something lacking in the historical evidence as well as in the logical attitude which requires such a position ? Devolution of functions is one thing; transmission of office is another. The Apostles were originally everything and then their functions were devolved, but as they themselves were never technically Deacons, Priests,

---

[1] By men like Bishop Gore, Canon Moberly, Rev. F. W. Puller, and many others.

[2] Bishop Lightfoot, Dr. Sanday, and many more.

[3] Dr. Ince makes the following acknowledgment:

"It must furthermore be honestly acknowledged that there are no directions in the New Testament which give to these officers the exclusive right of administering Church ordinances. . . . It was the Church itself which confined the administration of the Sacraments to those who were ministers of the Word, and yet reserved to itself the power of relaxing in case of necessity the universality of this regulation, as in the case of lay baptism" (*ut supra*, p. 10).

or Bishops, they could not transmit what they did not possess.   The
Apostles were unique in their characteristics and requirements, and could
not continue or transmit their office.   There is no proof that the Apostles
instituted the episcopate to perpetuate their own order.

Continuity is valuable, and no one wishes to destroy it or minimise its
importance, but the nature of continuity needs to be carefully stated.
Can we think it according to the genius of a spiritual religion to make
grace and sacraments depend on the outward laying on of hands ?[1]
Besides, the logical outcome of the extreme view is the Papacy, or else
episcopacy is for the diocese only and not for the Church.[2]

2. The questions connected with the ministry inevitably raise the
problem of present-day non-episcopalians, and this calls for careful study
along four lines.

(1) The consideration of the facts of history.   How far is the Church
to blame for at least some of the Nonconformist communities ?[3]—It is
no doubt true that many of the Puritan objections were utterly trivial
and frivolous, but at the same time it is impossible to approve of the
policy of Queen Elizabeth and Archbishop Whitgift.[4]

(2) The consideration of spiritual results.—It is impossible to avoid
observing the actual facts of the present day concerning the comparative
numbers and influence of various denominations.   It is well known that
all over the world there are non-episcopal Churches and missions in no
way inferior, and sometimes superior to those connected with episcopalian Communions.   Then the relative position of the various Churches
in the Colonies and Dependencies of the British Empire shows that the
Anglican Church is sometimes far behind others in membership and
missionary contributions.   How are we to account for these facts when
we consider such questions as to whether episcopacy is of the *esse* or *bene
esse* of the Church ?   How are we to explain the marvellous development

---

[1] "The well-known theory, that the continuity of God's grace in the Church is
externally secured by the Episcopal imposition of hands, that thus a conduit of grace,
reaching back to the Apostles, is preserved and prolonged, has the merit of definite
outline.   But it is questionable whether it has any other merit.   Not only does it seem
to embody a remarkably mechanical and unspiritual conception of God's grace, but
also it cannot produce sufficient evidence from the Apostolic writings to substantiate it.
All that the evidence allows us to say is, that the threefold ministry was the system
which the Church gradually developed as the representative organ of its corporate life"
(Blunt, *ut supra*, p. 147).
[2] Litton, *ut supra*, pp. 472 and 676.
[3] "The justification for much of the Nonconformity, which arose and increased in
the seventeenth and eighteenth centuries, was the fact that English Episcopacy did not,
on the whole, do its work well, and provide comprehensively for the spiritual needs
of the nation.   And, if it had continued to be untrue to its duty, it is arguable that
the English people would have been in the right to reject it altogether, as they had
rejected the Papal authority " (Blunt, *ut supra*, p. 114).
[4] Bishop Creighton, speaking of the Elizabethan Church, has said:
"It tended to lose the appearance of a free and self-governing body, and seemed
to be an instrument of the policy of the State.   Its pleadings and its arguments lost
half their weight because they were backed by coercive authority.   The dangerous
formula 'Obey the law' was introduced into the settlement of questions which concerned the relations of the individual conscience and God" (*Lectures and Addresses*).

of Churches which have no episcopate, and therefore, on this view, no channel of grace ? To ordinary observers it would seem to be impossible that by a theory of Apostolic Succession millions of the most intelligent and devoted followers of Christ in the world are to be cut off from any real recognition as part of the true Catholic Church. If the presence of the Holy Spirit is so manifest among these non-episcopal Christians, how can they possibly be rebellious against the will of God ? When we apply the test, " By their fruits ye shall know them," non-episcopal Christianity will often be found at least equal to that which claims to be the only true expression of the will of God. It is impossible to insist upon a precise form of Church government as the only true method unless it can justify itself by its works all over the world.

(3) The consideration of the meaning of the word " validity."—What precisely is to be understood by ministerial or sacramental validity ? If it be said that the demand is for assurance of grace, the question is at once raised, how this can be proved. Surely only by fruit in the life.[1] Even on the question of irregularity as distinct from invalidity the matter is by no means clear, because we have to face the question of what was the essential method of Ordination between A.D. 100 and A.D. 250.

(4) The consideration of what is meant by Schism.—In the New Testament the word invariably means separation *within*, not from the body of believers, and when this primary idea is applied to ecclesiastical matters the results are profoundly significant. Heresy in Scripture never bears its modern interpretation of false doctrine, but is a faction which divides the people of God. Its sinfulness lies not in that which divides, but in the division, and for this reason the forcing of any doctrine or practice as a form of Communion compels division and is a sin of heresy. This means that the schismatic is the one who raises barriers to communion which God has not raised, and thus the guilt of schism lies with those who impose the terms of fellowship, and not with the conscientious objector, who is thereby debarred from communion.[2]

[1] "Let us get rid of the expression 'validity' of Orders and Sacraments. Whether or no Orders and Sacraments are valid is after all something which we cannot settle. What we should ask is whether they are 'regular,' that is to say, whether a particular body of Christians correctly interprets the mind of Christ declared to us by His Church in the fulfilment of His command to celebrate the Sacraments and to send out messengers of His Gospel. . . . We have then to be sure not that the Sacraments of the Presbyterian bodies are valid, but that they are regular" (*Church Quarterly Review*, July 1908, p. 278).

[2] "What is the meaning of schism? The ordinary point of view of one body of Christians when speaking of schismatics is to suggest that they are themselves the Church and all the others schismatics, that is, persons who have separated themselves from it. Now historically that point of view cannot be held in any case. To an impartial observer it is quite impossible to say that the Eastern Church separated from the West, or the West from the East. They divided. A division was caused and a schism was created, that is to say, a division in a body; so, at the time of the Reformation, a schism was created, or rather many schisms were created. But it is not that this or that Church separated from the great body of the Church; a division was created in the body, sometimes large, sometimes small; and so in relation to ourselves and a body like the Wesleyans. And if this be the proper point of view it is equally important to recognise that the sin of schism does not probably in any case lie wholly

In the light of these considerations the problem of non-episcopal Christianity is not by any means so simple as is sometimes made out, and there is a real difference between pre-Tractarian and post-Tractarian Anglicanism on this point. Noncomformity was, of course, decidedly opposed before Tractarian days, but not on grounds of the necessity of episcopacy and succession, but only by reason of the sin of separatism. The exclusive view came in with Tractarianism, and to those who are not content with theory, but insist upon fact, it is impossible to conceive of Nonconformity with its overwhelming superiority in numbers, and its frequent equality (at least) in practical results all over the world, as ready to become absorbed into the Anglican Communion. It is for this reason that we insist upon the view laid down by Dr. Sanday in referring to the Society of Friends:—

" Any theory as to the nature of the Christian ministry must have its place for phenomena—for paradoxes, if we will—like these."[1]

3. The question of the ministry is vitally associated with the relation of the Church of England to the Church of Rome. From time to time we are urged not to do anything in the direction of non-episcopal Churches which might endanger the possibility of reunion with the Church of Rome and the Churches of the East. But quite apart from the simple but significant fact that the Churches of the East do not recognise even our Baptisms, to say nothing of our Orders and doctrine, the Church of Rome has within recent years made a pronouncement about Anglican Orders which it might have been thought would have been more than sufficient to prevent any effort, or even hope in that quarter, apart from the stultification of everything that is associated with our Church since the sixteenth century. The Church of Rome has a very simple method for Reunion, namely, the acceptance of the Papacy, and thereby absorption into the Roman Catholic system. It has been aptly said that the Church of Rome spurns any idea of being a sister Church, and insists that she is nothing else than the Mother of Churches. As long, therefore, as Rome is what she is, any thought of Reunion with her is wildly impossible.[2]

4. The key to the situation is undoubtedly found in what is known

on one side or the other. Neither Leo X nor Henry VIII can be considered entirely free from either moral or intellectual blame. Even the strongest admirers of Luther cannot acquit him of blame. We are not prepared to defend either the spiritual life of the Church of England in the eighteenth century, or the spiritual self-assertion of the Wesleyan movement. Schism means sin in the past and needs penitence and reparation in the future" (*Church Quarterly Review*, July 1908, pp. 278, 279).

[1] Sanday, *ut supra*, p. 68.

[2] Even Dr. Hamilton, who takes a definite Tractarian line on the subject of episcopacy, frankly admits that our first work is to consider the Protestant Churches, since these men are of the same blood and stock as ourselves:

"As these divisions were the last to be opened, so they must be the first to be healed; and when they are closed, reunion with Rome and the Churches of the East may come within the sphere of practical possibilities" (*The People of God*, Vol. II, Preface, p. iv.).

as Apostolic Succession. If this means simply a historical succession of ministers as a fact, thereby emphasising the corporate and continuous idea as distinct from individualism and separatism, there can be no quarrel with it. But this is not generally the case. The usual meaning is that the ministry has descended from the Apostles by a continuous transmission, and that this is the guarantee of grace in the Sacraments. But the latter doctrine is so vital that nothing but a plain Divine command could justify it, since, as it is usually understood, it is foreign to the Spirit of Christ and the New Testament.[1] It took shape in the second and third centuries when the world believed in the Divine right of kings. Authority was supposed to be mediated through the monarchs, and in them through the people, and this civil doctrine passed into the Church and soon took form in the idea of a line from the Apostles. But these times and ideas have passed. Authority is no longer a matter of Divine right either in King or in Bishop. The authority from Christ comes to the whole Church and not through any corporation of officials. If one Order endeavours to subject the whole Church to itself, whether that Order is papal, or episcopal, or presbyterian, the result will be spiritual disaster. The best way of meeting Apostolic Succession is a high doctrine of the Church. It is only by ignoring the Divine position of the Church that we can at all obtain a sacerdotal view of the ministry. There must be no isolation of any order of the ministry, as if this were the sole custodian of revelation. The Apostles were unique and the New Testament ministry was not originated by devolution from them. It was determined by spiritual gifts through the Spirit of God in the Church, so that the foundation of ministry is a gift, and both the call and the recognition of the gift were really spiritual, and together formed the authority for exercise. We find this in St. Paul's Epistles, and there is no trace of a man of gifts ever ordained to the ministry of them. But as spiritual gifts decreased and the stated ministry became more prominent, so there came a transition from the ministry of gifts to the ministry of the pastoral office. Yet there is nothing in the New Testament higher than Elders, and the New Testament *Episcopus* is a man with the function of the Elder. The Apostles were not officers, or rulers of the Church, and although at the end of the second century the Church was centralised in its chief Pastor, yet it was impossible to claim Apostolic Succession in the modern sense. Clement of Rome does not prove any transmission of the grace of Orders, and even Ignatius, while strong for episcopacy, nowhere connects the claim with any devolution from the Apostles. He is only urgent against disunion. Hence, primitive Christianity favours the Evangelical view of the Church and ministry. If episcopacy was for the purpose of unity, only under particular circumstances, then departure from it would not destroy essential unity, *e.g.* Sweden and Germany are both Lutheran and

---

[1] It led Bishop Creighton to quote and endorse a statement made to him that "if this view be correct since the third century, there has been no Church, but only two classes of men, one offering, the other accepting, grace" (Letter to Dr. W. F. Cobb).

Y

yet one is episcopal. The fact is that there is absolutely no proof of any such transmission as is involved in the use of the doctrine of Apostolic Succession. The first link is wanting, and there was no devolution. The earliest Bishops were regarded as the representatives of Christ, and the Presbyters as the representatives of the Apostles, according to Ignatius, and it is now generally admitted that episcopacy was a gradual evolution of the second century arising out of the needs of the Church. This process of development naturally raises the question whether episcopacy can possibly be regarded as an eternal institution, or whether it may not be treated as amenable to the Church that created or evolved it.

It has already been shown that the doctrine of Apostolic Succession was not known in the Church of England for nearly fifty years after the Reformation, and there is no doubt that the vital point at issue to-day is that which was raised by the Tractarian Movement, but never before in the Church of England, the question of sacramental grace associated with a sacerdotal priesthood. There does not seem to be room for compromise on this point. Either the priest is necessary for the consecration of the elements by which in some way the presence of the Lord becomes attached, or else the clergyman, as minister, sets apart the elements for the purpose of becoming symbols of our Lord's Body and Blood. The latter is the New Testament, the former the mediæval view. Recent scholarship tends more and more to show that on purely historical grounds it is impossible to maintain the doctrine of Apostolic Succession.[1] These admissions all point in the same direction, that the *crux* of the position is not any mere question of continuity, but of a sacerdotal ministry by which alone grace in the sacraments is safeguarded and guaranteed. Lightfoot's position stands untouched to-day by anything connected with scriptural exegesis or primitive Church history. This involves (a) the universality of the priesthood of all believers; (b) the ministry as an evolution not a devolution. If only we keep firm hold of the priesthood of all believers we shall find that it carries with it all essential authority and power for ministry. This was the source of all subsequent developments, and our conception of the Church and ministry will necessarily spring out of the prior idea of justification by faith leading to access to God.

Thus, until the vital question of what constitutes the ministry in the light of the New Testament is settled the Church of England will have no power to influence other Communions in the direction of reunion. But when we are prepared, following the Articles, to accept only that which is found in the New Testament as essential, and to emphasise only what is recorded there the difficulties will be reduced to a minimum, and the best guarantee provided of the Church as it should be in the sight of God and a means of blessing to mankind.

[1] E.g. Mr. Rawlinson, in *Foundations*; Dr. Headlam, *Prayer Book Dictionary*; Dr. Frere, *Church Quarterly Review*.

ARTICLE XXIV

Of speaking in the Congregation in such a tongue as the people understandeth.	*De precibus publicis dicendis in lingua vulgari.*
It is a thing plainly repugnant to the Word of God, and the custom of the Primitive Church, to have public prayer in the Church, or to minister the Sacraments, in a tongue not understanded of the people.	Lingua populo non intellecta, publicas in Ecclesia preces peragere, aut Sacramenta administrare, verbo Dei, et primitivæ Ecclesiæ consuetudini plane repugnat.

IMPORTANT EQUIVALENTS.

In the congregation   = *in Ecclesia.*
To have public prayer = *preces peragere.*

THE corresponding Article of 1553 had this title, *Agendum est in ecclesia lingua quæ sit populo nota.* ("Men must speak in the congregation in such tongue as the people understandeth.") The Article itself was as follows: *Decentissimum est et verbo Dei maxime congruit, ut nihil in Ecclesia publice legatur aut recitetur lingua populo ignota. Idque Paulus fieri vetuit nisi adesset qui interpretaretur.* ("It is most seemly and most agreeable to the Word of God, that in the congregation nothing be openly read or spoken in a tongue unknown to the people. The which thing Saint Paul did forbid, unless some were present that should declare the same.") Then, in 1563, the present Article was substituted in which, while the Latin contained the words "*et primitivæ Ecclesiæ,*" the words, "and the custom of the Primitive Church" were omitted. These, however, were inserted in 1571, in which year the present title was adopted. The Article in its present form was probably due to the action of the Council of Trent in September 1562, anathematising those who pleaded for the Mass in the vulgar tongue.

I.—THE TEACHING OF THE ARTICLE

1. The Practice described.—The Article refers to public prayer in the Church and the ministration of the Sacraments "in a tongue not understood of the people." The reference is, of course, to the mediæval custom of having Prayers and the Celebration of the Mass in Latin.

2. The Practice denounced.—This practice is opposed on two grounds. (*a*) As "a thing plainly repugnant to the Word of God." This is clear from the statement of St. Paul in 1 Cor. xiv. 14-17. The essential point was that not only the ordinary worshipper, but the casual visitor

should understand thoroughly what was being said. There is scarcely anything more striking in the New Testament than the emphasis on " edification " as one of the essential requirements of Christianity (1 Cor. xiv. 12, 26; Jas. ii. 1 ff.). (b) Against the custom of the primitive Church. This scarcely requires any notice, for not only are the ancient Liturgies in the languages of the people concerned, but the testimony of the Fathers is obviously in favour of the particular language of the people, and the necessity of the Service being in Latin is negatived by the simple fact that the language of the early Church even in Rome was Greek.

In 1553 our Reformers pleaded for οἰκοδομή, arguing that it was most fitting and agreeable to Scripture that nothing be openly read or spoken in a tongue unknown to the people. But now the Article goes further and condemns the opposite of this. The change from "unknown" (ignota) to " not understanded " (non intellecta) shows that the prohibition is concerned with either a foreign tongue, or even the mother-tongue unintelligently rendered. A tongue "not understood" obviously includes a voice that is not audible. This gives point to the rubrical directions found in the Prayer Book ordering "a loud voice," and " turning him to the people." It is noteworthy that Hooper in his Articles, which were influential on ours of 1553, spoke of " due and distinct pronunciation," as well as of the "vernacular."[1] The Ninth Homily in the Second Book, 1553, remarks that no public service ought to be rendered in a tongue unknown, or not understood of minister and people. In view of the Council of Trent defending the use of " a low tone " (submissa vox) as well as the prohibition of the vernacular, these references to " understanded " as well as " unknown " are undoubtedly significant.

II.—THE HISTORY OF THE PRACTICE[2]

The condemnation of the use of any foreign tongue had, as we have seen, special reference to the Latin used in the Middle Ages. This practice arose quite naturally when Latin was the universal language of the educated classes, and the origin was thus perfectly simple with no idea of developing into abuse. But by degrees Latin became practically a dead language, and this was especially the case when the Teutonic language came in, for the terms did not keep the Christian religion from the Latins. Unfortunately, however, this change was not provided for and Latin was retained. The reasons for this were that Latin remained the main universal tongue, and especially it was the language of the educated. The idea arose, too, that for the mass of the people it would conduce to reverence, and that seeing the mystic rites they would think more of them. Further, it was thought that a Latin Service was less open to popular criticism and judgment. Accordingly, the Reformation

[1] Hardwick, History of the Reformation, p. 322.
[2] Boultbee, The Theology of the Church of England, p. 205 f.; Gibson, The Thirty-nine Articles, p. 584.

set out with two great facts : a vernacular Bible and a vernacular Service, and in doing so set aside a practice which, however reasonable at first, had become wholly unwarranted. It is a lamentable fact that the Roman Catholic Church has felt it right to continue this practice in the interests of religion, for the vernacular might be used and Roman Catholicism remain exactly as it is. Indeed, the Roman Church has had to make concessions, by giving a vernacular Bible and certain vernacular Services. It is true that the Roman Bible Versions are inferior, but, still, they are Versions, and in the vernacular Litanies and Service Books there are translations with parallel columns. So far as these go they are good, but obviously they do not go far enough.

The Roman Catholic arguments in support of the Latin language do not carry any real weight.[1] The Council of Trent admits that the Mass contains a good deal of instruction for the faithful, and yet will not allow it to be celebrated everywhere in the vernacular. But if these prayers and sacraments do contain this help it is surely not right to deprive the people of it. It is clear from the usual method of defending the practice that it is associated with the Roman Catholic view of the sacrament of the Lord's Supper being something done apart from the worshipper and calling only for adoration apart from intelligent co-operation.

All this is entirely opposed to the New Testament conception of religion. Every true religion must rest on two things. First, that God can speak to man, and second, that man can speak to God. Revelation and response are thus the two pillars, and religion is a dialogue (Psa. civ. 34, LXX). It is for this reason that " edification " is so special a characteristic of the New Testament (Acts ix. 31 ; 1 Cor. viii. 1 ; x. 23; Eph. ii. 21 ; iv. 12 ; cf. 2 Cor. xii. 19 ; xiii. 10). Whether, therefore, we are concerned with preaching, or sacraments, or worship, or service, edification is the great Bible principle, and this is clearly brought out in the Prayer Book, for there are exhortations at all the Services. There is a remarkable fulness of the use of Scripture in Lessons, Psalms, Epistle, and Gospel, while the Sacraments are so associated with instruction that it is impossible to avoid the thought of true edification. Indeed, there is nothing in our public Services that does not in some way minister to this requirement. " Let all things be done unto edifying." Adherence on the part of our Church to this clear New Testament principle is another illustration of the fundamental difference between us and the Church of Rome, in regard to the essential features and methods of Christianity.

[1] Boultbee, *ut supra*, p. 207.

IV. THE HOUSEHOLD OF FAITH—*continued*

Corporate Religion

C. THE SACRAMENTS (Articles XXV–XXXI)

25. The Sacraments.

26. The Unworthiness of the Ministers, which Hinders not the Effect of the Sacrament.

27. Baptism.

28. The Lord's Supper.

29. The Wicked which eat not the Body of Christ in the Use of the Lord's Supper.

30. Both Kinds.

31. The one Oblation of Christ finished upon the Cross.

ARTICLES XXV-XXXI

THE SACRAMENTS

These Articles are concerned with the doctrine of the Sacraments and cover the entire field in the following way.

1. Articles XXV, XXVI. Sacraments in General.
2. Article XXVII. Baptism.
3. Articles XXVIII-XXXI. The Lord's Supper.

The doctrine of the Sacraments is closely connected with and really dependent on the doctrine of the Church. In the fullest sense of the term the Church means a community of those who are united to Christ, but the word is also used of all those who profess this union, and the Sacraments are connected with this visible association of Christ's professed followers. The Church came into existence through the Word preached and received by faith, and then followed Sacraments as visible expressions of membership in the Society of those who received the Word, and at the same time as Divine assurances and pledges of the fulfilment of the promises proclaimed in the Word.

The Word is thus central and supreme and calls for faith, and the Sacraments are always associated with the Word and therefore require faith. The minister is always the minister of " the Word and Sacraments." This is the relative position of the two, and is never reversed. There is nothing in the Word which is not implied and expressed in the Sacraments, and nothing in the Sacraments which is not interpreted and explained in the Word. The Word may act apart from the Sacraments, but the Sacraments never apart from the Word. The Word makes Christians through faith, the Sacraments make the Church through fellowship. The Word proclaims Christ to the ear, the Sacraments proclaim Him to the eye.

It is, therefore, important to keep Sacraments in the position assigned to them in the Bible. The Word of God naturally comes first as embodying the Divine revelation, to which believing souls are to respond. This is the supreme and all-inclusive means of grace, because it is the approach of God to the soul in the Person of our Lord Jesus Christ. Everything else is subsidiary to this, because it necessarily finds its warrant in the Divine promise and assurance. Whether, therefore, we think of prayer, or of the Sacraments, we know that it is only because the Word of God has given us a revelation that we are enabled to believe in the efficacy of these means of approach to God.[1]

In the Old Testament God's Word to Abraham was followed by the covenant of Circumcision, and God's Word to Israel by the covenant of the Passover. Both of these required faith in the Divine revelation on the part of the recipients, and in the same way in the New Testament the Gospel has associated with it two ordinances, Baptism and the Lord's Supper, both requiring faith in the Divine promise. These Sacraments signify and seal God's faithfulness to His promises and also our faith in Him. Christianity is the religion of promise; the Word is the instrument of the promise, and the Sacraments are the ratification.

Thus, the Sacraments are at once (a) expressions in act of what the Gospel is intended to be; (b) covenant rites in relation to God's promises; (c) expressions in visible form of our faith in God, Baptism implying the faith that accepts, and the Lord's Supper the faith that abides; (d) means of, and opportunity for the expression of fellowship in a social form between believers in Christ, Baptism being the Sacrament of initiation into the Society, and the Lord's Supper the Sacrament of continuation therein.

[1] This subject is clearly and ably treated in *The Ministry of the Word and Sacraments*, by the late Bishop of Carlisle (Dr. Diggle).

ARTICLE XXV

Of the Sacraments. | *De Sacramentis.*

Sacraments ordained of Christ be not only badges or tokens of Christian men's profession, but rather they be certain sure witnesses, and effectual signs of grace, and God's good will towards us, by the which He doth work invisibly in us, and doth not only quicken, but also strengthen and confirm our faith in Him.

There are two Sacraments ordained of Christ our Lord in the Gospel, that is to say, Baptism and the Supper of the Lord.

Those five commonly called Sacraments, that is to say, Confirmation, Penance, Orders, Matrimony and Extreme Unction, are not to be counted for Sacraments of the Gospel: being such as have grown partly of the corrupt following of the Apostles, partly are states of life allowed in the Scriptures; but yet have not like nature of Sacraments with Baptism and the Lord's Supper, for that they have not any visible sign or ceremony ordained of God.

The Sacraments were not ordained of Christ to be gazed upon, or to be carried about, but that we should duly use them. And in such only as worthily receive the same, they have a wholesome effect or operation: but they that receive them unworthily purchase to themselves damnation, as *Saint Paul* saith.

Sacramenta a Christo instituta non tantum sunt notæ professionis Christianorum, sed certa quædam potius testimonia, et efficacia signa gratiæ, atque bonæ in nos voluntatis Dei, per quæ invisibiliter ipse in nos operatur, nostramque fidem in se non solum excitat, verum etiam confirmat.

Duo a Christo Domino nostro in Evangelio instituta sunt Sacramenta, scilicet, Baptismus et Cœna Domini.

Quinque illa vulgo nominata Sacramenta, scilicet, Confirmatio, Pœnitentia, Ordo, Matrimonium, et Extrema Unctio, pro Sacramentis Evangelicis habenda non sunt: ut quæ partim a prava Apostolorum imitatione profluxerunt, partim vitæ status sunt in Scripturis quidem probati; sed Sacramentorum eandem cum Baptismo et Cœna Domini rationem non habentes, ut quæ signum aliquod visibile, seu cæremoniam a Deo institutam, non habeant.

Sacramenta non in hoc instituta sunt a Christo, ut spectarentur, aut circumferrentur, sed ut rite illis uteremur. Et in his duntaxat qui digne percipiunt, salutarem habent effectum: qui vero indigne percipiunt, damnationem, ut inquit *Paulus*, sibi ipsis acquirunt.

IMPORTANT EQUIVALENTS.

Badges or tokens	=	*notæ.*
Certain sure	=	*certæ quædam*
Rather	=	*potius.*
Witnesses	=	*testimonia.*
Effectual signs	=	*efficacia signa.*
Quicken	=	*excitat.*
Penance	=	*pœnitentia.*
Have grown	=	*profluxerunt.*
Following	=	*imitatione.*
Allowed	=	*probati.*
Nature	=	*rationem* (as in Article IX, etc.).
Duly	=	*rite.*
Receive	=	*percipiunt.*
Effect or operation	=	*effectum.*
Damnation	=	*damnationem.*
Purchase	=	*acquirunt.*

IT is very important to observe the exact wording of the corresponding Article of 1553, and to note the changes made in 1563 and 1571. In 1553 the Article was as follows :—

" Our Lord Jesus Christ hath knit together a company of new people with Sacraments, most few in number, most easy to be kept, most excellent in signification, as is Baptism and the Lord's Supper.

The Sacraments were not ordained by Christ that they should be gazed upon, or to be carried about, but that we should duly use them. And in such only as worthily receive the same they have an wholesome effect and operation, and yet not that of the work wrought (*ex opere operato*), as some men speak, which word as it is strange, and unknown to holy Scripture, so it gendereth no Godly but a very superstitious sense. But they that receive the Sacraments unworthily, purchase to themselves damnation as St. Paul saith.

Sacraments ordained by the Word of God be not only badges and tokens of Christian men's profession, but rather they be certain sure witnesses, and effectual signs of grace and God's good will toward us, by the which He doth work invisibly in us, and doth not only quicken, but also strengthen and confirm our faith in Him."

The Article was recast in 1563; the last clause of 1553 became the first; the present second and third clauses were added; and then the first clause of 1553 with omissions became the present fourth clause. All reference to *opus operatum* was omitted. In 1571 a slight change was made by the omission of any specific reference to the Sacrament of Penance towards the end of the third clause, which was made to read as it now stands.

Special attention should be given to the Latin equivalents for " badges," " effectual signs," " quicken," " duly."

A comparison of the Article of 1553 with the present Article shows a decided improvement, especially in the sequence of thought. The first paragraph of the old Article was taken practically from St. Augustine with certain modifications.[1] The present fourth paragraph (the second of 1553) seems to have been original with the English Reformers, though verbal parallels to it are available in most other Protestant Confessions. The present first paragraph (the third of 1553) is taken almost verbally from the Thirteen Articles of the Concordat of 1538, which in turn came from the Augsburg Confession. There are also several verbal coincidences with Augsburg : *notæ professionis ; signa et testimonia ; proposita ad excitandum.*

It will be seen from this that the present Article is helpful in its presentation of the true doctrine of the Sacraments. After defining a Sacrament and stating what New Testament rites are to be regarded as Sacraments, it proceeds to contrast the rites which the Church of Rome has called

[1] *Ep. Ad Januar.*

Sacramental, and then closes with emphasising the proper use, and indicating certain abuses in reference to the Sacraments.[1]

I.—THE TERM "SACRAMENT"

As this is a Latin word it has no history in the Apostolic and sub-Apostolic ages. It became current afterwards as the Latin rendering of μυστήριον. Thus, Eph. v. 32 was rendered *hoc est magnum sacramentum*. This, however, is an unfortunate and inaccurate representation of the Greek word, especially as μυστήριον is never applied to any external rite, and in the New Testament means something that was once a secret, but is now revealed. It is important to remember that μυστήριον never has the modern idea of "mysteriousness." The English word "mysteries" in connection with the Holy Communion has really nothing whatever to do with the Greek word, but is equivalent to the word "symbols." The word originally meant anything put aside as *sacred*, the earliest use being a law term, referring to the deposit of two parties before the hearing of a trial, the losing party forfeiting his for *sacred* purposes. It is thought that the deposit was called by this name either because of that or because it was put in a *sacred* place before the verdict. Then the word came to mean the civil suit or process itself, and subsequently it was used of the preliminary engagement or oath of the soldier before joining the standard, the final oath being *jusjurandum*. Lastly, the term was applied to any religious engagement, and this can be illustrated by the well-known reference in Pliny's letter to Trajan, where he speaks of Christians binding themselves with a *sacramentum* not to commit any crime or do anything wrong.

In the Christian Church the term was used very widely and applied to any sacred engagement or "mystery." Thus, the Creed taught to the catechumen was called *Sacramentum religionis*, and St. Augustine [2] speaks of all the *sacramenta* which are done by the minister, as exorcism, prayer, spiritual songs, thereby indicating all sacred ceremonies. Leo the Great speaks of the *sacramentum* of the heavenly warfare. But the word gradually assumed a more specific meaning. Perhaps the earliest trace of this is found in the words of Tertullian, *ad sacramenta baptismatatis et Eucharistiæ admittens*.[3] By the time of Chrysostom μυστήριον had acquired a more specific meaning, and in his Homily on 1 Corinthians he says that "a mystery" is seeing one thing and believing another. This is an approximation to our definition of a Sacrament as a visible sign of an invisible grace. St. Augustine[4] takes this up by saying that Sacraments are so called because one thing is seen and another is understood. But one expression of St. Augustine acquired great importance

---

[1] The one point of omission referring to the *opus operatum* theory, which had been condemned in the Article of 1553, will receive attention under a later section, and the true explanation of the omission indicated.

[2] *De Symbolo.*   [3] *Adv. Marcion*, IV, 34.   [4] Sermon, 272.

in the Reformation controversy and goes to the heart of the matter : *accedit verbum ad elementum et fit sacramentum.*[1] The importance of this was that it made the essence of a Sacrament not a sign only, but a word which gives the sign its significance, the word being, in St. Augustine's view, the Word of God.   And so when we come to the first systematic divine of the Middle Ages, Peter Lombard, a Sacrament is stated to be the visible form of an invisible grace : *invisibilis gratiæ visibilis forma ita signum est gratiæ Dei ut ipsius imaginem gerat.*   He also says that " there are two things in which a Sacrament consists, *verba et res,* as, for example, the invocation of the Trinity and water at Baptism."   To the same effect, Duns Scotus says : " A Sacrament is a sensible sign effectively signifying from a Divine institution the grace of God."

In the Middle Ages the word was applied to many ceremonies, and no question arose as to any precise number while this vagueness continued. But there seems to have been a clear idea based upon expressions found in Justin Martyr, Tertullian, and Augustine, that Baptism and the Lord's Supper were distinct from all the rest.   Thus, Augustine speaks of *gemina sacramenta,* not *duæ,* and elsewhere he represents it as an essential character of Christianity that the ordinances were few in number and easy to be observed.   So also Chrysostom, speaking of the blood and water that came from our Lord's side on the Cross, says that the Church exists by these two, and those who are introduced into the full knowledge of our faith know that while they are regenerated by water they are nourished by the Body and Blood.[2]   Even in the days of Augustine there was a growing sacredness for many ceremonies, and in the Middle Ages in the West from the seventh to the twelfth centuries the number varied from two upwards.   The special number of seven is first definitely stated by Peter Lombard, and yet after his date a great Schoolman, Alexander of Hales, distinguished the two Sacraments from the rest, much as our Church does, while Thomas Aquinas, who gave the Roman doctrine its chief development, refers to the two Sacraments as *quæ sunt potissima sacramenta.*   It is noteworthy that at the Council of Florence, 1439, amid the controversy of the Greek and Roman Churches, there was no real difference between them as to the number of the Ordinances called Sacraments.

Our Church now limits the term to two Ordinances which fulfil three requirements : (*a*) a visible sign ; (*b*) an invisible grace ; (*c*) ordained by Christ.   It should also be noted that throughout the Articles the word " Sacrament " is used strictly for the outward sign only.   In the same way, in the Catechism, when the child is asked, " What meanest thou by this *word* Sacrament ? " the answer is, " I mean an outward and visible sign *of* an inward and spiritual grace."   The sign is the Sacrament ; the grace of which the Sacrament is the sign is no part of it, but is the thing of which the Sacrament is the (1) sign, (2) means, and (3) pledge.   It is

[1] On St. John.   [2] On St. John.

sometimes said that the following answer in the Catechism, " How many parts are there in a Sacrament ? " " Two : the outward visible sign, and the inward spiritual grace," is contradictory of the former. But it is more likely that the word " Sacrament " is used in two different senses. Sometimes it means only the consecrated matter; at other times the entire administration of the Ordinance. It is in the former sense that the earlier question defines the meaning of the " word," while in the latter the " grace " and its " sign " are the two parts which make up the whole rite. It is not difficult, therefore, to understand the difference between a popular Catechism and the more accurate and theological scientific language of the Articles.

II.—THE NATURE OF SACRAMENTS

1. They are " badges or tokens " of Christian profession. This was the exclusive meaning attached to them by some parties in the sixteenth century. But while it is true, as seen to-day in the Mission Field and in the celebration of Holy Communion at home, it is inadequate, and so the Article proceeds further by saying that Sacraments are " not only badges or tokens."

2. They are " sure witnesses of grace." They speak to us ourselves as well as to others, testifying to the fact and reality of God's presence and grace in Christ.

3. They are " effectual signs of grace, and God's goodwill towards us." This view meets the two extremes : (a) against the view of Rome, which virtually denies the sign and identifies it with the thing signified; (b) against the defective view which regards a Sacrament as only a sign, or a bare sign. But it is important to note with great care the force of the adjective " effectual." An effectual sign which carries its own effect is effectual as a sign. In theological language a sign, signum, is a pledge, a seal, a promise, and Sacraments are effectual as such. The epithet does not destroy the substantive, or even change it, but only intensifies it. Sometimes it is said that " Sacraments effect what they signify." Everything, however, depends upon the mode,[1] for to " convey " in theological terminology refers to a legal deed, not to a channel or electric wire. Waterland says that a deed of conveyance is not the estate though it " conveys " it. The deed is not the property, but the guarantee of it.[2] As Hooker says :—

" Grace is a consequent of Sacraments, a thing which accompanieth them as their end, a benefit which they have received from God Himself, the Author of Sacraments, and not from any natural or supernatural quality in them."[3]

[1] Dimock, see Papers on the Eucharistic Presence, p. 689.
[2] Waterland, On the Eucharist, p. 131.
[3] Eccl. Pol., Bk. V, p. 57. See more fully Boultbee, ut supra, p. 218.

This phrase *efficacia signa* is also used to emphasise what is called the objective grace of the Sacraments apart from human faith. That grace must necessarily be objective first is assuredly true, but this does not mean that it is residential in the elements. All grace must at the outset be objective to the recipient.[1]

Notwithstanding the fact that the first paragraph of the Article in defining the Sacraments is drawn originally from the Augsburg Confession, it is urged that Cranmer " in 1538 improved upon the Lutheran doctrine by adding that they are effectual signs of grace," and that he retained " this phrase in spite of Swiss protests " in 1553.[2] It will be seen, however, that this argument is incorrect, for Luther himself used the term " effectual," and the phrase " efficacious signs of grace."[3] Thus, while Luther properly rejected the idea that the Sacraments effect Justification or confer grace apart from faith, he was equally clear with our Article that the Sacraments are " effectual signs of grace " to the believing recipient. In the same way, the Swiss or Reformed doctrine teaches the proper effect of Sacraments.[4] Further illustrations of the same identity of teaching between the Reformers can be adduced from the Scottish Confession of 1560.[5] All this clearly shows that the endeavour to distinguish between the Lutheran and Anglican doctrine in regard to *efficacia signa* falls to the ground. And so the epithet *efficacia* shows that the Sacraments are not mere signs, but signs which are also means of God's grace and favour.[6]

---

[1] "Whether the grace of the Holy Eucharist come to our souls by and through the elements or no, alike it is *objective*, as coming to us from without ourselves, and having existence independently of our own thoughts" (Bishop Moberly).

[2] B. J. Kidd, *The Thirty-nine Articles*, p. 36 f.

[3] "Thus it cannot be true that there is inherent in the Sacraments a power *effectual* to produce justification, or that they are *efficacious signs of grace*. These things are said in ignorance of the Divine Promise and to the great detriment of faith; *unless indeed* we call them *efficacious* in *this* sense, that if along with them there be unhesitating faith, they *do confer grace* most certainly and most *effectually*" (*De Capt. Bab.*; Primary Works by Wace and Buchheim, p. 191).

[4] The Second Swiss Confession (1536) said: "Wherefore we assert the Sacraments are not only badges of Christian fellowship, but also symbols of Divine grace, wherewith the ministers of the Lord co-operate unto that end which He Himself doth promise, offer, and *effect*; yet in such wise (like as we have said concerning the ministry of the word) that every power that bringeth salvation be ascribed unto the only Lord" (Section 20; Augusti, p. 99; Elberfeld, 1827).

And in the Third Helvetic Confession (1566), the denial of the "efficacy" of the Sacraments is expressly condemned: "Neither also do we approve the doctrine of them who talk about the Sacraments as of common signs, not hallowed or *effectual*" (Section 19; Augusti, p. 69).

[5] "Therefore we condemn the vanity of them who affirm that the Sacraments are nothing else than mere and bare signs," and after expounding their views of the Sacraments, go on: "But the whole of this, we say, results from a true faith which apprehendeth Jesus Christ, who alone doth make the Sacraments *effectual* unto us" (Section 21; Augusti, pp. 162, 163).

[6] "*Efficacia* does not necessitate a theory of simultaneity of time between the reception of the sign and of the thing signified. The word was in common use in the writings of Calvinistic divines, in combination with the obsignatory view of Baptism, as the seal of grace which was ante-baptismal" (See Mozley, *The Baptismal Controversy*, p. 359, Note; Dimock, *The Doctrine of the Sacraments*, p. 24).

A further proof of the truth of these statements is the fact that the Article speaks of Ṣacraments as effectual signs, not only of grace, but of " God's good will towards us." These last words clearly show the impossibility of regarding grace as something quasi-material, residing in the elements. God's good will means attitude, relationship. Sacraments are therefore analogous to those visible things in Scripture which are signs or pledges of God's favour and faithfulness, like circumcision, the Passover, the fleece, the brazen serpent, etc. As such, they are " sure witnesses and effectual signs " of Divine grace and favour.

III.—THE PURPOSE OF SACRAMENTS

The Article proceeds to state with great care the object and reason of Sacraments in the Divine economy.

1. By means of Sacraments God works invisibly in us. The Latin is particularly noteworthy, emphasising God as the Worker rather than the Sacrament itself : *ipse in nos operatur*.

2. This invisible working of God is for the twofold purpose of quickening and confirming faith. Here, again, the Latin equivalents help towards a true understanding of the purpose of Sacraments. To " quicken " in the Latin is *excitat*, which means, to arouse, stir up, not to create. Sacraments are intended to foster an existing faith, not to produce faith itself. The Word of God is intended for this latter purpose. Then, too, " strengthen and confirm " is a further explanation of the purpose of Sacraments, which strengthen the faith that already exists. Faith is thus aroused or stirred up by means of some object of sight or sense, but it is created in the first place by a word of promise from God (Rom. x. 17). It is important to notice at this point and elsewhere the connection of the Sacraments with faith. It is always so in Scripture. Thus properly the Homily defines Sacraments as " visible signs expressly commanded in the New Testament, whereunto is annexed the promise of true forgiveness of our sin, and of our holiness and joining in Christ."[1]

IV.—THE NUMBER OF SACRAMENTS

As already seen, the word was originally used in a very wide sense, expressive of any Christian symbol, and it was only during the Middle Ages that the tendency was seen to limit the number to seven, this becoming the formal doctrine of the Church of Rome at the Council of Trent, 1547. Everything, of course, depends upon our definition of the term, for if it is taken in its most ancient sense, then obviously it is impossible to limit the Sacraments to seven. If, however, the word is limited, as our Church does, to any rite instituted by Christ Himself, containing both an outward sign and an inward grace, then it is clear that only Baptism and the Lord's Supper come under the designation of

[1] Homily of Common Prayer and Sacraments.

Sacraments.   At the outset of the Reformation three Sacraments were mentioned by Luther and others, Baptism, the Lord's Supper, and Penance, or "Absolution," and this last idea persisted for some time, until at length it was seen that the Lutheran ordinance of Absolution was altogether different from the mediæval Sacrament of Penance.   But both in Germany and in England the three Sacraments were emphasised for several years up to the time of the Bishops' Book in 1537.   When Henry VIII issued the reactionary "King's Book," 1543, the mediæval view of seven Sacraments was once again taught.   On the repeal of the King's Book, 1547, Cranmer reverted to the Lutheran idea of three Sacraments.

It is interesting to observe that the last rubric in the Communion Service of the Prayer Book of 1552 spoke of "Sacraments and other Rites," apparently implying a wider meaning of the term, and in the Forty-two Articles of 1553, though Baptism and the Lord's Supper were spoken of as Sacraments, it is thought that there was an intention to refrain from denying the use of the word to other rites.   Yet, in the Catechism published in that year only two Sacraments are really recognised.   The wording of the *Reformatio Legum* should also be compared.[1]   At the revision of the Articles in 1563 our Church for the first time stated definitely that there are two Sacraments which fulfil the required definition, and that "the five commonly called Sacraments . . . are not to be counted for Sacraments of the Gospel."   And yet in the Second Book of the Homilies of the same date the wider term seems to be retained in harmony with the view of the early Church, though with a clear distinction between Baptism and the Lord's Supper and the other Ordinances.

"As for the number of them, if they should be considered according to the exact signification . . . there are but two, namely, Baptism and the Supper of the Lord. . . . And although there are retained by order of the Church of England, besides these two, certain other rites and ceremonies about the Institution of Ministers in the Church, Matrimony, Confirmation of Children by examining them of their knowledge in the Articles of Faith, and joining thereto the prayers of the Church for them, and likewise for Visitation of the Sick ; yet no man ought to take these for Sacraments in such signification and meaning as the Sacrament of Baptism and the Lord's Supper are ; but either for godly states of life, necessary in Christ's Church, and, therefore, worthy to be set forth by public action and solemnity by the ministry of the Church, or else judged to be such ordinances as may make for the instruction, comfort, and edification of Christ's Church."[2]

[1] "Ad sacramenti perfectionem tria concurrere debent.   Primum evidens est et illustris nota, quæ manifeste cerni possit.   Secundum est Dei promissum, quod externo signo nobis repræsentatur et plane confirmatur.   Tertium est Dei præceptum quo necessitas nobis imponitur, ista partim faciendi, partim commemorandi: quæ tria cum authoritate Scripturarum in Baptismo solum occurrant, et Eucharistia, nos hæc dua sola pro veris et propriis novi testamenti sacramentis ponimus" (*De Sacramentis*, Cap. II.)
[2] Homily of Common Prayer and Sacraments.
It is interesting to note that except a brief form of the first sentence the whole extract from the Homily given by Bishop Gibson (*The Thirty-nine Articles*, p. 600 f.) is an

The Article speaks of five ordinances " commonly called Sacraments " which, however, " are not to be counted for Sacraments of the Gospel." These are said to have grown partly from corruptions of Apostolic ideas, and are partly states of life approved of in Scripture, but, nevertheless, are not to be called Sacraments. The word " allowed " means " approved " (*probati*), and not merely the modern idea of " permitted." This clause was inserted in 1563, and was perhaps suggested by the Wurtemburg Confession. The question is often raised whether it is permissible to speak of these ordinances in any sense as Sacraments. Sometimes a distinction is made between the two as " Sacraments of the Gospel " and these five as " Sacraments of the Church." It is also urged that as the Article speaks of these five as " commonly called Sacraments " we may also use this term of them, even though they are not Sacraments of " like nature with Baptism and the Lord's Supper." Further, it is said that the Article is obscure because Confirmation is not a state of life, and if it is a " corrupt following of the Apostles " it ought not to be retained. Let us consider, first, the phrase " commonly called," which was used in 1563 as descriptive of the then usual name of these rites. The natural interpretation would seem to be that the phrase was employed for the purpose of correcting the error, and it is certainly noteworthy that wherever a similar phrase is found it indicates a current usage, and at the same time a recognition of inaccuracy. Thus, the Apostles' Creed is " commonly called " so, and the Athanasian Confession is " commonly called." Then, too, the Nativity of our Lord was " commonly called Christmas Day," and Article XXXI describes certain statements about sacrifices and Masses, in which it was " commonly said," etc. The natural and obvious meaning of such usage seems to be a discouragement of the application of the term " Sacraments " to these ordinances.

Then, too, as the five are admitted to be unlike in nature to Baptism and the Lord's Supper, the question at once arises whether they can be included in the sacramental definition involving (1) appointment by Christ, (2) an outward sign, and (3) an inward grace. As already noticed, if we once depart from this definition it is impossible to limit the idea of the Sacraments to seven.

In regard to the alleged obscurity of the Article, the explanation of the phrase, " corrupt following of the Apostles " obviously applies to Penance, Orders, and Extreme Unction, because none of these are Scriptural and all are characterised by error. Matrimony is also rightly described as " a state of life allowed in the Scriptures." The only question is as to Confirmation, and it is more than possible that in its mediæval meaning it is to be included in those which come from " the corrupt following of the Apostles," because the English Confirmation is entirely

nterpolation made by Queen Elizabeth after the Homily had been passed by the Convocation of Canterbury. It is therefore not quite adequate or accurate to quote that without adding the qualifying sentences of the Homily found in the quotation given above.—See Tomlinson, *The Prayer Book, Homilies, and Articles*, pp. 246–251.

z

different from the Roman. The two Confirmations have little or nothing in common, except the name. In the Roman Church the rite is intended to be administered to infants after Baptism, although the custom to-day in certain countries defers Confirmation until the age of seven. But in any case the candidates are not required to make any response on their own behalf. On the other hand, it is a vital point in the English Confirmation that the candidates should ratify and confirm their baptismal vows and unite in prayer for the Holy Spirit. So that it is quite accurate to speak of the Roman Catholic Confirmation as " a corrupt following of the Apostles," and Anglican Confirmation as " a state of life allowed in the Scriptures." Of course, strictly, Confirmation is a Service rather than " a state of life," but this is hardly worth mentioning in view of the inclusion of all these five Services in the Article, and is only referred to at all because of the way in which the Article is misused to-day. It is an interesting point in support of this view that at the Hampton Court Conference in 1604, " the Puritans complained that this phrase in the Articles involves a contradiction with the teaching of the Prayer Book, and that their complaint was dismissed as a mere cavil."[1]

The reason, as already stated, for rejecting these five, is that they do not fulfil the threefold definition found here and in the Catechism, they have " no visible sign or ceremony ordained of God." The nearest approach to this requirement is found in " Extreme Unction " because of the similarity of the scriptural anointing of the sick (Mark vi. 13 ; Jas. v. 13, 14). But it is obvious that " Extreme Unction " cannot be called a Sacrament since there is no evidence that our Lord instituted it, as such, or that the oil was intended as " an outward and visible sign of an inward and spiritual grace." Further, the Roman Catholic rite is altogether different from the Apostolic usage, since the anointing with oil was intended for the purpose of recovery as a medical remedy, while Extreme Unction is only administered when the person is not expected to recover.

It is sometimes said that the difference between us and the Church of Rome is comparatively small on this point,[2] but there are weighty reasons for believing that the difference is great, being one of things, not of words.[3] Bishop Andrewes has said :—

" For more than a thousand years the number of seven Sacraments was never heard of. How, then, can the belief in seven Sacraments be catholic, which means, always believed ? "

So also, Archbishop Bramhall says :—

" Our Church receives not the septenary number of the Sacraments, that being never so much as mentioned in any Scripture, council or creed, or father, or ancient author, but first divided in the twelfth century by Peter Lombard ;

[1] Cardwell, *History of Conferences*, p. 182; quoted in Gibson, *ut supra*, p. 604.
[2] Gibson, *ut supra*, p. 602.   [3] Boultbee, *ut supra*, p. 211 f.

decreed in the fifteenth century by Pope Eugenius IV, and established at Trent."[1]

Our definition of a Sacrament and that of Rome are practically the same, and so it is a question of evidence whether Christ did ordain the seven.[2] If the term Sacrament is quite general, why should it be limited to seven, as the Church of Rome does? This points to the need of clear definition and close application of the term.

" We are far from wishing to engage in verbal disputes, but the Council of Trent forbids the word to be taken in a lower sense, and maintains the seven to be *vere et proprie* Sacraments, and anathematises those who reckon fewer or more. To ascertain which party is in the right, we must define terms."[3]

Rome defines a Sacrament as " a sensible thing which by Divine institution causes as well as signifies holiness and righteousness."[4] By " sensible " is intended the element as the matter and the word as the form. When this definition is applied to the five rites or ceremonies, the Church of Rome teaches as follows.

1. Confirmation: Ordained by Christ; matter, chrism; word, " I sign thee," etc.

2. Penance: Ordained by Christ; quasi-material elements, acts of contrition, etc.; word, *ego te absolvo*.

3. Orders: Ordained by Christ; matter, cup and paten; word, " receive power to offer sacrifices," etc.

4. Matrimony: Christ raised it to the dignity of a Sacrament, but nothing else is explained by the Council of Trent.

5. Unction: ordained in the New Testament (Jas. v. 14); matter, oil; word, the utterances used for pardon.

Rome also teaches that Baptism, Confirmation, and Orders impress a character on the soul which is indelible.

The only one of these to which it is necessary to refer is Penance, for, as already observed, at this point there was some hesitation among the early Reformers, particularly Melanchthon. Luther, in 1520, in his " Babylonish Captivity of the Church," speaks of the great importance of the ministry of absolution and the promise annexed to it, but he restricted the word " Sacrament " to those ceremonies which have a visible sign, ordained by God, and for this reason absolution was not to be placed in the same category with Baptism and the Lord's Supper. But the controversy continued, and Hooker presented a complete statement of the different views held at the time.[5]

[1] Macbride, *Lectures on the Articles*, p. 431. "If anyone shall say that the Sacraments of the New Law were not all instituted by Jesus Christ our Lord, or that they are more or less than seven . . . let him be anathema" (Trent, Session VII, Canon 1).
[2] Boultbee, *ut supra*, p. 212.   [3] Macbride, *ut supra*, p. 433.
[4] Council of Trent.   [5] *Eccl. Pol.*, Bk. VI.

1. In the early Fathers we find the use of confession allowed and approved of, but not the system of auricular confession subsequently upheld by Rome. That Church teaches that the Sacrament of Penance is the only remedy for sin after Baptism, that confession (in secret) is an essential part of it, that God Himself cannot now forgive sins without the priest, and since forgiveness at the hands of the priest must arise from confession in the offender, confession is a matter of such necessity that unless it is performed either in deed or in desire the offender is excluded from pardon. As Hooker points out, these opinions have youth in their countenance, since antiquity never thought or dreamt of them. " This is the poison bag behind the adder's sting."

2. Calvin and those associated with him did not use private confession, but held the necessity of open confession for notorious offences, not for the remission of sins, but only in some sort to content the Church and to warn others.

3. The Lutheran position did not require open confession, though it was thought that men should at certain times confess their sins to God in the hearing of God's minister in order to receive encouragement and persuasion concerning the forgiveness of sins.

4. The Church of England provides public confession in the daily services and this answers to the purposes of the open confession practised on the Continent. For private confession and absolution the minister's authority to absolve is publicly taught and professed, but no such necessity is imposed upon the people to confess as if remission were otherwise impossible, nor is private confession pronounced unlawful or unprofitable, but only in respect of certain inconveniences which have been practically experienced. So that the Church of England hitherto has thought it the safer way to refer men's hideous crimes unto God and themselves only, yet not without special caution in regard to those who come to the Holy Communion and also for the comfort of such as are about to die.

After this treatment of the subject in general, Hooker proceeds to show more definitely the vital differences between us and Rome.[1]

1. Rome implies in the name of repentance much more than we do. We emphasise chiefly the true inward conversion of the heart, while they lay stress on works of external show.

2. We teach above all things that repentance, which is one and the same from the beginning of the world; they a sacramental penance of their own devising.

3. We labour to instruct men in such a manner that every wounded soul may learn how to heal itself; they on the contrary make all spiritual sores seem incurable unless the priest have a hand in them.

4. With us the remission of sins is a thing which is ascribed unto God, as proceeding from Himself and following immediately on true repentance, but that which we attribute to the virtue of repentance they impute to the Sacrament of Repentance, and having made repentance a Sacrament, and

---

[1] *Eccl. Pol.*, Bk. VI, Ch. II.

thinking of Sacraments as they do, they are found to make the ministry of the priest and their absolution the cause of that which God worketh.

In view of these considerations it does not seem possible to doubt that they are right who regard the difference between the Church of Rome and ourselves on the number of Sacraments as fundamental and vital.

V.—THE USE OF SACRAMENTS

1. The Article first speaks of an improper use. " The Sacraments were not ordained of Christ to be gazed upon, or to be carried about." This is a reference to mediæval abuses. The use of the plural " Sacraments " is of particular interest, since it shows that both ordinances are put on the same level, even though there has never been any thought of these improper uses in regard to the Sacrament of Baptism.[1] The Church of Rome tends to exalt the Holy Communion at the expense of Baptism by her liberal view of the latter, permitting anyone to baptise, and by her insistence on a priest at the former. Our Church places both Sacraments on a level of spiritual importance, each in its own place. There is no real difference between water and bread as elements of a Sacrament.

2. Then the Article emphasises the proper use. " But that we should duly use them." This, of course, refers to use according to the institution and command of Christ.

VI.—THE EFFECT OF SACRAMENTS

The Article clearly teaches that their effect is conditional on worthy reception. " And in such only as worthily receive the same they have a wholesome effect or operation; but they that receive them unworthily purchase to themselves damnation, as Saint Paul saith." It is noteworthy that St. Paul's language about the Lord's Supper (1 Cor. xi.) is here used in regard to both Sacraments. This distinction between worthy and unworthy reception is the key of the Anglican position. Spiritual efficacy is conditional, not absolute. Faith believes the promise, and the Sacrament seals or pledges the fulfilment, but without faith the Sacrament alone has no spiritual effect, except to condemnation (1 Cor. xi. 29). All the means of grace require faith in God on the part of the recipient if there is to be " a wholesome effect and operation." We are told of this in reference to the people of Israel, that God's word was unprofitable because of the absence of faith (Heb. iv. 2). In the same way prayer must be based upon belief in the promise of God (Jas. i. 5-7). It is, therefore, reasonable that this should be equally true in regard to the Sacraments.

---

[1] The suggestion made by Bishop Gibson (*ut supra*, p. 610, Note) that the plural may have been intended to refer to the two parts of the Eucharist (also endorsed by Tyrrell Green, *The Thirty-nine Articles and the Age of the Reformation*, p. 199), is obviously impossible, or at least most unlikely in view of the title of the Article and the fact that the plural is found in each of the other clauses. There is also no trace of any historical justification for the suggestion.

The cardinal error against which the Article stands is that Sacraments "contain" grace, that is, that grace resides in the elements by virtue of consecration, and that administration alone suffices to convey it to the soul. This is known as the *opus operatum* view, meaning that in the absence of any barrier (*obex*) the Sacraments invariably convey grace. Thus, on this interpretation, the only antecedent qualification is a negative one, the absence of sin, for no positive preparation is required.

The view of the Sacraments now criticised is associated with the Church of Rome, and has rightly been described as "one of the most difficult and complicated theories in her theology." Our great writer, Hooker, discusses this doctrine with his accustomed clearness, and in following his lead we shall be enabled to understand its true bearing. The earlier doctrine of the Roman Church was virtually identical with that of the New Testament in regard to the efficacy of the Sacraments. It was taught that God uses them for the purpose of bestowing His grace, but that such grace was given directly by God, and not, as it were, first located in the outward and visible sign, and then practically conveyed to us thereby. But the doctrine of the Roman Church became associated with the teaching of Thomas Aquinas, 1274, whose view was that the sacramental signs became divinely endowed or invested with a certain quality, and that God gave His grace to the recipient therein and thereby. This union was opposed by Duns Scotus and others, who showed very good reason that no Sacrament can, either by its own virtue, or by supernatural force given to it, be regarded as a cause to work grace, but that Sacraments are said to work grace because God Himself is present in the ministry of them, working that effect which proceeds wholly from Him without any real operation of theirs such as can enter into men's souls.

But the most important of all the questions which arose related to the proper condition of mind on the part of the recipient. From St. Augustine downward there continued strong assertions of the necessity of repentance and faith for the effectual reception of the Sacraments. Similarly St. Bernard of Clairvaux said that "the Sacrament without pious dispositions is death to the Sacraments, but these pious dispositions are life eternal to the recipient without the Sacrament." The other side emphasised the inherent virtue of the Sacrament, and that because of the tendency to draw a distinction between the Sacraments of the Old and New Covenants. It was urged that the Sacraments of the Old Covenant conveyed grace only by virtue of the coming Saviour and so only by faith in that Coming, but that the Sacraments of the New Covenant contained grace in themselves by virtue of the perfect Sacrifice of Christ. This was the original meaning of the phrase *ex opere operato*. But there was one exception to this *opus operatum* (the deed done), the performance of the ceremony, namely, that the recipient should not place a bar to the reception, *non ponere obicem*. Duns Scotus went so far as to say that the Sacraments confer grace by virtue of "the work wrought," so that there is no necessity of good motions, *bonus motus*, within the heart, but that in those acts of the Old Testament grace was not conferred in the simple absence of obstacle, but only by virtue of a good disposition in the heart by way of merit. Another Schoolman, Gabriel Biel, argued that the Sacraments are said to confer grace *ex opere operato*, in the sense that grace is conferred by the simple performance unless there is an obstacle of mortal sin, but that on the other hand the Sacraments of the Old Covenant confer grace *ex opere operante*, that is, the external ceremony was not sufficient, but good motions in the recipient were necessary for the bestowal of grace by God. These views gained the supremacy during the close of the Middle Ages, and it will at once be seen what great moral and spiritual dangers were revealed, making the Sacraments only magical ceremonies. This led to the abuses of solitary Masses. At length the Roman doctrine was formulated at Trent, which says that the seven Sacraments were instituted by our Lord. " If anyone shall say that the Sacraments of the New Law were not all instituted by Jesus Christ, or are more or fewer than seven, let him be anathema." " If anyone shall say that grace is not conferred *ex opere operato*, but that belief in the Divine promise alone suffices to obtain grace, let him be anathema."[1]

The abuses of this doctrine became so great that Roman controversialists were compelled to modify it, and this amounted to explaining it away. Bellarmine, one of the ablest and fairest, says : " The justification received by man in the Sacrament has many things concurrently. On the part of God, will; of Christ, His Passion; of the minister, authority; and of the recipient, honesty, will, faith, penitence, and finally external ceremony." Of all these that by which the grace of Justification is actively and instrumentally effected is the sole external ceremony, which is called the Sacrament, and this is called the *opus operatum*, so that the meaning of the Sacraments conferring grace *ex opere operato* is this, It confers grace by virtue of the instrumental action appointed by God for this purpose, and not by virtue of the merit of the celebrant or the recipient. The will, faith, and repentance are necessary requisites in an adult recipient as dispositions, not as active causes, for the dispositions are not the effectual cause of sacramental grace, but only remove the obstacles which would prevent the Sacrament exerting its ordinary effect, so that the Sacrament has its efficacy in children independent of those dispositions. This, it will be seen, is a considerable modification of the hard Roman view. There remained a dispute as to the requisite intention of the priest, which will be considered under the next Article, but in this respect in the midst of the Reformation the doctrine of the early Church as to Baptism was reasserted, Bellarmine saying that the intention required was to do what the Church does, and this he applied to the Church of Geneva, saying that the minister intends to do not his own view, but that of the whole Church.

The first cardinal point reasserted at the Reformation was the essential

[1] Session VII, Canon 8.

necessity of faith to a living Christianity and for a living participation of
Christ. The word *faith* with its correlative *God* is the turning-point of
the whole Reformation controversy, not merely the doctrine of Justification by faith, but in regard to the very nature of faith in answer to the
Word of God. This, it cannot be too strongly asserted, is the keystone
of the controversy. Faith is regarded as of supreme importance because
it is the only possible answer to a word or promise of God, and that characteristic of the Gospel which it embodies in the very word " Gospel " was
that which was mainly avowed by Luther and his successors. When,
therefore, it is said that the Reformers gave undue proportion to faith, it
only means faith in relation to God's Word, for there is no value in faith
itself, and no efficacy in a mere faculty of confidence. The Reformation
arose not out of this faculty of confidence, but out of a profound sense of
human weakness. Unless we keep these principles clear the true bearings
of the Reformation cannot be understood. But when this principle was
once asserted and realised the whole of the Roman doctrine of ceremonies,
producing their effect *ex opere operato*, fell to the ground, especially the
doctrine of the Schoolmen, that no *bonus motus* is required, which really
comes to this, that the promise of God has no claim to be believed.

It is this principle of faith which the terms of our Article emphasise
as the basis of blessing, and, as we have seen, our teaching is in essential
harmony with the Augsburg Confession. There is only one difference
between our statements and that of the Germans, by which our Reformers guarded against a possible danger which might arise, though that
was quite foreign to the minds of the Germans. While in essence the
declarations are the same, our Article, by emphasising the Sacraments as
effectual signs, *efficacia signa*, if worthily received, guards against the
error of making the Sacraments simple pledges of God's good will and
overlooking the fact that they are *means*, in the use of which God works
visibly in us. This is, of course, brought out quite clearly in the second
paragraph of the Augsburg Confession, but our Article has not separated
the two, and carries the meaning of the second clause in the word *efficacia*.
At the same time the Article guards by its form of expression against the
supposition in which the Roman Church indulged, that the Sacraments
work this grace themselves, for it says that God Himself works (*Ipse*),
and that efficacy depends on worthy reception.

The error about Sacraments being mere signs must not be thought to
be Zwinglian, for the Zwinglian error was that the Sacraments are pledges
on the part of *man*, and practically convey no Divine promise or message
at all. Zwingli regarded Sacraments as signs by which a man approves
himself to the Church as a disciple, or soldier, and the effect of Sacraments
is rather to give assurance of faith to the Church than any assurance to
the person himself, so that according to Zwingli Baptism is the man's
offering of himself to Christ, and thereby giving a pledge of his obedience,
or the parents giving a pledge to train the child in the faith, on which there
follows the blessing of God in response to this act of obedience. Now the

characteristic view of the Lutheran and our Churches is the message from God to the man and the child from God, that God has commanded His ministers to offer regeneration and blessing to all who will accept the message and obey. In the former case the Sacrament is primarily an act of man; in the latter an act of God. It was objected to the views of the early Reformers that there was an inconsistency in their saying that there was a promise of God, and faith on the part of man was needed in the Sacrament. But their answer was clear and simple, that the reason they required faith was because of God's promise, since without a promise there would be nothing to believe, while starting with the promise, man's part naturally follows, and as the argument develops it will be seen how this touches the fact of the other so-called Sacraments. The whole affair turned on the fact that these two Sacraments contained a Divine promise and that the others did not.

We may, therefore, notice the three views: (1) the Zwinglian, that Sacraments are primarily pledges on the part of man. This was absolutely rejected in the first words of the Article. (2) The Lutheran and our view, that they are sure witnesses and signs of grace and of God's good will towards us. (3) Then one further question arises, Have they merely the operation of promises acting simply like the preaching of God's Word, or have they a special grace conveyed in and through them? On this point our Church has followed the teaching, or interpreters of the teaching of Scripture, in the early Fathers, and in the early Reformers, like Luther and Melanchthon, as embodied in the Augsburg Confession.

The most serious error of the Roman Catholic view is that it tends to separate grace from God Himself and to make it a sort of deposit in the soul, a quasi-material element contained in a material element. But God's own life is received direct from God in the due fulfilment of His requirements. The Article teaches this in its emphasis on *Ipse*, and by saying that Sacraments are signs of God's " good will," which is certainly not in the elements. In the absence of any Divine revelation to this effect we cannot believe that grace, which is God's own life, resides in material elements, still less, that any application to the body can necessarily convey grace to the soul. Our Lord laid down this principle without any qualification (Mark vii. 18), and the application to Sacraments is too obvious to need further attention. The truth is that grace is relationship to God and needs a maintained attitude, not a residential locality. It is at this point that the Anglican and the Roman view of the Sacraments come into clear opposition. It is one thing to require a passive condition of not placing any bar in the way of Divine grace; it is quite another to demand the response of trustfulness towards God, as the soul expects grace directly from above. It is therefore of the greatest importance to have a clear view of the effect of Sacraments, and this is only possible by a careful comparison of the teaching of Rome with that of our Church. For this purpose we must quote again the Council of Trent, which says: " If anyone shall affirm that by the very Sacraments of the New Law this grace is not conferred *ex opere operato*, but that only belief in the Divine promise is sufficient to obtain grace, let him be accursed." On the other hand, our Catechism speaks of " Faith, whereby they steadfastly believe the promises of God made to them in that Sacrament." It is scarcely without significance that we thus use almost the exact words which the Church of Rome condemns.

There is perhaps nothing more necessary than clearness and definiteness as to the meaning of " grace " and " means of grace." By " grace " we are not to understand anything that can reside in certain material elements, and which can be conveyed to the recipients of those elements by the mere administration. Nor are we to understand by " grace " merely a Divine influence. According to the New Testament grace is the attitude and operation of God Himself working in believing hearts (Phil. ii. 13), and so " means of grace " signify the ways in which the Holy Spirit does His work in us, and, as such, these means are the divinely appointed ways through which God's presence and blessing are usually bestowed on our souls. They are the occasions and opportunities of Divine contact through faith. We can see this illustrated in our Lord's own Baptism when the Holy Spirit came direct from heaven and not in and through the water.

It is also necessary to remember that grace in the Sacraments differs in no way from grace at other times. Grace involves an attitude of Divine favour and a gift of the Divine life, and it is impossible to say that the Sacraments convey a special grace different in kind from ordinary grace.[1] It must never be forgotten that there is a serious ambiguity in the word " convey " which, as already pointed out, never means a mechanical, but only a legal instrument.[2] When this is thoroughly understood there need be no difficulty whatever as to the precise meaning of the value and method of Sacraments.[3]

It is sometimes argued that the omission of the *opus operatum* theory in 1563 indicates an intention to change the Anglican doctrine, or, at any rate, to avoid either the sanction or the condemnation of the phrase.[4] But a careful consideration of the circumstances connected with the phrase will enable us to see that the omission can be explained on very different grounds. Originally, the phrase, as used by the mediæval theologians, was meant to contrast the inevitable efficacy of the Sacra-

[1] Litton, *Introduction to Dogmatic Theology* (Second Edition), pp. 428–431.
[2] Litton, *ut supra*, pp. 425–427.
[3] "They are not physical but *moral instruments* of salvation. The manner of their necessity to life supernatural is not in all respects as food unto natural life, because they contain in *themselves* no vital force or efficacy. All receive not the grace of God which receive the sacraments of His grace" (Hooker, *Eccl. Pol.*, Bk. V, p. 57).
"The Romish doctrine of the *opus operatum* rests on the notion that the sacraments contain in themselves a physical virtue to heal the maladies of our nature as the medicines of the physician possess a power to heal those of the body; an apprehensive faith being as little needed in the one case as in the other. The sacraments thus become, not signs of spiritual life already existing or means of spiritual growth, but, by an inherent virtue, the instruments of implanting that life" (Litton, *ut supra*, p. 427).
[4] Gibson, *ut supra*, pp. 612–614.

ments in spite of the imperfection of the minister, the *opus operantis*. But the phrase came easily to be misunderstood as meaning *opus operatum*, implying that the subjective fitness of the recipient could not hinder the result. But the doctrine of Justification by faith raised a controversy which compelled the Church of Rome to repudiate the grosser understanding of the term, and the more correct attitude assumed by the Council of Trent may have led to the omission of words which cease to be of value when used in different senses. Under the pressure of reforming opinions certain Roman Catholic writers were compelled so to qualify the phrase *ex opere operato* as to remove from it " the very superstitious senses which it literally bears."[1] Under the circumstances of these ambiguities it is not surprising that the phrase was omitted in 1563.[2]

But the phrase is decidedly objectionable. First, it tends to emphasise the distinction between sign, grace (*res*) and virtue (*virtus*), making sign and grace independent of the recipient, and virtue dependent. But this distinction finds no warrant in Anglican formularies and involves the false mechanical understanding of the term " grace " already mentioned, which only came into the Anglican Church with the Tractarian Movement.[3] Then, too, the phrase assumes that the priest is *operans* in respect of the *grace* of the Sacrament, whereas he is only the *operans* of the *sign* of sacrament, the grace coming direct from God. The phrase was, therefore most wisely omitted because of the necessity of avoiding a term used by controversialists in different ways that no understanding could be arrived at. From another and opposite quarter the returning exiles after Mary's reign included men whose dread of attributing the inherent power of conveying grace to whomsoever the consecrated matter was applied led them almost to deny that in suitable subjects and under the required Divine covenantal conditions there could be any certainty of the gift of grace or any ground for that faith which steadfastly believes the promises of God made to us in a Sacrament. But the Gospel is the same to all, whether by speech or Sacrament, for in both the promises of God cannot be broken.[4] As, therefore, by 1563 the doctrine of superstition was adequately met by the word " duly," and as Article XXVI deals with the other problem of ministerial fitness, the phrase was omitted. But it is perhaps necessary to point out that the omission of a censure of a doctrine does not involve the approval of that doctrine. We know, for instance, that in 1553 several Articles condemned Anabaptist

---

[1] Von Hase, *Handbook to the Controversy with Rome*, Vol. II, pp. 154–157.

[2] "It should not, however, be forgotten that it is a phrase not free from ambiguities; that it has, no doubt, been sometimes used by those who taught a doctrine scarcely differing from the Reformed, and that it has accordingly been very wisely omitted from our Article" (Dimock, *The Doctrine of the Sacraments*, Ch. XX, p. 75; *Papers on the Eucharistic Presence*, p. 692).

[3] Archdeacon Wilberforce, from Aquinas. See *Protestant Dictionary*, Article, "Grace," p. 250, last paragraph.

[4] In the *Church Intelligencer* (June 1902, p. 85) will be found a declaration of doctrine made in 1559 by returning exiles. In this formula the words *opus operatum* were first dropped out, so that the omission was not due to any Romanising tendency.

views, and that these Articles were omitted in 1563, not because the errors were endorsed, but because there was no longer need to condemn them.   In the same way the omission of a reference to the mediæval *opus operatum* theory did not imply any approval of it, especially as it is clearly excluded by the insistence upon a worthy reception of the Sacraments and the teaching of the Catechism as to the requirement of repentance and faith.

It is now possible to see the principles reasserted and guarded by the Reformation.   Faith is necessary to participate in Christ, and is the only possible answer to God's revelation.   Consequently, the *opus operatum* falls entirely, for if no spiritual qualification is required then the Word of God has no claim on our belief.   Sacraments are messages from God to man with a special promise in them.   If there is no promise there can be nothing to believe, and without faith the promise is of none effect.   On the other hand, it is, of course, altogether incorrect to speak of faith as the cause of grace when it is only the channel or means.   This shows the necessity of guarding against errors from opposite directions.   We have to insist that the same use of the means of grace is spiritually unprofitable unless faith is associated with the grace.   We must also be equally careful to avoid the error that the various means of grace derive their power from the faith of the recipient, when, as a simple fact, they derive it from God Himself.   As it has been well put, faith " takes " the grace that God offers, but faith does not " make " that grace.

ARTICLE XXVI

Of the Unworthiness of the Ministers, which hinders not the effect of the Sacraments.

De vi Institutionum Divinarum quod eam non tollat malitia Ministrorum.

Although in the visible Church the evil be ever mingled with the good, and sometimes the evil have chief authority in the ministration of the Word and Sacraments; yet forasmuch as they do not the same in their own name, but in Christ's, and do minister by His commission and authority, we may use their Ministry, both in hearing the Word of God, and in the receiving of the Sacraments. Neither is the effect of Christ's ordinance taken away by their wickedness, nor the grace of God's gifts diminished from such as by faith and rightly do receive the Sacraments ministered unto them; which be effectual, because of Christ's institution and promise, although they be ministered by evil men.

Nevertheless it appertaineth to the discipline of the Church, that inquiry be made of evil Ministers, and that they be accused by those that have knowledge of their offences: and finally being found guilty, by just judgment be deposed.

Quamvis in Ecclesia visibili bonis mali semper sunt admixti, atque interdum ministerio Verbi et Sacramentorum administrationi præsint; tamen cum non suo, sed Christi nomine, agant, ejusque mandato et auctoritate ministrent, illorum ministerio uti licet, cum in verbo Dei audiendo, tum in Sacramentis percipiendis. Neque per illorum malitiam effectus institutorum Christi tollitur, aut gratia donorum Dei minuitur, quoad eos qui fide et rite sibi oblata percipiunt; quæ propter institutionem Christi et promissionem efficacia sunt, licet per malos administrentur.

Ad Ecclesiæ tamen disciplinam pertinet, ut in malos ministros inquiratur, accusenturque ab his, qui eorum flagitia noverint; atque tandem, justo convicti judicio deponantur.

IMPORTANT EQUIVALENTS.

Of the unworthiness of Ministers, which hinders not the effect of the Sacraments	= *De vi institutionum divinarum, quod eam non tollat malitia Ministrorum.*
Have chief authority	= *præsint.*
In receiving	= *percipiendis.*
From such as	= *quoad eos qui.*
Rightly	= *rite* (not *recte*).

THIS subject has exercised the Church at different ages, especially at the Reformation. If the Sacraments are associated with grace the question arose whether efficacy in any way depended on the one who administered them. The Article is derived from the Eighth Article of the Confession of Augsburg, with merely verbal alterations made in 1563 and 1571. The fact that this subject is included in both documents shows that the question was one of importance at the Reformation, and, as we shall see, the Article is directed definitely against the view which obtained at that time.

I.—THE TEACHING OF THE ARTICLE

Before looking at the precise purpose of the Article in the light of Church History it seems essential to consider its actual teaching.

365

1. The fact of evil in the Church is clearly recognised.—" Although in the visible Church the evil be ever mingled with the good, and sometimes the evil have chief authority in the ministration of the Word and Sacraments." The term " visible Church " is found here, as in Article XIX. This is a sad confession, not merely of evil being mingled with good, but even of evil sometimes having chief authority in the ministry of the Church. It seems impossible to doubt that this is a significant reminder of the state of the Church at and before the Reformation.

2. The assurance is given that grace is independent of personal character. —" Yet forasmuch as they do not the same in their own name, but in Christ's, and do minister by His commission and authority, we may use their ministry, both in hearing the Word of God, and in the receiving of the Sacraments. Neither is the effect of Christ's ordinance taken away by their wickedness, nor the grace of God's gifts diminished from such as by faith and rightly do receive the Sacraments ministered unto them ; which be effectual, because of Christ's institution and promise, although they be ministered by evil men." As ministry is exercised in the Name of Christ we may use it even though it be evil in character, and grace is not lost by reason of an evil ministry since the ordinances are effectual because of Christ's institution and promise whatever may be the instrumentality of administration.

3. The assertion of the duty of discipline is maintained.—" Nevertheless it appertaineth to the discipline of the Church, that enquiry be made of evil ministers, and that they be accused by those that have knowledge of their offences ; and finally being found guilty, by just judgment be deposed." This shows that an evil ministry is not to be tolerated even though grace is rightly regarded as independent of it.

II.—THE PURPOSE OF THE ARTICLE

1. The Article is clearly against the Anabaptist view that the ministry was not effective because of the bad lives of the priests. Reformation changes were often ostensibly accepted by Roman Catholics, and this led to some frank speaking on the part of Protestants, especially because of the prevalence of ignorance and immorality. The subject will best be understood by a brief review of the circumstances of earlier ages.

There had been sects in the Church from early times who maintained that the efficacy of the Sacraments depended upon the priest or minister. Tertullian said that heretics did not minister Baptism because they did not worship the same God as Christians. In Tertullian this view was associated with the error of Montanism, which was an attempt to realise in the external Church that which is only found in the invisible. Montanists believed themselves to be subjects of a special revelation of the Holy Spirit, and looked upon the visible Church as an impure and corrupt body. Cyprian soon afterwards, together with the African Bishops, denied the validity of Baptism by heretics and also by schismatics. It seems not unreasonable to think that Cyprian was misled on this subject by his great reverence for Tertullian, whom he called " Master." His principle was that Baptism by heretics was Baptism into another Gospel, and he urged that no man could have God for his Father who did not have the Church for his mother. He pressed this so far as to say that such Baptism begat children to the devil and not to God. He was opposed by Stephen of Rome, and although he found strong support in the African Church and parts of the Eastern Church, his views were quietly but completely over-ridden by the Church in general.

The next similar question, but one to be distinguished from it, was associated with the Donatists in the fourth century. The seeds were first sown by opposition to particular Bishops. A certain Cæcilianus was elected to Carthage, and his recognition was opposed on the ground of the person by whom he had been consecrated being a *Traditor*, one who had handed over his sacred books under pressure of persecution. As such, he was regarded in deadly sin and therefore could not convey the grace of Ordination. Donatus was the leader, and the result was a large sect, having four hundred Bishops. They refused all communion with the African Church, and rebaptised all who came from it to their own faction. This, therefore, is different from the former question as being concerned with the moral disqualification, while the former was official, and it goes beyond the question of our two Sacraments, for it refers to the grace of Orders, and meant that no grace was conferred by the Word and the Sacraments.[1]

The result of this controversy was to elicit from Augustine in particular a thorough treatment both as to moral and official disqualification, and he laid down in the broadest possible terms that the grace associated with ministerial functions is independent of the character of those who administer. He even says that it matters not how much worse the man is who administers. Chrysostom makes a similar pronouncement.

After that the question slumbered until it was revived in the Middle Ages by the gross lives of many of the Roman priests. This had such an effect that the reactionists are now often blamed, but wrongly. It was this that led to Wycliffe falling into the error of Cyprian, and the Council of Constance in denouncing him condemned his error of saying that nothing was valid unless morally sound. The great divines of the Roman Church maintained that the validity of the Sacraments did not depend on the validity of the officiating minister. Thomas Aquinas says that the minister acts instrumentally and not in virtue of his own authority, so that it is not required for the performance of the Sacrament that the minister should be in a state of charity; indeed, it is not necessary that he should have faith, since the ministration of an unbeliever would be valid. At the same time there was a difference among Roman divines as to whether *Intention* was not needed on the part of the priests. But Aquinas decided against it, saying that a due performance of the words

[1] Harold Browne, *Exposition of the Thirty-nine Articles*, p. 604.

and acts was sufficient. He taught that sacramental grace is directed chiefly to two objects; first, the removal of the defect in the soul left by past sins in so far as guilt remains, and, secondly, the perfection of the soul in those things which relate to the service of God in the Christian life.

The rigid view of personal morality as a condition of ministerial validity was asserted by several extreme Protestant sects at the Reformation. The Anabaptists revived a sort of Montanism, alleging that the Sacraments were not to be ministered by unworthy men.[1] The rise of this view led to great danger, and one of Hooker's controversies with Travers was as to salvation in the Roman Church, and so great was the feeling on both sides that many were disposed to deny salvation to any outside their own pale. It was this that led to the question being considered as early as the Confession of Augsburg.[2] The *Reformatio Legum* refers to the Anabaptist error.[3] Thus, the Augsburg Confession and our Article were substantially Articles of peace, that we do not " unchurch " anyone, but establish a principle of mutual charity.

It is impossible to avoid noting the truth that underlies these earnest protests. It is, or ought to be, spiritually intolerable to listen to and to receive Sacraments from those who are known to be living in any form of deliberate sin.

2. The question has been raised whether the Article was also intended to oppose the Roman doctrine of Intention. We have seen that the question of ministerial validity was touched upon in the Middle Ages, and it is thought that our Reformers may possibly have had reference to it. How far is the intention of the minister necessary to the validity of the Sacraments? Bishop Gibson is of opinion that our Article is not against the Roman doctrine of Intention. He states in most unequivocal terms that this idea is a mistake: " The language of the Article in no way bears on the doctrine, and it is difficult to see how it could ever have been thought to do so."[4] On the other hand, there is no little

---

[1] "The scandal was great in the eyes of many to find the law depriving them of the ministers they trusted, and commanding them to attend the Parish Church, served perhaps by a man who had conformed to every change of Henry, Edward, Mary, and Elizabeth, and whose morals and learning they equally held cheap. The Zurich Letters, published by the Parker Society, or the lives of Archbishops Parker and Grindal, will fully illustrate the intensity of this feeling. To such feelings the present Article might offer an answer theoretically and theologically true; but it could not control those instincts and sympathies which really govern the majority of mankind in such matters" (Boultbee, *The Theology of the Church of England*, p. 222).

[2] "Quanquam ecclesia proprie sit congregatio sanctorum, et vere credentium; tamen, cum in hac vita multi hypocritæ et mali admixti sint, licet uti sacramentis, quæ per malos administrantur, juxta vocem Christi: Sedent Scribæ et Pharisæi in cathedra Mosis, etc. Et sacramenta et verbum propter ordinationem et mandatum Christi sunt efficacia, etiamsi per malos exhibeantur. Damnant Donatistas et similes, qui negabant licere uti ministerio malorum in ecclesia, et sentiebant ministerium malorum inutile et inefficax esse."

[3] "Deinde ab Ecclesiæ corpore se ipsi segregant, et ad sacrosanctam Domini mensam cum aliis recusant accedere, seque dicunt detineri vel ministrorum improbitate, vel aliorum fratrum" (*De Hæresibus*, c. 15).

[4] Gibson, *The Thirty-nine Articles*, p. 617.

authority for believing that Intention was in view.[1] It is known that the decree of the Council of Trent on Intention dates from 1547, and Jewel argued on the subject against the Jesuit Harding. Harold Browne, while thinking that the Doctrine of Intention was probably not aimed at, holds that the Article virtually and effectively meets it.[2] Generally speaking, the principle of the Roman Church is that this Intention is necessary. Thus, Aquinas says that if a man does not intend to minister the Sacrament and only does it in mockery the validity is at an end. The Council of Trent anathematises those who say that the intention of the minister to do what the Church does is not required.[3] Subsequently a subtle distinction arose between internal and external Intention. The external Intention is the intention of the priest to administer the Sacrament in the customary form; the internal Intention is the intention to administer it in the sense of the Church. The only vital difference is as to the internal intention, and on this there is a difference in the Roman Church itself. The Ultramontane party has maintained the necessity of the internal intention, while the Gallican school have denied this. The difficulty was founded in the practice of the Middle Ages, when Hildebrand, in order to carry out his strict rules as to celibacy, said that the Eucharist administered by married priests was invalid. And another Pope (1691) expressly said that Baptism is invalid, however complete its form, if the priest has no intention to carry out the doctrine of the Church. This has been justly described as the most dreadful of all the Roman doctrines, for it makes a man uncertain whether he has received the grace for which he came. The doctrine was a weapon forged by Roman subtlety to neutralise agreement with the liberal doctrine of Stephen against Cyprian. Thus, they say in the case of our Anglican Orders that they cannot tell whether the one who consecrated Parker intended to do so. So that this Article which was perhaps originally meant solely as a protest against extreme Protestants at the Reformation, now really stands as a protest against the Roman doctrine of Intention. It is easy to see the necessity of this doctrine from the standpoint of the Church of Rome. If Sacraments work *ex opere operato* with no condition required; if in private Masses there is no communicant; since in infant Baptism there is no conscious reception, where is the spiritual value except as rites only? Consequently intention is needed since moral fitness in the ministry is not required by either side. But, as we have already seen, if Sacraments work *ex opere operato* they are mechanical only, and on the question raised by Rome as to the intention of

---

[1] This is held by Boultbee (*ut supra*, p. 223); Litton, *Introduction to Dogmatic Theology* (Second Edition), p. 427; Maclear and Williams, *Introduction to the Articles of the Church of England*, p. 313; Tyrrell Green, *The Thirty-nine Articles and the Age of the Reformation*, p. 203; the last-named points out that while previously to Trent the doctrine was merely a scholastic opinion it has Papal sanction as early as 1539.

[2] Harold Browne, *ut supra*, p. 608.

[3] "Si quis dixerit, in ministris, dum sacramenta conficiunt et conferunt, non requiri intentionem saltem faciendi, quod facit Ecclesia: anathema sit" (Concil. Trident., Session 7, Canon 11).

2A

doing what the Church does, the words of Hooker have often been
quoted :—

" What a man's private mind is, as we cannot know, so neither are we bound
to examine ; therefore, always in these cases the known intent of the Church
generally doth suffice, and where the contrary is not manifest, we may presume
that he which outwardly doth the work, hath inwardly the purpose of the
Church of God."[1]

The principle of our Article agrees with the line taken in the Augsburg Confession, that the Scribes sat in Moses' seat, and St. Paul refers
to the Gospel as the power of God, not of man. The whole question
largely depends upon our reason, for unless it is proved that God does
not confer the grace Himself none of us can be certain if grace is received.
We avoid all this by insisting on faith. Rome could not do this, and so
required intention, attaching to the priest an inward requirement or
qualification to do what the Church intended. In this way he becomes
indispensable to the Sacraments.

We must, therefore, carefully distinguish between official unfitness
and moral unworthiness, between public officers and private individuals,
between ministerial duty and spiritual efficacy. It is essential to exercise
discipline in regard to everything connected with evil, and yet it is
equally necessary to remember that personal moral unworthiness cannot
debar a soul from grace, or else we shall never have anything but uncertainty in view of our ignorance of the human heart. While, however,
we maintain very strongly the fundamental principles laid down in the
Article, yet it is equally true that unless the personal life of the clergy be
exemplary it is scarcely possible to expect blessing in the Church.[2]

[1] Hooker, *Eccl. Pol.*, Bk. V, Ch. LVIII, p. 3.
[2] "God may honour His own Sacraments and Word in spite of man's guilt; but it
is contrary to reason, to experience, to history, to Scripture, to suppose that an ungodly,
still less a vicious, ministry can issue in anything but an ungodly and corrupt state of
the people. No conspicuous work of grace has shown itself apart from a faithful,
devoted, prayerful administration of the word and ordinances of Christ" (Boultbee,
ut supra, p. 222 f.).

ARTICLE XXVII

<table>
<tr><td>Of Baptism.</td><td>De Baptismo.</td></tr>
</table>

Baptism is not only a sign of profession, and mark of difference, whereby Christian men are discerned from other that be not christened, but it is also a sign of Regeneration or New Birth, whereby, as by an instrument, they that receive Baptism rightly are grafted into the Church; the promises of forgiveness of sin, and of our adoption to be the sons of God by the Holy Ghost, are visibly signed and sealed; Faith is confirmed, and Grace increased by virtue of prayer unto God.

The Baptism of young children is in any wise to be retained in the Church, as most agreeable with the institution of Christ.

Baptismus non est tantum professionis signum, ac discriminis nota, qua Christiani a non Christianis discernantur, sed etiam est signum Regenerationis, per quod, tanquam per instrumentum, recte Baptismum suscipientes Ecclesiæ inseruntur; promissiones de remissione peccatorum, atque adoptione nostra in filios Dei per Spiritum Sanctum, visibiliter obsignantur; fides confirmatur, et vi divinæ invocationis gratia augetur.

Baptismus parvulorum omnino in Ecclesia retinendus est, ut qui cum Christi institutione optime congruat.

IMPORTANT EQUIVALENTS.

From other that be not christened	=	*a non Christianis.*
Of Regeneration or New Birth	=	*Regenerationis.*
Whereby	=	*per quod.*
As by an instrument	=	*tanquam per instrumentum* = legal advice.
Rightly	=	*recte.*
Are grafted into the Church	=	*Ecclesiæ inseruntur.*
To be the sons	=	*in filios.*
Are visibly signed and sealed	=	*visibiliter obsignantur.*
By virtue of prayer unto God	=	*vi divinæ invocationis.*
In any wise	=	*omnino.*
As most agreeable	=	*ut qui optime congruat.*

This represents the Article of 1553, with only slight verbal alterations. The last paragraph at that time was thus worded, " Mos Ecclesiæ baptizandi parvulos et laudandus est, et omnino in Ecclesia retinendus " —" The custom of the Church to christen young children is to be commended, and in any wise to be retained in the Church." In 1563 the Article had " sign and seal of our new birth," which was changed in 1571 to the present phrase, " sign of regeneration or new birth."

I.—THE MEANING OF BAPTISM IN SCRIPTURE

It is essential to consider this, first of all. What is the primary and original idea of Baptism as distinct from any results arising out of it ? As Scripture does not state or define this meaning we must derive it from usage. Three Baptisms are mentioned in the New Testament : Jewish (Heb. ix. 10) ; John the Baptist's ; Christian. There must, therefore,

371

be some common characteristic of all three with specific differences. Two Greek words are found in this connection: βάπτισμα, and βαπτισμός. The former is used for John's Baptism and Christian Baptism; the latter for the Jewish " washings " or " Baptisms " (Mark vii. 4; Luke xi. 38, 39; Heb. ix. 10). This word is never employed to describe the ordinance of Baptism in the Christian Church. Then, too, the English words " Baptism " and " Baptise " are literal renderings of the Greek, and require proper interpretation. Another difficulty is that one Greek preposition is associated with Baptism and yet has four renderings in English: *into* (Rom. vi. 3); *unto* (Matt. iii. 11); *for* (Acts ii. 39); *in* (Matt. xxviii. 19). The true idea of εἰς is " with a view to." In Acts ii. 38 we have ἐπί as well. It must be noted also that the verb βαπτίζειν, *baptise*, in reference to the individual who is to be baptised, is always found in the middle or passive voice, never in the active. " What doth hinder me from being baptized " (Acts viii. 36); " Repent and be baptized " (Acts ii. 38); " Arise, and be baptized " (Acts xxii. 16). From this it is clear that the Divine side of Baptism is primary, the minister being the representative of God. Baptism is thus fundamentally and primarily something from God to us, not from us to God.

But what is the common and what is the characteristic feature of each of these three New Testament " Baptisms " ?

1. In general, the idea is purification, or washing, a symbolical or ceremonial purification (Luke xi. 39; John iii. 25; 1 Pet. iii. 21).

2. Then each of these has a specific purpose in the washing, it is " with a view " to something (εἰς). The Jewish Baptism was with a view to Temple membership and worship; the Baptism of St. John was with a view to repentance and the coming of the Messiah; Christian Baptism was with a view to relationship with God in Christ.

3. A further characteristic is that of separation or designation for a specific purpose. Thus, the Jews used washing for the purpose of hallowing or consecrating their priests and Levites (Exod. xxix. 1, 4; Num. viii. 14), and so we read of " the water of separation " (Num. xix. 9). In the same way, the Israelites are said to have been baptised, that is separated, designated, separated for Moses (1 Cor. x. 2).

4. Thus, blending the word " Baptism," " washing," and the preposition, εἰς, " with a view to," we arrive at the thought of " washing with a purpose." The general idea is purification, the specific idea is designation.

When this is applied to Christian Baptism we see exactly what Scripture intends. " Whereunto then were ye baptized ? " (Acts xix. 3). " Baptizing them with a view to the Name " (Matt. xxviii. 19). So that Baptism is a Divine designation with a view to (*a*) remission (Acts ii. 38); (*b*) union (Matt. xxviii. 19). It is also noteworthy that Baptism always looks forward, not backward, and is connected with God's promises. It always possesses the element of futurity, " with a view to."

Thus, we observe that there is nothing in Scripture about the pro-

fession of faith in connection with Baptism; the Divine side is fundamental, and it must be kept so and made perfectly clear. Baptism implies
Divine designation. Confession of Christ is obviously not by Baptism
only, but throughout the entire life, and whenever there is confession in
Baptism it is accidental and no part of the essential meaning of the rite.
The soul can be designated for and consecrated to God altogether apart
from any profession before men. This will be found to be the case in
every instance in the New Testament, for nowhere is confession before
men taught, still less required.

II.—THE MEANING IN THE ARTICLE

It is clear from the foregoing consideration of Baptism that the statements in the Article are secondary rather than primary, referring to the
ecclesiastical rather than the purely personal aspects of the ordinance.

1. Baptism is a sign of Christian profession.—" A sign of profession,
and mark of difference, whereby Christian men are discerned from others
that be not christened." This idea of Baptism as the Divine mark of
Christians is an elementary view accepted by all, and it is seen in our
Baptismal Service, where the statement is made that " Baptism doth
represent to us our profession."

2. Baptism is a sign of regeneration.—" A sign of Regeneration or
New Birth." The word " sign," *signum*, has the same meaning as in
Article XXV, a pledge or seal. Circumcision was thus the seal of
Abraham's faith (Rom. iv. 11). Regeneration is explained as " New
Birth " and everything depends on the meaning of this word.[1] Attention should specially be called to the idea of birth, which is invariably
associated with Baptism. Much turns on the distinction between life
and birth, with the former of which Baptism is never connected either
in Scripture or in the Prayer Book.

3. Baptism is the instrument of introduction into the Church.—The
word " Whereby " has in the Latin the equivalent, *per quod, i.e. signum*;
it does not refer to the regeneration nor is anything implied as to this.
Per is also important, referring to instrumentality, not direct agency.
This has reference to the doctrine that God confers grace and not that
the Sacrament works *ex opere operato*, and the Latin is also important in
showing that *per quod* governs the whole of the remaining section down
to " God." The word " instrument," *instrumentum*, gives the idea of
" a legal instrument," " a deed of conveyance," so that Baptism " gives
as a deed gives, not as an electric wire gives."[2] The word *instrumentum*
was frequently used in the sixteenth century to express the Sacraments.[3]

[1] The subject can be studied in Dimock, *The Doctrine of the Sacraments*; Goode,
Infant Baptism; Mozley, *The Baptismal Controversy*.
[2] Bishop Moule, *English Church Teaching*, p. 98; cf. pp. 91, 95.
[3] Quotations can be seen in Hardwick, *History of the Articles of Religion*, p. 39 .

III.—THE CONDITION OF BAPTISM

The Article speaks of receiving Baptism " rightly," and the Latin
equivalent is important, *recte*, not *rite*. Comparison may be made with
Article XXVIII on the Lord's Supper, which is to be received " rightly
(*rite*), worthily, and by faith."   The word *rite* refers simply to the outward
ceremony, while *recte* includes inward dispositions as well.   Jerome's
words are sometimes quoted in this connection; " They that receive not
Baptism with perfect faith receive the water, but the Holy Ghost they
receive not."[1]   This principle can be illustrated from the Catechism:
" What is required of persons to be baptized ? "   " Repentance, whereby
they forsake sin ; and Faith, whereby they steadfastly believe the promises
of God made to them in that Sacrament."   So that in accordance with the
teaching of Article XXV the efficacy of Baptism is conditional on true,
that is, trustful reception.   No view of this Sacrament can be satisfactory
which does not account fully for the Baptisms recorded in the Acts.   Thus,
in chapter ii. 38, we read : " Repent, and be baptized every one of you
in the Name of Jesus Christ with a view to the remission of sins, and ye
shall receive the Holy Ghost."   In chapter viii. 13, Simon Magus was
baptised apparently without receiving the Holy Spirit.   In chapter x. 47,
Cornelius was baptised after he had received the Holy Spirit.   It is clear
from a careful consideration of these and other instances that Baptism is
associated with the promises of spiritual blessing and the introduction of
the recipient into the sphere of the Christian Church where those
blessings become available.[2]

IV.—THE EFFECTS OF BAPTISM

The Article then proceeds to show what precisely is accomplished by
Baptism.
   1. " Grafted into the Church."—This of course refers to those who
receive Baptism rightly (*recte*), and does not apply merely to Baptism as a
rite, because admission into the visible Church is not conditional on the
necessity of spiritual qualification but only on its profession.   The word
recte corresponds with the teaching of Acts ii. 38 ; 1 Cor. xii. 13 ; Gal.
iii. 26, 27.   If, however, the visible Church is to be understood it makes
the Baptism the rite of admission.
   2. The promises of forgiveness and adoption are signed and sealed.—
" The promises of the forgiveness of sin, and of our adoption to be the
sons of God by the Holy Ghost, are visibly signed and sealed."   This
connection of Baptism with promise is another illustration of the principle
laid down in Article XXV, that the Word of God as a Divine revelation

---

[1] Quoted in Goode, *ut supra*, p. 253.
[2] "Baptism, being a sacrament of the New Covenant, can effect nothing more than
that which is promised by the Covenant; and the revealed Covenant blessing of new
life is conditioned by repentance and faith" (Tait, *Lecture Outlines on the Thirty-nine
Articles*, p. 184).

intended to be met by the response of faith is the great underlying principle of all Sacraments (Acts ii. 38, 39; xxii. 16).[1] Special emphasis is evidently to be placed on the thought of visibility, " visibly signed and sealed," thereby giving the outward assurance by means of this ordinance that our sins are forgiven, and that we are adopted to be sons of God by the Holy Ghost. The words, " by the Holy Ghost," were first inserted in the English Version in 1563, though corresponding words were in the Latin text of 1553. In 1563 the clause was printed with a comma after " Ghost," so as to show that the reference was to the preceding adoption. This is the truth associated with Rom. viii. 14-16; Gal. iv. 5, 6. Some think, however, that the words " Holy Ghost " are to be taken in close connection with what follows. " By the Holy Ghost are visibly signed and sealed." But the English punctuation seems conclusive, to say nothing of the fact that the thought of the Holy Spirit doing a visible work is impossible and incredible. This latter view would therefore seem to be altogether unnatural.[2]

3. Faith is confirmed.—This shows that the faith is assumed to be already in existence before the ordinance, and the whole statement is another illustration of the necessity of faith for the purpose of receiving spiritual blessing.

4. Grace is increased.—" Grace increased by virtue of prayer unto God." Again it is to be observed that grace is presumably in existence before the administration, since increase alone is here mentioned. This corresponds exactly with the Latin of Article XXV, which speaks of Sacraments stirring up faith (*excitat*). The prayer in the Baptismal Service shows the same truth : " Increase this knowledge, and confirm this faith," referring to the recipients of the ordinance.

So we may say the Article affirms three things : (1) that Baptism is a sign of difference between Christians and other men ; (2) that it is a sign of regeneration or new birth ; (3) that it is an instrument of regeneration under five aspects ; (a) Incorporation with the Church ; (b) ratification of the promise of remission ; (c) ratification of the promise of adoption ; (d) strengthening of faith ; (e) increase of grace.

The doctrine of Baptism is best understood when we remember that God has made with man a covenant. This is the starting point of everything, for it not only implies that God has established a definite relation with Christians, but also that there are pledges of that covenant, the latter giving the Divine assurance, since without them there would only be on God's part an intention of goodwill and on ours an intention of trust. So that the Sacraments remain proofs and pledges of God's goodwill, and as personal covenants they are living witnesses of the Divine action of God in Christ. There can be no doubt that Baptism is the

[1] Dimock, *ut supra*, p. 44 ff.; Bishop Moule, *ut supra*, p. 101.
[2] For this question of punctuation see Gibson, *The Thirty-nine Articles*, p. 629 f.; Tyrrell Green, *The Thirty-nine Articles and the Age of the Reformation*, p. 211; Tait, *ut supra*, p. 181.

initiatory part of that covenant. On God's side it involves what is necessary for our life here and hereafter; pardon, adoption, the Holy Spirit, and everlasting life. These blessings are offered spontaneously and freely by God without any previous merit of ours, and are offered in themselves absolutely and not conditionally, though their nature is such that they cannot operate mechanically, and therefore require a response from us if they are to be enjoyed. There is a vital difference between offering a thing conditionally, and offering it absolutely while needing response to enjoy it. Following the Divine offer and pledge, we may regard Baptism as the formal act by which we embrace God's covenant, and it is the engrafting into that Church to which the promises belong. This is the meaning of our becoming or being made " members of Christ, children of God, and inheritors of the Kingdom of Heaven." Baptism introduces us into a new and special relation to Christ. It provides and guarantees a spiritual change in the condition of the recipient, but we must carefully distinguish between a change of spiritual relationship and a change of moral disposition. The words " new birth " suggest that Baptism introduced us into a new relation and new circumstances with the assurance of new power. But it is important to distinguish between this relation itself, which is regeneration, and the result of the relation, which is sanctification. Waterland says that regeneration is a renewal of the spiritual state at large, while renovation is a particular kind of renewal, namely, of the inward frame. Regeneration is therefore to be distinguished from renovation, and this distinction, though always observed in fact, has not always been observed in terminology, for men like Jeremy Taylor and Beveridge, while upholding what they believe to be Baptismal grace, yet spoke of the baptised as unregenerate, meaning that they were without renovation. This doctrine therefore involves the fact that the condition of the baptised is different from and superior to those who are unbaptised. It may be difficult in modern degeneracy to say that the baptised are better than the unbaptised, but speaking broadly it is so, for Baptism at least introduces the recipient to the sphere of the Church which on any view is decidedly higher and better than any sphere outside. In the case of adults repentance and faith are necessary prerequisites, and without these we must not expect the blessings of regeneration. But the reasons why they are requisite is not that they are necessary to contribute to the blessings, since God gives these unconditionally. They mean that our impenitence and unbelief can act as obstacles to God's grace. In regard to infants, while faith is personally impossible, they are accepted on the faith of their sureties, and it is on this ground that they are accepted just as are adults. But this subject will call for fuller consideration at a later stage.

V.—THE SUBJECTS OF BAPTISM

There is no question as to adults since they constitute the normal case, as seen in the New Testament from the Day of Pentecost onwards.

The Article therefore concentrates attention on the Baptism of children, and its carefully balanced and cautious statement calls for special notice. " The Baptism of young children is in any wise to be retained in the Church, as most agreeable with the institution of Christ." We have already seen that in 1553 this paragraph was worded somewhat differently : " The custom of the Church to christen young children is to be commended, and in any wise to be retained in the Church." This general, cautious, and yet definite statement is particularly valuable in view of modern teachings and tendencies in the direction of indiscriminate Baptism, and its position is in thorough harmony with the teaching of the Church through the ages.

" Is there any rule of the Universal Church compelling Infant Baptism ? When we consider that St. Augustine, son of a Christian mother, was not baptised until he was of full years, may we not accept the principle of freedom as regards Infant Baptism, especially in Missionary districts. There are many who are doubtful even of the advisability of indiscriminate Infant Baptism in some districts of England. Although we do not agree with them, it must be recognised that there is no Catholic rule compelling Infant Baptism."[1]

There are two questions which must be kept in view : (a) Why are Infants baptised ? (2) What are the results of Infant Baptism ? The Article is concerned with the former, and it is necessary to endeavour to justify the statement that the Baptism of young children is " most agreeable with the institution of Christ." We have seen that the meaning of Baptism is God's designation or consecration of the recipient for the purpose of entering into union with Him in a life of discipleship. Our Lord's commission (Matt. xxviii. 19, 20) was, " Go ye and make disciples of all nations, baptizing them . . . teaching them." A disciple is a learner, and as all disciples were to be baptised all the baptised were regarded as learners. So that the one question is whether children can be disciples or learners, whether the term is elastic enough to include them. There is nothing absurd or impossible in baptising an unconscious infant " with a view to " ($\epsilon\iota$ς) something unless profession of faith is an essential characteristic of Baptism, which, as we have seen, it is not. There is not a single passage in the New Testament which connects Baptism with the confession of Christ. Baptism, let it be said again, symbolises and expresses God's act to us. Assuming, therefore, that children can be disciples or learners, the following reasons may be adduced why young children should be regarded as fit subjects of Baptism, and their Baptism considered as " most agreeable with the institution of Christ."

1. There is, first of all, a much deeper question than the fitness of infants for Baptism. It is as to the exact relation of unconscious child-

---

[1] Article by Dr. Headlam, *Church Quarterly Review*, Vol. LXXVII, p. 418 (January 1914); see also *English Church Manual* on "Baptism," by Principal Grey.

hood to the Atonement of Christ. Whether we think of children dying or living, the fact is the same : what is the spiritual position of these infants in relation to our Lord ? Surely the truth is that all children are included in the great atoning sacrifice, and belong to Jesus Christ until they deliberately refuse Him. This is the great spiritual fact at the root of the practice of Infant Baptism. It is our testimony to the belief that childhood belongs to Christ and has its share in the great redemption. We baptise a child not in order to make it Christ's, but because it already belongs to Him by the purchase of His Sacrifice on Calvary. It would surely be strange if our Lord had no place for unconscious childhood in His plan of mercy and love for the race, for in view of the fact that so many die in infancy, perhaps at least half of the human race, it is surely impossible to think that they can be ignored entirely, and attention concentrated not on children but adults, with, it may be, experience of sin and wandering before receiving His love and grace.

2. In harmony with this we find the relation of God as the Father of unconscious childhood declared as early as the time of Abraham (Gen. xvii. 7). God then pledged Himself to be the God of Abraham and his seed, and this attitude of Divine Fatherhood has never been altered or modified through the centuries.

3. Another proof of this attitude is the ordinance of circumcision given to Abraham as a pledge of the Divine word. While circumcision was naturally used first of all of adults in the person of Abraham, and, as such, was the seal of an existing faith (Rom. iv. 11), it was also used for unconscious childhood when obviously it could not be the seal of faith. This modification of meaning when applied to children shows the position of childhood in the Abrahamic covenant of grace. It is entirely inadequate, and, indeed, inaccurate to speak of circumcision as merely the mark of Israelitish nationality, for in the case of pre-Mosaic circumcision, it is distinctly alluded to in connection with the Abrahamic covenant of grace. In the same way, Baptism to an adult Christian is the seal of an already existing faith, but to the little children of such an adult it is the pledge and seal of covenant blessings assured to the believer and his seed. The analogy is thus exact and complete.

4. In entire harmony with the foregoing we find little children entering into covenant with God, thereby showing the possibility of child-life having a true relation to God (Num. iii. 28 ; Deut. xxix. 10-12).

5. The attitude of our Lord to little children supports all that has been adduced. It is evident from His words and action (Mark x. 13-16) that little children are capable of spiritual blessing. His Divine words are the great charter of childhood. " Of such is the Kingdom of God " must mean in view of the context, " *such little children*," not, as is sometimes suggested, " such childlike natures," for this is the truth taught to the adults in the next verse. Our Lord first tells those around Him what children are in relation to things spiritual, and then solemnly tells the

adults that they too must become like little children if they would enter the Kingdom.

6. It is impossible to overlook the existence of households in the record of the early Church (Acts xvi. 15, 32, 34). Household Baptisms were prominent in the New Testament times, and although of course it is impossible to prove the existence of children, yet so general and inclusive a term was hardly likely to have been employed if the reference had been only to the Baptism of adults. If we should read nowadays of household Baptisms in the Mission Field it would be a fair inference that children were included. A study of the verses mentioned shows that there is a real unity between the head of the household and the members of it, and in the case of the jailer we are only told of his own personal faith (Acts xvi. 34, Greek) though all his house were immediately baptised. To the same effect are the words of St. Peter on the Day of Pentecost (Acts ii. 39), showing that children were still one with their parents in covenant blessings and promises.

7. The references to children in the Epistles are all along the same line of thought. St. Paul teaches plainly (1 Cor. vii. 14) that the children of Christian parents are in some way hallowed by reason of their parents' faith in Christ: " Else were your children unclean ; but now are they holy." There is no possible reference here to illegitimacy, but to what has been called relative or derived holiness, which would be changed in due course to personal holiness. The Apostle states the precious fact of the father's or mother's faith hallowing the little child as belonging to God.[1] Then, too, St. Paul's counsels to children (Eph. vi. 1-4 ; Col. iii. 20) assume their existence in the membership of the Church and their inclusion in " the saints and faithful " to whom the Epistles are addressed.

These are the grounds on which our Church finds her warrant for retaining the practice of Infant Baptism as in thorough harmony with the spirit and genius of Christianity, and when these considerations are given due weight, it is possible to see the futility of any argument urged on the ground that we have no command to administer Baptism to infants, an objection which would apply equally well to several other important and vital matters for which we have no command, though we have un-doubted inferences which warrant the practice. So also the objection that repentance and faith are required for Baptism does not affect the question of childhood, for while they are required for adult salvation apart from Baptism, no one would think of applying these conditions to the salvation of unconscious childhood. Those who bind up faith with Baptism in so absolute a way are curiously inconsistent in the case of adults who profess faith when they are baptised and are afterwards seen to have had no real trust in God. These are not baptised over again

---

[1] Lightfoot, *Notes on the Epistles of St. Paul*, says: " It enunciates the principles which lead to Infant Baptism; viz. that the child of Christian parents be treated as Christian."

when the real faith shows itself, and in such a case the person would be taught to enter spiritually into what his Baptism was intended to mean. This is exactly similar in principle to the position contended for in the case of children baptised in infancy, and then taught the spiritual meaning of their Baptism. It is sometimes argued that Infant Baptism necessarily implies infant participation in the Holy Communion, but this does not follow. There is such a thing as infant membership, as distinct from adult, and Holy Communion requires intelligence for the remembrance of Christ in a sense which Baptism certainly does not.

We therefore conclude that the practice of admitting infants into the visible Church of Christ with a view to their becoming possessed of all spiritual blessings is in accordance with the Word of God and with the revelation of His will. To the child Baptism is a constant reminder of God's attitude and covenant, and the designation of it in Baptism can be pressed as a motive to life and service. To the parent the Baptism of the child is a seal and pledge of God's acceptance, and this will elicit faith in the parent, and lead to the instruction of the child concerning Christian discipleship. The Kingdom of God is essentially a Kingdom of Promise, and every child introduced into the fellowship of the Church is introduced in virtue of the promise of God made to the children of believers. So that children are capable of relationship to Christ and of spiritual blessings. Baptism introduced them to the sphere where such opportunities are given while it also expresses a belief in the fact and possibility of blessing. On the basis of this assurance everything connected with the child is associated, and in due course the full realisation through faith in Christ will lead to all the blessings of the Christian covenant.[1]

VI.—THE EFFECTS OF INFANT BAPTISM

All the effects of Baptism mentioned in the Article are clearly applicable to adults only, for such statements as receiving " rightly," " forgiveness of sins," " adoption by the Holy Ghost," "faith confirmed," " grace increased" are all associated with adult, conscious life. And to grasp the doctrine of the Sacraments in its completeness we must view them as though all the conditions were present. This makes it essential to study the subject in the adult first of all. It is hardly without significance that nothing is mentioned in the Article as to the precise effects of Baptism on young children. But in view of the Baptismal services and the universal practice of Infant Baptism it is essential to consider the subject. Articles XXV, XXVI, XXVII are all clearly against the *opus operatum* theory, and yet the Baptismal Service has, "Seeing now that

[1] On the subject of Infant Baptism, see Litton, *Introduction to Dogmatic Theology* (Second Edition), p. 249; *English Church Teaching*, p. 103 f.; T. D. Hall, *Is Infant Baptism Scriptural?*, Barnes-Lawrence, *Infant Baptism*; D. H. D. Wilkinson, *Baptism : What saith the Scripture?*; Hubert Brooke, *Who, How, and Why Baptized?*. Although the Article does not discuss the method of Baptism, the subject will be found treated in an Additional Note, p. 521.

this child is regenerate "; and the Catechism also speaks of, " My Baptism, wherein I was made a member of Christ," etc. How are these to be reconciled ? The question largely turns on the interpretation of the word " Regeneration," and differences of opinion are almost wholly due to its ambiguity. There are three main views. They are difficult to describe in simple terms, but a consideration in detail will enable us to realise the distinctions.

1. Sacramental.—This interprets " I was made " as " I became," as in John i. 14, ἐγένετο. On this view grace enters the soul unless a bar is placed against it, and thus it is not the presence of our repentance and faith, but the absence of their opposites which constitutes fitness for grace. An adult may resist, but a babe cannot, and so the germ of life is planted in the child and this will develop if not stifled and abused. Now as this view is virtually identical with the *opus operatum* theory the following considerations need attention.

(*a*) Such a position is not only nowhere found in the Prayer Book and Articles as qualifying for Baptism, but it is virtually, if not actually, denied by the emphasis laid on the necessity of spiritual conditions.

(*b*) If it be said that at the Savoy Conference the Bishops in opposing the Puritans endorsed the theory of grace apart from the placing of a bar,[1] it should be pointed out that fifty years before that Conference the view was opposed by leading theologians of the day.[2]

(*c*) A mere negative condition cannot be regarded as the equivalent of a positive living faith.

(*d*) The Catechism, on the contrary, requires repentance and faith by the sureties, and it is on this ground, not on the absence of a bar, that the infant is allowed the Sacrament.

(*e*) Indiscriminate Baptism has never been allowed, although on this view it would be perfectly justified.[3]

2. Hypothetical.—This interprets " I was made " as " I was considered," as in 2 Cor. v. 21 (ἐποίησε); 1 John i. 10 (ποιοῦμεν). This gives " regeneration " its full spiritual meaning of a moral change of nature (2 Cor. v. 17), but regards the language of the service as that of

---

[1] Gibson, *ut supra*, p. 612.

[2] Abbott, Regius Professor of Divinity, Oxford, and Bishop Carleton of Llandaff.

[3] Bishop Gore in his Introduction to *Pastors and Teachers*, by the Bishop of Manchester, says :

"The Church does not baptise infants indiscriminately. She requires sponsors for their religious education; and the sponsors represent the responsibility of the Church for the infants who are being baptised. It is not too much to say that to baptise infants without real provision for their being brought up to know what their religious profession means tends to degrade the Sacrament into a charm. On this point we need the most serious reflection."

And an article in the *Church Times* (February 1908) entitled "Fencing the Font," says: "Those who advocate the indiscriminate Baptism of all children who can be gathered to the administration of the Sacrament have lost touch with the most essential feature of the Church's discipline. If they are to grow up in ignorance of Christianity, they had far better grow up unbaptised. Conversion will then be for them a more definite thing: how much fuller and richer than if they had a forgotten Baptism in their past, is known to those who have dealt with souls so placed."

faith and charity. All the conditions are assumed to be fulfilled, and so the blessings are assumed to be bestowed. In support of this position the following arguments are used.

(*a*) The whole Prayer Book is based on this assumption of sincerity.

(*b*) The Baptismal Service consists of two parts, or sides, involving covenant blessings : (1) offered (exhortations); (2) accepted (questions and answers); (3) sealed (act of Baptism); (4) followed (post-Baptismal prayers and exhortations).

(*c*) This view carefully emphasises the great principles connected with the Reformation position, that the ordinances are conditional, and that if children have a right to them they too must fulfil the conditions.[1]

3. Covenantal.—This interprets " I was made " by " I was put into a condition or sphere," as in Rom. v. 19, $\kappa \alpha \tau \epsilon \sigma \tau \acute{\alpha} \theta \eta \sigma \alpha \nu$. This means a change of covenant-head from Adam to Christ, and the acknowledgment of an already existing change of covenant head (1 Cor. vii. 14). The main arguments may be thus stated.

(*a*) This interprets " regeneration " by distinguishing life from birth. Birth is not life, but the introduction of a living being into a new state or world.

(*b*) Regeneration occurs twice in the New Testament. In St. Matt. xix. 28 it clearly means a new state or new circumstances. In Titus iii. 5 it is obviously distinguished from the renewing of the Holy Ghost. In the same way, St. John iii. 3 refers to birth, $\gamma \epsilon \nu \nu \eta \theta \hat{\eta}$ (Latin, *generatus*, conceived ; *natus*, born). Nicodemus seems to have understood the idea in this way. " How can a man be *born* ? " And in Article IX, where the Latin is *renatis*, the English word is " regenerated," while the English " believe and are baptised " finds its Latin equivalent in *renatis et credentibus*. According to this interpretation, therefore, regeneration is not equivalent to spiritual conversion.

(*c*) Baptism is always associated in the New Testament with birth, not with life. Birth is not a germ or seed of life, but the entrance of life into a new sphere, to enjoy privileges and to fulfil the functions of a life already possessed.

(*d*) If Baptism means the implantation of life for the first time, how are we to explain the existence of repentance and faith in an adult beforehand, since these are the marks of an existing life ? Yet this very person is prayed for at Baptism in regard to regeneration by water and the Holy Ghost. In harmony with this, this Article speaks of faith being confirmed and grace increased. So that " born of water," if it refers to Baptism, must mean the introduction into the Society of the visible Church, just as " born of the Spirit " means introduction into the spiritual Church (1 Cor. xii. 13).

(*e*) The only question is whether these two are always and necessarily

---

[1] This is the view declared in the well-known Gorham case, and in Goode's great work, *The Effects of Infant Baptism*. See also Mozley, *The Review of the Baptismal Controversy*, and *The Primitive Doctrine of Regeneration*. Cf. *English Church Teaching*, p. 104.

coincident. The Spirit is sovereign and cannot be tied to any outward rite depending on man for its performance. So that it is not necessarily the case that a man is introduced into the spiritual realm simply because he is introduced into the visible realm by Baptism.

(*f*) We can judge of the presence of spiritual life only by its manifestation, and the germ-theory of Baptism, which on the *opus operatum* view means the implantation of a seed of life that may lie dormant and then die or grow, is clearly inaccurate, since birth is not hidden or dormant life, but life visible and manifested. So that whether born of water or of Spirit, the effects must be perceptible. Hence, the grace may be imparted before, or at, or after the outward rite. We may charitably and hopefully presume its existence, but time alone will show whether in the adult or the child.

Reviewing these three interpretations, it is clear that the first is ruled out of our formularies as entirely opposed to the Church of England position, and the true view will probably blend the second and third ; the one for the sponsors and the other for the child. This meets all the needs, for even if the parents have no faith the child does not suffer entire loss because of the visible opportunity in the Church to which it is introduced.

If it should be asked why infants are baptised privately in view of death, the answer is to (*a*) insure Christian burial, (*b*) to assure of membership in the Christian Society. As to personal salvation, that depends on the Atonement of Christ. Baptism, as we have seen, looks towards introduction into a new world of fellowship, not towards eternal salvation. It is impossible to think that the Reformers would accept the *opus operatum* view here after denying it always elsewhere.

This general position can be justified on three grounds :—

(1) The views of the Reformers.—They undoubtedly held a doctrine of " Baptismal Regeneration," but it was not identical with that of Rome. The controversy which is now called " Baptismal Regeneration " they waged under the name of the " *Opus Operatum* Theory." They all believed Baptism to be the Sacrament of regeneration, but this was not so by the rite itself, but always as conditional and associated with the Gospel. An illustration of this is seen in the corresponding Sacrament of the Holy Communion. No Roman Catholic believes in the transubstantiation of water, or of the indwelling of the Spirit therein, and so the Holy Communion is exalted in that Church out of all proportion to Baptism. But the Reformers treated both Sacraments exactly in the same way. They used sacramental language, that is, they employed interchangeably the name of sign and thing, teaching that while all received blessing sacramentally, not all received it really. They thus distinguished between sacramental and spiritual regeneration. This is a well-known principle of Scripture which our Prayer Book follows in speaking of the sign and the thing signified in the same terms. St. Paul can speak of " the laver of regeneration," and St. Peter can say, " Baptism doth now save us," though both mean much more than the water. In illustration

of this view it may be pointed out that the leading Puritans never objected to the words, "Seeing now that this child is regenerate," nor did Baxter later on, because Whitgift had said that the Reformers taught that Sacraments did not contain, but only sealed grace. They never meant to declare dogmatically anything as to what is really received besides those signs which represent and bear the name of inward grace, and so the due administration of the Sacrament meant a formal and sacramental grant of privileges which make the recipients children of grace.

What, then, is the relationship of the sign to the thing signified? First, it is related to doctrine, as may be seen from the definition of the Homily already quoted, that Sacraments are visible signs "to which are annexed promises." The doctrine of the Gospel represents a written deed of conveyance, of which the Sacraments are the signs and seals. Second, the sign is related to grace as a pledge and seal, thereby correcting the view that the elements "contain" grace. Faith is, therefore, to exercise itself on the remembrance of Baptism. Parents are to make Baptism the starting-point for instruction in discipleship, reminding children of the pledge and seal. There would be no objection to this position if our faith were not so low, for to the Reformers these things were realities. We do not occupy ourselves sufficiently with the promises of God, although the Catechism speaks of "steadfastly believing the promises of God made in that Sacrament."

(2) Our Formularies.—Both the Articles and the Baptismal Service are intended to bring out the relation of Baptism to God's gift in the Gospel.[1] The word "mystical" always means "sacramental," "symbolical," and not necessarily "real," though, of course, the seal carries with it the promise and responsibility of grace. "Mystical" never means our modern idea of "mysterious," but always and only "figurative," though in such a way that the figure bodies forth a reality, as "the mystical Body of Christ." "Mystical" means "a figure to illustrate what is obscure, not to darken what is plain."[2]

There are thus two questions to be faced : (a) the meaning of "Wherein I was made," etc. ; (b) "All the elect people of God." We must find some principle which will explain and resolve both. The assumption of universal spiritual regeneration in the full sense would explain the former phrase, but not the latter. The only principle that will meet both sides is that which regards Baptism as introducing us to a new relation, as a seal of the covenant, and implying that the child will stand to the promise of the covenant. So that "Wherein I was made," etc., refers to privileges promised and sealed for the acceptance of faith. This is shown by the words, "Faith, whereby we steadfastly believe," etc., implying the ratification of a covenant grant. This is far more than any mere ecclesiastical sense and involves a real relation between sacramental and spiritual reception, a consecrated relationship of seals to the gift of grace. This view was approved of by English Reformers, by Foreign Reformers,

[1] Dimock, *ut supra*, p. 28.   [2] So, Boultbee.

by early Puritans, and was never questioned for fifty years after the Reformation. On 14th June 1552, just after the publication of the Second Prayer Book, Peter Martyr wrote to Bullinger that everything had been removed from the Prayer Book which could nourish superstition. This has an important bearing on the meaning of our Baptismal Service as finally settled in 1552.[1] It is, therefore, incorrect to say that our Service was imperfectly reformed, especially since the words, " Seeing now that this child is regenerate," date from 1552, which is usually regarded as the high-water mark of English Protestantism.[2] Nor is there any inconsistency between the teaching of the Prayer Book and the Articles.[3] The main point is the true relation of the Sacraments to the covenant of grace. Sacraments are not associated with the Gospel as unique channels of grace through the application of material elements, but are seals of the promises of the Gospel, the promises being restricted to those in whom the Spirit works. It must never be forgotten that the promises connected with the Sacraments are not different from the rest of the promises, but are the warp and woof of the New Testament revelation.

(3) The teaching of Scripture.—Each term in the Catechism is used in the Bible in a twofold sense: outward and inward; ecclesiastical and spiritual. We see this in regard to Israel (Rom. ii. 29; ix. 6). This twofold idea of membership in Christ can be seen in 1 Cor. xii. 27 compared with 1 Cor. vi. 15-18. The reference to children of God is equally clear. In the Old Testament all Jews were circumcised, and even Dives can speak of " Father Abraham " (Luke xvi. 24). Yet our Lord does not hesitate to associate them with their " father, the devil " (John viii. 44). To the same effect, the phrase, " Inheritor of the Kingdom of Heaven," has its earthly as well as its heavenly side, and so we have the twofold sense of opportunity and actuality. In the same way, Baptismal Regeneration is twofold. Regeneration is birth into the visible Church; conversion is birth into the Church invisible; death is birth into the Church of Paradise; resurrection is birth into the Church of Eternity. So that Baptism is the introduction of the recipient, whether adult or child, into a new condition or relation. It must not be overlooked that since the Puritan age Regeneration has come to mean renovation or conversion. But this was not the meaning of the Reformers, nor has the idea been changed in the Prayer Book. Israel as circumcised was a separate people, but within this area there was a smaller circle, the spiritual Israel, yet the former was always held responsible because of being in covenant relationship. Even without faith the seal of circumcision was a call to believe the act, so that a circumcised Jew was not merely a member of a visible community, but was in such a covenant relationship to God as ought to have been made into a spiritual reality.

---

[1] Dimock, *ut supra*, pp. 38, 42.
[2] Dimock, *ut supra*, pp. 33, Note, 35, 37.
[3] Dimock, *ut supra*, pp. 66, 157, Note.

And when Gentile proselytes were admitted they were called " regenerate," because they were introduced to the covenant and baptised. Thereby they obtained a relationship which the man was to accept in faith and make his own.

There is the same distinction between the visible and the invisible Church. The Epistles assume a spiritual position for the readers, and yet often utter warnings as to their actual condition. In the same way, Baptism represents a formal donation of a gift, which has to be appropriated by faith. How can a washing committed to the ministry of a man be a washing of regeneration in the full sense of spiritual blessing ? The whole question of grace and sacramental grace needs thorough consideration. Grace is not something infused or poured into the soul at certain times. Such a quasi-materialistic idea is not found in Scripture. Grace, as we have seen, is relationship to God, and the Sacraments imply the establishment of a relationship which did not exist before. When looked at in the light of the New Testament Sacraments are perfectly simple. They rest on the authority of Christ, and it is striking, perhaps it is also significant, that no promise of grace is actually attached to either, nor is the word " grace " ever found connected with Baptism or the Holy Communion.[1] Spiritual realities are due to believing obedience to whatever Christ enjoins. It is this, and this alone, that involves blessing.

It will be seen from this that the principle of Sacraments is that they *signify* something. The material element cannot produce a spiritual effect, which is only wrought by an agent of the same nature as itself, so that water is an agent for the body and not for the soul. This is doubtless why it is possible for St. Paul to speak as he does about Baptism (1 Cor. i. 14-17), since otherwise baptising would have been his highest ministerial function. It is untrue to say that God's appointment alone makes them efficacious unless we can show what that appointment really means. Even the blood of bulls and goats, though of Divine appointment, could not put away sin. Moral effects are only produced by moral means. The terms " channel " and " convey " are figures of speech only, unless we are to understand grace as like a material substance, conveyed through a material medium. Once again, we must remember that to "convey " is legal only, and involves no spiritual change apart from the act of him who is to be changed. When, therefore, we realise that grace is God's attitude of favour towards us we see that obviously it cannot reside in the material element.

The key to the right interpretation of the sacramental service is that the terms are to be understood in a sacramental sense, just as legal terms are to be understood in a legal sense. Baptismal regeneration means regeneration as related to Baptism. We have only to substitute " sacramental " to see this quite clearly. But to make it mean spiritual regeneration is to overlook the fact that the adjective is " Baptismal." And to be

---

[1] This could easily be proved by a reference to Bruder's or Moulton's *Concordance*.

sacramentally regenerate is to be regenerate *in foro ecclesiæ*, while to be spiritually regenerate is to be regenerate *in foro cœli*. So that "Wherein I was made" means sacramentally put into possession of the privileges of the Christian Church, and this is exactly what the Article says when it speaks of Baptism as "a sign of regeneration or New Birth."

It is, therefore, clear that the Reformers in their own books and also in the Formularies for which they are responsible, did not intend to condemn all doctrine of Baptismal Regeneration, but only the sense it has come to have to-day. They put the doctrine of Baptism into its true position in relation to the grace of the Gospel. They saw in it the seal of that gift, the real covenant donation of Divine grace, and they knew faith's acceptance of that gift as the beginning of the believer's new life. So that in the theology of the Reformation the controversy did not turn on the question whether there was or was not a true doctrine of Baptismal Regeneration, for the Reformers never hesitated to admit that Baptism is the Sacrament of Regeneration. The controversy hinged on the question whether there was or was not an inward and spiritual efficacy in the *opus operatum*, an administration apart from its connection with the Gospel of Christ, with the reconciliation of the soul to God, and the conversion of the heart to Christ. To this question the theology of the Reformation answered with a very decided negative.

This negative in denying universal, spiritual, inward efficacy in the mere administration can be proved by the following considerations:—

(*a*) By the word *recte* in Article XXVII.

(*b*) By the conditional doctrine of the Catechism, "Why, then, are infants baptised?"

(*c*) By the conditional character of the Baptismal Service.

(*d*) By the clear doctrine of the Homilies.

(*e*) By the spiritual dangers, as seen in Jewish history (Rom. ii. 25-29).

(*f*) By the refusal to assume necessary connection between sign and grace. This is not held in Holy Communion, or found in adult Baptism, or seen in such a case as that of Simon Magus. The fallacy as to the *opus operatum* view, which is now often called Baptismal Regeneration, is that those who hold it emphasise right administration, while our Church emphasises right reception.

(*g*) By the facts of the case. Our national life to-day is a positive proof that the spiritual efficacy does not invariably attach itself to Baptism

ARTICLE XXVIII

Of the Lord's Supper.

De Cœna Domini.

The Supper of the Lord is not only a sign of the love that Christians ought to have among themselves one to another, but rather it is a Sacrament of our Redemption by Christ's death: insomuch that to such as rightly, worthily, and with faith, receive the same, the Bread which we break is a partaking of the Body of Christ; and likewise the Cup of Blessing is a partaking of the Blood of Christ.

Transubstantiation, or the change of the substance of Bread and Wine in the Supper of the Lord, cannot be proved by Holy Writ; but is repugnant to the plain words of Scripture, overthroweth the nature of a Sacrament, and hath given occasion to many superstitions.

The Body of Christ is given, taken, and eaten, in the Supper, only after an heavenly and spiritual manner. And the mean whereby the Body of Christ is received and eaten in the Supper is Faith.

The Sacrament of the Lord's Supper was not by Christ's ordinance reserved, carried about, lifted up, or worshipped.

Cœna Domini non est tantum signum mutuæ benevolentiæ Christianorum inter sese, verum potius est Sacramentum nostræ per mortem Christi redemptionis: atque adeo rite, digne, et cum fide sumentibus, panis, quem frangimus, est communicatio corporis Christi; similiter poculum benedictionis est communicatio sanguinis Christi.

Panis et Vini Transubstantiatio in Eucharistia ex sacris literis probari non potest; sed apertis Scripturæ verbis adversatur, Sacramenti naturam evertit, et multarum superstitionum dedit occasionem.

Corpus Christi datur, accipitur, et manducatur in Cœna, tantum cœlesti et spirituali ratione. Medium autem, quo corpus Christi accipitur et manducatur in Cœna, fides est.

Sacramentum Eucharistiæ ex institutione Christi non servabatur, circumferebatur, elevabatur, nec adorabatur.

IMPORTANT EQUIVALENTS.

The Supper of the Lord	= *Cœna Domini.*
Ought to have	= [no Latin].
Rather	= *potius.*
Insomuch that	= *atque adeo.*
Rightly	= *rite.*
To such as receive	= *sumentibus.*
A partaking	= *communicatio.*
Or the change of the substance	= [no Latin].
In the plain words	= *apertis verbis.*
Is repugnant	= *adversatur.*
[Is] eaten	= *manducatur.*
Of the Lord's Supper	= *Eucharistiæ.*
Was not reserved	= *non servabatur.*
Was not carried about	= *non circumferebatur.*
Was not lifted up	= *non elevabatur.*
Was not worshipped	= *non adorabatur.*

HISTORY

THE present Article is in some respects materially different from the corresponding Article of 1553, and the changes call for special attention.

Article XXIX of 1553 did not contain the clause "overthroweth the nature of a Sacrament," which was added in 1563 and translated into "perverteth the nature of a Sacrament." The word "perverteth" was changed to "overthroweth" in 1571.

The third paragraph, "The Body of Christ is given," etc., was inserted in 1562 in place of a different one which was contained in the Article of 1553. This will need special attention at the proper place. According to Bishop Harold Browne, the clause was omitted and a new one substituted in Queen Elizabeth's reign, "lest persons inclined to the Lutheran belief might be too much offended by it; and many such were in the Church whom it was wished to conciliate."[1]

Several equivalents in the English and Latin Versions need special attention. (a) Paragraph 1. "Ought to have" is not in the Latin. (b) Paragraph 1. "Rightly, worthily, and with faith" is, "*rite, digne, et cum fide.*" (c) Paragraph 1. "Partaking" is "*communicatio.*" (d) Paragraph 2. "Or the change of the substance" is not found in the Latin.

I.—THE MEANING OF THE LORD'S SUPPER IN SCRIPTURE

1. This is the true starting-point, the discovery of what the Holy Communion means at its source, by a minute study of all the places where it is found. There are five passages: three records of the institution in the Synoptic Gospels, and St. Paul's references in 1 Cor. x. and xi. There is no other clear or even likely passage where the subject is mentioned or implied. Two titles may perhaps be regarded as scriptural; the Breaking of Bread (Acts ii. 42), and the Lord's Supper (1 Cor. xi. 20). Later on the word "Communion" (1 Cor. x. 16) and "Eucharist" are found, the latter being traced to Ignatius. But these are not found in Scripture as titles.

2. The Supper was instituted on the eve of our Lord's death, and was given only to disciples. This necessitates the enquiry as to what the disciples knew beforehand of that death. Generally, they knew the fact and a little of its meaning (Matt. xvi. 21).

3. But the main question is as to the interpretation of the great passage in St. John vi., which is often associated with the Holy Communion. What is the precise relation of this passage to the ordinance? The following points need consideration :—

(1) The discourse was spoken to unbelievers, not disciples, and at least a year before our Lord's death.

(2) The references to His death are all in absolutely universal terms, emphasising the necessity of participation by all without the slightest qualification (*vv.* 51, 53, 54, 56, 58).

(3) Our various bodily functions are treated as the best means of explaining our spiritual functions. These are not merely figures, but

[1] *Exposition of the Thirty-nine Articles,* p. 707.

analogies, like birth, sustenance, assimilation of food. We are taught that it is not sufficient merely to trust Christ, but there must be something in the spirit which corresponds to eating in the body, a reception of Him in our inmost soul until His will and nature become a part of ours, and, like food, strengthen all our faculties. There is nothing in our nature that so closely corresponds to this assimilation of Christ and our union with Him as eating and drinking, and it is, therefore, used here. If, then, we would feed on the Saviour and be in union with Him it is not enough to regard Him as our Teacher, or Master, or God; we must accept Him in the great act of His sacrifice as well. So that in the reception of Christ is included every part of His work for us. Primarily, it means spiritual feeding on the Atonement, since we must first be reconciled before we can do anything else. The result, fruit, or effect of our participation in the Atonement is fellowship with Him in union with His Body, and the outcome is a gracious vital presence of His Divine nature abiding in us. This general view is held by most of the ancient writers, however differently they may express it. They taught that Christ was primarily and properly our Bread of Life.[1] Of the Reformers Cranmer is the best representative, and he taught that the passage is not to be interpreted of oral eating in the Eucharist or of spiritual eating confined thereto, but of spiritual eating, whether in or out of the Eucharist. It means feeding on Christ's death and passion with the result that we have a mystical union with Him. Such spiritual eating is a privilege belonging to the Eucharist, so that the chapter is not foreign to the ordinance, but bears the same relation to it as the outward sign to the inward reality.

(4) In view of these facts a direct interpretation of the chapter in relation to the Holy Communion is obviously impossible, as the leading commentators agree. The relation is really one of universal to particular. It is not that the chapter refers to the Holy Communion, but the Holy Communion refers to it, or still better, both refer in different ways to the Cross. If the chapter is interpreted primarily of the Holy Communion, then the universal terms imply and require the necessity of participation in the Holy Communion by everyone for the purpose of receiving eternal life. As this is manifestly impossible and unthinkable, the interpretation which meets all the necessities of the case is the absolute requirement of participation in the Atoning Sacrifice of Christ. This admits of no exception or qualification, and there can be no doubt that the passage has in view the Atoning Sacrifice for the life of the world, and the necessity of individual and universal participation therein.[2]

4. The Passover associations with the institution of Holy Communion must be carefully studied. Whatever may be decided as to the exact date of the institution there is no doubt of the close association of the Lord's Supper with the Passover. Consider the following resemblances:—

[1] For the Fathers on St. John vi., see Waterland, *On the Eucharist.*
[2] See Bishop Moule, *What does John vi. mean?*

(1) The Passover was the memorial of a great deliverance from temporal bondage. The Eucharist was a memorial of spiritual redemption.

(2) The Passover prefigured the death of Christ before it was accomplished. The Eucharist was intended to look back upon the death as accomplished.

(3) The Passover was a covenant or federal rite between God and man. The Eucharist was associated with the New Covenant.

(4) No one was to eat of the Passover before circumcision. The Lord's Supper was only for disciples.

(5) The Passover was to continue as long as the Jewish law. The Eucharist is to continue " until He come."

(6) Total contempt of the Passover cut off a man from Jewish communion. No one can lightly ignore a Divine command of Christ.

(7) The Jew needed ceremonial cleansing for proper participation. The disciple at the Lord's Supper should be right with God and man.

(8) The Passover in our Lord's time was a feast only so far as individual houses were concerned, the actual sacrifice of the lamb having been made at the Temple. So with the Lord's Supper, the covenant action with the Passover refers to the feast only, since based on the Atonement of Christ our whole life is to be one continual festival (1 Cor. v. 7, Greek).[1]

5. The language used in the New Testament of the Lord's Supper must be studied with the greatest possible care.

(1) " He took bread and blessed."—God is the Object of this blessing, not the element, as the corresponding words " gave thanks " clearly show. Westcott points out that the word " bless " is never used directly of material objects as though conveying some special force. The blessing, therefore, was an acknowledgement of God as the Giver, the full phrase being to " bless God for the thing."[2]

(2) " This is My Body which is given for you."—The word " is " when used as a copula has no meaning apart from its context. It must be either literal or symbolical. This language corresponds exactly with that used at the Passover. " This is the bread of affliction which our ancestors ate in the land of Egypt."[3] It would be wise if writers remembered the language of Bishop Gore on this subject.

" It is, I venture to think, useless to argue with too great exactness about the word *is*. It describes very various kinds of identification. It is a sufficient warning against laying too much stress on it, that in one report our Lord is made to say, This cup is (not ' My Blood,' but) the new covenant in My blood. The copula, therefore, is clearly indeterminate."[4]

The words " which is being given on your behalf " must always be closely connected with the following phrase, " This is My Body," and

---

[1] *English Church Teaching*, p. 122 f.   [2] Westcott, *Hebrews*, pp. 203–205.
[3] Girdlestone, *Four Foundation Truths*, p. 57.   [4] Gore, *The Body of Christ*, p. 246.

" give " means " sacrificially to God," the reference obviously being to Calvary, not to the elements. The present tense is used for a future that is regarded as certain ; is to be.

(3) " This cup is the New Covenant in My Blood."—No one ever thinks of taking this literally, since such an interpretation would be senseless.

(4) " Which is shed for you and for many," that is " poured out on the Cross on your behalf."[1]

(5) " The New Covenant," that is, " claiming a part in the New Covenant which by My death I shall ratify." See Jer. xxxi. 31.

(6) " Remembrance."—The word (ἀνάμνησις) always means an act of the mind recalling and never an objective memorial (μνημόσυνον). The two Greek words for " remembrance " and " memorial " are never identical, but always carefully distinguished.[2]

(7) " Do this."—The force of the present tense in the Greek is " Do this again and again," i.e. " perform this action." It cannot possibly mean " Offer this."[3]

(8) " Fellowship " (1 Cor. x. 16).—The word is never used of participation (μετοχή), but partnership or fellowship. It refers to communion of persons with persons in one and the same thing, several persons all enjoying the same (1 John i. 7). The phrase " communion of the blood " is like " fellowship of the Spirit," referring to our partnership with one another in the same blessed reality.

(9) " Ye do shew " (1 Cor. xi. 26).—The word καταγγέλλειν means quite literally " pronounce " or " proclaim," and the indirect object of the verb is always man, never God. It cannot possibly mean " exhibit before God."[4] Attention has been called to the curious fact of mis-quotation of the English Version as " Shew forth the Lord's death." This is done in a well-known hymn, but the Apostle's allusion was evidently to the custom associated with the Passover which was " pronounced " or " proclaimed " in the sense of commemoration (Exod. xii. 26).

[1] Westcott, Life and Letters, Vol. II, p. 352, says: "'This is' must be taken in the same sense in 'This is My Body' as in 'This cup is the New Covenant.' It cannot be used of material identity. Cf. John xv. 1 ; the Lord is most really and yet not materially the True Vine."

[2] "A 'memorial' is something exterior to the person, which can generally be perceived by the senses; whereas the word translated 'remembrance' is a mental act, performed in, or by, or upon the mind. A 'memorial' may produce a 'remembrance,' but it is certainly not the mental effect or act itself" (Soames, The Priesthood of the New Covenant, p. 28). Readers of Marriott's Correspondence with Carter, and of his Memorials, will recall the strong plea made for a grammatical exegesis. The best authorities are perfectly clear against rendering the Greek term by the former word. Bishop Gore also admits this (The Body of Christ, (First Edition), p. 315).

[3] "To render the words 'Sacrifice this' is to violate the regular use of the word 'do' in the New Testament, and to import polemical considerations into words which do not in any degree involve or suggest them" (Bishop Ellicott on 1 Cor. xi. 25).
See also Plummer on St. Luke, p. 497 f.; Bishop Gore, ut supra; Westcott, Life and Letters, Vol. II, p. 353. This is also the rendering of the writers of the early Church and the compilers of the Ancient Liturgies.

[4] Perowne, The Doctrine of the Lord's Supper, p. 8; Marriott, Memorials, p. 207.

(10) "Unworthily . . . guilty . . . not discerning."—The verb
διακρίνειν is the same as in verses 29-31, implying a lack of true commemoration. There was no charge of idolatry, but by irreverence they
were guilty of offence against God.

(11) In 1 Cor. x. " table " is used for the Lord's Supper, though in the
same context " altar " is used for heathen sacrifices.[1]

(12) In Heb. xiii. 10, " We have an altar," the context is quite against
the idea of the Holy Communion.[2]

(13) In all the references to the Lord's Supper the two parts are kept
separate, implying the idea of Body and Blood separate in death. The
sole thought is the death of Christ. Blood could not enter into the
glorified humanity, so that the Holy Communion is always associated
with Christ's death, never with His glorification.[3]

(14) No distinction is drawn in the New Testament between the
institution and later occasions of the Holy Communion. Scripture
regards the first Communion as " a true Communion,"[4] and in no respect
did subsequent celebrations possess any spiritual difference, unless it be
by the power of Pentecost in degree of spiritual reception and realisation.
The gift of our Lord at the original institution was not different from

[1] "Some interpreters, from a comparison of 1 Cor. ix. 13, with x. 18, have inferred
that St. Paul recognises the designation of the Lord's table as an altar. On the contrary,
it is a speaking fact that in both passages he avoids using the term of the Lord's table,
though the language of the context might readily have suggested it to him, if he had
considered it appropriate. Nor does the argument in either case require or encourage
such a reference. In 1 Cor. ix. 13, 14, the Apostle writes: 'Know ye not that they
which wait at the altar are partakers of the altar? Even so hath the Lord ordained
that they which preach the Gospel should live of the Gospel!' The point of resemblance
in the two cases is the holding a sacred office; but the ministering at the altar is predicated only of the former. So also in 1 Cor. x. 18, e.g. the *altar* is named as common
to Jews and heathens, but the *table* only as common to Christians and heathens, i.e.
the Holy Eucharist is a banquet, but it is not a sacrifice (in the Jewish or heathen
sense of sacrifice") (Lightfoot, *Philippians*, "Essay on the Christian Ministry," p. 13).

[2] "In this stage of Christian literature there is not only no example of the application
of the word 'altar' to any concrete, material object as the Holy Table, but there is no
room for such an application" (Westcott, *Hebrews*, pp. 456, 458).

"The writer of the Epistle speaks of Christian sacrifices and of a Christian altar, but
the sacrifices are praise and thanksgiving and well-doing, the altar is apparently the
Cross of Christ. If the Christian ministry were a sacerdotal office, if the Holy Eucharist
were a sacerdotal act in the same sense in which the Jewish priesthood and the Jewish
sacrifice were sacerdotal, then his argument is faulty and his language misleading.
Though dwelling at great length on the Christian counterparts to the Jewish priests,
the Jewish altar, the Jewish sacrifice, he omits to mention the one office, the one place,
the one act, which on this showing would be their truest and liveliest counterparts in
the everyday worship of the Church of Christ" (Lightfoot, *ut supra*, p. 265).

[3] "One grave point I am utterly unable to understand—how 'the Body broken' and
'the Blood shed' can be identified with the Person of the Lord. I find no warrant in
our Prayer Book or ancient authorities for such an identification." "The circumstances
of the Institution are, we may say, spiritually reproduced. The Lord Himself offers
His Body given and His Blood shed. But these gifts are not either separately (as the
Council of Trent) or in combination Himself. It seems to me vital to guard against the
thought of the Person of the Lord in or under the form of bread and wine. From
this the greatest practical errors follow . . . " (The elements) "represent His human
nature as He lived and died for us under the conditions of earthly life" (Westcott,
Life and Letters, Vol. II, p. 351).

[4] Ellicott on 1 *Cor.* x. 16.

that bestowed by Him since. What He gave then He gives now, through His Body and Blood as shed in their spiritual force and efficacy, a gift offered to and received by faith alone.[1]

Thus, in the Holy Communion we may be said to have the whole Gospel in miniature : Christ for us, in us, with us, coming again. We recall Him, appropriate Him, confess Him, expect Him. The Gospel Supper appeals to intellect, heart, conscience, and soul.

As we review the place and meaning of the Lord's Supper in the primitive Christian life, we can readily understand its general conception and proper position. The very fact that so much of the teaching is incidental is a specially significant testimony to the proper interpretation. We may be sure that nothing that is not found in the New Testament can be regarded as essential, and we have only to remember some of the circumstances to realise what the Holy Communion meant. The place of institution was a house, not a Temple; the persons were ordinary Jews, not of the priestly line; the circumstances were associated with a family meal, a family gathering at the Passover time. It is surely impossible to imagine anything being of vital importance to the interpretation and administration of the Lord's Supper, which is not found plainly taught or clearly implied in the New Testament.[2]

III.—THE MEANING OF THE LORD'S SUPPER IN THE ARTICLE

In the first clause of the Article three aspects of the Lord's Supper are mentioned.

1. A sign of Christian love.—The social aspect of the Holy Communion ought to be carefully noted (1 Cor. x. 17), though, of course, by itself it is inadequate.

2. A Sacrament of our Redemption by Christ's death.—As we have observed already, *sacramentum* in the Articles always refers to the outward part, including word and action, as the *signum*. The Lord's Supper is thus a sign or symbol of Calvary. The Communion Service similarly speaks of " Holy mysteries, pledges of His love." The Lord's Supper is to the eye what the Word is to the ear.

3. A means of grace.—" Insomuch that to such as rightly, worthily, and with faith, receive the same, the Bread which we break is a partaking of the Body of Christ; and likewise the Cup of Blessing is a partaking of the Blood of Christ." The Lord's Supper " conveys " as in Article XXV. It is like a title-deed to those qualified to receive, for it is an opportunity for the appropriation of the spiritual efficacy. The teaching

---

[1] Plummer, Article, "Lord's Supper," Hastings' *Bible Dictionary*.

[2] For fuller consideration of the New Testament teaching, see Plummer on *St. Luke*, and Article, "Lord's Supper" in Hastings' *Bible Dictionary*; Ellicott, *Speaker's Commentary*, and *International Critical Commentary* on 1 Cor. x., xi.; two Articles on the "Lord's Supper" in Hastings' *Dictionary of Christ and the Gospels*; Barnes-Lawrence, *The Holy Communion*; the present writer's *A Sacrament of our Redemption*, Chs. I–V.

of the Catechism is in harmony with this statement: "What are the benefits whereof we are partakers thereby? The strengthening and refreshing of our souls by the Body and Blood of Christ, as our bodies are by the Bread and Wine."

III.—THE DOCTRINE OF TRANSUBSTANTIATION

1. The Definition.—Transubstantiation is explained in the English of the Article as "the change of the substance of Bread and Wine in the Supper of the Lord." It is necessary, therefore, to see how far this accords with the official teaching of the Roman Catholic Church.

(a) The Council of Trent teaches as follows:—

"Canon 1.—If any one shall deny that the body and blood, together with the soul and divinity of our Lord Jesus Christ, and, therefore entire Christ, are truly, really, and substantially contained in the Sacrament of the most holy Eucharist; and shall say that He is only in it as in a sign or in a figure, or virtually, let him be accursed. Canon 2.—If any one shall say that the substance of the bread and wine remains in the Sacrament of the most holy Eucharist, together with the body and blood of our Lord Jesus Christ; and shall deny that wonderful and singular conversion of the whole substance of the bread into the body, and of the whole substance of the wine into the blood, the outward forms of the bread and wine still remaining, which conversion the Catholic Church most aptly calls Transubstantiation, let him be accursed. Canon 3.—If any one shall deny that in the venerated Sacrament of the Eucharist, entire Christ is contained in each kind, and in each several particle of either kind when separated, let him be accursed. Canon 4.—If anyone shall say that, after consecration, the body and blood of our Lord Jesus Christ is only in the wonderful Sacrament of the Eucharist in use whilst it is taken, and not either before or after; and that the true body of the Lord does not remain in the hosts or particles which have been consecrated, and which are reserved or remain after the communion, let him be accursed."[1]

(b) The Creed of Pope Pius IV is in accordance with the above.

"I profess likewise, that in the Mass there is offered to God, a true, and proper, and propitiatory sacrifice for the living and for the dead. And that in the most holy Sacrifice of the Eucharist, there is, truly, really, and substantially, the body and blood, together with the soul and divinity of our Lord Jesus Christ: and that there is made a conversion of the whole substance of the bread into the body, and of the whole substance of the wine into the blood: which conversion the Catholic calls Transubstantiation."[2]

(c) In exact agreement with the above Canons and Creed the Catechism of the Council of Trent teaches thus:—

"But now the pastors must here explain, that not only the true body of Christ, and whatever appertains to the true mode of existence of a body, as the bones and

[1] Session 13.　　　　　　[2] Fifth Article.

nerves, but also that entire Christ, is contained in this Sacrament. . . . Because in the Sacrament of the Eucharist the whole substance of one thing passes into the whole substance of another, the word ' transubstantiation ' was rightly and wisely invented by our forefathers."

2. The History.—This calls for careful consideration.

(a) The wording of the Nonconformist Doddridge, " My God, and is Thy table spread," shows what liberty of language is possible when no thought of precise doctrine is in question. The language of the early Fathers was similarly free, inexact, and rhetorical, because there was no controversy. It is, therefore, necessary to take their statements with care because of the tendency of Oriental symbolism.[1] Their standpoints differed according to the needs of the times. On the other hand, it is equally necessary to be on our guard against minimising the teaching of the Fathers, especially because the heathen outside the Church were under a good deal of misapprehension as to the Sacraments.

(1) Ignatius stands alone in using the Lord's Supper against the Docetæ as a proof of the reality of our Lord's Body, but to show that we cannot take him literally the following words will suffice : " Renew yourself in faith, which is the Body of Christ, and in love, which is the Blood."[2]

(2) Irenæus spoke of a spiritual nature united to the elements and thus giving a power for resurrection.

(3) Clement of Alexandria and Origen speak of spiritual nourishment by spiritual food, but there is no sort of transubstantiation.

(4) Cyprian marks a change by the use of " priest " and " altar," and later on sacrificial terms were freely used.

(5) Athanasius shows himself in harmony with Clement and Origen, and after Nicæa we have one witness who is sufficient alone to carry the argument against transubstantiation in Theodoret in the fifth century.

(6) But as time went on the symbolism became transformed into literalism in growing ignorance of and real inability to enter into the spirituality of pure Christianity.

(b) The doctrine that the Bread and Wine are not figures, but the very Body and Blood of Christ was taught at the Second Council of Nicæa,

[1] "Several of the Fathers have spoken so strongly of eating the flesh and drinking the blood of Christ, that it is easy for an ingenious partisan to select passages from their works that shall seem to favour this doctrine; though others positively reject it as a preposterous conclusion. . . . I will merely refer to a decisive passage in Augustine, which must be taken as qualifying and explaining away any high-flown tropes and metaphors, which he may have used in his devotional works. 'If a passage be a precept either forbidding a crime, or enjoining an useful or charitable act, it is not figurative; but it is figurative if it seems to command a crime, or to forbid an useful or charitable act. When our Lord says, *Except ye eat the flesh of the Son of Man and drink His blood, ye have no life in you*, He appears to enjoin a crime. It *is therefore a figure*, teaching that we participate in the passion of the Lord, and we must sweetly and passionately treasure up in our memory, that His flesh was crucified and wounded for us'" (Macbride, *Lectures on the Articles*, p. 478 f.).
[2] *Ep ad Trall.*, Ch. VIII.

787, and by writers in the eighth and ninth centuries, but the full doctrine of corporal presence was first put forth by Paschasius Radbertus, 840, and after this time learning declined and superstition grew. He was much opposed by Ratramnus, or Bertram, to whom Bishop Ridley later on was largely indebted. The doctrine was also opposed by Berengarius in the eleventh century, who, however, did not maintain his opposition against the penal threats of Rome. The doctrine was introduced into England by Lanfranc in 1066, and at last it was decreed by the Lateran Council, 1215, the word " Transubstantiation " being either invented, or adopted from Peter of Blois. The decree of the Lateran Council was :—

" There is one universal church of the faithful, out of which no one at all is saved, in which Jesus Christ Himself is both Priest and Sacrifice, Whose body and blood are truly contained under the shapes (*sub speciebus*, kinds), of bread and wine in the Sacrament of the altar, having by the power of God been transubstantiated, the bread into His body and the wine into His blood, so that, for perfecting the mystery of union, we ourselves might receive of Him what He Himself received of us."

The Council of Trent finally established the doctrine, as stated above, and this continues to be the authorised and official doctrine of the Roman Church, and all study must, therefore, recur to the statements of the Council of Trent.

(*c*) This doctrine was one of those which was strongly and fundamentally opposed at the Reformation.

(1) Luther began by emphasising the truth of a Divine promise being attached to the Sacrament, necessitating faith for right reception. This emphasis on faith was his great point, but he never overlooked the real presence of Christ. He said that transubstantiation was a mere sophistical subtlety, and he thought nothing of it. This was the first stage of the Reformation, namely, that our Lord is present without defining the mode of the presence. But the matter could not remain thus, for all reference to the human body of Christ necessitated reasoning and argument. Luther urged that as Christ is on the right hand of God, and the right hand of God is everywhere, so Christ must be in or with the bread and wine, but he struggled against attaching any local relation of the body to the bread. Out of these conflicting statements two views prevailed among the Lutherans : one approached transubstantiation, and some phrases in the Augsburg Confession can hardly be said to differ from the Roman doctrine. Later on came consubstantiation, which it is difficult to define. It was associated with Luther's view of the ubiquity of our Lord's body, that as He is everywhere He must be given with the bread and wine, according to the literal interpretation of His words. But Lutheranism teaches that this occurs only at the moment of actual reception, that it is not so by virtue of consecration, and that it does not

continue after the reception. Nor is there any sacrifice of the Mass in
the Lutheran view. It will be seen from the history of Articles XXVIII
and XXIX that this Lutheran doctrine is no part of the English teaching.[1]

(2) Then other Reformers, like Carlstadt, Ecolampadius, and Zwingli,
broke away from this literalism to the allegorical view. The name of
Zwingli is generally regarded as expressing the commemorative view only,
though it is a matter of real question whether Zwingli held it himself.[2]
In any case, the view is not Anglican.

(3) The doctrine associated with Calvin is distinct from the other two
extremes, and teaches a presence which is such as does not involve attachment to the elements, or inclusion, or circumscription. According to
this the Spirit uses the elements through faith to unite us to Christ. By
many representative Churchmen this view is regarded as practically
identical with Anglican doctrine. It was certainly the view of Hooker,
but Bishop Moule makes one criticism, that Calvin associated the feeding
of the soul with our Lord's glorified humanity, which is not what our
Lord taught at the original institution.[3] Hooker's words are often quoted:
"The real presence of Christ's most blessed body and blood is not therefore
to be sought for in the Sacrament, but in the worthy receiver of the
Sacrament."[4]   And although in recent times attempts have been made to
show that these words do not represent the whole of Hooker's belief, the
result has not been convincing. Hooker's view is sometimes described as
that of a " virtual " presence only in the heart of the faithful recipient.[5]
But the word " virtual " is ambiguous and misleading. In modern phraseology it implies, " almost, but not really," but in connection with the
Lord's Supper, as taught by Calvin and Hooker, it refers to the " virtue,"
or " *virtus*," that is, the force of it.

(4) In the English Church to-day a view is held, though without the
word " Transubstantiation," that is practically identical with the teaching
of the Roman Church, and representative writers claim that there is no
essential difference between us and Rome on the Holy Communion.[6]
This makes it all the more important to consider with the greatest possible
care the reason why our Church rejects the Roman Catholic doctrine of
transubstantiation. Later on it will be necessary to enquire whether

[1] In 1892, Archbishop Temple, in his *Primary Charge*, said that it was difficult, if not
impossible, to distinguish between a doctrine held by certain extreme Anglicans and
the Lutheran doctrine of consubstantiation. But this view is now universally rejected
since those who hold the doctrine in the English Church deny any association with
consubstantiation, and the history of our Articles is, as we shall see, plainly opposed
to any identification of the Anglican and Lutheran doctrines.

[2] "The great Swiss Reformer, Zwingli, or Zwingel (who died 1531), is commonly
credited with having been a mere 'commemorationist.' The charge is baseless. He
held substantially the doctrine taught in the English Article (XXVIII). But writing
early in the history of the controversy on the Eucharist, he expressed himself sometimes incautiously" (see *Expositor*, Sixth Series, Vol. VIII, p. 161 f.; Bishop Moule.
The Supper of the Lord, p. 50, Note).

[3] Bishop Moule, *The Supper of the Lord*, p. 42 f.

[4] *Eccl. Pol.*, Bk. V, Section 67.

[5] Gibson, *The Thirty-nine Articles*, p. 663.

[6] Dr. Darwell Stone, *The Holy Communion*, p. 186.

there is any Catholic doctrine which, while not Roman, is distinct from the Reformed doctrine of Calvin and Hooker, involving a presence of our Lord as somehow attached to the elements by consecration.

3. The Rejection.—Transubstantiation is rejected by the Article on four grounds.

(a) It cannot be proved by Scripture.—This is clear from such passages as " that Rock was Christ " (1 Cor. x. 4); " I am the door " (John x. 7). As already seen, the interpretation which insists on the literalness of " This is My Body " defeats itself, especially when the full words are remembered, " This is My Body, which is given for you," thus clearly referring to the sacrifice of Calvary.

(b) It is repugnant to Scripture.—Christ was present at the time of the institution, and He spoke afterwards of " the fruit of the vine " (Matt. xxvi. 29). St. Paul similarly speaks of " bread " (1 Cor. x. 17 ; xi. 26). The only case of transubstantiation in the Gospels is the change of water into wine (John ii. 1-11), but the word in connection with the Holy Communion is " is," not " becomes."

(c) It overthrows the nature of a Sacrament.—The outward sign has gone, the doctrine of transubstantiation rests on a distinction between substance and accidents, between internal essence and visible properties. But this is impossible, since accidents are essentially characteristic.[1] In the case of digestion and corruption Aquinas said that the consecrated element was no longer the Body of Christ, but this really refutes the theory and involves a view practically equivalent to our own.

This phrase in the Article was adopted for the first time in 1563, after the Council of Trent had put forth its decree on Transubstantiation, and it was retained in 1571, doubtless with direct reference to it, for while it is untrue to say that Roman Catholics ever taught that the outward sign completely disappeared, nevertheless, the theory of Trent bids us disbelieve our senses and believe that in spite of them the bread has ceased to exist. Bishop Thirlwall[2] pointed out the fallacy, for " if a substance and its accidents are correlatives, it can no more be possible for the accidents to exist without the substance than the parts without their whole." It is impossible to conceive of a thing which neither senses nor imagination can realise. The word " there " is an adverb of place.

(d) It has been the cause of many superstitions. A large number of stories are associated with this doctrine, including cures, legends, processions, etc. The Festival of Corpus Christi dates only from the thirteenth century. It is a singular phenomenon in the Roman Catholic Church that the importance of the Ascension is minimised, and from the standpoint of transubstantiation this is consistent, for the early Church emphasised Ascension Day as being " the boundary of the dispensation of

---

[1] "The philosophy which holds that 'substance' has an existence of its own independently of its manifestations was never undisputed, and is now wholly out of date" (B. J. Kidd, The Thirty-nine Articles, p. 233).

[2] Charge, 1869.

Christ," and it was only when the theory of transubstantiation came in that the Festival of Corpus Christi was instituted. A nun dreamt of a breach in the moon through no Feast to the Sacrament being included in the Christian Year.[1]

IV.—THE DOCTRINE OF THE LORD'S SUPPER

The third clause, which embodies this teaching, was changed in 1563 from that which was found in the Article of 1553. The question is whether this change was intended as an alteration of doctrine. It is urged by some that this was undoubtedly the case.[2] By others it is argued with equal force that no such change was intended.[3] The question is one of historical fact, and it is important that nothing should be overlooked which will help towards arriving at the true meaning. But, first of all, it is essential to see what the paragraph itself contains when properly interpreted.

1. The fact of spiritual blessing.—"The Body of Christ is given, taken, and eaten, in the Supper." The phraseology is important, because the word "given" is sometimes used to support the view of a presence of Christ in the elements.[4] But the entire sentence must be considered in the light of what immediately follows.

2. The manner of spiritual blessing.—"Only after an heavenly and spiritual manner." The word "only" clearly refers to the entire statement that precedes, "given, taken, and eaten." The Body of Christ is not only taken and eaten after an heavenly manner, but is given in the same way. The gift must therefore surely be given by our Lord Himself, and this is implied not only by Cranmer and Jewel, but also by men who hold views similar to Calvin. Further, the very phrase of the Article is found in the smaller *Catechism* of Nowell, of whose doctrinal character and position there is no question.[5] These are the words of Nowell's *Catechism* :—

"The body and blood of Christ, which in the Lord's Supper are given to the faithful and are by them taken, eaten and drunken, only in a heavenly and spiritual manner, but yet in truth."

3. The channel of spiritual blessing.—"And the mean whereby the Body of Christ is received and eaten in the Supper is faith." This is in agreement with the teaching of clause one, already considered, and it may be illustrated by the rubric in the Service of the Communion of the Sick.

"But if a man, either by reason of extremity of sickness . . . or by any other just impediment, do not receive the Sacrament of Christ's Body and Blood, the

[1] Faber, Bk. III: "The Catholic Faith . . . does not rest on the Ascension but goes on to Corpus Christi."
[2] Gibson, *ut supra*, p. 644 f.
[3] Dimock, *Papers on the Eucharistic Presence*, p. 732.
[4] Gibson, *ut supra*, p. 661.   [5] Dimock, *ut supra*, pp. 732-740.

Curate shall instruct him, that if he do truly repent him of his sins, and steadfastly
believe that Jesus Christ hath suffered death upon the Cross for him, and shed His
Blood for his redemption, earnestly remembering the benefits he hath thereby,
and giving him hearty thanks therefore, he doth eat and drink the Body and Blood
of our Saviour Christ profitably to his Soul's health, although he do not receive
the Sacrament with his mouth."

Article XXIX also emphasises the same principle.

After considering the actual wording of the clause the historical circumstances call for careful study.

(a) Reference is frequently made to the statement that Bishop Geste
was the author of it.[1] This is intended in support of the view that the
presence is there, in the elements, independent of us, and Bishop Geste
suggested that the word "only" should be removed and the word
"profitably" be inserted, though this was not done. It may be rightly
asked whether the attempt by a Bishop to get the Prime Minister to alter
the Articles after failing to get Convocation to listen to his own arguments is a reason why we should accept such a writer as our guide to the
true interpretation. But the question is whether Geste was, after all,
the author, for we have this very sentence in Archbishop Parker's own
handwriting quite complete in that original draft which Parker (who is
well known as opposed to the Lutheran view of the "real and bodily
presence") brought with him to the Convocation of 1563, as Dr. Lamb
shows, and Geste tried in vain to alter this very wording. Further, the
Supreme Court in the trial, *Sheppard* v. *Bennett*, rejected Geste's statement as being no evidence at all.[2] Besides, as we shall see, Article XXIX
was inserted in 1571 against Geste's wish, and for some time he refused
to subscribe to the Articles, though afterwards he yielded. Another
Bishop, Cheney of Gloucester, being a Lutheran, could not subscribe at
all. Geste's views were in many respects peculiar, if not contradictory,
and they certainly were not representative of the English Church of his
day. He failed on every point, and had to subscribe to the very expressions
which he had privately denounced in his correspondence with Cecil. It
would seem as though his one object was to thwart Archbishop Parker's
determination to exclude consubstantiation from the teaching of the

[1] Gibson, *ut supra*, p. 661 f.
[2] "Gheast does not say that he was the 'compiler' of the Twenty-eighth Article, all
but one sentence of which had been in the Articles of 1552; and the context shows that
he used the word 'Article' only of this sentence, which, he says, was 'of mine own
penning.' Upon the faith of this letter, genuine or not, avowedly written for a personal
purpose ('for mine own purgation') is founded an exposition of the words 'only after a
heavenly and spiritual manner,' as meaning that though a man 'took Christ's Body in
his hand, received it with his mouth, and that corporally, naturally, really, substantially,
and carnally . . . yet did he not for all that see it, feel it, smell it, nor taste it.' Upon
this alleged exposition their Lordships feel themselves free to observe that the words,
'only after a heavenly and spiritual manner,' do not appear to contain or involve the
words 'corporally, naturally, and carnally,' but to exclude them; and that it is the
Article, and not the questionable comments of a doubtful letter written for personal
motives, which is binding on the clergy and this Court" (From the Judgment).

2C

Church of England, a determination which, as we shall see on Article XXIX, the Archbishop effectively accomplished.[1]

(*b*) The importance of this enquiry about Geste lies in the fact that in certain sections of the English Church to-day it is taught that the Body and Blood of our Lord are present in the Holy Communion by virtue of consecration,[2] and that therefore Christ our Lord present in the most holy Sacrament of the altar under the form of bread and wine is in it to be worshipped and adored.[3] In support of this view it is urged that the Anglican doctrine underwent some definite and fundamental changes between 1551 and 1604, that Cranmer in 1551 had become influenced by the Zwinglian school, that the Second Prayer Book of 1552 was intended to teach a merely figurative presence, and that in 1563 this Article, and in 1604 the addition to the Catechism so completely changed the Anglican doctrine that " they were now at the lowest estimate, patient of a Catholic interpretation, and contained nothing under cover of which the Zwinglianising party could honestly shelter themselves.   Moreover, they have since been supplemented by the clear teaching of the Church Catechism."   The conclusion drawn from all this is that " the opinions of the Edwardian Reformers, such as Cranmer and Ridley, on the subject of the Holy Communion, have nothing more than a historical interest for us . . . nor have their writings any claim to be regarded even as an *expositio contemporanea* of formularies, which, in their present form, belong to a later date, and to a time when much greater respect was shown to the ancient teaching of the Church."[4]

It ought to be said, however, that this summary almost wholly misrepresents the actual state of the case.   The matter is easily verifiable on historical grounds, and it is simply a question of fact.   In 1548, as seen in the Great Debate, Cranmer had already expressed a view of the Holy Communion identical with that which is now found in our Articles, and this was three years before he is said to have come under the influence of the Zwinglian school.   Consequently, it is inaccurate to say that he taught, or that the Prayer Book of 1552 taught, a merely figurative presence.   We have already seen that the change of the Article in 1563, made by one of Cranmer's disciples,[5] Archbishop Parker, did not involve any essential change, and the same thing is true of the addition to the Church Catechism, 1604, for the very answers now used to prove what is called " Catholic doctrine " are found in a longer form in Nowell's Catechism, which was of the definitely Reformed type.   Bishop Jacobson

---

[1] Goode, supplement to his work, *On the Eucharist*; Heurtley, *The Doctrine of the Church of England, touching the real objective Presence*; Dimock, *ut supra*, p. 665.

[2] Gibson, *ut supra*, pp. 661, 672.

[3] Declaration of English Church Union, 1900.

[4] Gibson, *ut supra*, pp. 642–647.

[5] It is also common knowledge that the views of all the Elizabethan Bishops, with the exception of the (Lutheran) views of Cheney and Geste, were identical with those of Cranmer.

says that " the additions made at the Hampton Court Conference were evidently abridged from it."[1]   It is difficult, if not impossible, to understand how otherwise the teaching of our Church concerning a definite spiritual presence and blessing could be expressed in order to distinguish the " Reformed " from the Lutheran view.[2]

We shall see still more clearly in Article XXIX that this doctrine of a presence of our Lord's Body and Blood by reason of consecration is no part of the doctrine of the English Church; indeed, it is absolutely opposed to the " Black Rubric," or " Declaration on Kneeling " that " the natural body and blood . . . are in heaven and not here."[3]

V.—ERRONEOUS USES OF THE LORD'S SUPPER

The Article closes by calling attention to certain observances which are regarded as incompatible with the ordinance of Christ.

1. Reservation.—In the time of Justin Martyr, the Lord's Supper was reserved for the absent and sick, the elements being taken at once to the houses ; an innocent and beautiful expression of unity and fellowship. But our Article has something very different in view.   The decrees of the Council of Trent were promulgated in October of 1551, and to this the paragraph in the Article is certainly due.   It has been said that the Article is " worded with the utmost care and with studied moderation. It cannot be said that any one of the practices is condemned or prohibited by it.   It only amounts to this : that none of them can claim to be part of the original Divine institution."[4]   But in view of the mediæval doctrine associated with the presence of Christ in the elements the clear statements of this Article, together with the equally clear order in the Rubric about the consumption of all the remaining consecrated elements,

---

[1] Preface to Nowell's *Catechism*, pp. 35, 36.

[2] "This answer in the Catechism makes no declaration whatever about the body and blood of Christ being verily and indeed contained or present under the forms of bread and wine at all, *i.e.* in the elements apart from reception.   It does declare that the body and blood are verily and indeed taken and received by the faithful in the Lord's Supper; it affirms a real and true, *i.e.* not imaginary or fictitious, reception, but only by the faithful.   It is in exact accordance with the Twenty-eighth Article, that 'to such as rightly, worthily, and with faith, receive the Sacrament, the bread which we break is a partaking of the body of Christ, and the cup of blessing is a partaking of the blood of Christ.'

"It has been abundantly shown by Dean Goode, in his work on the Eucharist, that all the accredited expositions of the Catechism interpret this answer as an assertion that the body and blood of Christ are received in this Sacrament by the faithful only, meaning by 'the faithful,' communicants who with a true penitent heart and lively faith receive the Holy Sacrament" (Ince, *Letter on the Real Presence*, p. 24 f.).

[3] The Invocation of the Holy Spirit on the Elements (included in the Scottish and American Prayer Books but deliberately omitted from the English Book) is sometimes said to indicate a belief in a Presence of Christ somehow attached to the Elements.   But quite apart from the significant absence of any such Invocation from the formularies of the English Church, it is now known beyond doubt that the primitive form of this Prayer was that the Holy Spirit might come upon the Communicant rather than upon the Elements (Woolley, *Liturgy of the Primitive Church*, pp. 93–120; Upton, *Outlines of Prayer Book History*, pp. 12–21).

[4] Gibson, *ut supra*, p. 665.

show that there can be very little question as to the meaning of our Church. The view that reservation is both condemned and prohibited was taken by all representative English theologians up to the time of the Tractarian movement; and even in the case of illness and the necessity of haste the occasions when there would be real need of reservation instead of the usual Service would be exceedingly rare.[1] The danger of any such reservation of the consecrated elements is too manifest to need much notice, for the inevitable tendency is to adore and worship Christ regarded as present therein.[2] Moreover, any cases of Communion in which the person would not be able to enter into even a shortened form of the Service would seem to imply the impossibility of the actual reception of the bread and wine, the case coming under the rubric in the Office of the Visitation of the Sick, dealing with the assured spiritual Communion of those who cannot partake of the elements.

2. Processions.—The Sacrament is not to be " carried about " or " lifted up." Elevation dates only from the eleventh century, and the Festival of Corpus Christi was removed from the Calendar in 1549.[3]

3. Adoration.—Nor is the Sacrament to be " worshipped." The elevation of the Host for adoration arose in the twelfth or thirteenth century, and, like the Festival of Corpus Christi, grew out of the doctrine of Transubstantiation. It is sometimes said that the adoration of Christ

---

[1] In the *Parish Magazine* of St. Martin's, Brighton, for October 1910, the vicar, Mr. Nugent, who practises Reservation in one kind for the sick, published a sermon on "The Real Presence," in which these words occur:

"Wherever the Holy Sacrament is, whether It is on the Altar at the time of Communion, or whether It is in the Tabernacle reserved for the sick, It is Jesus Christ Himself under that lowly form. As God He is everywhere, but as God-made man, He is in Heaven and in the Blessed Sacrament on the Altar. So you and I must adore Him in the Sacrament. We cannot do otherwise."

Another Brighton vicar, the Rev. Arthur Cocks of St. Bartholomew, resigned his living because he could not observe the Bishop's directions as to the reservation of the Sacrament, one of which was "that in the manner of reservation there is no encouragement of adoration or worship of the Sacrament." Mr. Cocks considered that this direction would involve "a dishonour to our Blessed Lord." Mr. Cocks subsequently left the Church of England for the Church of Rome with four other clergy and over one hundred lay people.

The decision of the Archbishops of Canterbury and York (Archbishop Temple and Archbishop Maclagan) was given in May 1900. They sat to consider the matter which had been referred to them for decision by three dioceses. The case of reservation was presented, witnesses were examined, and arguments advanced in support of the practice. The Archbishops took some nine months to consider the question, and they ruled absolutely that reservation is not legal in the Church of England. Archbishop Temple's words were these:

"I am obliged to decide that the Church of England does not at present allow reservation in any form."

Archbishop Maclagan: "I can come to no other decision than that it was deliberately abandoned at the time of the Reformation, and that it is not lawful for any individual clergyman to resume such practice in ministering to the souls committed to his charge." The late Bishop of London, Dr. Creighton, took the same line, and expressed the opinion that reservation was meant to be prohibited by the present rubrics (*Life*, Vol. II, pp. 310–313).

[2] See Meyrick, *Doctrine of the Holy Communion*, pp. 125, 133.

[3] Meyrick, *ut supra*, pp. 134–138; Bishop Drury, *Elevation in the Eucharist*.

present in the Sacrament cannot be prohibited,[1] but, of course, everything turns upon the meaning of the word " Sacrament," which in the Articles refers to the outward part of elements and word alone. It has been pointed out by a leading authority that no Eucharistic adoration existed for a thousand years after Christ, and while no Christian disputes the necessity of Christ's being adored wherever He is, yet when it is said that He is to be adored in the Sacrament " the question returns upon us whether ' Sacrament' means the visible symbols of His body and blood, or the whole rite in which He is undoubtedly present to the faithful communicant. In the latter sense we all adore Him."[2]

[1] Gibson, *ut supra*, p. 667.
[2] Canon Trevor, quoted by Dimock, *ut supra*, p. 136; see also p. 133; Meyrick, *ut supra*, pp. 139, 154.

ARTICLE XXIX

<table>
<tr><td>Of the Wicked which do not eat the Body of Christ in the use of the Lord's Supper.</td><td>De Manducatione Corporis Christi, et impios illud non manducare.</td></tr>
<tr><td>The Wicked, and such as be void of a lively faith, although they do carnally and visibly press with their teeth, as Saint Augustine saith, the Sacrament of the Body and Blood of Christ, yet in no wise are they partakers of Christ: but rather to their condemnation, do eat and drink the sign, or Sacrament, of so great a thing.</td><td>Impii, et fide viva destituti, licet carnaliter et visibiliter, ut Augustinus loquitur, corporis et sanguinis Christi Sacramentum dentibus premant, nullo tamen modo Christi participes efficiuntur: sed potius tantæ rei Sacramentum, seu symbolum, ad judicium sibi manducant et bibunt.</td></tr>
</table>

IMPORTANT EQUIVALENTS.

Of the wicked which eat not the Body of Christ in the use of the Lord's Supper	= *de manducatione corporis Christi, et imposi illud non manducare.*
The wicked	= *impii.*
Are partakers	= *participes efficiuntur.*
Sign	= *symbolum.*
To their condemnation	= *ad judicium sibi.*

THERE was nothing corresponding to this Article in 1553. It dates from 1563, and its history is so vitally important as to call for close study.

I.—THE HISTORY

It was introduced by Archbishop Parker in 1563 and accepted by Convocation, but subsequently struck out by the Queen. It is generally supposed that this was part of her policy to endeavour to conciliate the Lutherans. It certainly harmonises with the treatment of the " Black Rubric," and of the Ornaments Rubric in the Prayer Book of 1559. But in 1571 the Archbishop reinserted this Article, and then it was accepted by the Queen as well as Convocation. Parker evidently felt that Article XXVIII by itself was insufficient to meet the Lutheran view, and this will account for his insistence in making the point clear so as to exclude the Real Presence in the Lutheran sense. Bishop Geste, who, as we have seen, had evidently endeavoured to get an alteration in Article XXVIII, was now compelled to admit the fundamental difference between the Anglican and Lutheran doctrine.[1]

---

[1] Dugdale, *Life of Geste*, pp. 116, 147, 148; Dimock, *Papers on the Eucharistic Presence*, pp. 670–674. See also two articles in the *Churchman* for January 1920 and 1921 by W. Prescott Upton on the connection and significant contrast between our Articles and the Wurtemberg Confession.

II.—THE TEACHING

The statements of the Article do not admit of any doubt as to their meaning.

1. The wicked eat and drink the sign or Sacrament of the Body and Blood of Christ.—" The wicked, and such as be void of a lively faith, although they do carnally and visibly press with their teeth (as Saint Augustine saith) the Sacrament of the Body and Blood of Christ."

2. They do not partake of Christ Himself.—" Yet in no wise are they partakers of Christ." The Latin is particularly forceful, *nullo modo*.

3. They eat and drink the sign or Sacrament to their spiritual condemnation.—" But rather, to their condemnation, do eat and drink the sign or Sacrament of so great a thing." Thus, the Article is a corollary to Article XXVIII, because the teaching of the Church of Rome is that all receive, but all do not benefit. Efforts have been made to show that there is a distinction between the title and the Article, the title saying that the wicked do not eat the Body of Christ in the use of the Supper, while the Article says that the wicked are " in no wise partakers of Christ." It has, therefore, been suggested that the title does not say " receive not," but " eat not," and that the Article does not say the wicked are not partakers of the Body and Blood of Christ, but that they are not " partakers of Christ." This is an endeavour to show that while the wicked might receive the *sacramentum*, and what is called the *res sacramenti*, they could not receive the *virtus sacramenti*.[1] But this distinction between the inward part, *res*, and the benefit, *virtus*, of the Sacrament finds no place in Anglican theology; and, indeed, it would involve the fact of three parts in a Sacrament, which is contrary to our Catechism. The " thing signified " includes both the spiritual blessing and its benefit by participation.[2] This distinction between *signum*, *res* and *virtus* was the ordinary teaching of the Roman Catholic Church, as it is to this day, and it is obvious that the Article is not likely to maintain here what it so definitely denies, and even denounces, in Article XXVIII.[3] In view, therefore, of the circumstances of the introduction of the Article there is no reasonable doubt as to its meaning and purpose.[4] Proof of this can be adduced from representative writers of the time.[5] The Article is also directed specifically against Lutheranism, and in 1577 the *Formula Concordiæ* deliberately condemned its teaching almost in our very words.[6] It is also significant that the Anglican Articles have no place in the list of Lutheran Symbolics.[7]

[1] Maclear and Williams, *Introduction to the Articles of the Church of England*, pp. 348–350.
[2] Simpson, *The Thing Signified*, pp. 22–26.
[3] Dr. Kidd rightly says that this view is open to serious objections on three grounds: (*a*) From the history of the Article; (*b*) from its connection with Article XXVIII; (*c*) from other expressions in the Article itself. He adds that if it had been the natural interpretation Bishop Geste would have made no effort to get rid of the Article (Kidd, *The Thirty-nine Articles*, p. 237).
[4] Dimock, *ut supra*, pp. 615–617.   [5] Dimock, *ut supra*, pp. 618–640.
[6] Goode, *On the Eucharist*, p. 647; Dimock, *Vox Liturgiæ Anglicanæ*, p. xxii.
[7] So Schaff, quoted in Dimock, *ut supra*, p. xxiii.

As the Article quotes from St. Augustine and the true meaning has
been questioned, it is important to have the facts of the case in view.
The passage is from *Super. Joann.*, Tract 26 : " Qui non manet in
Christo et in quo non manet Christus procul dubio nec manducat
spiritualiter carnem ejus nec bibit ejus sanguinem *licet carnaliter et
visibiliter premat dentibus sacramentum corporis et sanguinis Christi* sed
magis tantæ rei sacramentum ad judicium sibi manducat et bibit." The
portions in italics are rejected by the Benedictine editors, and much controversy has been waged as to them. Archbishop Parker maintained his
point and adhered to them, and certainly it is unlikely that they were
added in the Middle Ages, though they might easily have been omitted.
They are as old as Bede and Alcuin, and even if spurious they do not
affect our Article.[1]

The one and only consideration is the proper interpretation of the
wording of the Article, whether these statements came from St. Augustine
or not.[2]

III.—THE DOCTRINE OF " PRESENCE "

The Church of England has avoided the term " Real Presence,"
because it is ambiguous and misleading. It does not date earlier than the
Middle Ages, and the Church has shown its wisdom in not using the
term, because it is difficult to conceive of a Real Presence of what is
locally absent. Presence is a relative word, expressive of a relation
between an object which is called present and the subject which is present.
It means " the application of the object to that faculty which is capable
of apprehending it." So that it has a twofold meaning according as the
thing referred to is corporal or spiritual. Corporal presence means
presence to the senses and spiritual presence means presence to the soul.
All presence is, therefore, " real," and a spiritual presence is none the
less real because it is spiritual. The crux of the question now at issue is
as to a presence in the elements by virtue of consecration, and in regard
to this the Church not only does not teach it, but teaches that which
implies the very opposite.[3] There is no need of a thing to be present in
order to be received, for the sun is present in efficacy though so far away.
It is the same with property, or even money. In like manner, the
Atonement is efficacious to-day although wrought centuries ago. We
must, therefore, estimate things in relation to their ability for enjoyment.

[1] Dimock, *Papers on the Eucharistic Presence*, pp. 676–686.
[2] "To affect the interpretation of the Article, it must be shown, not only what
St. Augustine's views are, but that at the time of the Reformation they were universally
felt, and by all confessed, to be clearly and unmistakably against what we contend for
as the natural meaning of our Article" (Dimock, *ut supra*, p. 681).
[3] "It will, perhaps, be said that the Church of England does not deny 'The Real
Presence'; but this is nothing to the purpose. She does not teach it: and if it were her
belief she would not have left a doctrine of such moment to be inferred by a very
doubtful process from statements which at best do not necessarily mean it" (Vogan,
True Doctrine of the Eucharist, p. 254).

So that the question is not one of the fact of a presence but of the mode ; not one of spiritual presence, but of local nearness (propinquity) ; not one of spiritual eating, but of oral eating (manducation). Bishop Gore considers that the question of a presence in the elements was " evaded " by those who drew up our formularies,[1] but in view of the profound differences between 1549 and 1552 it does not seem likely that the Reformers were men to " evade " such a question. It was far too acute and pressing to be overlooked, and it seems far truer to say that they avoided it and taught just the opposite.

Bishop Gibson[2] speaks of the necessity of the Body being " there " in order to be discerned. But can this mean to discern a presence in the elements ? What was the error against which St. Paul was writing ? If he had formerly taught them the presence of Christ in the elements, would they have been likely to turn the Service into a common meal in two or three years ? Would not the sin of idolatry have been far more likely ? If this had been his meaning, how much easier it would have been to say something like " This is sacrificial." The view of Bishop Gibson, as usual with a certain type of Churchman,[3] is marked by the fallacy of assuming that there can be no presence apart from attachment to the elements. Then, too, all this says nothing of the strict meaning of " discern," as used in the context.[4] The supreme test is as to what the wicked eat, and the view that Christ's Body being " there " is " offered " to the wicked, who is thus " brought in contact with it," but is unable to receive the food offered through want of faith is only another way of endeavouring to distinguish in mediæval fashion between *signum, res* and *virtus*. The teaching of the Article is plain, for it is absolutely impossible to conceive of anyone partaking of Christ without receiving spiritual benefit.[5]

Bishop Gibson also refers to Cranmer and Ridley admitting that " in some sense " the wicked may be said to " eat the Body." But the use of the term " sacramental " obviously means symbolical only, as many testimonies from the writings of Cranmer and Ridley amply prove.[6] For this reason no stress can be laid on the Prayer of Humble Access, as though it were possible " so to eat . . . that our sinful bodies " might

---

[1] Gore, *The Body of Christ*, p. 231.

[2] Gibson, *The Thirty-nine Articles*, p. 672.

[3] "If the Consecrated Bread and Wine are only in some relative symbolical sense the Body and Blood of Christ, it is a little difficult to see where the benefit of communicating or offering comes in" (Rev. T. I. Ball, *English Church Review*, Vol. V, p. 497).

[4] All the above is argued on the assumption that the text of the Authorised Version is correct, but if the Revised Version is read, and the words, "Not discerning the Body" are interpreted of the Church, the matter is quite clear. For an able treatment of this view see Barnes-Lawrence, *The Holy Communion*, pp. 137–213, and Simpson, *The Sacrament of the Gospel*, p. 52.

[5] No such eating is contemplated as a real eating which is not a beneficial eating also (Mozley, *Lectures, with other Theological Papers*, p. 205).

[6] "As for the ungodly and carnal, they may eat the bread and drink the wine, but with Christ Himself they have no communion nor company; and they neither eat His flesh nor drink His blood" (Cranmer, *The Lord's Supper*, p. 203).

not receive benefit.[1] It has been shown with abundant illustration that this interpretation of the phrase is meaningless and unwarranted. It is extraordinary that several authors should have pressed this view and made so much depend upon it, but Bishop Dowden is much nearer the historical truth when he says that, " It is plain that it is, to say the least, very hazardous to base a theological argument on the expression."[2]

It is sometimes said that modern teaching involving a presence of our Lord in some way attached to, or associated with the elements, is in the direct line of succession from the teaching of the Caroline divines. But this is not true to historical fact, as a reference to the work of these divines conclusively proves. Thus, one of the most representative of them, Bishop Cosin, speaks of the outward sign and the inward part as " united in time, though not in place."[3] And he also emphasises the great Reformation truth that apart from the proper use the sacramental signs are not Sacraments at all.[4] The whole subject may be summed up in the following words :—

" One thing is absolutely certain : It is no part of the doctrine of our Church that there is an adorable presence of Our Lord's body and blood *in* or *under* the forms of bread and wine. Such language is undiscoverable in the doctrinal standards of our Church, and wholly unknown to the Church of the early Fathers."[5]

[1] Gibson, *ut supra*, p. 675.
[2] Dowden, *Further Studies in the Prayer Book*, pp. 336-343; Dimock, *ut supra*, pp. 436-439.
[3] Cosin, *History of Popish Transubstantiation*, Ch. IV, Section 4.
[4] "We also deny that the elements still retain the nature of sacraments when not used according to divine institution, that is, given by Christ's ministers, and received by His people; so that Christ in the consecrated bread, ought not, cannot be kept and preserved to be carried about, because He is present only to communicants" (Cosin, *ut supra*, Ch. IV, Section 5).
The teaching of the Caroline divines was made clear in a series of valuable letters from the late Bishop of Edinburgh, Dr. Dowden, in the *Guardian*, for July, August, and September 1900, than which nothing could be more convincing as to their Eucharistic doctrine.
[5] Bishop Dowden, *Define Your Terms*, an address to the Diocesan Synod, 1900, p. 21.
By way of comparison, these words of a well-known Presbyterian divine may also be quoted, showing essential agreement between the doctrine of Calvin and Hooker, as represented by our Articles.
"There is, therefore, a most Real Presence of Christ in the Sacrament of the Supper on the pure Protestant view. . . . This view, to sum all up, knows of a symbolical Presence of Christ in the elements, a proclaimed Presence in the world, a mystical Presence in the ineffable union between Christ and the members of His spiritual body, and a gracious Presence in the power and plenitude of the gifts of His Spirit. Beyond this it will be difficult to show that Scripture recognises any other" (Orr, *The Real Presence*, p. 16).

ARTICLE XXX

Of both kinds.   *De utraque Specie.*

The Cup of the Lord is not to be denied to the Lay-people: for both the parts of the Lord's Sacrament, by Christ's ordinance and commandment, ought to be ministered to all Christian men alike.

Calix Domini laicis non est denegandus: utraque enim pars Dominici Sacramenti, ex Christi institutione et præcepto, omnibus Christianis ex æquo administrari debet.

IMPORTANT EQUIVALENTS.

Of both kinds	= *de utraque specie.*
Both parts	= *utraque pars.*
By Christ's ordinance	= *ex Christi institutione.*
Alike	= *ex æquo.*

In July 1562, when the Council of Trent reassembled, efforts were made to obtain sanction for Communion in both kinds, but instead Decrees and Canons were drawn up confirming the mediæval practice of Communion in one kind, and anathematising those who taught the opposite.

" (i) If any one shall say that by the precept of God, or by necessity of salvation, all and each of the faithful of Christ ought to receive both kinds of the most holy sacrament of the Eucharist : let him be anathema.

" (ii) If any one shall say that the holy Catholic Church was not induced by just causes and reasons to communicate under the species of bread only, laymen and clergy when not consecrating ; or has erred therein : let him be anathema.

" (iii) If any one shall deny that Christ, whole and entire, the fountain and author of all graces, is received under the one species of bread, because, as some falsely assert, He is not received according to the institution of Christ Himself under both kinds : let him be anathema."[1]

This Article was our reply. It dates from 1563, and was due to Archbishop Parker It was an interesting illustration of the increasingly strong Protestant attitude adopted at that date. Some modern writers

---

[1] "Si quis dixerit, ex Dei præcepto, vel necessitate salutis, omnes et singulos Christi fideles utramque speciem sanctissimi Eucharistiæ sacramenti sumere debere: anathema sit.

"Si quis dixerit, sanctam Ecclesiam Catholicam non justis causis et rationibus adductam fuisse ut laicos, atque etiam Clericos non conficientes, sub panis tantummodo specie communicaret, aut in eo errasse: anathema sit.

"Si quis negaverit, totum et integrum Christum omnium gratiarum fontem et auctorem, sub una panis specie sumi, quia, ut quidam falso asserunt, non secundum ipsius Christi constitutionem sub utraque specie sumatur: anathema sit" (Council of Trent).

favour the idea that during the first ten years of her reign Queen Elizabeth did her utmost to win the Roman Catholics.   But several strong
forms of expression in other Articles, including the insertion of an
Article like this, are convincing proofs to the contrary.   Elizabeth never
really attempted or even expected to conciliate the Romanists, but she
certainly did her utmost to unite Protestants in support of her Throne by
taking every step to conciliate the Lutherans.   This can be seen from
her action in regard to the " Black Rubric " and the Ornaments Rubric
in the Prayer Book of 1559, and in connection with Articles XXVIII
and XXIX in 1563.   But there is no historical proof of any ecclesiastical
or doctrinal movement to win Roman Catholics.

I.—THE HISTORY OF THE PRACTICE

It is generally thought that the withholding of the cup from the laity
arose from the carrying home of the elements in a superstitious way, but
the general rule of Communion in both kinds was so firmly established
that by the fifth century Decrees of Popes made the withholding of the
cup heretical.   Leo the Great informs the Bishops how to know the
Manichees who attend the Communion and yet refuse the cup.   Pope
Gelasius said that if any abstained from the cup they must abstain entirely.
But towards the end of the eleventh century the custom of withholding
the cup began to be observed very gradually, and Thomas Aquinas
justified it for fear of irreverence through spilling.   It is still more curious
that the custom of communicating in one kind was definitely condemned
by a Council in the eleventh century and by a Pope in the twelfth.   But
in the course of the next two centuries the custom gradually spread through
the West, and the Council of Constance, while stating that the custom
was not primitive, actually claimed power to refuse the cup, and even the
Communion in both kinds to the laity.   It is frankly admitted by leading
Roman Catholic authorities that Communion in both kinds was universal
until the twelfth century.   Cardinal Bona[1] admits that :—

" The faithful always and in all places, from the first beginnings of the Church
till the twelfth century, were used to communicate under the species of bread
and wine, and the use of the chalice began, little by little, to drop away in the
beginning of that century, and many bishops forbade it to the people to avoid
the risk of irreverence and spilling."

All the ancient Liturgies are quite clear on this subject, and the restoration of the cup was associated with the Reformation in Germany and
England.   We have seen the attitude of the Council of Trent on this
subject.

II.—ROMAN CATHOLIC REASONS FOR THE PRACTICE

While it is sometimes argued that fear of accident is an important
reason for the practice, there is no doubt that the chief reason is con-

[1] Quoted by Bingham, XV, v. 1.

nected with the doctrine of Transubstantiation. It is held that by the doctrine of " Concomitance " Christ is received in His entirety under the species of bread. This, as will be seen above, is the main line adopted by the Canons of Trent.

The other argument used is the claim of the Church to decree rites or ceremonies, urging that the power extends to this also.

> " Holy Mother Church, knowing this her authority in the administration of the sacraments, although the use of both kinds has, from the beginning of the Christian religion, not been unfrequent, yet in process of time that custom having already been widely changed—has, induced by weighty and just reasons, approved of this custom of communicating under one kind, and decreed that it should be held as a law, which it is not lawful to reprobate or change at pleasure, without the authority of the Church itself."[1]

III.—THE ANGLICAN POSITION

We take our stand on the institution of Christ, and both in the Catechism and in the Articles this is emphasised. It is impossible to argue that the custom is permissible from Scripture because the context of St. Paul's words is conclusive in support of Communion in both kinds (1 Cor. xi. 26, 27). The answer in the Catechism is as follows : " Bread and Wine, which the Lord hath commanded to be received." This simple statement is a striking illustration of the way in which our Church safeguards the true position by teaching young people positively apart from the controversy, as well as in the Article, that our Lord's ordinance and commandment settle the question.

Nor can we for a moment allow that the Church's power suffices to alter a Divine command. We fully recognise that the Church has " power to decree rites and ceremonies " (Article XX), but this cannot be extended to authorise anything " contrary to God's Word written," and Holy Scripture is too clear on this point to admit of any question (Matt. xxvi. 27).

The Council of Trent promised a further consideration of the matter at the earliest opportunity with a view to possible relaxation. It is sometimes said that the bread is often " dipped " now in the Roman Church, as it is in the Eastern Church, by the practice known as " intinction." But the Roman Church is officially bound by the decrees of Trent up to the present time, and nothing has been done by authority to relieve or modify the Tridentine decrees. It may be said without any hesitation that there is no practice in the Roman Catholic Church which is so difficult to defend.[2]

---

[1] "Quare agnoscens Sancta Mater Ecclesia hanc suam, in administratione sacramentorum auctoritatem, licet ab initio, Christianæ Religionis non infrequens utriusque speciei usus fuisset; tamen progressu temporis latissime jam mutata illa consuetudine, gravibus et justis causis adducta, hanc consuetudinem sub altera specie communicandi approbavit, et pro lege habendam decrevit: quam reprobare, aut sine ipsius ecclesiæ auctoritate pro libito mutare non licet" (Cap. II).

[2] See further Article, "Communion in one kind."—*Protestant Dictionary.*

ARTICLE XXXI

Of the one Oblation of Christ finished upon the Cross.

De unica Christi Oblatione in Cruce perfecta.

The offering of Christ once made, is the perfect redemption, propitiation, and satisfaction, for all the sins of the whole world, both original and actual; and there is none other satisfaction for sin, but that alone. Wherefore the sacrifices of Masses, in the which it was commonly said, that the priest did offer Christ for the quick and the dead, to have remission of pain or guilt, were blasphemous fables and dangerous deceits.

Oblatio Christi semel facta, perfecta est redemptio, propitiatio, et satisfactio pro omnibus peccatis totius mundi, tam originalibus quam actualibus; neque præter illam unicam est ulla alia pro peccatis expiatio. Unde Missarum sacrificia, quibus vulgo dicebatur, sacerdotem offerre Christum, in remissionem pœnæ, aut culpæ, pro vivis et defunctis, blasphema figmenta sunt, et perniciosæ imposturæ.

IMPORTANT EQUIVALENTS.

Of the one oblation	= *de unica oblatione.*
Once	= *semel.*
Satisfaction	= *satisfactio.*
Satisfaction for sin	= *pro peccatis expiatio.*
The sacrifices of Masses	= *missarum sacrificia.*
To have remission of pain or guilt	= *in remissionem pœnæ aut culpæ.*
Priest	= *sacerdotem.*
Dangerous deceits	= *perniciosæ imposturæ.*

THIS Article dates from 1553 with certain verbal alterations made in 1563 and 1571, which Bishop Gibson regards as "insignificant and immaterial,"[1] but which are considered by other authors to be both significant and material. This is a point that will demand special attention.

I.—THE DOCTRINE OF THE ATONEMENT

Although the mention of our Lord's sacrifice is made here with special reference to the second part of the Article, yet it is important in itself as one of four or five explicit statements in the Article on the subject. A careful comparison of these will give the Anglican doctrinal view of the Atonement. Article II : "Who truly suffered, was crucified, dead and buried, to reconcile His Father to us, and to be a sacrifice, not only for original guilt, but also for all actual sins of men." Article III : "Christ died for us." Article XV : "He came to be the Lamb without spot, who, by sacrifice of Himself once made, should take away the sins of the world." Article XXVIII : "Our redemption by Christ's death." The present Article : "The offering of Christ once made is that perfect

[1] Gibson, *The Thirty-nine Articles*, p. 687.

redemption, propitiation, and satisfaction, for all the sins of the whole world, both original and actual; and there is none other satisfaction for sin, but that alone." Of these, the statements in Articles II, XV, and XXXI, are the most important.

1. The Nature of the Atonement.—" The offering of Christ once made." The force of " once " should be particularly noted as meaning " once for all " (*semel*), answering to the New Testament words ἅπαξ, and ἐφάπαξ (Rom. vi. 10; Heb. vii. 27; ix. 12, 26, 27, 28; x. 10; 1 Pet. iii. 18).

2. The Purpose of the Atonement.—" Perfect redemption, propitiation, and satisfaction, for all the sins of the whole world, both original and actual." With this should be compared the statement of the Consecration Prayer in the Communion Office. " Who made there (by His one oblation of Himself once offered) a full, perfect, and sufficient sacrifice, oblation, and satisfaction, for the sins of the whole world." The words " offering," " redemption," and " propitiation " come from the New Testament, while " satisfaction " is a Latin term expressing an important aspect of the Atonement. It was first used by Anselm to indicate that the claims of Divine justice were met and satisfied in the Death of Christ. The distinction is again drawn, as in Article II, between original and actual sins (see also Articles IX and XV).

3. The Uniqueness of the Atonement.—" There is none other satisfaction for sin, but that alone." It is important to observe the force of " alone " which in the Latin is *unica*, not *una*, indicating the absolute uniqueness of our Lord's death in relation to sin.

II.—THE DOCTRINE OF MASSES[1]

1. Their Nature.—The Article describes what is to be condemned in these words: " The Priest did offer Christ for the quick and the dead, to have remission of pain or guilt." The word " pain " means " punishment " (*poenae*).

2. Their Description.—These sacrifices of Masses are said to be

---

[1] "Mass" or *Missa* is sometimes thought to be a corruption of *missio*. Originally it was the name for every part of Divine Service. The Service at which Catechumens were invited to be present was called *Missa Catechumen Orum*, and that at which the communicants were permitted to be present was called *Missa Fidelium*. As used by Roman Catholics, the word Mass denotes a Service of Holy Communion in their meaning of the Ordinance. The following words come from a recent book:
"'The Mass' or 'The Holy Mass' is the name used by the Roman Church and comes from the Latin *Missa*, which means 'dismissal—*Ite, missa est*,' being an intimation that those of the congregation who are not communicating may withdraw. Judged by itself, apart from its historical connection, little exception might be taken to its adoption, as a title, and yet for several reasons it ought not to be used by English Churchmen. In the first place, it is etymologically so unworthy as a description of the Lord's holy service. Secondly, it is historically condemned by our Church, in that it was definitely excluded in the Second Prayer Book (A.D. 1552). Thirdly, it is doctrinally confusing to many people as suggesting that the teaching of the Anglican and Roman Churches on the Holy Communion is identical, which, of course, it is not" (Bishop Denton Thompson, *The Holy Communion*, p. 9).

" blasphemous fables, and dangerous deceits." The Latin in its literalness is also noteworthy; " blasphemous figments and pernicious impostures."

3. Their Rejection.—" Wherefore." This word shows that the sacrifices of Masses are set aside because of the Atonement. The reference is evidently to some practices which were thought to be connected with the Atonement, and to imply the imperfection of Calvary.

III.—THE INTENTION OF THE ARTICLE

Bishop Gibson[1] argues that the Article does not refer to " the sacrifice of the Mass," but to " sacrifices of Masses," in connection with a current theory rather than with the formal statement of a doctrine. This contention is based on two grounds: (a) the words, " in which it was commonly said " (*vulgo dicebatur*), referring, it is urged, to some popular practice; (b) the decrees of Trent on " the sacrifice of the Mass " could not have been present to the minds of the revisers of 1553, since the subject was only considered at Trent in the autumn of 1562, nearly ten years later. For these two reasons it is maintained that the Article refers to popular teaching alone which was associated with very grave abuses.

The question at once arises whether this view is correct. It certainly is not the general Roman Catholic view, which holds that our Article is directed against their official " sacrifice of the Mass."[2] Dimock takes a view entirely opposed to Gibson, and the question is one of historical evidence and probability. The following points call for special consideration.

1. It will help towards a decision if the actual teaching of the Church of Rome is first of all stated. It is set out in full in Session XXII of the Council of Trent, where in chap. ii dealing with the sacrifice of the Mass this is said to be " propitiatory for the quick and the dead " (italicised words should be noted).

" And since in this divine sacrifice, which is performed in the Mass, *the same* Christ *is contained*, and is *bloodlessly immolated*, who *once* offered Himself bloodily upon the Cross ; and the holy council teaches that this sacrifice is *propitiatory*, and that by its means, if we approach God contrite and penitent, with a true heart, and a right faith, and with fear and reverence, we may obtain mercy, and grow in seasonable succour. For the Lord, *appeased by the oblation of this sacrifice*, granting grace and the gift of repentance, *remits even great crimes and sins.* There is *one* and the *same victim*, and the *same person*, who *now offers* by the *ministry* of the *priests*, who *then offered Himself upon the Cross* ; the *mode* of offering only being *different*. And the fruits of that bloody offering are *truly most abundantly received* through *this* offering, so far is it from derogating in any way from the former. Wherefore, it is properly offered according to the tradition of the Apostles, not only for the *sins, punishments, satisfactions,* and other *wants* of the living, but also for the *dead* in Christ, who are not yet fully purged."

---

[1] Gibson, *ut supra*, pp. 691–694. This is also the assertion of Newman in Tract XC.
[2] Moyes, *London Eucharistic Congress*, pp. 40, 46.

Canon 3.—" If any one shall say that the sacrifice of the Mass is only a sacrifice of praise and thanksgiving, or a bare *commemoration of* the sacrifice made upon the Cross, and that it is not *propitiatory*, or that it profits only the receiver, and that it ought not to be offered for the *living* and the *dead for their sins, pains, satisfactions, and other wants—let him be accursed.*"

Canon 4.—" If any one shall say that *blasphemy* is put upon the most holy sacrifice of Christ accomplished on the Cross by the sacrifice of the Mass, or that anything is detracted from the former by the latter, let him be anathema."

Canon 5.—If anyone shall say that it is an *imposture* to celebrate Masses in honour of the saints and for the purpose of obtaining their intercession with God, as the Church intends, let him be anathema."

This Session was held in 1562, when the Latin form of this Article had been in existence nearly ten years, and it may have been known to the Members of the Council, for both in the Article and in the Canon quoted above the word " imposture " (deceits) is found. But the true position of the Church of England is quite independent of any such assumption, however natural it may be.

2. In view of the foregoing statements of Roman doctrine it is hardly likely that popular opinion could have been so far astray in 1553, and that so definite a change of view was made between then and 1562, as is suggested in the wording of the decrees and canons of Trent. The phraseology is much too close to that of our Article to imply that our statements are directed only against some vague, floating and extreme notions.

3. In 1553 there was no authoritative Roman statement of the doctrine, though the general position was almost universally held. Under these circumstances the Article could not state it otherwise. It has been suggested that the past tense is used in the possible hope of some Roman reform.

4. At that date the question was whether the Council of Trent would condemn what our Article condemned, or uphold it. At the present time the question is whether Trent has, or has not, set its seal on the doctrine which our Article condemns.

5. The use of the plural cannot be said to possess much weight, since the Church of Rome frequently uses the plural of the Mass, and the Council of Trent does the same thing without any idea of making a doctrinal distinction. Masses (in the plural) are merely several instances of the same thing, Mass.[1]

---

[1] "The quibble which tries to distinguish between the terms 'sacrifice of the Mass' and 'sacrifices of Masses' on the ground that the Anglican article is directed against some mediæval *abuse*, and not against the use of the Mass in any sense whatever, has no foundation in history. The term 'sacrifices of Masses' was in common use then as now. It occurs in the decree of Union signed at Florence, A.D. 1438, both by Eastern and Western Bishops, which says, speaking of those who depart this life in venial sin, 'that their souls are cleansed after death by purgatorial pains; and in order that they may be relieved of these pains the suffrages of the faithful living profit them, namely, "the *sacrifices of Masses*," prayers, alms, and other works of piety.' The reform party were not ignorant of this decree, and if we compare it with the Anglican Article,

6. Nor can much, if anything, be argued from the phrase " commonly said," which can be found several times in the Prayer Book to denote ordinary popular practices and usages : *e.g.* " Commonly called Christmas Day."[1]

7. The first division of the Article teaching the all-sufficiency of the Atonement of Christ is clearly connected with the conclusion introduced by the " Wherefore " of the second part. So that the Article condemns all teaching inconsistent with the uniqueness and completeness of the sacrifice of Christ. The language of the first sentence of the Article clearly excludes even the possibility of any other propitiatory sacrifice than that which was offered once for all on Calvary, and in the light of what has been said of the decrees of Trent it is obvious that our Article rules out the sacrifice of the Mass. Further, the conclusion drawn in the second part of the Article actually uses the very words that were afterwards employed by the Council of Trent to describe the Mass, and it pronounces "sacrifices of Masses" to be "blasphemous fables and dangerous deceits." The Article, following Scripture, says, Christ was offered on the Cross " once for all " ; the Council of Trent teaches that there are as many offerings of Christ as there are Masses celebrated. Scripture and our Article say that Christ's offering is the one and all-sufficient propitiation for sin; Trent says that every Mass is a propitiatory sacrifice for sin. Surely nothing can be clearer than the condemnation of the sacrifice of the Mass by our Article, and its use of the plural is evidently intended to cover all the instances of celebration which are continually occurring, and to put them in contrast with and opposition to the uniqueness of Calvary. If words mean anything at all the Church of Rome by its teaching at Trent does derogate from the sufficiency of the Atonement of Christ on Calvary. All the Reformers were united in believing that she did, and succeeding writers are in agreement on this point.

8. If it be said that the language is so strong that it can only refer to gross corruption and not to the doctrine itself, it may be replied that, granted the belief of the Reformers, the language is not at all too strong, since three things are mentioned in connection with the sacrifices of Masses : (*a*) an offering of Christ ; (*b*) for the living and the dead ; (*c*) for remission of punishment or guilt. The question is whether the Council of Trent teaches this. It must be admitted that it does so, and for this reason "sacrifices of Masses" can be rightly described as

which says, 'Wherefore the sacrifices of Masses, in the which it was commonly said that the priest did offer Christ for the quick and the dead to have remission of pain or guilt,' were blasphemous fables and dangerous deceits,' there can be no doubt it was drawn up to deny explicitly the faith defined at Florence, both by East and West, and to assert instead the Lutheran teaching of Augsburg, from which are borrowed not only doctrines, but even the very words of the Anglican Articles. The true meaning of this Article, as a rejection of the ancient faith of the English Church, is made clear from the words of the *Homily concerning the Sacrament*: 'Take heed lest of the memory it be made *a sacrifice*, . . . Thou needest no other man's help, no other sacrifice, no *sacrificing priest, no Mass*'" (Father Breen, *The Church of Old England*, p. 47).

[1] See Tomlinson, *The Prayer Book, Homilies, and Articles*, p. 288.

"blasphemous fables and dangerous deceits." They are "fables" (Latin, *figmenta*, "inventions"), because they find no warrant in the Word of God, and come merely from man's device. They are "blasphemous," because they necessarily detract from the uniqueness and perfection of our Lord's Atonement. They are "deceits" (Latin, *imposturæ*, "cheats"), because they deceive men by professing to make a propitiation which they cannot possibly do. And they are "dangerous," because they encourage spiritual confidence in much that is untrue and impossible.

9. If the Article referred only to some gross error, why was it not referred to clearly in distinction from "the sacrifice of the Mass"? It is hardly likely that our Reformers would trouble to denounce mere popular and extreme errors which had been denounced even in the Roman Church itself.[1]

10. Cranmer and Ridley died for denying the Roman doctrine of Transubstantiation and the Mass; yet this was before the Council of Trent.

11. The word "altar" was omitted in the Prayer Book of 1552 and has never been replaced. This fact, together with the omission of the gift of the sacramental instruments and of the corresponding words from the Ordinal, seems to show that there was no intention of retaining a sacrificial element in connection with priestly acts and words.

12. As early as December 1551 certain Articles were submitted to the Council of Trent for discussion, dealing with Protestant denials on this very subject which it was expected were about to be condemned. It is possible that news came to our Reformers in 1553, but in any case the Council of Trent in 1562 clearly knew our Articles and also Jewel's Apology.[2]

13. The following facts should be carefully studied.

(a) In 1553 the Latin used the word "*figmenta*" and "*imposturæ*."

(b) In 1562 the Council of Trent denounced the denial of the "sacrifice of the Mass" as "*blasphemia*," and anathematised those who speak of Masses as an "imposture."

(c) In 1563 our Article added "*blasphema*" to "*figmenta*."

(d) In 1571 the English Version added "blasphemous."

14. In support of these contentions many quotations could be adduced from theologians of the Reformed Church. The following, by Cranmer, is of special importance by reason of his association with the Articles of 1553.

"The greatest blasphemy and injury that can be done against Christ, and yet universally used through the Popish Kingdom, is this, that the priests make their Mass a propitiatory sacrifice, to remit the sins as well of themselves as of others, both quick and dead, to whom they list to apply the same. Thus, under pretence of holiness, the Papistical priests have taken upon them to be Christ's successors,

---

[1] Dimock, *Dangerous Deceits*, p. 38.   [2] Dimock, *ut supra*, p. 67.

and to make such an oblation and sacrifice as never creature made but Christ alone, neither He made the same any more times than once, and that was by His death upon the Cross."[1]

To the same effect are the words of Cranmer's associate, Bishop Ridley, who calls the Mass :—

" A new blasphemous kind of sacrifice, to satisfy and pay the price of sins, both for the dead and the quick, to the great and intolerable contumely of Christ our Saviour, His death and passion ; which was, and is, the only sufficient and ever-lasting, available sacrifice, satisfactory for all the elect of God, from Adam the first, to the last that shall be born to the end of the world."[2]

15. These points all arise in connection with the actual history of the Prayer Book and Articles, and in confirmation of the position Newman's view should be carefully observed.   It is well known that he endeavoured to make out in Tract XC a view similar to that propounded by Bishop Gibson, but he entirely gave it up afterwards, and stated that our Article all along was directed against the central Roman doctrine of the Mass.[3] This is also the general view of the Church of Rome.[4]

Is it possible to regard these points as without significance ?   Surely they prove beyond all question that our Article refers, and can only refer, to the Roman doctrine of the " sacrifice of the Mass."

IV.—THE EUCHARISTIC SACRIFICE

It remains to consider what is meant by the phrase " Eucharistic Sacrifice."   It is evidently intended to mean some sacrifice which can be offered only at the time of the Holy Communion.

There seems to be no doubt that almost from the first the Holy Communion was spoken of under the name of an " offering," or " sacrifice." This is found either stated or implied in Clement of Rome,[5] and Justin

---

[1] Cranmer, *The True and Catholic Doctrine and Use of the Sacrament of the Lord's Supper* Bk. V, Ch. I.

[2] Ridley, *A Piteous Lamentation*, Works, p. 52.

[3] "The reasoning (viz., in Section 9 of his own Tract XC) is unsatisfactory. . . What the Article abjures as a lie is just that which the Pope and Council declare to be divine truth . . . nothing can come of the suggested distinction between Mass and Masses. . . . What, then, the Thirty-first Article repudiates is undeniably the central and most sacred doctrine of the Catholic religion, and so its wording has ever been read since it was drawn up." . . . "Masses for the quick and dead are not an abuse, but a distinct ordinance of the Church herself. . . . I do not see how it can be denied that the Article calls the sacrifice of the Mass itself, in all its private and solitary celebrations— to speak of no other—that is, in all its daily celebrations from year's end to year's end, *toto orbe terrarum*, a blasphemous fable" (Newman, *Via Media*, Vol. I, pp. 351-356).

[4] See Moyes, as above.

"Those who were responsible for it (Article XXXI) showed well enough by their actions—the destruction of altars, the cutting up of vestments . . . and their loathing of 'massing priests'—that subtleties of this kind never even entered their minds.   They hated the whole thing root and branch and said so" (R. H. Benson, *Non-Catholic Denominations*, p. 34).

[5] For a fuller discussion of this point given in summary above, see Dimock, *Missarum Sacrificia, Dangerous Deceits* ; Tomlinson, *ut supra*, p. 284.

Martyr, A.D. 190, the latter associating the Eucharist, as an oblation or sacrifice, with the passage in Malachi i. 10, 11. In Irenæus there are frequent references to the word, and Tertullian speaks of *panis oblationem*, and uses *offero* as signifying the whole ceremony. But during the second century we only hear of the oblation of gifts, not of the Body and Blood of Christ, which is of later date. Cyprian first gives a different meaning to the word and plainly speaks of the offering of Christ's blood, which must be understood as something subsequent to consecration. But what the early Fathers called the Memorial of Christ, Cyprian calls the Offering. Later Fathers adopted Cyprian's language, only explaining that they meant a solemn commemoration. Even Cyprian's language is not uniform.

The use of the word " altar " is not found associated with the Lord's Supper earlier than Tertullian,[1] and Westcott points out that such a usage would have been impossible during the second century.[2] This interpretation of the use of " offering " and " sacrifice " is also given by Bishop Harold Browne, who says that during this time " we find no certain reference to any offering in the Eucharist, except the offering of the bread and wine in the way of gifts or oblations to the service of God." And he also points out that the change of view in regard to the Eucharistic Sacrifice " does not expressly appear before the time of Cyprian," adding that if it had been believed before " it is certainly a most extraordinary example of silence and reserve that, for two centuries after Christ, they should never once have explained the sacrifice of the Eucharist in any manner, but either as an offering of first-fruits to God, . . . or else as an offering of praise and thanksgiving and spiritual worship."[3]

After the time of Cyprian, however, there is no doubt that writers frequently speak of the Eucharist as a sacrifice in the sense of our Lord's body and blood being commemorated and present and even offered. The Roman Catholics claim these statements in support of their own doctrine, though it is not at all clear that the meaning is identical. Certainly there is absolute silence among leading Church writers until the middle of the third century, and nothing in the writings after that date supports the view that a literal offering up of a literal sacrifice on the altar was contemplated. What seems quite clear is that the Eucharist was regarded as commemorative of the death of Christ and in this sense a commemorative sacrifice. The idea of gifts of bread and wine by the faithful and a sacrifice of prayer, and praise, and the offering of the communicants themselves, were of course kept in view, and then the thought of the Holy Communion as a memorial of Christ's sacrifice was made specially prominent. Beyond this it does not seem possible to go on any fair inter-

---

[1] "Tertullian, in whom we find both 'ara' used for the Holy Table, and '*summus sacerdos qui est episcopus*. Perhaps it would be impossible to find distinct earlier authority for either word" (Wordsworth, *The Ministry of Grace*, p. 133).

[2] "In this first stage of Christian literature there is not only no example of the application of the word θυσιαστήριον to any concrete, material object as the Holy Table, but there is no room for such an application" (Westcott, *Hebrews*, pp. 456, 458).

[3] Harold Browne, *Exposition of the Thirty-nine Articles*, p. 738 f.

pretation of the language of the Fathers of the first six centuries at least. Waterland has subjected the language of the Fathers of the early centuries to a thorough and most careful examination, and his conclusion is as follows :—

"The Fathers well understood that to make Christ's natural body the real sacrifice of the Eucharist would not only be absurd in reason, but highly presumptuous and profane ; and that to make the outward symbols a proper sacrifice, a material sacrifice, would be entirely contrary to Christian principles, degrading the Christian sacrifice into a Jewish one, yea, and making it much lower and meaner than the Jewish, both in value and dignity. The right way, therefore, was to make the sacrifice spiritual ; and it could be no other on Gospel principles."[1]

All this gives point to the important words of Boultbee that the student should be warned

"of the utter insecurity of relying upon isolated quotations from the Fathers, apart from an acquaintance with their phraseology, their habits of thought, and their mode of reasoning."[2]

And yet the modern and frequent use of the term "Eucharistic Sacrifice" calls for definite enquiry as to its meaning and character. In the Church of Rome the Eucharistic Sacrifice means the Mass.[3] When the doctrine of Transubstantiation had been set forth and defined it was easy to read into the new doctrine of the "sacrifice of the Mass" the language of the Fathers concerning the sacrifice and offering, and the definition of the "sacrifice of the Mass" in the Canons of the Council of Trent clearly states that the meaning is identical with Calvary and carries propitiatory effects : (1) for the whole Church ; (2) for the payee ; (3) for the priest. But this is not to be understood as a repetition, only a continuation of Calvary.

"If anyone shall say that in the Mass a true and proper sacrifice is not offered to God, let him be accursed."[4]

This view of Rome met with the strongest opposition from the Reformers of the sixteenth century, because they regarded it as detracting from the one perfect and sufficient sacrifice of our Lord on the Cross. German and English Reformers alike spoke in the plainest terms against this view, and it may be said, without any question, that in the sixteenth century the "sacrifice of the Mass" was the only Eucharistic Sacrifice really known.[5] And it can readily be understood why the Article uses

[1] Waterland, *On the Eucharist*, Ch. XII.
[2] Boultbee, *The Theology of the Church of England*, p. 272.
[3] Dearden, *Modern Romanism Examined*, p. 141.
[4] Council of Trent, Session XXII, Canon 1. See other Canons quoted above.
[5] "The whole substance of our sacrifice, which is frequented of the Church in the Lord's Supper, consisteth in prayers, praise, and giving of thanks, and in remembering

such plain language in speaking of what was universally regarded as a contradiction of the uniqueness of Calvary.[1]

It is, therefore, not surprising to read that " it must be admitted that the sacrificial aspect is not the prominent aspect of the Holy Eucharist dwelt upon in our Communion Office."[2] And the statements of Bishop Gore agree with this admission.

" No doubt there is some justification at first sight for saying that the New Testament does not suggest that the Eucharist is a sacrifice."

" On the subject of the Eucharistic sacrifice our Thirty-first Article only excludes any treatment of it which in any way suggests the insufficiency of the one offering of Christ. . . . Beyond this our formulas are silent."[3]

The dislocation of the Communion Office of 1549 in the Prayer Book of 1552, which still remains in our present Prayer Book, by which the sacrifice of praise and thanksgiving was put in a post-communion Collect instead of in the Consecration Prayer, is another proof of the way in which our Reformers did their utmost to dissociate the minds or the people from the mediæval sacrifice of the Mass. The omission of the word " altar " is, of course, another indication of the same purpose.

But notwithstanding all these facts the doctrine of the Eucharistic sacrifice is often taught in the English Church, a doctrine which, while rejecting the Roman view of associating the sacrifice with Christ's death, endeavours to connect it with our Lord's heavenly priesthood.[4] It is some-

and showing forth of that sacrifice once offered upon the altar of the Cross; that the same might continually be had in reverence by mystery, which, once only and no more, was offered for the price of our redemption" (Ridley, *Disputations at Oxford. Works*, Parker Society, p. 211).

[1] "It is readily acknowledged that there is a more favourable side on which the doctrine may be viewed. But I regret that I can by no means concur with Dr. Sanday in thinking it not impossible that the most favourable view may be reconciled with truth (see *Conception of Priesthood*, p. 87). However the sacrificial doctrine of the Mass may be minimised (and it is sometimes minimised to an extent which it is not easy to harmonise with Tridentine teaching), it is always a doctrine which requires the faith of a Real Presence of Christ on the altar, under the species, to be in some sense really offered as a sacrificial oblation (see *Eucharist considered in its Sacrificial Aspect*, p. 7; *Dangerous Deceits*, pp. 72, 73, 120–125; and *Doctrine of Sacerdotium*, p. 25). No heavy indictment brought against gross conceptions of the later mediæval doctrine of the sacrifice (see Gibson, *On Articles*, pp. 692 *et seq.*) can avail to turn away the condemnation of our Article XXXI from the doctrine itself to parasitical superstitions which were found adhering to it. Indeed, this truth stands confessed by one who once laboured hard to withstand it. It is Cardinal Newman who said, 'What the Thirty-First Article repudiates is undeniably the central and most sacred doctrine of the Catholic religion' (see *Missarum Sacrificia*, pp. 52, 58). And it is instructive to notice how Dr. Sanday's *eirenica* are regarded from the Romish point of view. Of his 'conception of sacrifice' it is said, 'this seems to us to be seeking peace through a confusion rather than through a clearer statement of contrary beliefs. . . . It might please the Protestant to know that he could use Catholic language without holding anything new; but for the Catholic it would be a retention of the ancient words with an abandonment of the ancient truth" (*The Month*, January 1899, p. 98). (Dimock, *The Sacerdotium of Christ*, p. 99, Note 2).

[2] Tyrrell Green, *The Thirty-nine Articles and the Age of the Reformation*, p. 258.

[3] Gore, *The Body of Christ*, p. 261.

[4] So Dr. Bright, in Bishop Gibson, *ut supra*, p. 691, and *Church Quarterly Review*, Vol. XLII, pp. 46–49.

what difficult to obtain a precise definition of this idea of the Eucharistic sacrifice, though it is intended to mean something associated exclusively with the Holy Communion. Various writers speak in different terms. One says that "it is the continual offering up to God of the Person of Jesus Christ in His body and blood. . . . We display to Him that precious body and blood. . . . Such an act is most truly a sacrifice."[1] Another defines it as "the presentation of the one holy sacrifice of Christ."[2] All that Bishop Gore can say is that it is "a feast upon a sacrifice, but the feast upon the sacrifice is the culmination of the sacri-·fice."[3] It is difficult, however, to see in what respect a feast can be even the culmination of a sacrifice, since in a sacrifice we give and in a feast we receive.

The problem, therefore, is as follows: (a) the Church of Rome is right in associating the Holy Communion with the death of Christ and wrong in making the Mass the continuation of Calvary. (b) Those in the English Church who teach as above are wrong in associating the Holy Communion with Christ in heaven, for everything in Scripture and the Prayer Book associates the Lord's Supper with the death of Christ, never with His life in heaven. The following considerations should be weighed in the study of this modern Anglican view:—

1. There is no trace of any such idea in the Ante-Nicene history.

2. Everything turns on what Christ is actually doing in heaven, and nothing in the New Testament gives the slightest warrant for believing that He is presenting before God the sacrifice once offered on the Cross. No such doctrine is to be discovered either in the New Testament or in the Prayer Book, and surely if Christ is offering Himself and His sacrifice in heaven, so important a fact would occupy a position of very definite prominence in the teaching of our Church. But it is nowhere to be found.[4]

3. What sacrifice is thus associated with our Lord above? Definition is absolutely necessary on so vital a point, and yet nothing can be found either in the New Testament or in the Prayer Book. The only language that can be adduced in this connection has already been considered in the Article on the Lord's Supper, and so it must suffice to say that τοῦτο ποιεῖτε cannot be rendered "offer this,"[5] or ἀνάμνησις, cannot be understood as a "memorial before God," and καταγγέλλετε cannot be rendered otherwise than "proclaim," with man, not God, as the object. It is therefore essential to discover what is our Lord's sacrificial act

[1] Mason, *The Faith of the Gospel*, pp. 327, 328.
[2] Hon. and Rev. J. G. Adderley, in *Goodwill*.
[3] Gore, *ut supra*, p. 261.
[4] Dimock, *The Christian Doctrine of Sacerdotium*, p. 13 f.
[5] It is surprising in the face of the best and almost the whole of modern scholarship that anyone can argue that these words mean "Make this your offering" (Tyrrell Green, *ut supra*, p. 255), or that another can say, "We do not see that any other explanation of the sacrificial view of the Eucharist is forthcoming" (*Church Quarterly Review*, July 1886, p. 328).

above, and what is really offered. There is only one answer from the New Testament and the Prayer Book : Nothing.

4. It is also essential to distinguish between sacrifice and sacrament. In the former God is the *terminus ad quem*, and in the latter He is the *terminus a quo*. The vital part of the sacrifice is the living will of the offerer (Heb. x. 10), and it is for this reason that sacrifice is associated with Christ's death, never with His life. If it should be said that Holy Communion is sacrificial at the moment of saying, " This is My Body," these words were not words of consecration at all and were uttered while the distribution or administration was proceeding. It has been shown that no " Catholic " form of consecration has ever existed,[1] and every particle of the bread and wine is intended to be consumed by man, not presented as a gift to God.

5. It may be said without any question that nowhere in Scripture is the idea of our Lord offering or pleading in heaven to be found.[2]

The Prayer Book, following the New Testament, has three sacrifices only. Those of ourselves (Rom. xii. 1) ; our gifts (Heb. xiii. 16) ; and our praises (Heb. xiii. 15). There is not even an oblation of the unconsecrated elements, as a comparison of the Rubric concerning these and the elements significantly shows.[3]

All this does not in the least set aside the primitive idea of sacrifice as applied either to the presentation of gifts to God or to the whole service of Communion. But the modern view is by no means identical or satisfied with these interpretations. So far as the English Church is concerned, no better expressed truth can be found than in the words of Bishop Bilson :

" Neither they nor I ever denied the Eucharist to be a sacrifice. The very name enforceth it to be the sacrifice of praise and thanksgiving, which is the true and lively sacrifice of the New Testament. The Lord's Table, in respect of His graces and mercies there proposed to us, is a heavenly banquet, which we must eat, and not sacrifice ; but the duties which He requireth at our hands, when we approach His Table, are sacrifices, not sacraments. As namely, to offer Him thanks and praises, faith and obedience, yea, our bodies and souls, to be living, holy, and acceptable sacrifices unto Him, which is our reasonable service."[4]

[1] Wordsworth, *ut supra*.

[2] "The modern conception of Christ pleading in heaven His Passion, 'offering His blood' on behalf of men, has no foundation in this Epistle. His glorified humanity is the eternal pledge of the absolute efficacy of His accomplished work. He pleads, as older writers truly expressed the thought, by His Presence on the Father's throne. Meanwhile, men on earth in union with Him enjoy continually through His Blood what was before the privilege of one man on one day in the year" (Westcott, *Hebrews*, p. 230).

"The words 'Still . . . His prevailing death He pleads,' have no apostolic warrant, and cannot even be reconciled with apostolic doctrine. . . . So far as the Atonement in relation to God is spoken of in any terms of time, the Bible seems to me to teach us to think of it as lying entirely in the past—a thing done 'once for all'" (*Life and Letters of F. J. A. Hort*, Vol. II, p. 213).

[3] Bishop Dowden, in an exhaustive Paper on "Our Alms and Oblations" in *Further Studies in the Prayer Book*, is conclusive on this point.

[4] Quoted in Waterland, *On the Eucharist*, p. 427.

This exegesis of the New Testament and the teaching of the Prayer Book are both clearly opposed to the Roman, and also to the modern Anglican, views of the Eucharistic Sacrifice.   In the Lord's Supper Christ is neither offered to God, nor for man, but He is offered to man in all the efficacy of His atoning sacrifice, to be received by faith.   It would be well if we could avoid ambiguous terms.   Even such a phrase as a " commemorative sacrifice " is ambiguous, for strictly, it is not this, but the commemoration of a sacrifice.[1]   If, however, the words " Eucharistic Sacrifice " mean some sacrifice which is offered only in and at the Lord's Supper, it is clear that no such idea is found either in the Bible or in the Prayer Book.[2]

[1] "You may as well call the Waterloo Banquet a memorial battle, as call the Lord's Supper a memorial sacrifice" (quoted by Bishop Moule, *The Supper of the Lord*, p. 37).
[2] For a fuller discussion of this subject reference may perhaps be permitted to the author's *A Sacrament of our Redemption*, Ch. XI, and his English Church Manual, *Our Lord's Work in Heaven*.

IV. THE HOUSEHOLD OF FAITH—*continued*

CORPORATE RELIGION

D. CHURCH DISCIPLINE (ARTICLES XXXII–XXXVI)

32. THE MARRIAGE OF PRIESTS.

33. EXCOMMUNICATE PERSONS, HOW THEY ARE TO BE AVOIDED.

34. THE TRADITIONS OF THE CHURCH.

35. THE HOMILIES.

36. CONSECRATION OF BISHOPS AND MINISTERS.

ARTICLE XXXII

Of the Marriage of Priests.	De Conjugio Sacerdotum.
Bishops, Priests, and Deacons are not commanded by God's Law, either to vow the estate of single life, or to abstain from marriage; therefore it is lawful also for them, as for all other Christian men, to marry at their own discretion, as they shall judge the same to serve better to godliness.	Epicopis, Presbyteris, et Diaconis nullo mandato divino præceptum est, ut aut cœlibatum voveant, aut a matrimonio abstineant. Licet igitur etiam illis, ut cæteris omnibus Christianis, ubi hoc ad pietatem magis facere judicaverint, pro suo arbitratu matrimonium contrahere.

IMPORTANT EQUIVALENTS.

Of Priests	= *Sacerdotum.*
Priests are not commanded by God's Law	= *Presbyteris nullo mandato divino præceptum est.*
The estate of single life	= *cœlibatum.*

SEVERAL questions of Church discipline naturally follow those on the Church, Ministry, and Sacraments. It is probable that the subject of this Article is to be closely connected with that of Article XXXI, because the duties of the priest in regard to Masses, etc., was thought to be incompatible with the position of marriage.

The corresponding Article of 1553 consisted of the first clause only of the present Article with the following title: *Cœlibatus ex verbo Dei præcipitur nemini*, " The estate of single life is commanded to no one by God's word." The Article itself was as follows: *Episcopis, Presbyteris, et Diaconis non est mandatum ut cœlibatum voveant, neque jure divino coguntur matrimonio abstinere.* " Bishops, Priests, and Deacons are not commanded to vow the state of single life without marriage; neither by God's law are they compelled to abstain from marriage." The second clause was added in 1563, giving a positive assertion instead of a merely negative argument in favour of the practice.[1] It has been suggested that this second clause was added because Queen Elizabeth, who was prejudiced against clerical marriages, had by the Twenty-ninth Injunction of 1559 put impediments in their way by alleging that

" There hath grown offence and some slander to the Church, by lack of *discreet* and sober behaviour in many ministers of the Church, both in choosing of their wives, and *indiscreet* living with them."[2]

[1] Hardwick, *History of the Articles of Religion*, p. 130.
[2] Cardwell, *Documentary Annals*, Vol. I, p. 192.

This wording may suggest the defence made in 1563 by means of this clause on clerical " discretion." In November 1563 the Council of Trent anathematised

" Whosoever shall say that clerks in holy orders, or regulars having solemnly professed chastity, can contract matrimony, and that the contract is valid notwithstanding the ecclesiastical law, or the vow."

I.—THE PURPOSE OF THE ARTICLE

It was, of course, directed against the Roman Catholic law of the celibacy of the clergy. It is curious that Rome should make marriage a Sacrament and yet deny it to priests. The application to Rome is probably the explanation of the word *sacerdotum* in the title of the Latin Version, though the Article itself includes all three Orders. It is sometimes urged that the use of this word proves the sacerdotal character of the ministry, that the Prayer Book term " priest " is intended for *sacerdos*.[1] But it ought to be obvious that the argument has no real weight. The Article includes Deacons under the general name of *sacerdotes*, but no one would argue from this that Deacons possess sacerdotal powers. It seems clear, therefore, that the term *sacerdotum* in the title is used in a general sense, and the Latin of the Article is clearly against the argument in its use of the term *presbyteris*, which is used to designate the second order of the ministry. In the same way, in Article XXXVI, the word " priests " is found in the Latin as *presbyterorum*. No argument can be drawn from Article XXXI, for the simple reason that the reference there is to Roman Catholic priests. One other point may perhaps be mentioned. This title, " *De Conjugio Sacerdotum*," actually occurs in German Reformed documents,[2] where the reference obviously cannot be to the sacerdotal character of the ministry.

The Article makes two statements : (*a*) there is no prohibition of clerical marriage in Scripture ; (*b*) it is lawful, if considered desirable, on proper grounds. Thus, our Church avoids the Roman error of forbidding clerical marriage altogether, and the Greek rule which requires marriage in the case of Presbyters as distinct from Bishops.

---

[1] "The use of the word *sacerdotum* shows how entirely the English Reformers repudiated the idea of a mere minister, and assumed that of a ἱερεύς or *sacerdos*. Had the word stood alone we might have supposed that it was a slip, but bearing in mind the employment of it in Article XXXI, we may suppose that it was no *incuria*, but intentionally done. If so, we have the identity of the priesthood before and after the Reformation asserted, just as actually we find maintained in the amended Statutes of Corpus Christi College, where it is held that the Fellows, 'though discharged from massing," were still of necessity to be Priests" (Forbes, *Explanation of the Thirty-nine Articles*, Vol. II, p. 264).

B. J. Kidd, *The Thirty-nine Articles*, p. 247, also says: "Note the retention of *sacerdos* as indicative of what is meant by 'priest.'"

It is interesting that Bishop Gibson, Maclear, and Tyrrell Green do not use this argument.

[2] *Augsburg Confession*, Part II, Section 2; Melanchthon's *Apology*, Section 11; Schmalcald, *Articles*, No. 11; see Von Hase, *Handbook to the Controversy with Rome*, pp. 21, 262, 334.

II.—THE HISTORY OF THE ARTICLE

It is clear that clergy married during the first three centuries, but there was a tendency quite early to prohibit marriage after Ordination, though so far as the West is concerned there seems to have been little or no difference in regard to marriage before or after Ordination.[1] By reason of persecution these early centuries constituted the heroic age of the Church, and the custom of celibacy grew, probably intensified by Gnosticism and Manicheeism, so that men left their wives after Ordination. It is significant, therefore, that the origin of clerical celibacy was heathen, not Christian, or Jewish. In 305 the Council of Elvira prohibited marriage for the first time, and when this was suggested at the Council of Nicæa, 325, it was objected to by Paphnutius, himself a celibate. Even in the fifth century, when it became customary for Bishops on appointment to cease living with their wives, the Bishop of Ptolemais would not leave his wife and was allowed to continue with her by his Metropolitan. The Council of Gangra, 350, anathematised all those who separated from their wives. The Trullan Council, 692,[2] made a distinction, and said that Bishops could not marry, but that priests might. This has had a bad effect on the Eastern Church, exalting the one position and depressing the other. This is substantially the law of the Greek Church to-day, which orders Priests to marry, but forbids Bishops. Priests may not marry a second time, and if a man marries after Ordination he has to forfeit his Orders.[3]

In the West the tendency was always towards celibacy, and Pope Siricius in the fourth century deposed those who claimed the right to marry. But concessions had to be made from time to time, and this went on up to the time of Hildebrand. In the Middle Ages he reorganised the Priesthood and found many Priests really married, and yet that grave abuses existed through the general rule of celibacy. His idea of supreme power made it essential for the clergy to be free of the Emperor, and so celibacy was insisted upon as the universal law. The Pope went so far as to say that if a Priest was married he could not administer a valid Sacrament. The result was that for five centuries there were great confusions and complications, mainly from financial matters, as a man came to the Church simply to live. Even Pope Pius II, 1464, admitted the need of alteration, but the reasons of Hildebrand continued most powerful. He opposed the idea of married Prince Bishops, since if they were married their Sees would tend to become heirlooms. He also urged that celibacy gave greater freedom from the world.

Clerical celibacy was introduced into England by Lanfranc, 1066, and Anselm, 1102, but it was impossible to enforce it, and clerical concubinage

[1] Wordsworth, *The Ministry of Grace*, p. 227.
[2] So called because held in the Trullan Hall of the Imperial Palace in Constantinople.
[3] Knetes, *Ordination and Matrimony in the Eastern Orthodox Church* (*Journal of Theological Studies*, April 1910).

became common. Wordsworth says that " at no time before the Reformation of the sixteenth century were the mass of the English clergy unmarried, though the position which their wives enjoyed was generally by no means an enviable one."[1] The Reformers saw the necessity of a change. Cranmer married his second wife just before his Consecration as Archbishop, but the Six Articles of 1539 were against it. In 1547 came a change introducing freedom. One of the Articles of Inquiry from the Archbishop of Canterbury was, " Whether any do contemn married priests, and for that they be married, will not receive the communion or other sacraments at their hands."[2] This position was confirmed by the Article of 1553, as stated above. In 1553, the first year of Queen Mary's reign, a letter reversed this rule and deprived all married Priests of their livings and commanded them to bring their wives within a fortnight in order that they might be divorced.[3] During this reign there were several Inquiries and Injunctions on the subject.[4] In 1559 came Elizabeth's Injunction, requiring every clergyman before marriage to obtain proper assurance from the Bishop and two Justices of the Peace,[5] and, as already noted, it is probable that this requirement led to the stronger statement inserted in the present Article.[6]

The Council of Trent, as we have seen, anathematises those who say that the clergy can marry, but it is significant that the Church of Rome yields on this point in connection with Uniate congregations.[7]

III.—THE CASE STATED

It is, of course, well known that Jewish priests married, and this was especially necessary in the case of the High Priest in order that his office might be continued in his family as an hereditary work. Our Lord's attitude to marriage carries a clear approval in regard to all His followers. St. Paul honours marriage, St. Peter was himself married, and the teaching of the Apostles is clearly that " marriage is honourable in all " (Heb. xiii. 4). Clerical marriage is obvious from such passages as 1 Tim. iii. 2, 12 ; Tit. i. 6 ; 1 Cor. ix. 5. Tertullian was married, and so were Hilary of Poictiers, Gregory of Nyssa, and others. Our complaint is against the universal imposition of celibacy ; its expediency

---

[1] Wordsworth, *ut supra*, p. 230.

[2] Cardwell, *ut supra*, Vol. I, p. 59.

[3] Cardwell, *ut supra*, Vol. I, p. 120.

[4] Cardwell, *ut supra*, Vol. II, Index (p. 447), s.v. Married Priests.

[5] Cardwell, *ut supra*, Vol. I, p. 224 f. The Queen never seems to have conquered her dislike to married clergy; see Cardwell, *ut supra*, Vol. I, p. 307.

[6] Ball (*The Orthodox Doctrine of the Church of England*, p. 241) is responsible for the following statements :

"The strong dislike of Elizabeth for wedded priests, combined with her desire to conciliate the reforming party, caused a very strange state of things to prevail during her reign; the clergy were allowed to marry, but their children were not accounted, legally, to be legitimate! This stigma on the offspring of the priesthood was not repealed until the reign of James I."

[7] Wordsworth, *ut supra*, p. 255.

in certain cases is fully admitted, and the Article lays down the principle
that clergymen are to consider the question in the light of " godliness."
It is not to be merely a matter of convenience or personal preference, but
that which shall serve the better to further their position as servants of
God. In the light of the Roman Catholic prohibition of marriage the
words of the Apostle are particularly significant (1 Tim. iv. 3). The
great rule of Scripture is that " it is not good for man to be alone," and
a celibate clergy tends to become a separate class away from the interests
and feelings of the people. Celibacy is sometimes favoured, and urged as
more excellent for spiritual work.[1] But not only is this without Scriptural
support, it has also against it the facts of history, which tend to show that
for spiritual and pastoral work in the New Testament sense the nature
of man is properly developed ordinarily through the influence of woman-
hood, and thereby he is enabled the better to do his work. It is, therefore, impossible to avoid the conclusion that compulsory celibacy is
" a constant blot and one of the most dangerous errors of the Roman
Church."[2]

[1] Gibson, *The Thirty-nine Articles*, p. 655.
[2] Wordsworth, *ut supra*, p. 251.
The present state of South America amply confirms this position. For a valuable,
historical, and practical statement of this subject the whole section in Bishop Wordsworth's *The Ministry of Grace*, pp. 206–256, should be studied. See also Lea, *Sacerdotal
Power in the Christian Church*; Hobhouse, *The Church and the World in Idea and in History*
(Bampton Lectures, pp. 69, 121); Hatch's Bampton Lectures, p. 159.

ARTICLE XXXIII

Of excommunicate Persons, how they are to be avoided.

De excommunicatis vitandis.

That person which by open denunciation of the Church is rightly cut off from the unity of the Church, and excommunicated, ought to be taken of the whole multitude of the faithful as an Heathen and Publican, until he be openly reconciled by penance, and received into the Church by a Judge that hath authority thereunto.

Qui per publicam Ecclesiæ denunciationem rite ab unitate Ecclesiæ præcisus est, et excommunicatus, is ab universa fidelium multitudine, donec per pœnitentiam publice reconciliatus fuerit arbitrio Judicis competentis, habendus est tanquam Ethnicus et Publicanus.

IMPORTANT EQUIVALENTS.

Of excommunicate persons, how they are to be avoided	= *de excommunicatis vitandis.*
Rightly cut off	= *rite præcisus.*
Heathen	= *Ethnicus.*
Penance	= *per pœnitentiam.*
That hath authority thereto	= *competentis.*

THE subject of Church discipline was the cause of great discussion and difference of opinion in the reign of Edward VI.[1] It was, therefore, natural that it should be included in the Articles, and this dates from 1553, with merely a change in the title which then read : " Excommunicate Persons are to be avoided."

I.—THE PURPOSE OF THE ARTICLE

It was felt necessary and wise to assert the right of the Church as a Society to exercise discipline and to exclude those who violated its laws. To be excommunicated was, of course, to be separated from the Communion of the visible Church.

II.—THE TEACHING OF THE ARTICLE

Various points are included in the claim made on behalf of the Church as a community.

1. The Fact of Discipline.—This is naturally assumed and is inherent in the existence of any Society.

2. The Method of Discipline.—Reference is made to " open denunciation of the Church," emphasis being placed upon the publicity of the action and its connection with the entire Society.

[1] Hardwick, *History of the Articles of Religion*, pp. 93, 105.

3. The Effect of Discipline.—The person thus dealt with is said to be
" rightly cut off from the unity of the Church and excommunicated."
The Latin equivalent for " rightly " is " *rite*," referring to due order and
emphasising the proper manner of doing the work, according to the
judgment of the Church.

4. The Attitude to Discipline.—The rest of the Church is to regard
the excommunicated person as " an Heathen and Publican," that is, one
who is outside the privileges of the Christian community. The allusion
is, of course, to our Lord's words in St. Matt. xviii. 17. The publican
was regarded as an offender then, but our Lord's attitude to the men
as a class suggests the true spirit of dealing with such cases.

5. The Purpose of Discipline.—This excommunication is intended
to produce ·reconciliation. " Until he be openly reconciled by penance,
and received into the Church by a Judge that hath authority thereunto."
Once again emphasis is laid on publicity, for the man is to be as openly
reconciled as he had been openly denounced. Penance (Latin, *pœnitentiam*) includes both the feelings of the offender, as he repents of his
wrongdoing, and the discipline required by the community as a condition
of his reinstatement. It will be observed that there is no definite statement as to the officer by whom the offender is to be restored. He is
merely described as " a judge that hath authority thereunto," the Latin
equivalent being " a competent judge." In the ordinary course of events
this would be a minister of the Church, though it is possible that the
Civil power is contemplated in connection with an Established Church.

III.—THE TEACHING OF SCRIPTURE

The subject of Christian discipline in Holy Scripture is one of importance. It may first be considered in the light of our Lord's teaching
in St. Matt. xviii. 15-18, where three principles are laid down : (*a*) in
the case of trespass between brethren the fault is first to be told between
the two parties with the hope of amicable arrangement (ver. 15) ; (*b*) if
this proves impracticable an effort is to be made in company with one or
two others, so that the situation may be clearly understood (ver. 16) ;
(*c*) then if this proves impossible the community in general is to be informed of what has happened, and if the offender will not listen to the
Society of God's people he is to be regarded as excommunicated, put
outside the pale of fellowship and privilege. These three proofs are confirmed by the solemn statement which vests Church discipline in the
community, " Verily I say unto you, Whatsoever ye shall bind on earth
shall be bound in heaven : and whatsoever ye shall loose on earth shall
be loosed in heaven " (ver. 18). These words are practically identical
with those spoken to St. Peter a little time before (Matt. xvi. 19). " Binding " and " loosing " were familiar Jewish terms for " prohibiting " and
" permitting,"[1] and refer to the power of the Christian community to

[1] John Lightfoot, *Horæ Hebraicæ*, on St. Matthew xvi. 19.

make regulations for its own life.[1] Similar teaching connected with Christian discipline is found in St. Paul's Epistles, and refers both to doctrine and practice (Rom. xvi. 17; 1 Cor. v. 2-7; 2 Cor. ii. 5-11; 1 Tim. i. 19, 20; 2 Thess. iii. 14; Tit. iii. 10; 2 John 10; 3 John 10). When St. Paul speaks of delivering someone to Satan (1 Tim. i. 20) he is doubtless referring to specific Apostolic power (cf. Acts xiii. 10); he implies something more than mere excommunication, and yet something less than death. It is natural that discipline would be considered more necessary while the Church was unformed, but at all times human nature needs some such influence.

IV.—THE HISTORY

As the Jewish religion was theocratic there was no difference between ecclesiastical and civil discipline. In the Old Testament discipline often involved death by God or man (Gen. xvii. 14; Exod. xxxi. 14). Later on the Jews exercised the power of excommunication (Numb. xii. 14, 15; Lev. xiii. 5, 6; Ezra x. 8), making distinctions between various offences. (*a*) The lightest sentence was separation for a month (נִדּוּי, ἀφορισμός); (*b*) the next severe form was excommunication from the assembly (חֵרֶם, ἀνάθεμα); (*c*) the severest of all was permanent separation from the community (שַׁמְּתָא). It is sometimes thought that our Lord's words in St. Luke vi. 22 correspond with these three stages, but according to a modern authority this is erroneous, for there were only two kinds of excommunication: temporary exclusion and permanent separation.[2]

The early Church naturally took over the idea of excommunication from the Jews (Luke vi. 22; John ix. 22; xii. 42; xvi. 21). In the early centuries the punishment was of three kinds: (*a*) admonition; (*b*) lesser excommunication from prayers and Eucharist, but not from the Church (ἀφορισμός); (*c*) greater excommunication (παντελὴς ἀφορισμός). There were also four orders of penitents: *flentes*, mourners; *audientes*, hearers; *substrati*, kneelers; *consistentes*, bystanders.[3] It was natural, with the New Testament before it, that the Church should emphasise discipline, and so the system grew up, though in its completeness it was apparently very seldom enforced.

The first to deal with the Church as a whole was Victor, Bishop of Rome, who took upon himself to excommunicate all those who did not observe Easter according to his rule. Tertullian refers to the exclusion of the Gnostic Valentinus, and of the heretic Marcion. The Council

---

[1] It is clear that the reference in this passage is to a power concerning things, not persons, a power given to the Society to make rules. See Bishop Wordsworth, *Letter to the Clergy of the Diocese of Salisbury*, p. 49 (Longmans, 1898).

[2] Schurer, *The Jewish People in the Time of Christ* (Second Edition), Vol. II, p. 60. Quoted in Bishop Gibson, *The Thirty-nine Articles*, p. 706, Note 2.

[3] Article, "Penitence," *Dictionary of Christian Antiquities*, Vol. II, p. 1591.

of Nicæa promulgated a decree excluding from Church fellowship for ten years, but giving Bishops the power of shortening the time. When a person was excommunicated by one Church he was regarded as excommunicated by all, for notices were given, and if any Church received him it was considered schismatical. But such excommunication did not annul his baptism or take away his civil or national rights, though the present Roman Catholic use is contrary to this. The trouble, of course, was that the early Church had no coercive power inherent in ecclesiastical authority, and the result was that before the Church became national the State had to be called in in the case of Paul of Samosata.

As superstition increased the Church was regarded as possessing some mysterious power which was worse than death itself. In the later centuries Papal interdicts were pronounced on nations for the fault of one individual, but these were unknown in the early Church and only began to be common in the twelfth century (e.g. King John's in 1206). They became weakened in the fourteenth, especially by the action of men like Wycliffe, and this was no doubt the reason why the Council of Trent guarded against their abuse. But the Roman Catholic doctrine of Penance renders the need of this general form of discipline very much less.[1] Private confession had superseded all other discipline.

Our Article has to do with Protestant opinion in the sixteenth century, and is not against the Church of Rome, except so far as emphasis is placed upon discipline being open. The Rubric after the Nicene Creed orders excommunications to be publicly read out in Church at that point. The Office for the Burial of the Dead is not to be used for those that die excommunicated, and there are similar Rubrics in regard to discipline connected with the Holy Communion. Canon 65 of 1604 provides directions for public denunciation of excommunicate persons, and Canon 85 includes in the duties of Churchwardens the keeping out of the Church of all such persons.[2]

The term "Erastianism" is often used to-day. It is derived from Erastus, a German physician, who died 1582. He said that the Church could only persuade, not enforce, and for this reason all ecclesiastical offences were to be dealt with by the civil authority, since the Church had no independent power. The Puritans went to the other extreme and taught that all power was spiritual. In 1645 a strong effort was made by the Presbyterians to exclude men from the Sacrament without any interference from the State, but Parliament saw the danger and refused to establish this *imperium in imperio*. The Anglican position recognises the Church as having no power over persons and property, and if the Church is independent of the State discipline would seem to be impracticable so far as these questions are concerned. The Church can frame any laws she likes, but the enforcement without the civil power

---

[1] For the history of discipline see Articles, "Excommunication" and "Penance," *Dictionary of Christian Antiquities*.

[2] See also Canons 2–8, 9–12, 109.

will naturally be difficult.   All that a Church can do is to exclude from ecclesiastical privileges and social intercourse.   Beyond this a spiritual community is necessarily impotent apart from any question that involves the law of the land.   It was the consciousness of this that led the Church to feel the need of some understanding for mutual assistance and control. Yet even when excommunication was enforced it was always intended for spiritual benefit and not for mere punishment.   In principle a Church is and must be independent of the State, and yet if that Church holds property it can only be by the laws of the State.

At the Reformation, when auricular confession was abandoned, public discipline was felt to be essential, and its absence is regretted in the Commination Service.   There is a wide feeling that more disciplinary power is necessary than we have at present.   We lost it by our own fault and by the terrible errors of former days.   Discipline was often regarded as one of the Notes of the Church.   Owing to the peculiar relations of Church and State in England Ecclesiastical Courts have practically no jurisdiction over the laity, and are therefore virtually obsolete.[1]

[1] Boultbee, *The Theology of the Church of England*, p. 278.   For the views of the Reformers on Church Discipline, see Harold Browne, *Exposition of the Thirty-nine Articles*, p. 766.

ARTICLE XXXIV

Of the Traditions of the Church.

It is not necessary that Traditions and Ceremonies be in all places one, and utterly like; for at all times they have been divers, and may be changed according to the diversities of countries, times, and men's manners, so that nothing be ordained against God's Word.

Whosoever through his private judgment, willingly and purposely, doth openly break the traditions and ceremonies of the Church, which be not repugnant to the Word of God, and be ordained and approved by common authority, ought to be rebuked openly, that others may fear to do the like, as he that offendeth against the common order of the Church, and hurteth the authority of the Magistrate, and woundeth the consciences of the weak brethren.

Every particular or national Church hath authority to ordain, change, and abolish ceremonies or rites of the Church, ordained only by man's authority, so that all things be done to edifying.

De Traditionibus Ecclesiasticis.

Traditiones atque Cæremonias easdem non omnino necessarium est esse ubique, aut prorsus consimiles: nam et variæ semper fuerunt, et mutari possunt, pro regionum, temporum, et morum diversitate, modo nihil contra verbum Dei instituatur.

Traditiones, et cæremonias Ecclesiasticas, quæ cum verbo Dei non pugnant, et sunt auctoritate publica institutæ atque probatæ, quisquis privato consilio volens, et data opera, publice violaverit, is, ut qui peccat in publicum ordinem Ecclesiæ, quique lædit auctoritatem Magistratus, et qui infirmorum fratrum conscientias vulnerat, publice, ut cæteri timeant, arguendus est.

Quælibet Ecclesia particularis sive nationalis auctoritatem habet instituendi mutandi, aut abrogandi cæremonias aut ritus Ecclesiasticos, humana tantum auctoritate institutos, modo omnia ad ædificationem fiant.

IMPORTANT EQUIVALENTS.

[No English]	= *omnino.*
Through his private judgment	= *privato consilio.*
Purposely	= *data opera.*
Openly	= *publice.*
Ought to be rebuked	= *arguendus est.*
Common order	= *publicum ordinem.*

THE first paragraph of this Article was evidently derived from the fifth of the Thirteen Articles of 1548 (The Concordat),[1] with the word " times " (*temporum*), added in 1563 for greater comprehensiveness. The last paragraph of the Article (referring to national Churches) was not in

---

[1] "Traditiones vero, et ritus, atque ceremoniæ, quæ vel ad decorem vel ordinem vel disciplinam Ecclesiæ ab hominibus sunt institutæ, non omnino necesse est ut eædem sint ubique aut prorsus similes. Hoc enim et variæ fuere, et variari possunt pro regionum et morum diversitate, ubi decus, ordo, et utilitas Ecclesiæ videbuntur postulare.

"Hæ enim et variæ fuere, et variari possunt pro regionum et morum diversitate, ubi decus decensque ordo principibus rectoribusque regionum videbuntur postulare; ita tamen ut nihil varietur aut instituatur contra verbum Dei manifestum" (Gibson, *The Thirty-nine Articles*, p. 717).

See Hardwick, *History of the Articles of Religion*, p. 264.

that of 1553, but was added in 1563. It is substantially (almost verbally) the same as the proposition laid down by the Reformers in their Debate with the Roman Marian Bishops in 1559.

This is a corollary of Article XX as to Ceremonial, and is a special application of it to the position of the Church of England in view of the attitude adopted by the Council of Trent to national Churches. It is also plainly directed against the excessive individualism of the extreme Protestant party. The Article still expresses the essential and fundamental position of the Anglican Church, as viewed from modern standpoints corresponding with those against which the Article was originally directed.

I.—THE TEACHING OF THE ARTICLE

1. The first principle laid down is that Traditions and Ceremonies need not be always alike. The reference is to practices just as Article VI applies to doctrine. The wording of the Article, expressing that " it is not necessary for Traditions and Ceremonies to be alike," is carefully guarded and suggests the desirability of uniformity wherever practicable. The teaching of the Article can be well illustrated by the prefatory matter of the Prayer Book. The third of the introductory addresses, " Of Ceremonies, why some be Abolished, and some Retained," is a full statement of the claim of the Church of England to change where necessary. Our Reformers could hardly help remembering the uniformity of the Western Church for centuries, and they doubtless regretted the necessity for change. The desirability of uniformity wherever possible is equally illustrated from the " Preface," and " Concerning the Service of the Church." It is a matter of simple fact that Traditions and Ceremonies have never been alike, and it is not going too far to say that they never will be. The history of the Church, as we shall see, has been, again and again, marked by change, according to differences of place, occasions, and circumstances. The one standard is Holy Scripture, for nothing is to be " ordained against God's Word." This, as already seen several times, was the great principle laid down at the Reformation.

2. At the same time the Article teaches with equal plainness the need of individual conformity. Wilful individualism is first described in very frank terms and then strongly deprecated on three grounds. No one through his private judgment is willingly, purposely, and openly to break Church traditions which are not unscriptural and are in common use. Any such deliberate breach constitutes a threefold offence: (a) against the common order of the Church; (b) against proper authority; (c) against weak consciences, leading them to do the same. The only question is as to what is scriptural, or " not repugnant to the Word of God," and at the same time supported by existing Church authority. All such breaches are to be subject to severe rebuke in order that others

may be prevented from doing likewise and causing untold confusion in the community.

3. Then the Article in its last clause proceeds to claim the right and power for national Churches to make such changes. There was of necessity no national Church in primitive times, and up to the sixteenth century the only real division was that of East and West.[1] But the exigencies of the Reformation necessitated national severances from Rome, and as a result Churches sprang up in the various nationalities which protested against the Roman dominion. In harmony, therefore, with the Reformation movement the Article claims that each such Church can "ordain, change, and abolish ceremonies or rites of the Church, ordained only by man's authority." Thus so long as they are only human and not divinely binding they can be altered, the one requirement being that of edification, "so that all things be done to edifying" (Rom. xiv. 19). This will mean that we are neither to adhere obstinately to anything ancient simply because it is ancient, nor rashly to introduce anything novel because it is new. In everything connected with ceremonies or rites the ruling principle of spiritual edification is to be kept in mind.

II.—THE HISTORY

The principles laid down in the Article can be amply justified by an appeal to primitive Church history, for diversity is clearly seen in the early Church. We know this from the story of Polycarp and Victor as to the date of the observance of Easter. The language of the great Liturgies is another illustration of the same diversity. Writers can also be adduced in support of this contention. Thus Tertullian (*De Corona Militis*) refers to many ceremonies formerly used, but subsequently discontinued, as, for example, the use of honey. To the same effect St. Augustine writes (*Ad Januarium*) about things which vary according to countries and places, like daily Communion, the Sabbath Fast, the Pax. Perhaps posture in prayer is the most notable instance of this principle of diversity. The Canons of Nicæa require standing in prayer, and to this day this custom is observed in the Eastern Church. So that after all the Puritans were really right, though perhaps they did not know that they were insisting upon what had been ordered by the Nicene Canon. As a further illustration of the way in which extremes meet, it may be mentioned that the Pope of Rome and Presbyterian Christians receive the Holy Communion in the sitting posture.[2] But as time went on uniformity became more and more the rule in the Western Church, although

---

[1] "Now that the Roman Empire is gone, and that all the laws which they made are at an end, with the authority that made them, it is a vain thing to pretend to keep up the ancient dignities of *Sees*, since the foundation upon which that was built is sunk and gone. Every empire, kingdom, or state, is an entire body within itself" (Burnet, *Exposition of the Thirty-nine Articles of the Church of England*, p. 451).

[2] Gibson, *ut supra*, pp. 517–519.

in England there was some diversity, as seen in the Sarum use. The Council of Trent has fixed the Roman use, though anciently there was a good deal of national liberty, with Gallican formularies in France, and the Ambrosian use in Milan.[1] The tendency to uniformity is useful, and should be encouraged as far as possible, and yet it contains its own perils which need to be watched. It is certainly incompetent for the Church of Rome to complain of variety, since, as Burnet says :—

" Of all the bodies of the world, the Church of Rome has the worst grace to reproach us for departing in some particulars from the ancient canons, since it was her ill conduct that had brought them all into desuetude."[2]

It was not surprising that at the Reformation there should be an inevitable rebound and reaction in Puritanism by an exaltation of rules to the position of principles. It was this difficulty that led to the great work of Hooker in which he showed the true nature of law, natural and spiritual, the place of Scripture in the Divine economy, and the particular application of these principles in the law of the Church of England.[3] In regard to matters of outward form, Hooker lays down four simple propositions. (1) Anything that can be shown to set forward godliness is to be accepted, notwithstanding slight inconveniences that may accrue. (2) In matters which do not suggest in themselves fitness, the judgment of antiquity may rightly weigh in their acceptance and retention. (3) Apart from Divine law, clear argument, and public inconvenience, the authority of the Church should rightly weigh with true followers of Christ. (4) If necessity or usefulness require, certain ceremonies may be dispensed with from time to time.[4] It would be difficult to deny the inherent reasonableness of this position as laid down by our great Church writer. The one thing to remember is that the Bible is essentially a book of principles, not of rules, and the supreme requirement is that amidst the varied and complex needs of life and worship no Church rule shall contravene a Bible principle. Apart from this there must necessarily be full liberty to " ordain, change, and abolish."

The wording of the Article on one point may naturally seem to be not only archaic, but altogether out of harmony with the freer conditions of life that obtain now as compared with the times when these formularies

---

[1] Maclear and Williams, *Introduction to the Articles of the Church of England*, p. 383, Note 1.

[2] Burnet, *ut supra*, p. 452.

[3] "The several societies of Christian men, unto every one of which the name of a Church is given, with addition betokening severalty, as the Church of Rome, Corinth, Ephesus, England, and so the rest, must be endued with correspondent general properties belonging unto them as they are public Christian societies. And of such properties common unto all societies Christian, it may not be denied that one of the very chiefest is Ecclesiastical Polity. . . . To our purpose the name of Church-Polity will better serve, because it containeth both government, and also whatsoever besides belongeth to the ordering of the Church in public" (Hooker, *Eccl. Pol.*, Bk. III, Ch. I). See also Hooker, *ut supra*, Bks. I–V.

[4] Hooker, *ut supra*, Bk. V, Ch. VI–IX.

were drawn up. It will suffice to show the true bearing of the Article on present-day life by quoting the wise words of one of our most able and thoughtful modern writers :—

" It need scarcely be observed to those who have read the history of the Church of England under the Tudor Sovereigns that the Thirty-fourth Article was very far from acknowledging the liberty of sects to organise themselves. The liberty which was claimed for the English State to organise the English Church was freely granted to Scotland, Saxony, or Geneva ; but more licence than this was not recognised in that age. Accordingly the *open rebuke*, as interpreted by the practice of the Tudors and Stuarts with regard to schismatics, included certain very severe personal results. Happily the Article itself is no warrant for these proceedings, and without difficulty adapts itself to the usage of a more tolerant age."[1]

III.—THE RELATION OF NATIONAL CHURCHES TO THE CHURCH CATHOLIC

This is a point of great importance at the present time. It is said by many to be impossible for a National Church to set aside anything that is truly " Catholic." It is, therefore, necessary to define as clearly as possible what we mean by a " National " Church and the Church " Catholic." What is a National Church ? In the general acceptation of the term it means a people organised for Christian worship under the Head of the State, or within the limits of the State. It is, of course, well known that the term " National " Church has never been anything else than nominal, for no Church has ever been literally coterminous with the nation. But for practical purposes the term is adequate to express the Christianity of England at the time of the Reformation, when the nation and the Church were virtually co-extensive, Convocation representing the clergy, Parliament the laity, and the two bodies together constituting the representation of the nation for ecclesiastical purposes. There is no question as to Faith, for, as we have seen, the supreme authority for the individual and the community is Holy Scripture (Article VI). What is often called in question at the present time is the right of a National Church to vary any tradition or ceremony which is regarded as " Catholic." But what is " Catholic " in reference to tradition ? One writer distinguishes between three kinds of tradition. (1) Divine Tradition, that is, some doctrine or ordinance, not recorded in Scripture, and yet believed to rest on Divine authority. The New Testament as a collection of divinely inspired writings is used to illustrate this point. (2) Apostolic Tradition, that is, doctrines or ordinances handed down " from the unwritten teachings of the Apostles." Instances of this are given, as the observance of the Lord's Day instead of the Sabbath, and the keeping of Lent. (3) Ecclesiastical Tradition, that is, doctrines or ordinances dating from post-Apostolic times, which rest solely on the authority of particular Churches. These may concern dogma, ritual, or morals. It

---

[1] Boultbee, *The Theology of the Church of England*, p. 173.

is urged that the Article is concerned with the third of these, Ecclesiastical Tradition, since " Divine Tradition is changeless," and the Anglican Church " has always strenuously repudiated any claim to interfere with Apostolic Tradition." Then, as to the third, it is said that its value will depend upon the extent to which it is in accordance with the well-known canon, *Quod semper, quod ubique, quod ab omnibus*, i.e. " That which has been accepted always, everywhere, and by all." It is added that a tradition which can fully stand this test can hardly be less than Apostolic in origin. One instance is given as an example of a tradition which will fully stand this test, the use of ecclesiastical vestments. [1]

It is necessary to state this position at length in order to give it proper consideration. The Church of England nowhere distinguishes tradition in this threefold way, nor does it regard acceptance of the New Testament as an instance of Divine Tradition. On the contrary, the way in which Scripture is treated in the Articles shows that it is considered to be our supreme authority received direct from our Lord and His Apostles. Then, too, there is no trace of any association of terms of equality of the observance of the Lord's Day and the keeping of the Lenten Fast as both due to " Apostolic Tradition " ; while as to the third distinction, the question at once arises whether the Vincentian Canon can possibly be applied to any " Tradition " or " Ceremony," such as is referred to in the Article. The very fact of ecclesiastical vestments being adduced in support of this Canon is a striking testimony to the impossibility of applying it, because it is a simple matter of history that these vestments have not been accepted " always, everywhere, and by all," but, on the contrary, they date from a period long after the time of the New Testament or the age of the primitive Church. It would seem, therefore, that this effort to distinguish between " National " and " Catholic " finds no warrant either in history or in the formularies of the Church of England.

Another attempt was made to elicit the true meaning of those who make this distinction when a question was asked of Lord Halifax at the Royal Commission on Ecclesiastical Discipline how he would distinguish between what is " Catholic " and what is " National " ? All that he was able to say was that Reservation being a matter of general consent was necessarily unchangeable, while Communion in both kinds was a matter on which change was possible. [2] It is obvious, however, that this does not carry us very far, nor does it give any clear principle by means of which " Catholic " and " National " may be distinguished.

Yet again an effort was made to arrive at a proper distinction. The Rev. Leighton Pullan expressed the opinion that if a Liberal Pope of Rome offered Anglican Churchmen terms there would inevitably be disruption unless it were declared that the Articles were not against any doctrine universally accepted at the time of the Great Schism, 1054, and

---

[1] Ball, *The Orthodox Doctrine of the Church of England*, pp. 247–250.
[2] *Report of the Royal Commission on Ecclesiastical Discipline*, Vol. III .p. 369.

that the practices of the Prayer Book could be legitimately identified with those of the Church of the eleventh century.[1] But here again, as it will be seen, there is a definite disregard of the events of the sixteenth century, which on any showing meant something in the way of a deliberate break with Rome. There seems to be no doubt that the reason why the last clause of the Article was added in 1563 was the attitude of the Papacy towards the English Crown and Church of that day.

It would, therefore, seem perfectly clear that this attempt to distinguish between what is " Catholic " and what is " National " is certain to fail, and that the only safe, indeed, the only possible ground, is to adhere closely to the teaching of the Article as it expresses and reflects the position of the Church of England at and since the sixteenth century. The wise words of Gregory the Great to Augustine are often quoted, and they express the great and eternal principle that customs may vary with " countries, times, and men's manners," the fundamental necessity being that " nothing be ordained against God's Word."[2]

All this makes it essential to consider with great care the frequent appeal to " Hear the Church." What does this mean ? In the Church of Rome the answer is clear. The authority is obvious and available. The Church is concentrated in the Pope, and everything required is an application of his authority. But there are those who reject the Pope, and yet emphasise the Church as no less authoritative. The Church is claimed to be the authority for doctrines and practices for life and ceremonial which are still said to be " Catholic." But, again, it must be asked what " Catholic " means ? No such authority exists. The Church as a whole has spoken in regard to very few points, and these are easily obtainable. For the first four centuries it was probably within the power of Christian men to obtain a true idea of general Church doctrines and practices, and our great Reformer, Jewel, issued his famous challenge in favour of our Church and against the Church of Rome, by appealing to the first six centuries, claiming that none of the distinctive Roman doctrines could be supported by the authority " of any old Catholic orator or father, or out of any old General Council, or out of the Holy Scriptures of God, or any one example of the primitive Church."[3] This, of course, does not mean that everything held and practised in the sixth century is binding now, for much has become impracticable and much has become universally disused. Still more, the Western Church since then has even

---

[1] *Ut supra*, Vol. II, p. 185.

[2] " Your fraternity know the custom of the Romish Church, wherein they remember that they have been brought up. But it is my decree, that what you have found in the Church of Rome, or the Gallican or any other that may more please Almighty God, you carefully choose the same: and the best constitutions that you can collect out of many Churches, pour into the Church of England, which is as yet new in the faith. For the customs are not to be loved for the country's sake, but the country for the customs' sake. Out of every particular Church, do you choose the things that are godly, religious, and good, and deposit them as customs in the minds of the English " (quoted in Kidd, *On the Articles*, p. 296).

[3] Jewel, *Apology*.

dared to add a clause to the Creed.   But beyond this there is now no " Church " to which we can appeal.   Dr. Sanday has said that :—

" From the date A.D. 451 onwards, the Christian world came to be so broken up into its several parts that the movement of the whole has practically lost its containing unity.   Although the formal separation of East and West was delayed, the development of each was continued on more and more divergent lines."[1]

Since then there have been other divisions, and if we are to have a union that is truly " Catholic " it is impossible to stop short with the views of the Greek, Roman, and Anglican Churches; we must appeal also to " some of the most vigorous and devoted Communions which the whole history of Christianity can show."[2]   The conclusion is that :—

" This supposed Catholic Church, to which appeal is made by the extreme High Churchmen of our day, is, except so far as it can be identified with the primitive Church, a phantom of the imagination."[3]

We return, therefore, to the true Anglican position of a constant and final appeal to Holy Scripture as the supreme rule of faith and practice, while heartily accepting everything that our Church prescribes in regard to traditions and ceremonies in the light of the principles set forth in this Article.

[1] Quoted in Wace, *Principles of the Reformation*, p. 241.
[2] Wace, *ut supra*, p. 243.
[3] Wace, *ut supra*, p. 243; see also p. 244.   The entire section on "Church Authority in Matters of Christian Faith and Practice" should be carefully studied, pp. 236–252.

ARTICLE XXXV

Of the Homilies.	*De Homiliis.*

The Second Book of Homilies, the several titles whereof we have joined under this Article, doth contain a godly and wholesome Doctrine, and necessary for these times, as doth the former Book of Homilies, which were set forth in the time of *Edward* the Sixth; and therefore we judge them to be read in Churches by the Ministers, diligently and distinctly, that they may be understanded of the people.

Tomus secundus Homiliarum, quarum singulos titulos huic articulo subjunximus, continet piam et salutarem doctrinam, et his temporibus necessariam, non minus quam prior Tomus Homiliarum, quæ editæ sunt tempore Edwardi Sexti: itaque eas in Ecclesiis per ministros diligenter et clare, ut a populo intelligi possint, recitandas esse judicavimus.

Of the Names of the Homilies.

1. *Of the right use of the Church.*
2. *Against peril of Idolatry.*
3. *Of repairing and keeping clean of Churches.*
4. *Of good Works : first of Fasting.*
5. *Against Gluttony and Drunkenness.*
6. *Against Excess of Apparel.*
7. *Of Prayer.*
8. *Of the Place and Time of Prayer.*
9. *That Common Prayers and Sacraments ought to be ministered in a known tongue.*
10. *Of the reverend estimation of God's Word.*
11. *Of Alms-doing.*
12. *Of the Nativity of Christ.*
13. *Of the Passion of Christ.*
14. *Of the Resurrection of Christ.*
15. *Of the worthy receiving of the Sacrament of the Body and Blood of Christ.*
16. *Of the Gifts of the Holy Ghost.*
17. *For the Rogation-days.*
18. *Of the state of Matrimony.*
19. *Of Repentance.*
20. *Against Idleness.*
21. *Against Rebellion.*

IMPORTANT EQUIVALENTS.

Book	= *Tomus.*
Godly and wholesome	= *piam et salutarem.*
As doth	= *non minus quam.*

THE corresponding Article XXXIV of 1553 necessarily recognised only the First Book of the Homilies, the Article being headed, "Homilies," and worded as follows : *Homiliæ nuper Ecclesiæ Anglicanæ per injunctiones regias traditæ atque commendatæ, piæ sunt atque salutares, doctrinamque ab omnibus amplectendam continent : quare populo diligenter, expedite, clareque recitandæ sunt.* "The Homilies of late given, and set out by the king's authority, be godly and wholesome, containing doctrine to be received of all men : and therefore are to be read to the people diligently, distinctly, and plainly." The Article in its present form is not found before the edition of 1571.

I.—THE HISTORY OF THE HOMILIES

Although preaching was one of the direct and immediate results of the Reformation it was difficult to obtain satisfactory preachers, owing to the incapacity of some, and the attachment of others to the mediæval religion. It was for this reason that sermons were provided which might be read to congregations, and these were called " Homilies." It would seem from an address of Cranmer to the Convocation of 1541 that even then there was an intention to provide Homilies for the purpose of instruction and to safeguard against error, but it is generally thought that if the book was prepared it was suppressed until after the death of Henry.[1]

The First Book was dated 31st July 1547, and was ordered to be read by clergymen to the people until further notice from the King. In connection with the Prayer Book of 1549 it was resolved to divide each of the Homilies into two parts, and to read one at a time, and a Rubric was accordingly placed in the Service. They were twelve in number : five doctrinal, and seven practical, and were probably in the main by Cranmer, and perhaps Ridley, though others have been suggested, including Bonner and Becon. The Second Book of the Homilies was published in 1562, having been referred to in the Injunctions of 1559. This was probably by Jewel, though the authorship is uncertain. The last Homily was due to a rebellion in the North of England in 1569, and was incorporated with the Second Book in 1571. The First Book of the Homilies was reprinted from time to time in separate form, and it was not until 1623 that the two books were incorporated in one volume.

It is not generally known that certain changes were made in the Homilies by Queen Elizabeth, the most important of them being the extension of the meaning of the word " Sacrament " in the Homily of Common Prayer, and another, the omission of a Declaration similar to that in Article XXIX denying that the wicked partake of Christ in the Lord's Supper.[2] But these changes were not sanctioned by Convocation, for this Article was subscribed in January 1563, while the Homilies, as altered by the Queen, were not published for several months afterwards.[3]

II.—THE TEACHING OF THE ARTICLE

1. The word " Homily " is derived from the Greek, ὁμιλία, meaning " conversation," " intercourse," from ὅμιλος, " a crowd." (See Luke xxiv. 14; Acts xx. 11; xxiv. 25; 1 Cor. xv. 33.) It was first used by writers of the fifth century to signify a simple discourse for people when there was no sermon.

[1] Tomlinson, The Prayer Book, Articles, and Homilies, p. 232.
[2] Mr. Gladstone (quoted in Tomlinson, ut supra, p. 253) remarks on this: "The point on which Elizabeth stands alone as far as I know is this, that she pursued her work from first to last mainly in opposition to the Church's rulers."
It is certainly interesting to realise that every one of the passages in our formularies on which modern extreme teaching has been based was due to the arbitrary and unconstitutional interference of Queen Elizabeth in opposition both to Convocation and Parliament. See on this action in reference to the Homilies, Tomlinson, ut supra, pp. 246–253.
[3] For the full history of the Homilies see Tomlinson, ut supra, Chs. IX, X, and Article, "The Homilies," Protestant Dictionary.

2. The character of Homilies is described as "godly and wholesome doctrine, and necessary for these times." The two reasons alluded to above warrant this statement. There were some clergy who were thought to favour the Church of Rome, and at the same time there was not a little illiteracy among the clergy. Thus, it was difficult to find competent preachers.

3. The direction given is that these Homilies were to be read "diligently and distinctly, that they may be understanded of the people." The insertion of this requirement is due to the fact that if the doctrine of the Homilies was disliked they were read unintelligibly or while murmuring or some other noise went on in Church.[1]

Later on, objections were raised to the Homilies by the Puritans,[2] but it would seem very slightly on doctrinal grounds. The main objection was to reading rather than preaching.[3] The only vital objection to doctrine, which came later than the last revision of 1571, was in connection with the subject of Predestination and falling from grace.[4]

4. The question of the obligation of the Homilies to-day is naturally raised by the Article, and it would seem correct to speak of this as general, not specific. But they are certainly valuable as illustrating the minds of the Reformers and the Revisers, and as such, they may be rightly called "semi-authoritative."[5] It has been very fairly argued that if the Article has any force at all "it must imply a general approval of the doctrines, as distinguished from any particular arguments used by the writers, or special illustrations or ideas adapted to those times."[6] Certainly in regard to the doctrine of Article XI there is the highest possible and most direct obligation as to the Homily of Justification.[7]

One question has been raised in connection with the obligation of the Homilies: What are we to understand as the true attitude of clergy to the Church of Rome? It is curious that opponents of and sympathisers with that Church both endeavour to find a warrant for their positions in the Article. With regard to the general attitude towards the Church of Rome, it is impossible not to agree with the opinion that the Homilies

[1] "The point of this order lies in the fact that the Homilies were resented by many of the old-fashioned clergy on the score of doctrine, who took their revenge by reading them unintelligibly" (B. J. Kidd, *The Thirty-nine Articles*, p. 256).
[2] Hardwick, *History of the Articles of Religion*, p. 209.
[3] Rogers, *On the Thirty-nine Articles*, p. 326.   [4] Hardwick, *ut supra*, p. 210.
[5] Harold Browne, *Exposition of the Thirty-nine Articles*, p. 777.
[6] Boultbee, *The Theology of the Church of England*, p. 282.
[7] "The Homilies I consider to have a peculiar value, as authorised Commentaries upon the Articles by those who formed and revised them, and who could not have been ignorant of their real meaning. To us of this distant age, they may be, from their brevity, sometimes obscure; and we must be aware of the tendency of preconceived opinions to distort the judgment, and to discover in a document which commands assent, a sense that was never intended. Cranmer puts this clue into our hands in summing up the short Article on Justification, with the hint, that 'it is more largely expressed in the Homily.' They also instruct the preacher rightly *to divide the word of truth*, and make the profound truths which unite in the accomplishment of man's salvation promote the edification of the least educated of his congregation" (Macbride, *Lectures on the Articles*, p. 516).

2 F

are valuable in throwing light upon sixteenth-century documents, " and may be useful for the instruction of our clergy and people in the doctrines of the Reformation."[1]   It is well known that Bishop Burnet expressed the view that since " there are so many of the Homilies that charge the Church of Rome with idolatry, no man who thinks that that Church is not guilty of idolatry can with a good conscience subscribe this Article."[2] To which it has been replied that

" Perhaps we may agree with Dr. Hey, rather than with Bishop Burnet, and hold that a person may fairly consider the Homilies to be a sound collection of religious instruction, who might yet shrink from calling the Roman Catholics idolaters."[3]

But certainly these words of Burnet are as timely and forcible to-day as ever :—

" If the nation should come to be quite out of the danger of falling back into Popery, it would not be so necessary to insist upon many of the subjects of the Homilies, as it was when they were first prepared."[4]

Another contention is that the Homilies actually teach the doctrine of the Real Presence in the Holy Communion, and that on this account we have no right to insist upon their Protestantism.

Newman made a great point of this in Tract XC, and in 1900 the Declaration made by the English Church Union quoted from the First Book of Homilies, " Of the due receiving of the Body and Blood of Christ under the form of bread and wine."   This was adduced in proof that the Church of England teaches the presence of Christ in the Sacrament under the form of bread and wine.   It is certainly surprising that a statement of this kind should have been made, because it has been shown again and again that this sentence is no part of a Homily.   It occurs in a Note appended to the First Book, promising that hereafter there would follow certain sermons, one of these being " Of the due receiving of Christ's blessed Body and Blood under the form of bread and wine."   It should be remembered that this First Book was published in July 1547, when the Act of the Six Articles was still in force, and while the Lord's Supper was described as " High Mass."   But this announcement was only a Royal Declaration and seems to have had no ecclesiastical sanction, and two years after, when the First Prayer Book of 1549 was issued, the name " High Mass " was changed for " The Celebration of the Communion " in this very Homily.   When the Second Book of Homilies was published in 1563 no sermon under the promised title was contained, but instead a sermon entitled, " On the Worthy Receiving and Reverent Esteeming of the Sacrament of the Body and Blood of Christ," teaching

---

[1] Harold Browne, *ut supra*, p. 777.
[2] Burnet, *On the Thirty-nine Articles*, p. 453.
[3] Harold Browne, *ut supra*, p. 777.
[4] Burnet, *ut supra*, p. 454.

which is directly opposed to that of the Declaration of the English Church Union. Cranmer himself shows that the expression found in the Note of 1547 is no part of the proper language of the Reformed Church, for he writes, " As concerning the form of doctrine used in this Church of England in the Holy Communion, that the Body and Blood of Christ be under the form of bread and wine—when you shall show the place where this form of words is expressed, then shall you purge yourselves of that which in the meantime I take to be a plain untruth." This was written in 1550.[1] It will be seen from this how impossible is the view set out in the Declaration of the English Church Union, and not the least testimony to its error and impossibility is the fact that the question is not referred to in most representative books on the Articles.

Reviewing the whole question of the character and obligation of the Homilies, it may at least be said that their study would be of value to the clergy for instruction in doctrine, while even their occasional and partial use would not be without profit even to-day.[2]

[1] Prebendary Meyrick's *Scriptural and Catholic Truth and Worship*, p. 206, from which the substance of the above explanation is taken, adds that the use of this formula as expressing a doctrine sanctioned by the Church of England, was brought in by Dr. Pusey, and still prevails in some quarters. Prebendary Meyrick adds a reference to a verse of a children's hymn where these words occur, and says that it is a translation from a hymn which called forth from Bishop Andrewes an indignant exclamation, "Let them 'worship the Deity hiding there under the species' made from a flour mill. Zion would shudder at that and utterly repudiate it."

[2] "The language of the Homilies is quaint, and the argument often tedious enough, but it is quite open to question whether the modern sermon is always an improvement on these old-fashioned but pertinent compositions" (Lightfoot, *Text Book of the Thirty-nine Articles*, p. 240).

ARTICLE XXXVI

Of Consecration of Bishops and Ministers.	*De Episcoporum et Ministrorum Consecratione.*
The Book of Consecration of Archbishops and Bishops, and Ordering of Priests and Deacons, lately set forth in the time of *Edward* the Sixth, and confirmed at the same time by authority of Parliament, doth contain all things necessary to such Consecration and Ordering: neither hath it anything, that of itself is superstitious and ungodly. And therefore whosoever are consecrated or ordered according to the rites of that Book, since the second year of the forenamed King *Edward* unto this time, or hereafter shall be consecrated or ordered according to the same rites; we decree all such to be rightly, orderly, and lawfully consecrated and ordered.	Libellus de Consecratione Archiepiscoporum et Episcoporum, et de Ordinatione Presbyterorum et Diaconorum, editus nuper temporibus *Edwardi VI*, et auctoritate Parliamenti illis ipsis temporibus confirmatus, omnia ad ejusmodi consecrationem et ordinationem necessaria continet; et nihil habet, quod ex se sit aut superstitiosum aut impium. Itaque quicunque juxta ritus illius Libri consecrati aut ordinati sunt, ab anno secundo prædicti regis *Edwardi* usque ad hoc tempus, aut in posterum juxta eosdem ritus consecrabuntur aut ordinabuntur, rite, atque ordine, atque legitime statuimus esse et fore consecratos et ordinatos.

IMPORTANT EQUIVALENTS.

Book	= *libellus.*
Set forth	= *editus.*
To be	= *esse et fore.*
Rightly, orderly, and lawfully	= *rite,*[1] *atque ordine, atque legitime.*

As Article XXIII gives the general teaching of our Church on the Ministry, so the present Article adds the specific instruction in regard to our form of the Ministry, consisting of the three Orders of Bishops, Priests, and Deacons. The corresponding Article, XXXV of 1553, was more general, and included a reference to the Prayer Book as well as to the Ordinal, both of which were stated to be scriptural, and therefore to be received. The title and exact wording are as follows :—

Of the Book of Prayers and Ceremonies of the Church of England.

" The Book which of very late time was given to the Church of England by the King's authority and the Parliament, containing the manner and form of praying, and ministering the Sacraments in the Church of England, likewise also the book of Ordering Ministers of the Church, set forth by the aforesaid authority, are godly, and in no point repugnant to the wholesome doctrine of the Gospel, but agreeable thereunto, furthering and beautifying the same not a little ; and, therefore, of all faithful members of the Church of England, and chiefly of the ministers of the word, they ought to be received and allowed with all readiness of mind, and thanksgiving, and to be commended to the people of God."

The Article was entirely re-cast when it appeared in its present form.

[1] *Rite* = correctly (in respect of form and manner). In Article XXV, *rite* is rendered "duly."

It is important to note what happened at each stage of the history in the sixteenth century.

1. No change was made in the Roman Catholic ritual of Ordination during the reign of Henry VIII, except the omission of the declaration of obedience to Rome.

2. But in 1549 the Pontifical was abandoned and a new form of Ordination was issued with the First Prayer Book, by which six men were consecrated Bishops. Although the Prayer Book and Ordinal are now one book, yet the fact that even to the present day the Ordinal has a separate title-page and preface shows that originally they were two distinct books. The First Prayer Book contained no Ordination Services, but these were provided later by the issue of what is generally called the First English Ordinal.

3. Both Prayer Book and Ordinal were revised in 1552 and superseded by the Second Prayer Book, and what is known as the Second Ordinal. These two books were connected with the Act of Uniformity, and although the Ordinal was in the Prayer Book it had its own title-page, and thus was strictly distinguished from the actual " Book of Common Prayer "; and the Act of Uniformity, 1552, distinguishes between the two. It was doubtless for this reason that Article XXXV of 1553 mentioned both the Book " Of Praying," and also the Book " Of Ordering."

4. These two books were, of course, suppressed by Mary, who repealed Edward's Acts of Uniformity, and re-established everything as it had been before the last year of Henry VIII. It has often been pointed out that this is a striking proof of the essential Roman Catholicism of Henry VIII, and altogether sets aside the popular Roman Catholic view that he is the founder of the English Church.

5. On Elizabeth's accession, 1558, Mary's Act was repealed, and the Second Prayer Book of Edward VI restored as the basis of revision. The Elizabethan Act speaks of the uniform order of Service at the death of Edward, which had been repealed by Queen Mary " to the great decay of the due honour and discomfort of the professors of the truth of Christ's religion." Then the Act of Mary was repealed " only concerning the said book," thereby leaving in strict legal force Mary's repeal of the rest of Edward's Protestant action. This at once raises the question as to the meaning of " the said book," because there was some doubt as to whether the Ordinal was included and intended. The authorities evidently considered the Ordinal of 1552 restored, because it was used at Parker's Consecration, and there is no record of any Consecration or Ordination being performed with any other form than that of 1552. But criticism was raised in regard to this point, that Elizabeth's Act did not expressly mention the Ordinal, and as a result those who were favourable to the Church of Rome maintained that the Ordinations and

Consecrations were invalid, because they held that the Ordinal of 1552 was still repealed by the Statute of Mary. This controversy was regarded as so important that it was felt necessary to make quite sure by the passing of an Act in 1566 to declare the validity of the Consecrations under the Ordinal of 1552, and to determine the use of it for the future.[1]

6. But, meanwhile, on the revision of the Articles in 1563, the present statement was put forth vindicating the validity of all Ordinations " since the second year of Edward VI," thereby including both the First and Second Ordinals. This made everything quite clear, and the validity of Protestant Ordinations was thus settled both in regard to the Second and also to the First Ordinal, under the latter of which two of Parker's consecrators had been consecrated in 1550.

7. The whole question was reviewed in 1662, when this Article received its last authorisation, and it is interesting that no change should have been made in the wording of the Article at that time even after the lapse of over a century. The only change made in 1662 was the requirement of Episcopal Ordination for the ministry, as seen in the preface, and one or two slight, but not fundamental, changes were made in the Ordinal itself.

II.—THE CHARACTER OF THE ORDINAL

1. The Ordinal is first described as that " lately set forth in the time of Edward the Sixth, and confirmed at the same time by the authority of Parliament." There is, of course, no doubt that it refers to the present Ordinal, which, with the exception of the addition to the preface, and the slight changes already referred to, is exactly the same as it was at that time.

2. The Ordinal is described as sufficient. " Doth contain all things necessary to such Consecration and Ordering." This is evidently directed against the Church of Rome, which has all along denied the sufficiency and therefore the validity of our Ordination. There are three main grounds taken by the Church of Rome.

(1) It is said that our Ordinal has no chrism and no delivery of the sacramental *instrumenta*. In accordance with this Queen Mary and Bonner made up what they regarded as deficiencies in those ordained under the Edwardian Ordinal by anointing their hands, and Pole similarly arranged for the delivery of the vessels and the use of the words referring to the offering of the sacrifice. To this we reply that there is no proof of these being required in Scripture for Ordination, and no indication that they were ever used in the early Church. Not only so, we go further, and point out that of the seven particulars included and made prominent in the mediæval Ordinal only one has been retained by our Church, and we alone of the Reformed Churches have done this. This one item being the words, " Receive ye the Holy Ghost, etc.," and the fact that these

---

[1] Hardwick, *History of the Articles of Religion*, p. 131, and Note 1.

come from Scripture make their retention and the omission of the other six all the more significant.[1]

(2) It is said that the Ordinal of 1553 had no words to distinguish Bishop from Priest. This is verbally true, the words " For the office of a Priest (or Bishop) in the Church of God," being inserted in 1662. But apart from this, the entire Service should be consulted, when there would be no doubt at all as to the precise purpose of the action. Even the Roman Ordinal itself is quite general.

(3) It is said that the Ordinal lacks Intention. The charge of invalidity, based on the history of the Elizabethan Ordinations, is now not mentioned by Roman Catholic authorities. It is evidently regarded as no longer a tenable position. The result is that everything is concentrated on the lack of Intention. Now public Intention must be judged by the Service itself, and this in turn must be tested by Scripture. It will, thereby, be seen what ministry our Church intends, and the decision will be in accordance therewith. We have obviously no right to think of any mere private Intention or any opinion of the Scriptural Intentions as essential. When this is clearly understood it will be seen at once that everything turns upon the character of the ministry. If the New Testament ministry means what the Church of Rome understands by it, namely a sacerdotal priesthood, then it is clear that our Orders are void in the eyes of Rome, but if, on the other hand, as we hold, the New Testament ministry is that of an evangelistic and pastoral Presbyterate, then our Ordinal is ample for the purpose. The various references to " sacrifice " in the Holy Communion Office clearly refer either to Calvary or to our spiritual sacrifices as believers ; never once to the Lord's Supper itself.

It would be well if all controversy were concentrated on this point ; viz., What is the true character of the primitive Christian ministry ? When this is settled all questions of Intention are at once resolved. It has been well said that Rome might find no difficulty in recognising our Orders if she held that the ministry was the episcopal Presbyterate of the New Testament. But as long as she requires Ordination for the purpose of exercising sacerdotal functions it is impossible for her to regard our ministers as equivalent to her priests.[2] It is, therefore, futile, and a waste of time to discuss questions of Intention in view of the

[1] Dimock, Article, "Ordinal," *Protestant Dictionary*, p. 474. The seven are:
"(1) Prefatory address, with statement of sacerdotal functions. (2) Delivery of *casula* (*i.e.* the *chasuble* which is the mass vestment) with a benediction containing the doctrines of Real Presence and of Transubstantiation. (3) Unction. (4) *Traditio instrumentorum*, with power to offer sacrifice and celebrate Masses. (5) The words (following the second imposition of hands), 'Accipe Spiritum Sanctum,' etc. (6) *Unfolding the casula*. (7) The final Blessing with the words, '*ut . . offeratis* placabiles hostias pro peccatis' " (*ut supra*, p. 474, Note 2).
[2] "Rome's doctrine of Orders involves the doctrine of *her* Real Presence, and of *her* Real Propitiatory oblation of Christ (really present on the altar) for the living and the dead. And this doctrine we hold and profess to belong to the class of 'blasphema figmenta, et perniciosæ imposturæ.' How, then, can our Orders be valid in her view? And how can we consistently desire that it should be otherwise ? " (Dimock, *Christian Doctrine of Sacerdotium*, p. 133).

fundamental difference between what is understood as ministry, for as long as this difference exists there cannot possibly be agreement between the two Churches.[1]

3. The Ordinal is stated to be Scriptural. "Neither hath it any thing that of itself is superstitious and ungodly." This is intended to meet an objection from the opposite quarter, the extreme Protestant party, who were subsequently called Puritans. The assumption of superstition and ungodliness is pretty certainly due to the presence in the Ordinal of the words of St. John xx. 22, 23 : "And when He had said this, He breathed on them, and saith unto them, Receive ye the Holy Ghost : Whosesoever sins ye remit, they are remitted unto them ; and whosesoever sins ye retain, they are retained." It should be, however, remembered that the difficulty is not a Prayer Book, but a Bible one, for, as we have already seen,[2] there is no reference in the words to the pronouncement of absolution in the Services, but to the proclamation of the Gospel of Forgiveness and its alternative. The words are thus a definite personal application to the one individual of the general authority given by our Lord to the whole Church, as represented in the Upper Room. Nor can the words, "Receive ye the Holy Ghost" come under this charge of ungodliness, since the words are merely the repetition of our Lord's commission and are most properly regarded as a prayer.[3] It is also noteworthy to recall once again that these words are not found in any Ordinal earlier than the thirteenth century.[4] So that in any case the words are not essential to the conferring of ministry. It will also help to clear thought if it is remembered that Ordination gives ministerial authority, the right to exercise ministry, not spiritual power, or the capability to do

---

[1] "It comes, then, simply to this: Can we surrender the principles for which the Anglican Church has steadily contended for the last 350 years? Or can we hold the doctrines of our Church, and, with a due regard for the ordinary and rational rules by which historical documents are interpreted, can we reconcile the sense of our historical and authoritative standards of doctrine with the authoritative doctrine of the Church of Rome? The only answer to each question is, *It is impossible*" (Bishop of Edinburgh, Address to Diocesan Synod, 1895, p. 9).

[2] See on Article XXIII, pp. 317, 320.

[3] For Hooker's defence of this form see *Eccl. Pol.*, Bk. V, Ch. LXXVII.

"The difference between such ordination and our Lord's ordaining of His first ministers recorded in St. John, xx. is this. In the latter case, Christ Himself, to whom the Spirit is given without measure, gave of that Spirit authoritatively to His disciples; and so, in giving, He breathed on them, as showing that the Spirit proceeded from Him. But, in the other case, our bishops presume not to breathe, nor did the Apostles before them; for they know that ordaining grace comes not from them, but from Christ, whose ministers they are; and so they simply, according to all Scriptural authority, use the outward rite of laying on of hands, in use of which they believe a blessing will assuredly come down from above" (Harold Browne, *Exposition of the Thirty-nine Articles*, p. 784).

"These words, *receive the Holy Ghost*, may be understood to be of the nature of a wish and prayer; as if it were said, *may thou receive the Holy Ghost*; and so it will better agree with what follows, *and be thou a faithful dispenser of the word and sacraments*. Or it may be observed, that in those sacred missions, the Church and Churchmen consider themselves as acting in the *name and person* of Christ" (Burnet, *On the Thirty-nine Articles*, p. 456).

[4] *Dictionary of Christian Antiquities*, Vol. II, p. 1513.

spiritual work. The latter naturally comes from prayer. Thus, the laying on of hands gives commission, and prayer is intended to suggest spiritual qualification. Further, the words " Whosesoever sins," etc., are clearly to be interpreted by the words which immediately follow : " And be thou a faithful dispenser of the Word of God and of His holy Sacraments." This, in general, is the Anglican reply to those who were, or are, tempted to speak of this part of the Ordinal as " manifest blasphemy."[1]

4. The Ordinal is declared to be valid. All who are consecrated and ordered according to this Book, whether past or future, are decreed to be " rightly, orderly, and lawfully consecrated and ordered." The Latin equivalent for " rightly " is *rite*, that is, in due form and manner. This is the Church of England claim, and it stands to-day as it has stood for over three centuries, maintaining that all Bishops consecrated and all clergy ordained under the Ordinals from 1549 onwards have been properly qualified to exercise their ministry. They were ordained " by public prayer, with imposition of hands," and thereby were " approved and admitted by lawful authority." Thus, these Orders have been " continued and reverently used and esteemed in the Church of England."

The subject of the validity of Anglican Orders was raised in 1896 by the effort of Lord Halifax and others, who desired to obtain a Declaration of the validity of Anglican Orders from the Pope of Rome. But the effort proved vain, and, instead, the Pope pronounced in unqualified terms the invalidity of our Orders. This was based on the usual Roman Catholic argument of lack of form, because there is no reference to the power to offer sacrifice, and lack of Intention, because our Ordinal is alleged to intend another than the Church idea of ministry. But this only raises again the question already considered, as to the character of the ministry. It is perfectly true that our ministry is intended to be something quite different from the idea of ministry which obtains in the Church of Rome, and as long as there is this fundamental cleavage any further discussion seems to be vain. We maintain that our ministry is scriptural and primitive, and, as such, fulfils all the requirements of scriptural lawfulness and spiritual validity. The action taken by our Church in the sixteenth century to remove from the Ordinal the various mediæval accretions clearly shows the significance of " these radical rejections by a Church professing such conservative principles."[2] And this leads to only one conclusion, that as long as we possess a true scriptural ministry and a true primitive idea of the functions of the New Testament Presbyterate, our Ordinal must stand condemned in the eyes of Rome, and so also must the Ordinations of the early Church. And so we conclude that :—

" It is impossible to study fairly the history of our Ordinal without seeing that

---

[1] Hardwick, *ut supra*, p. 210.
[2] Dimock, Article, "Ordinal," *Protestant Dictionary*, p. 477.

there is a doctrinal gulf between the Church of England and the Church of Rome."[1]

[1] Dimock, *ut supra*, p. 480.

: It is sometimes said that the Article asserts that there was "nothing superstitious or ungodly" in the Ordinal of 1550, and that as that Ordination Service was inserted in the Communion Service of the Prayer Book of 1549 we are compelled to believe that "there was nothing superstitious or ungodly" in that Book as well. It might have sufficed to refer to the history of the Article to show that any such definite approval of the First Prayer Book and First Ordinal was not intended by the revisers of 1563. Such an argument, if argument it can be called, overlooks the facts connected with the revision of 1662 by which we are now bound, for the last Act of Uniformity provides that subscription to this Article shall be understood to apply to the present Ordinal, just as before that time it had applied to the two Ordinals of Edward VI. And as to those who lived between the First Ordinal and the Ordinal of 1662, it may be pointed out that the greater number of Ordinations took place under the Second Ordinal, and the purpose of the Article is to vindicate the Ordinations under both Ordinals. As to the First Ordinal, the only possible application of the Article is that that Book contained nothing which was "of itself superstitious or ungodly." And this is literally true. Perhaps the greatest proof that no weight is to be attributed to this contention is the fact that it is not discussed in any representative modern books on the Articles, and is only found in those works which endeavour to discover some basis for the views which were altogether unknown in the Church of England before 1833. There can be no doubt that the question stands at present in the light of the Act of 1662, and points us to the belief that our present Ordinal "contains nothing superstitious and ungodly." (A full discussion of this point will be found in Tomlinson, *The Prayer Book, Articles, and Homilies*, Ch. XXII, p. 269).

IV. THE HOUSEHOLD OF FAITH—*continued*

CORPORATE RELIGION

E. CHURCH AND STATE (ARTICLES XXXVII-XXXIX)

37. THE CIVIL MAGISTRATES.

38. CHRISTIAN MEN'S GOODS, WHICH ARE NOT COMMON.

39. A CHRISTIAN MAN'S OATH.

ARTICLE XXXVII

| *Of the Civil Magistrates.* | *De Civilibus Magistratibus.* |

The Queen's Majesty hath the chief power in this realm of *England*, and other her dominions, unto whom the chief government of all estates of this realm, whether they be Ecclesiastical or Civil, in all causes doth appertain, and is not, nor ought to be, subject to any foreign jurisdiction.

Where we attribute to the Queen's Majesty the chief government, by which titles we understand the minds of some slanderous folks to be offended, we give not to our Princes the ministering either of God's Word, or of the Sacraments; the which thing the Injunctions also lately set forth by *Elizabeth* our Queen, do most plainly testify; but that only prerogative, which we see to have been given always to all godly Princes in Holy Scriptures by God Himself: that is, that they should rule all states and degrees committed to their charge by God, whether they be Ecclesiastical or Temporal, and restrain with the civil sword the stubborn and evildoers.

The Bishop of *Rome* hath no jurisdiction in this realm of *England*.

The Laws of the Realm may punish Christian men with death, for heinous and grievous offences.

It is lawful for Christian men, at the commandment of the Magistrate, to wear weapons, and serve in the wars.

Regia Majestas in hoc *Angliæ* regno, ac cæteris ejus dominiis, summam habet potestatem, ad quam omnium statuum hujus regni, sive illi Ecclesiastici sint sive Civiles, in omnibus causis suprema gubernatio pertinet, et nulli externæ jurisdictioni est subjecta, nec esse debet.

Cum Regiæ Majestati summam gubernationem tribuimus, quibus titulis intelligimus animos quorundam calumniatorum offendi, non damus Regibus nostris aut verbi Dei, aut Sacramentorum administrationem; quod etiam Injunctiones, ab *Elizabetha* Regina nostra nuper editæ, apertissime testantur; sed eam tantum prærogativam, quam in Sacris Scripturis a Deo ipso omnibus piis Principibus videmus semper fuisse attributam: hoc est, ut omnes status atque ordines fidei suæ a Deo commissos, sive illi Ecclesiastici sint sive Civiles, in officio contineant, et contumaces ac delinquentes gladio civili coerceant.

Romanus Pontifex nullam habet jurisdictionem in hoc regno *Angliæ*.

Leges Regni possunt Christianos, propter capitalia et gravia crimina, morte punire.

Christianis licet, ex mandato Magistratus, arma portare, et justa bella administrare.

IMPORTANT EQUIVALENTS.

King's Majesty	=	*Regia Majestas.*
Lately set forth	=	*nuper editæ.*
To their charge	=	*fidei suæ.*
Bishop of Rome	=	*Romanus Pontifex.*
The laws may punish	=	*leges possunt punire.*
Heinous offences	=	*capitalia crimina.*
To serve in the wars[1]	=	*justa bella administrare.*

So important were the changes made in this Article in 1563 that it may almost be said to have been reconstructed. Its present form is certainly a great improvement on the original. The first two paragraphs of the

---

[1] The English of the XLII had "lawful wars."

present Article date from 1563, and were substituted for a simple but strong assertion of the Royal Supremacy in the corresponding Article of 1553, which read as follows : *Rex Angliæ est supremum caput in terris, post Christum, Ecclesiæ Anglicanæ, et Hibernicæ.* " The King of England is supreme head in earth, next under Christ, of the Church of England and Ireland." The third clause, referring to the Bishop of Rome, remained unaltered. Then followed in 1553 a statement which was omitted in 1563 : *Magistratus civilis est a Deo ordinatus atque probatus : quamobrem illi non solum propter iram, sed etiam propter conscientiam obediendum est.* " The civil magistrate is ordained and allowed of God : wherefore we must obey him, not only for fear of punishment, but also for conscience' sake." The remainder of the Article in its present form has been unaltered, except for the very slight verbal alteration in 1571 of " the laws of the Realm," " *Leges Regni* " instead of " the Civil Laws," " *Leges civiles.*"

The object of the Article seems to have been threefold, dealing with the Royal Supremacy, the Papal Supremacy, and certain current objections to the right of the State to call upon Christian subjects to enter upon military service.

In view of the important questions arising out of the Article it seems well to look first of all at the Article itself in the way of a brief analysis, before considering its various points in detail.

I.—THE STATEMENTS OF THE ARTICLE

1. The Claim of the Royal Supremacy.—This is the teaching of the first clause, and it is put in two forms. (*a*) It extends to all estates of the realm, ecclesiastical and civil ; (*b*) it excludes all foreign jurisdiction.

2. The Meaning of the Royal Supremacy.—This is stated in the second section, and was due to " the minds of some slanderous folks." Both Roman Catholics and Puritans, from different standpoints, took exception to the chief government attributed to the Crown. (*a*) First, the meaning is stated negatively. It is not to be understood as giving to the Crown the ministry either of the Word or the Sacraments ; (*b*) Then it is stated positively. All that is to be understood is " that only prerogative, which we see to have been given always to all godly Princes in Holy Scriptures by God Himself." This reference to the Old Testament and the duty of Princes to rule all estates committed to their charge is, of course, to be understood in the light of the sixteenth century, when Church and State were regarded in a way as identical though from different standpoints.

3. The Denial of the Papal Supremacy.—The Latin equivalent of " Bishop " is *Pontifex*, and there seems to be no doubt that the denial is due to what has preceded in regard to the Royal Supremacy. The statement that the Bishop of Rome has no jurisdiction means that he has no

right to it, because it would imply usurpation of the authority of the Crown.[1]

4. Illustrations of Royal Supremacy.—Two matters are specifically mentioned in the Article as illustrating and expressing the extent to which the Royal Supremacy may be rightly understood to act: (*a*) the right of capital punishment; (*b*) the right of military service.

II.—THE ROYAL SUPREMACY

For the first three hundred years of the history of the Church, Christianity had necessarily no relation to earthly kings. When Constantine assumed authority people thought that all was well, and that the results would be advantageous to the Church. The fact was either forgotten or else ignored that he was not a Christian, and that his interposition carried with it serious consequences to the purity and liberty of the Church. But after the period of persecution the relief was so great that it was hardly surprising that Constantine's efforts were approved and welcomed. Added to this, it would seem as though the Church had forgotten the teaching of the New Testament concerning the Coming of the Lord, and had imbibed the idea that the Church was to penetrate and permeate with spiritual influence the whole world. All these things led to the acceptance of Constantine's interference, which, in the light of history, can hardly be regarded as otherwise than disastrous. Certainly tyranny was very often used, and for several centuries good and evil resulting from the relations of Church and State were only too evident. To this day in the East the State dominates the Church to such an extent that in Russia the State may be regarded as supreme.

In the West further complications arose through the growth of the Papacy of Rome, for what might have been regarded as a natural and legitimate primacy soon became a supremacy which resulted in tyranny. Temporal as well as spiritual power was claimed by the Pope, and it is not surprising that both Kings and Bishops felt the grievances of the position. The Reformation was essentially a reaction against this by the definite abjuring of the Roman Supremacy.

At this point, however, a difficulty naturally arose as to the transfer of power. Limiting ourselves to England, it is seen that the transfer of authority from the Pope to the King began about 1531, and Convocation was quite ready to accept this, regarding the King as Protector and Supreme Head, though with the qualifying clause " as far as the law of Christ permits."[2]

---

[1] It is significant that Bishop Forbes in his discussion of this sentence distinguishes between realm and Church. "Not in this Church of England, but in this realm," arguing that the question is civil only and not spiritual (*Explanation of the Thirty-nine Articles*, p. 773). This is a curious way of ignoring the statements of the Article which include ecclesiastical as well as civil causes.

[2] "Ecclesiæ, et cleri Anglicani, cujus singularem protectorem unicum et supremum dominum, et quantum per Christi legem licet, etiam supremum caput ipsius majestatem recognoscimus" (Gibson, *The Thirty-nine Articles*, p. 762, Note 1).

Following this date Parliament began to pass Acts restraining Papal jurisdiction and leading to an assertion of the Supremacy of the Crown, and in 1534 both clergy and Parliament accepted the position of the King as " Supreme Head." But the term " Head " was open to obvious objections, and was really only used by Henry to indicate the supersession of the authority of the Papacy. It was continued by Edward and Mary, but dropped by Mary on her marriage in 1554. When supremacy was restored by Elizabeth the term " Head " was altered to " Governor," and was explained by the Injunctions of 1559 as " Under God to have rule over all persons whether civil or ecclesiastical."[1] In this sense, therefore, there was a very definite alteration in the idea of the Royal Supremacy, and in the light of the Queen's action in regard to the first paragraph of Article XX, it is evident that while she insisted with characteristic firmness on governing the Church, yet she was equally strong about it being the Church and not the Crown which had " power to decree rites or ceremonies, and authority in controversies of faith." But the wise avoidance of the term " Head " by Elizabeth and the substitution of " Governor," while admirable in itself and particularly valuable for the prevention of ambiguity and confusion,[2] did not in the least affect the determination of Elizabeth to dominate everything, whether ecclesiastical or civil.

This power of the Crown was very ill-defined, and no one can doubt that it was arbitrarily used both by Elizabeth and the Stuarts, even although the Canons of 1603-4 say that Royal authority meant only such as had been given to Christian Princes in Scripture and the early Church. It was only ascertained and limited by the revolution of 1688.[3]

The connection between the Crown and the Church is naturally closer with an Establishment than with those who are free from it, for the civil power has more control over an Established Church. Thus the appeal to-day in England to Parliament tends to suggest a civil control rather than what Parliament was originally, the representation of the laity of the Church, and the confusion in the present day is due to the fact that Parliament no longer represents lay-Churchmen only, and because the powers of the Crown have passed to Parliament. While, therefore, it is true that " in the present day the Royal Supremacy signifies little more than the supremacy of the civil law and courts over ecclesiastical legislation and jurisdiction,"[4] yet it must never be forgotten that the essence of the Royal authority was the assertion of the supremacy of the lay power and not the interference of the State as such. Just as, before the

---

[1] Cardwell, *Documentary Annals*, Vol. I, p. 232. See also Index, s.v., Supremacy of Crown.

[2] "The Queen is unwilling to be addressed, either by word of mouth or in writing, as the head of the Church of England. For she seriously maintains that this honour is due to Christ alone, and cannot belong to any human being soever" (Jewel to Bullinger, *Zurich Letters*, Vol. I, p. 33).

[3] Boultbee, *The Theology of the Church of England*, p. 286.

[4] Boultbee, *ut supra*, p. 286.

Reformation, the supremacy of the Pope was regarded as the expression of the superiority of the clergy over the laity, so that supremacy of the Crown was intended in the opposite direction, to assert the independence and power of the laity. And this was actually the case as long as Parliament represented only the laity of the Church.[1]

It may be well, therefore, to state afresh the position of the Church of England. In theory the Monarch is the source of justice to all his subjects, and the supreme ruler of all classes of people, so that if anyone feels an injustice in any ecclesiastical or civil Court he has freedom to appeal to the Sovereign for redress.

The question has become acute in recent times in regard to what have been called " Spiritual Courts," by which is meant Courts representing the clergy only. Those who advocate this position are opposed to the Royal Supremacy as implying an undue encroachment of the civil on the ecclesiastical sphere because its decisions are made by a Court which is not ecclesiastical. It is, therefore, necessary to state briefly what has actually been the case since the time of the Reformation. During the reigns of Elizabeth, James I, and Charles I, jurisdiction was exercised by the Court of High Commission, consisting of Bishops and ecclesiastical lawyers. This Court was abolished just before the time of the Commonwealth and was never restored, its functions being transferred to a Court of Delegates appointed by the Sovereign. This was brought to an end in 1832, and a Committee of the Privy Council was appointed to exercise jurisdiction in all cases in which appeals apply to the Crown. The chief Judges of the Court are members of this Board, and for ecclesiastical purposes one Bishop at least must be included. The Court is called the " Judicial Committee of the Privy Council," and its function is judicial, not legislative. It has been rightly described as the Canon Law of the Church, and the position of the Church of England as an Established Church necessarily puts her under a restriction in regard to alteration of doctrine or ritual, no such alteration being possible without the consent of the State. It will be seen, therefore, that the difference in the Courts during the last three centuries has not involved any matter of essential principle, the difference being one of form.

At the foundation of the objection to the Judicial Committee of the Privy Council lies the old idea that the laity have no right to legislate on questions of doctrine and worship, which, it is urged, ought to be limited to the clergy. Added to this, there is the persistence of the unfortunate idea that the laity are somehow or other not the " Church," forgetful of the fact that the New Testament term from which we get the word " clergy " includes all the people of God (1 Pet. v. 3). It is, therefore, essential to insist upon the right and full meaning of the term " Church," as including both clergy and laity. To speak of a student entering the " Church " when the " Ministry " is meant, shows the fallacy of this position. The clergy were already members of the Church when lay-

[1] Harold Browne, *Exposition of the Thirty-nine Articles*, p. 802.

men, and no one can doubt that in Holy Scripture the government of the Church, as we have seen, is vested in the entire Christian community.

It must also never be overlooked that the English Reformation was pre-eminently a movement of the laity, as expressed by Parliament. The action and influence of individual clergymen like Cranmer, Latimer, and others, is, of course, undoubted, but speaking generally, it was not Convocation, but Parliament that took the lead in all matters connected with the Reformation. It is significant that Parliament, not Convocation, first gave the title of " Supreme Head " to the King in opposition to the Papacy.[1] The First Prayer Book of 1549 was prepared and authorised by the Crown and Parliament before being sanctioned by Convocation, and the First Ordinal was authorised, and these two books revised in the same way. Even Queen Mary re-established the pre-Reformation position by Parliament. When Elizabeth succeeded to the throne it was again Parliament that took the lead in the Reformation movement, and even the Prayer Book of 1604 was prepared and authorised by the Crown without the assent of either Parliament or Convocation. All these facts tend to show that the laity all along have taken a very definite part in the Reformation settlement.

It is, therefore, incorrect to say that

" the constitutional character of the supremacy of the Crown . . . does not differ in principle from that exercised by William I or Edward I, being in its essence the right of supervision over the administration of the Church, vested in the Crown as the champion of the Church, in order that the religious welfare of its subjects may be duly provided for."[2]

In reality there is a great difference in principle, because since the Reformation there has been no real question of the Crown championing the Church for the purpose of providing for the religious welfare of its subjects. On the contrary, the action of the Crown has been very largely exercised on behalf of the laity against the clergy. Then, too, the general question has been affected by the rejection of the Pope, and the claim that the Royal Supremacy affects all causes, both ecclesiastical and civil. There can be no doubt, therefore, that the Royal Supremacy, as exercised in the sixteenth century, was decidedly a " new thing,"[3] and was directed mainly against the supremacy of the Pope and for the purpose of insisting upon the liberty of England, both clergy and laity together, in regard to matters ecclesiastical.

Some illustrations from recent years may help to distinguish the issues more clearly and to state the truth of the position of the Church of England. In 1850 a circular was issued by three clergymen,[4] advocating certain changes in the meaning of the Royal Supremacy in matters eccle-

---

[1] In 1534.   [2] Wakeman, *Introduction to the History of the Church of England*, p. 321.
[3] "The supremacy itself was no new thing" (Gibson, *ut supra*, p. 771).
[4] Archdeacon Manning, Archdeacon Wilberforce (both of whom went over to the Church of Rome), and Dr. Mill of Cambridge.

siastical. These clergymen appealed for signatures to a document, stating that the meaning was not the supremacy of the Sovereign in all spiritual things or causes, but only "over the temporal accidents of spiritual things," whatever that might mean. The argument was that there was a distinction to be drawn between the Royal Supremacy as interpreted by the Articles and Canons of the Church, and as defined and established by Canon Law, the latter being said to give the Crown a power which was opposed to "the Divine office of the Universal Church as prescribed by the law of Christ." In reply to this appeal it was pointed out that there was no ground for this distinction, and the Statute Law gave the Crown supreme authority "as well in all spiritual and ecclesiastical things or causes as temporal," and that these very words were inserted in Canon 36 of 1603-4. It was also shown that even Convocation must obtain the sanction of the Crown to put forth any declaration, and that the Articles were first published under the authority of the Crown, while even the Book of Common Prayer was not brought before Convocation till the last revision of 1662, but was drawn up by Royal authority and enforced by the legislature. This has certainly been the acknowledged doctrine of our Church from the accession of Queen Elizabeth.[1] An additional proof of this position is seen when reference is made to the former practice of appealing to the Pope. It is said that the establishment of the Royal Supremacy was intended only to exclude foreign jurisdiction, but it is sometimes overlooked that the jurisdiction of the Crown was actually substituted for this foreign jurisdiction, thereby not merely abolishing the Papal Supremacy, but establishing the Royal Supremacy in its place. All appeals, therefore, which had formerly been made to the Pope were henceforward to be made to the Crown.

This position can be amply vindicated both from history and from the nature of the case. It is well known that in the fourth century the prevalence of Arianism among the clergy seriously endangered vital Christianity, and at that time if the Church and the clergy had been regarded as identical the consequences would have been very serious. Then, too, as there is no question whatever of the State making laws for the Church, but only interpreting the laws as they stand, it might reasonably be supposed that the supreme civil Governor was in every way fitted to mediate and moderate in matters of dispute. All that the Crown claims is the power of preventing the Church from being compelled to accept anything that a majority of the clergy might sanction, and also to prevent the laity being compelled to accept an interpretation being put upon the formularies of the Church, which is regarded as untrue to the doctrinal and national position of the Church. The idea that clerical legislation and interpretation necessarily carries truthfulness and accuracy is contradicted by much that has happened during the centuries. It was, therefore, not difficult to show that those who appealed for a change were really insisting upon something quite novel in the way of inter-

[1] See Jewel's *Apology*.

pretation, something that was neither Anglican nor Roman Catholic, and to which the names of "Catholic truth" and "Church principles." had been inaccurately and really unfairly given.[1]

More recent events show the impossibility of accepting the position of those who insist upon what they call a "Spiritual Court." It is well known that the Court of Arches, which is under the personal jurisdiction of the Archbishop of Canterbury, is a Spiritual Court. It will be remembered that the Lincoln Judgment by Archbishop Benson also came under the same category, and still later, Archbishops Temple and Maclagan issued certain opinions against Reservation and Incense. All these might well be called Spiritual Courts, and yet the decisions were in each case refused and opposed. Not only so, but on one occasion when the Archbishop of Canterbury deprived a clergyman for heresy, an appeal was made by those who supported him to the Privy Council, and the appeal was successful. Under these circumstances it would seem as though the plea for "Spiritual Courts" is as unreal in character as it certainly is untrue to all that we know of the history and genius of the Church of England. So long, therefore, as the Church of England is established it is essential for due freedom that a final appeal should be made to the King, and that all coercive jurisdiction should be regarded as coming from the State alone, that all men, clergy and laity, must remain subject to the law as it has been stated by various Acts of Parliament, and that in all ecclesiastical causes as well as civil every Churchman must be able to appeal to the "King as Supreme." If, and when, the time comes for Disestablishment, as it has come in Ireland and elsewhere, there is no doubt that the government of the Church will be vested in Synods as representative of the whole Church, and in this way the difficulty which some feel in regard to civil interference, and which others feel in regard to undue clerical interference, will find their proper solution.[2]

A brief consideration is necessary to the objection taken to the Article with special reference to the relation of Church and State. It is, of course, true that the Jewish Church was national, and the Christian Church is catholic in the sense of universal, and, as such, it is not necessarily bound up with an Establishment. The peculiar position of the Jewish Church in relation to the State, and in the light of God's purposes of redemption for the whole world, make it impossible to use Jewish Princes as illustrations of Christian Princes in the way that the Article does, a view that was adopted by Churchmen and Puritans alike. A far better interpretation of the right position between Church and State is found in such passages as Roms. xiii.; 1 Peter ii. 13-17. Then, too, the Jewish Church was theocratic in a way that the Christian Church never has been, or can be.

---

[1] The story of this Declaration and its criticism is taken in substance from the pamphlet by the late Dean Goode, *Reply to the Letter and Declaration Respecting the Royal Supremacy.*
[2] This general subject can be studied in Maitland, *Roman Canon Law in the Church of England*; Tomlinson, *Lay Judges*; Figgis, *Churches in the Modern State*; A. L. Smith, *Church and State in the Middle Ages*; Two Articles on "Canon Law," *Protestant Dictionary.*

It is, of course, easy to say that the influence of the State on the Church is injurious, and many Churchmen would be ready to admit this. But, on the other hand, Establishment is cherished by many because of its essential value as a national testimony to God. It must never be forgotten that Church and State are equally Divine in their proper places, though the distinction between them is vital and fundamental. As the State is based upon the law of compulsion involving outward adherence only, and the Church is based upon the law of love expressive of an inward willingness, it can easily be seen that with weapons so different the two can never be formally one. Indeed, they never have been, and whether we believe in Establishment or not, the precise spiritual relations of Church and State are quite clearly laid down in Holy Scripture. Many Churchmen make a great distinction between the Establishment of a Church *de novo* and the rejection of an existing Establishment. The former would probably not be accepted by anyone; the latter is thought by many to involve a serious rejection of God. The matter is one involving grave differences of view, and whatever may be the precise relation in the future between the English Church and the State there can be no doubt that, as in Scotland, there will be a definite and determined insistence upon the two great principles that the State shall not control the Church and that the clergy shall not control the laity.

III.—THE PAPAL SUPREMACY

The Article is quite clear that " the Bishop of Rome hath no jurisdiction in this realm of England," and this at once raises the question of the Papal Supremacy considered in relation to the past and also to the present. Roman Catholics themselves are not all agreed as to the precise power of the Papacy. The Gallican theory is that a General Council is supreme, the Pope being its mouthpiece. The Ultramontane view is that the Pope is supreme as the personal Head of the Church. Since 1870 the latter theory, known as Ultramontanism, has come more and more to the front, the tendency being to concentrate all authority in the Pope speaking *ex cathedra*.[1] The Roman arguments are mainly two in number.

1. The argument from Scripture.—First of all attention is called to the prominence of St. Peter in the Gospels, and this is easily and readily admitted, but prominence is not necessary for primacy, and the latter does not inevitably follow from the former. The words addressed to St. Peter in regard to authority in matters of Church discipline (Matt. xvi. 19) were afterwards addressed to the other disciples as well (Matt. xviii. 18) so that there was no monopoly of " binding " and " loosing." In view of other Scripture passages referring to the Apostle Peter it is difficult to see how the primacy can be fairly argued. Thus, he is sent

---

[1] For an outline of Barrow's great argument from his *Treatise of the Pope's Supremacy*, see Boultbee, *The Theology of the Church of England*, pp. 289–301.

by the other Apostles to Samaria (Acts viii. 14); he is compelled to explain his action in regard to Cornelius (Acts xi.); he does not occupy any leading or predominant position in the Council of Jerusalem (Acts xv. 6-35); and he is actually withstood at Antioch by St. Paul (Galatians ii.). These facts, together with St. Paul's claim to Apostolic equality (2 Cor. xii. 11), and St. Peter's own references to himself in his addresses and epistles, do not support the theory of primacy.

But the most important passage from Scripture is the well-known "Rock" passage: "Thou art Peter, and upon this rock I will build my Church" (Matt. xvi. 18). It is not at all certain that the reference is to Peter in person, especially if any distinction may be drawn between the two Greek words *Petros* and *Petra*. Perhaps the best exegetical suggestion is that the reference is neither to Peter only nor to his confession only, but to the man confessing, thereby including both the person and what he said.[1] This is in harmony with other references in Scripture to our Lord in relation to the Church (Eph. ii. 20; 1 Pet. ii. 1-5). It would almost seem as though the latter passage were the Apostle's own commentary on his Master's words. Then, too, no early Father interpreted the passage in the Roman Catholic way, and not a single Greek Father connected the position of the Bishop of Rome with the prominence given to St. Peter.[2]

There is no doubt that the authority and infallibility of the Pope are made to depend solely on this text, and practically all apologists for the Church of Rome make it prominent. If, therefore, in the words of a modern writer,[3] this foundation is mined, the Church resting upon it is shown to be the weakest of ecclesiastical structures. Now it is well known that at his ordination every Roman priest has to take a solemn oath of allegiance to the Creed of Pope Pius IV, and in this Creed these words appear concerning the Scriptures: "Neither will I take and interpret them otherwise than according to the unanimous consent of the Fathers." This "unanimous consent of the Fathers" fails entirely when applied to the text in question. This difference of opinion was forcibly shown at the Vatican Council of 1870 by the late Archbishop Kenrick of St. Louis, U.S.A. He was not permitted to deliver his speech, but it was

[1] Lindsay, *The Church and Ministry*, p. 25 f.
[2] "It is a marvellous thing that upon these words the Bishop of Rome should found his supremacy; for whether it be *super petram* or *Petrum*, all is one matter; it maketh nothing at all for the purpose to make a foundation of any such supremacy. For otherwise when Peter spake carnally to Christ (as in the same chapter a little following) Satan was his name, where Christ said, 'Go after me, Satan'; so that the name of Peter is no foundation for the supremacy, but as it is said in Scripture, *Fundati estis super fundamentum apostolorum et prophetarum*, that is, by participation (for godly participation giveth name of things,) he might be called the head of the Church, as the head of the river is called the head, because he was the first who made this confession of Christ, which is not an argument for dignity, but for the quality that was in the man" (Gardiner, *Sermon*, in 1548. Quoted in Hardwick, *History of the Articles of Religion*, p. 398).
[3] Rev. Arthur Galton, who himself went over to Rome and returned under the influence of this text.

afterwards printed at Naples, and he pointed out that the ancient Fathers gave no fewer than five interpretations of the word "rock." (1) The first declared that the Church was built on Peter, an interpretation endorsed by seventeen Fathers. (2) The second understood the words as referring to all the Apostles, Peter being simply the Primate. This was the opinion of eight Fathers. (3) The third interpretation asserted that the words applied to the faith which Peter professed, a view held by no less than forty-four Fathers, including some of the most important and representative. (4) The fourth interpretation declared that the words were to be understood of Jesus Christ, the Church being built on Him. This was the view of sixteen writers. (5) The fifth interpretation understood the term "rock" to apply to the faithful themselves, who, by believing on Christ, were made living stones in the temple of His body. This, however, was the opinion of very few. It is, therefore, clear that there is no such thing as "the unanimous consent of the Fathers" in regard to the interpretation of this text, and Archbishop Kenrick concluded his speech by saying that "if we are bound to follow the majority of the Fathers in this thing, then we are bound to hold for certain that by the 'rock' should be understood the faith professed by Peter, not Peter professing the faith." It is also noteworthy that no fewer than forty-four witnesses from among the Fathers are adduced by the Roman Catholic divine, Launay, to prove that by the "rock" is to be understood not Peter himself, but the faith which he professed.[1] It is also impossible to overlook the fact that in the Roman Missal itself the Collect for the Vigil of St. Peter and St. Paul's Day reads thus: "Grant, we beseech Thee, Almighty God, that Thou wouldest not suffer us, whom Thou established on the Rock of the Apostolic Confession, to be shaken by any disturbances."

It is doubtless true, as Hort points out, that "the most obvious interpretation of this famous phrase is the true one," that St. Peter himself, as the spokesman, interpreter, and leader of the rest, was the rock which Jesus Christ had in view.[2] But even if this were proved beyond all question it would still be necessary to require proof of authority to transmit the power, and this is, of course, wholly lacking. There is not the slightest hint given that Peter could transmit the authority to anyone, and, in particular, there is no suggestion whatever that any of the Bishops of Rome are to be considered as the "successors" of the Apostles. It is hardly without point, in view of present controversies, that though ample reference is made to Christians in Rome, and even to "Bishops" in other places, nothing is said of any "Bishop" as then existing in the Church at Rome. This assumption that Peter's authority can be transmitted depends upon another assumption, namely, that Bishops are "successors

---

[1] Included in these are Origen, Augustine, Chrysostom, and even Pope Gregory the Great, who in his Commentary on the Psalms says plainly: "The Son of God is the Rock from which Peter derived his name and on which He said He would build His Church."

[2] *Christian Ecclesia*, p. 16.

of the Apostles." But, as we have seen in our study of the Christian ministry, this is impossible. Apostleship required certain conditions (Acts i. 22; 1 Cor. xv. 7-9), and the moment such conditions were impossible Apostleship, as such, ceased to be. As already observed, we gladly recognise and emphasise continuity with Apostolic doctrine and life, but this is altogether different from what is understood as Apostolic Succession in the Episcopate. Ministerial continuity by means of the commission of Ordination is one thing, but continuity in the sense of Apostolic authority transmitted only by a particular line is quite another, and for the latter there is no Scriptural warrant at all. This being the case the great passage, on any interpretation, is to be limited to St. Peter, giving him that natural and rightful authority which we observe he used in the Acts of the Apostles, but not referring to anything beyond his personal and individual qualifications for the special work to which he had been called. The privileges are personal rather than official, and are necessarily limited to him, and are not capable of transmission to any " successor." The other passages which are sometimes adduced in support of this contention of St. Peter's primacy really do not touch the question at all, for St. Luke xxii. 31, 32 was at once a warning and an encouragement in view of the awful sin of denying his Master, and St. John xxi. 15-17 may be regarded as the complementary passage to the former, including a threefold reminder of the denial and a threefold restoration to his former position. Altogether, therefore, we may say without any hesitation that Scripture gives no warrant for identifying St. Peter's prominence with his primacy.

2. The argument from History.—Two points are involved here, and though they are distinct they may perhaps be considered together : (*a*) St. Peter's primacy; (*b*) St. Peter's Roman episcopacy. We may set aside as unnecessary to be discussed the question whether St. Peter was ever in Rome. There is nothing in the New Testament to warrant it and much that seems to be opposed to it, but tradition outside the New Testament seems to favour it, and it matters little whether we accept it or not.[1] It is, of course, perfectly clear that the Church of Rome was not founded by St. Peter; or, indeed, by any other Apostle, as the Epistle to the Romans clearly implies and teaches. With regard to the question whether St. Peter was ever in any sense of the word Bishop of Rome, history is quite clear that he was not. The idea curiously appears first in the second century heretical document, called the Clementine Homilies, which claim that Clement was the immediate successor of Peter, but Irenæus says that the Church in Rome was founded by Peter and Paul, and he gives Linus as the first Bishop. To the same effect is the testimony of Tertullian and the Apostolic Constitutions.[2] Later writers, like

---

[1] In the Bampton Lectures for 1913, *The Church of Rome in the First Century*, the Rev. G. Edmundson favours the view that St. Peter did go to Rome.

[2] Irenæus, *adv. Hær.*, Ch. III, p. 3; Tertullian, *de Præscript*, Ch. XXXII; *Apostolic Constitutions*, Bk. VII, Section 46.

Eusebius, Jerome, and Epiphanius, agree with this position. While, then, it is quite likely that the Apostle Peter reached Rome and was there put to death by martyrdom according to tradition,[1] there is no proof whatever that he remained, according to the Roman Catholic theory, twenty-five years as bishop, a position which is absolutely impossible according to chronology and historical grounds.

The view that St. Peter being Bishop of Rome was the natural and necessary Primate of that and of all other Churches is not only without support in Church history, but there is much against it. The well-known action and attitude of Polycarp against Anicetus in regard to the observance of Easter; the action of Irenæus against Victor; the opposition of Cyprian to Stephen; and the protest of Augustine against Celestinus, all show with unmistakable clearness the position of the Church of Rome among the other Churches. Not least of all is the protest of Gregory the Great against the use of the title of Universal Bishop for the chief pastor of the Roman Church, and he actually said that whoever should assume it should be regarded as the forerunner of Antichrist.[2]

Then, too, this primacy, and therefore supremacy, was never acknowledged in the Eastern Church; indeed, it could not have been admitted. The history of the early General Councils afford positive proof of this contention, since the Pope was not only not President, but until the Fourth Council was not at all influential in any of the decisions. The first step in the direction of the Roman supremacy seems to have been associated with the Council of Sardica, 347, when Athanasius naturally appealed to the Church of Rome to adjudicate, and the Canons of Sardica appointed the Pope as judge. But this was all new, and the Council was not a General Council. The idea, however, was fruitful, and developed into very much more by the time of Innocent III. Later on the political change from Rome to Constantinople gradually helped the Papacy. The Emperor had been called *Pontifex Maximus* in connection with the Pagan relation to Church and State, and when the Empire was transferred to Constantinople it was natural that the Bishop of Rome, as the chief person remaining in the city, should have transferred to him the Imperial title of *Pontifex Maximus*. But such a stupendous claim as is involved in the Roman supremacy ought to have an unquestioned historical basis, and it literally has none. The decretals in the Middle Ages which were used to support the Roman position are now admitted on all hands to have been forged.

Coming to our own country, it is sometimes said that England was in the Patriarchate of Rome. The very idea of a Patriarchate arose almost certainly from civil usage. A Bishop was regarded as presiding over

[1] Bishop Lightfoot holds that St. Peter reached Rome in A.D. 64, and was soon afterwards put to death in the Neronian Persecution (*Apostolic Fathers*, Part I, Vol. II, pp. 497, 498).
[2] Maclear and Williams, *Introduction to the Articles of the Church of England*, pp. 416–418.

παροικία (our " parish "); a Metropolitan over ἐπαρχία (our " province "); and a Patriarch over διοίκησις (our " diocese "). There were seven civil divisions in the East and seven in the West, and ecclesiastically there were one hundred and eighteen provinces with Patriarchates in their cities : Rome, Antioch, and Alexandria. All the others were primacies. But Rome had no power even over Milan, much less over Britain. There was a British Church before the coming of Augustine of Canterbury, and his mission did not and could not give jurisdiction to Rome. But gradually, especially through the action of Wilfrid and the results of the Norman Conquest, England became an integral part of the Roman Church until the Reformation. There were protests from time to time, but they were all civil, never ecclesiastical and spiritual.[1]

As the topstone of an ecclesiastical edifice the Papacy could be regarded as a natural evolution, and, as such, not essentially antichristian. It is only when the demand is made that this must be so and nothing else is right that it becomes impossible and intolerable on all grounds. Even the Reformers were at first ready to acknowledge the primacy of Rome, but only *jure humano*. But Rome would not be content with this, and transformed ecclesiastical development into Divine laws. Then, too, the question of primacy has not only developed into that of supremacy, but into the much more serious claim to infallibility, Rome insisting that the Pope is infallible when defining any question of faith or morals.[2]

In the doctrine of the Papacy we have the most signal example of the principle on which a spurious Catholicism proceeds, namely, the transformation of a natural ecclesiastical development into essential Divine laws of Christianity by means of a legal system. Two main ideas are at the root of this transformation. (1) The sacerdotal idea of the ministry,

---

[1] "Here again the Church of England, so far as *represented by its Synods*, acknowledged its identity with the Church of Rome; just as did the 'Determination' of 1413 above mentioned. When most independent of the civil power, the hierarchy of England owned itself bound by the laws of the Church of Rome and declared its authority derived from the Popes. This was near the eve of the Reformation.

"Thus we see the Church of England on its clerical side more and more separated from the civil power from the Conquest to the Reformation; more and more identifying itself with the Church of Rome from Henry I to the Reformation. The Crown had its share in encouraging Papal domination, from its being continually in need of the influence of the hierarchy; but Parliament, so far as its direct enactments went, resisted Papal usurpations, and was the only body in the Constitution that maintained a consistent attitude of independence in regard to the See of Rome" (Hole, *A Manual of Church History*, p. 113; see also pp. 28, 52, 72, 82).

[2] "Pastors and faithful of whatsoever right and dignity, as well individually as all together, are bound by the obligation of the hierarchical subordination, and of true obedience, not only in things pertaining to faith and morals, but also in those which relate to the discipline and regimen of the Church diffused throughout the entire world. . . . This is a doctrine of Catholic Truth, from which no one can deviate, and yet preserve faith and salvation. . . . Also we teach and declare the Pope to be the Supreme Judge of the Faithful, and that all causes relating to the ecclesiastical consideration may be referred to his judgment; the judicial sentence of the Apostolic See (than whose authority there is not a greater) may be revised by no one. Neither is it lawful for anyone to judge his judgment" (*Vatican Council*, Session IV, Ch. III).

involving mediation ; (2) the visibility of the Church as essential, with
the consequent need of a topstone.   It has often been pointed out that
Cyprian's view of the episcopate necessarily required the Papacy as the
culminating point of the ecclesiastical pyramid.[1]

And it is important to point out that it is futile to spend time on disproving the doctrine of Roman supremacy and infallibility if we leave
untouched the roots from which it sprang, for it would produce something
essentially like it if this form were abolished.   If any sacerdotal view of
the Church is held to be *jure divino*, it is impossible to take up a distinguishable position against Rome.   The idea of a Catholicism which is
not Roman is doomed to futility and destruction by the severe logic of
facts.   The only adequate safeguard against Roman supremacy is the
assertion of the great verities emphasised at the Reformation and embodied
in our Articles.[2]

IV.—ILLUSTRATIONS OF THE ROYAL SUPREMACY

The Article adduces two cases in which it is claimed that the Royal
Supremacy may be asserted over individual Christian lives.

1. The Lawfulness of Capital Punishment.—The inclusion of this
seems to be due to the fact that such a position was questioned in the
sixteenth century.   It is a recognition of authority, and is in harmony
with the primitive teaching of Gen. ix. 6.   It should be noted that the
question is stated as permissible, and does not touch the larger question
whether capital punishment is or is not advisable.

2. The Lawfulness of Military Service.—A distinction is to be drawn
here between defence and defiance.   The Article teaches that the exercise
of force is sometimes necessary, and that it is therefore lawful for Christian
men under proper authority to engage in military duties.   While, then,
the Article rightly opposes anything like anarchy on the part of Christian
men, it is impossible to question the well-known but rough words of the
American General, Sherman, that " War is hell."[3]   Here, again, there
seems to be no doubt that the teaching of the Article is directed against

---

[1] On these subjects see Fairbairn, *Catholicism, Roman and Anglican*, pp. 167–189;
Moyes, *London Eucharistic Congress*, p. 37 f.; Litton, *The Church of Christ*.

[2] Proof of this can be seen by a comparison of Bishop Gore's *Roman Catholic Claims*
with Dom Chapman's *Bishop Gore and Roman Catholic Claims*.   It must be frankly
confessed that the latter is easily victorious on almost every point.   Another illustration
is found in Littledale's *Plain Reasons against joining the Church of Rome*, in which the
plainest of all reasons is significantly omitted.   So also with Brinckman's *Notes on the
Papal Claims*.   For valuable books on the Roman Controversy see Dearden, *Modern
Romanism Examined* ; Von Hase, *Handbook to the Controversy with Rome*, Vols. I and II;
Salmon, *The Infallibility of the Church*; and *The Papal Council*, by Janus.

[3] On the subject of Christianity and War see Mozley, *University Sermons*, V ; Paget,
The Hallowing of War; Maclear and Williams, *ut supra*, p. 497; Martensen, *Christian
Ethics*, Section 2, pp. 233, 234; Hobhouse, *The Church and the World in Idea and in
History*, p. 13 f., 23.   *The Attitude of the Church towards War*, by Bishop H. E. Ryle
(Liverpool Lectures, No. 12), a brief but valuable summary of the history and true
position.

extremists in the sixteenth century who defied all civil authority and
opposed the lawfulness of war.[1]

The question of Christianity and War has naturally received special
attention through recent events, and the truth of the Article has been
seriously questioned.   But the distinction between wars of aggression
and defence remains valid, and the teaching of the Article, especially with
its Latin reading, *justa bella*, is undoubtedly in accord with the New
Testament principles of the Christian's relation and duty to the State.
Christianity does not remove us from interest in national life.   When
it is said that Christians are " not of this world " it does not mean " not
of this nation," for " world " and " nation " are not interchangeable
terms.   As Christians we share in national blessings and privileges, and
are as much part of the nation as are non-Christians.   Grace does not
destroy or set aside natural relationships, whether of the family or of the
State.   On the contrary, it sanctifies and uplifts them.   So that being
" under grace " is compatible with being " under government," and God
is as much the Ruler of nations as He ever was.   When St. Paul
showed patriotism in relation to Israel (Rom. ix. 14 ; x. 1) and claimed
the rights of Roman citizenship (Acts xvi. 37 ; xxii. 25-28), he was
not thereby disloyal to his Heavenly citizenship.

The War has helped us to understand certain aspects of New Testament teaching as never before.   Thus, while the law of the Sermon
on the Mount is clear in regard to individuals, it is not to be similarly
applied to personal responsibilities for others.   The law is plain that
envy, hatred, and malice are as absolutely wrong in nations as they are in
individuals, and so is revenge.   Not only so, but the very existence of war
is a clear proof that the law of God has somehow been broken, for if it
had been perfectly obeyed, it would have made war impossible.   But
when violence, aggression, and tyrannical cruelty are seen, the question
at once arises as to what Christianity requires of Christians.   As long as
the individual's own life is concerned, the matter is plain, but the problem
becomes acute when he is responsible for others.   The difficulty in some
minds is due to a confusion between retaliation and resistance.   The
former is unchristian ; the latter is not.   Resistance of evil may be and
often is a positive duty, for if a man or woman were to yield to pressure
in the face of certain aspects of evil, it would imply a weak and sinful
compliance.   There is also no essential distinction between police force
and military force, because in both instances force is exercised to resist
evil.   The kind and degree of resistance, or of the force required to
overcome it, are quite irrelevant to the issue, and if when a burglar
resists he gets maimed or killed, the householder or the policeman is not

---

[1] "Quin et Anabaptistarum profligandus est agrestis stupor, qui negant licere
Christianis magistratum gerere, quasi propterea Christus in terras descenderit, ut rerum
publicarum administrationem aboleret.   Imo vero Spiritus Sanctus statuit principes et
magistratus esse Dei ministros, ut benefactis favorem suum impartiant, et maleficia
suppliciis constringant ; quæ duo si rebus humanis abessent, maxima sequeretur omnium
rerum confusio" (*Reformatio Legum, De Hæresibus*, c. 13).

regarded as guilty of murder any more than the soldier is considered guilty on the battlefield. The contention that " Thou shalt not kill " is a prohibition of war is impossible, because the Jewish nation to which this command was given " had a strict military organisation constituted by the very authority from which the commandment came " (Dale).

When Christ said, " Resist not evil," He was stating in pithy, proverbial form the general principle of individual life. But to deduce from it a doctrine of universal non-resistance is to pervert the true meaning. If this verse is taken literally, why may not others be similarly interpreted ? (See St. Matt. v. 42 ; vi. 19.) As long as the wrongs inflicted are personal, the Christian's attitude is that of meekness, but when the wrong is done to others, resistance becomes a duty. The whole idea of St. Matt. v. 39 is personal and has no reference to war, or to civic affairs. So that in any world where men are not what they ought to be, some form of force will be necessary, and the Christian attitude to those who are aggressively brutal and unjust must be one of opposition and resistance in the highest interests of the community. Whenever, therefore, compulsory military service is the law of the land, it is impossible to doubt that Christians are justified in responding to the claim of the Government to take up arms in defence of the country. Government is still as much as ever the Divine method of maintaining order and putting down evil (Rom. xiii.).

It is sometimes said in opposition to this line that " all they that take the sword shall perish by the sword," and it is interpreted with literalness, as though it means that everyone who fights must necessarily be killed. But this is obviously not true, as history abundantly proves. Yet the principle of the words remains as our Lord intended it to be understood, and if the emphasis is placed on the word " take " the true idea will be seen. The words are directed against that spirit of militarism which aims at aggression merely for conquest.

We conclude, therefore, that it is not and cannot be a sin to be a soldier, for not only do we find to-day many of the most earnest Christians in the ranks, but the Bible nowhere condemns a soldier's life. Indeed, God Himself appeared before Joshua in military form (Josh. v. 21-23). Although it would be certainly wrong to say that the Bible approves of all wars, there are many aspects of war, and many different kinds of war. So that in regard to a Christian man voluntarily becoming a soldier, each must judge for himself according to his conscience in the light of Holy Scripture.

We may sum up the matter by pointing out that under certain conditions a Christian ought to be ready to draw and use the sword. He should do so when the rights of man are invaded, since no man lives to himself, but is part of a social order for which we are all responsible. A Christian man is justified in fighting when the righteousness of the cause is clear, for tyranny in its attempt to over-ride liberty is manifestly wrong in the sight of God. Then, too, war by Christians is justifiable when the resources of peace are really exhausted and the enemy still refuses to lay aside his tyranny and hatred. Once again, a Christian can legitimately enter into war when his individual conscience is clear. Our Lord always respected the rights of conscience, and when conscience is illuminated by the fundamental and essential truth of Holy Scripture, the matter must necessarily be left to the sincerity of the believer.

One other text has been much discussed during the recent War, namely, "Love your enemies," and again the need must be urged of distinguishing between personal and social attitudes; between individual life and corporate responsibility. No one questions for a moment that the command is absolutely binding on the individual, not, of course, as including pleasurable affection, but certainly as excluding all personal animosity and wish for evil. But the case is altogether different when the word is applied to an organised community, for other elements then enter into the problem which prevent us from using the precept to avoid hostility against national wrongdoing. The following words of the late Bishop of Durham in a letter to the *Spectator* make this distinction between the individual and the State clear and convincing :—

"There is no approach to a complete analogy between an organised community and a person, however much we may 'personify' the community. The State is not at all a personality : it is a great complex of personalities. It is such a complex that its organisation largely exists on purpose that the community may safeguard its personal components in their several interests and liberties, particularly its weaker components. From this point of view the State is morally right, is morally bound, to take indignant and resolute action when its members' lawful interests, of peace, security, liberty, are violated or forcibly threatened by another State. We are nowhere commanded by our Lord to love other people's enemies as such. Where others are concerned, as victims of wrong, a wholly new element enters the scene. We see a ruffian maltreat a woman, or a child. The aggressor, as such, is in no respect an object for our goodwill. He is an evil to be, by all possible means, quelled and also punished. And the State, when its member suffers violence and wrong, is called to act thus, as the third party interposing to protect and avenge another party."

It has been suggested that the attitude of the Pacifist is really due to the fallacy of believing that physical force is in itself an evil. This is certainly the weakness of several religious and philosophic systems, and is essentially the same as the old Gnostic position, that matter is evil and that only spiritual weapons are lawful. And yet, if matter and its force were created by God, it is impossible to say that these are evil *per se*, or that power, whether physical or intellectual or volitional, is inherently evil. As a matter of fact, this is often the only weapon that man can use to further his purpose. And so it may be concluded that the moral significance of force lies only in its use, and it is the unnecessary or cruel employment alone that is wrong. Force has to be used to slay an animal for food, and no one can say that this is wrong in itself, so long as our

employment is humane.   The same is obviously true in social, civic and
national affairs.   For this reason, it is contended that a war of defence for
the sake of righteousness and liberty is unquestionably justified, and, as
it has been well said, the true conclusion is not " peace at any price," but
righteousness at any cost.[1]

[1] "Ought Followers of the Galilean to be Pacifists?" by H. W. Magoun, *Bibliotheca
Sacra*, Vol. LXXIII, p. 55 (January 1916).

"We are Christians, servants of a religion of love which expresses itself equally by
gentleness and by force, never by supineness, never by hate.   Is a Christian less loving
when he seizes the bridle of a runaway horse, to save innocent bystanders from being
trampled under its hoofs?   He gives all for love, force, and reason freely flung into
the service of the right.   Has one forgotten Christ when one risks his life to restrain
a maniac crazed with disease and near to throttling an innocent neighbour?   Could
one's love, one's Christianity, be other than hypocrisy if one was not faithful unto death,
withholding no service called for?   Force directed to noble ends is not base.   Tiny
forces that wag tongue or pen in reasoning and persuasion are no more Christian
than the brute elemental force that launches a lifeboat.   Our religion may call for any
power we possess.   He who holds back any service in the hour of need does but lip
service to his God" ("America's Duty," by R. C. Cabot, *Outlook*, New York, 4th April
1917).

ARTICLE XXXVIII

Of Christian Men's Goods, which are not common.	*De illicita bonorum Communicatione.*
The riches and goods of Christians are not common, as touching the right, title, and possession of the same, as certain Anabaptists do falsely boast. Notwithstanding, every man ought, of such things as he possesseth, liberally to give alms to the poor, according to his ability.	Facultates et bona Christianorum non sunt communia, quoad jus et possessionem, ut quidam Anabaptistæ falso jactant. Debet tamen quisque de his quæ possidet, pro facultatum ratione, pauperibus eleemosynas benigne distribuere.

IMPORTANT EQUIVALENTS

Of Christian men's goods, which are not common. = *de illicita bonorum communicatione.*

Riches = *facultates.*

As touching the right, title, and possession = *quoad jus et possessionem.*

In 1553 and 1563 the title was *Christianorum bona non sunt communia,* " Christian men's goods are not common." The present titles date from 1571. The Latin is somewhat difficult to interpret. Dr. Hey suggests that it should be rendered, " Of the Unlawfulness of Acting as if all Goods were common." The Article is undoubtedly directed against certain extremists in the sixteenth century. The Reformers were obviously anxious to give the Church of Rome no handle for associating them with fanatical sects which arose in the age of the Reformation.

I.—THE TEACHING OF THE ARTICLE

1. The possessions of Christian men are not public property in regard to right, title, and possession.—This was the error of " certain Anabaptists " who were prevalent in England and on the Continent. The error is indicated in the *Reformatio Legum,*[1] and is also dealt with in more than one Confession of the Reformed Churches. In addition to the rejection of Infant Baptism the Anabaptists went to the extreme of abolishing all law and proclaiming the absolute equality of all Christian people. The outcome was fanaticism and Antinomianism, which led to terrible results. At the same time these extremes must not blind us to the fact that Anabaptism contained in it certain truths which found

[1] "Excludatur etiam ab eisdem Anabaptistis inducta bonorum et possessionum communitas, quam tantopere urgent, ut nemini quicquam relinquant proprium et suum. In quo mirabiliter loquuntur, cum furta prohiberi divina Scriptura cernant, et eleemosynas in utroque Testamento laudari videant, quas ex propriis facultatibus nostris elargimur; quorum sane neutrum consistere posset, nisi Christianis proprietas bonorum et possessionum suarum relinqueretur" (*De Hæresibus,* c. 14).

emphasis in opposition to the errors of Rome, and in spite of the deplorable excesses of certain forms of Anabaptism it is impossible to overlook the underlying truths of their position.[1]

2. The obligation of Christian giving proportionately to possession.— The word " alms " is singular, from the French, " elmes," based on the Greek, ἐλεημοσύνη.

II.—THE PRINCIPLES INVOLVED

Property as the fruit of industry is involved in the very notion of society as it exists by natural law, and if Christians have nothing of their own there can be no place for bounty and no necessity for liberality. It is important to bear in mind this essential and vital principle of the rightfulness of property when duly and legally obtained.[2] There is no proof that the action of the early Christians (Acts ii. 44 ; iv. 32) was anything more than a temporary expression of Christian fellowship, and certainly there is no proof of it ever being required as of Divine or permanent obligation. It is obvious that everything was purely voluntary and not compulsory (Acts v. 4). How can a man steal or covet his own ? What is the meaning of such phrases as " rich in this world " (1 Tim. vi. 17), and " this world's good " (1 John iii. 17) ?

The early Church after the time in the Acts, as seen in Justin Martyr and Tertullian, clearly shows that no such community of goods was in existence, and Clement of Alexandria wrote his Treatise, *Quis Dives Salvetur*, to show that there was no need for a Christian man to give up his possessions.

The insistence of the Article on almsgiving is, of course, one of the clearest Christian duties, and is found almost everywhere in the New Testament in precept and practice (Rom. xii. 13 ; 1 Tim. vi. 17-19 ; Heb. xiii. 16).[3]

The New Testament has three great principles of giving, and these call for careful attention and constant emphasis on the part of all who are required to teach. (*a*) A man is to give according as God hath prospered him (1 Cor. xvi. 2); (*b*) he is to give according to his ability (Acts xi. 29); (*c*) he is to give according to his heart's purpose (2 Cor. ix. 7). It is suggestive and significant of the true Christian life that in the last passage the word rendered " cheerful " is that from which we obtain the English word " hilarious." All the principles and methods of Christian giving may be carefully studied from St. Paul's two chapters, 2 Cor. viii.; ix. It will thus be seen that giving is to be " according to " (κατὰ) not " out of " (ἐκ). A man may easily give a very small amount " out of " his abundance, but this will not be Christian giving. He must

---

[1] For a full and discriminating discussion of Anabaptism, see Lindsay, *The History of the Reformation*, Vol. II, pp. 430–463; Forsyth, *Faith, Freedom, and the Future*, passim.

[2] For a careful study of this subject, see Clow, *Christ in the Social Order*; Flint, *Socialism* Ch. XI.

[3] The Eleventh Homily in the Second Book is on "Almsdoing."

give " according to " his abundance, or whatever he has.   The New Testament is thus true to its genius in avoiding all reference to a specific proportion like the Old Testament rule of the tithe.   In harmony with the essential feature of Christianity as a religion of principle, not of rule, it lays the burden upon the enlightened spiritual mind to give " according to " what is possessed, pointing out that giving is one of the most definite and searching proofs of the reality of the Christian life (1 John iv. 20, 21 ; iii. 17, 18).

ARTICLE XXXIX

Of a Christian Man's Oath.	*De jure jurando.*
As we confess that vain and rash swearing is forbidden Christian men by our Lord Jesus Christ, and *James* His Apostle; so we judge that Christian religion doth not prohibit, but that a man may swear when the Magistrate requireth, in a cause of faith and charity, so it be done, according to the Prophet's teaching, in justice, judgment, and truth.	Quemadmodum juramentum vanum et temerarium a Domino nostro Jesu Christo et Apostolo ejus *Jacobo*, Christianis hominibus interdictum esse fatemur; ita Christianorum religionem minime prohibere censemus, quin jubente magistratu, in causa fidei et charitatis jurare liceat, modo id fiat juxta Prophetæ doctrinam, in justitia, in judicio, et veritate.

IMPORTANT EQUIVALENTS.

Of a Christian man's oath	=	*de jure jurando.*
Christian religion	=	*Christianorum religionem.*
The prophet's teaching	=	*Prophetæ doctrinam.*

LIKE the last Article, this dates from 1553, though with a different title. Originally it was: *Licet Christianis jurare,* " Christian men may take an oath." This also is directed against the Anabaptists, who had imbibed the view that oath-taking, even in Courts of Justice, was wrong. The condemnation of this is also seen in the *Reformatio Legum.*[1]

I.—THE PROHIBITION

The Article frankly acknowledges that "vain and rash swearing is forbidden Christian men." The word "oath" comes from the Anglo-Saxon "ath," and means a solemn affirmation with appeal to God as to the truth of the declaration. This appeal implies at once the renunciation of the Divine favour and the imprecation of the Divine justice if the statements are proved to be false. Oaths are of two kinds: one asserts, simply stating something to be true ; the other promises, pledging the word in regard to truth. The latter would include such promises as what are known as the oath of allegiance, the oath of office, the oath of witnesses in Courts. The "vain and rash swearing" referred to in the Article doubtless has in view such passages as St. Matt. v. 33-37 ; St. James v. 12, and the vanity and rashness are clearly regarded as profane and irreverent, and therefore rightly forbidden because opposed to the true idea of the Gospel.

[1] "Præterea nec juramentorum Anabaptistæ legitimum relinquunt usum, in quo contra Scripturarum sententiam et veteris Testamenti patrum exempla, Pauli etiam Apostoli, imo Christi, imo Dei Patris procedunt; quorum juramenta sæpe sunt in sacris literis repetita" (*De Hæresibus,* c. 15).

II.—THE PERMISSION

The oath-taking that is claimed to be allowable is the solemn affirmation when required, and the Article rightly states that Christianity does not forbid such solemn statements when required by authority " in a cause of faith and charity." This kind of oath or solemn assertion is seen to be allowed and even ordered in Scripture (Deut. vi. 13). Our Lord Himself submitted to such without any question or objection (Matt. xxvi. 63). St. Paul often used it in connection with affirmations of the Gospel and of his own personal attitude (Rom. ix. 1 ; 2 Cor. i. 23 ; Gal. i. 20). It is also even recognised as associated with God Himself (Heb. vi. 16-18). It is evident, therefore, that such passages at once qualify, and in particular those in St. Matthew and St. James, and abundantly vindicate the practice of oath-taking in Courts of Justice, by solemnly appealing to the presence of God in support of statements made. The reference at the end of the Article lays down the principle of such taking of oaths. It must be done " according to the prophet's teaching, in justice, judgment, and truth." The allusion is to the words of Jeremiah (iv. 2). Granted these conditions, an oath is perfectly legitimate. It is no doubt correct that if men were always strictly truthful oaths would not be required, but in view of the presence of evil in the world the necessity of some solemn attestation seems inevitable, and for this purpose it is to be regarded as quite lawful and right for a Christian.[1]

[1] The Seventh Homily in the First Book is on the subject of "Swearing and Purgatory," where the passage from Jeremiah is quoted and explained.

CONCLUSION

In the light of the history and substance of the Articles several important questions remain for consideration.

It is sometimes argued that the Prayer Book and Articles are contradictory, and Pitt's words are often quoted, that the Church of England has a Popish Liturgy, an Arminian clergy and Calvinistic Articles. But notwithstanding its cleverness the statement is not only incorrect, but really reveals the ignorance of its author. There is no essential difference between the Prayer Book and the Articles, as the following facts show:

1. There was a distinct and considerable difference between Cranmer and some of the extreme Protestants of the sixteenth century, and he should not be identified with them.[1] Indeed, Cranmer's learning and balance of judgment are more evident to-day than ever.[2] And it is to Cranmer that we owe almost entirely both the Prayer Book and the Articles.

2. Archbishop Parker is known to have been a disciple and admirer of Cranmer,[3] and Parker's action in connection with Article XXIX shows the essential nature of his doctrine on the Holy Communion.

3. The essentially Protestant attitude of Jewel, Bishop of Salisbury, and final Editor of the Articles and a collaborator with Parker is well known.

4. The addition on the Sacraments made to the Catechism in 1604 did not involve any difference of doctrine, because the very wording of the questions and answers can be traced to Nowell's *Little Catechism*, a well-known Reformation document.[4]

---

[1] Hardwick, *ut supra*, p. 32.

[2] "Of the men, who were raised up to guide their country through the perils of that stormy crisis, and who finally succeeded in rebuilding for us what has proved itself a sanctuary not only from the malice of the Romanist, but also from a flood of Puritanical innovations, none was so illustrious and untiring as the primate of all England. After granting that the life of Cranmer was disfigured here and there by human blemishes; after granting that the caution and timidity of his nature had degenerated, on some rare occasions, into weakness and irresolution, he is still, if we regard him fairly as a whole, among the brightest worthies of his age: to him we are indebted, under God, for much of the sobriety of tone that marks the English Reformation, or in other words, for the accordance of our present system with the Apostolic models" (Hardwick, *ut supra*, p. 67 f.; see also pp. 68–70).

[3] Hardwick, *ut supra*, p. 118.

[4] Dimock, *Papers on the Eucharistic Presence*, pp. 289–429; Nowell's *Catechism* has been reprinted by Grove.

5. In 1662 no change whatever was made in the Articles, and it is well known that the reinsertion with a change of wording of the Black Rubric did not involve any change of doctrine on the Holy Communion ; indeed, the proposal emanated from the Puritan party.[1]

These facts are sufficient to show that there is no difference whatever between the Prayer Book and the Articles on points of doctrine, though there is naturally an obvious difference between the Book of Common Prayer and the Articles when they are considered in relation to their character and purpose. Thus the Act of Uniformity expressly restricts the clergy to " the use of the Book of Common Prayer," and this view is endorsed by the Act 23 of George II. And this use of the Prayer Book is based on the belief and affirmation that it does not contain anything " contrary to the Word of God." But with reference to the Articles the case is decidedly different, for these were drawn up as a test of doctrinal soundness for the clergy, and naturally the law requires an acknowledgement that they are " agreeable to the Word of God " and a declaration of " unfeigned assent " to them, while the original Act declared against the maintenance of " any doctrine contrary to them." Thus we see at once the natural difference between the assent required to the Book of Common Prayer and to the Articles. In the former case we are concerned with Formularies of devotion ; in the latter with a standard of belief. But it would be impossible to regard Formularies of devotion as providing an exact standard of faith such as we have in the Articles, and so all that is required concerning the Prayer Book is a declaration of belief that there is nothing in the Book contrary to Holy Scripture, while in regard to the Articles a declaration is required which shows that they were intended to be the standard of faith and test of orthodoxy. Not only, therefore, is there no contradiction between the two, as seen by their history, but, further, the essential difference of character and purpose is seen by the very different requirements from the clergy with respect to them. The Prayer Book is rightly regarded as an incomparable book of devotion, and as such it is to be valued and used, but the Articles, and not the Prayer Book, are the Church's confession of faith and the true test of essential Anglican doctrine on the matters included within their scope.

RELATION OF THE ARTICLES TO ROME

That the Articles were not intended to be merely pacificatory, but also a plain statement of the Anglican position against the Church of Rome ought to be clear from the Articles themselves. In addition to the original declarations in the Forty-two Articles of 1553, we have seen that a further anti-Roman sharpening was given to them in 1563. But it will be worth while to call attention in detail to the reference to Rome contained in the Articles.

---

[1] Dimock, *ut supra*, pp. 465–476. See also Perry, *English Church History*.

1. In Article XIX the Church of Rome is said to have erred not only in regard to Ceremonies, but also in matters of Faith.

2. In Articles VI, XX, XXI, XXII, there is an appeal to Holy Scripture as the sole and supreme standard of truth.

3. In Article XIV there is a plain reference to the Roman Catholic doctrine of " Works of Supererogation."

4. In Article XXII reference is made to the Romish doctrines of Purgatory, Indulgence, Veneration of Images and Relics, and Invocation of Saints.

5. Article XXIV teaches that public prayers are to be in the vernacular tongue.

6. Article XXV opposes the Roman Catholic view of the seven Sacraments and Processions of the Host.

7. Article XXVIII speaks definitely against Transubstantiation, Reservation, Elevation, Adoration of the Sacrament.

8. Article XXX refers to the Roman practice of withholding the cup from the laity.

9. Article XXXI speaks in the strongest terms against the " sacrifices of Masses " as derogatory to the sacrifice of Christ.

10. Article XXXII takes the opposite view of the Roman practice of the compulsory celibacy of the clergy.

11. Article XXXVI insists upon the validity of our Orders in opposition to Rome.

12. Article XXXVII states that the Bishop of Rome " hath no jurisdiction in this Realm of England."

13. Article XV in speaking of Christ alone as without sin is in opposition to the Immaculate Conception and sinlessness of the Virgin Mary.

14. Article XXIX involves opposition to the Roman doctrine of the Lord's Supper, in insisting that the wicked do not partake of the Body of Christ when they receive the elements.

Is it possible to avoid drawing the plain inference from all these statements that the Articles condemn in a very unmistakable way the essential doctrines of the Church of Rome ?

It might have been thought that this would have been more than sufficient to indicate the mind of the Anglican Church, but, strange to say, several attempts have been made to explain away this very obvious anti-Roman position by saying that the Articles had no intention of denouncing Roman official doctrine, but only certain extreme tenets of certain men in the mediæval Church of Rome. This means that when we read so often of Rome and " Romish " in the Articles we are to understand some extremists of the Middle Ages, though their very existence is quite mythical. The first of these attempts dates from the time of Charles I, when a Dominican monk, named Davenport, who wrote under the title of Franciscus à Sancta Clara, endeavoured to prove that the Articles could be interpreted so as to avoid the condemnation of Rome. His book is a curious illustration of intellectual ingenuity. The next attempt was made in the celebrated Tract XC of Dr. Newman, who took similar ground, especially in Articles XXII, XXVIII, XXIX, XXXI. He seems to have been inspired by Davenport's attempt, and endeavoured to distinguish between Roman and Catholic, urging that the Articles only denounced the former and not the latter. Such efforts justify the language of Archbishop Whately, who said :—

"To bring the Articles to bear such a sense as what Mr. Newman thought Catholic tradition required, was a task of no little difficulty. Indeed, he set such an example of hairsplitting and wiredrawing—of shuffling equivocation and dishonest garbling of quotations—as made the English people thoroughly ashamed that any man calling himself an Englishman, a gentleman, and a clergyman, should insult their understandings and consciences with such mean sophistry."[1]

It is not surprising that the Tract led to its condemnation by the Heads of Houses at Oxford, for

"Evading rather than explaining the sense of the Thirty-nine Articles and reconciling subscription to them with the adoption of errors which they were designed to counteract."

But in spite of Newman giving permission twenty years afterwards to republish the Tract, still later on in 1883 Newman came to see that his interpretation was impossible, and he frankly confessed it.[2] Since his day similar efforts have been made, but with little or no success in the light of the history of the sixteenth century which gave the Articles birth.[3] The words of Prebendary Meyrick are assuredly true that "we have the Thirty-nine Articles to serve as a permanent breakwater against the inrush of Mediævalism and Popery."[4]

---

[1] *Cautions for the Times*, p. 231.   [2] See on Article XXXI.

[3] By writers like Bishop Forbes, Rev. Vernon Staley, Dr. B. J. Kidd, Dr. Darwell Stone, Rev. T. A. Lacey, Rev. F. W. Puller, Rev. E. Tyrrell Green, and to some extent Bishop Gibson. As an illustration, the words of Bishop Forbes may be mentioned, which speak of Article XXXVII as referring to the absence of Papal jurisdiction in the "Realm" not in the "Church" of England, as if this distinction between Church and Realm could stand in the light of the well-known circumstances of the sixteenth century. But it is significant that most of the points emphasised by Newman in Tract XC find no allusion in Gibson's and Green's works, though they do elsewhere.

[4] *A Protestant Dictionary*, p. 44.

The view of a scholar who is outside our Church may also be cited: "Against the abuses and the errors of Rome there is no weakening or wavering of the Anglican protest. With all their halting between two opinions, their want of theological originality, their intentional incompleteness, they have been a noble bulwark of Protestant conviction, and possess a simple dignity and Catholicity of their own. Against their measured testimony, spoken with the formula of Trent as clearly in view as those of Lutheranism and Calvinism, even the interpretative casuistry and antiquarian imagination of the Oxford Movement urged their forces in vain. Their intention, their spirit, and their language are unquestionably Protestant" (Curtis, *History of Creeds and Confessions of Faith*, p. 182).

The facts connected with the Council of Trent, adduced above, point in the same direction.

Objection is sometimes raised to the Articles because it is said they are " in no sense a Creed." It is, of course, perfectly true that the Articles are not a Creed in the sense that the three Creeds mentioned in Article VIII are. But in view of the position of the English Church in relation to Rome, as expressed in the sixteenth century, the Articles have been set forth by our Church as a statement of Faith on the particular points with which they deal, and, as such, they are undoubtedly binding on clergy of the Church as expressive of Church of England doctrine. As already indicated, the various Reformed Churches in the sixteenth century were compelled to set out their own beliefs in opposition to Rome, and the Articles embodied the positive teaching of the Anglican Church on a number of vital and important points. A careful consideration of the statements of the Articles in connection with such subjects as the Nature of God, the Person and Work of Christ, the Holy Trinity, the Resurrection, the Nature of Sin, the Truth of Justification, the Necessity and Power of Good Works, and other similar doctrines, will show beyond all question what the Church of England holds and teaches on these fundamental questions, and it is impossible to charge the Articles with any vagueness or hesitation on these topics. Then, too, as it has been well pointed out, the Articles are studiously careful, balanced, and moderate in regard to many matters about which there have been differences of opinion among Christian people. If the language of the Articles on such subjects as Predestination, the Church, and the Ministry be examined it will be seen how cautious and wise are the statements, while rightly requiring for its own members certain general lines of truth. Further, it is impossible to overlook the remarkable balance and clearness in regard to the Sacraments. While insisting upon their Divine authority, the greatest possible care is taken to insist upon their value as means of grace, and at the same time the impossibility of regarding them as channels of blessing apart from definite faith in the promises of God. Nothing could be more definite than the teaching of the Articles concerning what is often called sacramental grace, that is, grace received in the due Scriptural use of these Divine ordinances.[1] From all this it is quite clear that the Articles are characterised by features that make them an admirable compendium of doctrine on the particular subjects treated.

THE PERMANENT VALUE OF THE ARTICLES[2]

The question is often raised whether Creeds and Confessions should be permitted to exist any longer, whether they have not had their day

[1] Prebendary Meyrick in the *Protestant Dictionary*, p. 42; and Bishop J. C. Ryle's *Knots Untied*, p. 63 ff.
[2] *Literature.*—Curtis, *History of Creeds and Confessions of Faith*, Chs. XXIII, XXIV (very important); Denney, *Jesus and the Gospel*, last chapter.

and ceased to be of service; whether, indeed, they are not hindrances to intellectual progress and checks on spiritual liberty. But it may be questioned whether this view possesses anything of real value to warrant it. The testimony derivable from Communions without Creeds and Confessions is not encouraging.[1] That a Church should know where it stands and that its teachers should have a clear idea of what they are to teach seem pretty evident propositions. Assuming, as we must, a settled, clear, and definite faith in God and truth, is it not natural to express it? Belief in God, in Christ, in the Holy Spirit—what is this but a Creed? Not only so, but it involves, however inchoately, an interpretation. Thought is inevitable and expression of thought equally so. Could anything be more dogmatic than modern science and modern rationalism? Even the agnostic must have a Creed. "No rational being can be Creedless," says Flint, and Herbert Spencer's words are well worth quoting again :—

" Religious creeds, which in one way or other occupy the sphere that rational interpretation seeks to occupy and fails, and fails the more the more it seeks, I have come to regard with a sympathy based on community of need : feeling that dissent from them results from inability to accept the solutions offered, joined with the wish that solutions could be found."[2]

Creeds and Confessions can be shown to have had a necessary place in the circumstances of the times in which they arose, and they bear testimony to the reality, force, and persistence of Christian truth and life.[3]

But it is, of course, essential that Creeds and Confessions should be continually made subject to the light of Scripture interpreted by growing Christian experience. John Robinson's words are true that " The Lord hath yet more light and truth to break forth from His Holy Word," and there is no reason why the Church should not revise her Formularies and adapt them to new needs. They are confessedly subordinate to Scripture, the supreme Rule of Faith, and fuller knowledge of the latter will naturally result in newer expressions of the former. The boast of *semper eadem* is a confession of spiritual sterility and stationariness. It may doubtless be wise and necessary to revise rarely and cautiously, but the principle of revision must be granted by all who know the genius of Christianity. As Creeds are based on Scripture, it is only natural that extension of the knowledge of the Bible should influence confessional expressions. The position that Creeds are sacrosanct and exempt from criticism is impossible, though at the same time the fact that Creeds come

[1] "The religious bodies which proclaim their freedom from dogma have not been overwhelmed by applications for admission to their membership" (Curtis, *ut supra*, p. 429).
[2] *Autobiography.* See Curtis, *ut supra*, p. 430.
[3] "It is in truth unthinkable that the vast aggregate of doctrinal symbols, evolved by the Church in all lands during nineteen centuries of intense activity, should have proceeded from any but a profoundly natural and honourable instinct in the soul of faith" (Curtis, *ut supra*, p. 432).

to us with the weight of authority will naturally make us pause long before either summarily rejecting or submitting them to serious modification. The problem on every side is difficult, but it exists and has to be faced.[1] We, therefore, rejoice and glory in a Creed and Confession as a guide, standard, and protection of the truth, while we claim a perfect right to revise its statements whenever necessary for spiritual light, life, and progress.[2]

ETHICS OF SUBSCRIPTION[3]

The question of subscription to Creeds and Articles is fraught with great and grave difficulties, and it was the consciousness of this that led to the endeavour made in 1865 to loosen the bonds and provide relief in a general rather than a detailed endorsement. What, then, are we to understand by assent to our Formularies ? Let us state it in the words of a modern writer :—

"Assent to a historic Creed or Group of Articles, under whatever formula, involves a reference, not merely to what is fondly termed the *plain meaning* of its sentences, but also to its historical meaning, purpose, background, and spirit."[4]

When this view is taken there need be no insuperable difficulty in arriving at the mind of the Church. The same view may be presented in the words of a Churchman :—

"A careful study of the Articles and the Prayer Book reveals the fact that Anglican Theology moves along certain definite and distinctive lines (see especially Articles VI, XI, XIX, XX, XXIII, XXV, XXIX, XXXI, XXXVI). These lines of doctrine distinguish it from Romanism on the one hand and from the extreme forms of Protestantism on the other. Subscription to the Articles should imply loyalty to these distinctive principles. It is not compatible with adherence to those opposing principles and practices which are distinctive of Rome on the one hand or of Anabaptism on the other. But within its own lines

---

[1] "How to change without loss of continuity, how to grow without loss of identity, how to be free in doctrine while clinging to a sacred past, how to meet the protean spirit of the times without bowing down to it, yet without alienating its rightful instincts and flouting its proper needs—these are the practical difficulties to the mind of a Church which would be true to the past, honest with the present, and helpful to the future" (Curtis, *ut supra*, p. 441).

[2] "Theology is a living science. The immense progress made in other departments of thought in the nineteenth century could not fail to show itself also in Theology. Biblical Criticism and Natural Science have thrown new light upon the problems of Theology. Men think in new categories, and it is inevitable that the definitions and propositions of the sixteenth century should be inadequate to express the best theological thought of our own day. But it is one thing to recognise the need for re-statement and quite another to put forth any re-statement which would command universal assent. This may be possible some day. When that day comes, let the task be taken in hand in humble dependence upon the guidance of the Spirit of God" (J. B. Harford, Article, "Articles of Religion," *The Prayer Book Dictionary*, p. 52).

[3] *Literature.*—Curtis, *ut supra*, Ch. XXV.

[4] Curtis, *ut supra*, p. 455.

there is scope for a genuine evolution of Anglican Theology in the light of present day knowledge."[1]

In the Gorham Judgment of 1850 the Court said that :—

" In all cases in which the Thirty-nine Articles, considered as a test, admit of different interpretations, it must be held that any sense of which the words fairly admit may be allowed, if that sense be not contradictory to something which the Church has elsewhere allowed or required."

Two recent incidents help to illustrate this. In October 1913, Bishop Gore wrote to *The Times* protesting against a statement of the President of the Baptist Union, in which the latter referred to the differences in the Church of England in spite of the fact that Churchmen used the same Prayer Book " and have signed the same Articles." The Bishop thereupon called attention to the fact that, as in 1865 the form of subscription was changed, it is now impossible to say that the clergy "sign the Articles." What they now do is to give a general assent to the doctrine contained in the three Formularies of the Articles, Prayer Book, and Ordinal. So that according to Bishop Gore it is impossible to describe this as " signing the Articles." On this, the then Bishop of Manchester, Dr. Knox, wrote, calling attention to the exact wording of the declaration made by ordinands and clergy about to be licensed or beneficed. The declaration refers not to doctrine in general, but to " the doctrine of the Church of England as therein set forth." Dr. Knox held that this distinction is important, because otherwise it might easily permit of some signing the declaration while holding *ex animo* all the doctrines of the Church of Rome, which doctrines they believe to be contained within the Anglican Formularies. Dr. Knox then added :—

" The very solemn questions put to ordinands imply that this Church and Realm has received and holds its own doctrine, and sacraments, and discipline, the said doctrine being ' set forth,' that is, honestly and definitely expounded in the Prayer Book and Articles. It is to this doctrine that assent is required, not to any form of doctrine loosely ' contained ' in those Formularies twisted to suit each man's taste as to what he chooses to believe."

All this illustrates and confirms the principle set forth above that assent involves a historical spirit. Bishops Knox and Henson are correct in emphasising the essential and characteristic features of Church of England doctrine as that to which the clergy are pledged, and as to the meaning of this there is no reasonable doubt. Whatever may have been the intention of those responsible for the change in 1865 as to the relaxation of subscription, it may be still questioned what precisely it does mean. The assertion that the doctrine is "agreeable to the Word of God " seems to leave the position practically very much as it was before. The

---

[1] J. B. Harford, *ut supra*, p. 52.

doctrine of the Church of England can only be found in its Formularies, and these are fundamentally the same as they were three centuries ago, and on the general subject it is impossible not to agree with the opinion that those who are called upon to preach the doctrines of the Church should be ready to proclaim them positively and heartily.[1] Nor does the Act of 1865 fundamentally alter the truth of our Church historian when he says :—

" Subscription to the Articles has been exacted with the hope of securing uniformity of doctrine in those churchmen who deliberately assume the office of public teachers. It accordingly involves their own appropriation of the Articles as the exponent of their individual opinions—so far, at least, as such opinions bear on subjects which have been determined by authority in that code of doctrine ; and, while pledging every clergyman to full and positive faith, subscription is the act by which he also formally renounces errors and corruptions which are there repudiated or proscribed."[2]

Creeds in the past have been either normative or apologetic. Apologetic Creeds will be needed to the end of time in order that Christianity may be stated in terms of current thought. Normative Creeds are mainly for the use of teachers, describing the limits in which they may and should move, and if they are regarded as landmarks, not as goals, they will always be useful, if not essential. One concluding caution may be given :—

" If the Creeds represent *Catholic* Doctrine, the Catechism contains elementary and the Articles more advanced *Anglican* Doctrine, and with these last may be grouped the incidental statements in the Prayer Book. It would be well if preachers and teachers avoided such expressions as ' The Church,' or ' The whole Church teaches . . .' when enunciating Doctrine not covered by these. What they affirm may be some truth contained in Scripture, or taught by the Primitive Church, but which has not found place in our Formularies ; but it may be some doubtful interpretation, or later tradition. It is, of course, perfectly legitimate to cite the Mediæval Church, or St. Thomas Aquinas, on points of Doctrine, but it is not legitimate to give forth *dicta* carrying no higher authority as if they had the endorsement of the whole Catholic Church, or the ratification of our own branch of it. Much prejudice against ' Church teaching ' would be

---

[1] "In an irreligious and latitudinarian age, an opinion was started, that the Articles were only Articles of peace, that is, that those who signed them only engaged not to contradict their assertions. This appears to me to be no better than a transparent fallacy, by which persons, whose worldly interest, as tutors or incumbents, required their conformity to this standard of doctrine, endeavoured to pacify their consciences. Such when they preach must at best be silent on tenets, on which they dissent from the judgment of the Church to which they profess to adhere; but what society would be satisfied with neutrality? Surely Churchmen have a right to demand, that the doctrines of their Church should not merely be not opposed, but that they should be explained and enforced" (Macbride, *Lectures on the Articles*, p. 36 f.).

[2] Hardwick, *ut supra*, p. 222. See also Article, "Subscription to Articles," *Protestant Dictionary*, p. 716 f.; *The Declaration of Assent*, by the late Bishop of Gloucester (Dr. Gibson).

avoided if those who speak for the Church would with more uniform care distinguish : (*a*) what all Christians agree to find in the New Testament ; (*b*) what the Catholic Church has enshrined in her Creeds ; (*c*) those elementary truths which have always been taught, and underlie the common worship, rites, and sacraments of the Church ; (*d*) that wider range of truth which the English Church has soberly and with restraint defined in her Articles and incidentally in the Prayer Book ; (*e*) such further truths drawn from Scripture as are agreeable to the foregoing ; (*f*) such alleged truths as at least appear to be at variance with Catholic or Anglican formularies, though a court of law would not necessarily regard them as excluded ; (*g*) Doctrines admitted to contravene both the letter and spirit of the formularies."[1]

[1] G. Harford, Article, "Doctrine," *The Prayer Book Dictionary*, p. 290.

APPENDIX

ARTICLE I.—THE PERSONALITY OF GOD

ONE of the most important questions, perhaps the most important, in modern theology is the Divine Personality, and that God is personal is, as already seen, the only possible position for theists. Modern investigation into the meaning of Personality should help in understanding and stating the theistic position more accurately and effectively. One line of thought tends to show that the old idea of isolation in personality is not correct, but that, on the contrary, personality can only be fully realised in association with other personalities. If this is correct, if human personality involves and implies fellowship, then it must be as true of the highest personality as of the lowest, and therefore of God as well as of man. How this may be can be studied in some valuable material now available. As an introduction an article should be read which appeared in the *London Quarterly Review* for April 1911 (Vol. I, Fifth Series, p. 280), entitled, "The Personality of God," by the Rev. A. T. Burbridge. In addition to the works referred to in this article reference should be made to the article on "The Trinity," by the Archbishop of Armagh in Hastings' *Dictionary of Christ and the Gospels*. See also *The Philosophy of Religion*, by Dr. Galloway. The subject may also be studied in the author's *The Holy Spirit of God* (chap. xviii).

ARTICLE II.—THE FATHERHOOD OF GOD

The question of the Atonement raises the problem of the relation of our Lord's sacrifice to the biblical doctrine of the Fatherhood of God. How are the two to be reconciled ? Is there not something incongruous in the thought of the attitude of fatherhood and that of a propitiatory sacrifice ? The solution of the problem will be found in a careful consideration of the true doctrine of the Divine Fatherhood.

I.—THE BIBLE TEACHING ON THE DIVINE FATHERHOOD

The terms Fatherhood of God and Brotherhood of Man are used freely in the present time, but often without due thought and care. It is, therefore, well to ask ourselves how far they contain truth and wherein they suggest what is untrue. The doctrine of the Fatherhood of God is not a truth of natural religion. We see the Divine power, providence, and glory in nature, but not Fatherhood. While love, goodness, truth, and providence are necessarily elements of Fatherhood, they do not belong solely thereto. For this reason men could hardly have imagined the Fatherhood of God, and as a fact they never did do so, for universal Fatherhood necessarily implies universal brotherhood, and such an idea was utterly alien from ancient thought.

In the Old Testament the Divine Fatherhood is found in connection with Israel only, and although it is seen quite clearly there, it is involved in and limited to the Divine covenant with the Hebrews (Exod. iv. 22 f. ; Deut. xiv. 1 ; Psa. lxxxix. 26). The reference in Psa. ciii. 13 is to similarity alone and not to relationship, and even so it is associated with pity and fear, not with love and fellowship. A nearer approach to the doctrine of universal Fatherhood may be seen in such passages as Isa. lxiii. 16 and lxiv. 8, but even there the thought is associated with the Divine Creatorship.

When we turn to the New Testament the doctrine of a Divine Fatherhood is absolutely clear. " The doctrine of the New Testament assumed such different proportions as almost to amount to a new revelation."[1] No longer is God regarded merely as calling forth awe and majesty, but also, and chiefly, is revealed in His nearness, fellowship, and love. God is seen to love man as a perfect Father loves His children (Rom. viii. 15, 16; 1 John iii. 1).

II.—THE MEANING OF THE DIVINE FATHERHOOD

It can only be understood properly in the light of human relationship, for to us all other senses than this must be derivative and metaphorical. It is true that the Divine Fatherhood is not exactly the same as human, and yet the applications of the Divine must be so related to the human as to give a true conception of God. Now the essence of Fatherhood is its relation to sonship, and *vice versa*. They are correlatives, and it is only in this mutual relationship that the terms have any intelligibility. This necessary relationship is always asserted in the New Testament in the various uses of the term " Father," and it is true universally, whatever may be the precise meaning of Fatherhood and sonship. If, for example, we speak of God's universal Fatherhood in creation, we at once think of its correlative in the universal sonship of humanity by creation. If we think of God's spiritual Fatherhood as potential we at once conceive of spiritual sonship as potential. And if we refer to the actual spiritual Fatherhood of God to believers we at once associate with this the actual sonship of believers. Thus there is a strict parallelism between Fatherhood and sonship at all points and in every sense. The idea that God is the Father of all men but that all are not sons is unthinkable.

[1] Sanday, Article, "God," Hastings' *Bible Dictionary*, p. 208.

There are three uses of Fatherhood in the New Testament. (*a*) God is described as the Father of our Lord Jesus Christ. This relationship between God the Father and God the Son is unique and exclusive, for in this Sonship no creature has a part. No one is " Son " as Christ is, and for this reason He never associates us with Himself by speaking of " Our Father." He always distinguishes between His Sonship and ourselves, as when He speaks of the Father of Me and the Father of you (John xx. 17). (*b*) God is also spoken of as the Father of the regenerate in Christ. All who believe in Christ as Saviour and Lord have the right to say, " Blessed be the God and Father of our Lord Jesus Christ," for their sonship is inseparable from the love wherewith the Father loves Christ (John i. 12 ; Rom. viii. 15 ; Gal. iii. 26). (*c*) He may be called the Father of man in general by reason of universal creation and benevolence. This must be the meaning of St. Paul's teaching at Athens, " Made of one [blood] ; we are also His offspring " (Acts xvii. 26, 28). In the first of these three instances the love of the Father for the Son is ineffable and infinite. In the second the love of God is peculiar to the saints as " in Christ." In the third the love of God extends to all mankind, " God so loved the world."

There is no real difference as to the first and second of these instances ; only as to the third, and yet even here the difference is not so much as to Fatherhood as to sonship. The question is whether all are sons in the same sense as God is Father. If this is so, are we to understand the sonship literally or figuratively ? In a word, is it possible to think of Fatherhood without sonship ? Now, to be sons there must be some resemblance to the father, and this can only be physical, or mental, or moral. Children are not created such, for creation by itself is not necessarily paternity. A creator is not a father simply because he has created, and in Scripture the sonship of creation is associated with the term " God," not with " Father." This may be seen in regard to angels (Job xxxviii. 7), and to Adam (Luke iii. 38).

It follows, therefore, that the true bond between son and father must be ethical, and since there is no such ethical bond between all men and God, the inevitable result is that sonship can only be a capacity or a possibility. Yet capacity is not sonship. The fundamental element is the experienced relation of children to a Heavenly Father. This is the truth which Jesus Christ lived, and it is only those who live in a similar manner as the children of the Father in heaven in whom this foundation is laid. This Christian character does not depend merely on the belief of the doctrine that God is the Father of us, but on the loving acceptance of that truth as the practical and controlling principle of our lives.

III.—THE NEW TESTAMENT REVELATION OF THE DIVINE FATHERHOOD

1. When we study the teaching of the New Testament on the Divine Fatherhood we must look first at the Gospels and then at the Epistles.

21

Omitting all references to Christ, there are only a few places in the Gospels where the term " The Father " is not limited to our Lord. Thus, in John iv. 21-23, it may be questioned whether the reference is to all men or to worshippers alone. For this reason we must decide by general New Testament usage. A careful consideration of the Sermon on the Mount will show that the application is to a specific body, the disciples, and not to all men (Matt. v. 1), and it may be said without question that in the Gospels there is no unequivocal statement of Universal Fatherhood. When we turn to the Epistles the nearest approach to Universal Fatherhood is found in Eph. iii. 14, 15; iv. 6; Heb. xii. 9. In the former two passages the context seems to indicate a reference clearly to the spiritual relationship of believers, while in the latter the antithesis between human and Divine Fatherhood is clear. In any case, it is noteworthy that the clearest teaching on this subject is found in St. Paul, not in Christ. It must surely be regarded as strange that our Lord's teaching is not clear on a point on which so many modern writers lay stress.

Similarly, in regard to sonship we must study both Gospels and Epistles. The Sermon on the Mount is quite clear about the necessity of ethical faithfulness in order to Divine sonship (Matt. v. 9, 45), while the teaching of the Fourth Gospel points beyond all question to a limited sonship (John i. 12). The only reference to universal sonship in the Gospels is found in connection with Adam (Luke iii. 38), and even this is associated with " God " not " Father." Outside the Gospels the nearest approach to universal sonship is found in the words of St. Paul in Acts xvii. 28, 29, but even here it is significant that the terms refer to kinship rather than to childhood, and to God not to the Father. Bishop Westcott remarks that " there is as far as it appears no case where a fellow-man, as man, is called a brother in the New Testament."[1] Thus what is understood as the brotherhood of humanity is not a New Testament idea, which is only concerned with a spiritual brotherhood in Christ.

The parable of the Prodigal Son is sometimes urged in support of the doctrine of universal Divine Fatherhood, and, indeed, it may be said to be almost the only warrant for it. It may be questioned, however, whether Christ was likely to contradict in the parable the rest of His clear teaching. Should not the teaching interpret the parable, not the parable the teaching? The parable is one of three indicative of God's attitude to men, or, rather, of Christ's vindication of Himself in opposition to the murmurings of the Pharisees (Luke xv. 1, 2). The three parables must be taken together if they are to be properly understood, but we do not think of God as a real shepherd in the first parable, or a real woman in the second. Indeed, the same lesson would have been taught in the third parable if the relationship of man and wife had been given. Then, too, the literalness defeats itself, for if the prodigal represents all men, who are to be understood by the elder brother and the citizens? The fact is

[1] *The Epistles of St. John*, p. 55.

that the parable turns on one point only, the attitude and action of Christ's pity and grace, and the omissions prove nothing, since there are other fundamental doctrines equally lacking, like Propitiation, Resurrection, the Holy Spirit, and the New Life. And thus, while the parable is evidently appropriate for its purpose, it is only a figure of speech and cannot be fairly used as the foundation of a metaphysical relation of God to man. To deduce a dogma from a figure of speech is perilous, for it is clear that the parable was not intended as a complete account of the principles and method of reconciliation. Thus the Father was not seeking the son, but only waiting for him, and the son, although a son by creation, had to repent and return as a lost sinner. His natural sonship did not suffice without these. If Christ intended Himself in all three by the figures of the Shepherd, the Woman, and the Father, the Fatherhood of God is entirely out of the question. But, on the other hand, if God the Father is intended, then there is no mention of Christ at all. Thus the argument is precarious, and it is quite impossible to infer that what is omitted is needless and what is inserted is complete.

It is, therefore, plain that while we may regard God as in one sense the Father of all men (by creation), in another and eternally vital sense we cannot, because His complete Fatherhood is only possible through Jesus Christ. The entrance of sin into the world severed the spiritual relationship between God and men as Father and children, and this fact is not usually taken into account by those who think of God as equally the Father of all. It is impossible to overlook our Lord's teaching about those who are " the children of the devil " (John viii. 41-44), thereby indicating a very definite limitation of Fatherhood. Besides, Fatherhood is not the sole idea of Godhead, as a careful consideration of the Bible as a whole clearly teaches. The judicial and kingly aspects must find their place, and, as already seen, Fatherhood and sonship are strictly correlative in every sense, for a Fatherhood without a sonship is unintelligible. It is also significant that Fatherhood in the New Testament is associated with holiness and fear (1 Pet. i. 17), and the only epithets ever used by our Lord in speaking of the Father were " holy " and " righteous " (John xvii. 11, 25). It is only possible to teach the universal Fatherhood of God by ignoring or rejecting the redemption of Christ, for men know the Father only through the work of the Son. " No man cometh unto the Father but by Me." " If ye had known Me, ye should have known My Father also." Universal Fatherhood and sonship tend to cut the cord of evangelistic work and make redemptive effort perilous. It suggests that there is no need of Atonement, for it tends to dispense with it, regarding sin as a trifle and God as good-natured and sentimental.

It is, therefore, essential to state that creation does not constitute men sons in the spiritual sense, for New Testament sonship is based on redemption and regeneration, while the doctrine of universal sonship rests either on a denial of the Fall, or on the assumption of universal regeneration, both of which are unwarranted by Scripture and experience. If the universal Fatherhood of God and the universal sonship of man are assumed, how is it that there is not a single clear instance of either truth in the New Testament ? Surely the truth of our adoption clearly shows that there is some state from which, and another state into which, men are taken. The very fact of " adoption " both socially and spiritually argues against the idea of an universal Fatherhood. By limiting the Fatherhood of God we secure its full meaning and value, for there is no solace or inspiration in telling a sinner that he is a child of God unless we mean that he is potentially one, and needs redemption and regeneration in order to become one in actual fact. Thus the Fatherhood of God has a place in the lives of those who have accepted Him in Christ, which it cannot possibly have in the life of humanity in general, and what is known as the " Brotherhood of Man " is in reality only a physical relationship, for men are brothers in spirit only when Christ is their life and God is their spiritual Father. When these truths are understood we see at once the true relationship and spiritual bearing of the Atonement of Christ on the New Testament doctrine of the Fatherhood of God.

ARTICLE VI.—BIBLE DIFFICULTIES

This question often affects our view of the authority and inspiration of Holy Scripture, and while it is impossible to deal with the subject in detail in the present work a few general suggestions may be offered. When once we have become convinced on adequate evidence that the Bible is the Word of God every difficulty found should be judged in the light of this antecedent conviction. In particular, the question should be considered whether difficulties are not inherent in the very fact of revelation. If the New Testament is the historic record of contemporary writers who were competent to testify to facts which they knew, their evidence ought to have full weight, as assuring us of the truth of the facts, and, as it has often been pointed out, since there was no secrecy, but full publicity by the circulation of these records among people who knew the facts, the Christians of the first century are really witnesses who corroborate the truth of the New Testament, a testimony often sealed by persecution and even death.

The supreme question for ordinary life is whether the Bible is trustworthy, for if so, the facts must be true, and if the historic proof is regarded as adequate, then no subsequent considerations ought to be allowed to counterbalance that proof, since no antecedent probability or improbability can affect this in the face of the evidence, so that the true position to be adopted is that difficulties are to be judged in the light of the evidence, and, as a great textual critic, Tregelles, says, " No difficulty connected with a proved fact can invalidate the fact itself." It is well known that if a scientist finds certain phenomena in nature involving variation from a great general law he does not thereupon abandon his general conclusion. Nor does a theist give up belief in a Creator because of the difficulties he observes in creation and nature. Since there are difficulties in nature and providence, and since revelation is presumably from the same source there may be difficulties there also. This is the great and convincing principle of Butler's Analogy. If the difficulties are not such as would invalidate the truthfulness of other writers they should have no more weight than in those cases. Further, the question continually arises whether the discrepancies are real or apparent, whether there is absolutely no explanation, or whether we only are unable to solve the problem. The words of Dean Farrar are noteworthy : " The widest learning and the acutest ingenuity of scepticism have never pointed to one complete and demonstrable error of fact or doctrine in the Old or New Testament."[1]

Thus it is correct to say that a Bible without difficulties would be itself the greatest difficulty of all, for such a work, presenting no problems and creating no perplexities, would impose a great strain on faith and really provide a weapon for scepticism. The difficulties of the Bible are usually divided into three classes : alleged discrepancies (a) with science; (b) with history; and (c) with ethics. In regard to the first, it will often be found that the discrepancy lies between some interpretation of Scripture and some theory of science, either or both of which may be incorrect, for the general harmony between the Bible and Science is as true as it is remarkable. The question of historical difficulties may be tested at many points in connection with Archæology, and both in regard to the Old and the New Testament, researches during the last fifty years have done much to confirm the truth of the statements of Scripture. The works of one writer, Sir William Ramsay, will suffice to indicate the truth of this contention. The ethical difficulties are chiefly concerned with the Old Testament and are largely due to the failure to recognise the progress of the revelation therein embodied.

Almost every difficulty can be solved by the consideration of the manifest advance of the Old Testament from the elementary to the complex, from the imperfect to the more perfect. Further considerations on this last point will be found in the author's *Methods of Bible Study*. It may also fairly be said that we are not called upon to answer every conceivable objection. It ought to be sufficient to prove the truth of Christianity, and this is very different from meeting all possible difficulties.

ARTICLE IX.—INFANT SALVATION

It is unfortunate that the problem of sinfulness has been closely and almost solely connected with children instead of adults. This complicates the situation when the question of guilt is considered. Most theories

[1] Article, "Inspiration," *Cassell's Biblical Educator*, Vol. I, p. 207.

turn on this point, but it is unwise to shift the emphasis from adults to children, of whom the Bible says so little. Like Baptism, sinfulness should be considered first in the adult, as referring to the normal condition, and only afterwards in children, as to whom the question of personal guilt in the common sense of the term cannot apply. The difficulty lies in the fact that children are sinners, involved in the sin of the race through the headship of Adam, while they are personally guiltless until they in conscious and wilful transgression make themselves personally responsible and liable.

The question of Infant Salvation has, therefore, naturally been prominent in discussions since the time of Augustine. To Augustine, infants dying after Baptism were saved, but if dying unbaptised they were lost, though incurring only the lighter punishment.[1] The explanation of this view is that Augustine is occupied with two lines of thought which he never reconciled : his doctrine of Grace and his doctrine of the Church.[2] One of these lines issued in the Reformation doctrine of Grace and the other found its development in the Roman Catholic theology of the Church.[3]

To the earliest of the Fathers salvation was by grace, and this included infants, but later the doctrine of grace became obscure, and the death of infants was regarded as an insoluble problem. As the Church and Kingdom tended to become identified in one visible organisation, the absolute necessity of Baptism for salvation was more and more emphasised, and thus infants who were not baptised could not be saved.[4] It was this view of the Church that Augustine inherited, and it led to his doctrine that no infant dying unbaptised could enter the Kingdom of Heaven. Pelagianism, with its denial of original sin and of punishment, nevertheless held that infants were outside the Kingdom of God, though obtaining eternal life. But the fundamental idea up to the time of Augustine was

[1] "This is the dark side of his soteriology. But it should be remembered that it was not his theology of grace, but the universal and traditional belief in the necessity of baptism for remission of sins, which he inherited in common with all of his time, that forced it upon him. The theology of grace was destined in the hands of his successors, who have rejoiced to confess that they were taught by him, to remove this stumbling-block also from Christian teaching; and if not to Augustine, it is to Augustine's theology that the Christian world owes its liberation from so terrible a tenet" (Warfield, *Two Studies in the History of Doctrine*, p. 137).
[2] "Augustine's doctrine of *the means of grace, i.e.* of the channels and circumstances of the conference of grace upon men, is the meeting point of two very dissimilar streams of thought—his doctrine of grace and his doctrine of the Church. Profound thinker as he was, within whose active mind was born an incredible multitude of the richest conceptions, he was not primarily a systematiser, and these divergent streams of thought rather conditioned each the purity of the other's development at this point than were thoroughly harmonised" (Warfield, *ut supra*, p. 135).
[3] "Despite the strong churchly element within the theology of Augustine, the development of which has produced the ecclesiasticism of Romish thought, it must be admitted that, on the side that is presented in the controversy against Pelagianism, it is in its essence distinctly anti-ecclesiastical. Its central thought was the immediate dependence of the individual on the grace of God in Jesus Christ" (Warfield, *ut supra*, p. 138)).
[4] Warfield, *ut supra*, p. 148.

that as saving grace could only come through baptism no unbaptised infant could be saved.

In the Middle Ages an endeavour was made to soften this severe doctrine under the influence of Semi-Pelagianism, and in the sixteenth century Roman Catholic writers advocated several opinions, though the general Roman Catholic view is that of the Council of Trent, which made Baptism necessary to salvation without any qualification.[1] This may be regarded as the usual Roman Catholic position to-day, though efforts have been made from time to time to mitigate it by the doctrine of Baptism by intention.

Luther's view was naturally affected by the general doctrine of grace and of the Church associated with the Reformation.[2] But this was connected with a doctrine of Baptism which emphasised its necessity for salvation, apart, of course, from special cases. Luther also emphasised a Baptism of intention. Yet Lutheran theologians have from the first differed considerably, and the idea suggested seems to be that of an unwillingness to speak definitely on the subject,[3] though without doing more than entertain a hope for the salvation of unbaptised infants.

The Anglican position needs careful attention because of the stages of growth among those who had to deal with the subject. In 1536 the Ten Articles explicitly taught that only baptised infants could be saved. "Infants and children dying in their infancy shall undoubtedly be saved thereby, and else not."[4]

This statement about the loss of all unbaptised infants is also found in what is known as the "Bishops' Book" of 1537. But in the "King's Book" of 1543 the final words, "and else not" are omitted. In the First Prayer Book of 1549, among the rubrics which precede the Order of Confirmation is the following :—

"And that no man shall think that any detriment shall come to children by deferring of their confirmation : he shall know for truth, that it is certain by God's Word, that children being baptised (if they depart out of this life in their infancy) are undoubtedly saved."

[1] "The Council of Trent thus made it renewed *de fide* that infants dying unbaptised incur damnation, though it left the way open for discussion as to the kind and amount of their punishment" (Warfield, *ut supra*, p. 155).
[2] "Men are not constituted members of Christ through the Church, but members of the Church through Christ: they are not made the members of Christ by baptism which the Church gives, but by faith, the gift of God; and baptism is the Church's recognition of this inner fact" (Warfield, *ut supra*, p. 166).
[3] "This cautious agnostic position has the best right to be called the historical Lutheran attitude on the subject. It is even the highest position thoroughly consistent with the genius of the Lutheran system and the stress which it lays on the means of grace. The drift in more modern times has, however, been decidedly in the direction of affirming the salvation of all that die in infancy, on grounds identical with those pleaded by this party from the beginning—the infinite mercy of God, the universality of the atonement, the inability of infants to resist grace, their guiltlessness of despising the ordinance, and the like" (Warfield, *ut supra*, p. 172).
[4] For the full text see Hardwick, *A History of the Articles of Religion*, p. 242.

In the Second Prayer Book of 1552 there was an alteration so as to make the latter portion read—

" That children being baptised have all things necessary for their salvation, and be undoubtedly saved."

No further alteration was made in the Prayer Book of 1559, but in the Prayer Book of 1662 the rubric was transferred to the end of the Order for the Public Baptism of Infants in the following form, which exists to-day :—

" It is certain by God's Word, that children which are baptised, dying before they commit actual sin, are undoubtedly saved."

It is noteworthy that the statement is not found in the Prayer Book used in the Protestant Episcopal Church in the United States. There does not seem to be any reason for supposing that the transference of the rubric from the Confirmation Service to that of Baptism in 1662 was intended to be reactionary. In the *Reformatio Legum* reference was made to the " scrupulous superstition " of the Roman Church in regard to the fate of infants dying unbaptised.[1] It is interesting and significant that this code of laws was, as we have seen, drawn up by a Commission presided over by Cranmer. In view of the Reformation doctrine that Baptism introduced the subject to a new sphere, it was natural to refer to infants as within that sphere, and it is never to be forgotten that extreme Reformers and the earliest Puritans raised no objection to the Prayer Book doctrine of regeneration, since, as already seen, it referred to the introduction into a new state or condition, not to the bestowal of a germ of life or a moral renovation in the modern sense. It should be noted that in the revision of 1552 the opening prayer in the Baptismal Office was brought practically into its present form, with the omission of the words, " And so save from perishing," and also a recasting of the entire tendency of the prayer. It is, therefore, not accurate to say that the Church of England expresses no hope for the salvation of infants who die unbaptised. It means that our formularies are limited to the simple statement about those who have presumably been brought within the covenant. The *Reformatio Legum* was issued by Archbishop Parker in 1571, and Becon, one of Cranmer's Chaplains, wrote very definitely and repeatedly on the subject of infant salvation in harmony with the statement of the *Reformatio Legum*. There seems to be no proof whatever that Cranmer ever changed his opinion.

The " Reformed " (or Swiss) view of this question was based on the

[1] "Illorum etiam impia videri debet scrupulosa superstitio, qui Dei gratiam et Spiritum Sanctum tantopere cum sacramentorum elementis colligant, ut plane affirment, nullum Christianorum infantem æternam salutem esse consecuturum, qui prius a morte fuerit occupatus, quam ad Baptismum adduci potuerit; quod longe secus habere judicamus" (*Reformatio Legum, De Baptismo*).

general doctrine of Divine grace, and was not limited by any idea of means of grace :—

" It is probable that Zwingli stood alone among the Reformers in his extension of salvation to all infants dying in infancy."[1]

But the question was involved in the doctrine of election and varied with different classes of Reformers. A few held Zwingli's view that death in infancy was one of the marks of election, and it is thought that Bishop Hooper was one of the earliest to adopt this position. At the very opposite extreme some few theologians holding that the only sure mark of election was faith taught that there was no real ground of conviction concerning the fate of infants. This position was subsequently condemned at the Synod of Dort. A third section held that all believers and their children are certainly saved, though the children of unbelievers, dying such, are certainly lost. Yet again, many held that not only was the salvation of the children of believers certain, but there was good reason for holding that as election and reprobation have no place in the unknown sphere of children, some infants of unbelievers were saved and some lost. But most adherents of the Reformed Churches held that the matter must be entirely left to the judgment of God, which would be just and holy. This view is found in conjunction with both hope and the absence of hope.[2] From all this it will be seen that the Reformed Churches have adopted practically the same position as that of the Church of England, apart from the question of baptism.

" The Reformed Confessions with characteristic caution refrain from all definition upon the negative side of this great question, and thus confine themselves to emphasising the gracious doctrine common to the whole body of Reformed thought."[3]

It will be seen, however, that, as mentioned above, the doctrine of infant salvation was involved in the doctrine of election, and the Reformed Churches held that the children of believers dying in infancy were saved, while declining to pronounce on the subject of the children of unbelievers. Later theologians, representing the Reformed Churches, seem to be united in the view that all who die in infancy are the children of God, not because of the absence of original sin, or freedom from guilt, but simply because God has chosen them in Christ.

But it may be pointed out that this view does not really solve the problem, and the best foundation for believing in the salvation of all infants is pretty certainly to be seen in the universality of the Atonement of Christ. No question of election should be allowed to enter. Infants

[1] Warfield, *ut supra*, p. 199.
[2] This sketch of Reformed views is summarised from Warfield's article, *ut supra*, pp. 203–211, to which this entire Note is deeply indebted.
[3] Warfield, *ut supra*, p. 213.

come into this world with the results of Adam's sin in them, and they are involved in the inherent sin of the race through the headship of our first parents. Whatever may be the meaning of St. Paul's word, " By the offence of one judgment was upon all men to condemnation," infants are assuredly included, but, on the other hand, they go out of this world equally associated with the work of the last Adam, the Lord from heaven. So that we can say of infants, " By the righteousness of One the free gift came upon all men to justification by Him." We must not forget that infants come into a world of grace as well as of sin, and the two parallel lines can never be overlooked. While there is, of course, no definite declaration in regard to the salvation of infants dying in infancy, all that we can infer from Scripture supports the view that they are saved on the ground of the Atonement of Christ, and this because although they were born in sin they were not actual transgressors of the Divine law.[1]

ARTICLE XIX.—THE WORD "CATHOLIC"

The Church of England, of course, distinguishes between particular Churches and the entire Church of Christ. The preface to the Prayer Book speaks of " the Church of England " and " the Catholick Church of Christ." The title of the Book of Common Prayer is to the same effect, and in Article XIX reference is made to particular Churches. The Preface to the Ordinal also has this important distinction. It is, therefore, essential to understand what is meant by the term " Catholic," as used in the Prayer Book.

Although the word is not found in Scripture, it is so familiar in phrases like " Catholic Church " and " Catholic Faith " that it calls for special notice, more particularly as it is often misunderstood. It comes from καθ' ὅλος, " throughout the whole," and its fundamental conception is universality ; but this idea has been variously applied in the use of the word " Catholic Church." The original idea was that of geographical diffusion. The meaning was simply that of universality as in the phrase, " Thy Holy Church universal." It indicated that Christianity was a religion intended for universal diffusion, that all men were eligible for membership. This is the meaning of the word when first used by Ignatius at the beginning of the second century, " Where Jesus Christ may be, there is the Catholic Church."[2] The word as thus used is essentially expressive of the supreme purpose of Christianity as a world-wide religion. The same idea is conveyed by the word when it appears

---

[1] This important subject can be studied in the valuable article by Warfield, already mentioned, and also in *The Buried Nations of the Infant Dead*, by Pratt (published by The Pratt Co., Hackensack, New Jersey, U.S.A.).

[2] Bishop Lightfoot, *Commentary on Ignatius* (Epistle to Smyrna, Ch. VIII, Note); Swete, *The Holy Catholic Church*, pp. 33–41.

next in the letter of the Church of Smyrna on the occasion of the martyrdom of Polycarp, addressed " To all the congregation of the Holy and Catholic Church in every place."[1]

This idea of universality was subsequently followed by the thought of *doctrinal purity and completeness* as a mark of Catholicity. By accurate and complete doctrine was understood that which most clearly adhered to the teaching of Christ and His Apostles. This extension of the meaning of the word was directed probably against Judaism, and certainly against heresy. The rise of heresies and schisms seemed to demand this application of the word to describe those who held fast to the complete truth of New Testament Christianity. As Lightfoot points out, the original meaning of the word was " universal " as opposed to " particular," and then later " orthodox " as opposed to " heretical." " The truth was the same everywhere, the heresies were partial, scattered, localised, isolated." We see this secondary meaning of the term as applied to doctrinal correctness and completeness in the phrase " the Catholic Faith."[2]

Still later came a third application of the term. Geographical explanation and doctrinal purity became expressed in *Church unity and fellowship*. At the outset fellowship was necessarily congregational; then it was widened to include associations of congregations in a town or district. Later came the idea of diocesan fellowship, and still later the fellowship connected with associations of dioceses called patriarchates. Last of all came the great divisions of Eastern and Western Christianity, each with its own view of Catholicity. The word " Catholic," as Greek by derivation, naturally came into use first in the East,[3] and did not appear in a Western Creed until nearly the end of the fifth century. Dr. Swete points out that the Church of Rome was long indifferent to the word, perhaps because she did not feel the need of support from the idea of Christian solidarity. There was a narrowness about its use by Rome, and it came to mean only those parts of Christendom that accepted the Roman supremacy. This was probably influenced by the idea of a State or Imperial Church as distinct from the sects which were not authorised by the Roman Government. In the East, Catholicity took the form of orthodox belief combined with the autonomy of certain Churches, while in the West it took the form of ecclesiastical unity in the Papacy. The Reformed Churches of the sixteenth century naturally adopted a position practically identical with that of Eastern Christendom in insisting upon the independence of particular Churches while preserving all the essentials of the Catholic Faith of Christendom.[4]

These three associated ideas of geographical diffusion, doctrinal purity, and ecclesiastical fellowship are all illustrated in the Prayer Book by the phrases, " the Catholic Faith," " the good estate of the Catholic Church," " all who profess and call themselves Christians," " all them that do

---

[1] Bishop Lightfoot, *ut supra.* [2] Swete, *ut supra*, p. 35. [3] Swete, *ut supra*, p. 38.
[4] Field, *Of the Church*, Vol. I, pp. 89, 90. See also, *Life of Archbishop Benson*, Vol. II, p. 624.

confess Thy Holy Name," " Thine elect in one communion and fellowship in the mystical body of Thy Son," " the Holy Catholic Church."

It will thus be seen that it involves a false antithesis to speak of Christians as either "Catholic" or "Protestant." The word "Protestant" is not
opposed to what is Catholic, but to what is distinctively Roman Catholic,
that is, to the perversion of Catholic truth and departure from true
Catholicity. The various Evangelical Reformed Churches, in accepting
those fundamental doctrines of the Christian Faith which are found in
the New Testament, rightly claim the true title of " Catholic "; and it is
noteworthy that in the Bidding Prayer these words occur, " Ye shall
pray for Christ's whole Catholic Church, that is, for the whole congregation of Christ's people dispersed throughout the world."[1]

So that we now have the interesting and significant feature of Evangelical Churches all over the world to-day returning to the original idea
of the word " Catholic " as expressed in Ignatius, " Where Jesus Christ
may be, there is the Catholic Church."[2]   The word is, therefore, most
appropriate as testifying to the world-wide extension of the Gospel in
the purpose of God. As Christianity is intended for all men, so all
Christians form the Catholic Church. The sole use of the term
" Catholic " by any one body of Christians is obviously a contradiction
in terms. The Church Catholic is the Church universal, not any one
Church, however large or well known. In its Catholicity all differences
and distinctions, whether of race or position or capacity, are unified and
utilised in the one fellowship of the saints in Christ Jesus.[3]

ARTICLE XXII.—PRAYERS FOR THE DEAD

It seems impossible to consider Purgatory without giving some attention to Prayers for the Dead. The statement is sometimes made that as
the Article in its original draft contained condemnation of Prayers for the
Dead, which was omitted before the Articles were published, " the
Church of England deliberately abstained from seeming to express any
condemnation of the practice of praying for the departed."[4]   But whatever may have been the cause of the omission, it may be questioned
whether this inference is warranted in view of the facts to be adduced.
The subject was one of great prominence at the time of the Reformation,

---

[1] Canons of 1604, No. 55.
[2] "For its theological content the *locus classicus* is the edict of the three Emperors—
Gratian, Valentinian II, and Theodosius, A.D. 380; 'we will that those who embrace
this (the Trinitarian) Creed be called Catholic Christians'; and in this sense the great
Churches of the Reformation, the Church of England among them, are Catholic"
(Review of Dr. Swete's book, *ut supra, Nation,* 11th December 1915).
[3] For a fuller description of the word and its bearing on several modern questions,
reference may be made to the author's *Catholic Faith,* pp. 340-360.
[4] Gibson, *The Thirty-nine Articles,* p. 538.

and it has obtained a good deal of attention in recent years. It is, therefore, a matter of real importance to discover what Holy Scripture and the
Church of England teach on the subject.

I.—THE MEANING OF PRAYERS FOR THE DEAD

Are they prayers for the unconverted dead ? This is not the case in
the Church of Rome. That Church holds as firmly as we do the finality
of this life as an opportunity for accepting or rejecting Christ. Nor is
it so, generally, in the case of Anglicans who pray for the dead. They,
too, realise the force of the appeal to " now " and " to-day " as the
accepted and only time of salvation. Prayer for the dead could be understood if we believed in another probation, in another opportunity after
this life, but this is not the teaching of the Romish Church or of the
majority of the extreme Anglicans. It should never be overlooked that
prayer for the dead does not necessarily involve belief in Purgatory.
Such prayer was offered ages before the doctrine of Purgatory arose,
and is practised to-day in the Greek Church, which rejects Purgatory
as Roman. Prayer for the dead implies belief in benefit accruing in
some way without any belief in mitigation of Purgatorial suffering.

The prayers must, therefore, be for the Christian dead. This is the
meaning of the practice in the Roman Church, and in the case of those
in the Anglican Church who adopt the custom. They both pray for
the converted dead and say, " May they rest in peace, and may light
perpetual shine on them."

But why should we pray for the Christian dead ? They are " with
Christ " (Phil. i. 23) in conscious fellowship. They are " present with
the Lord " (2 Cor. v. 8). They are " with Him in Paradise " (Luke
xxiii. 43). They are blessed, for " Blessed are the dead which die in the
Lord " (Rev. xiv. 13). The New Testament outlook concerning the
blessed dead is one of joy, peace and expectation ; we are to remember
their past life, imitate their faith, and praise God for them. It seems
to be unnecessary and even cruel to pray, " May they rest in peace," for
it reflects on their present peace, joy, and satisfaction in the immediate
presence of Christ our Lord.

II.—THE FOUNDATION OF PRAYERS FOR THE DEAD

Prayer must be based on God's Revelation. Prayer finds its warrant
in promise. It is evident that prayer, if it is to be real and definite, must
be based upon the Word of God as its warrant and encouragement. The
Bible is accordingly full of teaching on prayer. There are examples of
prayer, encouragements to prayer, models of prayer, and records of
answers to prayer. The Bible is the embodiment of God's revelation
in Christ, and as such it is at once the foundation and guide of our prayers.

God's revelation is thus the source and spring of our human response, and prayer is based on God's promises as revealed in His Word. At the same time Holy Scripture is the safeguard and limitation of all prayer, for it is obvious that we cannot pray for everything that might conceivably come into our minds, but only for those things that are included in the revealed will of God. Thus, when our Lord said, " Whatsoever ye shall ask the Father in My Name, He will give it you " (John xiv. 23), the " whatsoever " is limited by the phrase " in My Name," which teaches us that it is only as we ask *in union with God's revealed will* that we can really pray and be assured of answers. We can only pray definitely or satisfactorily in so far as we have the Divine warrant for praying. This practice must therefore be based, not on sentiment, but on Scripture. In a matter of this kind it ought to be clear that our desires are not a reliable guide. God, who is love, must understand our yearnings, and we may be sure He would not keep back anything profitable to us. And yet, as we shall see, there is not a single command or promise or example in Scripture. May we not argue fairly on this point from the silence of the Bible ? As God has not revealed Himself in regard to this matter it is impossible to pray with assurance, because prayer must be based on Revelation.

Revelation is clearly for this life. God's Word is almost silent as to the details of the future life, and absolutely silent as to any relation of prayer to that life. As to the unconverted, the present life is decisive and final in relation to opportunity; and as to the converted, while there is doubtless growth in the Kingdom of God in the state after death, as there must be to all eternity, yet no one syllable is to be found in God's Word to tell us that our prayers can either effect or affect that growth. If they see the face of Christ, they surely do not need our prayers. And our knowledge of that life is so small that prayer cannot be intelligent, only sentimental, uninformed. " Thy Kingdom come " is not prayer for the dead, because we say, " on earth as in Heaven." Prayer for others is bounded by this life, and after this, prayer is swallowed up in praise.

Prayer for the dead is, of course, quite intelligible on the Roman Catholic theory of Purgatory, though, as already seen, it is not inevitably bound up with it. If souls pass from here imperfect and need purification for eternal glory it is easy to understand how, according to Roman principles, prayer can be made for them. But with the rejection of the idea of a Purgatory, the practice of prayers for the dead tends to fall to the ground. But whether connected or not, the practice is not warranted by Scripture or our Church. Even those who associate prayers for the dead with the Communion of Saints are compelled to limit their prayers to the most general terms, and thereby entirely to alter the idea of prayer from the definite petitions and intercessions which we use on earth. The only justification of prayers for the dead would be to pray for them as definitely and pointedly as when they were here. But this would be to deny the teaching of the New Testament concerning their joy and blessedness in the presence of Christ.

The question then arises, Is there anything in the Bible which includes the Christian dead in our prayers ? Can we discover anything in Holy Scripture from which we may infer that prayer for the dead comes within the scope of the promise—" Whatsoever ye shall ask in My Name " ?

Can we find any instance of prayer for the dead in the Old Testament ? Not one.

Is there any example or precept as to prayer for the dead in the Gospels and in the life and works of our Lord ? Not one.

Can we discover any example or encouragement in the life of the early Church as recorded in the Acts of the Apostles ? Not one.

Is there to be found any clear testimony to prayer for the dead in the Apostolic Epistles ? Not one.

Is there any instance of prayer for the dead in the Revelation ? Not one.

The following passages are sometimes used to justify the practice :—

" Everyone shall be salted with fire, and every sacrifice shall be salted with salt " (Mark ix. 49). But what is here on the subject before us ? The text is clearly a symbolical statement concerning spiritual discipline in this life.

" The fire shall try every man's work of what sort it is " (1 Cor. iii. 13). But the whole passage clearly refers to the testing of Christian faithfulness at the judgment-seat of Christ ; there is not a hint of prayer for the dead.

" Baptised for the dead " (1 Cor. xv. 29). But whatever be the true interpretation, there is no reference to prayer.

" He went and preached unto the spirits in prison " (1 Pet. iii. 19). This passage, whatever it means, has no reference to the Christian dead, but to certain spirits " which sometime were disobedient."

" The Gospel was preached also to them that are dead " (1 Pet. iv. 6). Whatever interpretation we give to this passage, there is no reference to prayer for the Christian dead.

The only passage in the New Testament that can be adduced as a possible warrant is 2 Tim. i. 18. It is urged that Onesiphorus was dead when St. Paul wrote. The elements of the interpretation of this passage are somewhat as follows :—

(1) It is entirely uncertain whether Onesiphorus was alive or dead. No one can possibly decide one way or the other. This is not a very hopeful way of deriving an important doctrine from the passage.

(2) The assumption that he was dead is, therefore, entirely gratuitous. In 1 Cor. i. 16 and xvi. 15, compared with Romans xvi. 10, 11, we see that households can be referred to without the head of the house being dead.

(3) Then the view that Onesiphorus was dead probably runs foreign

to the context. If we compare verse 15, we see that some had forsaken St. Paul, but that Onesiphorus had not been ashamed of the prisoner and his chain (vv. 16-18); then Timothy is urged to the same boldness (cf. chap. ii. 1, " Therefore "). There is nothing here to warrant the idea of the death of Onesiphorus.

(4) Even supposing Onesiphorus was dead, it might be possible to express a wish like this for a friend without in the least admitting the principles on which prayer for the dead can be taken seriously. Dr. Swete, believing that Onesiphorus was dead, points out that, even so, the prayer is " for his acceptance in the day of Christ and not for his well-being in the intermediate life."[1]

Looking over the entire revelation of God we cannot help observing two things: (a) In the Levitical code, there are minute instructions as to all sorts of sacrifices, and yet, with sacrifices for the dead familiar all around in heathen religions, not a hint is given about them in the Mosaic law. (b) The New Testament, while so emphatic on the efficacy of prayer under all circumstances of life, never once extends the practice to the next world, even though often alluding to the dead and the future life.

From Scripture, therefore, the one fount of essential truth, we have no warrant, no foundation for Prayers for the Dead, but everything that looks in the opposite direction.

We have next to consider :—

III.—THE EARLY HISTORY OF PRAYERS FOR THE DEAD

It is generally thought that the Jews prayed for the dead, and that a passage in 2 Macc. xii. points in that direction. Jewish liturgies of the present day certainly have them. But it has been pointed out[2] that the passage in Maccabees does not necessarily involve Prayers for the Dead, nor is it certain that the present Jewish liturgies are of pre-Christian date. In any case, however, we have no record of our Lord and His Apostles observing such a custom, and it would be very precarious to base a Christian practice of such moment on merely Jewish grounds even if we were sure of them. Nor are we justified in arguing in support of the practice from Christ's silence.

In the Christian Church it is to be carefully noted that the earliest form of the phrase indicated by R.I.P. was not " requiescat," but " requiescit," which states the fact, " he rests in peace." The earliest inscriptions of the Catacombs, too, are " in pace," " in Christo," etc., without any prayer.[3] All primitive history points to the remarkable joy

[1] Swete, *The Holy Catholic Church.*
[2] C. H. H. Wright, *The Intermediate State*, pp. 28-43. See also an article in *The Expositor* for April 1915, by the Rev. J. W. Hunkin, which arrives independently at the same conclusion.
[3] De Rossi, *Inscriptiones Christianæ urbis Romæ septimo sæculo antiquiores*, Vol. I; B. Scott, *The Contents and Teachings of the Catacombs*, p. 159.

and definite certainty associated with Christian funerals, the thought of the beloved one being with the Lord overpowering all else. The future had no shadows, and praise, not prayer, was the attitude of these believers.

Dr. H. B. Swete, himself in favour of prayers for the dead, writes as follows :—

1. The first century has scarcely any evidence to offer. . . . The New Testament contains but one passage which can fairly be construed as a prayer for the dead. Early post-canonical writers are equally reticent. The letter of Clement contains petitions of all sorts . . . but makes no reference of any sort to the Christian dead.

2. This lack of evidence continues until past the middle of the second century. . . . It is certainly remarkable that nothing of the [same] kind occurs among the numerous inscriptions on Christian tombs in Phrygia, collected by Sir W. M. Ramsay.

3. It is at Carthage that prayers for the dead . . . are first seen. . . . Yet other Churches do not seem to have followed suit, and Origen's silence is " most remarkable."

4. The conclusion is that there is nothing to show communion for the departed during the Apostolic and sub-Apostolic periods.[1]

Surely this absolute silence to the end of the second century is impressive and significant. When prayers for the dead actually began in the Christian Church they were very simple and marked by a true reserve, because of our ignorance. They were merely prayers for the soul's rest, and that it might be placed at God's Right Hand. But the mind of man is impatient of restraint, and so something more definite was wanted to pray for. The order of thought and feeling seems to have been somewhat on this line, though, of course, not always definitely and consciously, nor all at once, but extending through several centuries : (1) Prayer implies need. (2) Need suggests imperfection. (3) Imperfection involves progress. (4) Progress indicates purification. (5) Purification demands suffering, and from this came the fully developed mediæval doctrine of Purgatory which, as we have seen, means purification based on the fact that the full penal consequences of sin are not all remitted in this life.

It is unnecessary to stay to discuss all this in detail, but this much may be said : (1) We can readily see how far it all is from New Testament simplicity ; and (2) Suffering is not necessarily remedial and purifying ; it often hardens. Joy is on the whole quite as purgative as suffering, and some would say that it is much more so.

This was the state of the case before the Reformation, and we are at once brought to :—

IV.—THE TEACHING OF THE CHURCH OF ENGLAND

This calls for our most careful attention and study, and we have to note the following stages of the history.

[1] *Journal of Theological Studies*, July 1907, p. 500.

2K

(*a*) In 1549 came the first Reformed Prayer Book, and in it were prayers for the dead, distinct and definite. The prayer now called the Prayer for the Church Militant was then headed, " Let us pray for the whole state of Christ's Church," and a petition for the departed was included in the prayer. There were also prayers for the dead in the Burial Service. But the Visitation Articles of 1549 which enforced this Prayer Book ordered " that no man maintain Purgatory . . . or any other such abuses and superstitions." So that our Reformers prohibited the doctrine of Purgatory while continuing to pray for the dead. This is proof that prayers for the dead are not necessarily connected with the Roman doctrine of Purgatory.

(*b*) In 1552, came the second Reformed Prayer Book. From this prayers for the dead were deliberately omitted, and the word " militant here in earth " added to the heading of the prayer. The Burial Service was altered in accordance with this so as to express the present joy of the holy dead, " with whom the souls of the faithful, after they are delivered from the burden of the flesh, are in joy and felicity." This change from 1549 deserves careful notice.

Bishop Drury[1] correctly calls this " the absence of direct and unambiguous prayer for the departed." But it is something more, for " what is quite certain is that direct and unequivocal utterances of prayer for the faithful departed were then removed and have never been restored."

One of the Homilies speaks in unmistakable plainness of the needlessness of prayers for the dead.

" Now, to entreat of that question, whether we ought to pray for them that are departed out of this world, or no ? Wherein, if we cleave only unto the Word of God, then must we needs grant that we have no commandment so to do. . . . Therefore, let us not deceive ourselves, thinking that either we may help other, or other may help us by their good and charitable prayers in time to come. . . . Neither let us dream any more that the souls of the dead are anything at all holpen by our prayers : but, as the Scripture teacheth us, let us think that the soul of man, passing out of the body, goeth straightways either to Heaven, or else to hell, whereof the one needeth no prayer, and the other is without redemption. The only purgatory wherein we must trust to be saved, is the death and blood of Christ, which if we apprehend with a true and stedfast faith, it purgeth and cleanseth us from all our sins, even as well as if He were now hanging upon the cross. . . . If this kind of purgation will not serve them, let them never hope to be released by other men's prayers, though they should continue therein unto the world's end. . . . Let us not, therefore, dream either of purgatory, or of prayer for the souls of them that be dead ; but let us earnestly and diligently pray for them which are expressly commanded in Holy Scripture, namely, for kings and rulers ; for ministers of God's holy word and sacraments ; for the saints of this world, otherwise called the faithful ; to be short, for all men living, be they never so great enemies to God and His people."[2]

---

[1] Dr. Drury, *Churchman*, January 1909, p. 21.   [2] The Homilies, pp. 337–340.

This was published within about twenty years of the Prayer Book of 1552. It will be noticed that the condemnation is of the practice *per se*, and not merely when associated with Purgatory. Bishop Drury says this shows the view that was taken by leading Elizabethan divines, and throws at least an important side-light on the facts already adduced.[1]

(*c*) In 1559 one of the reasons in Geste's letter to Cecil against the restoration of the Prayer Book of 1549 was that it contained prayers for the dead.[2]

(*d*) At the time of the revision of 1662 a proposal was made to omit the words " militant here in earth," and at one stage a prayer for the dead was actually inserted by some of the Revisers, but rejected by Convocation, and there the matter stands to this day, a thanksgiving for the departed alone being added.

This is the Church of England history on the subject, clear and definite, and surely capable of only one meaning.

In support of this position it can be shown that the Reformers and their immediate successors, men like Cranmer, Jewel, and Whitgift, all rejected prayer for the dead.[3]

It is said, however, that there are two passages where we pray for the dead.

(1) In the Post-Communion Collect.—" That we and all Thy whole Church may obtain remission of our sins and all other benefits of His passion." But surely the Church above has obtained " remission." These words were drawn up by the men who deliberately omitted prayers for the dead in 1552.

(2) " That with them we may be partakers of Thy heavenly kingdom." But this is a statement about *them*, and a prayer for *ourselves*. It is in the prayer for the *Church Militant*, and that phrase covers the whole prayer. We thank God for the departed; we do not pray for them.

Such is the Church of England history and doctrine. And if it be said, as it has been sometimes, that prayers for the dead have never been forbidden in the Church of England, we reply that this is true in word, but false in fact. What is the meaning of the changes made in 1552? Either they mean something or they do not. If they do not, or did not, why were they made? Indeed, we may ask what any of the Reformation changes meant? In the beginning of our Prayer Book we have, " Of Ceremonies, why some be Abolished, and some Retained." Prayer for the dead was one of those things that were abolished. Omission, therefore, clearly means prohibition. To say simply that a thing is " not forbidden " would justify almost anything that an individual clergyman might choose to adopt.

The former Archbishop of Canterbury (Dr. Davidson) distinguishes between private and public prayers for the dead, and says that the

---

[1] *Churchman, ut supra*, p. 28.   [2] Cardwell, *Conferences*, p. 52.
[3] Blakeney, *Book of Common Prayer, its History and Interpretation*, p. 457–458, edited 1866.

Church has deliberately excluded such from her Services.[1] Thus Bishop Andrewes had them in his private devotions, but cut them out of the public Service for the Consecration of Graveyards.[2]

In the course of a review of a book advocating prayers for the dead, the *Guardian* frankly admitted that the practice was only justifiable on the assumption that the condition of the departed is not fixed at the time of death. When the wording of the prayer at the Burial Service is remembered, " With whom the souls of the faithful, after they are delivered from the burden of the flesh, are in joy and felicity," it is not difficult to see the position of the Church about the state of the faithful at and after death. There is no doubt that the Prayer Book in its final form excluded all explicit prayers for the departed from the public Services. All Souls' Day has not been recognised by the Prayer Book, and was omitted at the Reformation from the Table of Feasts and the Calendar.[3] All this gives force to Bishop Drury's conclusion that " the statement that such prayers are nowhere forbidden (except in the Homilies) is not complete or fair unless the above fact [about the rejection of the practice proposed in 1662] is placed side by side with it."

We must not fail to notice how the New Testament meets the supposed demand for prayers for the dead.

V.—THE SAFEGUARD AGAINST PRAYERS FOR THE DEAD

(*a*) The New Testament generally is our best safeguard.

The burden there is on " now." The whole stress is on the *present*. We are to pray for others now, work for them now, endeavour to save them now. We intercede for them now because of their *need*. There is no revelation of need *then*, but just the opposite.

(*b*) The doctrine of Justification specifically is our perfect safeguard.

The root of prayers for the dead is failure to realise what Justification means. We are " accounted righteous before God " from the very moment we accept Christ. This Justification settles at once and for ever our position before God. Our spiritual standing is unchanged through life, and our title to heaven is at once and for ever given. Justification is not repeated, it is permanent, and this settles the question of heaven and God's presence once for all. We must ever remember that the Romish doctrine of Purgatory is not connected with Sanctification, but with Justification. It is not part of a process for making Christians holier, but a supplementary process rendered necessary because all the penal consequences are not remitted in this life. Purgatory is required because the debt is not fully discharged here. But what saith the Scripture ? " There is, therefore, no condemnation to them which are in Christ Jesus, who walk not after the flesh, but after the Spirit " (Rom.

[1] *Report of the Royal Commission on Ecclesiastical Discipline*, Vol. II, p. 408.
[2] See Dr. Drury, *Churchman, ut supra*, p. 28.
[3] *Report of the Royal Commission on Ecclesiastical Discipline*, Vol. IV, pp. 45-48; 1024.

viii. 1). If only we teach, preach, live, and enjoy that blessed truth we shall never use prayers for the dead.

VI.—RECENT DISCUSSIONS

The question has naturally obtained renewed attention through the War, and certain statements of representative Churchmen compel a fresh consideration of the position of the Bible and the Church of England. The Archbishop of Canterbury in a sermon on 2nd November 1914, and in his Diocesan Gazette, seems to have modified the view expressed in his evidence before the Royal Commission already quoted. While, on the one hand, he is strong against the danger of abuses, such as we find in the sixteenth century and continued in certain quarters to this day, yet on the other he is of opinion that there must be no discouragement of the " devout soul in prayer for the loved one out of sight." These words state the Archbishop's position from both standpoints :—

" My earnest wish is to be helpful, in this time of anxiety, strain and sorrow, to those who, in perfect loyalty to Church of England teaching, feel, and, I think, rightly feel, that they need not cease from reverent and trustful prayer on behalf of husband, son, or brother who has passed from the life we know and see into the larger life beyond.

" The subject of prayers definitely offered on behalf of those whose life on earth is ended is shrouded in so much mystery as to call for the utmost care and reserve on our part in handling it. ' God is in heaven and we upon earth ; therefore let our words be few.' The Church of England, it is hardly necessary to say, has nowhere declared it to be unlawful or erroneous to believe in the propriety and efficacy of such petitions. But as a consequence of exaggerated and superstitious teaching, and of grave misuse, our Church reverently, yet rigidly, excluded from prayers prescribed by authority for public and general use phrases which convey a definite prayer for the departed as distinguished from, or separated from, those now upon earth. For example, the words in our Order of the Holy Communion ' that we and all Thy whole Church may obtain remission of our sins,' were regarded by high contemporary authority as including the faithful who are beyond the grave, but it cannot be said that in their context they necessarily have that meaning. I desire loyally to maintain the distinction, markedly drawn by Bishop Andrewes and other great Anglican divines, between those beliefs, based upon definite Scriptural proof, the teaching of which is incorporated in our public formularies, and on the other hand opinions and beliefs which fall short of such definite proof. If the distinction be borne in mind, I have no doubt at all that prayers for the dead are permissible to loyal sons and daughters of our Church so long as they do not imply a condition of the departed which our Article XXII (' Of Purgatory ') has definitely condemned."

In the same direction are the words of the late Bishop of Durham (Dr. Moule) in his *Christus Consolator* (pp. 96-98), thereby marking a definite change from his *Outlines of Christian Doctrine* (p. 97), where, speaking of the arguments used in favour of prayer for the dead in the early

Church, as against " frequent criticism," he says : " These defences are inadequate, against the total silence of Scripture." The recent utterances of the Bishop are as follows :—

" Upon the grave and tender problem of prayer for the departed, the Bible, so I venture to think, after long reflection, is absolutely reserved. I cannot think, therefore, that the warrant for such prayer is a fact of revelation. Christians who so pray should have a reverent regard, when there is any occasion for such a feeling, for the misgivings of others, in whom, very probably, the thought of spiritual communion with their vanished ones is just as strong and warm as in themselves, and who continually greet them in the Lord, reaching them in Him through the veil. Only, they do not see the warrant for intercessory prayer for them.

" They do think, perhaps, and most justly, that at least the too easy use of such prayer may tend *to muffle* the divine appeals to man to seek salvation to-day.

" Misgivings about prayer for the dead are wholly justified, if the prayer in question means necessarily prayer for deliverance from gloom and pain, rather than a breath of loving aspiration sent after the spirit into its abode of light, asking, as a certainty may be asked for, for the perpetual growth in the emancipated being of the graces and the bliss of the heavenly rest, and its holy progress and education in the knowledge of its Lord. It is undoubted that such prayer for the departed is found in the fragmentary remains of very early Christian literature, certainly within half a century of the last apostles. Never there, nor ever in the inscriptions of the Roman catacombs, I think, does it suggest a purgatorial belief. It might almost be said to be, as regards its spirit, as much salutation and aspiration as petition. But in form it is prayer. And I for one cannot condemn such exercises of the soul, where reverent thought invites to it, in the private devotions of a Christian."[1]

These are significant utterances and indicate a desire (due to the circumstances of the War) to modify the Church of England rule about limiting prayer to that which can be definitely proved from Holy Scripture. Now while it is natural to feel intense sympathy with those who have lost loved ones in battle, the question must still be faced in the light of Holy Scripture, for it is part of the purpose of the Bible as the Word of God to guide, guard and control our natural desires and cravings. The following considerations must, therefore, be kept clearly and constantly in view.

1. When the Royal Commission on Ecclesiastical Discipline issued its Report in 1906 a chapter was devoted to the subject. The Commissioners stated that the Church of England had never formally condemned prayers for the dead, as distinguished from their public use in her services. Representative Divines of the Church, it was pointed out, have again and again protested against the necessity of a connection, such as is by Roman Catholic writers constantly assumed to exist, between the doctrine of Purgatory and prayers for the departed. The Commissioners at the

[1] Thess. iv. 14 (Footnote by Bishop Moule): "Its introduction into public worship is, in view of differing beliefs, another matter, on which I do not speak here."

same time made it clear that they dissociated themselves from all public services and prayers for the dead, concerning which evidence was given, according to their opinion, " significant of teaching which is entirely inconsistent with the teaching of the Church of England."

2. It is obvious on the Archbishop's admission in his sermon that " no explicit prayers for the departed at all were admitted into the public language of the Church, and people were taught to rely in these public offices upon that alone which can be definitely proved by Holy Scripture."

3. Then comes the enquiry whether the prayer recommended by the Archbishop is for the Christian or for the non-Christian dead. His words suggest the former, and, if so, the entire problem is raised of the relation of the Christian soul to God. If the soul has passed away as a believer, then its *title* to Heaven through Justification is assured, and prayer in such a case cannot be for anything else than growth in grace. But have we any warrant from Scripture for such a prayer ? To ask the question is to answer it. And is it logical to pray for anyone who is confessedly at peace in the presence of Christ ? It is generally admitted by advocates of the practice that it implies some need of purification.

4. But another question at once arises.—Is it possible in such circumstances as those of war to limit our prayers for the faithful departed ? Is there not an equally instinctive desire, indeed, a greater longing, to pray for those of whose salvation we are not certain ? But, if so, we are at once faced with the solemn and serious idea of a second probation, " the larger hope," and again the enquiry comes : Is this according to Scripture ? There is no doubt that prayers for the dead do imply a belief in some state of imperfection which needs to be removed, and it becomes a serious question whether the traditional limitation of prayers for the faithful departed can be maintained. As already seen, prayers for the dead did not arise out of Purgatory, but they have always been associated with that doctrine, and if once prayer is extended beyond the Christian dead, some form of Purgatory will assuredly be demanded.

Even the words of the Archbishop are not quite clear when he speaks of the one who has passed away still growing " in truer purity and in deepened reverence and love." This thought of a " truer purity " seems to imply that something in the Intermediate State can minister to a spiritual condition " truer " than that experienced below. But is not such an idea really a confusion between the soul's *title* to Heaven and its *place* there ? No one can question that prayer for the dead is associated in most minds with the thought of discipline after death. And in view of the fact that we know nothing about the condition of the departed, is it not fair to urge that we cannot pray for them with anything like the definiteness and assurance we enjoy in intercessory prayer for them while on earth ? If our prayers are to be at once satisfying to ourselves and pleasing to God, they ought to be strictly limited to the Divine revelation in Holy Scripture. The great danger is that by the practice of prayer we shall imply that there is some change of spiritual condition

between death and resurrection which we can effect by our intercession.[1]

Under all these circumstances, we would, therefore, again urge the
following considerations :—

(1) The importance and significance of the silence of the New Testament.—Nothing can be more remarkable than the way in which our
Lord and His Apostles never refer to prayer for the dead. " Blessed are
the dead which die in the Lord " (Rev. xi. 13). Observe Bishop Moule's
significant words :—

" The Bible . . . is absolutely reserved. I cannot think, therefore, that the
warrant for such prayer is a fact of revelation."

(2) The Witness of the Early Church.—Bishop Moule claims for
the practice a time " within half a century of the last Apostles." But
this, as we have seen, is not supported by Dr. Swete. A practice for
which there is no real proof earlier than the end of the second century,
the time of Tertullian, can hardly be called primitive, and, as Dr. Swete
has shown, prayer for the dead is certainly by no means prominent,
indeed scarcely noticeable at all, in the earliest Church.

(3) The history of the Church of England.—The changes in 1552
and 1662 tell their own story, and though there are a few who, like
Cosin, have intended prayer for the dead in some of the phrases of the
Prayer Book, no one can doubt that the balance of evidence is over-
whelmingly on the other side.

It is frequently urged that we pray for the dead when we ask in the
Church Militant Prayer, " That with them we may be partakers of
Thy heavenly Kingdom," and also in the words in the Burial Service,
" That we with all those who are departed in the true faith of Thy
Holy Name may have our perfect consummation and bliss." But it
may be asked : (a) How could this be the purpose of the Reformers when
such vital changes were made by these very men between 1549 and
1552 ? (b) Is this the real meaning of the words ? Surely " we with

[1] Dr. Wace, the late Dean of Canterbury, interprets the Archbishop's language in
the same way, for, after deprecating the introduction of "petitions which imply
suppositions respecting the condition of the soul in the Intermediate State, of which
Scripture tells us nothing," he says: "Even the Archbishop's language might give
some encouragement to such suppositions, when he speaks of praying 'for him . . .
who still lives and, as we may surely believe, still grows from strength to strength in
truer purity and in deepened reverence and love.' Then," Dr. Wace adds, "whoever
believes that does so without warrant of Scripture, and prayer based on such a belief
has no authority in revelation. The hope of the Christian is not that his soul will be
gradually purified after death, but that, in the words of the commendatory prayer in
the Service of the Visitation of the Sick, it may, in death itself, be washed in the blood
of that immaculate Lamb, and presented, when it leaves the body, 'pure and without
spot' unto God. Prayers, in short, which have any tinge of a purgatorial view are
unauthorised by Scripture, and inconsistent with a most blessed element of Evangelical
hope and faith." These words are all the more weighty, because Dr. Wace favours
prayer to the extent of commendation of the departed to God and that the fulfilment
of the Divine promises for the Judgment Day may be realisd (*The War and the Gospel*,
p. 225 f.).

them " is different from " they with us." Their position is clear, for they are " departed in the faith and fear of God," but " we " are still here. Further, if the Church Militant Prayer is to have this interpretation, it will imply that participation in the Kingdom of Heaven by the faithful departed is, somehow or other, dependent on our lives; " give *us* grace . . . that (*they*) may be partakers." The absurdity of such an idea hardly needs to be mentioned. But if the statement is properly interpreted to be equivalent to " like them we," there is a perfect balance of thought and expression. And if, as it has been well said, we wish to go with a person, it implies that the person is assuredly going.

(4) Our ignorance of the future state and, therefore, the impossibility of intelligent prayer.—What do we really know of the future life? Practically nothing; and at the same time absolutely nothing in regard to any bearing of our prayers thereon. How, then, can we be of service to the dead by prayers for them? Either our prayers benefit them or they do not. To limit prayer for the departed to " a breath of loving aspiration sent after the spirit into its abode of light " is hardly likely to be adequate and satisfying to those who are accustomed to the practice.

(5) May we not also enquire whether the War, with all its strain and stress, great as they are, can really make such a change as is involved in praying for the departed? If the practice was wrong before, it must still be wrong, while if it is right now, it must have been right before. Such a revolution as is here implied cannot be justified even by the War.

For further study, see *The Intermediate State*, by Dr. C. H. H. Wright; *The Blessed Dead: Do They Need Our Prayers?* by H. Falloon; *Prayers for the Dead*, by Bishop Drury.

ARTICLE XXVII.—THE MODE OF BAPTISM

Although the Article is not concerned with the method of baptism it is impossible to avoid a reference to it in view of modern controversies. The rubric in the Baptismal Office places immersion first, but allows pouring as an alternative.

" If they shall certify him that the child may well endure it he shall dip it in the water discreetly and warily. . . . But if they certify that the child is weak it shall suffice to pour water upon it."

And yet it is clear that the use of the word " dip " does not necessarily mean what is usually understood as immersion, for in the case of the baptism of those of riper years the person to be baptised is to stand by the font, and then the clergyman " shall dip him in the water, or pour water upon him." From this it is clear that " dipping " may mean partial or total, and, strictly, partial dipping is described as immersion, and total dipping by submersion. It is the latter, submersion, that is held by Baptists to be the only right mode, and it is this that calls for special consideration.

The word used for " Baptism " is βαπτιζω, not βαπτω, and as the latter means " to dip," but is never used for the ordinance of baptism, it is clear that we must derive the significance of the former word from the usage. The word βαπτω is used three times only in the New Testament: (1) The dipping of the tip of the finger of Lazarus in water (Luke xvi. 24); (2) Our Lord's dipping of the sop which He gave to Judas (John xiii. 26); (3) The Lord's vesture dipped in blood (Rev. xix. 13). But it is noteworthy that there is a difference of reading in this last passage, and the Revised Version favours the reading " sprinkled " instead of " dipped."

The various arguments drawn from the Old Testament, the Apocrypha, Classical Greek, and the New Testament can be studied in the author's *The Catholic Faith* (p. 402 ff.).

Christian History and Archæology afford no evidence that the early Christians thought they could not be baptised except by immersion. The only evidence we possess on the point is found in a well-known passage in the Didache (chap. vii) which runs thus :—

" Now concerning Baptism, thus baptise ye ; having first uttered all these things, baptise unto the Name of the Father, and of the Son, and of the Holy Spirit, in living water. But if thou hast not living water baptise in other water ; and if thou canst not in cold, then in warm ; but if thou hast neither, pour water upon the head thrice unto the Name of the Father and Son and Holy Spirit."

This passage shows that dipping in running water rather than in a baptistery was the method preferred by early Christians, but it shows with equal clearness that dipping was a question of preference and not of necessity. Surely this expresses the true Apostolic spirit, and to insist upon one precise method as necessary to baptism is not only untrue to all that we know of usage, but also out of all harmony with the true conception of the Christian religion.

ARTICLE XXVIII.—THE HISTORY OF ANGLICAN DOCTRINE ON THE HOLY COMMUNION

It is sometimes urged that the Prayer Book and Articles are not in harmony on the doctrine of the Holy Communion, and this makes it imperative to give special attention to the history associated with the various Revisions of the Prayer Book and Articles. There are eight periods to be studied. The First Prayer Book of 1549 ; the Second Prayer Book of 1552 ; the Forty-two Articles of 1553 ; the Elizabethan Prayer Book of 1559; the Thirty-eight Articles of 1563; the Thirty-nine Articles of 1571; the Additions to the Catechism in 1604; and the last Revision of the Prayer Book in 1662.

The fundamental changes between the Prayer Books of 1549 and 1552 are universally recognised, and it is also admitted that in 1559 the Prayer Book of 1552, not that of 1549, was adopted as the basis. The question is whether at and since 1559 any of the changes made essentially altered the Anglican doctrine. Bishop Gibson thinks this has happened.[1] But other authorities are equally clear that fundamental doctrine has been uniform throughout.[2] If any such changes have taken place their character must be clearly stated. The vital problem is whether there is any doctrine which can be called " Catholic " without being Roman, which is essentially identical with the Reformed doctrine of Calvin, which Hooker believed and accepted. This is the question which has to be faced.

I.—THE PRAYER BOOK OF 1559

While adopting the Second Prayer Book of 1552 as the basis of the Elizabethan Revision, the " Black Rubric " was omitted. By some this is regarded as a mere technicality, by others as due to a deliberate effort on the part of Queen Elizabeth to win the Lutherans. In connection with this the difficulty about the Ornaments Rubric and the blending of the words of administration found respectively in the Prayer Books of 1549 and 1552 must be considered. It is now generally recognised that in the action of the Queen and her advisers in 1559 the Roman Catholics were not really in view, but only the desire and determination of the Queen to plant herself more firmly on the Throne by uniting all Protestants, and therefore removing from the Prayer Book anything which might seem to oppose the distinctive Lutheran view.

II.—THE ARTICLES OF 1563

As already noticed above, the third paragraph of Article XXVIII was changed, and Article XXIX, while accepted by Archbishop Parker at Convocation, was refused by the Queen. But this Royal action did not involve any essential change, since Parker was a disciple of Cranmer and held strongly the Reformed (or Swiss), not the Lutheran doctrine.[3] Once again, there is no proof of an endeavour to conciliate Rome, because several significant alterations were made in the Articles at this time which resulted in their becoming more anti-Roman than even in 1552.

---

[1] *The Thirty-nine Articles*, pp. 643–647.
[2] Simpson, *The Thing Signified* (Second Edition); Griffith Thomas, *A Sacrament of our Redemption*, pp. 53–79.
[3] Griffith Thomas, *ut supra*, pp. 64–70.

III.—THE ARTICLES OF 1571

In 1563 Bishop Guest claimed to be the author of the new paragraph of Article XXVIII, though, as we have seen, these very words are found in Archbishop Parker's own draft.   Guest desired to make it possible for Lutherans, like Bishop Cheney, to accept the Articles. Bishop Gibson lays great stress on Guest's claim to this authorship, but the Judges in the Bennett Judgment practically set it aside as either impossible or unworthy of notice.   But in 1571 Archbishop Parker obtained the reinsertion of Article XXIX, which was accepted by the Queen, and thereupon Guest admitted that Lutheranism was henceforward impossible.   Somehow or other he brought himself to sign the Articles, but Bishop Cheney did not do so.   In 1577 the Lutheran Church definitely denounced the doctrine taught in Article XXIX, and almost used our very words in so doing.

IV.—THE CATECHISM OF 1604

In the sacramental addition to the Catechism Bishop Gibson sees a further endeavour to return to a more " Catholic " doctrine on the Holy Communion.[1]   And this contention is alleged by other writers of the same school.   But it is overlooked that these Questions and Answers come almost verbally from Nowell's *Catechism*, which is known to be a thoroughly Protestant document of the Reformed, not Lutheran, type.[2]   And several modern writers urge strongly that no fundamental change was made by these additions.[3]

V.—THE PRAYER BOOK OF 1662

The only point to be considered here is the re-insertion of the " Black Rubric " with the verbal change from " real " to " corporal."   It is sometimes argued that this involves a significant and vital change of doctrine.   The question is solely one of evidence.   It was the Puritans who requested the re-insertion of the Rubric, and there is no evidence of any change of doctrine being intended by those who replaced it in the Prayer Book.   The change of terminology was necessary, because the word " real " in the sixteenth century meant the same as the word " corporal " in the seventeenth.[4]   To have inserted the Rubric with the word " real " would have led to misunderstanding, since men like Jeremy Taylor used it to express the presence of a definite Protestant and anti-

[1] *The Thirty-nine Articles*, p. 647.
[2] Dimock, *Papers on the Eucharistic Presence*, p. 306.
[3] Simpson, *The Thing Signified*.
[4] Dean Aldrich.

Roman type.[1] The Rubric really turns on the statement that our Lord's Body is in heaven, not here, and this remained unchanged.

In view of these facts, and it is admitted that they represent in summary the whole of what was done at various times, it is clear that no change of Anglican doctrine was made from 1552 onwards, but that it has remained uniform throughout.

SPECIAL NOTE ON ESCHATOLOGY

It is well known that in 1553 there were four Articles dealing with questions connected with "The Last Things," and while the Church of England is not now committed to any of the statements contained in those Articles, reference may be made to them as included in the Forty-two Articles of 1553 as indicating what was then believed concerning eschatological problems. The subject of "The Last Things," although not included in the doctrinal statements of the Anglican formularies, has naturally occupied very great attention during the last century, but all that can be done here is to indicate in general the views that are held and to refer to some of the more important works upon the subject.

There is, perhaps, no topic on which it is more necessary to keep strictly to the exact words and meaning of Holy Scripture without attempting to draw inferences beyond those which strict exegesis allows. We must carefully examine first the language and then the teaching of Scripture before drawing any conclusions. It is important to study first of all the various words and phrases connected with the future; indeed, it is only by means of the widest possible induction of Scripture passages that we can expect to arrive at a clear idea of its meaning.

1. The great hope set forth in the New Testament is the Coming of the Lord. "From thence He shall come to judge the quick and the dead." Two works for study are *Ecce Venit*, by A. J. Gordon, and *Jesus is Coming*, by W. E. Blackstone. The precise interpretation of the Apocalypse in regard to the future will be found according to the Historical School in *Daniel and the Revelation*, by Tanner, and according to the Futurist School in *Lectures on the Apocalypse*, by Seiss.

2. The question of future punishment is associated with three general lines of interpretation :—(a) Universalism, implying the hope of universal restitution. For this reference can be made to *Salvator Mundi*, by Cox; *Restitution of All Things*, by Jukes; and *Eternal Hope*, by Farrar. (b) Annihilation, teaching that the wicked will be destroyed and only those who are in Christ will have eternal life. For this the books are *Life in Christ*, by Edward White; *Our Growing Creed*, by W. D. Maclaren.

---

[1] Bishop Moule, *Pledges of His Love*, p. 143; Tomlinson, *Prayer Book, Articles, and Homilies*, p. 264; Soames, *The Real Presence*, pp. 9, 12 f.; Griffith Thomas, *ut supra*, pp. 75–78.

(*c*) Everlasting Punishment.   This is regarded as the orthodox view according to the New Testament.   The best work on this, as indeed on the general subject, is *The Christian Doctrine of Immortality*, by Salmond. (*d*) Another view which endeavours to harmonise the idea of everlasting punishment with the non-eternity of sin will be found stated and discussed in *The Eternal Saviour-Judge*, by R. L. Clarke ; *Reason and Revelation* (chap. xii), by Illingworth ; *Sin, a Problem of To-day* (the last pages), by Orr ; *World Without End*, and *Veins of Silver*, by Garratt ; and *The Victory of Love*, by T. R. Birks.   Two small and little known , but weighty discussions will be found in *The Gospel in Hades*, and *Hades, or Heaven ?* by R. W. Harden (Combridge & Co., Dublin).   Valuable criticisms of the various modern theories will be found in *Human Destiny*, by Sir Robert Anderson, and *Immortality*, by Dr. H. R. Mackintosh. There are also several articles on the different topics included in Eschatology in the *International Standard Bible Encyclopædia*.

A BRIEF SELECTION OF BOOKS FOR FURTHER STUDY

HOLY COMMUNION.

ANGUS, S., *The Religious Quests of the Græco-Roman World* (Chapters VIII to XIV).

BARNES-LAWRENCE, A. E., *The Holy Communion.*

BURKITT, F. C., *Eucharist and Sacrifice.*

CRANMER, ABP., *The Lord's Supper*, with an Introduction by H. Wace.

CRANMER, ABP., *On the Lord's Supper* (Cranmer's Works, Parker Society).

DIMOCK, N., *Doctrine of the Lord's Supper.*

DIMOCK, N., *Doctrine of the Sacraments.*

DIMOCK, N., *Notes on the Round Table Conference on the Doctrine of the Holy Communion and its Expression in Ritual.*

DIMOCK, N., *Our One Priest on High.*

DIMOCK, N., *Papers on the Eucharistic Presence.*

DRURY, T. W., *Elevation in the Eucharist : Its History and Rationale.*

GOODE, W., *The Nature of Christ's Presence in the Eucharist.*

HARRIS, G. H., Essay in *The Inner Life.* See also Appendix by Bishop Jeune.

KENNETT, R. H., *The Last Supper.*

MACGREGOR, C. H. C., *Eucharistic Origins.*

MEYRICK, F., *Doctrine of the Church of England on the Holy Communion.*

MOULE, H. C. G., *Ridley on the Lord's Supper.*

PAIGE COX, W. L., *Communion or Mass* in " Anglican Essays."

PAIGE COX, W. L., *The Heavenly Priesthood of Our Lord.*

PEROWNE, T. T., *Our High Priest in Heaven.*

QUICK, O. C., *The Christian Sacraments.*

SCOTT, C. ANDERSON, *The Church : its Worship and Sacraments.*

SCUDAMORE, W. E., *The Communion of the Laity.*

SCUDAMORE, W. E., *Notitia Eucharistica.*

TAIT, A. J., *The Heavenly Session of our Lord.*

TAIT, A. J., *The Nature and Function of the Sacraments.*

TEMPLE, W., *Christus Veritas.*

THOMAS, W. H. GRIFFITH, *A Sacrament of our Redemption.*

VOGAN, *The True Doctrine of the Eucharist.*

WATERLAND, D., *The Doctrine of the Eucharist.*

REPORT of the *Fulham Round Table Conference on the Doctrine of the Holy Communion and its Expression in Ritual*, 1900.

THE CHURCH AND MINISTRY.

BLUNT, A. W. F., *Studies in Apostolic Christianity.*

CARTER, C. SYDNEY, *Ministerial Commission.*

DIMOCK, N., *The Sacerdotium of Christ.*

DIMOCK, N., *The Christian Doctrine of Sacerdotium.*
DIMOCK, N., *Christian Unity.*
DULLES, *The True Church.*
GIBSON, BP., On Articles XXIII and XXXVI.
GORE, BP., *The Church and Ministry.*
GORE, BP., *Orders and Unity.*
GWATKIN, H. M., *Early Church History.*
HATCH, *Organization of the Early Christian Churches.*
HEADLAM, BP. A. C., *The Church of England.*
HEADLAM, BP. A. C., *The Doctrine of the Church and Christian Reunion.*
HENSON, BP. HENSLEY, *Godly Union and Concord.*
HENSON, BP. HENSLEY, *Westminster Sermon.*
HENSON, BP. HENSLEY, *The Road to Unity.*
HENSON, BP. HENSLEY, *The Relation of the Church of England to the other National Churches.*
HORT, F. J. A., *Christian Ecclesia.*
HORT, F. J. A., *Judaistic Christianity.*
HUNKIN, J. W., *Episcopal Ordination and Confirmation in Relation to Inter-Communion and Reunion.*
LIGHTFOOT, BP., *Essay on the Christian Ministry.*
LINDSAY, *The Church and Ministry in the Early Centuries* (Presbyterian).
LITTON, E. A., *The Church of Christ.*
MOBERLY, R. C., *Ministerial Priesthood.*
MOULE, H. C. G., *Outlines of Christian Doctrine.*
SALMON, A. L., *The Infallibility of the Church.*
SANDAY, W., *The Conception of Priesthood.*
STREETER, B. H., *The Primitive Church.*
WORDSWORTH, BP. J., *The Ministry of Grace.*

BAPTISM.

BARNES-LAWRENCE, A. E., *Infant Baptism.*
CLEMANCE, CLEMENT, *Baptism : Its Meaning : and Its Place in Christian Ordinances.* An Exposition and Defence.
EDWARDS, *Candid Reasons for Renouncing the Principles of Antipædobaptism.*
GOODE, W., *The Effects of Baptism in the case of Infants.*
GORHAM, *Efficacy of Baptism.*
MOZLEY, *On the Primitive Doctrine of Baptismal Regeneration.*
MOZLEY, *A Review of the Baptismal Controversy.*
WALL, W., *History of Infant Baptism.*
WILKINSON, *Baptism : What Saith the Scripture ?*

THE RESURRECTION.

LATHAM, H., *The Risen Master.*
ORR, JAMES, *The Resurrection of Jesus.*
MILLIGAN, W., *The Resurrection of Our Lord.*
MOULE, H. C. G., *Jesus and the Resurrection.*

WACE, HENRY, *The Story of the Resurrection.*
WESTCOTT, BP., *The Revelation of the Risen Lord.*
WESTCOTT, BP., *The Gospel of the Resurrection.*

GENERAL.

BICKNELL, E. J., *A Theological Introduction to the Thirty-nine Articles of the Church of England.*
BROWN, W. A., *Christian Theology in Outline.*
BROWNE, BP. HAROLD, *Exposition of the Thirty-nine Articles.*
BURNET, BP., *On the Thirty-nine Articles.*
CARTER, C. S., *The Anglican Via Media.*
CLARKE, W. N., *Outline of Christian Theology.*
CLOQUET, *An Exposition of the Thirty-nine Articles.*
CURTIS, O. A., *The Christian Faith.*
DALE, R. W., *Christian Doctrine.*
DENNEY, J., *Studies in Theology.*
EVANS, *The Great Doctrines of the Bible.*
GIBSON, BP., *The Thirty-nine Articles.*
GREEN, *The Thirty-nine Articles and the Age of the Reformation.*
HARDWICK, C., *A History of the Articles of Religion.*
JONES, *The Teaching of the Articles.*
KIDD, B. J., *The Thirty-nine Articles.*
LIDGETT, J. S., *The Christian Religion.*
LITTON, E. A., *Introduction to Dogmatic Theology.*
MACBETH, *Notes on the Articles.*
MACLEAR AND WILLIAMS, *Introduction to the Articles of the Church of England.*
MARTENSEN, BP., *Christian Dogmatics.*
PEAKE, A. S., *Christianity, Its Nature and Truth.*
ROGERS, *On the Thirty-nine Articles* (Parker Society).
STEARNS, *Present Day Theology.*
STRONG, A., *Manual of Theology.*
TAIT, A. J., *Lecture Outlines on the Thirty-nine Articles.*
TERRY, *Biblical Dogmatics.*
VAN OOSTERZEE, *Christian Dogmatics.*
WILSON, *Present Day Theology.*
By Various Authors (Essays)—
   Religion and the Modern Mind.
   The Faith of Centuries.
   The Ancient Faith in Modern Light.

2L

INDEX

Divine, 33-42
Human, 39-40
Nazianzen, Gregory, 294
Nestorianism, 41, 86, 292
Newman and the Articles, lvii; 189,
274, 298, 420, 450, 488
New Testament, 108-113. See *Canon*
Nicæa, Council of, xxxiv; 30, 94, 95,
148, 273, 292, 304, 305, 437
Nicene Creed, 95, 98, 146, 147, 148,
149
Novatians, 231

Oaths, Article XXXIX, 483-484
Oblation, Christ's one, Article XXXI,
414. See *Death of Christ* and
Atonement
Old Testament, Article VII, 134-145.
See *Testament*
Omnipotence, Divine, 16
Omnipresence, Divine, 17, 18
Ontological Argument for God, 6
Opus operatum, xliv; 358-364, 383
Orders, Validity of our, 335, 457
Ordinal, Article XXXVI, 452-458
Origen, 106, 114, 178, 301, 305, 396
Original Righteousness, 155, 156
Original Sin, 156-160. See *Sin*
Ornaments Rubric, xlvi; 523
Orr, Dr., 250
Ousia, 30

Pantheism, 17, 27
Papal Supremacy, xxxvii; 469-475
Pardons, Article XXII, 304
Roman Doctrine of Indulgences,
303, 304
Parker, Archbishop, and Articles, xliii-
xlv, xlvii, lv, 523, 524; on
Justification, 184,189; Authority,
281-282; the Lord's Supper, 401-
402; and the Wicked, 406, 408;
Both Kinds, 411
Parliament, Church and, 464-466
Passover, The, 391
Paul of Samosata, 37
Paul III, Pope, xxxi
Paul VII, Pope, 291
Paul, St., and Doctrine of Justification,
186-194, 201

And St. James, 205-206
Pelagianism, 160-161, 178, 201, 242,
245
Penance, xxxvii; 352-356, 437
Perichoresis, or Co-inherence, 31
Perseverance, Final, 236-257
Personality, Divine, 18, 19, 495
of Holy Spirit, 21, 95
Personal Religion, Articles on, 153
Person of Christ, 32
Person, the theological term, 30, 31
Peter, Supremacy of, Article XXXVII,
469-473
Philo, 35, 113
Pius IV, Pope, xxxiii; 306, 395
Pliny, 347
Pneumatomachi, the, 93
Polytheism, 18
Prayer Book, Articles and, 485-486,
522-525
Prayer for the Dead, 303, 508-521
Meaning, 509
Basis, 509-512
History, 512-513
Anglican Doctrine, 513-516
Safeguard, 516
Recent Discussions, 517
Predestination, Article XVII, 236-257
Outline of Article, 237-238
Nature, 238-239
Proof, 239
Effect, 240
Safeguard, 241
History, 241
Problem, 244
Ecclesiastical Arminianism, 245-246
Calvinism, 246-247
Scripture, 250-257
Presence, Doctrine of, 408-410, 450-
451
Priesthood, 316-323
Priest, the term, 316-323
Private Judgment, 289-290
Procession of Holy Spirit, 94-96
Processions of Sacrament, 357, 404
Protestantism, in Articles, lvii, lviii
Punishment, Capital, 475
Purgatory, Article XXII, 298-310,
510, 514
Roman Catholic Doctrine, 300